Transcendence and Phenomenology

Major criticism of phenomenology in relation tto theology

John Milbank

See pages 312 - 14

His critism is based on pure phenomenology isolating the finite. The later Husserl thinks more in terms of transcendental intersubjectivity where the finite is not comprehensible in its own terms.

The Veritas Series

Belief and Metaphysics
Edited by Conor Cunningham and Peter M. Candler, Jr

Proposing Theology
John Milbank

Tayloring Reformed Epistemology:
Charles Taylor, Alvin Plantinga and the de jure Challenge to
Christian Belief
Deane-Peter Baker

Theology, Psychoanalysis, Trauma
Marcus Pound

Transcendence and Phenomenology
Edited by Conor Cunningham and Peter M. Candler, Jr

VERITAS

Transcendence and Phenomenology

Edited by

Conor Cunningham

and

Peter M. Candler, Jr

scm press

in association with

The Centre of Theology and Philosophy
University of Nottingham
2007

© Conor Cunningham and Peter M. Candler, Jr 2007

The Authors have asserted their right under the Copyright,
Designs and Patents Act, 1988, to be identified as the
Authors of this Work

British Library Cataloguing in Publication data

A catalogue record for this book is available
from the British Library

Hardback 978 0 334 04 151 1
Paperback 978 0 334 04143 6

First published in 2007 by SCM Press
13–17 Long Lane,
London EC1A 9PN

www.scm-canterburypress.co.uk

SCM Press is a division of
SCM-Canterbury Press Ltd

Typeset by Regent Typesetting, London
Printed and bound in Great Britain by
MPG Books Ltd, Bodmin, Cornwall

In memoriam
Michel Henry
10 January 1922 – 3 July 2002

Caro salutis est cardo
Tertullian

In the depth of its night, our flesh is God
Michel Henry

Contents

Centre of Theology and Philosophy   xi

Veritas Series Introduction   xiii

Foreword by H.E. Paul Cardinal Poupard   xv

Acknowledgements   xix

Contributors   xxi

1   Perception, Transcendence and the Experience
    of God   1
    Jean-Yves Lacoste

2   Originary Inauthenticity – On Heidegger's *Sein
    und Zeit*   21
    Simon Critchley

3   'And There Shall Be No More Boredom':
    Problems with Overcoming Metaphysics in
    Heidegger, Levinas and Marion   50
    Joeri Schrijvers

4   Postmodern Philosophy and Jean-Luc Marion's
    Eucharistic Realism   84
    Philipp W. Rosemann

5   Husserlian Approaches to the Icon and the Idol   111
    Javier Carreño

6   Obscure Habit: Preambles to a Phenomenology
    of Christian Existence   134
    Jeffrey Bloechl

Contents

7 Doubled Reflection: Gadamer, Aesthetics and the Question of Spiritual Experience 151
Nicholas Davey

8 From Description to Doxology: The Dogmatic Bases of Christian Vision 174
Nathan R. Kerr

9 Original Immanence according to Michel Henry: The Intuition of Religion 201
Jean Leclercq

10 The World without the Lie 227
Karl Hefty

11 Phenomenology of Life 241
Michel Henry
Translated by Nick Hanlon

12 Suspending the Natural Attitude: Transcendence and Immanence from Thomas Aquinas to Michel Henry 260
Conor Cunningham

13 The Thomistic Telescope: Truth and Identity 288
John Milbank

14 Sacramental Aesthetics: Between Word and Flesh 334
Richard Kearney

15 Heidegger, Dilthey and 'the Being-Question': Towards a Critical Appraisal of Heidegger's Use of Hermeneutic Phenomenology 370
Cyril McDonnell

16 Love of Enemies for a Lover of Wisdom, or, Can a Phenomenologist be a Philosopher? 404
Felix Ó Murchadha

17 Anamnesis as Alterity? 421
Ian Leask

Contents

18 'The Words of the Oracle': Merleau-Ponty and
the 'Philosophy of Freudianism'   434
Mauro Carbone

19 On the Critiques of Pairing and Appresentation
in Merleau-Ponty and Levinas   448
Timothy Mooney

20 Towards An Ethically Inspired Fundamental or
First Theology   495
Michael Purcell

Sources and Acknowledgements   525
Name and Subject Index   527

Centre of Theology and Philosophy

www.theologyphilosophycentre.co.uk

Every doctrine which does not reach the one thing necessary, every separated philosophy, will remain deceived by false appearances. It will be a doctrine, it will not be Philosophy.
Maurice Blondel, 1861–1949

This book series is the product of the work carried out at the Centre of Theology and Philosophy, at the University of Nottingham.

The COTP is a research-led institution organized at the interstices of theology and philosophy. It is founded on the conviction that these two disciplines cannot be adequately understood or further developed, save with reference to each other. This is true in historical terms, since we cannot comprehend our Western cultural legacy unless we acknowledge the interaction of the Hebraic and Hellenic traditions. It is also true conceptually, since reasoning is not fully separable from faith and hope, or conceptual reflection from revelatory disclosure. The reverse also holds, in either case.

The Centre is concerned with:

- The historical interaction between theology and philosophy.
- The current relation between the two disciplines.
- Attempts to overcome the analytic/Continental divide in philosophy.
- The question of the status of 'metaphysics'. Is the term used equivocally? Is it now at an end? Or have twentieth-century attempts to have a post-metaphysical philosophy themselves come to and end?
- The construction of a rich Catholic humanism.

I am very glad to be associated with the endeavours of this extremely important Centre that helps to further work of

xi

enormous importance. Among its concerns is the question whether modernity is more an interim than a completion – an interim between a pre-modernity in which the porosity between theology and philosophy was granted, perhaps taken for granted, and a postmodernity where their porosity must be unclogged and enacted anew. Through the work of leading theologians of international stature and philosophers whose writings bear on this porosity, the Centre offers an exciting forum to advance in diverse ways this challenging and entirely needful, and cutting-edge work.

Professor William Desmond (Leuven)

VERITAS

Series Introduction

'. . . the truth will set you free.' (John 8.32)

Pontius Pilate said to Christ, 'What is truth?' And Jesus
remained silent. In much contemporary discourse, Pilate's question has been taken to mark the absolute boundary of human
thought. Beyond this boundary, it is often suggested, is an intellectual hinterland into which we must not venture. This terrain
is an agnosticism of thought: because truth cannot be possessed,
it must not be spoken. Thus, it is argued that the defenders of
'truth' in our day are often traffickers in ideology, merchants of
counterfeits, or anti-liberal. They are, because it is somewhat
taken for granted that Nietzsche's word is final: truth is the
domain of tyranny.

Is this indeed the case, or might another vision of truth offer
itself? The ancient Greeks named the love of wisdom *philia*, or
friendship. The one who would become wise, they argued,
would be a 'friend of truth'. For both philosophy and theology
might be conceived as schools in the friendship of truth, as a
kind of relation. For like friendship, truth is as much discovered
as it is made. If truth is then so elusive, if its domain is *terra
incognita*, perhaps this is because it arrives to us – unannounced
– as gift, as a person, and not some thing.

The aim of the Veritas book series is to publish incisive and
original current scholarly work that inhabits 'the between' and
'the beyond' of theology and philosophy. These volumes will all
share a common aspiration to transcend the institutional
divorce in which these two disciplines often find themselves,
and to engage questions of pressing concern to both philosophers and theologians in such a way as to reinvigorate both
disciplines with a kind of interdisciplinary desire, often so

absent in contemporary academe. In a word, these volumes represent collective efforts in the befriending of truth, doing so beyond the simulacra of pretend tolerance, the violent, yet insipid reasoning of liberalism that asks with Pilate, What is truth? – expecting a consensus of non-commitment; one that encourages the commodification of the mind, now sedated by the civil service of career, ministered by the frightened patrons of position.

The series will therefore consist of two 'wings': 1, original monographs; and 2, essay collections on a range of topics in theology and philosophy. The latter will principally be the products of the annual conferences of the Centre of Theology and Philosophy (www.theologyphilosophycentre.co.uk)

Conor Cunningham
Peter Candler
Series editors

Foreword

BY PAUL CARDINAL POUPARD

Twenty-five years ago, Pope John Paul II established the Pontifical Council for Culture, citing as a motivation his desire to create a body dedicated to promoting the great objectives that the
Second Vatican Ecumenical Council had proposed regarding the
relations between the Church and culture (*Lettera di creazione*,
20 May 1982). The Pastoral Constitution on the Church in the
Contemporary World, *Gaudium et spes*, had in fact dedicated
an entire chapter to culture, noting particularly its fundamental
importance for the full development of the human person, the
many links between the message of salvation and culture, the
reciprocal enrichment of the Church and different cultures, as
well as the necessity for believers to understand in depth the way
of thinking and feeling of other men and women of their time.

It is evident that diverse philosophies are at the heart of different cultures. But not every philosophy can truly be considered to be at the service of the dignity of the human person,
which, as revealed by the Word of God, is the ultimate measure
for the Church's discernment. No more so than today is the
drama of our times the crisis of cultures as manifest in the vary-
ing philosophical bases of contemporary societies; the schism of
reason from faith, the trend of believing without reason as seen
in many sects, the rejection of wisdom, and successive waves of
pensiero debole have flourished in an era in which theology and
philosophy have followed diverse and often dividing paths. The
result is clear for all to see: the denigration of the full dignity of
the human person. When Pope Benedict XVI reminded the

Church gathered in Aparecida, Brazil, that not every culture is equally open to the transcendent, his concern was for the impact of the processes of secularization which do not favour the full development of human dignity including each person's religious potential.

Indeed, the Church, as Good Samaritan, responds with the enduring appeal to search for truth, in which 'philosophy has the great responsibility of forming thought and culture' (*Fides et Ratio*, 6). The culture in which each of us is immersed must become the privileged forum for the meeting between philosophy and theology, in which the fullness of our nature, including the religious dimension, are understood as open to the transcendent. This is why, when Rector of the Catholic Institute in Paris, directing my *Grand Dictionnaire des Religions,* I asked Hans Urs von Balthasar to write what became a famous article on 'Religious Truth', in which he chose to begin with the *fait religieux* as a subjective phenomenon inherent to the human person (cf. *Vérité religieuse*, Presses Universitaires de France, 1993). Conscious of his original difference, the human person, essentially *homo religiosus*, radically refuses to be satisfied by finite and terrestrial goods. Von Balthasar cited as evidence of this the failure to eliminate the religious factor in communist countries. Today we should cite the re-awareness of the religious factor in materialist cultures, despite the best efforts of the secularists to suppress, ignore or deny this. But the phenomenon of the subjective religious factor, expressed timelessly in religious desire for the transcendent, is also an occasion to express the distinctiveness of Christianity, which is built not on the product of a transcendental projection of our need and desire, but the necessarily objective truth of Trinitarian Love, the first Love, which came before all things, and is the source of our new culture of Christian humanism.

The editors of this volume are to be applauded for putting together in a liberating manner the themes of Phenomenology and Transcendence, within an interdisciplinary setting, stimulating articles from the new men and women of culture, under the perspective of Revelation, to pursue that search for the

Truth, at the service of the human person whose daily reality cannot but be engaged with the Transcendent.

Paul Cardinal Poupard
President of the Pontifical Council for Culture
30 May 2007

Acknowledgements

This volume is the result of the Centre of Theology and Philosophy's first annual conference, which took place in September 2005. We would very much like to take this opportunity to thank all those who helped to make that event the great success that it turned out to be, and in addition those who gifted their support to the launch of the Centre:

Rt Revd Malcolm McMahon OP, Msgr Javier Martínez, Most Revd Dr Robin Eames, Fr Jean-Yves Lacoste, Crystal Cunningham, Alan Ford, Philip Goodchild, Karen Kilby, Alison Milbank, Mary Elmer, Janet Longley, Peter Watts, Richard Bailey, Rosie Fraser, and Richard Rouse. Also, the Rt Revd Donal Murray's speech for the official opening of the Centre was truly inspiring, and set the tone for the rest of the conference. Our very special thanks go to His Eminence Paul Cardinal Poupard, without whose support and encouragement the conference would have been a rather duller affair, if not impossible.

We would also take this opportunity to thank those who gave financial support to the conference: The British Academy, Archbishop Chrysostomos, and Graeme Paxton of Strategic Resource Group.

With regard to this volume, we would like to thank Barbara Laing, Mary Matthews, Hannah Ward, Anthony Paul Smith (who prepared the index), all at Red Roof Designs, especially Sara Cunningham-Bell, Murray Bell, and Eric Lee, and a very special thanks to Patrick Riches, without whom this volume would have been impossible.

Acknowledgements

Lastly, we would like to thank John Milbank, whose intelligence, support, enthusiasm, and willingness to put his hand to any task, no matter how menial, was an inspiration.

This volume is dedicated to the memory of Michel Henry, a true genius.

Contributors

Jeffery Bloechl is Associate Professor of Philosophy at the College of the Holy Cross in Worcester, Massachusetts. He has published widely in contemporary European philosophy, philosophy of religion, and fundamental ethics. He is the author of *Liturgy of the Neighbor* (2000), the editor of *Religious Experience and the End of Metaphysics* (2003) and *The Face of the Other and the Trace of God: Essays on the Philosophy of Emmanuel Levinas* (2000), and is founding series editor of *Levinas Studies: An Annual Review*.

Mauro Carbone is Professor of Aesthetics at the State University of Milan, Italy, and the author of *Il sensibile e l'eccedente. Mondo estetico, arte, pensiero* (1996), *La visibilité de l'invisible: Merleau-Ponty entre Cézanne et Proust* (2001), *The Thinking of the Sensible: Merleau-Ponty's A-Philosophy* (2004), *Una deformazione senza precedenti. Marcel Proust e le idee sensibili* (2004), and the co-author, with David Michael Levin, of *La carne e la voce. In dialogo tra estetica ed etica, Di alcuni motivi in Marcel Proust* (1998). Professor Carbone is the founder and a co-editor of the journal *Chiasmi International. Trilingual Studies concerning Merleau-Ponty's Thought*.

Javier Carreño is a doctoral scholar at the Husserl Archives: International Centre for Phenomenological Research, at the Catholic University of Louvain. He writes on Husserl's phenomenology of phantasy and pertinent issues in the philosophy of literature and in the philosophy of religion. He holds a Master's degree in philosophy from Louvain, and a Bachelor's degree in Philosophy and Literature from the University of Dallas.

Simon Critchley is Professor of Philosophy at the New School for Social Research in New York City and at the University of Essex. He is author of many books, most recently *Infinitely Demanding* (2007) and *The Book of Dead Philosophers* (forthcoming).

Conor Cunningham is lecturer in Theology at the University of Nottingham, and is Assistant Director of the Centre of Theology and Philosophy. He is author of *Genealogy of Nihilism* (2002), which has now been translated into Spanish, and the forthcoming *Evolution: Darwin's Pious Idea* (*Interventions* series, Eerdmans, 2008). Along with Peter Candler, he is the series editor of the *Veritas* series(SCM-Press) and *Interventions* series (Eerdmans)

Nicholas Davey is Professor of Philosophy and Dean of Humanities at the University of Dundee. His principal research interests are in aesthetics and hermeneutics. He has published widely in the field of Continental Philosophy, aesthetics and hermeneutic theory. His most recent book is *Unquiet Understanding, Gadamer and Philosophical Hermeneutics* (2006). He is currently working on a study of hermeneutics and aesthetics, which will appear under the title *Seeing Otherwise*.

Karl Hefty is a PhD student in Philosophy of Religion and Theology at the University of Chicago. He is writing a dissertation on Michel Henry, Maine de Biran and others.

Michel Henry was a French philosopher and novelist. He wrote five novels and a great many philosophical works, and lectured at universities in France, Belgium, the USA, and Japan. His works include *L'essence de la manifestation* (1963), *La généalogie de la psychanalyse* (1985), *La Barbarie* (1987), *Phénoménologie matérielle* (1990), *C'est moi la vérité* (1998),

Voir l'invisible: Sur Kandinsky (1998), *Incarnation. Une philosophie de la chair* (2000), and *Paroles du Christ* (2002). Michel Henry died in July 2002; it is to his memory that this volume is dedicated.

Richard Kearney is Professor of Philosophy at Boston College and University College Dublin. He is the author of numerous books on modern philosophy and culture, including *Dialogues with Contemporary Continental Thinkers* (1984), *The Poetics of Modernity* (1998), *The God Who May Be: A Hermeneutics of Religion* (2001), *Strangers, Gods and Monsters: Ideas of Otherness* (2002), *Debates in Continental Philosophy: Richard Kearney in Conversation with Contemporary Thinkers* (2004), and *The Wake of Imagination* (2005), and as well as two novels and a volume of poetry. His books have been translated into many European languages.

Nathan R. Kerr is Assistant Professor of Philosophy and Theology at Trevecca Nazarene University in Nashville, Tennessee. He is the author of several essays and articles including, most recently, 'St. Anselm: *Theoria* and the Doctrinal Logic of Perfection'. He is currently completing a book project on apocalyptic, history, and the politics of Christian mission.

Jean-Yves Lacoste is a Roman Catholic Priest, theologian and world-renowned phenomenologist, a Life Fellow of Clare College, Cambridge, and a Visiting Professor at the University of Chicago. His many publications include *Le Monde et l'absence d'oeuvre* (2000); *Note sur le temps: Essai sur les raisons de la mémoire et de l'espérance* (1990); *Expérience et absolu: Questions disputées sur l'humanité de l'homme* (1989); (*Experience and the Absolute: Disputed Questions on the Humanity of Man*, 2004); *Narnia, monde théologique?: Théologie anonyme et christologie pseudonyme* (2005); and *Presence et Parousie* (2006). He is editor of the acclaimed *Dictionnaire critique de théologie* (1998). Fr Lacoste is also writing the foreword to the forthcoming English translation of

Contributors

Michel Henry's *Parole du Christ*, to be published in the *Interventions* series (Eerdmans). He lives in Paris.

Ian Leask is a lecturer in philosophy at the Mater Dei Institute, Dublin. He enjoyed a formation in Scholastic Philosophy at Queen's, Belfast, and he has published widely in the history of philosophy and on Continental Philosophy. His publications include *Questions of Platonism* (2000) and he is the joint editor of the collection *Givenness and God: Questions of Jean-Luc Marion*, published by Fordham in 2005.

Jean Leclercq holds degrees in philology and theology. He received his doctorate of philosophy from the Catholic University of Louvain, where he is now a professor of the history of philosophy and the philosophy of religion. His research is concentrated specifically on French philosophy from the nineteenth to the twenty-first centuries, but also on the relationship between literature, theology and philosophy. He is currently the Director of the Centre d'archives Maurice Blondel (at Louvain-la-Neuve), and is also responsible for the newly arrived Michel Henry archives, deposited at Louvain University in May 2006.

Cyril McDonnell is lecturer in the Department of Philosophy in the National University Ireland, Maynooth, and tutor in philosophy with the National Distance Education Centre at Dublin City University. His areas of interest are Brentano, Husserl, Heidegger, Levinas, and the development of hermeneutics from Schleiermacher via Dilthey to Heidegger and Levinas.

John Milbank has taught at the universities of Cambridge and Virginia, and is currently Professor of Politics, Religion, and Ethics at the University of Nottingham, where he is also Director of the Centre of Theology and Philosophy. He is author of numerous articles and books, many of which have been translated into a number of languages. His most notable works include *Theology and Social Theory* (1990, 2nd edition, 2006), *The Word Made Strange* (1997), *Truth in Aquinas*, with

Contributors

Catherine Pickstock (2000), *Being Reconciled* (2003), *The Suspended Middle* (2005), and the forthcoming volume *Proposing Theology* (Veritas, SCM, 2007). Professor Milbank is series editor of *Radical Orthodoxy* (Routledge) and *Illuminations* (Blackwell).

Timothy Mooney was educated at University College Dublin and the University of Essex. He is currently Senior Lecturer in Philosophy at University College Dublin. He has co-edited *The Phenomenology Reader* with Dermot Moran (2002), and has published numerous articles in the areas of phenomenology, deconstruction and process thought.

Felix Ó Murchadha lectures in philosophy at the National University of Ireland, Galway. He studied philosophy and history for his primary degree and continued his studies in philosophy at University College Galway, University College Dublin, McMaster University (Canada) and Bergische Universität Wuppertal (Germany). He has taught in Canada, Germany, and Ireland and has published in German and English.

Michael Purcell is Senior Lecturer in Systematic Theology at the University of Edinburgh. He has published many articles, and is the author of *Levinas and Theology* (2006), *Mystery and Method: The Other in Rahner and Levinas* (1998).

Philipp W. Rosemann is Associate Professor of Philosophy at the University of Dallas. He works at the intersection of medieval thought and Continental philosophy. He is the author of a Lacanian reading of the thought of Thomas Aquinas, *Omne ens est aliquid: introduction à la lecture du "système" philosophique de saint Thomas d'Aquin* (1996), and of *Understanding Scholastic Thought with Foucault* (1999). His most recent books are an introduction to the theology of Peter Lombard (2004) and a study of how medieval and early modern theology developed in the commentaries on Peter

Lombard's famous *Book of Sentences*, entitled *The Story of a Great Medieval Book: Peter Lombard's "Sentences"* (2007). Professor Rosemann is completing a volume entitled *Transgression* for the *Interventions* series (Eerdmans).

Joeri Schrijvers holds Master's degrees in Philosophy and in Theology from the Catholic Univeristy of Louvain. He is now a doctor in theology, and working as a Postdoctoral Fellow of the Research Foundation-Flanders (FWO-V) in the research group 'Theology in a Postmodern Context' at the Department of Systematic Theology, Louvain. He has published articles on Jean-Yves Lacoste, Jean-Luc Marion, and Emmanuel Levinas.

1. Perception, Transcendence and the Experience of God

JEAN-YVES LACOSTE

God is admittedly no thing.

And when he dares be present in the world as a thing (Hegel uses the word 'thing' about the Catholic conception of the Eucharist), he does so in the sense perception perceives only as a *sacramentum*: the *res* is unperceivable.

These two inaugural sentences are not meant to suggest that a phenomenology of perception has no relevance for us. And to show that in fact it does have relevance, I propose a few steps towards a concept of divine transcendence. I shall show, first, that sense perception, in the Husserlian account, deals organically with transcendence. I shall then observe that the realm of phenomena is larger than the realm of perceived entities, and ask a few questions about what appears to us in affective experiences. Finally I will suggest one or two things about the way God appears while transcending his present apparition.

Res semper major

Two points are remarkable in Husserl's account of perception in the 1905–06 lectures on epistemology.[1] The first is that

---

1 See E. Husserl, *Wahrnehmung und Aufmerksamkeit: Texte aus dem Nachlass*, XXXVIII *Gesammelte Werke*, ed. T. Vongher and R. Giuliani (Dordrecht: Springer, 2004), pp. 3–67.

perception is an authentic acquaintance with things. The second is that the nature of things makes it humanly impossible to come to any total or perfect perception.

No reader of the *Logical Investigations* may feel any surprise when taught that perception deals with things themselves and, therefore, that we can be (in a most anti-Russellian fashion) acquainted with things. In the Husserlian treatment of perception there is no need to 'describe' a cube in order to know it. We see the cube, though sensation 'presents' only part of it to us. No need, let us be more precise, to *say* that 'the object which is now visible to me is a cube'. The cube is here 'in the flesh', *leib-haft da*. And yet what is presented here and now is not the whole thing. It is the thing as a (here-and-now) visible entity: when I say that I see the cube, or rather the cat or the pipe, I admit implicitly that I do not touch or smell them – and that my perception is alarmingly partial. But when I claim that I do see the cat or the pipe, my claim is phenomenologically (that is, philosophically) justified, as it would be justified if I did not see the cat or the pipe. One must go further. 'Perception' does not denote a punctual experience; rather it denotes what we might call perceiving life, or a slice of life. There are punctual or quasi-punctual perceptions: Husserl uses the example of a flash of lightning illuminating a landscape at night. But we perceive in time; and we can say that time is given to us ('us' means here the addition of consciousness and a sensory apparatus) to enable what Husserl calls 'synthetic' perception. I am seeing a house from a distance, and then near, and then nearer, I can eventually walk around the house, etc. Moreover, perspectives, different distances etc., all that is not to be considered as constituting different discrete perceptions, but as moments to be synthesized in a global perception. I am right to say that I see the house when I see it from afar, as well as when I walk around it. But we need no phenomenology, and only some common sense, to remark that one can see the same thing differently – in Husserlian terminology, one sees differently, but with the same *Wahrnehmungssinn,* in different acts of perception endowed with the same reference or denotation. Perceiving is a synthesis of 'adequate' and 'inadequate' perception. In the experience we are briefly describing, it is the synthesis of a present perception of the thing as it is now presented to us by sensation and of past perceptions of the thing as presented to us by memory. And in non-temporal (that is, not necessarily temporal) perception, it is the synthesis of what is now presented to us by sensation and what it 'alludes to' ('symbolic' perception) – I see an armchair, but its back is not adequately perceived.

This leads us to the second point. The wholly adequate perception, viz. the perceiving act the content of which would be the whole of the thing, or the whole of its perceivable reality (perception of atoms is impossible, and Husserl knew this) is an ideal and only an ideal. We can try to describe it and prove that ideality is no impossibility. This assertion needs to be qualified, though. The comprehensive experience of an object, in fact, has only the possibility of an infinite experience. And even if we admit that almost no perception is strictly instantaneous, and therefore that perception, as a synthesis, involves sensation, memory, and even expectation, it will be wise not to embark upon the task of comprehensive perception without a previous knowledge that what is perceived now will perhaps be forgotten, or distorted by memory, when we perceive another aspect of the same thing. Sensations present fragments of reality. Perception synthesizes these fragments. But the temporal limits of perception are obvious. Fink in his sixth *Cartesian Meditation*, pictures an ego, or a consciousness, endowed with the power of perceiving comprehensively – this over-dimensioned transcendental ego is nonetheless no human ego (a fact Fink readily admits). Contrariwise, Husserl's concept and description of consciousness, in 1905–06 (and later, indeed) are the concept and the description of human consciousness. And such a consciousness cannot be acquainted (Husserl speaks of *Bekanntheit*) with the whole of the thing (or the whole of the perceivable thing). We are well acquainted with many things: our cat, our pipe etc. But even with these old acquaintances, no eschatology of perception is conceivable. No *human* eschatology of perception.

3

This allows us to introduce cautiously a concept of transcendence. The word is absent from the 1905–06 lectures, where Husserl only reminds us that nothing appears except to consciousness, and that we cannot describe what does not appear to us – and this leads to the classical Husserlian concept of transcendence. We shall easily concede that there is no phenomenology without phenomena, and it will look tautological. But is it? The case of perception proves that it is not, or more precisely that 'appearing' is more than 'being presented by our senses'. Perception precisely deals simultaneously with what appears (what is presented by our senses) and what does not appear (what is not presented by our senses). We perceive the cube and not the 'side', *Seite,* of the cube, which is now visible to us. And as soon as we have said that we perceive the cube, though we do not perceive it 'adequately', we must add that the invisible is part of what we perceive. We do not see the invisible. But we perceive the invisible: the visible refers ('symbolically') to the invisible. Perceiving what is presented by sensation and what is presented symbolically must not be confused. I was perceiving a computer while writing this essay: a computer, and not the part of the computer my eyes and hands allowed me to perceive adequately. This, let us add, was a unitary perception: 'adequate' and 'symbolic' perception must neither be confused not be separated. And nonetheless it was an incomplete perception. The computer was partly appearing, partly unappearing. But the experience was in no way frustrating: we are natively used to the fact of things being never adequately perceived.

All this means that we are natively familiar with the fact of things always transcending their actual phenomenality. Most of the furniture of the universe is now absent from the field of my consciousness, and this does not matter. But what appears to me is partially absent as well, and this does matter. This does matter because it discloses a major law in the logic of experience. This law may be spelled out shortly: perceptive experience deals simultaneously with the phenomenal and the non-phenomenal. Or, more adequately: perceptive experience deals also with the non-perceived. Let us here take a closer look.

First point: we perceive more than our senses present to us. Describing implies necessarily a knowledge of the invisible (the inaudible, etc.), and this knowledge is granted to us by the visible. That is, the visible lets the invisible appear. Second point: one ought to be careful not to demand too exact a knowledge of the invisible (the inaudible, etc.). Husserl is careful to remark, in English, that the logic of *belief* is never far from the logic of perception. No visual sensation does present to me now, the back of my chair. I sit on it, and have sensation plus perception of its back. And yet I quite normally believe that this limited perception allows me to be conscious of sitting on the chair I normally sit on when working with my computer. But in so far as perception only is involved, this is belief. (I can reason and come to the conclusion that it is 'justified as true belief' – but this is another problem.) The first epistemological fact, in Husserlian terms, is well known, 'the originary ground of belief': it describes our relation to phenomena as well as our relation to non-phenomena. We have gone further in our reading of perception. What we face in the case of the non-appearing is a second-order belief. The first-order belief is that there are things outside the field of consciousness. The second-order belief is that what appears to us lets the non-phenomenal appear as well. It seems that Janicaud made a major phenomenological blunder when he assumed that phenomenology deals only with the visible (the audible, etc.), and that the play of sensory 'matter' and intentional 'form' gives access to the visible and the visible only.[2] No phenomenon, indeed, without a quasi-apparition of the non-phenomenon. Or in other words: there is no perception of the visible without a co-perception of the invisible. Or again: perception grasps – *Auffassung* – simultaneously the visible and the invisible.

This is not enough, and one could easily object to my assumptions. The so-called 'symbolic' perception or quasi-perception

2 D. Janicaud, 'The Theological Turn of French Phenomenology' in Janicaud *et al.* (eds), *Phenomenology and the 'Theological Turn': The French Debate* (New York: Fordham University Press, 2000), pp. 16–103.

of the invisible may turn out to be a non-perception. What I perceive as a cube may very well not be a cube. What I perceive from afar as a house may very well turn out to be a theatre setting. Verification, of course, is (almost) always possible: I just need to have a closer, longer look at things. But what am I doing when I am having this closer look? It seems I am refusing tacitly a fundamental phenomenological law, namely the primacy of intuition. 'As much intuition as possible, as less understanding as possible.' But if we have a closer look at what is going on when I have a closer look, we shall easily come to a counter-conclusion: to have access to the thing, I must have understood that perception (not only sensation but perception as well) may perpetually deceive me. Therefore, more intuition is needed. And thus, we are driven back to perception as a temporal process. And if such a process is 'required', we must conclude that the invisible has very often to become visible to be perceived.

'Transcendence', therefore, sounds like the apt word. Experience (one at least, perception) is fragmentary. Not only because it deals only with this or that, but also because this or that appears always partially, and appears in such a way that perception may perpetually be deceived. Things are here and appear 'in the flesh'. But to be faithful to what sensation presents to consciousness, 'signs' and 'symbols' must be interpreted (the interpretation is tacit and intuitive, of course) with care or 'flair'. Does what is presented to me point to the presence of a house? No hasty 'conclusion' is allowed.[3] Signs and symbols may always be pseudo-signs and pseudo-symbols. And we may eventually take leave of pure perception, and ask reasoning to come to the help of the party, to decipher them.

These are no grounds for despair. We believe originarily in the transcendent existence of the world and of things in the

---

3 'Conclusion' means here what it can mean, according the late Husserl (namely in *Experience and Judgment*), in the case of ante-predicative experience. There is no need to add that *Experience and Judgment*, though Landgrebe edited the work in 1939, uses much earlier manuscripts.

world, and we know originarily, or natively, that perceptive comprehension is forbidden to us. Each perceptive experience, therefore, provides us with an opportunity to acknowledge its fragmentary nature (I feel the chair I am sitting on, I do not see it, etc.), to acknowledge that the thing transcends what is presented to me here and now. In this way we have already noticed that we cannot rely on the time which is given to us. Everything available to sensation transcends perception. Everything is critical of my perception of it: *res semper major*.

Fühlen von etwas

This was not a conclusion but my first point. And let me hasten to add that phenomenology is definitely not to be reduced to a theory of sense perception. Phenomenology deals with phenomena, and it belongs to the definition of the phenomenon that it 'appears'. But what does 'appearing' mean? A quick look back at the distinction between what is 'presented' to consciousness and what is 'grasped' by consciousness will be enough to prove that the field of phenomenality is wider than the field of perceivable entities. Things appear, but other entities appear, that is, are presented to consciousness in one way or another. Numbers appear, though they are devoid of any perceptibility. Values appear (something Scheler is not the only phenomenologist to have noted). The ego appears to itself (always partially, and we do not need a psychoanalyst to say so). And if it is phenomenologically axiomatic that consciousness is always intentional, the 'aboutness' of consciousness implies that perceivable entities are only one subset among the set of appearing entities; and that proves that non-perceivable entities are as transcendent to consciousness as perceivable entities are. I began with remarks borrowed from Husserl's 1905–06 lectures; my last observations lead us back to the *Logical Investigations* and even to the *Philosophy of Arithmetics*. (And, as a matter of fact, Husserl never forgot, even in his last works, that he had written the *Logical Investigations*.)

Phenomenology started its career with an anti-psychologism battle-cry. And although the 'thing' came later, in the post-Second World War Heidegger, to receive a highly determined and idiosyncratic meaning, its Husserlian meaning is under-determined through and through: a value is a 'thing'; a number is a 'thing'; the Other Man is a 'thing'; etc. Things so appear to consciousness (this is a redundancy, of course: appearing is appearing to consciousness). Things, on the other hand, are not products of consciousness. A logical law is not a psychological law. A number is not reducible to my awareness that 2+2=4. The *modus ponens* or number 2, when they appear to me, is of course immanent to consciousness. But beware! Their existence in the field of consciousness is pseudo-existence (a non-Husserlian term), and the originary task of phenomenology is to stick to their real, extra-psychological existence.

I have just made use of a very broad concept of existence, and said that numbers, logical laws, values etc. 'existed'. This was unobjectionable, for one reason: numbers and values have the same right to appear to us that cats and pipes also have. Segregation here would be a bad starting point, because phenomenology is interested in all phenomena, however they appear to us. This may be eventually objectionable, though, and I have just said why: because there is not a unique and uniform way of appearing. The cat appears to me, the logical law appears to me (we have only, to make such an assertion, to purify 'appearing' from all visual connotation). But I perceive the cat, and I do not perceive the logical law (I can perceive logical symbols, but there is no need to prove that they are not the logical law). In both cases, the cat and the *modus ponens*, I can speak of acquaintance, *Bekanntheit* (Russell, by the way, is ready to speak of 'acquaintance' in the case of certain math-ematical objects). What is self-evident, though, is that we are dealing here and there with very different modes of phenomen-ality. And if there are different modes of phenomenality, we need only to take one step in order to suggest that there are different modes of phenomenality because there are different modes of being.

And here, a differentiated concept of existence becomes necessary. If I may take leave of Husserl for a few instants, let me remark that Heidegger has names and concepts for many modes of being; for 'existence', which is the mode of being proper to humanity; for 'life', which is the mode of being proper to the animal; for 'being-at-hand', which is the mode of being proper to objects; and for 'subsistence', which is the mode of being proper to mathematical objects. The list is Heidegger's, and in no way exhaustive (what of the mode of being proper to the angels, or to God?). But it is certainly sufficient for our purpose. Let us say, then, that number 2 subsists, and that the pipe is 'objectively present':[4] two very different entities, two very different modes of being. We have already noticed that the pipe does not appear as number 2 appears. Conclusion, therefore: each mode of being has its own mode of phenomenality. I am sorry, here, to be immensely trivial. My conclusion is not to be found *expressis verbis* in the Husserlian corpus, but it is a well-known Husserlian axiom that 'to any fundamental form of objectivity . . . belongs a fundamental form of self-evidence'. And as self-evidence is a property of phenomena, I am adding nothing to my sources. A pity. I shall not have to be pitied, though, if we remark that this has its bearings on the phenomenological status of transcendence. Here and there, in the realm of perception or in the realm of non-perceivable phenomena, we are facing transcendence: transcendence of the number, transcendence of the pipe, etc. But do we exactly deal with transcendence, singular? If I am right, we do not: we deal with transcendences, plural. The pipe and the cat are out there, but nobody will believe that numbers are out there – nobody, even the most aggressive Platonist among philosophers of mathematics. There is no place to locate numbers. They subsist

---

4 'Objective presence' translates *Vorhandenheit* in J. Stambaugh's translation of *Sein und Zeit* (Albany, NY: SUNY Press, 1996). Robinson and Macquarrie say 'presence at-hand'. Martin Heidegger, *Being and Time*, tr. J. Macquarrie and E. Robinson (New York: Harper & Row, 1962).

nowhere, and first of all not in our mind. As Desanti once said, 'mathematics belong neither to the earth nor to heaven'. And this electivity of mathematical objects is a mode of transcendence, more precisely a mode of transcendence mathematical entities do not share with any other set of entities. Modes of being, plural, modes of appearing, plural, modes of transcendence, plural. I think that my conclusions, though I have argued quickly, are only a short gloss in the margins of Husserl.

Let me hasten to add that I have bracketed an embarrassing case. We have assumed, while having a first glance at phenomenality, that phenomenality was a property of the other – and, for that matter, of any other. And therefore, no theory of phenomenality could be constructed without the help of a concept of transcendence. But what about myself? That I am acquainted with myself is obvious (which does not imply that I am perfectly acquainted with myself). That any experience of some other thing is a co-experience of myself is also obvious. But though things keep appearing to me, they appear in the sphere of immanence of consciousness (an elementary fact which will eventually enable me to describe them faithfully without the slightest interest for their transcendent reality – one speaks of 'reduction' in the case of such descriptions). That the transcendent becomes immanent in so far as it acquires phenomenality raises no major problem or no problem at all. One could call perception to the dock and suggest that the unachievable task of perceiving provides us with an argument in favour of the transcendence of things. The question is still here, nonetheless: can we say that the self appears to himself? Existence of course can always appear to existence (in the Heideggerian *Fürsorge*, in the Levinasian 'epiphany', etc.). More humbly, intersubjectivity (in the Husserlian sense) is always possible. And here and there, an other man appears as criticizing his (always possible) reduction to the status of the intentional object. But do I appear to myself? As I have just said, I am certainly acquainted with myself. I can also perceive myself. Pain, for instance, enters the field of consciousness as well as a pipe or a tune enter it. Perceiving, suffering, feeling etc.: wherever consciousness is present, intentionality is also present, and no intentionality is deprived of an object – of course.

I do not claim to have given an answer to the problem of 'self-appearing'. But we have noticed at least a telling case: the case of feeling. When we speak of feeling, a fortunate native speaker of German will have two concepts at his or her disposal: *Gefühl*, that is, absolute feeling ('I am feeling well') and *Fühlen von etwas*, that is, intentional feeling, feeling endowed with an object – for instance a 'value', if we agree here with Scheler. We are feeling well, or we are feeling alone, or we are feeling a pain, or we are feeling that this music is beautiful, or we are feeling that this behaviour is morally shocking, etc.: we can legitimately use the same word. We are affected by music 'as' we are affected by a toothache and as we are affected, to give a non-Schelerian and non-Husserlian example, by the threats of nothingness as disclosed by anxiety. Scheler, nonetheless, makes an important point when he proposes his distinction between *Gefühl* and *Fühlen von etwas*. To the concept of feeling, it does not belong to have an object. Heidegger, to come back to him, distinguishes fear – which is always *fear-of* – and anxiety, which has no object. We can disagree and argue that anxiety has no object only because it has no limited object – but that it has as its object a reality (nothingness) that transcends all objectivity. But never mind (here). The unforgettable lesson we have to receive, not from a *consensus phenomenologorum* which we could not trace, but at least from the main tenets of all phenomenology, is fairly clear: between 'intentional' and 'non-intentional' feeling, we ought to draw a dividing line, but we are unfortunately unable to do so.

Am I feeling 'something'? A preliminary answer is that some entities can only be felt ('aesthetic' values are the best example), and/or that affection ('affection', to translate Heidegger's *Befindlichkeit*[5]) has a genuine cognitive power. This unfortunately is not enough, and we must add that this cognitive power

---

5 I follow Emmanuel Martineau, as we ought all to do. See his *Etre et temps* (Paris: Authentica, 1985), p. 310.

is not something we can rely on whatever appears to us. Values, for instance, are remarkably vague entities which, in most cases, appear only to the member of this or that community: Schönberg's music will not appear to the musically uneducated as it appears to a modern music addict; and what appears to me as wicked will not appear as morally evil to the standard Islamic terrorist. Values, moreover, can be deprived of any phenomenality. The philistine, looking at a work of art, may very well perceive only an object among all objects and feel nothing except the presence of an object to be compared with any other – and which is not more 'valuable' than any other. And which is more, what I feel may be only myself, or rather my being an existing entity, that is, my being-in-the-world, in one or another way. Feeling at ease, feeling lonely, feeling anxious, these affective tonalities disclose nothing except myself (and we can claim, at least, to know here how to understand the problem of 'self-appearing'). Affection may be cognitive – I readily admit that it is. But this does not mean that things or entities perpetually affect me. I may be affected by myself or by the world (and both may be equivalent). Being affected, therefore, may very well mean becoming acquainted with this or that. But it may also mean being acquainted with myself and/or the world. And if affection disclosed purely our finiteness to us, as it does in the phenomenon of anxiety, it will inevitably lead us not to be affected by the work of art which is now presented to us, but which we do not 'let appear' as it is. I am anxious, and therefore I feel 'nothing'. Feeling 'nothing', viz. the paradoxical presence of nothingness, I do feel indeed. And in so far as I do feel, I cannot co-feel, if I may say so, what I am only able to see or to hear. Values, thus, perhaps appear to us, but we have also to make them appear to us. And this task, which belongs roughly to 'attention', requires often more than attention: one needs more than attention to get rid of anxiety and let the work of art appear to us as a work of art and not as an object among all objects.

Again, do I feel 'something', or do I feel myself as (in most cases but certainly not in all cases) being-in-the-world? We very often cannot decide. We certainly would like to decide whether what happens in us comes from us (from a sphere of radical immanence) or transcends us. It would be unwise, though, to become the preys of some 'phenomenological purism'. What appears to us in the course of our affective life, and when we scrutinize this life, is rarely pure presentation of the self and his world to himself, or pure presentation of a transcendent entity to the self. There are cases of pure presentation: perfect attention to the work of art will bracket everything but the work of art and its appearing. But there are cases when we cannot have a sure opinion about what is appearing to us – and these cases are certainly more interesting for us today. I may feel something, I may feel the transcendental conditions of experience (that is, what Heidegger calls the 'world'), I may be affected by the world while hearing this or that, but I cannot both feel myself as being-in-the-world and feel some transcendent entity. And, which is worse, I very often cannot decide what the 'meaning' (the Husserlian *Sinn*) of my feeling is. Before Husserl, Meinong had noticed that emotions 'presented' something to consciousness. It must be clear, by now, that the case of sense perception and the case of emotive perception are not analogical. The disanalogy is obvious. In the first case, we can always give a name to the object of our experience. In the second, we cannot do it always. A pity for W. Alston, who would like to convince us that 'Christian Mystical Experience' (his words) is as reliable as sense perception and perfectly analogous to it.[6]

Parousia

It is high time to ask whether we can make room for the Absolute, or God (as German idealism is dead, we can use safely the concept of the Absolute), in the problematic we have

---

6 W. P. Alston, *Perceiving God: The Epistemology of Religious Experience* (Ithaca and London: Cornell, 1991). For a better understanding of Alston's argument, see his *The Reliability of Sense Perception* (Ithaca and London: Cornell, 1993).

sketched. A preliminary question must be answered: can God 'appear' to us, or be 'presented' to us, viz. to consciousness? Can a phenomenal 'content' have the Absolute as its definite 'reference', *Sinn*? And, therefore, can we be acquainted (is *Bekanntheit* possible) with the Absolute? Let us not forget that acquaintance, in phenomenological terms, is an offspring of intuition and not of a discursive-conceptual work. And let us remember that in the mainstream of the Christian tradition (the one I know reasonably well), intuition of God, 'vision', is an eschatological event: that here and now we do not see, but believe (if we are wise enough to do so). What of these objections and of their consequences?

We may give a first and negative answer. Some experiences, of the emotive variety, claim to have God as their object. And against them, we can easily develop a strategy akin to John of the Cross: 'if you feel, this is not God'. This is a good strategy, and it leads to an important point. What we feel in 'religious' experiences may be described as the sacred, or the (Heideggerian) proximity of 'divine beings', more adequately than the Absolute. And even the chief believer in the existence of a *sensus divinus* innate in human beings is careful to say that this sixth sense allows us to know for sure that there is a God, and not that we feel it. To John of the Cross and his followers (myself included), though, we may nonetheless object that we have no right to forbid the Absolute from appearing to us, and from doing so in the realm of affection. I concede that the God of Abraham, Isaac and Jacob cannot be conceived of as a potential intentional object. But we have a right to describe, first, and then a right to have a respectable concept of divine transcendence. A well-known God cannot appear to us: the God known as Wholly Other – probably Plotinus' *thatéron,* certainly not Augustine's *valde aliud*, of course the modern *ganz Anderes*. And it is very unfortunate for Otto's descriptions (and, as a matter of fact, for Barth's early theology) that they can find names, concepts and contents of experience to identify the presence or proximity of this God. A Wholly Other God, after all, ought to appear as 'numinous' and yet beyond the numinous, as fascinating and yet as beyond all fascination, etc. He ought to appear as Other and Non-Other, *valde aliud* and *non aliud*. He ought to criticize every experience that claims to be an experience 'of God' (he does it in Barth, of course – and he does it in Balthasar, who, very surprisingly, bores us with *das Ganz Andere* throughout his best small book[7]). And this suggests that the concept of abstract otherness, or abstract transcendence, can leads us nowhere. I am not reneging on what I have just said, or said elsewhere; the ambiguity of feelings and emotions is still perfectly valid. Can God nonetheless, despite the disanalogy between perception and affection, appear to us, if I may say so, 'in the flesh'? I think we can argue in favour of this hypothesis.

In an all-important passage of *Being and Time*, Heidegger describes affection, *Befindlichkeit*, as endowed with cognitive abilities. He then praises Scheler for having rediscovered these abilities, following impulses by Augustine and Blaise Pascal. And there, in footnote 3 to section 29, he quotes both Augustine and Pascal. According to Augustine, *non intratur in veritatem nisi per caritatem*:[8] one does not reach truth except through love. And according to Pascal, who develops Augustine's maxim, 'in the case we are speaking of human things, it is said to be necessary to know them before we can love . . . But the saints, on the contrary, when they speak of divine things, say we must love them before we know them, and that we enter into truth only through charity.'[9] We can prove *ab absurdo* the rightness of the argument. Could God appear to us and not be loved? Can we figure an experience of a non-lovable God? Otto's *mysterium tremendum et fascinosum*, admittedly, is no lovable object. The primal experience in Schleiermacher's *Christian Faith* (that is, the feeling of absolute dependence) makes no

---

7 See *Glaubhaft is nur Liebe* (Einsiedeln: Johannes Verlag, 1963). A surprising thing in a book devoted to proving the kind of cognoscibility belonging to a God who reveals himself.

8 Augustine, *Contra Faustum Manichaeum libri triginta tres, Opera Omnia*, PL 42, 32.18.

9 *Sein und Zeit*, tr. Stambaugh, pp. 403–4.

room for love. And I am ready to admit that in such experiences, if we stick to interpreting them from a theological point of view, God hides himself more than he discloses himself. What I have just said, nonetheless, was no slip of the tongue, and I intend to suggest that God can appear, paradoxically, as a hidden God – or more precisely, that it belongs to God's disclosure that his hiddenness is ever greater.

Let us say, first, that all varieties of 'religious experience' are vague occurrences, the affective 'content' of which does not allow us to decide whether the religious person is facing God or an idol, or rather God or the sacred, as immanent to the Heideggerian 'Fourfold'. And let us suggest that it is illegitimate to believe that some criterion or some conceptual distinction (for instance, Levinas's distinction between the 'sacred' and the 'holy') could allow us always to draw a boundary between experiences which 'grasp' in some way the Absolute and experiences which fail to do so. Here again, one cannot interpret the logic of feeling if one does not perceive this intrinsic vagueness. In many cases, of course, our object is not vague: to take an example, 'pagan spiritualities', which are by no means dead, are not disclosures of God however – they disclose the earth, both in the precise Heideggerian meaning of the word and in the simple, non-conceptual meaning contemporary pagans give to the same word. In many other cases, though, and these are the theoretically challenging cases, vagueness is essential to experience. Such experiences are certainly 'religious'. But do they stand under the protection of God? We cannot exclude the possibility that the experience into which Schleiermacher was initiating the reader of his *Speeches* can disclose God in some way – but we cannot exclude the possibility that this experience hides God more than it discloses him. This is our problem.

Nevertheless, let me suggest, and this is my second point, that it belongs to any truthful experience of God to be infinitely partial. This is a truism. Truisms may be useful, though. The old motto, *Deus semper major,* has an eschatological meaning: though generations of Latin theologians have used the word, we shall never be *comprehensores*. It has also a historic content, and we shall focus on it. Let us say, then, that a partial experience of God is nonetheless an experience of God. Properly understood (that is, with a generous use of the principle of charity), Schleiermacher's 'feeling of absolute dependence' presents God to the subject of this feeling: partly, but adequately. But the relgous or Christian person, does not learn from affection only: Scriptures and creeds teach us more than affection does. But we are feeling animals, all presence is meant to be felt and, as I have said, the God we would deprive of the right to be felt would be a weak God. If God is to be thought as the Infinite, a very apt concept in our context, his disclosure cannot be a parousia. Disclosure nonetheless, and disclosure in the field of affective life, must be accepted as a perpetual possibility. Most disclosures after all are partial – any analysis of intersubjectivity would provide us with ample material.

The idea of a process of disclosure-and-hiding, or hiding-in-disclosure, then, ought not to raise any theoretical problem. Sense perception 'grasps', but wholly 'adequate' sense perception is only an ideal. Aesthetic emotion 'grasps' the beauty of a work of art, but it does not take possession of it once for all. And if no experience can make the Absolute available to us, though the Absolute may be truly presented to us here or there, then God's hyperbolic transcendence may be elucidated, *juxta modum,* as we elucidate any transcendence – that is, any non-divine transcendence provides us with a pre-understanding of divine transcendence. Another suggestion: should we not say that we have to wait until God is (affectively) present to us to know clearly what transcendence means after the Husserlian breakthrough? This second suggestion is probably the right one. I have spoken of God being here 'in the flesh', and this was no allusion to an incarnation. It meant, simply, that we might be conscious of his presence and no other – which God may appear to us, not according to the laws of theophanies, but in the modest way of his presence being felt. Peter's presence does not provide me with a 'comprehensive' affective knowledge of Peter: I just know that this one is Peter; I am acquainted with him though I keep discovering new aspects of his personality, etc. Peter is visible and God is invisible. But in both cases, we are not dealing with an apocalyptic disclosure of any sort. It will take years to become 'perfectly acquainted' with Peter, if it is possible at all. And can we say it is possible to become 'perfectly acquainted' with God?

We are again back to the problem of 'phenomenology and the invisible', with the surprising conclusion that a phenomenology which would deal exclusively with what is presented to consciousness would be a short-lived enterprise. We have come to say that the Absolute may be felt as present – the Absolute in the flesh – but that his presence is no parousia. The God 'the heart can feel' (the words are Pascal's) is therefore both present and absent. It would not raise any difficulty, moreover, to prove that our feeling of his absence grows in proportion with our feeling of his presence: to paraphrase loosely the Fourth Lateran Council,[10] to prove that *non potest praesentia sentiri, quin etiam major sit absentia sentienda.* No 'God' is at our disposal except the idol. And the fact that the heart may feel both God's presence and absence, and always a greater absence, is the cornerstone of all hermeneutics of so-called 'religious experiences'. God is unfelt more than he is felt. Anticipations of his eschatological presence, that is, his parousia, may very well be granted to privileged witnesses. But in the everydayness proper to our experience of God, we have to be satisfied with sheer non-eschatological presence. This does not mean, of course, that we have to bracket all *knowledge* of God being immensely more than we feel he is, or to bracket all desire to 'see' what is presently 'invisible', viz. to feel what is presently out of reach of affection. God's presence, in so far as 'presence' is understood as present to the 'heart', is essentially frustrating. Anticipations may be enjoyed, but the God whose presence we

---

10 See the Fourth Lateran Council (1215) document *Constitutiones,* 2: *De errore abbatis Iochim.* For the Latin text with English translation, see N. P. Tanner (ed.), *Decrees of the Ecumenical Councils,* vol. 1: *Nicaea I to Lateran V* (London: Sheed & Ward; Washington: Georgetown University Press, 1990), pp. 231–3.

enjoy is more to be desired than to be enjoyed. And consequent quietism (though I do not think any historical form of quietism has been that consequent) could be accused of ignoring the way the Absolute is presented to us, both in disclosure and in hiddenness.

We perceive houses, though only part of the house is adequately presented to us. We feel the presence of God, though nothing more than presence, and no parousia, is given to us. We shall be wise not to think that the *mysterium tremendum et fascinosum* is equivalent to the mystery of God (might an experience of a faceless mystery be an experience of God?). We shall concede, perhaps, that a 'feeling of absolute dependence' is a sure index of the presence of God: and this will mean that Schleiermacher's God discloses himself when he is present as the Almighty. We shall not concede, of course, that God is only (or first of all) presented to us as the Almighty. And we shall certainly refuse the right for any particular kind of experience to be paradigmatic of an affective experience of God. God is not *only* the Almighty – this is the *articulus stantis et cadentis* of any theology (not only Schcleiermacher's) with a starting point in affective experience. It is true; nonetheless, that God only is the Almighty. But we cannot spell it out in both a philosophically and theologically respectable way if we do not confess the essential partiality of affective life.

And so we are back to the logic of love and the paradoxical priority of love over knowledge. It is not necessary to insist on an elementary fact: love is affective, but affection cannot be reduced to the experience of love. The same Heidegger who quotes Augustine and Pascal on the cognitive power of this precise affective experience – *love* – does not describe in the following sections of *Being and Time* any experience involving 'love' or 'charité'. Nor does Heidegger feel any need to mention the love of God. This is a puzzle for the historian of philosophy, and we have no time here to solve it. But we can make suggestions (and it will not be detrimental if they turn out to be at least partly correct).

The first is that love desires what theology calls 'vision', and

what we have called 'parousia' – nothing less. This sounds innocent. But does it not imply that love knows, or feels, precisely,
that God's presence in the world is only presence, and that more
than presence is needed to give rest? Love, needless to say, is
intentional through and through. I do not love: I love Peter,
Paul or God (or the three of them together, of course). If I love
Peter, I desire Peter's presence (and we must admit that this
desire, too, is doomed to be frustrated: Peter's presence is not
parousiac, *pace* Levinas). But, more importantly, if I love God
as he is present to me in the world, I can but know that he transcends every 'side' – every Husserlian *Seite* – of himself that is
here disclosed to me now.

A second point, or a corollary, is that we can refuse implicitly
the transcendence of God and, therefore, love an idol. Could we
not suspect that realized eschatology, in all its forms, from
Hegel to Bultmann, is guilty of idol-worship? Hegel's knowledge of God is unsurpassable. Bultmann's experience of God
is unsurpassable. Here and there, no room for a *desiderium
videndi Deum,* no acknowledgement of God's ever greater
divinity: a fact which proves, perhaps, that Hegel and Bultmann
know no other love of God than an *amor Dei intellectualis* – or
that they love theology more than God. And if we think that
God is *offenbar,* and/or when we have no room left for hope, I
suspect, again, that idolatry is not far off.

A third point, then, by way of a rough conclusion: God may
be presented to us in intentional affective experiences is both *de
jure* and *de facto*. That God, or the 'divine god', criticizes all
affective grasps, is a matter of common sense. And that he is
affectively present to us in a non-parousiac way is also a trivial
matter of fact. To say it more simply: God's phenomenality
cannot be understood if we do not understand that God
transcends his phenomenality. Parousia, to be sure, does not
contradict presence. But we cannot understand divine presence,
that is, that this presence is divine, if we do not look for
parousia. And I suggest that love only understands, first that
presence is presence, and second that presence is *only* presence.

2. Originary Inauthenticity – On Heidegger's *Sein und Zeit*[1]

SIMON CRITCHLEY

> *The past beats within me, like a second heart.*
> John Banville, *The Sea*

Although its author still invites controversy and polemic, and its theses invite much misunderstanding, there is no doubting the originality and massive influence of Heidegger's *Sein und Zeit*, first published in 1927. Some would argue that it is the most important work of philosophy published in the twentieth century. In this paper, I will attempt to give a reinterpretation of Heidegger's *Sein und Zeit* through an internal commentary of the text in its own terms rather than through some sort of external and potentially reductive reading. I will do this by

---

1 This paper was first presented at the American Philosophical Association, Eastern Division, December 2005, 'Perspectives in Analytic and Continental Philosophy'. All references to *Sein und Zeit* (hereafter *SuZ*) are to the pagination of the 15th edition (Niemeyer, Tübingen, 1984), which can be found in the margins of English translations of the text. Allow me a brief word of explanation about this paper. It is the revised and still unfinished version of a paper first published in 2002, called 'Enigma Variations: An Interpretation of Heidegger's *Sein und Zeit*', *Ratio*, 15.2 (June 2002), pp. 154–75. I had long wanted to go back to it as I became unhappy with the formulation of certain of my claims, particularly towards the end of the original paper. While I feel that the basic line of interpretation is still plausible, a year of intensive Heidegger teaching at the New School for Social Research in 2005 gave me the occasion to revise my views.

focusing on two phrases that provide a clue to what is going on in *Sein und Zeit*: *Dasein ist geworfener Entwurf* and *Dasein existiert faktisch* ('*Dasein* is thrown projection' and '*Dasein* exists factically'). I begin by trying to show how an interpretation of these phrases can help to clarify Heidegger's philosophical claim about what it means to be human. I then try to explain why it is that, in a couple of important passages in *Sein und Zeit*, Heidegger describes thrown projection as an *enigma*. I trace the use of enigma in *Sein und Zeit*, and try and show how and why the relations between Heidegger's central conceptual pairings – state-of-mind (*Befindlichkeit*) and understanding (*Verstehen*), thrownness and projection, facticity and existentiality – are described by Heidegger as enigmatic. My thesis is that at the heart of *Sein und Zeit*, that is, at the heart of the central claim of the *Dasein*-analytic as to the temporal character of thrown-projective being-in-the-world, there lies an enigmatic a priori. That is to say, there is something resiliently opaque at the basis of the constitution of *Dasein*'s being-in-the-world which both resists phenomenological description and which is that in relation to which the phenomenologist describes. In the more critical part of the paper, I try to show with more precision how this notion of the enigmatic a priori changes the basic experience of understanding *Sein und Zeit*. I explore this in relation to three examples that are absolutely central to the argument of Division II: death, conscience and temporality. I seek to read Heidegger's analyses of each of these concepts against the grain in order to bring into view much more resilient notions of facticity and thrownness that place in doubt the move to existentiality, projection and authenticity. This is the perspective that I will describe as *originary inauthenticity*. As will become clear in due course, this line of interpretation has significant consequences for how we might consider the political consequences of Heidegger's work, in particular – and infamously – the question of his political commitment to National Socialism in 1933.

* * *

There are two phrases that provide a clue to what is going on in *Sein und Zeit*: *Dasein ist geworfener Entwurf* and *Dasein existiert faktisch*. That is, *Dasein* – Heidegger's word for the person or human being – has a double, or articulated structure: it is at once thrown and the projection or throwing-off of thrownness. Yet it is a throwing *off* – which is how I interpret the privative *Ent-* in *Ent-Wurf* – that remains *in* the throw. As Heidegger puts it, *Dasein im Wurf bleibt* (*SuZ* 179). *Dasein* is always sucked into the turbulence of its own projection. *Dasein* is the name of a recoiling movement that unfolds only to fold back on itself. Its existentiality, its projective being-ahead-of-itself, is determined through and through by facticity, it is always already thrown in a world, and in a world, moreover, ontically determined in terms of fallenness: the tranquillized bustle of *das Man* ('the one' or 'the they'). This movement of thrown throwing off or factical existence is the structure of *Sorge*, the care that defines the being of *Dasein* in *Sein und Zeit*. Heidegger summarizes the structure of care with enigmatic formulae, such as 'Dasein ist befindliches Verstehen' ('*Dasein* is state-of-minded, or disposed understanding', *SuZ* 260); or again, 'Jedes Verstehen hat seine Stimmung. Jede Befindlichkeit ist verstehend' ('Every understanding has its mood. Every state-of-mind or disposition understands', *SuZ* 335). The principal thesis of the published portion of *Sein und Zeit* is that the meaning of care, where meaning is defined as that upon which (*das Woraufhin*, *SuZ* 324) the thrown throwing off of *Dasein* takes place, is temporality (*Zeitlichkeit*). Simply stated, the meaning of the being of *Dasein* is time. With the term temporality, Heidegger seeks to capture the passage from authentic to inauthentic time and back again. That is, the masterfulness of what Heidegger calls 'ecstatic' temporality, consummated in the notion of the *Augenblick* (moment of vision, or blink of the eye) always falls back into the passive awaiting (*Gewärtigen*, *SuZ* 337) of inauthentic time. Thrown projection or factical existing is ultimately the activity of *Dasein*'s temporalizing, its *Zeitigung*, an articulated, recoiling movement, between sinking away in the dullness of the everyday and momentarily gaining mastery over the everyday by not choosing *das Man* as one's hero.

Once this structure begins to become clear, then it can also be seen that thrown projection or factical existing defines the concept of truth. For Heidegger, truth is also a double or articulated movement of concealment and unconcealment that he finds lodged in the Greek term *aletheia*. In Paragraph 44, the famous discussion of truth in *Sein und Zeit* (with an important emphasis that goes missing in the Macquarrie and Robinson translation), Heidegger writes:

> Die existenzial-ontologische Bedingung dafür, daß das In-der-Welt-sein durch 'Wahrheit' und 'Unwahrheit' bestimmt ist, liegt in *der* Seinsverfassung des Daseins, die wir als *geworfenen Entwurf* kennzeichneten. (*SuZ* 223)

> (The existential-ontological condition for being-in-the-world being determined through 'truth' and 'untruth' lies in *the* [the italics, and hence the linguistic and conceptual force of the definite article is missing in Macquarrie and Robinson] constitution of the Being of Dasein that we have designated as *thrown projection*.)

That is, the condition of possibility for the play of truth and untruth in *aletheia* is the claim for *Dasein* as thrown projection. In his later work, however, Heidegger always wants to read *Sein und Zeit* from the perspective of what he calls 'the history of being' (*Seinsgeschichte*) by claiming that the 'lethic' element in truth already implies an insight into *Seinsvergessenheit*, the forgetfulness or oblivion of being. Therefore, although Heidegger will admit in his later work that *Sein und Zeit* expresses itself metaphysically, it already implies an insight into the history of being and thereby into what he calls 'the overcoming of metaphysics' (*die Überwindung der Metaphysik*). This is how – in a manner that I always find questionable because of the complete assurance with which Heidegger feels himself able to shape and control the interpretation of his work – Heidegger continually seeks to preserve the unity of what he calls his *Denkweg*, his path of thought. To use Heidegger's own idiom from a manuscript on nihilism from the late 1940s, we might say that the basic experience (*die Grunderfahrung*) of *Sein und Zeit* is this belonging together of facticity and existence, of thrownness and projection, of fallenness and surmounting. It remains a hypothesis to be confirmed or disconfirmed by future research as to whether this is the basic experience of Heidegger's work as a whole.[2]

So, what is the being of being human for Heidegger? Or, in so far as the human being is understood as *Dasein* whose essence lies in *Existenz,* what is the nature of existence? It is care as a temporally articulated movement of thrown throwing off or factical existing. My concern here consists in working out why Heidegger describes this structure as an *enigma* and what might be the implications of this claim for an interpretation of *Sein und Zeit.* Once the claim for *Dasein* as thrown projection is introduced in Paragraph 31 on *Verstehen* (*SuZ* 148), which is also where the word enigma makes its most significant entry into *Sein und Zeit,* then the rest of the book is simply the deepening or nuancing of this structure, like a leitmotif in Wagner, moving through a series of variations. Let's call them 'enigma variations', to use an English rather than a German example, Elgar rather than Wagner. What fascinates me in *Sein und Zeit* is what I would call the spinning or oscillating movement of these variations, where Heidegger tries to capture this enigma in a series of oxymoronic formulations: *Dasein existiert faktisch, Dasein ist Geworfener Entwurf, Dasein ist befindliche Verstehen, Jedes Verstehen hat seine Stimmung, Jede Befindlichket ist verstehend, 'Dasein ist in der Wahrheit' sagt gleichursprünglich ... 'Dasein ist in der Unwahrheit'*, etc. etc. (*'Dasein*

---

2 In this regard, see the interesting *Beilagen* to 'Das Wesen des Nihilismus', in *Metaphysik und Nihilismus*, Gesamtausgabe vol. 67 (Frankfurt a.M: Klostermann, 1999), pp. 259–67. See especially, pp. 265–6, where Heidegger claims that the essence of nihilism in *Sein und Zeit* is located in the thought of *das Verfallen*, which is the condition of possibility for the surmounting (*Überstieg*) of that fallenness.

is in the truth' simultaneously says . . . '*Dasein* is in the untruth', *SuZ* 222). As I shall try and make clear presently, the thought which is spinning out or being spun out in *Sein und Zeit* is that of *Dasein* as the enigma of a temporal stretch, an almost rhythmical movement or *kinesis* of factical existing that is so obvious, so absolutely and completely obvious, that it is quite obscure. As Wittgenstein notes, 'The aspects of things that are most important for us are hidden because of their simplicity and everydayness (*Alltäglichkeit*). (One is unable to notice something – because it is always before one's eyes.)'[3]

The word *Rätsel,* enigma or riddle, kept catching my eye when reading certain key passages from *Sein und Zeit,* so I decided to try and follow its usage systematically. I have found at least eleven places where the words enigma (*Rätsel*), enigmatic (*Rätselhaftig*) and enigmaticity (*Rätselhaftigkeit*) are used in *Sein und Zeit* (*SuZ* 4, 136, 137, 148[x2], 371, 381, 387, 389, 392, 425), and I will examine these below. The word enigma also appears in Heidegger's later work, in particular in his 1942 lecture course on 'Der Ister', which I discuss elsewhere.[4]

Returning to *Sein und Zeit,* in the opening paragraph Heidegger writes that 'in jedem Verhalten und Sein zu Seiendem als Seiendem apriori ein Rätsel liegt' (*SuZ* 4). That is, in every comporting oneself to beings, or intentional relation to things, there lies an a priori enigma. This claim already begins to strike a rather dissonant note with the formulation of the phenomenological notion of the a priori in the first draft of *Sein und Zeit* in the 1925 *Prolegomena zur Geschichte des Zeitbegriffs* that I discuss in detail elsewhere, where the a priori is that which shows itself in what Husserl calls 'categorial intuition'.[5] It would seem that the intentional comportment of the phenomenologist

3 L. Wittgenstein, *Philosophical Investigations*, tr. G. E. M. Anscombe (Oxford: Blackwell, 1958), no. 129.

4 M. Heidegger, *Hölderlins Hymne 'Der Ister'* (Frankfurt a.M: Klostermann, 1984). I discuss the latter in 'Enigma Variations', pp. 158–9.

5 See 'Heidegger for Beginners' in J. Faulconer and M. Wrathall (eds), *Appropriating Heidegger* (Cambridge: Cambridge University Press, 2000), pp. 101–18.

directs itself towards, and itself arises out of, something that eludes phenomenological manifestation. This 'something' is what I call the *enigmatic a priori*.

However, the form that this enigmatic a priori takes in *Sein und Zeit* becomes much more striking in Paragraphs 29 and 31, on *Stimmung, Befindlichkeit* and *Verstehen*. Heidegger writes that *Stimmung* (mood) brings *Dasein* to 'the That of its There' ('das Daß seines Da') in a way that stares back at it with an inexorable enigmaticity ('in unerbittlicher Rätselhaftigkeit entgegenstarrt', *SuZ* 136). Let me clarify this point. Heidegger's initial claim in *Sein und Zeit* is that *Dasein* is the being for whom being is an issue. In Division I, Chapter 5, the claim is that the being which is an issue for *Dasein* is the being of its 'there', the disclosure of its *Da*. (*SuZ* 133). Thus, *Dasein* is fundamentally characterized by the capacity for disclosure (*Erschlossenheit*). Or, better, *Dasein* itself *is* the clearing that discloses, '. . . es selbst die Lichtung *ist . . . das Dasein ist seine Erschlossenheit* (*SuZ* 133). As Tom Sheehan points out, this is what Jean Beaufret had in mind in translating *Dasein* as *l'ouverture*, which we might render as 'the open*ed*ness' to convey the idea that *Dasein* is always already the space of its disclosure.[6] Indeed, rather than thinking of *Dasein* as being-there as opposed to here, we might think of being-in-the-world as an openedness which is neither here nor there, but both at once.

Heidegger's claim in Paragraph 29 is that the way in which *Dasein* is its 'there' is caught with the notion of *Befindlichkeit*, namely that *Dasein* is disclosed as already having found oneself somewhere. The means of disclosure for this *Befindlichkeit* is *Stimmung*; namely, that I always find myself in some sort of mood: I am attentive, distracted, indifferent, anxious, bored or whatever. Therefore, *Dasein*'s primary form of disclosure is affective, and this affective disclosure reveals *Dasein* as *thrown* or delivered over to its existence, its 'there'. Therefore, what

---

6 See T. Sheehan, 'Kehre and Ereignis: A Prolegomenon to *Introduction to Metaphysics*', unpublished typescript. J. Beaufret, *Entretiens avec Frédéric de Towarnicki* (Paris: PUF, 1992), pp. 17, 26, 28.

stares inexorably in the face of *Dasein* is the enigma of its thrownness, the fact that I am, and that I am disclosed somewhere in a particular mood. This fact is like a riddle that I can see but cannot solve.

Perhaps the most thought-provoking usage of enigma in *Sein und Zeit* occurs just a little further on in the text, at the end of Paragraph 31, where Heidegger summarizes the discussion of *Befindlichkeit* and *Verstehen* by introducing the idea of *Dasein* as thrown projection in a series of sentences that enact the very enigma that is being described:

> Befindlichkeit und Verstehen charakterisieren als Existenzialen die ursprüngliche Erschlossenheit des In-der-Welt-seins. In der Weise der Gestimmtheit 'sieht' das Dasein Möglichkeiten aus denen her es ist. Im entwerfenden Erschließen solcher Möglichkeiten ist es je schon gestimmt. Der Entwurf der eigensten Seinkönnens ist dem Faktum der Geworfenheit in das Da überantwortet. Wird mit der Explikation der existenzialen Verfassung des Seins des Da im Sinne des geworfenen Entwurfs das Sein des Daseins nicht rätselfhafter? In der Tat. Wir müssen erst die volle Rätselhaftigkeit dieses Seins heraustreten lassen, wenn auch nur, um an seiner 'Lösung' in echter Weise scheitern zu können und die Frage nach dem Sein des geworfenen-entwerfenden In-der-Welt-seins erneut zu stellen. (*SuZ* 148)

Let me closely paraphrase rather than translate this passage, as the precision of Heidegger's conceptual expression is difficult to render literally. The first sentence simply summarizes the conclusions of the opening Paragraphs of Chapter 5, namely that the disclosedness of being-in-the-world is constituted through the existentials of *Befindlichkeit* and *Verstehen*. Let's call them (B) and (V). But the following three sentences enact this conclusion in the form of a series of conceptually pallindromic statements:

1 In its being-attuned in a mood (B), *Dasein* 'sees' possibilities (V).

2 In the projective disclosure of such possibilities (V), *Dasein* is already attuned in a mood (B).
3 Therefore, the projection of *Dasein*'s ownmost potentiality-for-being (V) is delivered over to the *Faktum* of thrownness into a there (B).

Enigmatic indeed! But, Heidegger insists, the full enigmaticity (*Rätselhaftigkeit*) of this enigma must be allowed to emerge, even if this all comes to naught, founders, is wrecked, or shatters into smithereens, which are various connotations of the phrase *scheitern zu können*. So although Heidegger adds that out of such a wreckage might come a new formulation (*erneut zu stellen*) of the question of thrown-projective being-in-the-world, the disruptive force of the enigma is such as to lead to a breakdown over any phenomenological 'solution' (*Lösung*) to the riddle of *Dasein*.

Turning now to Division II of *Sein und Zeit*, the word enigma appears on the final page of the Chapter 4, 'Temporality and Everydayness', and four times in Chapter 5, 'Temporality and Historicality', and once in Chapter 6 on time-reckoning and the genesis of our ordinary understanding of time (*SuZ* 389, 392, 425). I would like to look in detail at one further appearance of enigma, which occurs just after the temporal *Wiederholung* or recapitulation of the analytic of inauthenticity. Heidegger says that *Dasein* can for a moment – *für den Augenblick* – master the everyday, but never extinguish it (*den Alltag meistern, obzwar nie auslöschen*). He continues:

Was in der faktischen Ausgelegtheit des Daseins *ontisch* so bekannt ist, daß wir dessen nicht einmal achten, birgt existenzial-ontologisch Rätsel über Rätsel in sich. Der 'natürliche' Horizont für den ersten Ansatz der existentialen Analytik des Daseins ist *nur scheinbar selbstverständlich* (*SuZ* 371)

(What is ontically so familiar in the factical interpretedness of *Dasein* that we never pay any heed to it, conceals enigma after enigma in itself existential-ontologically. The 'natural'

29

horizon for the first starting point of the existential analytic is *only seemingly self-evident.*)

That is to say, the existential analytic renders enigmatic the everyday ontic fundament of life, what Husserl calls the natural attitude, what Plato calls the realm of *doxa*. But, and this is crucial, Heidegger does not say that the existential analytic overcomes or permanently brackets out the natural attitude of ontic life, it does not achieve some permanent breakout from the Platonic cave.[7] Rather, as Heidegger points out a few lines prior to the above-cited passage, 'Die Alltäglichkeit bestimmt das Dasein auch dann, wenn es sich nicht das Man als 'Helden' gewählt hat' (*SuZ* 371). That is, even when I have not chosen *das Man* as my hero, when I choose to become authentically who I am, the everyday is not extinguished, it is rather rendered enigmatic or uncanny. That which is ontically so familiar hides enigma after enigma ontologically. Or, in the words of the opening paragraph of the existential analytic, 'The ontically nearest and familiar is the ontologically furthest' (*SuZ* 43). The existential analytic of *Dasein* seems to return ceaselessly to the enigma from which it begins, an enigma which, in Heidegger's words, shatters the seeming self-evidence of any natural attitude from which phenomenology might begin in order to force the philosopher to formulate anew the question of being-in-the-world. That is, Heidegger transforms the beginning point of phenomenology from the self-evidence of the natural attitude to the enigma of a *Faktum*, the fact *that* one is; philosophy begins with the riddle of the completely obvious.

So, my thesis is that at the heart of *Sein und Zeit*, that is, at the heart of the central claim of the *Dasein*-analytic as to the

---

7 This phrase is Rüdiger Safranski's, which he uses to describe the undoubted Platonism of Heidegger's political commitment in 1933. See *Ein Meister aus Deutschland: Heidegger und seine Zeit* (Munich: Hanser, 1994). On the question of the enigma of the everyday in Heidegger, see M. Haar, 'L'enigme de la quotidieneté' in J.-P. Cometti and D. Janicaud (eds), *Être et Temps de Martin Heidegger: Questions de méthode et voies de recherché* (Marseille: Sud, 1989), pp. 213–25.

temporal character of thrown-projective being-in-the-world, there lies an enigmatic a priori, a fundamental opacity that both seems to resist phenomenological description and is that in relation to which the phenomenologist describes. As such, in Kantian terms, we might say that the enigmatic a priori is not only transcendentally constitutive, it is also regulative. It is not only descriptive, or rather a limit to the activity of phenomenological description, but also normative, functioning like an imperative in the philosophical analysis of being-in-the-world. Philosophy must attempt to be equal to the enigma of our being-in-the-world, while knowing all the time that it cannot. My question will now be: what does this fact entail for our reading of *Sein und Zeit*?

* * *

Heidegger defines 'phenomenon' as *was sich zeigt*, what shows itself, and the phenomena that show themselves in *Sein und Zeit* are not empirical facts, but rather the a priori structures of *Dasein*'s being-in-the-world – the existentials (*SuZ* 31). However, if a phenomenon is what shows itself, then an enigma by definition is what does not show itself. It is like a mirror in which all we see is our reflection scratching its chin in perplexity. An enigma is something we see, but do not see through. We might therefore, at the very least, wonder why the vast and sometimes cumbersome machinery of Heidegger's phenomenological apparatus should bring us face to face with an a priori enigma, with a riddle that we cannot solve. We might be even further perplexed that the riddle here is nothing particularly complex, like the final insoluble clue in a tricky crossword puzzle. On the contrary, the riddle here is that of absolute obviousness, the sheer facticity of what is under our noses, the everyday in all its palpable plainness and banality. Yet, it is this riddling quality of the obvious as the very matter or *Sache* of phenomenology that interests me here.

I began by saying that there are two formulae that provide a clue to understanding what takes place in *Sein und Zeit*: *Dasein existiert faktisch* and *Dasein ist geworfener Entwurf*.

Ultimately, I would like to *modify* the way we hear the formulations, 'thrown projection' or 'factical existing', by placing the emphasis on the *thrown* and the *factical* rather than on projection and existence.[8] That is, on my interpretation, *Dasein* is fundamentally a *thrown* throwing off, a *factical* existing. It should be noted that what is continually appealed to in Heidegger, in *Sein und Zeit* and even more so in the later work, is a change in our capacity for hearing, that is, whether we *hinhören auf* or listen away to *das Man*, or whether we *hören auf* or hear the appeal that *Dasein* makes to itself (*SuZ* 271 – *inter alia Sein und Zeit* can be understood in musical terms, as an immense treatise on sound, hearing and rhythm). It is my hope that a change in the way we hear these key formulae will produce aspect change in the way we understand the project of fundamental ontology.

I will begin to spell out this aspect change presently, but it should first be asked: why is it necessary? It is necessary, in my view, in order to move our understanding of *Sein und Zeit* away from the heroic political pathos of authenticity, consummated in the discussions of fate and destiny in the infamous Paragraph 74 on 'The Basic Constitution of Historicity'. As Karl Löwith was the first to learn when he met with Heidegger in Rome and Frascati in 1936, although he has subsequently been followed by other scholars, the concept of *historicity* (*Geschichtlichkeit*) is the link between fundamental ontology and Heidegger's political commitment to National Socialism in 1933.[9] Let me

---

8 *Modifikation* is an absolutely key concept in *Sein und Zeit*. See, for example, the claim that authentic being-one's-self is an '*existentiell modification of the "they" – of the "they" as an essential existentiale*' (*SuZ* 130). A claim that is simply and flatly inverted in the Second Division, where Heidegger amnesiacally writes: 'It has been shown [but where exactly? SC] that proximally and for the most part Dasein is *not* itself but is lost in the they-self, which is an existentiell modification of the authentic self' (*SuZ* 317). Is the authentic a modification of the inauthentic, or is it the other way around? Heidegger makes noises of both sorts.

9 See K. Löwith's essay in *The Heidegger Controversy*, ed. R.Wolin (Cambridge, MA: MIT Press, 1993). To my mind, the systematic

try and briefly restate the argument as prima facie the connection between historicity and politics will be far from obvious for many readers.

Dasein's authentic anticipation of its death is called 'fate' (*Schicksal*) by Heidegger and this is designated as the originary historicizing or happening (*Geschehen*) of *Dasein* (*SuZ* 384). Heidegger's claim in Division II, Chapter 5 is that the condition of possibility for any authentic understanding of history lies in *Dasein*'s historicity, which means the self-understanding of the temporal character of being human, i.e. finitude. So, to repeat: the meaning of the Being of *Dasein* is temporality, and the meaning of temporality is finitude (*SuZ* 331). *Dasein*'s authentic self-understanding of finitude is 'fate', and this originary historicizing is the condition of possibility for any authentic relation to history, by which Heidegger means 'world historical historicizing' (*SuZ* 19), or indeed for any science of history. It is clear that political events, such as revolutions, the founding of a state or general social transformations, would qualify as world historical events for Heidegger.

Now, it was established in Division I, Chapter 4, that *Dasein* is always already *Mitsein*. That is, the a priori condition of being-in-the-world is being together with others in that world. As is well known, the everyday, social actuality of this a priori condition of *Mitsein* is called *das Man* by Heidegger, and this is determined as inauthentic because in such everyday experience *Dasein* is not truly itself, but is, as it were, lived through by the

---

connection between fundamental ontology and National Socialism was convincingly established by Philippe Lacoue-Labarthe in his 'Transcendence Ends in Politics', *Typography* (Cambridge, MA: Harvard University Press, 1989), and also at greater length in his *Heidegger, Art and Politics*, tr. C. Turner (Oxford: Blackwell, 1990). The same argument has been stated much more polemically and in extraordinary scholarly detail by Johannes Fritsche in *Historical Destiny and National Socialism in Heidegger's* Being and Time (Berkeley: University of California Press, 1999). About the discussion of historicity, Fritsche claims, 'Section 74 of Heidegger's *Being and Time* is as brilliant a summary of revolutionary rightist politics as one could wish for' (p. xii).

customs and conventions of the existing social world. Now, returning more closely to the argument of Paragraph 74, if fateful, authentic *Dasein* is always already *Mitsein*, then such historicizing has to be what Heidegger calls co-historicizing (*Mitgeschehen, SuZ* 384). An authentic individual life, Heidegger would seem to be suggesting, cannot be led in isolation and opposition to the shared life of the community. The question therefore arises: what is the *authentic* mode of being together with others? What is an authentic *Mitdasein* that escapes or masters the inauthenticity of *das Man*? Heideger writes, fatefully in my view, 'Wenn aber das schicksalhafte Dasein als In-der-Welt-sein wesenhaft im Mitsein mit Anderen existiert, ist sein Geschehen ein Mitgeschehen und bestimmt als *Geschick*' ('But if fateful *Dasein* as being-in-the-world essentially exists in being-with with others, its historicizing is a co-historicizing and is determined as *destiny*'). So, destiny is the authentic historicizing that I share with others in so far as my individual fate is always already bound up with the collective destiny of the community to which I belong. Heidegger goes on, 'Im Miteinandersein in derselben Welt und in der Entschlossenheit für bestimmte Möglichkeiten sind die Schicksale im vornhinein schon geleitet. In der Mitteilung und im Kampf wird die Macht des Geschickes erst frei' ('The fates are already guided from the front in the being-with-one-another in the same world and in the resoluteness for determinate possibilities. The power of destiny first becomes free in communication and struggle', *SuZ* 384). So, the fates of authentic, individual *Dasein*s are 'guided from the front' by the destiny of the collective, a destiny that first becomes free for itself or self-conscious in the activity of communication and struggle. Obviously, the word *Kampf* has acquired some rather unfortunate political connotations between the period that saw the publication of *Sein und Zeit* and the present. But that is not the worst of it. Heidegger completes this run of thought with the following words, 'Damit bezeichnen wir das Geschehen der Gemeinschaft, des Volkes' ('In this way, we designate the historicizing of the community, of the people', *SuZ* 384). So, the authentic communal mode of

Mitsein that masters the inauthenticity of *das Man* is *das Volk*, the people. In my view, it is the possible political realization of a resolute and authentic *Volk* in opposition to the inauthentic nihilism of social modernity that Heidegger identified as 'the inner truth and greatness' ('der inneren Wahrheit und Größe') of National Socialism just a few years later in *Einführung in die Metaphysik* in 1935. Despite the horrors of Nazi Germany, Heidegger – to the understandable consternation of the young Habermas writing on Heidegger in his first published essay – stubbornly refused to revise his judgement on 'the inner truth and greatness' when the 1935 lectures were published in 1953.[10]

There is, I believe, a systematic philosophical basis to Heidegger's political commitment, which is due to the specific way in which Heidegger develops the concept of authenticity in Division II of *Sein und Zeit* and which culminates in the concept of *das Volk*. That is, the only way in which Heidegger can conceive of an authentic mode of human being-together or community, is in terms of the unity of a specific people, a particular nation, and it is the political expression of this possibility that Heidegger saw in National Socialism in 1933. In other words, as Hannah Arendt obliquely implied throughout her work, Heidegger is incapable of thinking the *plurality* of human being-together as a positive political possibility. Plurality is always determined negatively as *das Man*, as the averageness and levelling down that constitutes what Heidegger calls, between scare quotes, 'publicness' ('die Öffentlichkeit', *SuZ* 127). In my view, the urgent task of Heidegger interpretation – provided, of course, that one is not a Nazi and provided one is still in the business of thinking, as I do, that Heidegger is a great philosopher – is to try and defuse the systematic link between Heidegger's philosophy and his politics. As should have become clear, the key concept for establishing the link between philosophy and politics is authenticity and this is what I want to

---

10 See M. Heidegger, *Einführung in die Metaphysik* (Tübingen: Niemeyer, 1953), p. 152; and J. Habermas, 'Mit Heidegger gegen Heidegger denken. Zur Veröffentlichung von Vorlesungen aus dem Jahre 1935', *Frankfurter Allgemeine Zeitung*, 25 July 1953, pp. 67–75.

question by developing the notion of what I call *originary in-authenticity*, a possibility of interpretation that is available, if somewhat latent, in *Sein und Zeit*.[11]

* * *

Let me try and explain myself by going back to the key concept of *Befindlichkeit*: state-of-mind, attunement or what William Richardson nicely translates as 'already-having-found-oneself-there-ness'. Heidegger's claim is that I always already find myself attuned in a *Stimmung*, a mood or affective disposition. Such a mood discloses me as *geworfen*, as thrown into the 'there' (*Da*) of my being-in-the-world. For Heidegger, these three terms – *Befindlichkeit, Stimmung*, and *Geworfenheit* – are interconnected in bringing out the nature of facticity. As is well known, Heidegger's early work is a hermeneutics of facticity, a description of the everyday ways in which the human being exists. In being disposed in a mood, Heidegger writes that *Dasein* is satiated or weary (*überdrüssig*) with itself, and as such its being becomes manifest as a burden or load (*eine Last*) to be taken up. The burdensome character of one's being, the sheer weight of the 'that-it-is' (*Das es ist*) of existence, is something that I seek to evade. Heidegger writes, 'Im Ausweichen selbst ist das Da erschlossenes' ('In evasion itself is the there disclosed', *SuZ* 135). This is fascinating, because Heidegger is claiming that the being of *Dasein*'s *Da*, the there of its being-in-the-world, is disclosed in the movement that seeks to evade it. Evasion discloses that which it evades. It is precisely in the human being's turning away (*Abkehr*) from itself that the nature of existence first becomes manifest. I find myself as I flee

---

11 Let me add that I find it curious, to say the least, that certain interpretations or borrowings from Heidegger that would want to distance themselves decisively from any stain of National Socialism often deploy the concept of authenticity in an unquestioned manner. In my view, this is somewhat problematic. I am thinking in particular of the work of Charles Guignon (see *On Being Authentic* (London: Routledge, 2004) and Charles Taylor (see *The Ethics of Authenticity* (Cambridge, MA: Harvard University Press, 1992)).

myself and I flee myself because I find myself. Heidegger seems to rather enjoy the paradox 'gefunden in einem Finden, das nicht so sehr einem direkten Suchen, sondern einem Fliehen entspricht' ('found in a finding that corresponds not so much to a direct seeking, but to a fleeing', *SuZ* 135). What is elicited in this turning away of *Dasein* from itself is the facticity of *Dasein*'s being delivered over to itself (*Faktizität der Überant-wortung*) and it is this that Heidegger intends by the term thrownness, *Geworfenheit*.

The concept of *Befindlichkeit* reveals the thrown nature of *Dasein* in its falling movement of turning away from itself. But two paragraphs later in *Sein und Zeit*, Heidegger will contrast this movement of evasion with the concept of *Verstehen*, under-stood as ability-to-be, which is linked to the concepts of *Entwurf* (projection) and *Möglichkeit* (possibility). That is, *Dasein* is not just thrown into the world, it can throw off that thrownness in a movement of projection where it seizes hold of its possibilities-to-be, what Heidegger calls from the opening words of the existential analytic, *Seinsweisen*, ways to be. This movement of projection is the very experience of *freedom* for Heidegger. *Dasein* is a thrown project – but where Heidegger will place the emphasis on projection, possibility and freedom as the essential elements in the movement towards authenticity, I would like to propose another possible trajectory of the existential analytic of *Sein und Zeit*, namely originary inauthenticity.

The thought behind the notion of originary inauthenticity is that human existence is fundamentally shaped in relation to a brute facticity or thrownness which cannot be mastered through any existential projection. Authenticity always slips back into a prior inauthenticity from which it cannot escape but which it would like to evade. As we saw above, it is in this movement of evasion, or the self's turning away from itself, that *Dasein*'s embeddedness in factical existence is disclosed. From the perspective of originary inauthenticity, human existence is something that is first and foremost experienced as a burden, a weight, as something to which I am riveted without being able to know why or know further. Inauthentic existence has the

character of an irreducible and intractable *thatness*, what
Heidegger called above '*das Daß seines Da*'. I feel myself bound
to 'the that of my there', the sheer *Faktum* of my facticity, in a
way that invites some sort of response.

Now, and this is where my proposed aspect change begins to
kick in, the nature of this response will not, as it is in Division II
of *Sein und Zeit*, be the authentic and heroic *decision* of existence that comes into the simplicity of its *Schicksal* by 'shattering
itself against death', as Heidegger rather dramatically puts it
(*SuZ* 385). The response will not be the heroic mastery of the
everyday in the authentic present of what Heidegger calls
the *Augenblick* (the moment of vision), which produces an
experience of what he calls ecstasy (*Ekstase*) and rapture
(*Entrückung*) (*SuZ* 338). On the contrary, the response to the
Faktum of my finitude is a more passive and less heroic decision,
a decision made in the face of a facticity whose demand can
never be mastered and which faces me like a riddle or enigma
that I cannot solve. As I try to show elsewhere, such a fact calls
for comic acknowledgement rather than tragic affirmation.[12]

Dasein is, as Heidegger writes in his extraordinary pages on
guilt, a thrown basis (*ein geworfene Grund*). As this basis,
Dasein continually lags behind itself, 'Being a basis (*Grund-
seiend*), that is to say existing as thrown (*als geworfenes
existierend* – another of Heidegger's enigmatic formulae),
Dasein constantly lags behind its possibilities' (*SuZ* 284). The
experience of guilt reveals the being of being human as a lack, as
something wanting. In the light of these remarks, we might say
that the self is not the ecstasy of a heroic leap towards authenticity energized by the experience of anxiety and being-towards-
death. Such would be the reading of the existential analytic –
and I do not doubt that this may well have been Heidegger's
intention – that sees its goal in a form of *autarky*: self-sufficien-

___
12 See the final chapter of my *On Humour* (London and New York:
Routledge, 2002), pp. 93–111; and 'Displacing the Tragic-Heroic
Paradigm in Philosophy and Psychoanalysis' in *Ethics, Politics,
Subjectivity* (London and New York: Verso, 1999), pp. 217–38.

cy, self-mastery or what Heidegger calls in Paragraph 64, 'self-constancy' ('Die Ständigkeit des Selbst', *SuZ* 323). Rather, on my view, the self's fundamental self-relation is to an unmasterable thrownness, the burden of a facticity that weighs me down without my ever being able to fully pick it up. Expressed temporally, one's self-relation is not the authentic living present of the moment of vision, but rather a delay with respect to oneself that is perhaps best expressed in the experience of fatigue or weariness. I project or throw off a thrownness that catches me in its throw and inverts the movement of possibility. As such, the present continually lags behind itself. I am always too late to meet my fate. I would like to think that Heidegger might have had this in mind at the end of *Sein und Zeit* when he writes of bringing us face to face with 'the ontological enigma of the movement of historicizing in general' (*SuZ* 389).

It is my hope that if one follows my proposed aspect change from a heroics of authenticity to an originary inauthenticity then a good deal changes in how one views the project of *Sein und Zeit* and its political consequences. My main point is that both aspects are available to an attentive reading and this is why the young Habermas was right in suggesting that it is necessary to think both with Heidegger and against Heidegger. However, the completion of such a reading is a considerable task whose fulfilment will have to be postponed to the future. In the remainder of this paper, I would just like to sketch how we might begin this task by briefly examining three central concepts from Division II: death, conscience and temporality.

* * *

First, I think that the notion of originary inauthenticity places in question what Heidegger sees as the non-relational character of the experience of finitude in the death-analysis in Division II, Chapter 1 of *Sein und Zeit*. You will recall that there are four criteria in Heidegger's full existential-ontological conception of death. It is *unbezüglich, gewiß, unbestimmt* and *unüberholbar*: non-relational, certain, indefinite and not to be outstripped. It is only the first of these criteria that I would take issue with, as the other three are true, if banal: (i) it is certain we are going to die; (ii) the instant of our death is indefinite, that is, we don't know when it is going to happen; and (iii) it is pretty damn important. However, if the first of the criteria falls, then the whole picture changes.

Heidegger insists on the non-relational character of death because for him, crucially, 'der Tod ontologisch durch Jemeinigkeit und Existenz konstituiert wird' ('Death is ontologically constituted through mineness and existence', *SuZ* 240). Therefore, dying for an other (*sterben für*) would simply be to sacrifice oneself (*sich opfern*) for an other, or to substitute (*ersetzten*, *SuZ* 239) myself for another. Thus, the fundamental experience of finitude is non-relational, and all relationality is rendered secondary because of the primacy of *Jemeinigkeit*.

Now, I just think this is wrong. It is wrong empirically and normatively. I would want to oppose it with the thought of the *fundamentally relational character of finitude*, namely that death is first and foremost experienced in a relation to the death or dying of the other and others, in being-with the dying in a caring way, and in grieving after they are dead. Yet, such relationality is not a relation of understanding: the other's dying is not like placing an intuition under a concept. It is not a relation of subsumption, in Kantian terms a reflective rather than a determinate judgement. In other words, the experience of finitude opens up in relation to a brute *Faktum* that escapes my understanding or the reach of my criteria. Deliberately twisting Heidegger's example from Paragraph 47, I would say that the fundamental experience of finitude is rather like being a 'student of pathological anatomy' where the dead other 'ist ein *lebloses* materielles Ding' ('a *lifeless* material thing', *SuZ* 238). With all the terrible lucidity of grief, one watches the person one loves – parent, partner or child – die and become a lifeless material thing. That is, there is a thing – a corpse – at the heart of the experience of finitude. This is why I mourn. Antigone understood this well, it seems to me, staring at the lifeless material thing of her dead brother and demanding justice. Authentic *Dasein* does not mourn. One might even say that authenticity is constituted by making the act of mourning secondary to *Dasein*'s *Jemeinigkeit*. Heidegger writes, shockingly in my view, 'We do not experience the death of others in a genuine sense; at most we are just "there alongside" (*nur "dabei"*)' (*SuZ* 239).

If death and finitude are fundamentally relational, that is, if they are constituted in a relation to a lifeless material thing whom I love and this thing casts a long mournful shadow across the self that undoes that self's authenticity, then this would also lead me to question a distinction that is fundamental to Heidegger's death-analysis. Heidegger makes the following threefold distinction:

1 dying, *Sterben*, which is proper to *Dasein*; which is the very mark of *Dasein*'s ownness and its possibility of authenticity;
2 perishing, *Verenden*, which is confined to plants and animals; and
3 demise, *Ableben*, which Heidegger calls a *Zwischenphänomen* between these two extremes, and which characterizes the inauthentic death of *Dasein* (*SuZ* 247).

Now, although one cannot be certain whether animals simply perish – 'if a lion could talk, we could not understand him' – I have my doubts, particularly when one thinks of domestic pets and higher mammals. Thus, I think one should at the very least leave open the possibility that certain animals die, that they undergo *Sterben* and not just *Verenden*. I also doubt whether human beings are incapable of perishing, of dying like a dog, as Kafka's fiction and the facts of famine, war and global poverty insistently remind us. And what of those persons who die at the end of a mentally debilitating disease, or who die while being in what is termed 'a permanently vegetative state'? Do they cease to be human on Heidegger's account? I see no other option. But, more importantly, if finitude is fundamentally relational, that is, if it is by definition a relation to the *Faktum* of an other who exceeds my powers of projection, then *the only authentic death is inauthentic*. That is, on my account, an authentic relation to death is not constituted through mineness, but rather through otherness. Death enters the world not through my own *timor mortis*, but rather through my relation to the other's dying, perhaps even through my relation to the other's fear, which I try to assuage as best I can. It is this notion of an essentially inauthentic relation to death that both Maurice Blanchot and Emmanuel Levinas have in mind when reversing Heidegger's dictum that 'death is the possibility of impossibility' into 'death is the impossibility of possibility' (*SuZ* 262). I have power neither over the other's death nor my own. Death is not a possibility of *Dasein*, but rather describes an empirical and normative limit to all possibility and to my fateful powers of projection. My relation to finitude limits my potentiality and my ability to be (*Seinkönnen*). In my view, the experience of finitude impotentializes the self and disables the healthy virility of authentic *Dasein*.

* * *

Once this relational picture of finitude is in place, the picture of conscience would also have to change significantly. I have come to think – against some long-held prejudices about Division II – that the discussion of conscience is one of the most explosive and interesting parts of *Sein und Zeit*, and we have already had occasion to discuss certain passages above. Of course, the analysis of conscience follows on logically from the death analysis, being the concrete ontic-existentiell testimony or attestation (*Zeugnis, SuZ* 267) for the formal ontologico-existential claim about death. Death is ontological, conscience is ontic. Indeed, the word testimony might detain us more than it has done in reading *Sein und Zeit*. Testimony evokes both a notion of witnessing as testifying to something or someone, and also expresses a link to evidence and verification, where Heidegger is seeking in conscience the concrete ontic evidence for the formal ontological claim about death, a question which resolves itself relativistically in the key concept of 'Situation' (*SuZ* 299–300).

My point here is simple: if death is non-relational for Heidegger, then also a fortiori conscience is non-relational.

Heidegger writes, in italics, *'In conscience Dasein calls itself'* (*'Das Dasein ruft im Gewissen sich selbst'*, SuZ 275). That is, although in conscience it is as though the call of conscience were an alien voice (*eine fremde Stimme*, SuZ 277) that comes *über mich*, such a call, although it is not planned, really comes *aus mir*. Its source is the self. As Heidegger insists in differentiating his concept of conscience from the 'vulgar' one, what is attested to in conscience is *Dasein*'s ownmost or most proper ability to be (*eigensten Seinkönnen*, SuZ 295). Authentic *Dasein* calls to itself in conscience, and it does this not in the mode of chattering to itself, but rather in discretion (*Verschwiegenheit*) and silence (*Schweigen*). This behaviour is what Heidegger calls resoluteness (*Entschlossenheit*), which is then defined as the *'authentic Selfhood'* of *Dasein* (*SuZ* 298). Heidegger completes this train of thought in a slightly troubling fashion by claiming that when *Dasein* has authentically individuated itself in conscience, 'it can become the 'conscience' of others (*zum 'Gewissen' der Anderen werden*). Only by authentically being-their-selves in resoluteness can people authentically be with one another' (*SuZ* 298). Once again, the condition of possibility for collective authenticity or community is the mineness of individual conscience.

This brings me to my question: is conscience non-relational? It would seem to me that a consideration of Freud, in particular his essays on Narcissism and 'Mourning and Melancholia', might throw some helpful light on Heidegger's concept of conscience.[13] The Freudian thought I would like to retain is that of conscience as the psychical imprint, interior mark, or agency, for a series of transferential relations to the other: ego ideal, paternal super-ego, maternal imago, or whatever. Conscience is the *Über-Ich* that stands *über mich*, it is the super-ego that stands over against me. The point is that a Freudian concept of conscience is essentially relational. Furthermore, in analytic experience it is the place of the hostile super-ego that the analyst

---

13 See volume 11 of the Penguin Freud, *On Metapsychology* (Harmondsworth: Penguin, 1984), pp. 163ff.

has to occupy in order to break down the symptom that is the occasion of the patient's suffering. Conceived in this way, the appeal made by conscience would not be *Dasein* calling to itself or even the voice of the friend that every *Dasein* carries within it (*SuZ* 163). If that were so, then *Dasein* would have to be its own best friend, which is a rather solipsistic, indeed slightly sad, state of affairs. Even worse, I would want to avoid Heidegger's suggestion that the authentic self can become the conscience of others in some sort of presumptuous and potentially dominating way.

On my picture, conscience is the ontic testimony of a certain splitting or undoing of the self in relation to a *Faktum* that it cannot assimilate, the lifeless material thing of the experience of mourning and grief that the self carries within itself and which denies it from achieving self-mastery. It is this failure of autarky that makes the self relational. The call of conscience is a voice within me whose source is not myself, but is an other's voice that calls me to respond. Pushing this slightly further, the relational experience of conscience calls me to a responsibility for the other that one might consider ethical. In other words, a relational and arguably ethical experience of conscience only becomes possible by being inauthentic, that is, in recognizing that I am not the conscience of others, but rather that it is those others who call me to have a conscience.

It would here be a question of reading Freud's concept of narcissism, as a splitting of the self into conflictual agencies (the division of ego, super-ego and id in what is usually called the second topography) back into *Sein und Zeit*. If authentic *Dasein* cannot mourn, because its fundamental relation to finitude is a self-relation, then I think this is because, to put it in psycho-analytic terms, it has not entered into the relational experience of transference. Transference is a relation to an other whom I face, but whom I cannot completely know, whom my criteria cannot reach. Such a face-to-face relation is described by Levinas with the adjective 'ethical'. Of course, *Mitsein* is being-with-another, but it is standing shoulder to shoulder with those others in what Heidegger calls in one passage 'eigentliche

Verbundenheit' ('*authentic* alliance or being-bound-together', *SuZ* 122). Such alliance might well be said to be the camaraderie that induces the political virtue of solidarity, but it is not a face-to-face relation and as such, in my view, is ethically impoverished. I sometimes think that authentic *Mitsein* is a little like being in church, it is a congregational 'being-together-with-others' where we vibrate together as one body in song and prayer. Pleasant as it doubtless must be, such is not the only way of being with others.

* * *

If we begin to hear thrown projection as *thrown* projection, and factical existence as *factical* existence, then I think Heidegger's claims about temporality – the very meaning of being – would also have to be revised, away from the primacy of the future and towards the primacy of the past. To recall, Heidegger's claim in his discussion of temporality is that there are three 'ecstases' of time: the future (*Zukunft*) that is revealed in the anticipation of death, the past or 'having-been-ness' (*Gewesenheit*) that is opened in the notion of conscience, guilt and resoluteness, and the present or 'waiting-towards' (*Gegen-wart*) that is grasped in the moment of vision (*Augenblick*), or taking action in the Situation. The claim is that *Dasein is* the movement of this temporalization, and that this movement *is* finitude: 'Die ursprüngliche Zeit ist endlich' ('Primordial time is finite', *SuZ* 331).

Now, although Heidegger insists that the structure of ecstatic temporality possesses a unity, the primary meaning of temporality is the future (*SuZ* 327). As Heidegger writes, 'Zeitlichkeit zeitigt sich ursprünglich aus der Zukunft' ('Temporality temporalizes itself primordially out of the future', *SuZ* 331). That is, it is the anticipatory experience of being-towards-death that makes possible the *Gewesenheit* of the past and the *Augenblick* of the present. For Heidegger, the *Augenblick* is the authentic present which is consummated in a vision of resolute rapture (*Entrückung, SuZ* 338), where *Dasein* is literally carried away (*ent-rückt*) in an experience of ecstasy. Rapture, which we encountered above in the discussion of authentic *Mitsein*, is a word that worries me, not least because of the way in which *raptus* seems like a plundering of the past, some sort of rape of memory. If we approach *Sein und Zeit* in terms of the aspect change that I am proposing, and we emphasize the thrownness in thrown projection and the facticity in factical existence, then this would entail the primacy of the past over the future. This past is one's rather messy, indeed often opaque, personal and cultural history. In my view, it is this personal and cultural thrownness that pulls me back from any rapture of the present into a lag that I can never make up and which I can only assemble into a *fate* on the basis of a delusional and pernicious notion of historicity, and into a *destiny* on the basis of a congregational interpretation of that delusion.

On the contrary, from the perspective developed in this paper, the unfolding future always folds back into the experience of an irredeemable past, a past that constitutes the present as always having a delay with respect to itself. Now is not the now when I say 'now'. My relation to the present is one where I am always trying – and failing – to catch up with myself. As such, then, I do not rise up rapturously or affirmatively into time, becoming, as Nietzsche exclaimed on the verge of madness, 'all the names in history'. No, I wait, I await. Time passes. For Heidegger, this is the passive awaiting (*Gewärtigen*) of inauthentic time. Of course, such a passive awaiting might make the self fatigued, sleepy even. As such, in the experience of fatigue, the river of time begins to flow backwards, away from the future and the resolute rapture of the present, and towards a past that I can never make present, but which I dramatize involuntarily in the life of dreams. True, I can always interpret my dreams or, better, get another to interpret them for me. But what Freud calls the navel of the dream, its source, its facticity, always escapes me, like an enigma.

Conclusion

In closing, let me try and identify three consequences that can be drawn from the reading of *Sein und Zeit* that I have tried to offer in this paper.

(1) The critique of authenticity, particularly with regard to social and political life, permits a revalorization of inauthentic social existence as something to be judged positively and not seen in terms of categories such as falling. Although Heidegger insists again and again – indeed, the man doth protest too much methinks – that his concepts of falling, thrownness and inauthenticity do not and should not imply any moral critique of the modern world, there is no way around the feeling of Heidegger's lip curling as he describes the levelled-down life of the 'great mass', or – in some twisted echo of Lenin or Kautsky – the 'real dictatorship of the 'they''. Such a dictatorship is evidenced in the life of levelled down 'publicness', in reading 'newspapers' and using 'public transport', where 'every Other is like the next' (*SuZ* 126–7). However, if we view Heidegger's descriptions from the perspective of originary inauthenticity, then a good deal changes. For example, when Heidegger writes that in the world of 'the they', 'Everyone is an other and no one is himself', or indeed when he says that the 'who' of everyday *Dasein* is *Niemand,* nobody, then such phrases might be otherwise interpreted (*SuZ* 128). If we are, indeed, others to ourselves in social existence, if we are even nobody in particular, then this could well provide the basis for a thinking of sociality that would not be organized in terms of the goals of authenticity, autarky or communitarian solidarity. Reading *Sein und Zeit* from the perspective of inauthenticity might allow us to see social life as constituted in relations of radical dependence on others. I am nobody in particular and nor are you, and in so far as we are both using 'public transport' to get to work, then our interactions are based on a shared dependence and even civility. I might pick up and read the 'newspaper' that you leave on the seat and we might even exchange a few courteous words about the dreadful terrorist explosion that happened the previous

day.[14] The point is that *das Man* need not be seen as an inauthentic or levelled-down 'publicness' that requires the authenticity of *das Volk*. We might simply abandon the latter and affirm the former. This leads to my second point.

(2) On my interpretation of *Sein und Zeit*, the core of the existential analytic is not the heroic, non-relational and constant self who achieves authentic wholeness through anticipatory resoluteness. On the contrary, sociality begins with an inauthentic self who is formed through a relational experience of finitude and conscience. This is not an autarkic and unified self that can rise up to meet its fate, but a self defined through its relations of dependence on others, a self that only *is* through its relations to others and which always arrives too late to meet its fate, it is a comic rather than a tragic self. Indeed, such an essentially inauthentic self might not enjoy the robust health of authentic *Dasein*; it might be uneasy with itself, even unwell (the possibility of a sick *Dasein* never seems to have occurred to Heidegger). Such a self might be less an individual than a 'dividual', divided against itself in the experience of conscience. In a key passage from the analysis of *Mitsein,* Heidegger writes, 'because *Dasein*'s being is being-with, in its understanding of being already lies the understanding of the Other (*das Verständnis Anderer*)' (*SuZ* 123). For Heidegger, the relation to the other is based on understanding, whose condition of possibility is the understanding of being. However, if we privilege the inauthentic and relational self, then this is not a self that can claim to understand the other, but is rather a self who is directed towards the other in a way that is neither based in understanding nor culminates in understanding. Perhaps the other person is simply that being that I have to acknowledge as refractory to the categories of my understanding, as exceeding my powers of projection or the reach of my criteria, but together with whom I am thrown into a social world where we

---

14 I first wrote that sentence on 8 July in Central London, on the morning after the terrorist attacks.

can engage with each other based on relations of respect and trust. Perhaps it is such an inauthentic self that is truly ethical.

(3) The temporality of such a relational self would not be primarily orientated towards the future, a future that culminates in the rapturous 'moment of vision' through what I see as a redemption of the past, understood as one's 'having-been-ness'. On the contrary, such an inauthentic, relational self would be organized in relation to a past for which it is responsible, but which it cannot redeem, a past that constitutes the self without the self constituting or reconstituting it. It is in this way, perhaps, that we might be able to push the existential analytic towards the issue of responsibility for the past, even a guilty responsibility for a past that cannot be fully made present and for that very reason will not let go and cannot be passed over in silence.

What I hope to have done in this paper is to begin to think about how we might approach Heidegger's existential analytic in a way that frees it from what I see as its tragic-heroic pathos of individual and collective authenticity, but in a way that is hopefully not based on a strategic or reductive external interpretation, but a possible internal reading that derives from the central theses and basic experience of *Sein und Zeit*.

3. 'And There Shall Be No More Boredom': Problems with Overcoming Metaphysics in Heidegger, Levinas and Marion

JOERI SCHRIJVERS

'The end of metaphysics', it seems, has become a slogan, and one often supposes it to be achieved by the simple act of saying these words. As if, however burdened we were with the troubling message issuing from Nietzsche and Heidegger, we were – suddenly – able to tear off the shadows of the metaphysical God, and free ourselves from that terrible metaphysics that has caused us to misrepresent the relation with God. Thereto we embrace particularity; we are hiding in stories – albeit most often in negative theological clothing. We are eager to grant our narrative its limits, and thereby, we like to believe, its openness to otherness. In this essay, I want to question this pretension to overcome metaphysics, by pointing to the limits of its enterprise.

This article portrays the way in which particularity makes its appearance in contemporary philosophy. Heidegger, Levinas and Marion are called upon to seize this turn to particularity and singularity. It is true that these three figures all frame their thought around that which might counter the reckoning with beings and objects. Philosophy, they argue, has preferred controllable, foreseeable and 'present-at-hand' objects. Heidegger's *Being and Time* was concerned precisely with showing how our particular being-in-the-world hardly encounters objects at all. In our dealings with things ready-to-hand that Heidegger sought to describe, one can interpret the critique of metaphysics as a critique of the tendency to regard 'objects' and 'objectivity' as the sole way to acquire truth. The critique of metaphysics can therefore also be seen as a critique of the scientific world-view, that is, as a critique of science as the sole path to truth about the supposedly external world, as a critique of the thought that science is able to provide an adequate and transparent account of the world 'as it is in itself'. Marion, then, tries to differentiate between the 'safety' of constituting and constituted objects and the surprising novelty of the saturated phenomenon. Levinas, as is well known, attacked the widespread western adage that 'knowledge is power' by pointing to the Other as that instance which both resists and makes possible the adequation on which knowledge thrives. It is in this sense that all these thinkers are querying for an alternative account of our particular and historical encounter with world to the one that, in philosophy, came to be known as the correspondence theory of truth: truth is *adaequatio rei et intellectus*, the correspondence between the thing in itself and the thing as it is thought or represented.

Our aim in this article is twofold: on the one hand, we will depict the manner in which Heidegger, Levinas and Marion try to surpass this narrow view of attaining truth, by, respectively 'being,' 'the Other' and 'givenness', but, on the other hand, we hope to provide some evidence as to why these attempts seem not to succeed. Indeed, we will show how in all three of these thinkers the thought of an adequate and transparent view on particularity can, after all, be obtained. It, therefore, appears that *we can surpass metaphysics only by presupposing it*, that is, by never being able to surpass it. It is this paradox, we will contend, that needs to be thought through, and which forces one to handle the phrase 'overcoming metaphysics' not only with the greatest care, but also with suspicion. Hence the title of this chapter: it is somewhat stretching Levinas's contention in *Otherwise than Being* that the encounter with the other liberates one from boredom.[1] It is, indeed, in theses like this that a return of metaphysics might be suspected. We would like to gain an understanding for the view that 'overcoming meta-physics' might itself be yet another metaphysical convulsion, another way to retreat in 'illusion, intoxication and artificial paradises'.[2] Thus, one must question metaphysics as much as its supposed overcoming.

The article closes with the consequences this 'overcoming' of metaphysics might have for theology. It is indeed barely noticed that Heidegger and Levinas *share* a similar disdain for the theological enterprise. Therefore, my question is: does the turn to the particularity of being in a world necessarily entail reluctance towards theology? Or, alternatively, can particularity serve as an impetus to rephrase theological questioning? Is the existential analytic of Heidegger, as much as it reopens the question of being, not equally important to reopen the question of God, that is, of God's incarnation?

Heidegger: Dasein, Metaphysics and Dasein's Metaphysics

Already in *Being and Time*, Heidegger launched an attack on the idea of *truth as adaequatio* or, as contemporary thought contends, truth as representation. This correspondence between the thing in itself and the thing-as-it-is-thought is said to have as its presupposition being-in-the-world.[3] Truth as correspondence,

---

1 E. Levinas, *Otherwise than Being, or Beyond Essence*, tr. A. Lingis (Duquesne: Duquesne University Press, 2002), p. 124, 'Substitution frees the subject from ennui, that is, from the enchainment to itself.'

An earlier version of this paper appeared in '"And there shall be no more Boredom": Metaphysics and Particularity in Contemporary Philosophy (Heidegger, Levinas, and Marion)' in L. Boeve, M. Lamberigts and T. Merrigan (eds), *Theology and the Quest for Truth* (BETL 202) (Leuven: Peeters, 2006), pp. 259–83.

2 Levinas, *Otherwise than Being*, p. 192, n. 21.

3 M. Heidegger, *Being and Time*, tr. J. Macquarrie and E. Robinson (New York: Harper & Row, 1962), pp. 262ff. All further references are to this translation.

according to Heidegger, rests upon something like a condition of possibility that Heidegger calls '"true" in a still more primordial sense'.[4]

Truth as correspondence tends to forget that, for something to be true in this way, this something must first *appear* or *show itself* – phenomenologically – to be true. Phenomenology investigates, not primarily the judgement, but the appearing of a particular appearance of which we, then, can predicate something of something. For instance, for a judgement – say, 'the table is brown' – to be able to correspond to a certain state of affairs, it is first necessary that this table show and reveal itself as brown. For something to reveal itself, however, it has to occur within *Dasein*'s comprehension of being-in-the-world. Truth, therefore, presupposes *Dasein*: it is only as and to *Dasein* that something can show itself as true or that something (i.e. the table) is uncovered as brown. This 'discovery' is possible only since to be *Dasein* is essentially 'uncovering' (*Entdecken*), since to be *Dasein* is already dwelling among beings (*Entdecktheit*, uncoveredness). However, this 'uncovering' is not at *Dasein*'s disposal, since it is possible only on the basis of a more primordial disclosedness of the world that gives a particular existence (*Dasein*) to itself in the mode of uncovering being. *Dasein*, thus, presupposes truth. *Dasein* is already 'in the truth', it is thrown – *Geworfen* – into truth, that is, I (and every individual existence) am thrown into the disclosure of being, which is always and already disclosing a certain world.

Heidegger is quick to point out that the 'truth' of this being-thrown into a world does not mean that *Dasein* is, or has, from time immemorial, been 'introduced to all the truth'.[5] Rather, Heidegger tries to convey that this being-thrown into the disclosedness of world is always and already twofold: not only do I understand my own being-uncovering in terms of the world,

---

4 Heidegger, *Being and Time*, pp. 263ff. See for the German, *Sein und Zeit* (Tübingen: Niemeyer, 2001), pp. 220ff. Compare however, ibid., p. 184, where Heidegger asks *why* beings would be understood, 'if they are disclosed in accordance with their condition of possibility'.

5 Heidegger, *Being and Time*, p. 263.

and from out of (an imitation of) the behaviour of others, but also from out of my ownmost disclosing of world. It is important to note that Heidegger does not *oppose* – in a dialectical fashion – *Eigentlichkeit* ('authenticity') and *Uneigenlichkeit* ('inauthenticity') as unconcealment over against concealment. The first is not, and can never be, a permanent state of *Dasein*, since being proper with respect to, for instance, this table necessarily entails that one is improper towards other beings in the room. The second, inauthenticity, is not the total absence of unconcealment. To be sure, the inauthenticity of 'the They' is a concealment, but it is a concealment that does not notice its own concealment. On the contrary, it regards this comportment toward beings as the only way to relate to being-in-the world: 'idle talk . . . develops an undifferentiated kind of intelligibility, for which nothing is closed off any longer'.[6] The fallenness of 'the They', therefore, seems to consist in a certain temptation to conceive of its comportment towards beings as a total and transparent unconcealment.[7] The conclusion seems to be that, for Heidegger, 'authenticity' or a proper comportment towards the being of beings cannot be conceived of as the total absence or the privation of everything improper, whereas the simple and plain *Verfallen* (fallenness), out of which the proper comportment emerges, does not notice its own concealment and regards therefore its comportment to beings, as for instance, the table, as the total absence of anything that would be a concealment.

An example: suppose I look at this table, and then say to you 'this table is brown'. What is happening? I convey something about something to you. You look at the table, shrug your shoulders and agree. But the very fact that you agree, Heidegger is implying, is dependent upon two things: first, upon the fact that in and through the assertion 'the table is brown', I commu-

---

6 Heidegger, *Being and Time*, p. 213.

7 Compare Heidegger, *Being and Time*, p. 217, 'Curiosity, for which nothing is closed off, and idle talk, for which there is nothing not understood, provide themselves . . . with the guarantee of a "life" which, supposedly, is genuinely "lively".'

nicate myself as being a *Dasein* that always and already dwells among beings that are ready-to-hand, and second, that in and through my communication of this assertion you as well bring yourself into your awareness of a being as being-uncovering of entities within-the-world. The conclusion seems to be that, for Heidegger, truth does not so much reside in the judgement or in the assertion, taken by itself, but in speech, in our speaking together of being always and already thrown into a world, that is, both in that its being-with is, as we have discussed already, 'limited to a determinate circle of others' and 'alongside a definite range of entities within-the-world'.[8] This is so because, at the moment of the assertion and our agreement, the uncoveredness of the table is still preserved. It is this preservation of the uncoveredness of this individual table as a brown table that accounts for the fact that the judgement or the assertion relates and corresponds to the entity about which it is an assertion.

Yet Heidegger stresses that for the judgement 'the table is brown' to be true, it is not necessary that one bring oneself face to face with the table, that one, as Husserl would say, has to experience the table 'in person'. After all, it is possible to speak about this table (or, of course, anything else) in a proper manner while not being near to the table. What matters to Heidegger seems to be a certain modification in the understanding of the relation between the assertion and the entity being spoken of. That there is this relation, one will recall, stems from the uncoveredness of the table, which is preserved in the assertion. However, once asserted, the judgement becomes 'as it were ready-to-hand which can be taken up and spoken [of] again'.[9] It is here that the tendency to fall as a peculiar relation to the uncoveredness of a being comes into play. As one will recall, 'the They' is portrayed by Heidegger as doing what everyone does, speaking about that which everyone speaks

---

8 Respectively M. Heidegger, *Einleitung in die Philosophie* (Frankfurt am Main: Vittorio Klostermann, 1996), p. 334, 'Mitsein mit Anderen ist eingeschränkt auf einen bestimmten Umkreis' (my translation), and *Being and Time*, p. 264.

9 Heidegger, *Being and Time*, p. 266.

about, reading what others have read and so on.[10] In Paragraph 44 of *Being and Time*, Heidegger understands the being-uncovering of the They as 'the absorption in something that has been said', that is, 'that which has been expressed as such takes over Being-towards those entities which have been uncovered in the assertion'.[11] Thus, in the idle talk of the They the relation between the assertion and that which is spoken of changes: no longer is the assertion 'the table is brown' something that occurs within in a world and in our speaking of entities within-the-world, in its stead 'the table is brown', and the relation between the assertion and that of which it speaks, becomes present-at-hand. The uncoveredness that was preserved in the utterance is substituted for a scientific and logical understanding of the utterance: 'Uncoveredness of something becomes the present-at-hand conformity of *one* thing which is present-at-hand – the assertion expressed – *to* something else which is present-at-hand – the entity under discussion.'[12] In this way, 'the uncoveredness (truth) becomes, for its part, a relationship between things that are present-at-hand (*intellectus et res*) – a relationship that is present-at-hand itself',[13] or, as it is stated in *Introduction to Metaphysics,* 'truth loosens itself, as it were, from beings, this can go so far that saying again becomes mere hearsay'.[14] What worries Heidegger here is that philosophy, instead of reflecting upon being in a particular world, returns to the Cartesian and thus mathematical understanding of world as, say, a collection of things present-at-hand, a collection of objects that can be adequately defined and, above all, represented correctly by a subject. Philosophy, again, reflects upon present-at-hand beings, and does not even ask what being, that is, what being-in-a-world might mean. Philosophy, turning to

---

10 Heidegger, *Being and Time*, pp. 153–68 and 210–24.

11 Heidegger, *Being and Time*, p. 267.

12 Heidegger, *Being and Time*, p. 267.

13 Heidegger, *Being and Time*, p. 267.

14 M. Heidegger, *Introduction to Metaphysics*, tr. G. Fried and R. Polt (New Haven: Yale University Press, 2000), p. 198. All further references are to this translation.

Heidegger's critique of Descartes at the beginning of *Being and Time*, 'prescribes for the world its "real" Being'.[15]

In his later works, as is well known, Heidegger pondered the experience of being that the Greeks entertained. For this, he returned to the understanding of *physis*, as 'a manner and mode of becoming present'.[16] But how then do beings become present and how are they uncovered? Beings come into the open (or they withhold themselves). If they appear, this simultaneously entails that they have a certain look (idea), which is both how a being 'presents itself to us, re-presents itself and as such stands before us' and *that* something that comes to presence indeed is coming to presence or presence*s*.[17] The table, for instance, presents itself, but both in the sense *that* there 'is' this table and in the sense of *what* the table essentially is, i.e. a brown plateau having four legs. The look – *idea* – or what a being shows itself to be, is equated with its being: *that* there is (this) being in this or that way is substituted for 'that which comes to presence in the whatness of the look'.[18] A being is determined thereby from out of its lying present as *a* being for a subject: a table is what it is because it shows itself most often as a brown plateau with four legs. The being of the being table is that it 'is' as being a plateau with four legs; the 'real' being of a being is held in thought, rather than encountered from out of a particular event. The 'idea' or essence determines how the being of the table will come into presence, namely, as a being that lies present for a subject. The consequence is that the very fact *that* a being is able to lie present for a subject is considered to be secondary. Herein lies the birth of the so-called modern subject: a being is if and only if it (a) shows itself *to* a subject, and (b) if this subject can determine both that a being shows itself at all

---

15 Heidegger, *Being and Time*, p. 129.

16 M. Heidegger, 'On the Essence and Concept of *Physis* in Aristotle's *Physics* B, 1' in M. Heidegger, *Pathmarks*, tr. T. Sheehan, ed. W. McNeill (Cambridge: Cambridge University Press, 1998), pp. 183–230, p. 200.

17 For that which follows, see Heidegger, *Introduction to Metaphysics*, pp. 190ff. The citation is taken from p. 192.

18 Heidegger, *Introduction to Metaphysics*, p. 193.

and what this being shows itself to be like, that is, if the subject can re-present the being of a being *for itself* as if it was an object.

Thus, metaphysics loosens this second sense of becoming-present from the first sense, and detaches the 'look' that a being gives 'to us' from the becoming-present of a being itself. In metaphysics, this what-ness – *essentia, hupokeimenon, subiectum* – becomes the norm and the criterion for anything to show up. That the table is brown, for instance, is no longer inferred from the fact that the table presents itself from out of a world, but it is because the table has this or that essence – chemical elements that produce a certain pigment – that this table *must* be brown. Metaphysics retains of the becoming-present of being(s) merely the 'whatness' of a being and understands the very appearing of a particular being, its 'thatness,' always and already from out of its 'whatness'. Therefore, this whatness or essence comes to determine also how beings in particular appear, that is, they will always and already appear as a privation, a fall and defect over against the whatness that 'is most in being about beings'.[19] It is, according to Heidegger, Plato who develops this metaphysical pattern for the first time: now 'beings themselves, which previously hold sway sink to the level of that what Plato calls *mē on* – that which really should not be and really *is* not either – because beings always deform the idea, the pure look, by actualizing it, insofar as they incorporate in matter'.[20] For Plato, it is the pure abstracted look that matters, the material being is only a deformed, inferior copy of the being as it is held in thought. Thus, now that which appears, that which makes an appearance is but a seeming and a defect, in short, a fall over against the 'whatness' of the particular being which 'is now what *really* is'[21] – Derrida *avant la lettre*! Here is what Heidegger understands by metaphysics: essentially the

---

19 Heidegger, *Introduction to Metaphysics*, p. 196. The German has 'das Seiendste am Seienden'; see M. Heidegger, *Einführung in die Metaphysik* (Tübingen: Niemeyer, 1958), p. 140.

20 Heidegger, *Introduction to Metaphysics*, p. 196.

21 Heidegger, *Introduction to Metaphysics*, p. 196.

appearance of a range of distinctions or of a cleft in that which, for the Greeks prior to Plato, originally *belonged together*, namely, and among others, being and becoming or being and thinking. Whereas for the Greeks the being of beings is to be traced from out of the manifold appearances of beings, metaphysics distinguishes between the inferior appearance of a being in time and in materiality and the 'permanent presence' of the essence of a being that does not appear, but can be held in thinking. It is here that one must understand that Heidegger would not subscribe to Derrida's thesis of a 'metaphysics of presence'. Heidegger does not dismiss all presence of beings, but is rather looking for a more original (phenomenological?) account of the presence of beings in their very presencing or coming into presence in being and in time. This is what Michel Haar suggests: 'metaphysics is not linked to presence as such, but rather to its permanent character, and its disgust of all finitude, that is to say, to its forgetting of temporality.'[22] Whereas for the Greeks being and thinking belong together in the sense that being *needs* the *noein* or apprehension of human beings so that 'apprehension also necessarily occurs along with appearance',[23] in metaphysics 'thinking sets itself against Being in such a way that Being is re-presented to thinking, and constantly stands against thinking like an ob-ject'.[24] Being and thinking no longer belong together and call for one another, but thinking assumes dominance over being in that the representation of the essence of a being decides over the appearance of beings. The appearance of a being does no longer give rise to thought; rather a being *is* only in so far as it can be represented in thinking. To conclude, it is important to note that, in this sense, the metaphysical appearance of such a cleft is always worked out from out of a privative term: for instance, 'becoming' appears over against being as something that really should not be and is

---

22 M. Haar, *La philosophie française entre phénoménologie et métaphysique* (Paris: PUF, 1999), pp. 1–9, p. 6.

23 Heidegger, *Introduction to Metaphysics*, p. 148.

24 Heidegger, *Introduction to Metaphysics*, p. 123.

therefore, from the perspective of being, proclaimed as something that in reality *is* not either.

How does all this relate to Christianity? Not only do we have here the means to grapple with what Heidegger understood as ontotheology – 'God' as the uncaused cause and unmoved mover who founds or holds together the (immaterial) essences of diverse material (but imperfect) beings – but also one can understand Heidegger here as a thinker who is careful not to think of our particular being-in-the-world as a defect, or, to use theology's terminology, as a fallen or sinful creature that has to deplore its own status. Rather Heidegger is concerned to retrieve from this conception of a being's appearing and appearance as a defect a more original openness toward being. This new conception would no longer regard the becoming-present of a being merely as a defect. The seeming of every appearance of a being is not something that really should not be, but the appearance of such a seeming necessarily belongs to the way in which (a) being itself makes itself known to human beings. This seeming, then, need not be understood in a privative manner, as something that should not be. It is part and parcel of this more original truth – *aletheia* as the event of being – that tries to think through that which, according to Heidegger, Aristotle already understood, namely, that *Dasein* 'can *either* conceal *or* unconceal' and that this double possibility is distinctive of the truthfulness of *Dasein*'s existence.[25] To return to our example: it is not that the seeming and the appearance of the table must be opposed to an adequate judgement, to, say, a scientific and 'correct' understanding of the table. It is, rather, the other way around: such a scientific understanding is only possible since (un)concealment is already in play. It is not that the judgement unconceals the 'essence' of the table, and is 'more true' than all the rest we would like to say about tables, for instance in poetry. Both are possible only on the basis of authentic and inauthentic (un)concealment, which, in turn, is possible on the basis of *Dasein*'s being-thrown-in-the-world as concealing and

---

25 See Heidegger, *Being and Time*, p. 268. Heidegger's italics.

unconcealing. What happens in the distinction between ready-to-hand and present-at-hand judgements is that in the latter the reference to this particular being, and to *Dasein*'s relation toward this being, is interpreted in a metaphysical way: when judgement becomes the locus of truth, this judgement is always and already an utterance about something that lies present (as objects lie present) to someone – the subject – to which this object always and already *only* can lie present and to which this object can only present itself as present-at-hand. What is overlooked is that the 'truth of the truth of the judgement' lies in *Dasein*'s appropriating it in its own way – which always is both concealing *and* unconcealing, improper and proper. In short, that *Dasein* has to be – or, rather *is* – its own *Entdecken* from out of a particular world is no longer taken into view.

But can it be? Heidegger's own account of overcoming metaphysics is a complex one. He seems to be sure, though, that one can only surmise what this 'overcoming' might be, if one understands metaphysics *from within*. The famous *Schritt zurück* tells us precisely that: the step back out of metaphysics occurs only when metaphysics is properly understood. On the other hand, whether this 'overcoming' can ever succeed is not clear. Not only is the appearance of 'ground' (the movement which seeks to found finitude in an infinite and unfounded instance) portrayed as a 'perhaps necessary illusion of foundation',[26] but it is also confirmed that 'fallenness is a natural condition of *Dasein*'.[27] Throwness and falling are constitutive for *Dasein*'s being-in-the-world. As such, they account for what Heidegger has called the inauthentic manner of being-in-the-world. We have already noted that this inauthenticity deals only with beings in their presence rather than with their becoming-present, and that it therefore has lost sight of the being of this or that being. In other words, the openness towards being is closed off in favour of a disclosing of beings, which, in turn, is

26 Heidegger, *Introduction to Metaphysics*, p. 3.

27 See M. Heidegger, *Vier Seminäre* (Frankfurt am Main: Vittorio Klosterman, 1977), p. 100, 'Das ontologisch verstandene "Verfallen" ist sogar der Naturzustand des Daseins . . .'. My translation.

regarded as the only possible way of relating to being. It is, at least in *Being and Time*, not sure whether this inauthentic manner is something that can be overcome. Indeed, authenticity is not a permanent state of *Dasein* opposed to the metaphysical nature of inauthenticity and throwness. Rather, it 'has its moments': for instance, angst, sickness, boredom and death.[28] In these moments – similar to Kierkegaard's *kairos* – the tendency of fallenness to understand itself out of the world and out of beings disappears, but only to show, or to make appear, that *Dasein* already has to be its world, that is, has to be its openness toward the world and toward being; in short, and more familiar terms, what is revealed is that this *Dasein* is the being that has to be its own being as a being-with others and entities within-the-world. The inauthentic tendency is not brought to a halt, but what now appears is that its unconcealing is, in fact, at the same time, concealing – a comportment toward particular beings. Angst and death, one could say, make *Dasein*'s openness appear – its *Entdecken, Entwurf, Erschlossenheit* – as such, that is, as entailing the double possibility of concealing and unconcealing: its relation to (its own) being. But since this authentic way is not a permanent *Zustand* of *Dasein*, some have argued that angst and death only show the inevitable character of fallenness.[29] However, to look at it in this way *already* presupposes that this fallenness has to be conceived of as a defect to be overcome which, as we have shown above, is not at all what Heidegger intended. Rather, and instead of deploring the inevitability of fallenness as such, one should ponder whether the tendency to regard the appearance of beings to be a defect, that is, the tendency to regard fallenness and throwness

---

28 It is barely noticed that Heidegger, at least at one place in *Being and Time*, regarded sickness as playing a similar role to that of death; see *Being and Time*, p. 291. On boredom, see M. Heidegger, *Die Grundbegriffe der Metaphysik: Welt – Endlichkeit – Einsamkeit* (Frankfurt am Main: Vittorio Klostermann, 2004).

29 As Rudi Visker does in *Truth and Singularity* (Dordrecht: Kluwer Academic Publishers, 1999), pp. 23–46, and pp. 55ff.

to be a privation, as 'that which really should not be' is inevitable.

It is not clear whether Heidegger, at least in 1927, succeeded in doing this. Indeed, if one can maintain that Heidegger was seeking to disclose another way of comporting toward being, it is highly disturbing precisely how he reached this conclusion. Thrownness is part and parcel of being-in-the-world, and it is characteristic of thrownness that it is disclosed 'more or less plainly and impressively'.[30] Thus, the disclosing of thrownness admits of degrees: it is either disclosed totally or in a lesser manner. This point needs, of course, to be proven. It is Heidegger himself who, though through a single occurrence, delivers this proof. Those instances that make our being-in-the-world appear seem like a sort of maximum of disclosed-ness. So, for instance, angst is accompanied by the selfsame of 'the disclosure and the disclosed',[31] which is, in both cases, the (possibility of) being-in-the-world as such. Indeed, that which is disclosed is the same as that what which discloses, i.e. being-in-the-world or *Dasein* as such. However, does not such a maximum intimate the return of truth as correspondence or at least the thesis that *Dasein*'s facticity can be taken into view adequately?[32]

Before pondering what this recurrence might mean for theology, and more importantly, faith, we shall now turn briefly to the accounts of Levinas and Marion. Indeed, if one wants to overcome metaphysics, and if this means to overcome, first of all, the theory of truth as adequation, one should be wary of yet another recurrence of this theory. In Levinas, we will show, it is the Other who coincides with him- or herself and who,

---

30 Heidegger, *Being and Time*, p. 315.

31 Heidegger, *Being and Time*, p. 233, see *Sein und Zeit*, p. 188, 'die existenziale Selbigkeit des Erschließens mit dem Erschlossenen'; *Being and Time*, p. 233.

32 One should not too quickly object that such a return loses its sense in a philosophy where the *intellectus* is substituted for the affective *Befindlichkeit* and *Verstehen*. The thesis that an object can be represented adequately by the subject is as questionable as the thesis that our affective states would be available to us in a transparent manner.

therefore, is able to tear the subject out of its *situatedness* –
Levinas's term for *Geworfenheit*. In Marion, on the other hand,
the gifted is, time and again, defined as the sum of his or her
responses toward givenness.

Levinas: Another Metaphysics? The Metaphysics of the Other

This section sketches how Levinas undertakes an enquiry similar to Heidegger. We will focus on two main issues: first,
Levinas's insistence that all knowledge entails the correspondence theory of truth, that is, in his terms, the reduction of the
other to the same, and second, Levinas's concern that this
primacy of the theoretical attitude devalues both human beings
and God.

For Levinas, all knowledge – especially that of being – exposes
a will to power or a reduction of the Other to the same. To
return once again to our example: how does the table appear to
consciousness? Strictly speaking, I only perceive two or at times
three legs of it. That I still refer to the table as a table arises from
the fact that I, according to Husserl, constitute its fourth leg.
But, precisely, this constitution is a mental act that already
presupposes what a table in general has to look like, for
instance, as a plateau with four legs. Thus, constitution presupposes an essence of the table, and this essence, in turn, functions
as the horizon that secures the unity or univocity of tables in
general. However, this essence of the table already precludes
certain tables to appear – one need only think of certain designer
tables. Of course, this is a rather innocent example, but one can
think of other instances in which this reduction occurs. When,
for instance, human beings came to be defined as *animal ration-
ale*, this idea of the essence of human beings could not prevent
that *certain* women and men were excluded from this definition.

For Levinas, however, there is one instance that always
escapes this violent reduction. That instance, of course, is *the
face of the other*. The face of the other questions consciousness'

mode of procedure: consciousness proceeds through reducing otherness to the same, that is, through an operation of knowledge that reduces a phenomenon to that which it can adequately describe and define or represent of the phenomenon. In the face-to-face encounter with the other, Levinas contends, consciousness is put into question. It cannot make sense of the other, since this otherness of the other, the transcendence of the human person, resists all identification or adequation. The other's face is not reducible to some common characteristics, or 'form', that this particular other would share with others.[33] Hence according to what would be Levinas's account of racism:[34] racism reduces black persons to their being black, to his or her form or visible attributes. This, however, is to commit an injustice towards the black person's face, his or her being a unique individual. The black person is reduced to being 'nothing other' than his or her blackness. Note that, if racism proceeds thus, it almost automatically extends to all black men and women: since you, as a black person, are nothing other than your blackness, all other black persons are merely instantiations and instances of this essence 'blackness', and thus you will be racist against these others as well. For, if one black person can be reduced to his or her participation in 'being black', the racist will also reduce all the other black persons to what they share with or have in common with this one particular other to whom he or she is being racist. In a Levinasian vein, one could therefore portray *the 'end' of metaphysics as the end of thinking about anything or anyone in general*, since the dignity of a human being, for Levinas, does not lie in being a member of a particular community, a determinate context, but precisely in being irreducible to that context. Thus, Levinas sets out an opposition

---

33 See, for instance, E. Levinas, *Totality and Infinity*, tr. A. Lingis (Duquesne: Duquesne University Press, 2002), p. 66, '[T]he manifestation of a face over and beyond form. Form – incessantly betraying its own manifestation, congealing into a plastic form, for it is adequate to the same – alienates the exteriority of the other.'

34 The example is taken from Visker, *Truth and Singularity*, pp. 328–9 and 349. I will come back to this example below.

between the (invisible) face and the (visible) form of the human person, between the manifestation, the revelation and the epiphany of the face, and the ordinary phenomenality of objects and beings, between the 'pure signification'[35] of the encounter with the other and the 'impure' appearance of a form, already contaminated with the phenomenality essential to being. While the former is an inadequation par excellence, the appearance of the latter is conditioned by the correspondence between the concept and the phenomenon in question. While the former manifests itself 'independently of every position we would have taken in this regard',[36] the latter is dependent precisely on the position that the subject assumes over and against the objective phenomenon (just as the table can only appear to a subject over and against the horizon of a table in general).

However, we need to question how Levinas maintains this distinction. It might be that the failure of adequation with regard to the face is in turn dependent on the correspondence theory of truth, since after all the manifestation of a face entails 'a coinciding of the expressed with him who expresses'.[37] Thus, it seems that one can escape the (metaphysical) correspondence theory of truth only by presupposing it. But what does Levinas mean? The face to face with the other originates, as we have seen, in language. In expression, that which is manifested coincides with the one manifesting herself. On one condition, however: that the one manifesting herself attends to its own manifestation, that is, is able to correct its own manifestation. According to Levinas, the Saying always differs from the said.[38] For example, if I see someone crying, it is not me who decides on the meaning of the tears of the Other, the truth of these tears has to be communicated by him or her. It is only in discourse that the transcendence of the Other makes its appearance – but only to

---

35 Levinas, *Otherwise than Being*, p. 143.

36 Levinas, *Totality and Infinity*, p. 65.

37 See Levinas, *Totality and Infinity*, p. 66, with parallels on p. 296, 'in expression the manifestation and the manifested coincide', and p. 262, 'an essential coinciding of the existent and the signifier'.

38 Levinas, *Otherwise than Being*, pp. 45–51, 153–62.

disappear, to leave its trace. The Other can tell me that his or her tears are faked, since he or she is rehearsing for a play, but he or she can just as well retrieve even this statement on a later occasion. Thus, it is not *what* the Other says that is the trace of transcendence, but the fact that she speaks and that she, in this way, is always able to retrieve *what* she has said, in short, able to *teach* me,[39] in the sense of revealing to me something which I do not already know. Teaching in this sense is for Levinas the mark of transcendence, the mark of the other's height – an absolute difference different from all other, ontic, differences between the other and I.[40] Thus, the transcendence of the other lies in his or her being always other and always different from that which is said, in his or her irreducibility to the form of the said.[41] However, this difference is, in one way or another, subordinated to the possibility that the one speaking coincides with that which is said. Thus, if there is a difference between the face (the Saying) and the form (the said) it can only be so because the one instance that makes a difference – the other – is excepted from this difference: the other can coincide with herself, and is, therefore, able to point me to the difference between her saying and her said. It seems, therefore, that the difference between the Saying and the said can only be maintained if this difference is measured by the possible adequation between the one manifesting and that which she manifests. One might surmise, therefore, that it is, at least for the Levinas of *Totality and Infinity*, not me who is the modern subject, but the Other. Here is not the place to tackle all these questions, but suffice it to say that the return of truth as

---

39 See for instance Levinas, *Totality and Infinity*, p. 51.

40 I take the expression from Jean-Marc Narbonne (and W. Hankey), *Lévinas et l'héritage grec suivi de Cent ans de néoplatonisme en France* (Laval: Presses de l'Université, 2004), p. 63.

41 In expression, the Other is supposed to 'break through all the . . . generalities of Being, to spread out in its "form" the totality of its "content," finally abolishing the distinction between form and content'; see Levinas, *Totality and Infinity*, p. 51. The frequent recurrence, for instance, in quarrels of formulas as 'Did I say that?' or 'I did not say that!' might be elucidated thus.

mere more 'adequate to the same' might point to the fact that 'overcoming metaphysics' may not be as easy a task as it nowadays sometimes seems.

In the next section we will therefore point to a critique of Levinas that is encountered in the works of both Marion and Visker. Visker argues for a reconsidering of the relation between the face and the form. Marion is concerned with the individuation of the other over and against the neutral horizon of Levinasian ethics.

A Significant Other? From the Other to the Individual

Levinas is quite clear on the distinction between the face and the form, both in *Totality and Infinity* and in *Otherwise than Being*. Consider the following quote, taken from the former book: 'the alterity of the Other does not depend on any quality that would distinguish him from me, for a distinction of this nature would precisely imply between us that community of genus which already nullifies alterity'.[42] Hence there is a distinction between the transcendence of the other and the (Husserlian) transcendence of the object. For the difference between different objects is possible only on the basis of the (different) qualities that emerge from within a community of genus, just as we are able to distinguish between a brown and a black table from out of the shared horizon of a table in general. *Otherwise than Being* will underline the non-phenomenal character of the other as well: 'the neighbor does not stand in a form, like an object abides in the plasticity of an aspect, a profile or an open series of aspects, which overflows each of them without destroying the adequation of the act of consciousness',[43] for if he or she would appear in a form and be reduced to the *Abschattungen* and adumbrations the reducing I performs in face of the object, the glory of the face would become a phenomenon *as every other phenomenon* and enter into conjunction with the very subject to

---

42 Levinas, *Totality and Infinity*, p. 194.
43 Levinas, *Otherwise than Being*, p. 87.

which it appears and which closes itself and the other up in finitude and immanence.[44] To be sure, the face *can* be treated as every other phenomenon, and it is precisely in this reduction of the other to his or her visible properties that the possibility of racism and sexism resides.

Although we will see Marion arguing for the individuation of the other below, it is noteworthy that he, in his own way, rehearses Levinas's distinction between the face and the form. According to Marion indeed, one should distinguish between the flesh ('la chair') and the body ('le corps'): whereas I am exposed as an object in medical examination or in surgery, the erotic flesh-to-flesh, according to Marion, is to be conceived of as the pendant of the ethical face-to-face.[45] This strict distinction between the face and the form or between the flesh and the body, however, might suffer from the spiritualization Derrida detected in contemporary philosophy: 'by putting the flesh everywhere, one risks vitalizing, psychologizing, spiritualizing and interiorizing everything, even there where one speaks of a non-possession and of an alterity of the "flesh."'[46] A similar objection could be raised against Marion's configuration of God's crossing of being in *God without Being*. Most commentaries have focused on Marion's endeavour to go beyond Heidegger's ontological difference. Little attention has been paid, however, to what Marion regards as God's indifference to ontic differences.[47] Though this is a profound religious thought (indeed, it should not matter for God whether you are black or white), it remains to be considered whether or not our

44 Cf. Levinas, *Otherwise than Being*, p. 144.

45 Cf. J.-L. Marion, *Le phénomène érotique: Six méditations* (Paris: Grasset, 2003), pp. 178–90.

46 J. Derrida, *Le Toucher, Jean-Luc Nancy* (Paris: Galilée, 2000), p. 267. I take (and translate) the citation from Robert Esposito, 'Chair et corps dans la déconstruction du christianisme' in F. Guibal and J. C. Martin (eds), *Sens en tous sens: Autour des travaux de Jean-Luc Nancy* (Paris: Galilée, 2004), pp. 153–64, p. 154.

47 Cf. J.-L. Marion, *God without Being: Hors-Texte*, tr. T. A. Carlson (Chicago and London: The University of Chicago Press, 1991), pp. 88–9, '[the] indifference to the difference between beings'.

blackness or whiteness does matter for *our* relation towards God or the other person. It is this question that will concern us in that which follows, for if I really may not 'notice the color of [the other's] eyes', not even that 'his pupils are black as holes', how then can I 'see' his face?[48] The question can be posed in another way: is Levinas's account of the alterity of the other apt to encounter a *singular* other, that is, 'able to welcome the Other in his or her ethnic identity'?[49] What if this particular other does not speak Greek or Hebrew, and speaks, perhaps, only a 'babbling language, like . . . the discourse of a stranger *shut up in his maternal language*'?[50]

In this section, therefore, we would like to trace a few criticisms of Levinas's distinction between the face and the form, for, if we are right when contending that the end of metaphysics implies that one refrains from thinking of anything or anyone in general, then one should ask whether the Levinasian other itself refuses all such generalization.

Visker, for instance, develops the idea that a 'more correct

---

48 Respectively: E. Levinas, *Ethics and Infinity: Conversations with Philippe Nemo*, tr. R. A. Cohen (Pittsburgh: Duquesne University Press, 1985), p. 85, and J.-L. Marion, *Being Given: Toward a Phenomenology of Givenness*, tr. J. Kosky (Stanford: Stanford Univeristy Press, 2002), p. 232.

49 R. Bernasconi, 'Who is my Neighbor? Questioning the Generosity of Western Thought' in *Ethics and Responsibility in the Phenomenological Tradition* (Pittsburgh: Duquesne University, 1992), pp. 2–31, p. 22. For this question, see also J.-L. Marion, 'From the Other to the Individual' in R. Schwartz (ed.), *Transcendence: Philosophy, Literature, and Theology Approach the Beyond* (New York: Routledge, 2004), pp. 43–59, esp. p. 49, 'It remains no less a necessity, even and especially in ethics, if one claims to have access to a face, to accede to *his* face, thus to identify him as such, to particularize the face, to individuate it,' and p. 54, where Marion asks whether one can be responsible for the universal at all.

50 Levinas, *Otherwise than Being*, p. 143. I am referring here to a rather perplexing statement of Levinas: 'I often say, though it's a dangerous thing to say publicly, that humanity consists of the Bible and the Greeks: all the rest – all the exotic – is dance'; see also for further references, Bernasconi, 'Who is my Neighbor?' p. 14.

phenomenological description of the alterity of the Other'[51] would amount to a reconsideration of the relation between the face and the form, for the dignity of the human being might not lie in him or her being an abstract man or woman without context, but rather in his or her being *not without* context. This is why an Afro-American 'is angry not just with those who discriminate against him because of his color, [but also] with those who respect him notwithstanding his color'.[52] It seems, therefore, that Levinas somewhat underestimates the attachment of human beings towards that with which they identify, and here is another reason why the axiom running from *Totality and Infinity* to *Otherwise than Being*, namely the reduction of everything in being to being but an expression of an (injust) *conatus essendi*, is itself, perhaps, an injustice towards the Other. To develop this claim, one might reconsider Levinas's argument that the face is strictly distinct from the works in which it expresses itself.[53] For the works *of* the other are, perhaps, not merely egoistic and economic reductions of otherness to the same, but rather seem to contribute to the other's otherness in a particular way. Just as Afro-American women and men would be angry if I would say to them that I respect them regardless of their skin colour, so too the other would be treated unjustly if I would pay no attention at all to that which he or she does to make a living or to 'persevere in his or her being'. It is in this way that Levinas seems to disregard the attachment of human beings to that with which they identify themselves, and does not even consider that the ontological enjoyment in the 'making a living' might just as well 'enter into the way of existing of the exterior being'.[54]

---

51 R. Visker, *The Inhuman Condition: Looking for Difference after Levinas and Heidegger* (Dordrecht: Kluwer Academic Publishers, 2004), p. 14.

52 Visker, *Truth and Singularity*, p. 349.

53 Levinas, *Totality and Infinity*, pp. 66–7, 175–83.

54 See Levinas, *Totality and Infinity*, p. 35. It is not difficult to come up with examples of this. One should ponder, perhaps, why in the case of a first encounter with a stranger the first questions to be asked most often concern the other's name and his or her profession.

This brutal and sweeping claim that turns all identification into an egoistic complaisance of oneself also bears on what one often finds praised as Levinasian ethics, for this ethics suffers perhaps from that which Finkielkraut remarks of the doctor without frontiers, who 'is too busy filling the hungry mouth with rice, to still have time to listen to what it is trying to say'.[55] Here an ethics solely based on an asymmetry between the Other and I seems to encounter its limits, for how could an ethics does not concern itself with the other's movement towards me[56] ever make room for Finkielkraut's objection? Indeed, what if the other demands water and all my hands have to give to him is bread? One should ponder indeed whether an ethics appropriate to the individual is not another ethics than the one Levinas advances, since Levinasian ethics is almost exclusively focused on the relief of the other's basic needs. The signification that is supposedly before culture turns into an attending to the other that is an ethics *only* of 'nourishing, clothing, [and] lodging'.[57] But, to misuse a New Testament phrase, one does not live by bread alone. It is here, therefore, that the Heideggerian analysis of solicitude (*Fürsorge*) as a care for-the-other might be invoked to balance Levinas' ethics, not only because solicitude incorporates the concern 'with food and clothing, and the nursing of the sick body',[58] but especially because solicitude in its authentic mode does not take away the care of the other for

---

55 A. Finkielkraut, *La humanité perdue: essai sur le XXe siècle* (Paris, Seuil, 1996), p. 128, as cited in Visker, *The Inhuman Condition*, p. 160. The few instances in which Levinas gives a positive meaning to non-verbal language may not be able to counter these objections. For Levinas on non-verbal language (and thus certainly a nuance on the strict distinction between face and form), importantly, in both *Totality and Infinity* and *Otherwise than Being*: respectively p. 262, 'the whole body – a hand or a curve of the shoulder – can express as a face', and p. 85, 'skin . . . is always a modification of the face'. See also p. 192, n. 27, 'the unity of the face and the skin'.

56 See Levinas, *Otherwise than Being*, p. 84.

57 Levinas, *Otherwise than Being*, p. 77.

58 Heidegger, *Being and Time*, p. 158.

him – leaping in for him as when one, as a parent, would do the child's homework – but rather 'gives it back to him authentically as such for the first time'[59] – as when one would take the time to teach the child the matter at hand so as to prepare it to do the homework itself. Most important for our concern here, however, is how Heidegger defines this authentic care for the other: it is an authentic care because it pertains to the care for the existence of the human being *in toto* and not only, as is the case in Levinas's ethics, to a 'what' or to the basic needs with which he is concerned.[60]

All this might entail that the encounter with the other is not so much 'without context' as Levinas contends, and that, if one wants to take our particular being-in-the-world seriously, one best not dream of a 'total transparence'[61] in these matters, for an ethics that wants to be truly an ethics might need to take into account not only that the care for the other is *in each case mine*, but also that the ethics to be followed might be different from one ethnic group to another or from one individual to another, and that, therefore, the appropriate response to the other is *in each case different*.

Marion envisages a passageway to the particular and singular other through the question of love. There are, of course, good reasons for this, because perhaps only love permits and demands the individuation of the other.[62] In this way, love is always love of *this* particular other. With the question of love, Marion seems to open a path for thought that goes beyond Levinas's almost exclusive attention to ethics. Already in *Prolegomena to Charity*, Marion manifests a certain reluctance towards the universality of Levinasian ethics and the Kantian resonances

---

59 Heidegger, *Being and Time*, p. 159.

60 Heidegger, *Being and Time*. We are indebted here to Jean-Luc Marion's lecture, 'Levinas and Heidegger: The Care for the Other and Substitution', given at the conference *The Exorbitant: Levinas between Jews and Christians*, 17–19 April 2004, Notre Dame, Indiana, forthcoming in a volume edited by Kevin Hart.

61 Levinas, *Totality and Infinity*, p. 182.

62 Marion, *Being Given*, p. 324.

thereof.[63] Both the Kantian respect for the other as an end in itself or the Levinasian responsibility for the other concern the other human being in general. In this sense, ethics is always and already the neutralization of the particular other. I am not responsible for this rather than that other, I am responsible for every other human being to the extent that he or she is merely an instantiation of the face:

> paradoxically, the moral law – which states that the other man must always count as an end and not as a means – never uses the face of an individualized other except as a means for accomplishing the universal. The injunction of obligation toward the other leads, in reality, to the neutralization of the other as such [comme *tel*].[64]

The objection can be repeated in face of Levinas's other, for 'the face itself neutralizes unsubstitutable individuality: I do not find myself responsible for *this* other as much as this other admits of being reduced to a face *in general*.'[65] One should ponder, however, whether this notion of a 'face in general' is not in itself a metaphysical notion, robbed from all things finite and temporal, for if this or that other can only impose an ethical claim on me because of his or her being an actualization of the face in general, how are we to determine the status of this face-in-general? Is it that one leaps from the particularity of this face to the essence of a face in general or – the other way around – that the concept of a face 'in general' determines beforehand how this or that particular other will appeal to me? Here, then, one

---

63 See J.-L. Marion, *Prolegomena to Charity*, tr. S. E. Lewis (New York: Fordham Univeristy Press, 2002), pp. 90–101, and also Marion, 'From the Other to the Individual', pp. 50–2. Note that whereas the former text distinguishes between Kant and Levinas's ethics, the latter text interprets Levinas's ethics in a Kantian fashion.

64 Marion, *Prolegomena to Charity*, pp. 92–3; *Prolegomènes à la charité* (Paris: Ed. La Différence, 1986), p. 112.

65 Marion, *Prolegomena to Charity*, p. 94 mod.; *Prolegomènes à la charité*, p. 114.

finds reasons to doubt that the appeal is always and everywhere ethical, and why ethics might be yet another usurpation of our particular being-in-the-world. It is because of these intimations of Levinas's inability to attain the other as an individual that I fully subscribe to Marion's turn to the individual (*haeccitas*),[66] and to the conclusion of *Le phénomène érotique*:

> strictly speaking . . . one should never speak of the face in general, nor of the other in general, but only of *this* other, with *this* face – in the sense that one never envisages a universal face or a face that we all have in common, but it is always *this* face that opposes me *this* alterity.[67]

Given, however, Marion's insistence on an appeal in general that, because it is considered to be the 'pure form of the appeal', incorporates all possible other appealing instances, whether it be God, the other, self-affection or difference,[68] one should ask whether the sketch of the other as an individual that one finds in Marion's thinking about love is not fundamentally at odds with the phenomenological project of *Reduction and Givenness* and *Being Given*. One should, therefore, take not only Derrida's claim 'that there is more than appeal'[69] seriously, but also ask why and to what extent Marion's configuration of the *adonné* is incompatible with the turn to the individual evoked here. Both questions deserve to be posed: for the account of the *adonné* as the one who receives him- or herself from that which he or she receives makes no mention at all of the sexual difference

---

66 Cf. Marion, *Prolegomena to Charity*, p. 95, 'Haeccitas passes beyond beingness [*l'étantite*] in general, but also beyond that which, in the injunction and responsibility, falls under the universal, and thus the Neuter.'

67 Marion, *Le phénomène érotique*, p. 160. Marion's italics.

68 See for this Marion, *Reduction and Givenness: Investigations of Husserl, Heidegger, and Phenomenology*, tr. T. A. Carlson (Evanston: Northwestern University Press, 1998), p. 202.

69 J. Derrida and J.-L. Nancy, 'Responsabilité – du sens à venir' in *Sens en tous sens*, ed. Guibal and Martin, pp. 165–200, p. 184.

between men and women, and in this sense seems to disregard all questions on the differences in the manner of receiving between men and women. There is no place to develop this here, but the question at least hints at the fact that Marion's phenomenology is substituting the face-in-general for the *adonné*-in-general. The next section, therefore, will focus on the *mathematical* manner with which Marion describes the *adonné* in order to point to the incompatibility of the human being as an *adonné* with the account of the human being from out of his or her *haeccitas*.

Marion: Responding ad infinitum?

Marion shares with Levinas the concern of thinking through, after metaphysics, the death of God. For both, the death of the metaphysical God is the opportunity for a renewed consideration of whether and how 'God' can appear in philosophy. Both will maintain, as Heidegger had done before, a strict distinction between philosophical and theological discourse. However, one can argue that Marion presents a radicalized version of Levinas's philosophy: 'one should generalize to each being given the status of beyond being-ness'.[70] This is, in fact, what his *magnum opus*, *Being Given*, sets out to do. Givenness gives itself in every phenomenon as a non-metaphysical present (gift). Phenomena come into being, but without that being determining essentially this or that particular being. Phenomena always exceed the gaze of the subject that tries to constitute it as an object; that is, it exceeds attempts to describe it adequately. Take, for example, the saturated phenomenon of the event. No one has seen the battle of Waterloo.[71] The event cannot be described adequately, but appeals to a multiplication of views that altogether forbid constituting it as one single object. Saturated phenomena have no essence, no constant presence to which one can constantly and confidently refer, but appeal to

---

70 J.-L. Marion, *Le visible et le révélé* (Paris: Cerf, 2005), p. 88.
71 Cf. Marion, *Being Given*, pp. 228–9.

the subject to align itself to its appearance. This appearance is a gift: therefore, it cannot be, as was the case with the correspondence theory of truth, foreseen – the presence of this or that chemical element predicts that the table must be brown – its invisible present arrives a surprise, unforeseen, as when one suddenly notices that the brown of this particular table here resembles the table in one's parents house. This non-essential character of the gift extends to all phenomena: though to some extent everything that happens to the subject can be considered to be an object, this object-like character never suffices to explain the unforeseeability of what comes to us as a gift: an echograph makes the birth of a child to a certain extent foreseeable, at least for the doctors, but this anticipation of its birth cannot annul the fact that this birth will be lived, at least by the parents, as unforeseeable.[72] The birth of the child, and for that matter all phenomena, give themselves as an event and summon the subject to receive itself from that which it receives. Hence Marion's thought that, for phenomena to appear, they require an individuation: the phenomena give their selves when giving themselves. The birth of my child is, at least for me, a *singular* event. Moreover, this event singularizes me as the gifted, its happening happens to give me to myself as the one who is given, in and through the reception of the birth, to the child: I am now given to the child as a father, and this is what individuates me. Therefore, the gifted plays a secondary role toward givenness: it is already a response to an appeal. It pertains to the gifted, however, to show or to make appear what is given to him or her: the appeal shows itself in the response of him or her to whom it is given. However, the generalization of the *epekeina tes ousias* requires one to consider the appeal anew. Herein lies Marion's critique of Levinas.[73] It is, according to Marion, not clear

---

72 This example is taken from E. Falque, 'Phénoménologie de l'extraordinaire', *Philosophie* 78 (2003), pp. 52–76, p. 62.

73 For this critique, see J.-L. Marion, 'The Voice without Name: Homage to Levinas' in J. Bloechl (ed.), *The Face of the Other and the Trace of God: Essays on the Philosophy of Emmanuel Levinas* (New York: Fordham University Press, 2000), pp. 224–42, esp. pp. 226–8.

whether the appeal of the face in Levinas comes from the other or from God. This *à Dieu* even risks to name that which cannot be named, to suppress the anonymity and ambiguity of the appeal, in short, 'to dissolve the very thing [it was] to protect'.[74] Hence Marion's insistence on the pure form of the appeal, that cannot be identified, that is, thus, radically anonymous, and that, if it was to be identified, could only be named inappropriately, since pertaining to the limited and finite response of the *adonné*.

What concerns us here is, however, that there is an appeal, and one cannot not respond to this 'always already there interpellation'.[75] This is why Marion can determine human beings as follows: 'the history of the gifted is due to the *sum* of its responses'.[76] Such an almost mathematical understanding of phenomena is by no means a single occurrence in Marion's phenomenology: not only the event, of which Marion insists so much that it resists all unification, seems to allow for a kind of teleology ad infinitum of which the *telos* nevertheless receives a determination as 'the *sum* of the agreements and disagreements among subjects',[77] the painting as well could in principle be adequately represented, if only one could make 'sum of all that which all have seen, see, and will see there'.[78] It is, however, the definition of the human being as the sum of his or her responses that shows itself to be particularly revealing of what one could call an objectification of the subject. Indeed, *what* is this sum and who or what is going to determine it? In any case, that such a sum of responses is possible shows that the overcoming of the metaphysical adequation may not have succeeded. Indeed, simply the fact of stating that such a sum could be envisaged seems to imply the recurrence of a God's-eye

---

74 Marion, 'The Voice without Name', p. 227.
75 Marion, *Being Given*, p. 217 mod.
76 Marion, *Being Given*, p. 295.
77 Marion, *Being Given*, p. 229.
78 J.-L. Marion, *In Excess: Studies of Saturated Phenomena*, tr. R. Horner and V. Berraud (New York: Fordham University Press, 2002), p. 72.

point of view, that is, the thought that someone or something can oversee the totality of my responses. One could agree that this sum of my responses is obtained at the occasion of my death. However, since it is considered to be an endless hermeneutics, the responses of those that respond to my death would have to be included in the sum of my responses. This sum of responses is therefore, in this world, always to be deferred and postponed. Therefore, one can surmise whether an instance 'not of this world', distant from the world,[79] could oversee the sum of my responses. A God's eye point of view indeed!

Towards a Theology of Incarnation: The Consequences of Overcoming Metaphysics for Faith and Theology

We have seen that Heidegger, although keen to keep our openness to being open, has recourse to the concept of adequation to define this 'proper' openness: there are moments when that which is disclosed is the same as that which is disclosing itself. Levinas responds that this openness towards being is already filled in by the other, and that it is this other that coincides with him- or herself, for that which is spoken is the same as the one speaking. And, if it is not the same, the being that speaks can at least correct itself, thus pointing to an eventual, a 'possible' adequation. Marion, in turn, responds to Levinas, that this filling-in is filling in too much, and that therefore there is no reason to prefer the other, instead of something without name.

It is well known that Heidegger had a somewhat peculiar relation to Christianity, and that he, more often than not, claimed philosophy to be thoroughly atheistic. In *The Metaphysical Foundations of Logic*, however, Heidegger asks: 'might not the presumably ontic faith in God be at bottom godlessness? And might not the genuine metaphysician be more religious than the usual faithful, than the members of a "church" or even the

---

79 Cf. Marion, *God without Being*, pp. 83–4.

"theologians" of every confession?'[80] This conclusion hopes therefore to show that, 'after' metaphysics, the link between faith and atheism in all three thinkers is tightened to such an extent that one might even ask whether atheism does not genuinely belong to faith of any kind. In the later *Introduction to Metaphysics*, Heidegger develops a similar mode of procedure towards the question of faith. 'Anyone for whom the Bible is divine revelation and truth has the answer to the question "Why are there beings at all instead of nothing?" before it is even asked.'[81] However, even here Heidegger keeps open the possibility of an authentic questioning, even in matters of faith. For faith, of course, has no answer, only faith. For faith to be a mode of questioning, it must, according to Heidegger, rid itself not only of the answer that God as Creator answers for the existence of beings, not only of the agreement to adhere to a doctrine somehow handed down, but, most importantly, 'continually expose itself to the possibility of unfaith'.[82]

Surprisingly, we find Levinas saying the very same thing. For instance, in his *Entre nous*, he writes: 'The ambiguity of transcendence – and thus the interplay of the soul going from atheism to faith and from faith to atheism – [is] the original mode of God's presence.'[83] One might even surmise in Marion's phenomenology a similar critical stance towards dogmatics. It is indeed difficult to see how the emphasis on God's incomprehensibility can be reconciled with the Church as the guarantee of truth. Here we agree with Robyn Horner who states that (Marion's) phenomenology does open onto theology, but that the theology 'that emerges from this opening cannot rest secure

---

80 The citation is taken from M. Heidegger, *The Metaphysical Foundations of Logic*, tr. M. Heim (Bloomington: Indiana University Press, 1984), p. 165, as cited by R. Bernasconi, *Heidegger in Question: The Art of Existing* (New Jersey: Humanities Press International, 1993), p. 37.

81 Heidegger, *Introduction to Metaphysics*, p. 7.

82 Heidegger, *Introduction to Metaphysics*, pp. 7–8.

83 E. Levinas, 'Un Dieu Homme?' in his *Entre Nous, Essais sur le penser à l'Autre* (Paris: Grasset, 1991), pp. 69–76, p. 72.

in dogma', since 'the hardening of dogma betrays transcendence'.[84]

The overcoming of metaphysics thus not only means that we cannot consider faith to be an object that is freely at our disposal, or, as Marion would put it, an 'idiotic prolepsis of a blunt certitude'.[85] It might also mean that we, when and if theologians, have to lose our faith in order to, in one way or another, gain it. It is worth noting that this supposed overcoming of metaphysics also entails not only the end of rational theology, as explained above, but also that of natural theology. This is obvious, for instance, in Levinas's rejection of theodicy. 'God' cannot be invoked to explain (or to justify) the suffering of human beings. God is no longer to be viewed as the 'reason' or 'cause' of humanity's violence and miseries, since God is transcendent to history. Every attempt to explain history on the basis of the will of God is, according to Levinas, an infliction towards precisely the victims of that history and, most often, such an attempt cannot prevent this God becoming 'a protector of all the egoisms'.[86] Heidegger would argue that developing a theology on the basis of, for example, the natural sciences disregards the fact that these sciences are already indebted to the metaphysical theory of truth as correspondence. These sciences are therefore ontic, and deal with being only in terms of beings. Therefore, they cannot instruct us on what it means to be, and even less on how God might come into being.

This means that faith is not primarily dogmatic, but ethical (Levinas) and pragmatic (Marion), a faith moreover 'in which it is no longer a matter of naming or attributing something to something, but of aiming in the direction of . . . of relating to . . . of comporting oneself toward . . . of reckoning with'.[87] It is not that this faith would become purely and solely pragmatic; it

---

84 R. Horner, 'The Betrayal of Transcendence' in R. Schwartz, (ed.) *Transcendence: Philosophy, Literature, and Theology Approach the Beyond*, pp. 61–79, p. 75.

85 Marion, *God without Being*, p. 71.

86 Levinas, *Otherwise than Being*, p. 161.

87 Marion, *In Excess*, pp. 144–5.

is the admission of the fact that the debate of whether or not a referent applies to this faith can only begin in and through precisely such a pragmatic stance, in which faith first and foremost has become a question. This is the reversal: theology can no longer start with the assertion that 'God is . . .', it can only start in prayer or in ethics, as if a *fides qua* without the blunt beforehand certitude of *fides quae*, as if only in the faithful stance of the *fides qua* a genuine *fides quae* might be able to be discerned. This, therefore, seems to be the lesson to be learned from Heidegger, Levinas and Marion.

But, then again, is it? Have we not shown how all three of them have recourse to the concept of a (possible) adequation to make acceptable their respective accounts of overcoming metaphysics? Indeed, matters are more complicated still. We have seen how both Levinas and Marion try to institute an invisible instance that accounts for our being-in-the-world. For Levinas, the other does not and cannot appear 'in' the world. For Marion, that which is shown of givenness through the *adonné* is not 'of' the world. For both, then, a certain distance from the world and its history is the condition of the correct interpretation of this world. That there is no metaphysical 'otherworldliness' involved does not mean, however, that the metaphysical mode of procedure has been surpassed. Indeed, both have recourse to the metaphysical theory of truth as correspondence to justify such an instance distinct and distant from the world. This might mean that we, philosophers and theologians alike, have not yet succeeded in thinking particularity otherwise than as a fall. For Marion, givenness 'arrives' in the world from a distance which is not of this world, but which could only be given. This again seemed to imply that there is an instance that could obtain an adequate sight of the *adonné*, that could oversee the sum of my responses, as if I was only an object, transparent to whatever kind of subject.

Is not the attempt to signify particularity and facticity fully by an otherwise than being *in se* a metaphysical endeavour? Does not the attempt to make facticity 'in general' signify fully through an *epekeina tēs ousias already* presuppose that the signification of particularity is given in an incomplete and imperfect manner? Trying to think facticity otherwise than as a fall: that, therefore, is the way to overcome metaphysics. However, the lessons learned from these philosophers seem equally to instruct us that we lack the means to do so. It is possible, on the other hand, that these means come to us from theology. Indeed, as James K. A. Smith says, 'an incarnational paradigm operates on the basis of an affirmation of finitude'.[88] However, we need to be wary of interpreting this incarnation in a symbolic manner as Smith sometimes seems to do. After Levinas, and his devastating critique of symbolism, an account such as that of Smith somehow seems to beg the question. An incarnational paradigm does not ask whether 'there is any way to "say" that which *exceeds* and resists language'.[89] Rather it asks whether, from the part of finitude, it can still be maintained that there *is* something *exterior* to language. Only then, the question of incarnation really becomes the question of God, even when it is already a question posed to God.

---

88 Here I agree with J. K. A. Smith, *Speech and Theology: Language and the Logic of Incarnation* (London: Routledge, 2002), p. 156.

89 Smith, *Speech and Theology*, p. 9 *et passim*. My italics.

4. Postmodern Philosophy and Jean-Luc Marion's Eucharistic Realism

PHILIPP W. ROSEMANN

In his encyclical *Fides et Ratio,* John Paul II spoke of the considerable ambiguities that attach to the term 'postmodernism'. It is not clear when exactly modernity should be considered to have come to a close and to have given rise to a fundamentally different historical period; moreover, there is dispute as to whether the advent of postmodernity should be regarded as a positive or a negative development. 'One thing, however, is certain,' the Holy Father continues:

> the currents of thought which claim to be postmodern merit appropriate attention. According to some of them, the time of certainties is irrevocably past, and the human being must now learn to live in a horizon of total absence of meaning, where everything is provisional and ephemeral. In their destructive critique of every certitude, several authors have failed to make crucial distinctions and have called into question the certitudes of faith. This nihilism has been justified in a sense by the terrible experience of evil which has marked our age. Such a dramatic experience has ensured the collapse of rationalist optimism, which viewed history as the triumphant progress of reason.[1]

---

1 John Paul II, *Encyclical Letter Fides et Ratio: On the Relationship*

In this essay, I should like to offer a contribution to the fair-minded assessment of postmodernism which *Fides et Ratio* calls for. I am by no means the first Catholic thinker to attempt such a dialogue. In recent years a number of Christian philosophers have set out to develop a postmodern articulation of the faith – just as the Church Fathers and medieval thinkers took up the task of rethinking the tradition in the light of the intellectual challenges that confronted them in their own day. One of the most respected and sophisticated postmodern Catholic thinkers is Jean-Luc Marion, who teaches at the Sorbonne in Paris and at the University of Chicago. In the context of the present volume, I shall comment upon one of the central themes of Marion's thought, a topic that has preoccupied him since his very first publications: the theology of the Eucharist.

But first, a brief introduction to the postmodern movement is in order.

What is Postmodern Philosophy?

Fides et Ratio draws attention to three central characteristics of postmodern thought. According to the encyclical, the latter typically engages in (1) *destructive critique* of certitude and meaning, indeed so much so that it frequently results in (2) utter *nihilism*. These tendencies are to be understood as (3) a *reaction to the collapse of modern rationalism*, which for many has become untenable given the experience of evil in the modern age. Let us further examine these characteristics.

Modernity is a complex phenomenon to which it is obviously not possible to do justice in a few sentences. Nonetheless, there can be little doubt that modern thinkers tended to espouse an excessive rationalism – excessive in the sense of regarding reason as a goal in itself. To be sure, premodern philosophy and theology recognized reason as a defining feature of the human

---

between Faith and Reason (Boston: Pauline Books and Media, 1998), para. 91.

being; this feature, however, was seen as ordered towards a higher good, one not reducible to human reason. Plato, for example, held that human life finds its ultimate fulfilment only in contemplation of the Good, which he considered to transcend human knowledge and indeed Being itself. For Christianity, human beings are made in the image and likeness of God. This means that human existence does not have its centre in itself, but in that of which it is the image: God and his inner-trinitarian life. The tension between image and exemplar sets in motion a dynamism that longs to find ultimate completion in the beatific vision, its end or *telos*. Since this *telos* is not reducible to human reason, neither is, ultimately, the human being itself. It longs for more than itself, for more than it can comprehend.

Modernity, by contrast, recognizes no goal and no limit – no *telos* – outside the unfolding of human reason. Thus, self-regulated rational progress is the ultimate goal of the modern age. Progress is no longer aimed at anything that sets limits to reason, at anything where the rational movement would naturally come to an end (such as the Platonic Good or the beatific vision, which are understood as completing human nature). Rather, it is limitless and shapeless: without form, as traditional metaphysical language would put it. As reason unfolds in ever-accelerating, self-propelling motion, it absorbs everything in the demands of progress; that which cannot be so assimilated is marginalized or destroyed.

Philosophically, this vertiginous dynamic is perhaps most impressively evidenced in the preface to Hegel's *Lectures on the Philosophy of World History*. In this remarkable text, Hegel systematically reduces all aspects of reality to Reason or Spirit: human history, which he believes follows an inherently rational, predictable course; faith, in which he allows for no element of mystery that could not be penetrated by the light of Reason; and even God and divine providence.[2] Yet the totalizing

---

2 See G. W. Friedrich, *Introduction: Reason in History*, tr. H. B. Nisbet (Cambridge: Cambridge University Press, 1975), pp. 25–43.

tendencies of modern reason are not limited to the theoretical sphere: most tellingly, in the same preface Hegel vehemently defends colonialism, arguing that peoples whose way of life does not correspond to his conception of reason possess no culture, history and state worthy of the name. They must therefore be 'civilized', that is, absorbed into western rationality, or wiped out. About the native population of North America, Hegel writes that, 'after the Europeans had landed there, the natives were gradually destroyed by the breath of European activity . . . Culturally inferior nations such as these are gradually eroded through contact with more advanced nations.'[3] Perhaps, in writing of the 'terrible experience of evil which has marked our age', the Holy Father had in mind not only the Holocaust and the wars of the twentieth century, but also the exploitation of the European colonies and brutal destruction of their cultures. Often, however, the perils of modernity are considerably more subtle. Martin Heidegger has provided an incisive philosophical analysis of the structures of technological capitalism, suggesting that it aims at nothing but ever-increasing efficiency: thus, both subject and object are dissolved in structures that increasingly elude human direction and for which there is nothing that could not be turned into a 'resource' for further growth.[4] To cite a topical example, in medical research involving human foetal tissue, even the human being itself is no longer regarded as an end in itself, but rather as a mere means for 'progress'.

The main thrust of postmodernism is directed precisely at such totalizing rationalism. Against the modern presumption according to which nothing is opaque to reason (conceived as calculative, technological and autonomous), postmodern thinkers emphasize the irreducibility of that which is 'other' than rationality. In this manner, Kierkegaard set out to defend

---

3 Hegel, *Lectures on the Philosophy of World History*, p. 163.
4 See esp. M. Heidegger, 'The Question Concerning Technology' in D. Farrell Krell (ed.), *Basic Writings* (New York: HarperCollins, 1993), pp. 311–41.

the integrity of faith; Nietzsche maintained that a high price has to be paid for the repression of the irrational, destructive, 'Dionysian' forces in human life; Foucault argued that reason is subject to history, rather than vice versa, as Hegel had claimed – so that there exists no universal Reason but only particular incommensurable rationalities; and Derrida argues that language, far from being the obedient tool of reason, subverts any attempt to construct stable, unambiguous meaning: all human speaking remains on the way to a completion that is always 'deferred' (*différance*). From these examples, it is obvious what *Fides et Ratio* means when it refers to a postmodern loss of certitude. Justified as the postmodern critique of modern excesses may be, it often remains a mere counter-image of modernity, negating the latter without being able to point to meaning-ful alternatives. The result is nihilism.

This nihilism is all the more serious as its implications reach far beyond the modern age. Since Nietzsche, postmodern thought has pursued a 'destructive critique' of modernity that has sought the roots of the modern predicament in the development of the western tradition from its earliest beginnings. This critique reached its paradigmatic form in Heidegger's philosophy. For Heidegger, the 'task of thinking', as he called it, consisted less in the construction of philosophical systems than in the 'destruction' (*Destruktion*) of the western tradition, which for him had found its logical culmination in modernity. It is important to note, however, that for Heidegger and his postmodern disciples, 'destruction' is not synonymous with 'destroying'. Rather, Heidegger understands 'de-struction' etymologically, as the painstaking 'un-building' (from the Latin *de-struere*) of the layers of thought that have, since Presocratic times, gradually led to a rationality which, instead of 'listening to' the mystery of Being, is merely interested in mastering beings.[5]

---

5 On the notion of 'destruction' in Heidegger, see *Being and Time*, tr. J. Macquarrie and E. Robinson (New York: Harper Collins, 1962), para. 6, pp. 41–9.

For Heidegger, such 'forgetfulness of Being' – of the mystery of the All – is inextricably tied to a metaphysics of presence. Since the ancient Greeks western thought has privileged vision as access to reality, rather than, for example, the much more humble sense of hearing.[6] We imagine even abstract things as though we could see them. In contemporary English, for example, we constantly use phrases like 'I see' or 'let me throw some light on this issue', rather than expressing such ideas through other kinds of metaphors ('I hear'? 'I touch'?). But in order for a thing to be available to sight, it needs to be relatively static; any dynamism in which it may be engaged has to be arrested. This is why western metaphysics has always regarded stable presence as the paradigm of being, rather than flux, process, dynamism. Even the Greeks themselves – as the later Heidegger concedes against a position he maintained earlier on in his career – no longer understood the implications of the etymology of the Greek word for truth, *alētheia*.[7] *Alētheia* is composed of the word *lēthē*, 'forgetting', and the alpha privative (*a*- meaning *non-*, *un-*). Thus, in the Greek language, truth, etymologically understood, was not simply some (static) state of affairs, but a process of 'un-forgetting', in which something previously not present to the observer emerges into presence. Had being been conceived in this manner as a dynamism in which an initially hidden, 'mysterious' element is given to man (like a blossom bursting into bloom), perhaps western philosophy would not have culminated in modern technology.

---

6 Genuine hearing requires listening, that is to say, careful attention to the source of sound – sound that is highly transient, unlike objects of vision. On Heidegger's critique of the philosophical root-metaphor of vision, see the brief remarks in my article, 'Heidegger's Transcendental History', *Journal of the History of Philosophy* 40 (2002), pp. 501–23, esp. p. 510.

7 See M. Heidegger, 'The End of Philosophy and the Task of Thinking' in *Basic Writings*, pp. 431–49, esp. p. 447.

Christian Postmodernism?

Generally, postmodern thinkers do not exempt the Christian tradition from their destructive critique of western metaphysics. For many – such as Heidegger – the Christian God forms an integral part of the metaphysics of mastery: God, as cause of Being, ensures the availability of reality to reason. Nietzsche, for his part, sees nothing more in the Christian faith than an attempt to repress the wild forces of Dionysian life in superficial morality. Against the background of such fundamental critique, what constructive dialogue can there be between postmodernism and Christianity?

Christian postmodernists take the critiques of Nietzsche, Heidegger and their contemporary disciples very seriously. The metaphysics of presence, totalizing rationality and mastery of beings, coupled with a forgetfulness of Being, represent genuine dangers, which are at the root of many of the ills that affect the global civilization of the twenty-first century. But how deeply is the western tradition infected by these dangers? There is considerable disagreement about this question. Some, such as the influential Anglo-Catholic movement known as Radical Orthodoxy, deny that the seeds of the problems of modernity were sown in antiquity, and perceive a radical break between premodernity and the modern age.[8] In his early work on Heidegger and St Thomas, John Caputo, an American Derridean who is Roman Catholic, accepted much of Heidegger's critique of the western tradition, but maintained that Thomistic metaphysics remains exempt from it: St Thomas did not 'forget' the difference between beings and Being.[9] Jean-Luc Marion has been quite hesitant on the status of Thomism, sometimes criticizing, sometimes commending St Thomas' thought.[10]

---

8 This is the position of Catherine Pickstock in *After Writing: On the Liturgical Consummation of Philosophy* (Oxford: Blackwell, 1998).

9 See J. D. Caputo, *Heidegger and Aquinas: An Essay on Overcoming Metaphysics* (New York: Fordham University Press, 1982). Caputo formulates his conclusions on pp. 283–4.

10 On this point, the differences in emphasis between the French edi-

Whatever side is taken on the status of premodern thought, and of Thomistic metaphysics in particular, one point seems to be agreed upon by Christian postmodernists: a philosophico-theological articulation of the Christian faith must be cautious to avoid the pitfalls of modern rationalism. Authentically Christian thought can therefore learn much from the destructive analyses of postmodern philosophers. Indeed, it faces the task of critically examining the Christian tradition itself, with the goal of identifying elements of that tradition which may unwittingly have succumbed to the metaphysics of presence, while emphasizing those aspects of the tradition that are most immune to any form of subtle intellectual idolatry. In this context, it should come as no surprise that many contemporary Christian philosophers and theologians have rediscovered the strengths of Neoplatonism, with its consistent emphasis upon the mystery of the divine in its transcendence of both Being and knowledge.[11]

Jean-Luc Marion

Born in 1946, Jean-Luc Marion entered the philosophical scene in the 1970s as an expert on Descartes. Following in the footsteps of one of his 'masters',[12] Étienne Gilson, Marion devoted several influential books to the topic of Descartes' relationship and indebtedness to the tradition. For, although Descartes famously declared the need to create a blank slate, a tabula rasa,

---

tion of *God without Being* and its English translation are well known. See esp. J.-L. Marion, *God without Being*, tr. T. A. Carlson (Chicago and London: University of Chicago Press, 1992), pp. xxii–xxiv.

11 Werner Beierwaltes has been one of the foremost proponents of a dialogue between Neoplatonism and contemporary thought; see, for example, *Platonismus und Idealismus* (Frankfurt am Main: Klostermann, 2nd edn, 2004), and *Denken des Einen: Studien zur neuplatonischen Philosophie und ihrer Wirkungsgeschichte* (Frankfurt am Main: Klostermann, 1985).

12 Marion, *God without Being*, p. xix.

in order to free philosophical reflection from the prejudices of the past, Gilson demonstrated that his thought was deeply rooted in the philosophy of his late Scholastic predecessors. In *Sur l'ontologie grise de Descartes* ('On the Grey Ontology of Descartes'), Marion expanded upon Gilson's insights by showing how Descartes' philosophy was based upon a systematic subversion and redefinition of Aristotelian concepts.[13] Still more spectacularly, *Sur la théologie blanche de Descartes* ('On the Blank Theology of Descartes') presented Descartes as a Christian thinker in the tradition of negative theology: far from being some kind of closet atheist, Marion argued, Descartes was fundamentally motivated by a genuine desire to save God's transcendence from the dangers of late Scholastic metaphysics and modern mathematical science.[14] With these and other groundbreaking publications, Marion quickly won recognition as one of the leading experts on the founder of modern philosophy. The relevance of Marion's theses, however, is not limited to the interpretation of Descartes. What is at stake is nothing less than the meaning of the philosophical project of modernity. According to Marion, modernity (at least in its Cartesian form) is grounded less in a deliberate rejection of Christianity than in a (misguided and problematic?) attempt to defend it.

While making a name for himself through his rereading of Descartes, Marion produced a steady flow of explicitly Christian, and indeed theological, writings. One of the first essays he ever published was devoted to the contemplation of the Blessed Sacrament: entitled 'La splendeur de la contemplation eucharistique' ('The Splendour of Eucharistic Contemplation'), it appeared in the year 1969 in *Résurrection*, the review of a French Catholic lay movement which was founded by Fr

---

13 J.-L. Marion, *Sur l'ontologie grise de Descartes: science cartésienne et savoir aristotélicien dans les 'Regulae'* (Paris: Vrin 1(975), 4th edn, 2000).

14 J.-L. Marion, *Sur la théologie blanche de Descartes: analogie, création des vérités éternelles, fondement* (Paris: Presses Universitaires de France (1981) rev. edn, 1991).

Maxime Charles (1908–93).[15] Fr Charles served as chaplain of the Sorbonne between 1944 and 1959, creating the influential Centre Richelieu there, which quickly became a vibrant centre of Catholic intellectual life. Later, until 1985, he was rector of Sacré-Cœur at Montmartre. After Fr Charles's death, some of his sermons were published in book form, under a title that is significant in our context: *Guide de l'adoration eucharistique*, 'Guide to Eucharistic Adoration'.[16]

Marion elaborated on the reflections that appeared in 1969 in several subsequent articles on the theology of the Eucharist; these culminated in Chapters 5 and 6 of *God without Being*. It is no exaggeration to say that Marion's thought is eucharistic in its very core. About all this, more in a moment. Three important books, *L'idole et la distance* ('The Idol and Distance'),[17] *Dieu sans l'être* ('God without Being')[18] and *Prolégomènes à la charité* ('Prolegomena to Charity'),[19] also belong to Marion's early Christian writings. They show a thinker profoundly influenced by the negative theology and mysticism of the Greek Fathers, especially Pseudo-Dionysius the Areopagite; but also a contemporary philosopher in dialogue with Nietzsche and Heidegger.

More recently, towards the end of the 1980s, Marion's

---

15 J.-L. Marion, 'La splendeur de la contemplation eucharistique', *Résurrection* 31 (1969), pp. 84–8.

16 M. Charles, *Guide de l'adoration eucharistique* (Paris: OEIL, 2002). For a recent monograph on Fr Charles, one may consult Samuel Pruvot, *Monseigneur Charles, aumônier à la Sorbonne, 1944–59* (Paris: Éditions du Cerf, 2002).

17 J.-L. Marion, *L'idole et la distance: cinq études* (Paris: Grasset, 1977; 3rd edn, Paris: Librarie générale française, 1991). English translation: *The Idol and Distance: Five Studies*, tr. T. A. Carlson (New York: Fordham University Press, 2001).

18 Marion, *Dieu sans l'être* (Paris: Fayard, 1982; 2nd edn, Presses Universitaires de France, 1991). For the English translation, see n. 10 above.

19 J.-L. Marion, *Prolégomènes à la charité* (2nd edn, Paris: Éditions de la Différence, 1986, 1991). English translation: *Prolegomena to Charity*, tr. S. E. Lewis (New York: Fordham University Press, 2002).

thought has acquired a third axis: phenomenology. From its beginnings in Husserl, phenomenology has wrestled with the problems of the modern turn to the subject and, in particular, Kantian transcendentalism. Husserl's famous battle-cry was *Zu den Sachen selbst!* ('To the things themselves!'). Is it at all possible – and if so, how – to come to know things as they are themselves, abstracting from the question of how their appearances are processed and formed by human rationality? More technically put, what is the pure 'givenness' of phenomena? If Marion's first writings, on Descartes, treated of the beginnings of modernity, his publications on phenomenology address the possibility of emerging from it – not by means of a simple (and simplistic) rejection, but by *working through* modern thought to its own logical conclusions. Thus, phenomenology ultimately calls for the possibility of a phenomenon or of phenomena that determine the conditions of their own givenness. In books such as *Réduction et donation* ('Reduction and Givenness'),[20] *Étant donné* ('Being Given'),[21] and, most recently, *Le phénomène érotique* ('The Erotic Phenomenon'),[22] Marion has examined this possibility. As with his research on Descartes, his work on phenomenology has earned Marion a reputation as one of the finest experts in this field. Yet the ultimate inspiration of this work is, once again, Christian. Unless the 'saturated phenomenon' exists – a phenomenon that makes us humans what we are, rather than being made and formed by us, by human rationality – there can be no God; or, more precisely, all discourse on God,

---

20 Marion, *Réduction et donation: recherches sur Husserl, Heidegger et la phénoménologie* (Paris: Presses Universitaires de France, 1989). English translation: *Reduction and Givenness: Investigations of Husserl, Heidegger, and Phenomenology*, tr. T. A. Carlson (Evanston, Ill.: Northwestern University Press, 1998).

21 J.-L. Marion, *Étant donné: essai d'une phénoménologie de la donation* (Paris: Presses Universitaires de France (1997), 2nd edn, 1998). English translation: *Being Given: Toward a Phenomenology of Givenness*, tr. J. L. Kosky (Stanford, CA: Stanford University Press, 2002).

22 J.-L. Marion, *Le phénomène érotique: six méditations* (Paris: Grasset, 2003).

all theo-logy, would in the last analysis remain idolatrous.[23] It would impose human categories upon God, instead of allowing itself to be formed by an experience of the divine. For Marion, love or charity is the saturated phenomenon par excellence.

Jean-Luc Marion's Eucharistic Realism

Many of the important issues of postmodern thought that were discussed in the previous sections converge in Marion's theology of the Eucharist.[24] From his very first publications on the subject, Marion has emphasized the need to avoid two different yet dialectically related modern 'idolatries'. Both arise from mistaken conceptions of the real presence. The first calls into question liturgical practices (such as perpetual adoration and

---

23 For the concept of 'saturated phenomenon', see Marion, *De surcroît: études sur les phénomènes saturés* (Paris: Presses Universitaires de France, 2001). English translation: *In Excess: Studies of Saturated Phenomena*, tr. R. Horner and V. Berraud (New York: Fordham University Press, 2002).

24 Marion's publications on the theology of the Eucharist include the following titles: 'La splendeur de la contemplation eucharistique', *Résurrection* 31 (1969), pp. 84–8; 'Présence et distance. Remarques sur l'implication réciproque de la contemplation eucharistique et de la presence réelle', *Résurrection* 43–44 (1974), pp. 31–58; 'Le présent et le don', *Revue catholique internationale Communio* 2:6 (1977). The last article was revised for *Dieu sans l'être* (1982), in which it appeared as chapter 6 (pp. 225–58). In addition, *Dieu sans l'être* contains a chapter (no. 5) entitled, 'Du site eucharistique de la théologie' (pp. 197–222). Both chapters are of course included in the English translation of *Dieu sans l'être*. I have not seen 'La splendeur de la contemplation eucharistique' in *La politique de la mystique: hommage à Mgr. Maxime Charles* (Limoges: Éditions Criterion, 1984), pp. 17–28.

The later articles from this list often expand upon the argument of the earlier ones, although there are also some shifts of emphasis. For the purposes of the present essay, I shall attempt to distil a systematic theology of the Eucharist from Marion's publications on the subject. I shall not address the question of developments in Marion's thought.

My sincere thanks are due to Monsieur Georges Théry, of the journal *Résurrection*, for sending me photocopies of Professor Marion's articles.

eucharistic processions) that appear to reduce the Blessed Sacrament to a 'thing'. Such practices, the argument goes, reflect a misguided metaphysicization of the eucharistic mystery: 'the substantial presence . . . fixes and congeals the person in a permanent, manipulable, and delimited thing that is at our disposal'.[25] Against the background of what we have said about the metaphysics of presence and its concomitant forgetfulness of Being, it is clear why Marion concedes: 'the objection is very profound'.[26] This does not mean, however, that he rejects the liturgical practices that are at issue here; far from it. Rather, he is suggesting that, in order to understand and fully to appreciate eucharistic contemplation, we need an appropriate conception of the real presence.

The second idolatry concerning the Eucharist aims to avoid the shortcomings highlighted by the first, yet fails due to a similarly insufficient understanding of the real presence. Marion attributes this conception to certain 'liberal' theologies; for instance, the Dutch Catechism and Fr Edward Schillebeeckx.[27] For these theologies, the Eucharist is above all a meal through which Christ becomes present in the consciousness of the community. There is no reification of Christ in this conception, but only at the price of moving the real presence into the human subject. Christ is now no longer received as a gift through the priest who speaks the words of consecration *in persona Christi*; rather, Christ's presence is dependent upon the state of mind of the community itself. Attempting to avoid one idolatry, the 'liberal' theology of the Eucharist thus produces another.

In his own publications on the Eucharist, Marion responds to the contemporary crisis in eucharistic practice and theory by means of reflections that are both fully orthodox and take into consideration many of the concerns of postmodern philosophy. His reflections centre upon a dialectical analysis of the two terms that figure in the expression 'real presence'. For Marion,

---

25 Marion, *God without Being*, p. 164 (= *Dieu sans l'être*, pp. 229–30); translation amended.
26 Marion, 'Présence et distance', p. 31.
27 See Marion, 'Présence et distance', p. 50 n. 1.

'reality' and 'presence' designate two closely related yet distinct aspects of Christ's body and blood in the Blessed Sacrament.

The reality of Christ in the Eucharist

The term 'reality' is derived from the Latin word *res*, 'thing'. When the Church speaks of a 'real' presence, it thereby indicates that in the Eucharist God has become a 'thing', indeed an 'object'.[28] Now according to Marion, the reality of Christ's body and blood in the Eucharist is not without precedent in the economy of salvation, rather constituting the culmination of a progressively more intense, 'palpable' self-manifestation of the Infinite within the finite.[29] Out of infinite love, God has manifested himself in creation, at least to those capable of looking at creation with open eyes. Furthermore, he has spoken through his prophets, who have left us a text, sacred Scripture, through which we may discover him – if we have faith. Still more radically, the Word has become incarnate, in a complete unification of infinite, divine and finite, human nature; yet even the divinity of Christ is open to doubt by unbelievers. Finally, and most dramatically, the outpouring of God's love has permitted the mystery of transubstantiation, in which the Son of God enters our finite world in the form of lowly food. Here, the danger of misunderstanding is at its highest.

In each of these stages of self-manifestation or theophany,[30] God embraces and penetrates the material world more thoroughly in order to offer us his love. Each of these forms of self-manifestation represents a completely gratuitous gift (*don*).

---

28 In para. 15, the *Encyclical Letter Ecclesia de Eucharistia: On the Eucharist in Its Relationship to the Church* (Boston: Pauline Books and Media, 2003) quotes Paul VI, who used the expression 'objective reality' to describe the real presence. It is crucial to interpret the term 'objective' correctly, that is, not according to the categories of modern epistemology.

29 For the following argument, see Marion, 'La splendeur', p. 86 and 'Présence et distance', pp. 38–9.

30 Marion uses this term in 'La splendeur', p. 86.

In each of these theophanies, God can also be said freely to 'abandon' his divinity in order to communicate his love. In the incarnation and in the Eucharist, however, this 'abandonment' (*abandon*) becomes extreme: in the former, Christ abandons his life for our salvation, subjecting himself to humiliation, torture and death; in the latter, God's 'gift of self goes right to the point where He abandons Himself as a thing'.[31]

God's *aban-don* (gift-abandonment)[32] on the one hand serves to show us his boundless love. On the other hand, by 'abandoning' himself, God freely exposes himself to the risk of not being recognized in his divinity. This risk is due to the fact that in each of his theophanies, there remains a distance between the Infinite and the finite.[33] Creation is not God but a sign of its Creator. Scripture is not God's unmediated voice, but his revelation through inspired prophets and apostles; it is a text that requires interpretation. Even in the incarnation, the difference between divine and human nature is not abolished. Christ is not merely a sign of God, he *is* God; yet he is also human. Similarly, in the Eucharist, the reality of Christ is conjoined to the species of bread and wine, which ensure a certain limited persistence of the finite (even though only as accidents). In each of these cases, the finite is never simply absorbed into the Infinite. In each of these cases, we therefore remain *free* to misread and misinterpret God's self-manifestation. The world around us does not *have to* be viewed as creation; it can be understood as material 'stuff' completely explicable through the laws of physics. Scripture, too, is open to the possibility of being read as an

---

31 Marion, 'Présence et distance', p. 39: 'le don de soi va jusqu'à l'abandon de soi comme d'une chose'. I suspect that 'comme d'une chose' is a misprint and that the text should read 'comme une chose'. 'Présence et distance' contains an unusually large number of typographical errors, no doubt due to the semi-professional mode of publication of *Résurrection*.

32 On the topic of 'Transubstantiation as Mystery of Abandonment', see Marion, 'Présence et distance', pp. 34–41.

33 See Marion, 'Présence et distance', p. 44; *God without Being*, p. 169.

interesting historical document, rather than as the word of God. In this case, it is regarded as a sign without (divine) referent. Alternatively, the referent can be absorbed into the sign; for in Judaism, God has become 'a kind of prisoner'[34] of a legalistically interpreted text. Again, Christ does not force us to receive him as the Son of God; he can be – and of course has been – considered as merely a fascinating and inspiring historical figure. Those who crucified him saw in him a political and religious threat. As for the Eucharist, it is susceptible to being misunderstood as nothing more than a childish and perhaps even sinister superstition. Indeed, in the Eucharist, 'the possibility that one disrespect the person in it'[35] becomes an extreme danger – one that is not even unknown in Catholic circles, and which is closely related to the two idolatries mentioned earlier on. Despite its considerable theoretical interest, the reader of Marion's work on the Eucharist senses that it is above all inspired by sincere piety, that is to say, by a desire to promote liturgical and contemplative practices which will restore to the Blessed Sacrament all the reverence that it is due.

From reality to presence

We have to acknowledge that there obtains an irreducible distance between the reality of Christ's body and blood in the Eucharist, on the one hand, and his presence in this sacrament on the other. This distance is in complete accordance with the structure of God's self-revelation in creation, in Scripture and even in the incarnation. However, 'the more [God's] reality lowers itself, the more is it necessary to deepen the gaze that perceives the brilliance of [his] presence. The more the gift of God realizes itself without reserve [*sans retour*], the more is it able to be rejected.'[36] Therefore, it is our 'gaze', our approach to reality, which needs to be modified so that we may become able

---

34 Marion, 'La splendeur', p. 86.
35 Marion, 'Présence et distance', p. 42.
36 Marion, 'La splendeur', p. 86.

to discern the presence of God in it: 'the distance which separates and unites 'reality' and presence corresponds to the economy of our conversion'.[37] Note that, according to Marion, both the reality and the presence of Christ in the Eucharist exist 'independently of our mind[s]';[38] it is the *distance* between them that is due to the finitude and imperfection – in a word, to the fallenness – of the human gaze.[39]

In *God without Being*, Marion has developed a helpful distinction to describe two kinds of 'gaze' (*regard*), two kinds of viewing the real: the idol and the icon. The idol, according to Marion, 'consigns the divine to the measure of the human gaze'. An 'invisible mirror', it allows man to grasp reality only according to the depth of his own intention.[40] The idol can be the result of an authentic religious experience; thus, veneration of, say, a river indicates less an absence of religious feeling than the critical shortcomings of the latter. The human being, not expecting the divine to transcend a certain measure, fails to 'transpierce visible things'[41] in order to discover the divine in a dimension that exceeds them. 'God', the idolatrous god, thus remains subject to man. The icon, by contrast, 'does not result from a vision but provokes one'.[42] Or, to use the language of phenomenology, rather than being determined by human conditions for the possibility of perception and knowledge, the icon itself determines, 'starting from itself and itself alone, the conditions of its reality'.[43] The icon makes man, rather than being made by man. The reality experienced as icon shapes the human being's gaze, breaks through the circle of reflexivity, and transforms man in(to) its own image.

---

37 Marion, 'La splendeur', p. 88.

38 John Paul II, *Encyclical Letter Ecclesia de Eucharistia*, para. 15.

39 See Marion, 'La splendeur', p. 88: 'Le monde n'est séparé de Dieu que pour autant que notre regard ne réunit point encore en une seule évidence la présence et la 'réalité' du Christ.'

40 Marion, *God without Being*, p. 14 (= *Dieu sans l'être*, p. 24).

41 Marion, *God without Being*, p. 11 (20).

42 Marion, *God without Being*, p. 17 (28).

43 Marion, *God without Being*, p. 171 (241).

The question, then, becomes one of how the Eucharist can be approached iconically. In the Eucharist seen as an idol, a human being will discover nothing more than a wafer or, perhaps, a sign of Christ's presence in the community. In this manner, such a person will fail to acknowledge that there is a distance between the reality of Christ and his presence in the Eucharist, between the species of bread and wine and the divine person. This distance calls for conversion, for a training of the spiritual eye, as it were, as a result of which the believer will increasingly be able to see 'through' the accidents of bread and wine to Christ, who appears 'behind' them, as the substance of the Eucharist.

The temporality of Christ's eucharistic presence

The difference between the idolatrous and the iconic approaches to the mystery of the Eucharist entails a distinction between two modes of 'temporalization'. Marion terms these modes, respectively, 'metaphysical' and 'Christic' temporality.[44] His analyses on this subject are closely modelled upon the distinction between authentic and inauthentic time which Heidegger presented in *Sein und Zeit*. Marion himself explicitly acknowledges his indebtedness to Heidegger at this crucial point of theological reflection:

> According to *Sein und Zeit*, in fact, metaphysics deploys an *'ordinary conception of time'* . . . through metaphysics, being is deployed in its Being only as long as its manipulable and assured availability endures. The presence available in the present – as the *here and now* – guarantees the permanence where spirit maintains a hold on being . . . This ontological overdetermination of a primacy of the present leads to a double reduction of the future and of the past: the one finishes and the other begins as soon as the present begins or finishes. Their respective temporalities count only negatively,

---

44 Marion, *God without Being*, pp. 169–72 (239–42).

as a double non-present, even a double non-time . . . What separates a good number of Christians from a theologically correct (if not adequate) comprehension of the Eucharistic present has to do with nothing less than the *'ordinary conception of time'* and hence with the metaphysical discourse of presence.[45]

Marion's move to invoke Heideggerian categories in the elucidation of one of the central mysteries of the faith is just as bold, I would suggest, as the use of Neoplatonic philosophy by the Church Fathers or the creative adaptation of Aristotelian philosophy by the theologians of the Middle Ages. We tend to take it for granted today that the faith can be expounded in terms of substance and person, participation, matter and form, and similar categories. These concepts, however, have nothing inherently Christian about them. They were derived from pagan sources by successive generations of Christian thinkers who had the faith, vision and courage to engage in fruitful dialogue with the intellectual currents of their times. Our time is the post-modern age, and as Christians we have nothing to fear from the likes of Nietzsche, Heidegger, Foucault and Lacan. Indeed, the religious impulses of postmodern thought are not difficult to discern beneath a surface of agnosticism or even atheism.[46] Our task, then, is to deepen the Christian intellectual tradition once again, by learning the philosophical language of our day.

But let us return to the passage just quoted. Christ's presence in the Eucharist is not exhausted by his objectification in the 'bread' and 'wine', an objectification through which he becomes available in the here and now like a thing – with the concomitant dangers of profanation that we discussed earlier on. For a 'theologically correct' comprehension of the Eucharist, such a meta-

---

45 Marion, *God without Being*, pp. 170, 181 (239f., 256f.); translation amended.

46 The literature on this topic is growing. The following volume may serve as a good introduction: I. N. Bulhof and L. ten Kate (eds), *Flight of the Gods: Philosophical Perspectives on Negative Theology* (New York: Fordham University Press, 2000).

physical conception of time should be left behind in favour of a properly Christic perspective. This perspective must avoid any reductionism in which the present appears, in the final analysis, as the only dimension of time, such that the past is construed as the no-longer-present and the future as the not-yet-present. In this inauthentic (and un-Christic!) mode of temporalization, human beings live primarily in the present, rather than building the present out of the past into the future.

What could such an authentically Christian mode of temporalization mean in connection with the Eucharist? To this question, Marion responds that 'the present must be understood first as a gift that is given'[47] – given precisely by the past and the future. The Eucharist is, in its first mode of temporalization, a memorial: 'Do this in remembrance of me' (Luke 22.19). However, this memorial does not have the purpose of reminding the Christian community of Christ's life, death and resurrection, as for example the Dutch Catechism teaches.[48] Marion asks ironically: '[W]ould we be 'Christians' if we had forgotten them?'[49] Rather, it is a matter of 'making an appeal, in the name of a past event, to ~~God~~, in order that He recall an engagement (a covenant) that determines the instant presently given to the believing community'.[50] Marion thus views the Eucharist as taking up and perfecting the Jewish practice of praising God for the deeds whereby he confirmed his covenant with the people of Israel: 'This cup that is poured out for you is the new covenant in my blood' (Luke 22.20; cf. Mark 14.24). Just as on the cross, Christ abandoned his life to the Father, so the priest celebrates the Eucharist in order to appeal to the Father that Christ may come again in glory so that the promise of eternal life may be

---

47 Marion, *God without Being*, p. 171 (242).

48 See Marion, *God without Being*, p. 229 n. 18. The topic of the Eucharist as memorial is developed more fully in 'Présence et distance', pp. 46–9.

49 Marion, *God without Being*, p. 173 (244).

50 Marion, *God without Being*, p. 172 (243f.); capitalization adjusted. Marion uses the typographic convention of striking through the word 'God' in order to indicate a non-idolatrous conception of God.

fulfilled. The daily 're-presentation'[51] of Christ's sacrifice – to use terminology from *Ecclesia de Eucharistia* – does not have the purpose of adding anything to the work of redemption, which was completed on the cross; rather, the Eucharist defines the present as being situated within the distance, in the interstice, between Christ's self-giving to the Father, for our salvation, and his second coming. The presence of Christ in the Eucharist renews God's pledge of Christ's full presence that we eagerly await. In this way, the present, far from being self-sufficient, derives its meaning from the past.

And from the future! From the very nature of the Eucharist as memorial, its eschatological dimension has already become apparent. The two are, in fact, inextricable in their connection. For the cross, as the culmination and fulfilment of the covenant, holds the promise of the parousia: 'I tell you, I will never again drink of this fruit of the vine until that day when I drink it new with you in my Father's kingdom' (Matt. 26.29; cf. Mark 14.25). According to a 'properly Christian temporality',[52] then, the present is constituted in the dynamic tension between the past and the future; it is 'anticipation concretely lived'[53] (*epektasis*; cf. Phil. 3.13) of the fulfilment of God's promise.

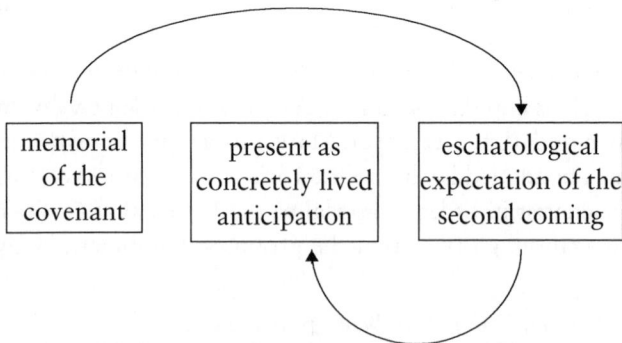

memorial of the covenant	present as concretely lived anticipation	eschatological expectation of the second coming

The structure of Christic temporality

---

51 John Paul II, *Encyclical Letter Ecclesia de Eucharistia*, para. 11, para. 15.

52 Marion, *God without Being*, p. 181 (256).

53 Marion, *God without Being*, p. 174 (246).

There are consequences to this Christian, non-metaphysical understanding of the present. Most importantly, the present of the Christian life appears as a gift of God's love. Outside of this love, the present descends into meaninglessness: 'Each instant of time sinks into vanity . . . if we do not endeavour to render the Eucharistic Body present in it.'[54] In this context, one should not forget that Jean-Luc Marion is the author of a book entitled *God without Being*, in which he outlines a form of postmodern Christian thought that is strongly influenced by the negative theology of Pseudo-Dionysius. Marion believes, with much of the Christian tradition, that Love is the first name of God, and not Being. The world receives its Being from Love; the world does not possess Being and, subsequently, God's love is added to it. Without love, therefore, the world stands in danger of sinking back into nothingness – a thesis, by the way, that Marion illustrates through brilliant phenomenological descriptions of the effects of melancholy.[55]

It is necessary, therefore, to revise our ordinary understanding of reality. The 'really real' is not, as modern philosophy has taught us, that which stands before us in neutral 'presence-to-hand' (*Vorhandenheit*, as Heidegger says in *Sein und Zeit*). Such presence in the frozen 'here and now' is, in fact, secondary and derivative. From a Christian point of view – and here Marion revises and deepens Heidegger's insights – 'only that attains to the status of reality which seems "mystical" to the ordinary gaze'.[56] We have previously seen that the term 'reality' derives from the Latin word *res*, 'thing'. The theological tradition has sometimes employed the term *res* to designate the matter of the sacraments, such as water in baptism, or bread and wine in the case of the Eucharist. Interestingly, however, there is a certain ambiguity in the use of the term *res*, such that it can also refer to the ultimate meaning of each sacrament: the ultimate 'thing' of penance, for example, is the remission of

---

54 Marion, 'Présence et distance', p. 50.
55 See Marion, *God without Being*, ch. 4.
56 Marion, *God without Being*, p. 180 (256); translation amended.

sins.[57] In the theology of the Eucharist, the 'thing' in this latter sense has traditionally been considered to possess two dimensions: the first *res* of the Eucharist is the body and blood of Christ, whereas the second *res* is the Church, or Christ's ecclesiastical body. Marion comments:

> The bread and wine consecrated and transubstantiated into the Body and Blood are valid as *res* – Christ really given in the Eucharistic present – but, at the same time, they still remain a *sacramentum* [a sacramental sign] with respect to the ecclesiastical body of Christ, the Church which they aim at and construct; only this ecclesiastical Body should be called purely *res*.[58]

What is 'really real', then, from a properly Christian point of view, are not the 'bread' and 'wine' – they are surface, though a tempting surface for our 'naturally blind gaze'.[59] The iconic gaze, the gaze informed by God's gift of charity, does not see bread and wine, but rather Christ in person. More than that: the iconic gaze perceives the kingdom of God, which already exists, albeit imperfectly, in his Church. Thus, the reality and presence of Christ are reconciled: Christ's presence in the Eucharist *is* reality. The Eucharist calls us to a transformation of the real: leaving behind the lowly 'bread' and 'wine', we are called to ascend to that which is revealed in them. In this life, however, this ascent will never be complete: the distance between the reality and presence of Christ – a distance that God has completely traversed since the passion and the resurrection –

---

57 Marion does not discuss this ambiguity of the term *res*, on which one may read ch. 7 of my book, *Peter Lombard* (Oxford/New York: Oxford University Press, 2004, pp. 144–78). Marion's principal source on the premodern theology of the Eucharist is the work of Fr Henri de Lubac SJ, especially *Corpus mysticum: l'Eucharistie et l'Église au moyen âge. Étude historique* (Paris: Aubier-Montaigne, 2nd edn, 1949).

58 Marion, *God without Being*, p. 180 (255); translation amended.

59 Marion, *God without Being*, p. 180 (255).

remains, for us, a call to constant conversion, a 'conversion that requires the time of our entire lives'.[60]

Marion on the Eucharistic Site of Theology

We have already seen that, according to Marion, the tension between the divine reality and presence in the Eucharist – a tension that exists but for the human eye – is paradigmatic of the structure of all creation, understood as theophany: God's self-revelation is not without a moment of concealment. It is as though all of creation possesses the nature of a sign or a text, which requires interpretation for its proper meaning to emerge. Another way of framing this insight is to say that, for us in this life, all presence of the divine remains irreducibly tied to re-presentation: we do not live in the immediate presence of God that is characteristic of the beatific vision. The Eucharist, however, is a very special and privileged sign, for in the Blessed Sacrament the sign and that which it signifies coincide:

> Thus, only the coincidence of that which signifies (the 'bread') and of that which is signified in it (thing, referent) – of Him who signifies Himself in it – is able to privilege a signification ('body of Christ'), because only this coincidence, which imposes presence in the nexus of signs of the Word, transcends the insignificant and reciprocal circularity of that nexus.[61]

What Marion is attempting to explain in this rather technical passage is, in the end, quite simple: in all the signs that God has given us to manifest himself, he himself is not present in person. Creation does not contain God, nor does the text of Scripture. We may dissect creation and interpret Scripture as much as we want, we will never discover more in them than *signs* of the

---

60 Marion, 'La splendeur', p. 88.
61 Marion, 'Présence et distance', p. 38.

divine; we will never be able to move from signs of the Word to the Word himself. That, precisely, is different in the Eucharist, in which the Word signifies himself through the bread and wine accidents, yet is also genuinely present as substance.

Catherine Pickstock has criticized Marion's conception of the Eucharist because she believes that 'he insists on the idea of presence outside the sign'. Pickstock counters: 'So, whereas, for Marion, the Eucharist is something extra-linguistic which *makes up* or compensates for the deathliness of language, it is on the contrary the case that the Eucharist situates us more inside language than ever.'[62] I think that this criticism is not justified. As is obvious from the passage just quoted, according to Marion the Eucharist does not render God present outside the sign: such un-represented presence is something that can occur only in the beatific vision. The coincidence of sign and presence of which Marion speaks in the case of the Eucharist is not tantamount to the abolition of the sign.

Pickstock's mistaken impression that, for Marion, the Eucharist is something extra-linguistic stems from his discussion of the relationship between theology and the celebration of the Eucharist. Marion understands the theologian as, first and foremost, an interpreter of Scripture. But how can the theologian overcome the 'gap'[63] that exists in Scripture between the text and the event of which it speaks – between the words and the Word? Furthermore, how can he or she become an iconic theologian, one who refrains from imposing merely human meanings on the text instead of letting it speak for itself? The question again becomes one of how the phenomenon – in this case, the text of Scripture – can determine, 'starting from itself and itself alone, the conditions of its reality'.[64] This requires a radical turning away from the modern subject, to (one might say) the 'sub-ject'; for it requires a subjection to the text of Scripture: 'To do theology is not to speak the language of gods

---

62 Pickstock, *After Writing*, pp. 256 and 262, respectively.
63 Marion, *God without Being*, p. 145 (205).
64 Marion, *God without Being*, p. 171 (241).

or of [an idolatrous] "God," but to let the Word speak us.'[65] Such being-spoken-by-the-Word occurs paradigmatically when the priest, *in persona Christi*, pronounces the words of conse-cration: 'the Eucharist offers the only correct hermeneutic site where the Word can be said in person in the blessing' – *où le Verbe se dit en personne dans la bénédiction.*[66] The French original is more radical than its English translation, for in French *se dire* suggests that, in the words of consecration, agency has passed from the priest to Christ, who 'says Himself' in the blessing.

All of theology, then, must centre upon the abandonment of human agency which occurs at the central moment of the Eucharist. Theology is a matter of conforming oneself increas-ingly to the Word, by contemplating the words of God in Scripture. Marion thus thinks theology in the most traditional manner, and that is, mystically. Theology is not a science, he declares, but rather a process of conversion: the theologian must be holy. '[T]heology cannot aim at any other progress than its own conversion to the Word.'[67]

And another consequence follows from Marion's eucharistic conception of theology: '*only the bishop*', who possesses the fullness of the priesthood, '*merits, in the full sense, the title of theologian*'.[68] To be sure, the bishop may delegate the tasks of the theological hermeneutic. Any theologian, however, who breaks the ties of communion with his bishop, *ipso facto* for-sakes the eucharistic site of theology and thus loses the legiti-macy of speaking theologically. With this thesis, Marion does not mean to defend theological 'conservatism' but simply formulates a *conditio sine qua non* of any theological discourse that is to be more than a sophisticated form of idolatry. The indissociable tie between theology and the Eucharist does not negate the freedom of thought or the legitimate, and indeed necessary, multiplicity of theologies. In a very Augustinian vein,

---

65 Marion, *God without Being*, p. 143 (202).
66 Marion, *God without Being*, p. 153 (215).
67 Marion, *God without Being*, p. 158 (221). Italics in the original.
68 Marion, *God without Being*, p. 153 (215). Italics in the original.

Marion affirms: 'The multiplicity of theologies – if these indeed Eucharistically merit *theo*logical status – ensues as necessarily from the unspeakable infinity of the Word as does the infinity of Eucharists.'[69] We will never be able completely to close the gap between the text of Scripture and the divine persons of whom it speaks; but in our theological words, we can again and again utter our desire to live, one day, in the full presence of the Word. Thus the Eucharist, rather than detaching us from the text of Scripture, immerses us ever more deeply in it.[70]

---

69 Marion, *God without Being*, p. 157 (220); capitalization adjusted. The theme concerning the impossibility of exhausting the infinity of meaning that the divine author has deposited in Scripture appears in many Christian writers, from Pseudo-Dionysius and Augustine to John Scottus Eriugena.

70 This article first appeared in Maurice Hogan SSC and James McEvoy (eds), *The Mystery of Faith: Reflections on the Encyclical Ecclesia de Eucharistia* (Blackrock, Co. Dublin: Columba Press, 2005), pp. 224–44. Thanks are due to Columba Press for the permission to reuse it.

5. Husserlian Approaches to the Icon and the Idol

JAVIER CARREÑO

*'I will cleanse you from all your impurities and from all your idols.
I will give you a new heart and put a new spirit in you.'* (Ezek. 36.25)

The use of images in religion – whether according to the traditions which permit certain images, sometimes called icons, as divine revelations whose veneration glorifies God and sanctifies humanity; or according to the traditions which warn against idols, whose characterization as divinely inspired images is not only false but also perilously misleading – alike entails the same tantalizing problem. How is it possible for a 'carved' image depicting a religious subject to be worshipped as if the divine was really and actually present therein? Is it veritably the case that the believer engaged in such acts of devotion mistakes the image for what is depicted in it?

One long-standing explanation – which we typify as intellectualistic – holds that image-worship is the aftermath of the *confusion* of the divine with its cultic image – a confusion that is symptomatic of an eminently *rational* failure. According to this explanation, only a primitive form of life in the pits of deception can worship an image, a human-made artifact, and take it for the divine itself. How such deception can be sustained may be a matter of lacking the proper metaphysical distinctions between divine and finite being: 'They pray to these statues,' said Heraclitus, at the dawn of western thought, 'as if one were to carry on a conversation with houses, not recognizing the true nature of gods or demi-gods.'[1] But it could also be that within a given culture the limited acquaintance with images turns them into wondrous and extraordinary objects; their rarity not only conditions the worshipper's credulity, but also accentuates the risk of being positively deceived by them. The believer is thus tricked by the image and takes it for its original, as happens with perceptual illusions and hallucinations.

However, this intellectualistic explanation of the phenomenon loses credibility at least on account of the structure of conscious representation it presupposes.[2] Taking our point of departure in a phenomenologically inspired theory of images, such as the one proposed by Edmund Husserl in manuscripts recently published in English translation,[3] we challenge the intellectualist thesis of *confusion* operative in image-worship. On the basis of this clarification, we seek a new point of entry into the phenomenon of image-worship – this time, though, not

---

1 Fragment 5. In G. S. Kirk and J. E. Raven (eds), *The Presocratic Philosophers: A Critical History with a Selection of Texts* (Cambridge: Cambridge University Press, 1971), p. 211.

2 That the intellectualistic explanation of icons and idols lacks a convincing theory of representation is also suggested by some passages in L. Wittgenstein's *Remarks on Frazer's Golden Bough*, tr. R. Rhees (Atlantic Highlands: Humanities, 1979): 'Imagination is not like a painted picture or a three-dimensional model, but a complicated structure of heterogeneous elements: words and pictures. We shall then not think of operating with written or oral signs as something to be contrasted with the operation with "mental images" of the events' (p. 7e). Edmund Husserl, however, will take us in a direction opposite to Wittgenstein – i.e. precisely contrasting signitive and imaginative consciousness. Husserl will agree that there is a complication to imagination which is not of the kind found in 'a painted picture'; but whether the account of conscious implication to which Husserl will lead us is analogous to 'words and pictures' is not the case.

3 E. Husserl, *Phantasie, Bildbewusstsein, Erinnerung: Zur Phänomenologie der Anschaulichen Vergegenwärtigung. Texte aus dem Nachlass (1891–1925)*, *Hua XXIII*, Herausgegeben von E. Marbach (The Hague, Boston, London: Martinus Nijhoff, 1980). English translation: *Phantasy, Image Consciousness, and Memory (1898–1925)*, tr. J. Brough (Dordrecht, Boston, London: Springer, 2005). Henceforth *Hua XXIII*, followed by German and English pagination numbers.

by dwelling on the structure of physical images, but rather by turning to Husserl's description of the subject's commerce with fictions. In doing so, image-worship reveals itself as an experience that necessitates determinate cultural context-clues as well as the wilful, imaginary engagement of the worshipper.

distinctive features

The Lineaments of Husserlian Image-Consciousness

Let us begin by sketching the revolutionary understanding of images originally proposed by phenomenology. Already in his groundbreaking work, the *Logische Untersuchungen*,[4] Husserl is critical of the long-standing psychological and/or epistemological tradition which claims that real objects cannot be given in perception as they really are, but can only and always be given as conglomerates of sensuous contents, which one may name representations, or images. According to this representationalist tradition – which Husserl calls the *Bildertheorie* – when sensations corresponding to the real object are immanently present in consciousness, one genuinely experiences a perceptual representation. In contrast, when the sensations contained in consciousness do not correspond to the real objects, the sensations amount to phantasms, for they represent not a real but an imaginary object. Deceptions and illusions are also cases where immanent sensations do not correspond to really existing objects; thus, imagination becomes associated with these and other experiences (i.e. hallucinations and mirages) whose claim to represent reality is compromised. But this is not

---

4 Cf. E. Husserl, *Logische Untersuchungen* 'Untersuchungen zur Phänomenologie und Theorie der Erkenntnis', Zweiter Band, Erster Teil, Hua XIX/1, Zweiter Teil, Hua XIX/2, Text der 1 und der 2. Auflage ergänzt durch Annotationen und Bleiblätter aus dem Handexemplar. Herausgegeben von Ursula Panzer (The Hague, Boston, Lancaster: Martinus Nijhoff, 1984). English translation: *Logical Investigations*, vols 1 and 2, tr. J. N. Findlay, from the second German edition (London and New York: Routledge, 1970, reprinted 2001). Especially see *LU* V, appendix to § 11 and § 20.

the only way in which the *Bildertheorie* helps the intellectual-istic reading of image-worship by suggesting that one may possibly be deceived by one's imagination. Worse still is the implication that, since representations are psychic phenomena, they are subjected solely to psychological laws and subjective conditionings. Image-worship would then be tantamount not only to a failed rational discernment between the image and what it images, but just as possibly to a psychological disturb-ance.

Husserl strongly objects to this *Bildertheorie*, and the kernel of his multiple objections is the claim that no account of con-sciousness on the basis of images or mental representations can prove what, in fact, is the very axiom of conscious life, perceptual or otherwise, namely, intentionality. By this term we designate the fact that consciousness is not only aware of its objects, but in fact it is *directed* towards them in a pregnant sense; and this directionality is not articulated by the merely conscious contents themselves. Here are some arguments on behalf of Husserl's opposition to the *Bildertheorie*: (1) Accord-ing to the doctrine of the *Logische Untersuchungen*, in outer perception I do not *mean or intend* immanent contents, but rather, I *mean* real objects: when I see the tree in the garden, I do not intend my tree-representation, but the tree in question. Immanent contents such as colour sensations or sounds may animate my perception of the object – but the object and the contents have at no point been mistaken and in fact, in the case of outer perception, can *never* be identical because the object, unlike the contents, is transcendent to my consciousness: the tree is an object which can never give itself exhaustively in my perceiving of it, and can therefore never be 'contained' by my consciousness. (2) This concept of conscious 'containment' of the object is once again refuted by Husserl when challenging a second claim of the *Bildertheorie*, namely, its insistence that our thoughts must always be tied to images or mental representa-tions (and, a fortiori, also ruled by the psychophysical laws governing such contents). For especially our use of language flies in the face of this description of conscious thought: I can think of a regular thousand-sided object, for example, and intend it merely signitively or emptily, without the accompaniment of any thousand-sided mental representation; I can express myself meaningfully and be understood when speaking about this thousand-sided object, even though I may not have 'in mind' a thousand-sided representation (and if I do, it is indistinguishable from a circle, which is again another problem for the representationalist). (3) The *Bildertheorie* supposes that representations or mental images do duty for the real object on the basis of some resemblance; but if the real object can never be given in perception, *nothing* guarantees this resemblance. In such a case it would be more consistent to assume, as Husserl's master Franz Brentano did, that outer perception is always *false* – i.e. its perceptual representations have no resemblance whatsoever with the things themselves – and that, at best, representations are mere signs for real objects. (4) Besides, 'resemblance' and 'image' are by no means synonymous: Napoleon resembles his portrait, but he does not portray his portrait; and this is hardly a trivial observation. For on the one hand it rebuts the representationalist's claim that we constantly confuse the immanently perceived contents with the things themselves on the grounds of their inherent resemblance (which is impossible to demonstrate because of the supposed inaccessibility of the thing itself); and on the other hand it refutes the intellectualist who claims that image worship occurs as the confusion of an object for another because of their mutual resemblance.

In short, by reintroducing the question of conscious intentionality, Husserl has made a beginning in the refutation of the bias of *presence* – namely, the claim that an object has to be somehow *present* 'in' consciousness for one to be conscious of it. In epistemological/psychological models like the *Bildertheorie*, only immanent contents are present, and they alone dictate *what* occurs in consciousness. Intentionality, on the other hand, compels us to protest at this inherent passivity vis-à-vis sensuous contents and to give consciousness its due not only for distinguishing between object and content, but also for intertwining the one and the other such that the content is interpreted or apprehended (*aufgefasst*) as the perceptual, imaginal or signitive representative of an object. As the American phenomenologist Robert Sokolowski has aptly put it:

> Only because we have become the kind of being that uses names, only because we have come to distinguish between a thing and the presence of the thing, can we take something as a picture of that thing: then we achieve the presence of the thing without having the thing itself there.[5]

The challenge befitting a phenomenology of image-consciousness, however, is to describe how this wonder occurs – i.e. that we have an intuitive experience of an object that is absent. In fact image-consciousness entails not one but three different objects (only one of which needs to be real), intertwined by two different constitutive moments.[6] On the one hand there is a physical object, a thing which Husserl calls (i) the physical image (*das physische Bild*) – say, a canvas made out of a given cloth, cut in certain dimensions and marked by oil, watercolour or paint-spots. On the other hand, when beholding a painting, something *other* than plain brushstrokes appears: we recognize an image – more specifically, an (ii) image-object (*das Bild-objekt*). These two objects (i and ii) are intertwined in a relation of constitutive foundation, such that the contents are apprehended *as* an image; and yet, the image-object remains transcendent and irreducible to its physical component; the original

---

5 R. Sokolowski, *Pictures, Quotations, and Distinctions: Fourteen Essays in Phenomenology* (Notre Dame and London: University of Notre Dame Press, 1992), pp. 23–24.

6 As Husserl says, '[T]he constitution of the image as image [*das Bild als solches*] takes place in a peculiar intentional consciousness, whose *inner* character, whose specifically peculiar mode of apperception [*Apperzeptionweise*], not only constitutes what we call image-representation [*bildlich Vorstellen*] as such, but also, through its particular inner determinateness, constitutes the image-representation of this or that definite object' (*Hua XIX/2* 436–7/II 125).

canvas of Da Vinci's *Leda and the Swan* is lost, for example, but the image has survived in Cesare da Sesto's copy of it. In turn, an image both resembles and differs from *what* is imaged by it, so we can further distinguish a third object, namely (iii), the subject of the image. It is this subject which is constitutively given by an image. When we behold, for example, Raphael's *Sistine Madonna* at the Gemäldegalerie Dresden,[7] we do not see something resembling a woman holding a child – but rather, we *see* a woman holding a child, the Madonna and the child Jesus, as if there, in the frame.

The constitutive intertwining of the three objects is sustained, paradoxically, by their being in mutual conflict. Thus, the image-object (ii) resists becoming (i) mere colour spots on the canvas: the image is no real object, since it stands in obvious discontinuity with its perceptual surroundings – the frame and the wall, in the sense that the frame is no actual window looking onto another room behind the wall. Conflict also emerges because the Madonna and the child Jesus themselves (iii) may not appear in real life with the glossy oleo colours with which Raphael pictorially renders them (ii). In virtue of these conflicts, the viewer is not inclined to take the imaged subject (iii) to really exist 'inside' the frame (i) – even though one freely sees the subject (iii) *as if it were there*. In other words, an image is not a perceptual illusion, and the viewer is not *disenchanted or disappointed* by the picture in the sense in which an illusion can disappoint. A simple example can bring this point home: what from a distance seemed like a farmer taking care of his crops turns out to be an ingenious scarecrow. We would naturally say that the scarecrow is a relatively sophisticated depiction of a farmer – but, technically speaking, this appreciation is not correct: the scarecrow aims at *being apprehended as* a really existing object, i.e. the farmer. Pictures, paintings and sculptures, in contrast, do not aim to be taken for actually existing objects. For although one perceives their colours and shades, *what* is intuited in apprehending these contents is consciously

---

7 This is one of Husserl's own examples; cf. *Hua XXIII* 506/607.

taken as absent. Therefore, contrary to the intellectualist suspicion, images and illusions are *faux amis*; not only is there no family resemblance between the two, but in fact, they belong to different fields of experience, namely, imagination and perception.

There is one objection to this account that is much a propos to the issue of icons and idols. We claimed that in picture-consciousness there is a tension between the image-object (ii) and the image-subject (iii). But can this tension be maintained whenever the image-subject is something invented, something that does not genuinely exist? This problem of the 'objectless' representation, which plays an important role in Husserl's early thought, is addressed by emphasizing the transcendence of the intended object to consciousness.[8] To be sure, this transcendence is not established by the factual 'existence' or 'non-existence' of the object, since 'existence' is not a part or element of an object that could come to intuition; it is not, as Kant would say, a predicate or part of the concept of anything. Transcendence here, rather, refers to the objective possibility or impossibility to be fully given in pure intuition, and on that score, even when the image-subject (iii) does not exist, it loses none of its transcendence. This transcendence is every bit at stake whenever two persons intend an existing object or even a fictitious character in a novel (say, *Don Quixote*), of whom two persons may give non-coinciding pictorial renditions (for example, Dorés' rendering versus Picasso's). Ultimately this transcendence makes sense of another fact raised as a puzzle to image-worship, namely, the fact that the worshipper is not troubled by descriptive discrepancies between one and another representation of the same religious subject.[9]

---

8 For a helpful presentation of the transcendence of objects to their representation in Husserl, cf. D. Zahavi, 'Intentionality and the representative theory of perception', *Man and World* 27 (1994), pp. 37–47.

9 Here, however, a new problem is formulated. For the early Husserl a constituted, objective resemblance holds between the image-object and its image-subject, which is teleologically oriented towards an ideal of givenness – i.e. perfect resemblance. Iconic figures, in contrast, may offer

Phantasy and Self-Displacement

We are nevertheless still at a loss as to how to describe the exceptional enticement of the icon and the idol – the fact that they receive worship befitting to the divine. Indeed, how is it possible for the believer to react adoringly to images when she knows their image-subject is at the same time absent, that is, not perceptually given *in the flesh*? We will suggest a first step towards an answer by considering a decisive development in Husserl's thought on imagination.

*   *   *

In the period following the publication of the *Logische Untersuchungen*, Husserl pays careful attention to a class of experiences where objects are intuitively given even though they are not actually before oneself, not even as physical images (i). To this class he dons the name of presentifications[10] (*Vergegenwärtigungen*) and he distinguishes it from another class, comprehending perception, where the object is not only given as intuitive but also as actually existing before oneself in the present, and which he calls presentiations (*Gegenwärtigungen*). Imagination (*Phantasie*), as the intuitive giving of an absent object whose thetic character – its existence or non-existence – is not an issue, belongs to the former class; but so does memory as well, understood as the intuitive giving of an object which is not actually present before oneself but was perceptually given in a past 'present'.

---

not just incompatible but downright contradictory renderings of the same intended object, which leads to suppose that religious images must also be in keeping with a symbolic order that on occasion makes up for these intuitive discrepancies.

10 Regrettably, even though 'representation' would be a more colloquial translation of this German term into English, it is in some contexts potentially misleading, which is why Husserlian commentators have opted for introducing the neologism of 'presentiation' or 'presentification' (after the French *se présentifier*). See D. Cairns, *Guide for Translating Husserl* (The Hague: Martinus Nijhoff, 1973).

*bring a thing to presence

Husserl seeks a point of entry into both phenomena by reverting to the model of the physical image-apprehension above: he supposes imagination and memory to be structurally analogous to pictorial representations or images by means of which an object is presented, but *not* as being actually present before oneself. While perception gives its object intuitively and straightforwardly, imagination and memory give their object in virtue of an image-apprehension that stands apart from perception on account of its idiosyncratic tripartite objectivity.

However, this solution, much in accordance with the doctrine of conscious apprehension of the *Logische Untersuchungen*, is overpowered by insurmountable problems pointing to a representationalist inheritance still latent in this groundbreaking work.[11] An unfolding of these problems now would take us too far from our current concern, but it suffices to mention that there is nothing in consciousness that could play the analogous role of the physical image (i), that is, a present content/object intuitively giving an absent object; there are no such mental objects 'in' consciousness. Further, talk of sensuous contents 'in' consciousness prior to or independently from a conscious apprehension leads to unresolved ambiguities, precisely because no such contents are ever met *without* an apprehension; consciousness is consciousness *through and through*. Paradoxically, then, in imagination (*Phantasie*) there is nothing like 'images' (*Bilder*), so that image-consciousness (*Bildbewusstsein*) and what we now term *phantasy*[12] are in fact also *faux*

---

11 For a more detailed analysis of Husserl's transition in his consideration of imagination from the model of image-consciousness to that of memory, see J. Jansen's 'Phantasy's Systematic Place in Husserl's Work: On the Condition of Possibility for a Phenomenology of Experience' in R. Bernet, D. Welton and G. Zavota (eds), *Edmund Husserl: Critical Assessments of Leading Philosophers*, vol. III, *The Nexus of Phenomena: Intentionality, Perception, and Temporality* (London and New York: Routledge, 2005), pp. 221–43.

12 We use this English rendition not only to avoid the seeming contradiction that would ensue from claiming that there are no 'images' in 'imagination' but also to avoid the sense of 'inventing' or 'concocting' unlikely objects expressed by terms such as fancy or fantasy.

amis. The new point of entry into the life of phantasy has to be found not in comparison to image-consciousness but in comparison to memory as the intuitive consciousness of the past.

When remembering something, obviously I do not perceive this object in the present, but neither do I merely presentiate it 'floating before me' by means of some sensuous content; for the object's merely sensuous, intuitive givenness would not sufficiently characterize my consciousness of it as the remembrance of something having happened in the past rather than actually happening before me. The difference between perceptual and memorial givenness has to be located in the fact that whereas perception gives an impressional consciousness of the object in the present, conscious memory can give the object only in a reproductive consciousness. In other words the remembrance of an object *entails* the reproduction (*Reproduktion*) of the previous perceptual consciousness that enjoyed the object. But what this conscious implication means deserves careful consideration. Husserl is not saying that in an act of memory we have a case of reflection, that is, of an act reflecting on another act that must be equally present. No: memory is a *direct* unmediated consciousness, and when enjoying a remembered object we do not execute another act, e.g. the perception; but to be a consciousness *of the past* means to consciously implicate the past act of perception. This is, in brief, what Husserl means by the claim that we can only be impressionally conscious of the perceptual present, while in memory we are reproductively conscious of the past.

The upshot that interests us about this description of memory is that, when remembering, there is what Husserl calls a displacement (*Versetzung*) of the conscious self. In conscious remembrance, there is a present, *experiencing* consciousness that must be displaced to allow for the reproductive consciousness of the *experienced* past. Every act of remembrance therefore entails a split of the ego (*Ichspaltung*), i.e. between a remembering, actual 'I' and an entailed, remembered 'I'. This displacement of self, however, occurs also in the context of an identity: I recognize these experiences, these past events, as belonging to the single experiential nexus where I am also in the present; there is an identity of myself with my past, thanks to conscious remembrance.

How do things stand with what Husserl calls phantasy? We also reckon phantasy as an intuitive, wilful, reproductive experience where the presentation of an object entails the reproduction of a perceptual consciousness – even though the 're' of 'reproduction' in this case does not implicate any prior, actual, perceptual consciousness. What is the upshot of this distinction? Phantasy does entail the perception of an object, but the entailed, reproduced perception is neither past, nor present, nor future. I am conscious of the phantasy object as if it were perceived, but this does not mean that the object has been perceived or is perceived, or will be perceived, and so on. Consequently, phantasy objects have a claim to be original and *sui generis* rather than inauthentic and derivative vis-à-vis perceived objects.

In phantasy too we meet a displacement of the self: on the one hand there is the 'phantasying' self implicating a phantasied, reproduced perceptual consciousness of the object. Let us note the difference in givenness between remembering and phantasying. When we remember, the object is indefatigably given with the consciousness of having been in the past. In contrast, when we reproduce a phantasy object, this absent object is consciously given not as 'having been perceived' but 'as if it were perceived'. And while in memory the remembering and remembered selves are identifiable, in phantasy the split selves *cannot* be identified. They do *not* belong at all to the same nexus of conscious experience the way the remembering and the remembered selves do. I cannot, for example, phantasy before me a genie and claim that I am also perceiving it; I can only say that I am presentiating the genie as if it were present.[13] I could venture

_____

13 Cf. *Hua XXIII*, p. 505/606, 'We say correctly, and yet again incorrectly: In mere phantasy we do not believe. In phantasy we do not carry out any positing, but it would be incorrect to say that consciousness of being is not to be found here in any sense. On the contrary, it is

the hypothesis that the genie would genuinely appear if I ran into Aladdin's lamp and rubbed it; but if that *ever* happened, and I perceived the genie, I could not then also claim that I would intuit him both perceptually and imaginatively at the same time. In the final analysis, phantasy objects cannot *not be absent* from the real, actual world.

The displacement of phantasizing and phantasied selves, therefore, yields a veritable doubling of intentional life: an irreducible, radical alterity at the core of consciousness. This radical alterity is archetypical in that it comes with a mixture of wealth and poverty. Freely and wilfully I furnish phantasy worlds, each of them allowing me to escape the monopoly of the single, perceptually given world. Yet this releasement is evanescent, for phantasy objects cannot be integrated as phantasies into the life of the real I (*Real-Ich*). It is well known too that phantasies have a protean mode of manifestation, a frailty that cannot eclipse the perceptual life indefinitely. Just as a man cannot 'live in' the past given to him by memory but only episodically relive it, so also a man cannot perpetually 'live in' fictions.

* * *

Not all phantasy self-displacements resemble day-dreaming – a state of private reverie that does not call for the attention of others. Phantasy can also be founded on eminently public, perceptual phenomena, such as it occurs in the aesthetic experience of drama. Dramatic fictions are founded on the perception of a stage with its props and actors; and yet, the theatrical play is not reducible to the mere perceptual intuition of these objects. Here too there is phantasy displacement of both the actors and the public. As Jorge Luis Borges once put it, the actor 'plays at being another before a gathering of people who play at taking

---

to be found in every sense in which it occurs in and characterizes actual experience, "except" that every sense and every form of this consciousness has, so to speak, been emasculated, has taken on the impotent "as if" of phantasy.'

him for that other person'.[14] If we now turn to this issue apparently unrelated to the adoration of religious images, it will not be to make the preposterous claim that the latter phenomena are merely histrionic. Rather, our intention is to grasp the role of phantasy self-displacement with which we can, in turn, revisit the worship of images.

The tantalizing suggestion that Husserl draws on the few notes that he makes on the phenomenology of drama (especially text N 18 and relevant appendixes of *Husserliana XXIII*) is that art consists not only of perceptual or reproductive phantasies; at least in part, art must also consist of *non-intuitive phantasies*.[15] But if phantasy has been understood from the beginning as a sensuous, intuitive consciousness, how can we account for this *non-intuitiveness*?

The answer will readily become available through exemplification. Take the case of the actor representing Hamlet on stage. Considering what Husserl has said on image-consciousness, one would say that the actor is a depiction or a portrayal of the Prince of Denmark.[16] However, Husserl notices that 'acting' in drama is quite different from 'portraying'. The spectator does not intend the actor as a merely didactic depiction of Hamlet, but as the performance, the role-playing of an *other* who is no longer merely intended as absent. For Hamlet *is* imaginarily before the spectator, *in a dramatic image* to be sure, but not as a portrayal of an absently intended subject. The fictitious character has become *present*, and yet not as a perceptual illusion, but as *fiction*.

---

14 From 'Everything and Nothing' in J. L. Borges, *Labyrinths: Selected Stories and Other Writings*, ed. D. A. Yates and J. E. Irby (New York: New Directions, 1962), p. 248. Cited in K. L. Walton, 'Fearing Fictions' in P. Lamarque and S. H. Olsen (eds), *Aesthetics and the Philosophy of Art – The Analytic Tradition: An Anthology* (Oxford: Blackwell, 2004), p. 311.

15 Cf. *Hua XXIII*, 514/616.

16 I concur with the interpretation of the phantasy self-displacement of the actor, as well as of the phenomenological account of catharsis, of Sokolowski's worthy reading of the *Hua XXIII* texts in his *Pictures*, esp. pp. 18ff.

This peculiar appearance is indebted, as we have mentioned, to the interplay between two parties playing mutually corresponding roles. The first is the theatrical cast or ensemble: each actor stepping on stage *displaces his- or herself and phantasies his- or herself* on stage *as if he or she were*, for example, Hamlet, Ophelia, and so on. This displacement is what role-playing is genuinely about; that is, it is not sufficient for the actor to wear a costume, in the sense that he obviously does this too while on backstage: he must stop, as it were, *being himself* (e.g. Lawrence Olivier) and appear on stage *as* Hamlet. The second party is the audience; each spectator must wilfully displace herself, phantasying herself into the world of the play and, on the level of phantasy, interact with it. Thus, she sympathizes with the fictive characters, witnesses their story, for example, their tragedies, and sheds tears for them while all along not dealing with these as real objects or persons (unless she wishes to comment on the actors or the production as such). In a pregnant sense, the spectator responds to the destinies of the heroes in ways that would not be fitting to real people in actual situations; she can, for example, feel pity and fear for Hamlet as he dies, and yet she will not call for help as one should when someone is veritably dying before oneself.

Of the props that recreate the environs of Ellsinore Castle, one could say that there is intuitive, perceptual phantasy: as props, they are images for objects in the fictitious world of the play. But of the essential self-displacement which animates dramatic fiction both on the side of the actor and of his public, there is no intuition.[17]

Drama thus raises the following phenomenological challenge. Husserl insists that phantasy consciousness requires my

---

17 To speak Husserlian: not all images in drama 'depict' fictions, and thus, it is worth distinguishing between pictoriality (*Bildlichkeit*) and depictability (*Abbildlichkeit*). Objects in a play that serve as depictions of objects in the fictitious world fall under the rubric of a play's depictability. Phantasy self-displacements which animate fictional characters while neither adding nor taking away from the intuitive element of an image fall under the rubric of pictoriality.

free and wilful engagement. As one reader has put it, 'nothing in reality can force me to contemplate an irreal object (for example the image-object (ii) of a painting)'.[18] And yet, at the same time, if a given culture lacks knowledge of the *specific* attitude required for the aesthetic experience of drama – the execution of the phantasy self-displacement of which we have spoken – the unreal object will *also* be missed. For example, a child with little acquaintance with drama may suffer distress and disappointment upon learning that Peter Pan does not really exist, and cannot really fly; the disappointment is indicative that the child has experienced the man hung by thin threads and pretending to be someone else initially as a perception which has turned out to be illusory. But someone better acquainted with drama will not experience this kind of disappointment; he may be disappointed by, for example, poor acting, but *not* by the fact that what he contemplated was nothing real. To what can we ascribe the difference between the frustrated child and the spectator who has enjoyed the drama? The answer will not be the pedestrian claim that since children have more imagination than grown-ups they are therefore more easily deceived by images. The difference, rather, is that in the latter case the spectator knows the peculiar disposition befitting drama, and willingly effectuates the phantasy displacement which permits the aesthetic experience. The phenomenological account of theatre, therefore, cannot do without the requirement of this disposition made available through culture.[19]

---

18 R. Bernet, *Conscience et Existence: Perspectives Phénoménologiques* (Paris : PUF, 2004), p. 108. A relevant section of this work on Husserl's phenomenology of phantasy has appeared in English translation: 'Consciousness of the Absent and the Fictitious', *Proceedings of the 35th Annual Meeting of the Husserl Circle at the University College Dublin*, tr. B. Vassilicos (Dublin: Humanities Institute of Ireland, 2005), pp. 139–52. For this quote, p. 143.

19 Cf. *Hua XXIII*, 510/611. This point has also been brilliantly illustrated by Jorge Luis Borges in his short story, 'La busca de Averroes' (in *El Aleph* (Madrid: Alianza, 2000), pp. 104–17). The plot of this tale deals with Averroes' failure to understand what Aristotle meant by tragedy and comedy (Averroes takes these terms to mean, respectively,

Clues for Approaching Divine Images

Image worship has a very long and rich history across cultures which we cannot purport to address here comprehensively. Our present efforts, rather, will only be limited to elaborating the following suggestion on the basis of Husserl's phenomenology of phantasy. Just as the aesthetic experience of drama necessitates both (1) the wilful engagement and displacement of both actor and spectator, and (2) the execution of the appropriate attitude, so also the worship of images requires both (a) mutual engagement of the divine and the human, as well as (b) the execution of a specific religious attitude.

In making these suggestions we depart from Husserl, who does not deal with cultic images in this fashion. For sure, he uses images with religious themes regularly in order to exemplify the structure of image-consciousness. But the sporadic analyses he devoted to cultic images as cultic basically fall in line with the concern that such images, if taken merely as images, may not only falsify our understanding of the divine as not-of-the-world but also raise an obstacle to the religious relation with God. More precisely, the obstacle lies in that images command one's regard from without, while the genuine locus to encounter the divine lies within.[20]

---

panegyrics and satires). He comes to no better understanding of these terms after fellow Arab travellers (themselves ignorant about the culture of drama) give him precise descriptions of mysterious 'illusion houses' (i.e. theatres) in distant lands. That Averroes misses the point has nothing to do with a lack of intelligence, but it has everything to do with living in a culture which has not cultivated the adequate attitude for drama.

20 Cf. one of Husserl's unpublished manuscripts, labelled MS E III 9/22a <27 XI 31>, available at the Husserl Archives of Leuven and for whose access I thank the director of the archives, Prof. Dr Rudolf Bernet and his assistant Dr Thomas Vongehr. A relevant part of this text has been translated and published by Louis Dupré ('Husserl's Thought on God and Faith', *Philosophy and Phenomenological Research*, XXIX, 2 (1968), pp. 201–15), as follows: 'All cultic images are images and at the same time they are not images, for as soon as God is represented as

We do not purport to enter this discussion regarding the advantages and disadvantages of prayer with images. Instead, we want to pursue the comparison and contrast between the aesthetic and the religious, as suggested above. A first obvious resemblance between the two phenomena is that neither the religious worshipper nor the aesthetic spectator take the image as a mere depiction, that is, of religious themes. Arguably, when the religious image is taken for a mere depiction, it is not yet treated as an object of worship, just as a work of art, when taken as a mere depiction, is not yet aesthetically experienced. As Van der Leeuw reminds us, 'the religious character of art is not conditioned by its subject but by its purpose'.[21]

Also, it is thanks to a cultural or religious awareness or sensibility that the image in question can be experienced as *more than* a mere depiction. But a certain challenge is raised by the description of this awareness. With regards to drama we indicated that the spectator not only had to engage the play *already* with the acknowledgement of its fictional character, but also displace himself *into* the world of the play. With regards to the adoration of religious images, the spectator must begin with the acknowledgement of its *sacred* character, and while displacing himself so as to contemplate the divine image, he must precisely *not* disengage himself, his *real* self from the act of adoration.

Let us see now how this paradoxical displacement and identification plays out in a determinate context. If we take our bearings from the richly iconographic tradition of the Eastern Church,[22] we may spot these two seemingly contradictory ele-

---

"Father," worldly, real, with the structure of a real father, God is no longer represented as God . . . Each image directs one's view *from without*, but the truly actual relation to God is interior, it is an attitude of prayer' (p. 215).

21 G. Van der Leeuw, *Sacred and Profane Beauty: The Holy in Art*, tr. D. E. Green (New York: Holt, Rinehart and Winston, 1963), p. 157.

22 For an authoritative overview of the Orthodox understanding of iconography, in ways that are not only theologically but also phenomenologically enriching, I would like to refer to L. Ouspenski and V. Lossky's introductory articles to their text *The Meaning of Icons* (New York: St Vladimir's Press, 1982).

ments at play. On the one hand the image-worshipper begins with the awareness that he is facing not an aesthetic work of art but a *sacred* image. How this sacredness is present is inextricably linked to its mysterious origin. According to this tradition, the iconographer himself is to fulfil seemingly contradictory demands; he himself needs not be holy, and yet he must be engaged in an act which is eminently sacred (for the icon is a work of prayer). To this avail he must fast and pray before he paints the icon, while he paints it, and once it is painted, he must use it for prayer. Yet it is not his fasting and praying which make his work holy. On the contrary, the purpose of this ascetic behaviour is for the iconographer to genuinely and truly *displace himself* so that the icon becomes not the work of his wilful imagination but, rather, the work of obedience to the divine inspiration of the Holy Spirit. The iconographer is thus the painter, but the author of the image is the divine – hence the fact that the iconographer does not *sign* the icon. Fitting to the logic of the divine spirit permeating the icon, it is considered a religious act to touch the latter, just as one would do with a relic.[23] This detail is quite telling: it suggests that the iconographic canons are not in place as if it were always out of faithful resemblance to the original that the image becomes holy. More relevant than to their documentary value, icons owe their sacredness to the *fiat* of the divine which places *his* own image through the iconographer. Neither this relationship of displacement, nor, as we have seen, the imaginative displacements of actor and spectator, are given intuitively.

It remains to be asked, however, how the worship of icons differs from the aesthetic experience, since we have suggested that a different kind of self-displacement is found at work in the religious practice. To get to the heart of this difference, let us first consider the specific purpose of icons. According to

---

23 I borrow this thoughtful liaison from Prof. Dr Paul Moyaert of the Katholieke Universiteit, Leuven, who has recently published his research on this topic. See his *Iconen en beeldvererin: godsdienst als symbolische praktijk* (Nijmegen: Sun, 2007).

iconophilic traditions, the worship of icons not only gives glory to God, as he wishes to be glorified, also in his angels and saints, but also helps the human being's call to become Christ-like. The same tradition claims, however, that it is *not* merely by contemplating or adoring icons that a person becomes Christ-like, but by prayer and works of love. How do we address this tension, this simultaneous wealth and poverty of icons? The adoration of religious images, as much as the making of such images, requires the voluntary self-displacement of the painter and of the community from the stance of the strictly perceiving subject in rapport with the world of real objects. The perceptual and the imaginary world here remain irreducible to one another, and yet the act of adoration is not tantamount to the mere disengagement of our perceptual selves, for these latter *too* must carry on in real life the work of glorification which already begins in prayer with icons. By being described as windows to paradise, icons not only offer a view of the *escathon* which is endless glory, but by the same token, they beckon the worshipper to give glory to the divine in act and deed, in the present rather than just in mere imagination.

Hence the contrast between the actor and the iconographer: between the actor and his *dramatis personae* there is an irreducible alterity and separation. Only Hamlet, and not Lawrence Olivier, will be tainted by his murderous actions. And the public, in turn, will become engaged by Shakespeare's fiction on the basis of phantasy. But religious acts cannot tolerate that the worshipper be just a *dramatis personae* or an imaginative participant who merely disengages his or her real self. This is why it is not enough for the iconographer merely to phantasy in order to paint the icon, since in such case the initiative would come from himself alone and rely on nothing else. Rather, by obedience and ascetic sacrifice, the iconographer genuinely disengages himself so as to be, paradoxically, veritably engaged *by* the divine. Both iconographer and worshipper must displace themselves, not to be marginalized by the religious event but precisely in order to be genuinely taken up by it.

The Ensuing Problem of the Idol

We conclude the pursuit of these suggestions by delineating a problem that remains emblematic of the limitations of a phenomenology of image-worship, namely, how to account for the equally religious denunciation of (certain) images as idols, i.e. representations of false gods. Our study of Husserl's phantasy has countered the suggestion that idols are *fictions*, in the sense of artistic fictions; for the attitude of worship as we have described it has not only a different structure but also presents a different set of cultural presuppositions than does an aesthetic experience. One would seem to be compelled to return to a scenario that we thought long left behind, namely, the possibility that the image-worshipper has indeed *confused* the image for the object intended in it.

On this score we refer to the *via media* that Robert Sokolowski briefly offers to this problem. His point of departure, like ours, is the correlation between an appeal and a response to an appeal which is characteristic of aesthetic consciousness as much as of religious worship: 'In the picture the [pictured] object makes an appeal to whatever in us responds to what is presenced.'[24] Sometimes, however, this appeal may overpower certain conscious distinctions:

> In some extreme cases, the power of picturing can cause some viewers to lose the sense of the detachment of the image from the original; they may believe that the actions performed on the image affect what is imaged in it. An idol becomes the actual presence of a demon or a deity, a voodoo doll can be a way of influencing the human being it depicts. Even persons can become embodiments of spirits; masks and costumes reinforce this confusion of a pictorial with a direct presence.[25]

In such way, claims Sokolowski, a ritual identification occurs in idolatrous cults, probably also as a result of the limited

---

24 Sokolowski, *Pictures, Quotations, and Distinctions*, p. 21.
25 Sokolowski, *Pictures, Quotations, and Distinctions*, pp. 21–2.

acquaintance not only with images but also with the essential distinction between an image and what has been imaged. The apparition of an unreal object in the continua of real, perceptual objects may have been, for primitive peoples, disquieting: 'all depictions may well have been disturbingly like the actual presence of what they depict'.[26] In contrast, iconography, as developed in the wake of the Council of Nicea (AD 787), emerges on the basis of both the strong distinction between the image and the imaged, as well as the acknowledgement that, as epiphanies of the divine, icons participate in the life of their subject.

On some scores this position is agreeable without catering to intellectualistic readings of the phenomenon. The element of scarcity of images, and the fascination that images must have attracted in virtue of their rarity, is not to be underestimated, and neither are we to reject that the cultural/philosophical absence of the distinction between image-object and subject is not without an impact on their effective distinction. Yet this account does not articulate the possibility that cultures with idolatrous rituals (up until today) may also be well acquainted with the non-ritualistic uses of images.[27] Further, we are left with the problem of how such a confusion between image and imaged object can be maintained for generations without the surfacing of the realization of such obvious experiential discordance. The implication of this scenario is that, since image-consciousness is still a wilful, free act, and yet, since the idolaters constantly fail to make the distinction between image and imaged, then, in fact, they are able to hallucinate at will – a possibility that Husserl categorically rejects.

We revert therefore to our original position: in acts of image-consciousness there is no confusion between the image and the imaged, because image-consciousness is clearly distinct from perception. This is not to say that we never confuse fiction and

---

26 Sokolowski, *Pictures, Quotations, and Distinctions*, p. 22.

27 I refer here again to G. Van der Leeuw's discussion of primitive art and ornaments, *Sacred and Profane Beauty*, pp. 155ff.

reality. Confusions may sometimes emerge, as when, in a state of tiresomeness, I may take something imagined for a past event. Memories are not fail-safe. But such exceptional situations rather than foiling the irreducibility of reality and fiction, only give more evidence to Husserl's claim that phantasy has a greater family resemblance to memory than to illusion. We are thus further prevented from thinking that idols emerge as the usurpation of a memory by a phantasy, as if by dint of the wonder of the image the idolater would be capable of tampering with his memory of having carved the image.

And just as we have found substantial differences between the aesthetic experience of drama and the worship of icons, the same differences obtain vis-à-vis the worship of idols. This is not to say that there are no differences between icons and idols. But precisely the language of icons and idols finds no longer its point of entry in phenomenology, but in theology, since it makes reference to the divine manifestation which interrupts and displaces the subject's way of life in ways that could not have occurred by dint of imagination.

6. Obscure Habit: Preambles to a Phenomenology of Christian Existence

JEFFREY BLOECHL

I

I take my bearings from two brief passages. The first is found in Heidegger's 1927 lecture course on *The Basic Problems of Phenomenology*:

> *For Husserl* the phenomenological reduction . . . is the method of leading phenomenological vision from the natural attitude of the human being whose life is involved in the world of things and persons back to the transcendental life of consciousness and its noetic-noematic experiences, in which objects are constituted as correlates of consciousness. *For us* phenomenological reduction means leading phenomenological vision back from the apprehension of a being, whatever may be the character of that apprehension, to the understanding of the being of this being.[1]

The second comes from John of the Cross's *Ascent of Mount Carmel*:

> Faith, the theologians say, is a certain and obscure habit of soul (*un hábito del alma cierto y oscuro*). It is an obscure

---

1 M. Heidegger, *Basic Problems of Phenomenology*, tr. A. Hofstadter (Bloomington: Indiana University Press, 1982), p. 21.

habit because it brings us to believe divinely revealed truths which transcend every natural light and infinitely exceed all human understanding. As a result the excessive light of faith bestowed on man is a darkness for him, because a brighter light will eclipse and suppress a dimmer one.[2]

Each passage calls for some elaboration.

First, following Heidegger I consider *phenomenology* as the final determination of philosophy as a form of seeing, whether of the things that present themselves to be seen (Husserl) or according to an openness by which being is comprehended as beings (Heidegger). That said, one cannot be reminded too soon or too often that phenomenology, already in Husserl's lectures on the inner consciousness of time, is well aware of dimensions of experience and existence that are anterior to seeing. Still, when even these dimensions are developed as the horizon within which things show up and become known, the primacy of appearing and thus seeing is confirmed. Let me underscore at least one crucial implication: for phenomenology, it is possible to speak of knowledge and the truth of a thing only within the limits in which that thing first gives itself to be seen.[3]

Second, evidently enough, faith such as John of the Cross defines it must exempt itself from these conditions. But this is

---

2 John of the Cross, *The Ascent of Mount Carmel*, II, 3, tr. K. Kavanaugh and O. Rodriguez (Washington, DC: Institute of Carmelite Studies Publications, 1979), p. 110. Though 'the theologians' are not named here, they would seem to include Thomas Aquinas (*STh* II–II, q. 4, a. 1): 'the intellect of the believer is convinced by Divine authority, so as to assent to what it sees not. Accordingly if anyone would reduce the foregoing words to the form of a definition, he may say that "faith is a habit of the mind, whereby eternal life is begun in us, making the intellect assent to what is non-apparent [*non apparentibus*]".'

3 The *locus classicus* is E. Husserl, *Ideas for a Pure Phenomenology and a Phenomenological Philosophy*, Book I, § 24, tr. F. Kersten (Dordrecht: Kluwer, 1982): 'every originary presentive intuition is a legitimizing source of knowledge; everything offered to us in "intuition" in an originary way (that is, in its personal [*leibhaft*] reality) must be received simply as what is presented, but also only within the limits in which it is thus presented.'

not to say that he considers understanding, or for that matter imagination, is therefore wholly *unreliable*. Rather, the faculties of the mind are said to provide access to a natural knowledge that is by definition *limited*, whereas faith attends to that which is by definition unlimited and thus greater. Here then is the first instance of the religious claim long recognized to challenge phenomenological research: the life of faith transpires in relation with a *transcendence* that surpasses all possible limits and, as the medievals would have it, embodies all conceivable perfections. The Christian God, which will be the only God holding my attention on this occasion, exceeds and absolves himself from any possible image or idea we may have of him; such a God is unknowable as such, or in Anselm's sense unthinkable (God is *aliquid quo maius cogitari nequit – Proslogion* I). This is plainly how we are to interpret the mystic's key symbols: the light of faith is not less than ordinary light by which natural reason knows the things of the world, but to the contrary exceeds that ordinary light with a brilliance beyond capture in any focus. Natural reason, it may thus seem, is born in a focusing of the eyes that lessens the glare of a light that is, according to a word that seems not to have lost its currency, 'supernatural'.

What will it mean for phenomenology to seek an understanding of divine transcendence only within the limits in which it presents itself to be seen? To begin with, it will mean describing or interpreting the life of faith – of the structures and modalities of consciousness in which the believer experiences God – without assuming either that God truly exists or that God does not. Husserl, at least, has been clear enough about this: phenomenology has nothing to say about the existence of the God confessed in faith.[4] One can only investigate the form of life that makes such a confession, and ask whether elements of it might testify to a dimension beyond capture within any horizon. The difficulty of the task should not be exaggerated, real though it is: one must approach the pertinent examples in a manner that

---

4 See Husserl, *Ideas for a Pure Phenomenology*, Book I, § 58, pp. 133–4.

is especially attentive to *precisely those inner possibilities that are most difficult to grasp and express in concepts.*

On these terms, incidentally, the merit of the phenomeno-logical approach will *also* be confirmed, it seems to me, in its capacity to resist and even correct for the impoverishing effects of an approach that is too quickly inclined to draw all findings into a system. After all, true progress in understanding the facts of experience occurs first of all at the level of observation, which for its part is dependent on the excellence of the best available method (and the range of available material). If, as I think, phenomenological method has provided us with an excellent means of description or interpretation, then there is every reason to suppose that it may eventually contribute to a richer and deeper understanding of the full range of human experi-ence, including – why not? – the experience that belongs to Christian faith.

II

Let us now try to get closer to the things themselves. To claim an experience of anything at all is at the same time to claim a relation with it. When it is a matter of something or someone moving in accord with the discernible order of being, the rela-tion may be cognized through reflection and argument. When, however, it is a matter of the source for actions or interventions that do not seem to belong entirely to the discernible order of being, the relation is approached in what is more properly called *faith* – which is to say in an attitude of listening to the self-revelation of that source. On this conception – still minimal, to be sure – faith is present already in an attitude that merely *senses* that things are moved from beyond all under-standing. One may think here of Greek religion, where Heraclitus, for instance, recognizes the provenance of decisions that are ultimately unfathomable: 'The god whose oracle is at Delphi neither speaks nor conceals, but gives signs' (fragment B 18; see also, e.g., Pindar, fragment 50). But the Christian

Scriptures enjoin a bolder faith, opening the believer to events that go all the way promising us liberation from the necessity of being (Rom. 11.25). This would be how to understand the Good News: as the genuine possibility of salvation (Matt. 8.22, Mark 10.52, Luke 7.50), of perfect happiness (Matt. 5) and lasting purity of heart (Acts 15.9) – in short, of victory over the sinfulness and suffering that otherwise clings to us in this world.

This attitude is easily rendered in phenomenological terms: Christian faith nourishes a distinctive way of being in the world, and it so belongs to this way that it immediately contests the limits of being in the world. With this in mind, it is hardly of any use to repeat the well-known passage from Hebrews 11.1 – 'Faith is the substance of things hoped for, and the evidence of things unseen' – except perhaps in order to note how phenomenology prepares us to understand it: perfect fulfilment, contradicting our very finitude, cannot be known in this life, or at least not according to the structures of experience and existence that seem to prevail there. And yet, when the believer nonetheless lives in view of such an extraordinary possibility, in many cases steadfastly, he claims for himself a kind of knowing that is somehow received from beyond our insertion in the world.

Faith thus presents itself as somehow resting beneath or outside the world in which the believer nonetheless assuredly does live and move. Its 'posture,' if one may conceive of it this way, displays an openness to a fulfilment that has not yet fully arrived in the world. Most fundamentally, act and movement of faith testify: they give evidence – if there is evidence to be had – of a meaning whose complete realization lies always in the future, but which nonetheless casts its light over everything else that enters experience. Of course, this much can be said of any proposition at all, to the degree that it expresses a basic trust founding one's being in the world. Each of us, whether or not a believer in any god, faces and give meaning to each new moment as it arrives from the future, according to an inner confidence in some original principle. Yet it should not be forgotten that Christian faith claims to found and gives meaning to the believer's world *without belonging entirely to it*. Faith is not simply one instance of a general condition, whether psychological or existential. The fact that it assents to God, the absolute-beyond-all-relativity, sets it apart from basic trust in oneself, one's primary caretakers, or one's most beloved, all of which are conditioned by their finitude and all of which, as the psychoanalysts remind us, have their own interests. And after all, the life of faith can burn with a desire that threatens to consume those other, different forms of trust.[5] It is therefore not enough to say, with Bernhard Welte, that Christian faith may be distinguished from other forms of basic trust by its force and audacity[6] – not enough to draw attention to its struggle against our attachment to the things of this world, and thus to the agony that mounts as faith itself intensifies – unless one also recognizes all of that as the expression of an attitude that seems to open onto being-in-the-world as if from before or outside it. Needless to say, this claim for a pre-ontological attitude appears to present the phenomenologist with a conception of the human that cannot be contained within the limits of what Heidegger calls *Dasein*.

Let us try to understand this better. When it is said that faith welcomes the revelation of possibilities otherwise unseen and opens to a future otherwise unhoped for, all that is achieved is a better understanding of what it means to say that faith entrusts one to a mysterious promise. And when it is said that the believer's faith in the promise *founds an entire way of being*,

5 One will find an existential-psychological analysis of faith, desire and basic trust in P. Moyaert, 'On Faith and the Experience of Transcendence: An Existential Reflection on Negative Theology' in I. Bulhof and L. ten Kate, *Flight of the Gods: Philosophical Perspectives on Negative Theology* (New York: Fordham University Press, 2001), pp. 374–82.
6 B. Welte, *Was ist Glauben? Gedanken zur Religionsphilosophie* (Freiburg: Herder, 1982), p. 43. The limitations of this view are confirmed a few pages later, when Welte recognizes Nietzsche's equally audacious, but reactionary thought of man as the rival of God. To thus reduce faith to a single form of spiritual audacity is to confine it solely within the range of our being, without adequate attention to a transcendence that is essential.

this serves only as a reminder of the fact that one does not have faith in a promise without having somehow understood and accepted some of what it means. Yet when a believer speaks of 'knowing' that she is saved there is evidently more involved than the mere understanding of an idea. Those who have faith in the promise of salvation and perfect happiness – faith in the promise of beatitude – know enough of what that means to wish that it be fulfilled, and indeed enough to commit themselves to making ready for it. Faith is not only a knowing but also a desiring, or perhaps a knowing that is already animated by a desiring. The theologian captures these things well when she tells us that faith is, at heart, a foretaste (*praegustatio*) of a future fulfilment. It is an informed longing for the moment in which one will at last know a perfect goodness that, in this life, is always yet to come.[7]

As the heart of faith, a foretaste of beatitude must be the defining attitude of Christian being in the world, and thus an elemental structure of the living relation with God. Not that God appears directly in the relation, as a manifest interlocutor: a foretaste of perfect happiness and salvation is only the pang of hunger felt in one who still desires more of what God has promised, and indeed what he himself wants most – only the mark, therefore, of nonconformity between the believer's own situation and the situation that God holds out for him. The promise, let us note, calls forth desire and movement; desire and movement respond to that call. And in the soul that discovers itself capable of hearing the call and responding to it – finds itself disposed to move in desire towards a transcendent goodness – one might be tempted to see the trace of a God who desires us to desire him.

That sort of thought is certainly at home in some of the classical Christian texts – Augustine's *De Trinitate*, for instance, or Bonaventure's *Itinerarium* – but in such cases an analysis of the

---

7 Thomas Aquinas, e.g., *In III Sententia*, d. 23, q. 2, art. 1, ad. 4. The importance of this conception has been impressed on me in several conversations with Jean-Yves Lacoste.

soul is bound up inextricably with speculation on the divine, so that a psychology of the former is never without some influence by a metaphysics of the latter. It is both the advantage and the disadvantage of phenomenology that it must address the same thesis on the soul – that it is animated by a desire for God that gives witness of God's desire for us – within a more restricted, existential inquiry: by what primordial condition will the soul have been prepared to not only hear a divine word promising salvation, and not only wish that the latter might indeed be realized, but also accept that word as indeed true, as the revelation of the truth of our humanity? The quest is as evident as it is necessary: in the phenomenological approach to Christian faith one cannot be content with a characterization of its proper attitude (or attunement) as 'foretaste', and cannot be content with a basic definition of the religious desire that animates it, but must seek some account of the seed of even *their* possibility in what can only be called a 'receptivity' to the divine word that is already in place, as it were, anterior to the various forms of its lived expression. And this is to say that the inquiry would have to move beneath the basic elements of any Christian anthropology. The latter, moreover, will receive its proper definition only from the inquiry that is in fact interested in the very thing it presupposes: again, receptivity to God. In short, what has sometimes been called 'Christian man' is of interest here only as the expression of what it means for God to be, as it were, received into human consciousness.

At this point, it is difficult not to think of an analogous move in the philosophy of Heidegger. In *Being and Time* (§ 10) the matter is stated quite negatively: anthropology, whether Greek or Christian, approaches the human according to an objective definition – rendering it, in Heidegger's lexicon, present-to-hand (*Vorhanden*) – without feeling any need to ask about the being of the human and still less about being as being. A slightly more positive account of this position is developed in later essays, with regard to the general notion of 'humanism' and the concept of *humanitas* that it promotes. '"Humanism" . . . should we decide to retain the word, henceforth means: the essence of man *is* essential for the truth of being, [but only] in such a way that what matters is not man simply as such.'[8] What matters *for Heidegger* is of course the question of the meaning of being, most immediately because for him our relation with being is presupposed by our relation with everything else. This proposition awaits and indeed resists the notion, not without its own phenomenological support, that the basic elements of Christian *humanitas* are best grasped as an expression of an anterior relation with God. Are the historical and cultural forms of being Christian most fundamentally an expression of a primordial relation with being, or of a primordial relation with God? Heidegger himself puts a fine point on the difficulty when, in the same context I have been citing, he contends that our prior understanding of being determines how we comprehend the being of God.[9] Now this would not necessarily mean that God is *only* a being, an *individuum* limited by some *principium individuationis* (and still less that God does not exist), but it does suggest that the relation with being diverges from the relation with God.

Here, unfortunately, the challenge posed by Heidegger brings with it a corollary problem: it is not clear, even among the relatively few who have interested themselves in these things, whether our relation to being must be *opposed* to our relation with God, or is only *distinct* from it. To be sure, the believer is in the world and thus has a relation with being. But one still wants to know whether this flatly obstructs the relation with God, so that the divine must break into being with a certain violence, or only accompanies the relation with God, and perhaps sometimes as the medium of religious witness. The possibility of such a debate is already enough to serve notice that one cannot ask where or how a receptivity to God might be embedded in human being without also asking, sooner or later, whether that receptivity would actually be at odds with our being.

---

8 M. Heidegger, 'Letter on Humanism' in *Pathmarks*, tr. W. McNeill (Cambirdge: Cambridge University Press, 1998), p. 263.

9 Heidegger, 'Letter on Humanism', pp. 266–7.

For theologians, this is recognizably a new form of a rather old problem: in the philosophy of Heidegger, the classical notion of being *coram Deo* is now confronted by a forceful argument for the secular nature of being as such. Phenomenology would thus have us understand the problem this way: in order for being-in-the-world to include the possibility of being-in-the-world-*toward*-God, there must already be a receptivity to the divine that is not strictly occluded by being – and not, moreover, cancelled by our innate tendency to care first for ourselves. The notion is both inevitable and precarious: it is *inevitable* because without it Christian faith does not evidently transcend the drama of being and beings; it is *precarious* because we are thus given to think that in faith what matters most transpires outside being and thus, one would think, without the possibility of ever coming to light as such.

This recalls the claims of the mystic, and it is mysticism that henceforth gives philosophy the most to think about.

III

If one returns to John of the Cross after listening to Heidegger, it is with a single interest especially in mind: perhaps in the experience of the mystic, who seeks the perfect form of the human relation with God, it will be possible to recognize and clarify a faith that might elude comprehension by ontology. But this already calls for an immediate precaution. Mysticism, let us not forget, does not comprise the whole of Christian faith any more than does morality or ritual. This does not mean that mysticism is somehow alien to those other elements, or for that matter that it is independent of the biblical and sacramental substrate that they share. Still, the abundance of scriptural and historical references in *The Ascent of Mount Carmel* or *The Dark Night of the Soul* do not merely confirm a certain orthodoxy; they are also marks of the noetic content of the experiences that the author wishes to describe. Let us go slowly: if the first expression of those experiences is *poetic* (if the treatise interprets the poems, and not vice versa), and if the poetry admits even approximate translation into theological language, then the experiences themselves are to some degree framed theologically from the outset. Perhaps this is all too obvious, but it requires us to think that the mystic always sees and desires in a particular way: that is, John of the Cross does not see or desire beyond all definition, even when it is a matter of a God that he himself considers 'incomprehensible'.

The idea that mysticism might nonetheless reveal something about the nature of Christian faith as such can be found in at least two features of the John of the Cross's texts. Initially, and still in line with the theological parameters of the sanjuanist perspective, it is clear that he addresses spiritual adepts who wish to advance in the faith that they already sense transcends natural reason. In short, the text leads one to a deeper understanding of Christian faith, and not to a wholly different one. Second, one cannot overlook the numerous instances in which that path is described as one of *recollection*, in the sense of an awakening and a return to original conditions. Of the dozen or so instances of this expression in the two major works, three may be cited as broadly indicative:

1 Already at an early stage along the way, it is to be understood that in prayer 'the soul recollects itself in the presence of God, [entering] upon an act of general, loving, peaceful, and tranquil knowledge, drinking wisdom and love and delight'.[10]
2 In a more general sense, it may be said that ' . . . the Holy Spirit illumines the intellect that is recollected, and He illumines it according to the mode of its recollection, and the intellect can find no better recollection than in faith, and thus the Holy Spirit will not illumine it in any other recollection than in faith'.[11]
3 At the pinnacle of the ascent, one must envision ' . . . the highest recollection, a recollection which consists in the concen-

---

10 John of the Cross, *The Ascent of Mount Carmel*, II, 14, 2, p. 143.
11 John of the Cross, *The Ascent of Mount Carmel*, II, 29, 6, p. 205.

tration of all the faculties on the incomprehensible Good and the withdrawal of them from all apprehensible things'.[12]

Whether or not these passages are fully congruent with the Platonic and Neoplatonic influences that certainly come to mind,[13] they are highly suggestive of a discipline that remains affirmative even while it is also purgative, of a faith that endeavours to purge itself from everything qualifying or compromising its bond with God. One knows the terms in which the *Ascent* describes the journey towards God: the mystic progresses first through the *night of the senses*, in which the soul detaches itself from the gratifications offered by material goods, and then through the *night of the spirit*, in which the soul also detaches itself from the gratifications even of spiritual goods. What this comes down to, finally, cannot be a departure from the world and its conditions, for the mystic never makes such a claim and if he did the phenomenologist would surely not concede it. What mystical life promotes is rather a redefinition of one's attitude in the world as well as, of course, about the world. Whereas previously one had lost oneself in the immediate concerns of everyday life or perhaps the distracting wiles of the ego, now one begins to see the relation with God that has been there all along. Considered as a *spiritual exercise* directed to such a vision, the *Ascent* centres on what John of the Cross sometimes calls the 'stilling' of the senses and of the faculties of the soul (memory, intellect, will), not so much negating them as neutralizing them, or, better, suspending their active movement.

---

12 John of the Cross, *The Ascent of Mount Carmel*, III, 4, 2, p. 221.

13 Key passages include, e.g., *Phaedo* 69c and 72e–78b and *Enneads* V.7, 33. Apart from that, it should be noted that all three passages that I have cited, and indeed all pertinent instances in John of the Cross's major works, employ one or another form of *recoger*. Having been unable to determine the philosophical heritage and connotation of that word for mid-sixteenth-century Spanish letters, I can only contrast its apparent sense of retrieval with the sense of retrospection and remembering investing *recordar* – and observe that the latter sense is certainly *not* a good definition of Platonic anamnesis.

Considered with a view to its *end*, it thus seeks the perfect receptivity to God that would be fully exposed only in this stillness that has abandoned every form of activity, whether by sensation, memory, intellect or will.

If one leaves aside the mystic's overtly theological language for a moment, one may note that this stillness and its receptivity define an extraordinary approach to perfect intimacy between the finite human spirit and the infinite of which it feels itself a part. For John of the Cross, this state represents the fulfilment of a movement that belongs to the very nature of the soul: unable to remain satisfied with limited goods, the soul empties itself of them and even of its tendency to trust the faculties that offer them, always in the name of a greater goodness and a more perfect happiness. That said, there is no mistaking the outcome and what must pass as the discovery: inevitably, the believer is left alone with the desire that has moved him all this way, and of course with a deep awareness that what he wants most lies beyond the reach of his own powers.

A final concern. One might easily suppose that this situation of powerlessness will draw the believer into melancholia, which is in fact the slow death of one's desire: desire withdraws from every external object, back into itself, feeding on its own distance from any possible satisfaction. But in the *Ascent of Mount Carmel* this is precisely not the fate of the mature believer: unlike the melancholic, those who are advanced in the life of faith never abandon their desire for God – that is, they do not wish to remain in unfulfilled desire, and indeed live in hope that one day they will not.[14] This is an important difference, for what clearly distinguishes the situation of the believer from that of the melancholic is an ongoing faith that satisfaction which has been promised will indeed come, albeit essentially *in its own time*. Mystical experience is thoroughly eschatological, and it thus also entails a heightened sense of the foretaste that has already been identified as a mark of the distinctively Christian attitude.

---

14 John of the Cross, *The Ascent of Mount Carmel*, II, 13, 6, p. 141.

Hence the claim: over and against everything that leads one to think, or feel, that the finitude conditions of mundane life come first, there is always a bond with the divine already established in the very possibility of inordinate religious desire; and this bond is always ready to be awakened in those who hear the call of that inordinate desire, as the voice of conscience making me one with what I truly am. What the mystic dramatically 'recollects' is the inexplicability of the soul without the God who creates it, *and* the unknowability of such a God without its expression in the soul. Metaphysically, one may speak here of a belonging-together of the finite and the infinite, and the ungroundedness of their relation. Theologically, one returns to the idea of profound agreement between the soul's love of God and God's love of the soul. Phenomenologically, one is compelled to think that the believer's primordial receptivity to God resides *in that love itself*, and now somehow as its antecedent cause. Christian faith proposes that the soul is always already in love with God, whether one realizes it or not.

IV

All of this suggests that the primordial receptivity to God that is proper to Christian faith, as a distinct mode of being-in-the-world, may be defined by a twofold affirmation anterior to any act that expresses it. This would not be the affirmation of free movement – not the affirmation made by one whose identity is already assured in some prior determination – but rather an affirmation in which identity is always already determined before any question of acting on its basis – an *Ur-affirmation*, perhaps. I repeat: Christian life is rooted simultaneously in an affirmation of God as loving Creator and an affirmation of the soul as created and called to love in turn. This has been the point where the metaphysics of charity sees its chance with Heidegger, and with any philosopher of being, contending that love is prior to being and beings, and that the 'things' of love transcend their being. The resulting critical perspective is so familiar that it needs no commentary here: before being is comprehended as beings according to *Dasein*'s care for its own existence, it is given in love (J.-L. Marion). Faith 'knows' this, it is argued, and in faith the believer may enjoy being as a gift. In faith, then, the things we encounter have a richness and may be known with a passion that must, in comparison, appear lacking in those who are not open to their divine source.

One may hesitate before such proposals, and not only in allegiance to a certain phenomenology. After all, nothing in them actually rules out the possibility of still taking a thing as a phenomenon and not as a gift. Moreover, this must be possible even for the believer, since one can hardly live in a constant state of religious awareness. The life of faith, one will have to admit, certainly includes moments – often long moments – when one falls short of experiencing the world, or even oneself, as God-given. And then, of course, one meets the world and things as such (or as given, in Husserl's sense), without any intimation of a transcendent source for their meaning. Would it not be precisely this that phenomenology, which is not theology, investigates when attending to what it calls 'the things themselves'?

But apart from any religious assurance for the possibility of phenomenology – an assurance that, to be sure, phenomenology has not felt compelled to seek – the fact that a believer can experience something like *abandonment* to the world alone also opens the way to a better understanding of the condition of faith, as being *in-the-world*-toward-God. One might have seen it earlier: in the life of Christian faith 'being-in-the-world' designates the possibility and perhaps even the inevitability of *not* realizing perfect intimacy with God by one's own efforts, though it also designates the situation in which one nonetheless tries, and indeed makes progress. I venture to recall the relevant theological principle: perfect intimacy with God, salvation, beatitude and the other names for what faith desires, are truly possible only with what the tradition calls the resurrection at the end of time. Failing that, until then, the life of faith necessarily admits a secularity in which one may well hear and answer the call of the divine, making it the centre of one's being, but in which one may also fail to hear it, or hear it but fail to respond effectively, so that it becomes senseless, distant and empty.

It is not difficult to imagine the figure in which the call is heard and the response is apt, though our psychologies and sociologies makes us uncertain about particular cases. In the *pilgrim* one may witness a ceaseless movement – spiritual, if not also physical – whose dominant affect is joy and not anxiety, and whose restlessness thus cannot be reduced to a flight from one's own death. The pilgrim is in the world but not wholly of the world, yet her movement, her itinerance is not for all of that 'free-play'. There is labour in Christian faith, in being-in-the-world-toward-God. *Strange* labour: one freely carries on without any of the usual proof that one's aim will ever be achieved, and sometimes what one seeks does come after all, but precisely in a moment of rest.

Need it be stated that the name for this condition – the name for the power by which an absurd task is animated by joy, and by which the impossible cannot be ruled out – is 'grace'? By grace alone would freedom be more than natural movement and more than the circulation of self-transcendence among things and in an environment. By grace, too, labour exceeds the economy of exchange, living on hope and not mere expectation. Graced freedom presents itself as capable of more than it could know, and its efforts appear to lead towards more than it could ever calculate or project.

It is of course this notion of grace, of a supernatural surplus, infusing nature, as its necessary supplement, so that it is somehow more than itself alone, that must finally clarify John of the Cross's sense of a 'habit' that is certain and yet also obscure. From that perspective, it is the central, and indeed perhaps only, problem for a phenomenological account of Christian faith. Essential for faith, it is, however, unintelligible for phenomenology – which, let us not forget, steps back from it in order to see it. Could it be that phenomenology will get closest to grace – closest to thing itself – precisely by recognizing that it cannot be made to appear? If so, it will have spoken best about grace, and in that line best about faith, too, when it has demonstrated with all its considerable rigour that in this case it sees nothing more than what a believer will insist are only silhouettes.

7. Doubled Reflection: Gadamer, Aesthetics and the Question of Spiritual Experience

NICHOLAS DAVEY

Introduction

This essay focuses on a doubled reflection concerning a problem shared by Gadamer's hermeneutical aesthetics and contemporary theology. The focal issue concerns a mutual need to establish a secure grounding for subjective experience. Kant's metaphysical scepticism offered a profound challenge to both aesthetics and theology: if either discipline is to avoid banishment to the realms of arbitrary subjective preference and irrational belief, a new grounding is required. The question Kant's subjectivization of aesthetics poses for Gadamer is how to demonstrate that the intensely subjective nature of aesthetic experience has a worth because it is both grounded in and reflects a level of being which transcends subjective consciousness. Gadamer invariably insists that to start with subjectivity is to miss the point. To secure the cognitive claim of aesthetic experience requires reaching beyond subjectivity to grasp the substantiality that informs it (*TM* 302).[1] Kant's metaphysical scepticism offers the same challenge to the cognitive status of spiritual experience within theology. McIntosh argues that

---

1 H.-G. Gadamer, *Truth and Method* (London: Sheed and Ward, 1989), p. 302. Further references to this text will be referred as *TM* and will be followed by the appropriate page number.

while no one would want to discount the significance of experiential phenomena in the spiritual life, if these are seen as the defining features then spirituality seems to lose its theological voice. It is reduced to being only an expression of human subjectivity. The analysis of spirituality solely in terms of such subjectivity washes out the theological implications of the transformation a subject can undergo in such experience.[2] What the theologian von Balthasar says of art in this context can also be said of spiritual experience. The subjectivization of art has the consequence of rendering 'the enjoyment of art and art itself' as a 'trivialised detached and peculiar pleasure, which leads to nothing else'. Its part in the whole experience of humankind is left unexplained.[3] The counter argument that Gadamer and McIntosh put is that in order to secure the cognitive content of both aesthetic and spiritual experience, they need to be brought under the wider cultural and religious horizons that underpin them. Von Balthasar's comment that 'aesthetics must abandon itself and go in search of new categories'[4] not only has a clear relevance for Gadamer but it also indicates the precise nature of the task facing those who would defend the significant content of spiritual experience.

This paper will explore the symmetry between Gadamer's and McIntosh's attempt to strip aesthetic and spiritual experiences of their subjectivist connotations and restore to inward experience its proper cognitive status. Our purpose is not merely to note this implicit symmetry but to make use of it. We suggest that whereas the ontological turn in modern hermeneutics was in part a response to the methodological challenges posed by nineteenth-century theological and philological studies, so now that hermeneutical response can in its turn offer theology an

---

2 M. A. McIntosh, *Mystical Theology: The Integrity of Spirituality and Theology* (Oxford: Blackwell, 2006), p. 9.

3 S. Hampshire, *Thought and Action* (London: Chatto and Windus, 1959), p. 246.

4 H. U. von Balthasar, *Theo-Drama: Theological Dramatic Theory*, vol. 1, *Prolegomena*, tr. G. Harrison (San Francisco: Ignatius Press, 1998), pp. 16–17.

answer to the problem of subjectivism in its renewed debate about the status of spiritual experience. That Gadamer's philosophical hermeneutics and his aesthetics are informed by and can now inform theological debate is indicative of a doubled reflection or recursive loop in the historical unfolding of key debates within both sets of disciplines. Modern hermeneutics has its roots in biblical scholarship. As the works of Manfred Franck, Peter Szondi and Andrew Bowie amply demonstrate, the influence of the Protestant theologian Schleiermacher upon modern hermeneutics is enormous.[5] He was among the first to promote an argument central to the *Sprachsphilosophie* of Heidegger and Gadamer: 'Language never begins to form itself through science, but via general communication/exchange; science comes to this only later, and only brings an expansion, not a new creation in language.'[6] Just as Schleiermacher's theological orientation has shaped the language horizon of post-Heideggerian hermeneutics, so the responses that hermeneutic theory developed to methodological difficulties within both theology and other interpretive disciplines now reflect back into theology and in particular offer a solution to key issues surrounding the status of subjective (spiritual) experience. Heidegger's ontological turn is renowned. Understanding is no longer treated as an epistemic issue but as a question of being. Discussion shifts from treating understanding as the activity of a subject to approaching it as a mode of being in which different subjects reflect and participate.[7] Gadamer renders Heidegger's

---

5 M. Franck, *Das individuelle Allgemeine: Textstrukturierung und Interpretation nach Schleiermacher*, vol. 1, Aufl. edn (Frankfurt am Main: Suhrkamp, 1971); Peter Szondi, *Introduction to Literary Hermeneutics* (Cambridge: Cambridge University Press, 1995); A. Bowie, *Aesthetics and Subjectivity from Kant to Nietzsche* (Manchester: Manchester University Press, 1990).

6 F. Schleiermacher, *Dialectic*, cited by A. Bowie in *The Cambridge Companion to Friedrich Schleiermacher*, ed. J. Marina (Cambridge: Cambridge University Press, 2005), p. 89.

7 For an excellent discussion of Heidegger's ontological turn, see P. Ricouer, *Hermeneutics and the Human Sciences* (Cambridge: Cambridge University Press, 1981), part 1.

ontological stance less abstract by changing the ground of hermeneutic operation. His emphasis is not so much upon a theory of being but upon an account of how subjects acquire their initial interpretive orientation by participating in linguistic and cultural horizons which, though they always transcend individual subjects, do not exist apart from them. Gadamer articulates his stratagem in Hegelian terms.

> All self-knowledge arises from what is historically pre-given, what with Hegel we call 'substance', because it underlies all subjective intentions and actions, and hence both prescribes and limits every possibility for understanding any tradition whatsoever in its historical alterity. This almost defines the aim of philosophical hermeneutics: its task is to retrace the path of Hegel's phenomenology of mind until we discover in all that is subjective the substantiality that determines it. (*TM* 302)

This stratagem enables Gadamer to win back the cognitive content of aesthetic experience. Rather than regarding the latter as the product of human consciousness per se, he is able to treat consciousness as an expressive medium exhibiting aspects of the substantialities that sustain it. The recursive loop in the reasoning is evident. Just as subjectivity is informed by the historical substantialities in which it is grounded, so they in turn reveal themselves in the subjective experiences they shape. Subjectivity and its underlying substantialities co-inhere. The theologian Wolfhart Pannenberg captures this figure of recursive reasoning perfectly in his book *Theology and the Philosophy of Science*:

> Insistence on the primacy of the understanding of meaning as a disclosure of life even in its religious and universal-historical dimensions does not mean a restriction to a merely subjective hermeneutic because the totality of meaning in experience always transcends the meanings apprehended in intention. For the same reason, the objective understanding of meaning in history which in its movement breaks open

subjectively attributed meaning does not appear as something alien to subjectivity. On the contrary the subjective
experience of meaning is drawn by its own action, if it does
not close itself to reflection, into the movement of history
which analyses its contents and its truth.[8]

Such recursive looping is deployed by Gadamer to resist the
subjectivization (marginalization) of aesthetic experience. We
shall argue that Gadamer's stratagem could also be employed
within theology to counter the subjectivization of spiritual
experience. With this image of hermeneutic reflection doubling
back on its origins, let us turn to Gadamer's critique of aesthetic
subjectivization.

AVE, VERUM: Gadamer's Hermeneutical Reappropriation of Aesthetics

Contrary to the view that aesthetic experience is merely an
expression of subjective preference, Gadamer's *Truth and
Method* makes a fundamental claim: artworks address us. Their
address involves a type of truth-claim. If and when an artwork
'speaks', we find ourselves truly addressed in the sense that we
cannot turn our back on its claim. A true or genuine claim
demands a response such that to refuse it is to become disingenuous. When an artwork speaks, we experience a 'concre-
tion of meaning' (*TM* 397). Its subject matter addresses us on its
terms, directly, and according to the expectancies of our interpretations. The artwork 'happens', it addresses us irrespective
of our willing and doing. Before the artwork, 'subjectivity and
self-consciousness' fall away and we are confronted by its
address.[9] We no longer ask what it means. We no longer interpret it, or rather, when an aspect of its meaning reveals itself,

---

8 W. Pannenberg, *Theology and the Philosophy of Science*, tr. F.
McDonagh (London: Darton, Longman & Todd, 1976), p. 205.

9 See Gadamer's Foreword to J. Grondin, *Introduction to Philosophical Hermeneutics* (Albany, State University of New York Press,
1994), p. x.

interpretation cancels itself (see *TM* 465). The spectator's open-ness to the artwork's address is a confession of vulnerability: something that matters is being discussed or put in question. We cannot turn away from art's address because it is capable of both implicating our self-understanding and placing it at risk. A hermeneutical approach to art demands rethinking the scope and character of aesthetics. Gadamer argues, 'Aesthetics has to be absorbed into hermeneutics . . . hermeneutics must be so determined as that it does justice to the experience of art' (*TM* 144, 116, 164).

Gadamer's and von Balthasar's call for a new framework for aesthetics is no idiosyncrasy but an eloquent response to shift-ing paradigms of thought within modern European philosophy. Both are the intellectual heirs of the arguments of another citizen of Königsberg, the theologian and philosopher Georg Hamann (1730–88). Hamann's passionate defence of the singularity of experience and his refusal to accept that neither reason nor science were the sole arbiters of truth, initiates an intellectual resistance to the Enlightenment's privileging of reason and theory which Gadamer's aesthetics sharpens and continues.[10] This resistance fuels a key misunderstanding of recent hermeneutics and aesthetics. That they abjure reason and science as the principal arbiters of truth does not imply that they are irrational. To the contrary, the value of Gadamer's hermeneutics lies in its ability to show how aesthetic judge-ments can indeed be inherently *reasonable* without conforming to method. What may, indeed, be irrational is the deliberate devaluation of alternative ways of approaching truth and truthfulness. As Bjorn Ramberg has argued, 'scientism is not bad because it gets the world wrong . . . but because it renders us subject to certain forms of oppression', namely those which seek to exclude ways of looking at things that are not amenable to the methods of the natural sciences.[11] The recursive

---

10 I. Berlin, *The Magus of the North: J. G. Hamann and the Origins of Modern Irrationalism* (London: John Murray, 1993).

11 Ramberg cited by Bowie in *The Cambridge Companion to Friedrich Schleiermacher*, p. 88.

stratagem which Gadamer deploys against the subjectivization of aesthetic experience is a device which aims to insure that aesthetic experience is not marginalized by commitments to an epistemological framework more suited to operations within the natural science. It endeavours to do this by animating a recursive loop which constantly refers the part (the subjective expression) to the whole (the substantiality that informs it) and the whole (the underlying tradition or series of hermeneutic involvements) to the part (the individual utterance through which an aspect of the whole finds expression). It is the argument of this paper that the recursive stratagem which enables Gadamer to free aesthetic experience from subjectivism, establishes an intellectual manoeuvre capable of saving spiritual experience from the same corrosive prejudices.

We shall now turn to Mark McIntosh's defence of spiritual experience which is eloquently offered in his book *Mystical Theology*.[12] His argument will be divided into the following themes: 'Repositioning the subjective', 'The autonomy of the spiritual', 'Spiritual experience as encounter', 'Spiritual experience and wisdom', 'Spiritual openness'. Discussion of each theme will be set against a comparison of Gadamer's reasoning.

Speaking the Truth: McIntosh on Recovering the Theological Status of Spiritual Experience

Repositioning the subjective

McIntosh argues that any academic defence of spiritual experience must overcome the prevalent tendency to treat it merely as an expression of a private state of inner transcendence experienced by the self.[13] To approach spiritual experience in this way is to lock it in what Gadamer refers to as 'the impotence of subjectivity' (*TM* 489). Religious and academic institutions

---

12 See note 2 above.
13 McIntosh *Mystical Theology*, p. 22.

sometimes deliberately conspire to contain spiritual experience in this way in order to marginalize its inconvenient claims to legitimacy. Such containment has other dangers.

> The problem with this separation (of spiritual experience) from theology is that it tends to disorientate spirituality, to deprive it of some stable communal goal and reference, and hence render it susceptible to the idols, compulsions or fears of the individual. There is another danger as well. The intensity of mystical experience can easily lead to a kind of absolutism that oppresses the lives of mystics themselves or of cultures receptive to them.[14]

The congruence with Gadamer's reasoning concerning the subjectivization of aesthetic experience is striking. Stressing the subjectivity of a conscious state prioritizes its incommunicable intensity rather than its transmittable content. Gadamer is above all interested in the transmittable content, that is, how subjective experience manifests in an individual manner realities that underlie it. If, on the one hand, private aesthetic experience and the subject matters of art and, on the other, spiritual experience and theology are separated, both parties suffer. Aesthetic and spiritual experiences become potentially ever more decadent if they are separated from 'some stable goal and reference'. Furthermore, the collective knowledge held in art and religious tradition becomes increasingly remote unless it is instantiated in individual experience. McIntosh insists, therefore, that 'every spiritual consciousness *must* be contextualized and appraised in terms of its context (since) claims to a putatively absolute experience, free from the interpretive matrix of one's cultural location are always problematic'.[15] In a way that Gadamer would agree with, McIntosh argues that 'the whole scheme of inner subjectivity by which modernity has tended to interpret spirituality may need to be relinquished in favour of a more

---

14 McIntosh, *Mystical Theology*, p. 14.
15 McIntosh, *Mystical Theology*, p. 14.

embodied and contextual model'.[16] It is surprising that McIntosh does not invoke religious tradition as a basis for establishing the embodied and contextual foundations of spiritual experience. Spiritual experience may be *de novo* psychologically speaking but in terms of its hermeneutic context, it rarely if ever is.

The autonomy of the spiritual

McIntosh concedes that one strategy for bringing spiritual experience back into theological debate is to treat it phenomenally. The intellectual tactic here is straightforward. It disregards the insightful claims of spiritual experience and treats its emergence as indicative of something else, i.e. a socio-political phenomenon. The move has a certain persuasiveness.

> This approach is immensely attractive, first because it permits the study of spirituality purely in terms of the human sciences, and hence seems to legitimize spirituality in the politics of academia. Furthermore its openness to an implicit commonality among religions is beguilingly ecumenical and modern.[17]

McIntosh is aware of the pitfalls of the procedure: by treating spiritual experience as a sign or symptom of a social process, the experience is from the subject's point of view bleached of its theological implications. It is treated not as significant in itself but for what it reveals of other processes. The claim of the experience itself is not addressed. To the contrary, such experience is taken as a means to an end, as evidence for another cultural (sociological) discourse. From the point of view of the subject of the experience, to know that my experience is indicative of a certain class or gender disposition is certainly interesting but it has no direct bearing on what addresses me from within that experience. It is worth noting that Gadamer is

---

16 McIntosh, *Mystical Theology*, p. 22.
17 McIntosh, *Mystical Theology*, p. 9.

acutely aware of the same issue with regard to aesthetic experience.

Gadamer's approach to art is anti-representationalist. To treat art as a representation of something beyond the work is to reduce the work to being a secondary vehicle of what it represents. Hegel's definition of the beautiful as the 'sensuous appearing of the Idea' presumes, for example, that aesthetic experience reaches beyond the specific type of appearance to an underlying idea. Aesthetic experience becomes the expectation of a semantic fulfilment. Once the idea behind the appearance is grasped, 'the whole of its meaning would have been understood once and for all and thus brought in to our possession so to speak'. The work of art becomes a carrier of meaning, to be abandoned once the lead story has been grasped. To treat aesthetic experience as a signifier of something else is in effect to say that aesthetic experience is self-negating on two counts. If an art work successfully brings to mind the idea within it, the work is surpassed. Aesthetic experience becomes a means to philosophy. Gadamer's opposition to aesthetic idealism is supported by the claim that art 'cannot be satisfactorily translated in terms of conceptual knowledge'.[18] A work does not simply refer to a meaning independent of itself. Its meaning is not to be grasped in such a way that it can be simply transferred to another idiom. Indeed, because it invites many meanings, an artwork acquires an ideality of possible meanings which cannot be obviated by any possible realization.[19] The work has, therefore, an autonomy which cannot be substituted by anything else, or, to put it another way, the work is always in excess of its readings, its meanings are always more than its interpretations. To reduce the work to being a sign of something else not only diminishes its autonomy but reduces the meaning it is able to generate from within itself. Such a reduction displaces and, at worst, silences the inner meaning. We can see then that by

---

18 H.-G. Gadamer, *The Relevance of the Beautiful* (Cambridge: University of Cambridge Press, 1986), p. 69.

19 Gadamer, *The Relevance of the Beautiful*, p. 146.

default, Gadamer eloquently puts the case in favour of the autonomy of spiritual experience.

Spiritual experience as encounter

A further consequence of subjectivizing spiritual experience is its denigration as an indulgent escapism which avoids the reality of the other. McIntosh argues that spirituality entails a discovery of the 'self' precisely in its encounter with the divine and human other, an encounter which does not allow the self to reside in a reassuring self-image nor to languish in the prison of a false social construction of itself.[20]

> Understood in this sense, spirituality as the transformation and discovery of the self always happens in encounter, it is an activity constantly stirred up and sustained by the other who calls one out of one's 'self' and into the truth of one's mission in life, out of provisionality and into the adventure of incarnation.[21]

This suggests that far from being introverted or solipsistic, spiritual experience is inherently oriented towards discovery, towards new perceptions and new understandings of reality, and is, hence, intimately related to theology.[22] McIntosh argues that the focal points of spirituality are not the states of inner transcendence experienced by the self, but rather the patterns, structures and images that embody the beckoning of the other and the response this invitation evokes.[23] Spirituality is not a retreat into isolation but allows the individual to grow into a new matrix of relations. It is this beckoning of the other (and the response this beckoning elicits in us) that draws us from provisional existence into real life.[24] Spiritual experience

---

20 McIntosh, *Mystical Theology*, p. 5.
21 McIntosh, *Mystical Theology*, p. 6.
22 McIntosh, *Mystical Theology*, p. 6.
23 McIntosh, *Mystical Theology*, p. 22.
24 McIntosh, *Mystical Theology*, p. 22.

demands risk: it asks that our categories for understanding and experiencing reality be given over to – and perhaps be transformed by the reality of the other who is always beyond oneself.[25] The shifting patterns of self-understanding initiated by such experience are invariably the result of an ongoing awakening, a troubling, by the call of the other.[26] Spirituality is never about a silent absorption in a putative 'inner self' but is rather the activity of being drawn into an encounter with the other.[27] Spiritual experience is to be understood as a transforming process into a new network of relationships in which the subject continually loses itself in order to find itself.[28] The parallel with Gadamer's reasoning is striking.

The primary thrust of Gadamer's hermeneutical reappropriation of aesthetics is to free aesthetic experience from being reduced to the hedonism of aesthetic consciousness and thereby save it from being condemned as nothing more than a sequence of pleasurable mental states. Such condemnation deprives aesthetic experience of significant content by isolating the subject from the historical and cultural substantialities upon which the worthwhileness of experience depend. In other words, it encourages the false view that aesthetic experience is an entirely private affair. This, for Gadamer, it manifestly is not. Aesthetic experience is a dialogical encounter with another who speaks through art or with the otherness of art. In aesthetic experience we are addressed. When a work 'speaks' we are truly addressed, we are dialogically open to its address and therefore also open to the possibilities of translation and transcendence. Such openness is not without risk, the risk of transforming one's self-understanding and hence one's relations with others. Aesthetic experience shares with spiritual experience the fact that it entails transformative relations not just with other persons but also with the hermeneutical or religious realities that underlie them. Spiritual experience is not immersion in an inner

---

25 McIntosh, *Mystical Theology*, p. 152.
26 McIntosh, *Mystical Theology*, p. 140.
27 McIntosh, *Mystical Theology*, p. 153.
28 McIntosh, *Mystical Theology*, pp. 9–10.

state but a genuine attempt to negotiate what underlies the realities that underlie it.[29] McIntosh notes:

> The mystics themselves appear to be fascinated not by their own feelings but by something felt, by someone from without becoming present within. As a perceptual phenomenon, the mystical state no doubt testifies to a magnificent capacity of human consciousness. But this matters less to the mystic than who or what appears on the perceptual field. Consciousness is valuable not because of what it is but because of the other that it can experience as not identical with itself or at its disposal.[30]

This is in line with Karl Rahner's remark that it is not a question of naming or describing the reality that underlies spiritual experience as such but rather of trying to say something about the experience one has had of that reality.[31]

Spiritual experience and wisdom

The centrifugal impetus of aesthetic and spiritual experience impel one towards the dialogical other. This promises the possibility of hermeneutic translation and transcendence but it also entails the risk of being interrogated by the very reality one has broken through to. Once again, McIntosh's and Gadamer's arguments are mutually informative. McIntosh speaks of spiritual experience as a form of 'breakthrough' to the 'living self-disclosing ground of my own understanding'.[32] He goes on:

> The contemplative act is not in the first instance a moment of especially excited feelings, though these may be involved; it is

---

29 See D. Marmion and M. E. Hines (eds), *The Cambridge Companion to Karl Rahner* (Cambridge: Cambridge University Press, 2005), p. 230.

30 McIntosh, *Mystical Theology*, p. 22.

31 See *The Cambridge Companion to Karl Rahner*, p. 304.

32 McIntosh, *Mystical Theology*, p. 9.

rather an event of being grasped by the self-disclosure of wisdom. Contemplation is not particularly concerned with the inner states of the contemplative (however interesting, unusual and worthy of study they may be in their own right), but with the breaking through of wisdom into the contemplative's consciousness. This is one of those subtle differences that matters enormously. First because it makes clear that the whole event of contemplation is not primarily something that one does but that one is invited into. Second, to speak of contemplation as the breaking through of wisdom makes clear that the event of contemplation issues in new *understanding*, a new encounter with wisdom.[33]

It is plain that the attainment of wisdom is complex. It may involve the abandonment of previous assumptions in the sense of them being expanded or surpassed but it may also demand the renunciation of cherished assumptions that the experience of wisdom exposes as wanting. Embracing the discipline of spiritual experience is to accept a ready openness to the possibility of having all one's expectancies transformed, challenged or overturned. Thus spiritual experience, like aesthetic experience, demands a willingness to submit to the reality of what transcends one. McIntosh speaks of spirituality as a fundamental willingness to face what is real rather than the projected fears or wishes of the ego.[34] Gadamer would agree. It is not hedonistic states that are at the root of aesthetic experience but the hermeneutical reality of the subject-matters (*Sachen*) that ground the interrogative thrust of aesthetic experience. McIntosh continues almost in the same vein:

> The real is never an abstraction, but living truth that calls for response. To avoid this call, to prefer the security of a putatively self-constructed world, is a kind of dishonesty. This dishonesty is not simply a neotic error with regard to the

---

33 McIntosh, *Mystical Theology*, pp. 12 and 15.
34 McIntosh, *Mystical Theology*, p. 28.

truth of things. Rather it consists in doing things an injustice – violating them in their very being, refusing to be honest with them, refusing to deal with them honourably. From this perspective, spirituality is embedded in the very structure of reality, because everything that exists calls and beckons toward honest relationship; I exist humanly in my truthful encounters with the real. And at the heart of these encounters always lies encounter with the One who is the continual source of reality – both what I think of as my own reality and what I am drawn out of myself to encounter honestly as the reality of the other. So we could say that 'I' come to exist and to know by relating to reality in ways that do not attempt to control reality for my own devices. This is an 'act of correct, converted intelligence, intelligence that identifies as its primary interest the objective service of reality, not the service of the thinking subject'.[35]

McIntosh speaks as we have seen of the wisdom that emerges from engagement with the other and its attendant risks. Gadamer does so as well but by emphasizing the centripetal rather than the centrifugal dynamic of the encounter.

It is certainly the case that Gadamer's conception of aesthetic experience can transform our outward grasp of a subject-matter but that very transformation can reveal something of the all too human limits of our understanding: 'Experience is initially always experience of negation: something is not what we supposed it be' (*TM* 354). 'Every experience worthy of the name thwarts an expectation' (*TM* 357). 'Experience . . . involves disappointments of one's expectations' (*TM* 356). The aesthetic experience may, then, reveal more of what we thought we were acquainted with and offer a greater completeness to our grasp of something else, but this self-same experience brings something additional. It offers an insight into how we may have

---

35 McIntosh, *Mystical Theology*, p. 29, quoting Simone Weil, 'Come With Me' in *The Simone Weil Reader*, ed. George A. Panichas (Kisco, NY: Mayer Bell, 1977), pp. 410–11.

been initially deceived by an experience. It reveals the limited nature of our understanding and exposes the folly of planning and future expectations. Indeed, Gadamer sees the very negativity of experience as a pathway which also breaks through to a clear form of wisdom:

> What a person has to learn through suffering (the negativity of experience) is not this or that particular thing, but insight into the limitations of humanity, into the absoluteness of the barrier that separates man from the divine. It is ultimately a religious insight. (*TM* 357)

Such order of insight does not offer a glimpse of another order of existence nor even a better knowledge of things in this world. What it offers or rather opens us out on to is 'the real', the absolutely finite nature of both our understanding and our being: 'Experience teaches us to acknowledge the real' (*TM* 357). McIntosh's words, 'I exist humanly in my truthful encounters with the real,' perfectly summarize Gadamer's experiential account of the breakthrough into transformative wisdom.[36] It is not a penetration of things that is at issue 'but an exalted, wondering "exploration of wisdom"' itself.[37]

Spiritual openness

We have argued above that openness to the other is a central aspect of both spiritual and aesthetic experience. Such openness is neither momentary nor occasional but the result of prolonged discipline and experience. In short, openness and responsiveness to spiritual experience is indistinguishable from an acquired posture or hermeneutic poise.[38] Gadamer's remark that 'the essence of what is called spirit lies in the ability *to move* within the horizon of an open future and an unrepeatable' sug-

---

36 McIntosh, *Mystical Theology*, p. 39.
37 McIntosh, *Mystical Theology*, p. 72.
38 N. Davey, *Unquiet Understanding* (New York: Albany State University Press, 2006), p. 214.

gests that there is no definitive spiritual state or understanding, no final or ultimate revelation.[39] It is always a question of letting go of the past and of allowing what one has acquired from past experience to be probed and tested by the future. Such arguments are central to philosophical hermeneutics: understanding is always open, there is always something more to be said about a *Sache* (subject-matter), and a work of art is never complete in that the interpretive interactions which help constitute it are always ongoing. The hermeneutic poise is, in effect, a way of life. McIntosh pursues a similar line of reasoning.

Spiritual experience is not meant to fill theology's logical gaps with devotional material. To the opposite, he argues, 'Spirituality calls theology to an honesty about the difficulty of understanding what is unfathomable . . . that "suspended wonder" . . . an openness to what is never a puzzle to be solved but always a mystery to be lived.'[40] Here McIntosh touches upon a point which is fundamental not just to theology but to understanding within the humanities.

Mysteries are not subject to the methodological solutions which problems are. A problem denotes a difficulty demanding a solution. Mysteries can only be understood more deeply. They are not to be explained away but are to be discerned as an ever present limit to our understanding. They invoke the hermeneutical insight that to the extent to which there is always more to be said or understood about a subject matter, understanding is indeed without limit. Gadamer contends that precisely because our experiences of truthfulness, of beauty or of love cannot be fully objectified in language, it is necessary to seek out the appropriate words for them. When such words *work*, they open speculative pathways into a deeper understanding of what they attempt to address. To turn away from the difficulty of finding such words or to refuse the attempt on the grounds that only apodictic speech is legitimate, demeans and impoverishes the

---

39 H.-G. Gadamer, *The Relevance of the Beautiful and Other Essays* (Cambridge: Cambridge University Press, 1986), p. 10.

40 McIntosh, *Mystical Theology*, p. 15.

complexities of human experience. It is also to spurn in nihilistic fashion what human life and learning depend on, namely, the ceaseless endeavour to extend and deepen experience. In the words of Andrew Louth, 'the desire to make all reasoning explicit manifests a dislike of evidence, varied, minute, complicated and a desire for something producible, striking, decisive; such a desire is really irrational, as it fails to understand the realities of human behaviour and action'.[41] However, the key point remains. Openness to the mystery of the subject-matters which circumscribe our existence, whether aesthetic or theological, demands a way of life constantly tempered and adjusted by the experiences that constitute its being. Aesthetic and spiritual experience are attached to a way of life rather than to a broad analytic technique or interpretive procedure.

That aesthetic and spiritual experience betray, in effect, a way of life that aims at nothing outside itself only its own self-transformation is implicit in Gadamer's argument that 'the truth of experience always implies an orientation toward new experience' (*TM* 355). As he aptly remarks, 'The dialectic of experience has its proper fulfilment not in definitive knowledge but in the openness to experience that is made possible by experience itself' (*TM* 355). The argument is mirrored in McIntosh's reasoning. What makes spiritual experience important is not that it offers another order of experience but that it is a call to further and new frameworks of experience. Gadamer's and McIntosh's accounts of the essential openness of aesthetic and spiritual experience are, in effect, notes towards *'practices for the transformation of experience' itself.*

In a certain respect, acquiring such openness is willingly to seek dispossession of oneself. As a mode of being, the disciplines of spirituality and aesthetic response are open to formative encounters with the other and otherness. Gadamer describes this encounter as dialogical and McIntosh moves in the same direction. What I think of as my own reality and what I am, is

---

41 A. Louth, *Discerning the Mystery* (Oxford: Clarendon Press, 1983).

drawn out of myself to encounter honestly the reality of the other.[42]

'I' come to exist and to know by relating to reality in ways that do not attempt to control reality for my own devices. This is an 'act of correct, converted intelligence, intelligence that identifies as its primary interest the objective service of reality, not the service of the thinking subject'.[43]

This demands an honest relationship to the call of reality and requires not just observation but a bestowal of life, a practice of love towards the reality of the other. In a sense, reality calls this loving response forth from us; or we could say that the reality of the other calls us out from our moment of selfhood into a new form of life.[44]

The call to be responsive to that which is, in effect, out of ourselves is entirely consistent with the claim that 'hermeneutics is a passion'.[45] Aesthetic and hermeneutical experience entails openness to what happens to us. Weinsheimer puts it well when he remarks, 'An interpretation occurs to me.'[46] When insight occurs to us, it is then that we understand. As a flash of Enlightenment, the epiphany of understanding is not something we do but something that happens to us.[47] Hermeneutic philosophy considers understanding not as subjective behaviour but as a response to and a being involved with and carried away by the reality of the other. A similar pattern of reasoning is pursued by McIntosh. It is not so much *I* who know but rather that 'the known' has drawn me into an encounter with itself: 'knowing reality is associated more with the intimacy, even the desire, that runs between knower and known . . . and less with our

---

42 McIntosh, *Mystical Theology*, p. 29.

43 McIntosh, *Mystical Theology*, p. 29.

44 McIntosh, *Mystical Theology*, p. 29.

45 J. Weinsheimer, *Philosophical Hermeneutics and Literary Theory* (New Haven: Yale University Press, 1991), p. 40.

46 Weinsheimer, *Philosophical Hermeneutics*, p. 35.

47 Weinsheimer, *Philosophical Hermeneutics*, p. 40.

modern conception of a scientific analysis of manipulable objects by the knower'. For McIntosh what reveals itself to us in spiritual experience as knowledge is not really our own act at all, but an event in which I yield myself to what makes itself known to me.[48] However, as Gadamer insists, such giving of oneself over to the otherness of the other or of the real is 'anything but a privative condition, for it arises from devoting one's full attention to the matter at hand, and this is the spectator's own positive accomplishment' (*TM* 126). A spectator's aesthetic distance may entail an ecstatic self-forgetfulness but 'what rends him from himself at the same time gives him back the whole of his being' (*TM* 128). McIntosh follows a similar path of argument. Calls for spiritual detachment are not proposed as 'higher' experiences preferable to other types of experiences. Detachment is not itself an experience alongside others but *practice for the transformation of experience*.[49] Its pattern is inherently self-dispossessive and yet self-constitutive in its dispossession-for-the-other.[50]

Conclusion. The Transformative Nature of Aesthetic and Spiritual Experience

An area of significant complementarity between Gadamer's approach to aesthetic experience and McIntosh's account of spiritual experience concerns the transformative capacity of meaning within both types of experience. Both thinkers are wedded to a presentational account of meaning: the meaning of both forms of experience resides within them and is not dependent upon anything external to them. McIntosh contends that the meaningfulness of mystical texts does not reside in whatever experiences might lie behind the text or might even be evoked in the reader but, rather, in the shape of a new interpretive frame-

---

48 McIntosh, *Mystical Theology*, p. 70.
49 McIntosh, *Mystical Theology*, p. 135.
50 McIntosh, *Mystical Theology*, p. 135.

work posed for the reader by the text.[51] The movement of interpretation is never back to a putative experience behind the
text.[52] Gadamer's hermeneutic stratagem is notably the same.

Gadamer aims to release the meaning held within the artwork and our experience of it. A work does not simply refer to
a meaning which is independent of it. Its meaning is not to be
grasped in such a way that it can be simply transferred to
another idiom. The work has an autonomy of meaning which
cannot be substituted by anything else. Gadamer's conception
of art is presentational (*darstellen*) rather then representational
(*vorstellen*). In the essay 'Wort und Bild' (1992), he claims that
he tries 'to undermine the idea that the picture is a mere copy'.[53]
As a work does not represent anything other than itself, the
meanings it carries only come to the fore in its self-presentation.
Yet the emergent meaning is never given in its entirety nor obviated by any realization. This is consistent with the *eventual*
nature of art. 'When a work of art truly takes hold of us, it is not
an object that stands opposite us which we look at in hope of
seeing through it to an intended conceptual meaning . . . The
work is an *Ereigniss* – an event that "appropriates us" to itself.
The work of art consists in its being open in a limitless way
to ever new integrations of meaning'[54] and, furthermore, 'the
inexhaustibility that distinguishes the language of art from all
translation into concepts rests on an excess of meaning'.[55]
Gadamer's stance concerning the presentational nature of
meaning is in accord with the stance adopted by McIntosh.
However, we are in danger of missing the key point here.

The meanings which come forward autonomously in our
engagement with artworks and spiritual texts do indeed address
us but they do not address us in a vacuum: the meanings which

---

51 McIntosh, *Mystical Theology*, p. 135.

52 McIntosh, *Mystical Theology*, p. 142.

53 H.-G. Gadamer, *Gesammelte Schriften* (Tübingen: J. C. B. Mohr,
1993), Band 8, p. 374.

54 H.-G. Gadamer, *Philosophical Hermeneutics* (Berkeley: University
of Califirnia Press, 1977), p. 96.

55 Gadamer, *Philosophical Hermeneutics*, p. 102.

emerge from artwork and text address us in terms of what we already know, indeed, are capable of transforming what we know. McIntosh argues that 'once one has learned not to take the patterns of the text as a description, then the text can function as a new theological *gestalt*, a hermeneutical field within which everything is seen in a new light and is charged with a new resonance'.[56] The theological text or artwork are thus not important for what they state or manifest in isolation but for what they achieve as 'hermeneutic key' capable of opening and transforming a huge treasury of meaning which is already in our pre-understanding. In short, the artistic and spiritual insight gain meaning not so much because of what they assert themselves but because of their ability to transform the matrix of meanings and associations which shape our implicit cultural horizons. McIntosh puts the point well when he comments that 'all this points us to a crucial hermeneutical insight: mystical texts are more adequately understood not as descriptions of experiences but as a call towards a new framework for having any experiences whatsoever', 'as a matrix of symbols which serves to re-contextualize one's experiences entirely'.[57] The equivalent contention in Gadamer's thought is the transformation-into-structure argument (*TM* 110ff.). The artwork and the claim it has upon us are not so much significant in themselves but are significant because of their capacity to transform our entire horizon of understanding. Here lies a clue to the transformative meaning of both aesthetic and spiritual experience. On one level, it is ridiculous to ask for the meaning of such experiences since there is no end to them. None of these experiences point definitively outside themselves in such a way as to enable us to say that *that* is their meaning. However, as we have argued, the attentiveness and openness which is integral to these experiences is more to do with a disciplined poise or receptiveness to those moments which can be truly momentous, to those occasions when a specific aesthetic or spiritual experience can

---

56 McIntosh, *Mystical Theology*, p. 143.
57 McIntosh, *Mystical Theology*, p. 135.

transform the matrix of symbols and orientations which encapsulate our existence. Transformation and transcendence is what aesthetic and spiritual experience achieves: that alone is their meaning and hermeneutical significance and, most important, it is a significance which restores their proper cognitive content.

We have, in conclusion, argued that it is the recursive looping in Gadamer's argument which moves attention away from the subjective to the substantialities that underlie it and then back to the subjective again, that proves decisive. The manoeuvre enables him to reveal how subjective states are capable of transcending themselves by pointing towards the horizons of tradition which are their ground. This does not diminish the importance of subjective experience. In fact, it might be argued that the manoeuvre gives additional significance. Subjective experience becomes a vehicle through which the substantialities underlying experience achieve phenomenal expression. Gadamer uses the manoeuvre with some success in retrieving the cognitive content of aesthetic (subjective) experience and it is a move which McIntosh's defence of spiritual experience could well benefit from. On the other hand, McIntosh's conception of the meaning of spiritual experience as that which transforms an entire framework of experience has a relevance for aesthetic experience and hermeneutics generally of which Gadamer might have taken fuller account.

8. From Description to Doxology: The Dogmatic Bases of Christian Vision

NATHAN R. KERR

Introduction

In what follows, I should like to reprise the question of the phenomenology–theology differend, first broached by Martin Heidegger in his address 'Phenomenology and Theology',[1] and posed anew most recently by Dominique Janicaud in his influential *Le tournant théologique de la phénoménologie français*.[2] I will endeavour to do so, however, from the perspective of *theology* proper, that is, by seeking to expound the *dogmatic* bases of Christian vision. I will argue that in so far as Christian vision is to be doxologically determined by the grace of the one triune God revealed pre-eminently in the single visible that is Jesus Christ, then such vision cannot be accommodated by the phenomenological reduction to a more original and unconditioned givenness, nor can it be theologically accounted for via

---

1 M. Heidegger, 'Phenomenology and Theology', tr. J. G. Hart, J. Maraldo and W. McNeil, in *Pathmarks*, ed. W. McNeil (Cambridge: Cambridge University Press, 1998), pp. 39–62.

2 D. Janicaud, *Le tournant théologique de la phénoménologie français* (Paris: Éditions de l'Éclat, 1991); translated as 'The Theological Turn of French Phenomenology', tr. B. G. Prusak, in *Phenomenology and the 'Theological Turn'* (New York: Fordham University Press, 2000), pp. 1–103.

the methods of cognitive description. My contention will be that a theological turn from *within* phenomenology, whereby theology is rendered simply a 'higher phenomenology', is at best disingenuous and at worst obfuscatory, in that it supplants the revelatory bases of Christian vision with a more general epistemology of manifestation, and so short-circuits the task of doxology by rendering theology as yet another mode of description.

In the first main section of this essay, I will examine, in Emmanuel Levinas, one exemplar of the so-called 'turn' to transcendence among recent French phenomenologists. Having shown that such a turn can only speciously be called 'theological',[3] methodologically predicated as it is upon the presumed phenomenal (and cognitive) insuperability of this world as it is given to appearance, I shall proceed to ask to what extent recent attempts to correlate theology with phenomenology around the question of 'Being' are right to discern in Christian doctrine a theo-ontological description of human perception. I will argue that, just so long as this 'theological' account of perception continues to be sought mainly according to an original phenomenal impetus to transcendence, it offers an account of Christian vision and faith that remain partly reducible to an immanentist (and independently neutral) phenomenological method. In the final section, I shall contend that only by returning, for reasons of catechism and proclamation, to a more rigorously *dogmatic* account of its revelatory bases, will Christian theology be able to articulate a 'doctrine of seeing' (von Balthasar) whose doxological account of Christian vision positively surpasses the ultimate epistemological sovereignty of phenomenological 'description'.

---

3 My use of the term 'theology' and its cognates throughout this essay is intended to refer only to the theology of the Judaeo-Christian tradition.

Phenomenology and the 'Theological Turn'

I want to begin by calling into question the a priori applicability to theology of the two 'traits' which Dominique Janicaud supposes make up phenomenology's 'theological turn': 'the rupture with immanent phenomenality' and 'the opening to the invisible, to the Other, to a pure givenness, or to an archi-revelation'.[4] Presumably, Janicaud too would insist, as his discussion of Merleau-Ponty vis-à-vis Levinas demonstrates, that these moves are not theological in-themselves, but only in so far as they are made under phenomenological pretences and without 'methodological clarification', as a means of leaving-off from phenomenality 'in a quest for divine transcendence'.[5] However, two initial observations can be made at this point. First, as Janicaud at no point undertakes an inquiry into what precisely 'theology' is, he is left with the quite banal assumption that theology's pre-eminent task is the 'quest for divine transcendence'. This allows Janicaud to take it for granted that Emmanuel Levinas's tendency to privilege one single phenomenon vis-à-vis the totality of being, or Michel Henry's proclamation of an auto-affective life-world counter to this totality, or Jean-Luc Marion's quest to found phenomena in a pure givenness, are manoeuvres automatically native to theology itself. Second, whatever these thinkers might mean to say constructively, Janicaud's haste to label their moves 'theological' obscures their importance as stringent critics of the doctrinaire phenomenological method that Janicaud purportedly takes for granted, and ignores the sense in which their evocation of the notion of transcendence is itself methodologically heuristic, deployed for the sake of attending to a more originary *phenomenological* excess that immanentist phenomenology has itself obscured.

This point can be made well with reference to Emmanuel Levinas, as one prime exemplar of this so-called 'theological

---

4 Janicaud, *'Theolgical Turn'*, p. 17. Hereafter cited as *TT*.
5 Janicaud, *TT*, pp. 17, 70.

turn' in phenomenology.[6] The question has to do with the degree to which Levinas's 'unconditional affirmation of transcendence' really is theological, and in what sense it might *not* be theological for explicitly phenomenological (that is, methodologically descriptive) reasons. Indeed, I contend that if in Levinas there is an occlusion of what Janicaud calls 'the patient interrogation of the visible',[7] it occurs on strictly methodological grounds, in as much as the structures of Levinas's turn are meant to describe more fully an originary call of transcendence that lies at the very heart of all perception. Thus, writing late in his career, in an essay entitled 'Transcendence and Intelligibility',[8] Levinas proposes to stay true to the 'formal' structure of phenomenology by opposing the 'phenomenologies of immanence' found in Husserl and Heidegger with 'another phenomenology', a 'phenomenology of transcendence' which proceeds by way of 'the destruction of the phenomenology of appearance

---

6 I am well aware that Janicaud's treatment and critique of this theological turn is not aimed at Levinas alone, but also, in addition to Marion, is directed towards Jean-François Courtine, Jean-Louis Chrétien, Michel Henry and, to a lesser extent and for different reasons, Paul Ricoeur. While it may appear natural and right that I would have chosen to engage Janicaud's reading of one of these latter figures, in so far as they are all more or less what one might call 'Christian' philosophers, and in my opinion represent more rigorous and nuanced versions of the turn to transcendence in French phenomenology, I have chosen to engage his reading of Levinas for methodological reasons. For what Janicaud sees as holding these thinkers together as phenomenologists in their theological turn is their *methodological* failures and heresies; he has no problem with their attempts to develop a new philosophical approach to God or the transcendent Other, nor with their attempts to do something like a 'Christian' philosophy. He only wishes that they would stop calling it 'phenomenology.' In so far as he sees Levinas as the key source of these failures, in his express disregard for phenomenology's proper methodological 'neutrality' (*TT*, pp. 35–49), engagement with him at this point is especially appropriate.

7 *TT*, p. 26.

8 E. Levinas, 'Transcendence and Intelligibility' (1984) in A. T. Peperzak, S. Critchley and R. Bernasconi (eds), *Basic Philosophical Writings* (Bloomington: Indiana Univiversity Press, 1996), pp. 149–59.

and of knowledge'. Certainly, then, we should take Levinas at his word when he states in the preface to *Totalité et Infinité* that 'the presentation and development of the notions employed owe everything to the phenomenological method'.[9]

But in what sense is this the case? Of course, there is the commonly repeated observation that this occurs for Levinas via the strategic privileging of transcendence over immanence. But what is rather less commonly understood is the way in which Levinas's turn to the notion of transcendence *necessitates* his retention of the key methodological procedures and aims of phenomenology proper: *description* is retained under the guise of Levinas's account of the 'relation without relation' of an original Other, which is the 'height' of experience; *intentionality* occurs under the guise of revelation *kath 'auto*; and the *epoché* is upheld through the suspension of cognitive intuition, or 'vision', in favour of the call of the invisible. All three of these moves presuppose a certain 'reduction' (though Levinas will not employ the term), in that the inbreaking intention of the Other (*l'aplomb*) allows one phenomenologically to be 'led back' or 'led out' to a primary, original relation with the non-thematizable. The point is this: Levinas is classically in line with the initial impulse of all phenomenal description, viz. to recapture and to describe the original, native impulse of givenness inscribed within the immediate phenomena of consciousness. That this impulse is *ethical* for Levinas simply means that there is a primordial duty that coincides with my phenomenologically described worldliness. One is right to argue then (as Derrida first did[10]) that Levinas is not so much doing away with Husserlian phenomenology, as he is ruining it by reinventing it, by showing how the methodological procedures of description and intentionality, when taken with their proper rigour, actually uncover an original, (non-)violent relation with the Other.

---

9 E. Levinas, *Totality and Infinity: An Essay on Exteriority* (Pittsburgh: Duquesne University Press, 1969), p. 28. Hereafter cited as *TI*.

10 J. Derrida, 'Violence and Metaphysics: An Essay on the Thought of Emmanuel Levinas' in *Writing and Difference*, tr. A. Bass (Chicago: University of Chicago Press, 1978), pp. 79–153.

For the question that Levinas wants to ask in the wake of Husserl is this: if phenomenology proceeds on the basis of a certain intentional relation to what is given to me, and if this thing that is given is not-me, is other, then must there not be something about that other that escapes or overflows my intentional consciousness, and so is in-adequate to consciousness' task of adequation? And instead of merely 'bracketing' that excess, would not phenomenology *qua* phenomenology be compelled – responsible, called – to *describe* it as inadequate, as other, as transcendent?

It is thus a methodological point that Levinas is making when in a famous text written in response to Derrida he says: 'It is the meaning of the beyond, of transcendence, and not ethics, that our study is pursuing.'[11] Levinas clarifies just how this is so in relation to Heidegger and the question of ontology: A true relationship to *a* being, to 'beings as such, as pure beings', presupposes a plenitudinous and original 'depth' that the encompassing, horizonal gaze of 'fundamental ontology' cannot capture.[12] Not only can the reflexive gaze of ontology not capture this transcendence, but this transcendence is the very condition for such a gaze to get underway. The relation with the Other is 'an original relation', which functions 'as the condition of any conscious grasp'.[13] Indeed, as Levinas sees it, to 'do' phenomenology is in the first place to be confronted by this original alterity.[14] This is the whole upshot of *Totality and*

---

11 E. Levinas, 'God and Philosophy' tr. R. A. Cohen and A. Lingis in S. Hand (ed.), *The Levinas Reader* (Oxford: Blackwell, 1989), p. 188, n. 15. Levinas continues: '[The study] finds its meaning in ethics.' I take this to mean that Levinas's project is not a description of the ethical so much as a performance of the conviction that genuine phenomenological description of transcendence can only succeed on an ethical basis, via an ethical commitment to the Other. Ethics transforms the way one 'sees' (*TI* 29), and it is this new ethical 'optics' that *Totality and Infinity* wants to sketch out.

12 E. Levinas, 'Is Ontology Fundamental?' (1951) in *Basic Philosophical Writings*, p. 10.

13 Levinas, 'Is Ontology Fundamental?', p. 6.

14 Levinas, 'Transcendence and Intelligibility', p. 158.

Infinity: to reduce a being – any being – to our conscious intention, to understand this being against a preconceived horizon of Being, is already to have come up against its alterity, which means that phenomenology as Husserl and Heidegger have conceived it can only proceed by 'grasping being out of nothing or reducing it to nothing, removing it from its alterity'.[15] In seeking to describe that which appears to it, the phenomenology of immanence has only succeeded in obfuscating that originary event which precisely makes such appearance possible, and so has failed to be true to its own founding principle, viz. the description of pre-predicative experience. Thus, Levinas's 'turn' to transcendence is part and parcel for Levinas of remaining methodologically committed to phenomenology's ambition of describing the originary impulse at the heart of all phenomenal disclosure.

And yet, it is equally the case that this turn to transcendence occurs for Levinas only on the basis of a prior determination of what it is possible 'to see'. The turn to transcendence comes only after the destruction – or exhaustion – of immanent phenomenality. Consequently, it is possible to argue that Levinas's positive ethical project is based entirely upon this negative move, and results from carrying through to its logical conclusion the methodological task of immanent phenomenological description. One can see how this is the case, by drawing attention to the fact that what gets suspended in Levinas's phenomenology of transcendence are the dual tasks of conceptual intentionality: ontology and vision. 'Vision', for Levinas, is defined as 'an adequation of the idea with the being, a comprehension that encompasses' (*TI* 34). 'Encompassing' as such is a horizonal concept; what appears is precisely *envisaged* by an aim or intention.[16] The 'adequation' of vision on this scheme

---

15 Levinas, *TI*, pp. 27, 44.

16 Taking our cue from the French verb *viser*, which means 'to aim at' or 'to be directed at'. What I have to say here regarding Levinas applies also, on my view, to Jean-Luc Marion, who plays on the French verb *viser* to suggest that 'the vis*able*' is that upon which our visual aim settles, so as to admit of no beyond. See J.-L. Marion, *God Without*

gets construed as the task of the intentive I; vision occurs as a kind of active project, inasmuch as it is the task of the 'seeing' I to identify what appears to it with the primal, eidetic content it has schematized from the outset. 'To see', it would seem, is what it means 'to be I', which is for the ego to exist 'in identifying itself, in recovering its identity through all that happens to it' (*TI* 36). Vision is thus an inherently egological exercise, a task that is of a piece with 'the primordial work of identification' (*TI* 36–8). *Ipso facto*, vision as comprehension links up with knowledge as ontological cognition; the 'luminous horizon' of eidetic consciousness (Husserl) or being (Heidegger) secures vision itself as the condition of the essence of what can be given to me in phenomena (*TI* 44–5). Such knowledge is, one might say, a rigorous application of the phenomenological *epoché*; it is the 'suspension' of alterity itself (*TI* 38). And this in turn gives rise to the now famous indictment of Heideggerian fundamental ontology as a discourse which seeks always (albeit in a phenomenological mode already inscribed by Husserl) to reduce transcendence to immanence, and to inscribe alterity within the same (*TI* 45–6).[17]

The upshot of this is that a phenomenological project that begins with the call of invisibility, one that views the intentional process as starting *from* the Other, as from *beyond* being, can only be such that the response to this call is one of dis-interestedness (*désintéressement*) (*TI* 35, 50), thereby effecting an essential break with ontology. The desire for the invisible is concomitant with a sacrifice of being for the Other (*TI* 63), which sacrifice means simply that the project of the conscious 'I', which is that of the constitution of being or essence itself, is 'interrupted' by a more primordial intention that comes from without. And this intention initiates a more radical *epoché*, a suspension that leads, according to Levinas, to the very

---

Being: Hors-Texte, tr. T. A. Carlson (Chicago and London: University of Chicago Press, 1991), pp. 26–7.

17 Thus, in knowledge as comprehension, the other 'is somehow betrayed, surrenders, is given in the horizon in which it loses itself and appears, lays itself open to grasp, becomes a concept' (*TI* 43–44).

'destruction' of being-itself (the irony of Levinas echoing Heidegger's *Destruktion* here should not be missed).[18] So, in a collection of essays that addresses the question of 'God' in relation to themes from across his *oeuvre*, and that articulates the contours of what he calls 'a phenomenology of the idea of the Infinite',[19] we find Levinas describing this interruption by the Other as 'the *epoché* opened by disinteredness',[20] which is a 'suspension of essence' as a suspension of one's own intentional consciousness through its displacement in response to the 'intentional' demand of the Other.[21] But this suspension of ontology or essence is equally a suspension of what is given to vision.[22] To say this is to admit that the essence of what we see – its very being – can in no way be bound up with our desire for the infinite, or with the task of responding appropriately to the call of the infinite in the vein of a particular phenomenological methodology. For it is not these methodological devices, per se, but rather their circumscribed usage within a transcendental horizon, that forces phenomenology to cover over an original signification, and so to run aground.

Consequently, precisely by way of his rigorous commitment to the phenomenological method, Levinas leaves in place certain fixed immanentist assumptions about being, about what one sees, and about the given *datum* of the world itself: (1) that the essence of what is seen is there to be exhausted by the intentional consciousness; and (2) that what is genuinely other, what is transcendent as such, has to do with an 'existence' that is 'beyond' essence, and so inassimilable by this intentional 'I' according to which all visible essence is co-ordinated. That is,

---

18 See E. Levinas, 'Preface to the German Translation of *Totality and Infinity*' in *Entre Nous: On Thinking-of-the-Other*, tr. M. B. Smith and B. Harshav (New York: Columbia University Press, 1998), p. 199.

19 E. Levinas, *Of God Who Comes to Mind*, tr. B. Bergo (Stanford: Stanford University Press, 1998), p. xiv.

20 Levinas, *Of God Who Comes to Mind*, p. 5.

21 Levinas, *Of God Who Comes to Mind*, pp. 10–11. Levinas describes the 'ontological interruption' of this *epoché* as a 'dislocation' from the totality that is tantamount to a 'departure from being' (pp. 8–9).

22 Levinas, *Of God Who Comes to Mind*, p. xii.

Levinas is able to think transcendence only by leaving in place the transcendental assumptions of being according to which Husserl and Heidegger proceed. In an important transitional essay from 1965, Levinas remarks that '[t]he Other can . . . not appear without renouncing his radical alterity, without entering into an order',[23] and this because God for Levinas, who is 'the original form of "transcendence"', and whose perpetual with-drawal is the condition for the Other's alterity,[24] is 'separate from the adventure of being which occurs in phenomena and in immanence'.[25] It would thus seem that to note in Levinas's turn to transcendence an unequivocal turn to 'theology' would be to obscure the *phenomenological* impetus for his work, and to miss the way in which he employs the phenomenological method to negotiate an aporia that he locates at the very heart of the phenomenology of immanence.[26] Indeed, the word 'God' in Levinas's work, from beginning to end, is intended only to signify the 'phenomenological concreteness' of this aporia, an aporia to which phenomenology can only attend by placing itself in the service of 'first philosophy' as the dis-inter-estedness of ethics.[27] His appeal to transcendence is not, manifestly, an appeal to a divine domain behind this world, which requires one speculatively to capitulate to 'saintly discourses and lofty dogmas', as Janicaud supposes (*TT* 27; translation slightly altered). Even if the word 'God' to which Levinas does appeal is 'nothing less than the God of the biblical tradition' (*TT* 27), we need simply to remind ourselves that for Levinas the 'God of the Bible' is meant only to signify 'the beyond being, trans-cendence',[28] which is not, on the face of it at least, a strictly

---

23 E. Levinas, 'Enigma and Phenomenon' (1965) in *Basic Philo-sophical Writings*, p. 68.

24 See Levinas, 'Trace of the Other', pp. 356–9.

25 Levinas, 'Enigma and Phenomenon', p. 71.

26 See 'From Consciousness to Wakefulness: Starting from Husserl' in Levinas, *Of God Who Comes to Mind*, pp. 15–32.

27 See Foreword in Levinas, *Of God Who Comes to Mind*, pp. xi-xv; Levinas, 'God and Philosophy', p. 184.

28 Levinas, 'God and Philosophy', p. 168.

theological assertion. To say 'God' for Levinas is above all else to testify to an ethical demand, which is the site of all 'real', genuine experience, and so is the site of all true philosophy, as such.[29]

To conclude this section, then: not only is it wrong to view Levinas's turn to transcendence as marking a departure from rigorous phenomenological method, but such a phenomenological construal of transcendence turns out to be harmful to a Christian theological account of being and vision. For no positive ontological content can be given to the name 'God' in Levinas's work. 'God' for Levinas is one whose transcendence is that of an Other separate from the adventure of being which occurs in phenomena and in immanence, and whose appearance is negatively conditioned from the outset by this immanental ontology. Levinas's 'God' serves as a foil to negotiate the aporia of immanence, and so functions as a mere cipher for describing an a priori intentional project.[30]

---

29 Levinas, 'God and Philosophy', pp. 184–6 and *passim*.

30 As Phillip Blond has shown, a similar conclusion could be drawn with respect to Jean-Luc Marion's phenomenological project, in so far as transcendence finds its meaning for Marion in the privileging of a single phenomenon (the icon) vis-à-vis immanent phenomenality, as such. Clearly, for Blond, this transcendence, or in-visibility, still takes finite intentionality as its measure, even if now only negatively. One might argue here that Marion's reduction to a (more purely revelatory) 'givenness' is nonetheless more 'theological' than Levinas's reduction to the ethical face of the Other, in so far as it allows one to speak phenomenologically of God's 'appearance' as such. But one need only point up that such appearance is for Marion purely a matter of epistemology to realize that Marion's 'God' (and we can now say 'Christ') appears as yet another cipher for negotiating the phenomenological aporia of immanent cognition. See Marion's treatment of Jesus Christ as the phenomenon of revelation in J.-L. Marion, *Being Given: Toward a Phenomenology of Givenness*, tr. J. L. Kosky (Stanford: Stanford University Press, 2002), pp. 236–41. Cf. P. Blond, 'Introduction: Theology Before Philosophy' in P. Blond (ed.), *Post-Secular Philosophy: Between Philosophy and Theology* (London: Routledge, 1998), pp. 34–8.

Theo-Ontology as 'Higher Phenomenology'

In the previous section, I have shown that there are indeed good reasons not to take traditional phenomenological accounts of transcendence as necessarily marking a 'theological turn', and so *de jure* providing the basis for an account of Christian vision. It remains for us to ask, then, whether there can in fact be a genuinely *theological* turn within phenomenology? In this section, I want to investigate one possible way forward with regards to this question, by way of reference to recent attempts to proffer a more robustly *ontological* and *participatory* account of divine transcendence. At the same time, I should like to pose some tentative questions with respect to the Christian *dogmatic* bases of these attempts, and to show in what ways I think this approach still retains the tendency to reduce revelation to a species of phenomenological manifestation, and so arbitrarily to cognize the focal object of Christian vision.

In the wake of John Milbank's influential essay, 'Only Theology Overcomes Metaphysics',[31] recent thinkers favouring his turn to a renewed *analogia entis*, such as Phillip Blond, have sought a theological correlation with phenomenology around the question of 'Being', rather than that of 'givenness', 'experience', 'affection', etc. Blond especially, as a theologian, has an obvious interest in maintaining the revelatory basis of theological perception, and so of properly expounding the doctrinal locus of Christian vision. Consequently, Blond's is an attempt to build a theory of human perception entirely upon Christology, or upon the Christian doctrine of the incarnate *Logos*.[32]

---

31 J. Milbank, 'Only Theology Overcomes Metaphysics' in *The Word Made Strange: Theology, Language, Culture* (Oxford: Blackwell, 1997), pp. 36–52.

32 See P. Blond, 'The Primacy of Theology and the Question of Perception' in P. Heelas (ed.), *Religion, Modernity and Postmodernity* (Oxford: Blackwell, 1998), pp. 285–313; P. Blond, 'Perception: From Modern Painting to the Vision in Christ' in J. Milbank, C. Pickstock and G. Ward (eds), *Radical Orthodoxy: A New Theology* (London: Routledge, 1999); P. Blond, 'Theology and Perception', *Modern Theology* 14.4 (October 1998), pp. 523–34.

Blond's argument is that Christology alone describes the excessive, transcendent dimension of all perception as such, and therefore provides an account for us of the highest possibility of this given, visible world.

According to Blond, the key failure of most phenomenological appeals to transcendence (like those of Levinas and Marion) is that they collude all too easily with the classical phenomenological denial of God to being and vision.[33] Because such appeals are still too parasitic upon a factical onticity that posits a transcendental immanence as the ground or possibility for any transcendence, the phenomenological notion of transcendence as classically conceived cannot account for the divine dimension *of* being, and so cannot attain to the theological dimension of perception at the heart of all immanental disclosure. Phenomenological perception fails to attain to theological perception on account of a *failed conception of transcendence*, and this failed conception of transcendence is, in turn, a *failure of ontology*. Rather than constituting a 'theological turn' in phenomenology, it turns out that the construals of transcendence in Levinas and Marion, just as much as those of Husserl and Heidegger, actually prevent such a turn from occurring. For Blond, Levinas and Marion are simply further exemplars of the way in which phenomenology fails at its own game, in that its own unquestioned ontological assumptions disallow a final *theological* reduction to the conditioning of immanence by transcendence, and so to the originary transcendent impulse at the heart of all of visible being. Phenomenology as such cannot account for what Maurice Merleau-Ponty calls 'the invisible *of* this world';[34] it does not remain true to *la foi perceptive*, which says simply that at the heart of all we perceive, of all that is manifest to us, lies an experience whose essence our vision cannot possibly envelope.[35] With this notion of 'perceptual

---

33 On this point, see especially P. Blond, 'Emmanuel Levinas: God and Phenomenology' in *Post-Secular Philosophy*, pp. 195–228.

34 M. Merleau-Ponty, *Le Visible et L'Invisible*, ed. C. Lefort (Paris: Editions Gallimard, 1964), p. 198.

35 Merleau-Ponty, *Le Visible et L'Invisible*, pp. 17, 75, 147.

faith', Merleau-Ponty's positive affirmation of 'natural' human vision in the face of an inexhaustible dimension of invisibility supplies Blond with the possibility of describing the *ontological* dimension of transcendence at the heart of all immanence, and of all perception as such.

But herein lies the key, according to Blond. For if, as Merleau-Ponty maintains, phenomenology is methodologically bound by this perceptual faith, this original transcendence, this initial invisibility, then phenomenology is methodologically bound to *'become instead a theology'*.[36] For, as Blond puts it, only Christianity, with its insistence upon 'the permeation of creation by the logos and supremely with the incarnation of the word into flesh', is able to supply the ontology by which 'perception is granted its fullest range'.[37] What Christianity supplies, that is, is an *analogical* ontology according to which perception of *God* occurs neither according to the univocalist terms of an ontotheology, nor as a phenomenological description of the possibility of a God 'beyond' or 'without' being, but rather as coincident with a *theo*-ontological *percipi* at the heart of all vision. It is thus according to a certain original theophanic quality given with all phenomena that we are able to see God, and only as such are we then able truly to say that we are seeing the things themselves, in their eidetic fullness, as their essence just is continually to surpass themselves in the direction of an ideal form to be realized. Christian theological perception alone thus allows one to 'see' beyond the arbitrarily imagined ontological limits set to immanent vision by classical phenomenology.

All of this hinges upon Blond's christological reworking of Merleau-Ponty's category of 'perceptual faith'. 'Phenomenology

---

36 Blond, 'Primacy of Theology', p. 311 (my emphasis). Certainly, Blond's appeal to Merleau-Ponty here is not unironic, considering Janicaud's evocation of Merleau-Ponty's work as a supreme instance of doctrinaire phenomenological rigour, vis-à-vis those of the 'theological turn' whom he indicts for lacking such rigour.

37 Blond, 'Primacy of Theology', p. 309.

becomes theology because "the reality is Christ".[38] At this point, however, it is incumbent upon us to ask just what this 'reality' is: How is it that Christ is determinative of phenomenal reality? Certainly, Blond would answer 'faith in Jesus Christ', the proper description of which theology alone can give. And indeed Blond himself makes clear that the analogical *percipi* is granted to us only through the faith which believes that perception itself is excessive and self-transcendent in response to God's prior revelation in the world.[39] At this point, one would expect Blond, as a theologian, to turn his attention to faith's object, Jesus Christ, and to expound the *visio Dei* that is unfolded in the life, death and resurrection of Jesus of Nazareth, as alone determinative of what it is that Christian faith 'sees'. But this is manifestly what Blond does *not* do. He opts rather to explore the perceiving subject as the site of a universal, a priori 'perceptual faith'. Treating *la foi perceptive* as an intrinsic, essential dynamic of being human, Blond makes the believing human subject the focal object of his theological inquiry, and in turn introduces Christ into the discussion as a modifying feature or directional motif within the basic structure of perceptual faith. Thus, for Blond, faith, after Christ, names for us 'a new faculty of perception', a new 'subjectivity not blinded by its own potency'.[40] On this score, faith is simply the trust that in all perceptual disclosure as such we are given the 'creative power' (as Blond puts it in a recent essay[41]) to 'envision' God through the 'world' that we aesthetically produce via our own self-transcending perceptions. Divine 'grace', moreover, is the condition for the 'discharge' of this creative power, and such grace comes to us via a transcendent gratuity that our world is paradoxically

38 Blond, 'Primacy of Theology', p. 311.

39 Blond, 'Primacy of Theology', pp. 289–90; Blond, 'Theology and Perception', pp. 532–3; Blond, 'Perception', pp. 238–9.

40 Blond, 'Perception', p. 232.

41 P. Blond, 'The Politics of the Eye: Toward a Theological Materialism' in C. Davis, J. Milbank and S. Zizek (eds), *Theology and the Political: The New Debate* (Durham: Duke University Press, 2005), p. 459.

understood to carry or to convey *within itself* from the outset. The crucial question to be asked here is whether Blond wrongly supposes that the Christian theological account of 'faith in Jesus Christ' naturally can be examined in terms consonant with Merleau-Ponty's secular phenomenological account of *la foi perceptive*, such that the essential content of Christian revelation reduces simply to a more intense affirmation of the presence of a certain dimension of invisibility at the heart of all 'natural' visibility as providing sufficient guidance for what we 'see'. When this occurs, one is certainly right to ask whether the Christian revelation has been evacuated of its uniquely *dogmatic* and *confessional* content, in favour of a more generally available *phenomenological* description. That is, has theology been displaced from an objectively dogmatic account of what God has done (and 'sees') for us in Christ, to an account of what Christian doctrine can describe with respect to what it is possible for a certain perceptual faith to see? Is it enough simply to understand theology's task as the restoration of God to human cognition, and to open up transcendence to the possibility of human perception itself?[42] These questions are sufficient to record the suspicion that Blond is involved *not* in a (more purely biblical and revelatory) account of the new creation that the Christic 'phenomenon' gives us to see, *theologically*, but rather that he expounds Christian doctrine – in this case, Christology – within a privileged *phenomenological* framework.

To substantiate this suspicion: consider the way in which Blond submits the Christic phenomenon to a kind of phenomenological reduction. This reduction is especially evident in what it is that Blond understands that we have been given to 'see' in Jesus Christ, viz. a given, transcendent dimension to all human perception as such. In effect, the Christic phenomenon is simply the phenomenological culmination and expression of the created world's own revelatory dimension,[43] as that which grants us that our own 'highest attempted descriptions might actually

---

42 See Blond, 'Primacy of Theology', pp. 286–7.
43 Blond, 'Perception', p. 235.

be the case'.[44] In this way, it is hard to imagine how what we see in Jesus Christ, according to Blond, is not in fact simply a function of our own given capacities of perception. Indeed, as Blond himself admits, it is *we* who 'color-in the adumbrations and transcendent shapes of the invisible and make it seen'; the invisible functions phenomenologically by 'calling forth from us a contribution such that we might make it so, and make manifest that it is so'.[45] Precisely by granting to human vision itself a certain immanent operation and capacity for perceptual determination, Blond's passage from phenomenology to theology – that is, from the given capacity for human perception to the gift of divine revelation – is forced to double back upon itself as a return to phenomenology, such that what we perceive of the gift of revelation is nevertheless reducible to a function of our given capacities for perception. In so far as the 'reality' that is Christ represents 'the fulfillment of the highest human possibility',[46] this reality refers back to *la foi perceptive* understood as an intrinsic, essential dynamic of being human, which can be called upon to achieve a salvific relation to transcendent and worldly reality. In other words, while he views the invisible excess of all immanent visibility as a transcendent revelatory (and redemptive) event, Blond reads the theological content of this event back onto the structures of the given perceiving subject, and is therefore forced to read the event of revelation as a function of the subjective, perceptual faith of this general worldly economy – albeit as this economy functions according to its 'highest power'.[47] This allows him to conceive of the Christian *Logos* as some kind of absolute originary, and the incarnate *Logos* itself as a transcendent ideality, which permeates all of creation and so is specifiable (at least in principle) without reference to Jesus Christ at all.[48]

---

44 Blond, 'Theology and Perception', p. 532.

45 Blond, 'Perception', p. 240.

46 Blond, 'Primacy of Theology', p. 311.

47 Blond, 'Perception', p. 237.

48 See Blond, 'Perception', p. 235; Blond, 'Primacy of Theology', p. 309.

There are, then, as it turns out, genuine grounds upon which to be suspicious of any account of theological perception the apogee of which is simply the rendering of theology as a 'higher phenomenology', and which remains content with describing the theological task as 'an entirely new account of human possibility'.[49] My main suspicion, moreover, has been registered with regards to the assumption that one can adequately account for the fullness of theological perception generally, and of Christian vision specifically, by way of this or that appeal to transcendence within a phenomenological account of human perception. For in so far as such appeals remain bound to the assumptions of phenomenology proper, they cannot but construe transcendence in such a way as to always take the description of *human* perception as its measure. Thus, the theological task is reduced to that of determining how it is that *this* given world describes God for us, and Christian doctrine becomes merely the instrument for such description.[50]

In the end, the problem for theology, as I see it, is that there is a hiatus with regard to the *dogmatic* work of theology when phenomenological approaches to divine transcendence and theological vision like Blond's are carried out. When Blond passes to theology, and to the quest, after all, for a genuine perception of transcendence, an attempt is made to pass beyond immanent cognition to faith grounded in revelation. Yet herein arises the hiatus, for the content of this revelation for faith is attained by reference back to the cognitive human performance, and not the gratuitous operation of the one trinitarian God, as such, but to the world conceived in the mode of a revelatory economy.[51] As a result, Blond's phenomenological passage to

---

49 Blond, 'Primacy of Theology', p. 305.

50 See Blond, 'Theology and Perception', pp. 530, 532.

51 One example of this could be to note the way in which truncated treatment of the trinitarian operations leaves us with a crypto-modalistic understanding of the work of the Father and Son with relation to the created world. For Blond, to be created is automatically to stand in a 'mediated alignment with the Creator', and so to reveal immediately one's origin in God the Father. Then, given the created world's fall into

theology doubles back upon itself, such that strict phenomenological method dominates the entire doctrinal performance
throughout. The irony is that the more Blond reduces Christian
theology to a matter of perceptual cognition, the more he
narrowly associates the task of Christology with the quest
for a more adequate epistemology, and thereby encourages an
improperly 'forensic' account of Christ's person and work,
which turns upon the human subject, and her mis-cognition of
God in the world. However, this runs entirely contrary to
Blond's initial concern to associate Christian doctrine itself
with an entirely new metaphysic, and an ontology unburdened
by the arbitrary strictures of immanence. And yet, in so far
as this Christian ontology remains for Blond a modality of
phenomenological *description*, it cannot (despite Blond's intentions) altogether escape the pitfalls of cognitive adequation, and
the desire to discern the proper ratio between the knower and
the thing known, between immanence and transcendence.[52]

---

sin, which is a misalignment of our cognition of the world in relation to
God, the Son must take flesh in the event of the incarnation so as to
restore creation to its mediatory relation to the Father. See Blond,
'Perception', p. 239. This *reads* modalistically because Blond appears to
have elevated the question of the created world's mediatory participation in God above that of the triune God's immanent intra-trinitarian
operations within the order of theology proper, and so has doctrinally
reduced the question of theological perception to that of the question of
creation's mediatory role, as such. This is ultimately a methodological
problem for Blond. Because he has assumed that to pursue the fullness of
theological vision is to pursue the immanent, given possibilities of created (and creative) human perception, he thereby assumes that the notion
of a transcendent gratuity, given at the origin – as the *excess* – of all finite
human perception, is theologically adequate to describe what that God
gives us to see.

52 Of course, Blond will insist that in so far as this knowledge is *theological*, there is always *more* of God to be known, such that our knowledge is always asymmetrical. We are always 'catching-up' to God, as it
were; and so God cannot be 'comprehended'. The problem, however,
arises when Blond suggests that such 'asymmetry' is there as a given phenomenal *excess* to be *described*. This leads him to begin speaking of the
ways in which the created world and human perception are *adequate* to

Indeed, it is the metaphysically Christic dimension of Blond's project that I would like in some sense to uphold. Though I would want to do so by insisting that this metaphysic is not itself phenomenologically deducible. That is, we do not attain the vision of the new world in Christ simply by discerning 'in amidst the fractures and disjunctures of a secular world' a 'transcendence and invisibility at the heart of all things', which Christian theology then 'describes' as a 'truer origin';[53] we do not attain this vision simply by showing that the Christian perceptual faith is best able to secure the given ontological meaning of this immanent world, through the delineation of a more phenomenologically adequate notion of transcendence. The Christian vision is not at all to be attained, but purely received, as a vision so inscribed 'in Christ' that we have nothing to do but to proclaim and celebrate the *transfiguration* of this world through the ongoing passage of God's ever-coming glory, as our truest reality. But this means that we must indeed expound how Christian faith teaches us to see *otherwise* than in the phenomenological mode of cognitive description.

Towards a Doxological Vision

In the foregoing, I have suggested that accounts of transcendence which serve merely ontologically to negotiate the aporias of immanental perception, are duty-bound to think transcendence *purely* phenomenologically, as a matter of cognitive *description*. At the same time, I have argued that when an attempt is made to pass from phenomenology to theology, and to an account of that vision specific to Christian faith, theology is right to take Christology as its perceptual basis. And yet, where christological doctrine is itself deployed simply in service of a 'higher

---

this asymmetry, and to begin seeking the proper measure according to which human knowledge and perception 'fulfil' or 'complete' God's intentions for the created order, by discerning in its own perceptions 'the mind and work of God'. See Blond, 'Politics of the Eye', pp. 456–61.

53 Blond, 'Primacy of Theology', p. 311.

phenomenology', the tendency is to subject Christ himself to an independent reduction from without, and to cast Christian theology as simply a matter of describing differently that which universal humanity is everywhere and always already given 'to see'. Contrariwise, in this final section I want to propose the passage from phenomenology to theology as a passage not from one to another mode of description, but as *a passage from description to doxology*, and to do this by asking again in what sense Christology provides the normative matrix for Christian vision. In doing so, I will be shifting the idiomatic register from 'transcendence' to 'eschatology', as more distinctive to the theological vision that is given 'in Christ'.

Where Christology is deployed in service of theology as a 'higher phenomenology', and as the basis for retrieving God for human cognition, the tendency is to begin with the question '*What?*' As in '*What* reality does this phenomenon present to us?' or, 'What *concept* or *principle* adequately describes this phenomenon for us?' However, as Dietrich Bonhoeffer has so eloquently stated, the real christological question is not a question of the 'What?' or the 'How?', but of '*Who?*'[54] As in 'Who is this man?' (Matt. 21.10); 'Who do you say that I am?' (Mark 8.29); 'Who will deliver us from this body of death?' (Rom. 7.24). The Christological question directs us to the question of 'Who?' To say this is not only to say that Jesus Christ is the single reality in whom 'all things hold together' (Col. 1.17), but that he is this as the single one whom we *worship*, whom we *name* as Lord, 'to the glory of God the Father' (Phil. 2.9–11).[55]

---

54 D. Bonhoeffer, *Christ the Center*, tr. E. H. Robertson (San Francisco: Harper, 1978), pp. 27–37. It is interesting to note that for Bonhoeffer, it is only in asking 'who' Jesus Christ is that we are genuinely asking the question of 'transcendence'. For the theological question 'who' this one is is a question that can only properly come *from God* (pp. 30–1).

55 On the significance of 'naming' Jesus as a work of liturgy and doxology, see my 'The Logic of the Name of Jesus: Derridian Nomination and the Radical Alterity of Theology', *ARC, The Journal of the Faculty of Religious Studies, McGill University* 31 (2003), pp. 53–73.

The secret of the 'What?' is hidden in the 'Who?'; doxology precedes description. In faith, our life is nothing but the praise of
Jesus Christ, whose eschatological coming in glory is itself the
fullness of vision (1 Pet. 1.3–9).

It is in light of this question, the question of the 'Who?' that
Jesus names, and of the *doxa* that this question commits us to,
that it is appropriate to speak phenomenologically, as Jean-
Yves Lacoste does, of the 'irreducibility' of Christology, of Jesus
Christ's 'indescribability' as a mere reprisal of the phenomenological question of the origin of human perception.[56] For, if as
Lacoste understands it, Jesus' life is but the revelation of the
filial distance of the Son from the Father, in the appearance of a
single human being radically dispossessed by his own future
coming in glory,[57] the time of which belongs to the Father alone
(Mark 13.32), then this appearance is uninferrable from the
'natural' world as such, nor can it be described by means of a
reduction to an original *givenness* in this world. (Hence,
Lacoste's oft-repeated refrain that 'the originary is not the
eschaton'.[58]) What we are given in Christ is not simply the
means of describing the origin of our being-in-the-world; rather
we have revealed to us the *distance* that separates us from our
origin (which distance just *is* the being of God in Christ), as well
as the revelation of our own true being, now an eschatological

---

56 J.-Y. Lacoste, *Note sure le temps: Essai sur les raisons de la
mémoire et de l'espérance* (Paris: Presses Universitaires de France, 1990),
p. 121.

57 Lacoste, *Note*, pp. 177–80.

58 See J.-Y. Lacoste, *Experience and the Absolute: Disputed
Questions on the Humanity of Man*, tr. M. Raftery-Skehan (New York:
Fordham University Press, 2004), p. 90; see also Lacoste, *Note*, p. 121:
'Il n'y aurait pas de commencement la ou l'accomplissement serait
codonne avec l'origine. Ajoutons a cette verite d'evidence que l'ecart qui
separe la theologie de l'origine de l'achevement est theologiquement
celui qui separe la theologie de l'alliance de la christologie . . . Le dernier
mot n'est pas la reprise identique de l'origine. La fin n'est pas le retour du
commencement. Et l'alliance "nouvelle" ne sera pas deductible de l'alliance "ancienne": *la christologie est irreductible, et inedite.*'

being-in-vocation,[59] by which we are called out of nothingness and into the praise of the trinitarian God. Such praise is *christologically* grounded, in that in addition to being a praise directed *to* Christ as the second person of the Trinity, it is also a praise that is for us alone proleptically realized in the life, death and resurrection of Jesus of Nazareth. To begin to say, then, that Christian vision is doxological, is to say that its sole object of vision is the personal structure of being in the complete, historical Jesus Christ.[60]

* * *

It should come as no surprise, then, that the constellation of terms the New Testament (and particularly the Johannine literature) uses to denote Christian 'seeing' – *phanizo, phaneroo, phainoo, deknumi*, and their cognates – are almost entirely focused around the appearance of Jesus Christ in this world. 'Visibility' for the Christian comes into play not as an alternative mode of describing *what* the truth of the world is, but rather as the personal and historical instantiation of *who* the truth is. Christian vision in Christ is thus reoriented *not* around a 'world' which we are all simply given 'to see', but rather around the singular phenomenal reality of Jesus of Nazareth's life and ministry – a set of concrete works, deeds, signs and wonders, and fleshly enactments[61] – by which the person of Christ sets himself over against any mode of perception that would divert one from the vision of his life, death and

---

59 On the crucial difference between 'being-in-the-world' and 'being-in-vocation', which is also a distinction between 'being-in-fact' and 'being-before-God', or between the 'empirical I' and the 'eschatological I', see esp. Lacoste, *Experience and the Absolute*, pp. 55–98.

60 Lacoste, *Note*, p. 122.

61 This is particularly the case with respect to the Gospel of John and the Johannine Epistles. See especially the references to Jesus' 'signs' and 'wonders' in John 2.18; 5.20; 10.32, as well as the reference to Jesus' 'appearance' in the flesh through his works of 'love' in 1 John 1.2; 3.5, 8; 4.9; John 14.21.

resurrection in this world.[62] It is as if for faith, *all* that is to be seen is the light and life that are Jesus Christ. The point here is that for Christian faith this singular phenomenon does not appear in such a way as to range itself as one alternative visible among all other visibles, but as the single visible which is alone available for Christian faith. And herein lies the importance of stressing the sense in which the 'perceptual faith' of the Christian is from beginning to end an explicit *pistis Iesou Christou* (and so, a faith grounded in the dogmatic question of *who* Jesus Christ is): when every alternative mode of human 'vision' is refused to her who is confronted by the gospel grace of Jesus Christ, she in fact learns – is *taught* – that she will never again see 'the world', except as to see it in the doxological reception of and participation in the eschatological rule and reign of Jesus Christ, which reign just *is* the free exchange of glory between Father and Son, made ever new in the concrete love of the Spirit.

It is for this reason that Lacoste, in speaking of the 'Christological sense of the eschaton', speaks concomitantly of the 'eschatological sense of ipseity'.[63] There is an irreducible 'eschatological reserve'[64] to the Christic revelation of God's glory, a reserve into which we ourselves are inscribed. 'In Christ', there is no glory that is not received ever anew from the Father; and there is no grace that does not dispossess[65] humanity of its pretension to somehow house its definitive reality within itself. To say this is to say that in the grace of Christ we are indeed

---

62 In John 10.32 and 1 John 3.8, e.g., Jesus is said to 'show himself' particularly in order to encounter unfaith and to overcome the visible works of Satan. And John's Gospel especially iterates the sense is which the 'light' that is Jesus Christ is most fully light as it shines in the 'darkness' of the sin and evil of this fallen world (see John 1.5ff.; 3.19ff.).

63 See Lacoste, *Note*, pp. 119–22, 201.

64 Lacoste, *Experience and the Absolute*, p. 117.

65 On the idea of 'grace' as 'dispossession', I am as much indebted to Stanislas Breton as to Jean-Yves Lacoste. See Stanislas Breton, *The Word and the Cross*, tr. J. Porter (New York: Fordham University Press, 2002), *passim*. Cf. Lacoste, *Experience and the Absolute*, pp. 168–94.

bereft of any stable categories by which to 'describe' who we are, as *given*, in-ourselves. Thus it is not to be missed that Paul, for instance, everywhere he speaks of what is given us to be 'seen' in Christ, speaks of Jesus being made visible in 'mortal flesh', so that in him we might be made to see the passing away of what is seen, as itself the continual grace and promise of what is unseen: 'an eternal weight of glory beyond all measure' (see 2 Cor. 4). As crucified in mortal flesh, the phenomenality of Jesus Christ thus adjudicates all that is 'seen', as alone being seen for what it truly 'is' under the singular sign of his cruciform life, a life lived from the outset as the reception of a gift, and as an unqualified openness to the surprisingly new – *resurrection*. To 'see' doxologically is thus to have our perceptions, our words, our lives, hallowed out by this cruciform manifestation of glory. To say this, furthermore, is to say that our world only ever 'is' through an existence that is formally doxological, that is, as borne along by the dispossessive reception and passing on of the gift of glory that *is* the *life* of the God-man Jesus Christ.

And herein, especially, is where the perceptual difference between 'description' and 'doxology' lies for Christian vision. For description can only get underway by referring back to a *given* world, stable in its being-seen, *originarily*, and prior to its cognitive reception. Doxology, on the other hand, is that life in which God is celebrated and praised, from the outset, as the passage of pure grace, and in which the world only ever 'is' as constituted by the pure *reception* of that grace. Description always comes too late; it is a step removed, as it were, from what we see. Praise and celebration, if they are to occur in such a schema, occur only as a delayed reflex of description; as such, a residue of what we see must necessarily 'remain' prior to and outside of our descriptions of and praise of God's glory. In doxology, though, our vision is *constituted* by praise; there is only ever a world for the Christian to see, in so far as this world *is* a doxological offering, a supplication to God for the full coming of Christ in glory. *This is what it means to 'see' doxologically: it is to confess that the world that is God's good creation is not simply there as a world to be envisaged with our* eyes; *it is to confess that we only really have eyes to see in the reception of God's gift of glory, and that we only ever see in the passing on of that glory in the form of praise.* To put it another way: The phenomenality of Jesus Christ is one in which the descriptive link between our own perceptual intentions and the manifestation of God's glory has been broken, since God's glory is 'seen' through the miracle of resurrection alone, and not through the efficacy of our cognitive descriptions.

In all of this the Christian theologian seeks neither to abolish phenomenology, nor to ignore its descriptions, nor to deny that faith itself bears a measure of knowledge, all of which would be absurd. Certainly, phenomenological description is an eminent possibility for humanity, and is one of the surest ways of securing the truth of our own perceptions. But in so far as her task is that of praise, of being borne along in God's *doxa* by the grace of continual reception, the theologian must insist that description is only possible where doxology breaks down, for only where such a breakdown of praise occurs, are we able to presume a *given* world that we then must place in descriptive correlation to God. Indeed, the doxo-logic of praise precedes and surpasses the onto-logic of description; for prior to our own projects of perception stands God's doxological vision in Christ. Such doxological vision is certainly unthinkable for anyone who presumes the phenomenal insuperability of this world *as given*, and for whom being-in-this-given-world provides the sole categories for describing our being-before-God. To this the theologian can only respond that while the theologian-cum-phenomenologist may yet be right to claim that human perception itself is given the possibility of seeing the invisible in the visible, and of discerning a measure of transcendence in immanence, it still remains that the time of the eschaton – as the fullness of resurrection – belongs to the Father alone, which alone is the time in which we shall see, *as we have been seen by God.*

'As it is, we do not see everything in subjection to him. But *we do see Jesus*, revealing the grace of God by tasting death for everyone' (Heb. 2.8–9). *'But we do see Jesus.'* This is the vision that the theologian *proclaims*. This alone is what the believer is given to see; and yet this vision alone enables us to go ahead proleptically with the theological work of praise. Which work itself is the truly redemptive, and not merely descriptive, approach to human perception.

> The eye with which I see, is the eye with which God sees me.
> (Meister Eckhart)

9. Original Immanence according to Michel Henry: The Intuition of Religion

JEAN LECLERCQ

Translated by Patrick Riches

Pour Simon

Que pouvons-nous faire ? Nous écrier avec l'un des grands penseurs
de ce temps : 'Seul un dieu peut encore nous sauver!' Mais ce dieu
habite en nous, il est la vie qui ne cesse de nous donner à nous-mêmes
avec ses prescriptions insurmontables, qui ne cesse, malgré le tumulte,
de faire entendre sa voix. Peut-être est-ce aux intellectuels et aux
philosophes de l'entendre, de ne plus se précipiter aveuglément dans les
voies ouvertes par le savoir scientifique, de se souvenir et de dire qu'il
en existe un autre, plus ancien et plus essentiel, et qui, en effet, peut seul
aujourd'hui nous sauver.[1]

Introduction: Of Phenomenology and Archaeology

In an interview published in the January 2000 issue of
Philosophique,[2] Michel Henry appealed to what was then his as
yet unpublished book, *Incarnation* (a profound inquiry on the
subject of 'pathetic inter-subjectivity'). There Henry succumbed
to the temptation to situate this forthcoming work within the
overall continuity of his intellectual oeuvre. To honour the

---

1 M. Henry, 'L'éthique et la crise de la culture contemporaine' in
Phénoménologie de la vie, 4: Sur l'éthique et la religion (Paris: PUF,
2004), pp. 38–9.

2 The text is reprinted in M. Henry, *Entretiens* (Arles: Sulliver, 2005),
pp. 113–23.

rigour of his argument, we will insist, that in relation to his early work on Maine de Biran, Henry's vocabulary has indeed changed, to the measure that 'the sequence of history' has become that of gospel and patristic texts, and in so far as he is now intent on formulating 'a phenomenology or an archae-ology of flesh' in which Christianity becomes the object of an inquiry that radicalizes the project of phenomenology. Why? Because the incarnation precedes the flesh: 'elle est un avant la chair'. Henceforth the question will be that of 'before the "I"' (*avant le moi*). The question of knowing will now be that of 'how the 'I' comes to be itself'. And this it will be claimed is phi-losophy's necessity against which there cannot be a challenge, not even in the name of criticism. A necessity Michel Henry posits in this way:

> The philosopher is not condemned to refer to texts that belong to a canonical corpus of revered philosophy, delin-eated once and for all. The essential intuitions of philosophy can be found elsewhere, in poetry, literature, in spiritual texts whether religious or not. In the initial passages of [the Gospel of] John, for example, the *Prologue* expresses nothing other than the process of this auto-generation of life as the genera-tion in itself of a First living Self in which it reveals itself and experiences itself to itself.[3]

Certainly the Greek critique persists, to which this essay will return in conclusion where it will be argued Michel Henry introduces a nuance into his own discourse. Indeed this critique is interior to the conflict between the dualism of Platonism and

---

3 M. Henry, 'Eux en moi: une phenomenology' in *Phénoménologie de la vie, 1: De la phénoménologie* (Paris: PUF, 2003), p. 208. [Whenever possible the references to Henry's texts here follow the exist-ing English translation (where the translation is modified it has been noted); for convenience the reference to the original French is given fol-lowing the English. However, because most of Henry's work is as yet untranslated, the majority of the references are to the original texts and the translations are proper to the present translation of Leclercq's essay (Trans.).]

the schematics of Christianity. But within these arguments there is, within the Henrian analysis, a clear thread of continuity connecting his philosophical oeuvre. The continuity is related to *Phénoménologie matérielle*, and the research there on the 'substance of life', a discussion bound to the temporalization of the Husserelian notion of impression. The continuity is equally one with Henry's programmatic text, *L'Essence de la manifestation*, from which his research leads on to 'Archi-flesh', 'Archi-pathos' and 'the flesh of love', through which he shows that 'love cannot be reduced to an empty or formal gaze that simply falls upon what passes in the world', and in so far as 'Archi-flesh is the thickness of life', it is that which manifests itself in the whole of Henry's recovery of reflection and his research on anguish from 1963 and following. This is so much the case that this thread of continuity is picked up in a gesture of unification in the magisterial question of Henry's *Philosophie et phénoménologie du corps*, the question of the knowledge of what is 'more dense or more real than the gaze' (*de plus dense, de plus réel, qu'un regard*)?[4] – in this way the thread of the continuity of his thought is similarly retrieved in all its philosophical acuity.

Material phenomenology of course! Always! Now more than ever. But from now on it will be practised as an explicit archaeology in the measure to which 'that which lies before is essential'. It is in this mode that Michel Henry's philosophy has changed: it is 'no longer an archaeology of the human sciences but an archaeology of flesh'. What is more, he adds to his discourse the development of a 'genealogy' of auto-revelation.[5] This evidences that 'nothing of ourselves is explained in the end by objectivity. We are not worldly beings because in the world there is no Life.' From this, a profoundly unified oeuvre

---

4 M. Henry, *Philosophie et phénoménologie du corps* (Paris: PUF, 1997), p. 258.

5 See here the programmatic note on p. 45 in M. Henry, *The Essence of Manifestation*, tr. G. Etkorn (The Hague, Netherlands: Martinus Nijhoff, 1973); p. 58 in *L'Essence de la manifestation* (Paris: PUF, 1963).

emerges, an oeuvre assuredly haunted by a capacity to think through the articulation of the sense between the individual and the absolute, but never marked by the pretext of a 'turn'. This decisive passage of *L'Essence de la manifestation* will never be repudiated:

> belief whereby it [i.e. religious consciousness] defines itself is not flight from reality but the immediate grasp of it; *it is the original experience of the Being constitutive of Being and of its structure [l'expérience originelle de l'être constitutive de l'être lui-même et de sa structure].* 'To believe', says Kafka, 'means to set free the indestructible in ourselves, or more exactly, to free oneself, or still more exactly: to be indestructible, or still more exactly: to be.' The ontological identity of Being and belief (*Glauben ist Sein*) is the constant theme of all religious thought which lives such thought and expresses it as the correlative heterogeneity of Being and knowledge.[6]

And we can add to this the dazzling analysis of the 'two worlds' of Kafka in *L'Essence de la manifestation*, and the echo of this 1963 discovery nearly forty years later, in the passionate exegesis of the duplicity of language in *Paroles du Christ* (a programmatic work of rare philosophical and intellectual exigency to which we will return).

L'Essence de la manifestation: The incompatibility of Being's eidetic and knowledge

From the time of *L'Essence de la manifestation*, the subjectivity evoked by Michel Henry is sealed by the mark of a particular life, by the individual and the real. This is achieved in terms of a radical immanence according to which 'transcendence rests upon immanence'.[7] This 'rest' is so great that transcendence is

---

6 Henry, *The Essence of Manifestation*, p. 406; French: *L'Essence de la manifestation*, pp. 509–10.

7 Henry, *The Essence*: English at p. 41; French at p. 52.

figured, by its very nature, as astonishingly never anterior to anything; which is to say that transcendence does not depend upon a hermeneutic that, sooner or later, must be envisaged to take into account an understanding or a scheme of thought (*l'arraisonner*), rather immanence is seeing that which is considered as 'saturated', 'revealed' or 'manifested'. There is here a strong intuition that spreads throughout the whole work, so that when opening the Third Section of *L'Essence de la manifestation*, Michel Henry can resume his labour through a radical formula: 'The essence of transcendence resides in immanence.'[8] To which he adds this particularly necessary comment:

> In the positivity of the latter, not in the simple fact that transcendence does not assume its own manifestation, we must look for the reason for this hiding, if there is such a reason, and we must look for it in such a way that the making evident of this reason, identical to the essence, would then belong to the clarification of the essence and to its internal structure.[9]

It seems therefore, that from the beginning of his philosophical work, archaeological research is primary, notably in the collection of originary data. Michel Henry writes:

> The Being of the ego is truth [*L'être de l'ego est la vérité*]. Not that truth which is possible only through transcendence and as the very work of transcendence, but a truth higher in origin, more ancient, and without which transcendence itself would not be. To such a truth, which is not different from the ego itself and which constitutes its very *Being* [*son être même*], we give the name originary truth. It is only when it is capable of going to the origin that the problem of truth proves to be identical to that of the ego.[10]

Consequently everything is revelation, all manifestation is reconstituted by means of the immanence of life itself. Therefore:

---

8 Henry, *The Essence*: English at p. 380; French at p. 379.

9 Henry, *The Essence*: English at p. 380; French at p. 379.

10 Henry, *The Essence*: English at pp. 37–8; French at p. 48.

An immanent revelation is an internal experience. It is neces-sarily invested with a monadic form. It is within the eidetic structure of the originary truth that the ipseity of the ego is rooted. An internal experience understood as an originary revelation which is accomplished in a sphere of radical immanence exists by itself, without any context, without the support of any exterior and 'real' Being, it is itself precisely an 'existence', or better, existence itself, which it is well to think of under the rubric of 'human reality'. Such an existence owes nothing to transcendence, rather it precedes it and makes it possible. More originary than the truth of Being is the truth of man [Plus originaire que la vérité de l'être est la vérité de l'homme].[11]

There is no hermeneutic here, there is only the exigence of sensing what is conceivable as real by an interior life, that is, through understanding reality's invisibility and inexpressibility. This is what guides the whole thematic of auto-affection 'by' oneself and 'of' oneself. This 'by' and 'of' oneself is what is more originary.

This is what constitutes the essence of feeling, the essence of affectivity as such: self-feeling by self, in such a way that feel-ing is not something which feels itself, this or that feeling, at one time this one, at another time that one, but precisely the fact of self-feeling by a self considered in itself in the effective-ness of its phenomenological realization, namely, in its real-ity. As such, as this phenomenologically effective 'self-feeling self', constitutive of essence and rendering it possible, feeling does not differ from the essence; affectivity is the original essence of revelation.[12]

---

11 Henry, *The Essence*: English at p. 41 (translation lightly modi-fied); French at p. 53.
12 Henry, *The Essence*: English at pp. 462–3 (translation lightly modified); French at p. 578.

The invisible can therefore be grasped 'as' the essence of life, in so far as it is not in the world that one finds the 'the original immanence of transcendent life'.[13] Here the whole enterprise of historical philosophy finds itself radically shaken:

> *If negation included in the concept of the invisible is not that of phenomenality but determines the mode according to which phenomenality phenomenalizes itself originally and helps us to conceive the concept,* the claim of seeking the origin of all knowledge in the visible and its powers, a claim which was explicitly formulated by Kant and which in fact dominates the entire development of Western philosophy, loses its rights and is reversed . . . *The invisible is not merely revelation in itself through and through, it rather defines the nature of revelation.*[14]

One ought here to note the Henrian sensibility of the invisible, which must be understood as the 'primitive and positive mode by which the impression is self-experienced through an insurmountable passivity with regard to the self, and it is in this way that it is, in this impressionable immediation [*immédiation impressionnelle*] constitutive of its reality'.[15] We are therefore not speaking of 'unreality', 'illusion' or of a 'fantastic otherworldliness', rather the invisible designates reality as such. Much later Michel Henry writes:

> If one considers a different phenomenon such as suffering, it must be admitted that it does not appear as exterior, rather it is bound to the self in its own pathos which the Self cannot put at a distance from itself. Life is incapable of this putting at a distance and it is in this sense that revelation differs totally from the world. For in the world everything is put at a

---

13 Henry, *The Essence*: English at p. 392; French at p. 493.

14 Henry, *The Essence*: English at p. 439; French at p. 551.

15 M. Henry, 'Incarnation' in *Phénoménologie de la vie. De la phénoménologie*, p. 168.

distance from the self, because as long as it is seen as included in the world it is seen as if through a glass window [*où tout est mis à distance de soi y compris nous-mêmes en tant qu'êtres du monde qui pouvons nous voir dans une glace*]. But life – our anguish and our suffering – can never be seen from the exterior. One must therefore problematise the objective and the subjective. These two modes of revelation are fundamentally different, for the subjective is an adhesion to the self of that which cannot be undone and which cannot represent its own suffering [*le subjectif étant cette adhésion à soi dont on ne peut se défaire et qui fait qu'on ne peut se représenter sa souffrance*].[16]

However, if life possesses this quality of silent invisibility, and if a radical and material phenomenology uniquely dispenses with recourse to worldliness and the ek-static (*ek-statique*), how then is one to speak of this life and how is one to think of this phenomenology? In fact the response is in the rejection of every idealism and every intentionality. For to move toward the fundamental knowledge of life, which will be a pathetic language, a 'language of pathos', is to move towards a knowledge of the experience of life as that which is not uniquely mine, singular and individual, but is rather absolute life, in the sense of the articulation posited in *L'Essence de la manifestation*. To this end, the whole work of philosophy reveals itself in insisting on the disclosure of the excessive attention paid to the unique form of appearing under the mode of exteriority (the world, the gaze, the distant, the ek-static, the transcendent). This is true of western philosophy and even of Husserl.

One must therefore understand that it is important, within this archaeological gesture, to institute a 'historical' phenomenology, in order to point out that this is a new mode of phenomenology that will be qualified above all as 'radical' and 'material': a radicalization of the phenomenological reduction. And a phenomenology that will be 'material' will be a phe-

---

16 Henry, *Entretiens*, p. 139.

nomenology of 'Life' in the flesh, a phenomenology of this subjective body experienced (*ce corps subjectif éprouvé*). The focal
point of this phenomenology will therefore be the mode of the
manifestation of Life. From this will proceed the constant
denunciation of the 'confusion' of the appearance of the world
with all appearing that points to the phenomenology of Life, to
the radical immanence of living. In this way a passage is foraged
from intentional phenomenology (which establishes the object
and founds it in the world) toward 'the' phenomenology of life.
As Michel Henry explains:

> To the appearance of the world we oppose point by point the
> revelation proper to life. Which means that the world unveils
> 'outside-of-the-self', in such a way that all that it unveils is
> exterior, other, different. The first decisive trait of the revela-
> tion of life is that it does not bear within itself any gap and so
> is never different from the self, and is never revealed apart
> from itself. Life is self-revealing. Life is an auto-revelation.
> Auto-revelation, when it is about life, means two things.
> First, it means that it is life that accomplishes the work of
> revelation, and that it is therefore anything but anonymous
> and blind. And second, it means that that which is revealed is
> itself. The revelation of life and that which is revealed by it
> are one.[17]

Within this framework, Michel Henry argues that what is
'essential is appearance and so Being cannot be perceived except
within this appearing'. The privilege accorded to intentionality
therefore occludes 'a more fundamental appearing', an appearing that is 'truly fundamental to Being proper'. This, Michel
Henry calls the 'transcendental Life'; it is that which is affective
of an 'original revelation' and 'the essence of life itself'.[18] He
writes: 'the central question of phenomenology, the one of
phenomenality or appearance considered in itself, has received

---

17 Henry, 'Eux en moi: une phenomenology', p. 199.
18 Henry, *Entretiens*, p. 56.

a unilateral response which we do not share'.[19] Therefore the phenomenology of radical immanence is a phenomenology that precedes every relation of the word and every ecstatic inclination, consequently it gives attention to the fundamental import of appearance itself, to transcendental life, to that which is not affected by biological life or the processes of biology. In this way, with regards to the two different modes of appearing – Being (in its ek-static dimension) and life (in its auto-revelation) – one can say that appearing is 'omni-present to itself', according to a non-ek-static (*non ek-statique*) conception of time that is necessarily a time of 'plenitude', a time 'which is always real and which never implicates only a part of myself in so far as what is unreal has passed or is to come'.[20]

Attentiveness to this critique of intentionality must be retained, especially when it touches on the question of the other,[21] and more particularly in the measure to which it permits us to evoke the theme of community and inter-subjectivity. For precisely on this point the discussion is bound to Husserl in the three relative presuppositions to the life of the other. The first presupposition is that the other is not given except under the modality of the experience of an 'I'; that is, in so far as he is the other in me, which means that the other is given in and by intentionality. On a second presupposition one notes the decisive importance for the Henrian analysis played by analogy, in the measure to which it accomplishes something 'which is not other but which is aimed at as other, not by the real other but the other of thought, the noetic of the other, which is to say the other as noetic, the other reduced to a sensibility, a sense of being other, the other in the mode of "as", of *als*, a quasi-other'.[22] Lastly, the third presupposition extends the first two under the modality of necessity and universalism, in so far as

---

19 Henry, 'Eux en moi: une phenomenology', p. 197.

20 Henry, *Entretiens*, p. 57.

21 M. Henry, 'Réflexions sur la *cinquième Méditation cartésienne* de Husserl' in *Husserl-Ausgabe und Husserl-Forschung* (Ijsseling: Kluwer Academic Publishers, 1990), pp. 107–23.

22 Henry, 'Réflexions sur la *cinquième Méditation cartésienne*, p. 108.

'the other is necessarily given in me . . . out of me, as something transcendent'. Here a precision is brought to bear that 're-covers' intentional donation and donation in me, which Michel Henry states to be 'decisive but un-thought by the Husserlian analysis of the other and perhaps by the whole of his philosophy in general'.[23]

The reproach of Michel Henry against this decisive Husserl-ian advance is that it does not take into account the notion of 'sym-pathy', precisely in its pathetic form, because it is overly centred by the discourse of intentionality. Henry writes:

> If the particular is in truth particular to me, to the ego, only the nature of the ego can say and define what is particular to it. Is not then the particular, in as much as it is particular to the ego, the ego itself? But it is this thesis that Husserl has already set aside in his preliminary analysis and which he will set aside without relent leading him to conduct analyses according to a solipsism . . . Husserl therefore needs to dis-sociate the ego and, on the other hand, that which is particu-lar to it even if he has nothing else to say otherwise of the particular, if not that which is particular to the ego. In any case the cleavage is between the ego and whatever is particu-lar to it, their essential connection in the definition of the particular is at the same time their necessary dissociation, rejected by a solipsism which needs to be made the theme of an explicit problematic that has no other part.[24]

These two radical critiques of the Husserlian project come down to two decisive points: the emphasis on intentionality; and, as a corollary, the forgetfulness of the pathetic dimension of inter-subjectivity. In effect, the 'other' is the object of the ontological reduction that exhibits and constitutes the body in the sphere of the appearance of the 'I', and above all in the form of a phenomenology of perception. But the question is this: how

---

23 Henry, 'Réflexions sur la *cinquième Méditation cartésienne*, p. 109.
24 Henry, 'Réflexions sur la *cinquième Méditation cartésienne*, p. 110.

many more are needed to know that which in itself will be an experience of other in which perception will not play a role? In this way Michel Henry recalls that the experience of the other presupposes a plurality of subjects and relations between them, and here relation is forced onto the plane of ipseity – that which makes up the essence of each of these subjects – and which is not of the order of the world, but rather of the order of life. This means one must recognize the impossibility of relating to a self within the exteriority of the world, it cannot happen except in life, except in view of the experience of life. And so Henry can advance this essential thesis:

> There is no life without a living Self in which this life is itself experienced, and so no Self that is not engendered in life as that in which it becomes life. As such the first condition of every experience of the other is posited. And this means that *such an experience is always that which makes an other me similar to him* – an *alter ego* – and insofar as this relation is to myself, all of me is not possible except in the accomplishment of this radical process of immanent life and its self-engendering by that process.[25]

In this way Michel Henry insists on not confounding the ipseity of the Self and the individuality of a thing, which is a product of the categories of the world (space, time, relation, identity, etc.). In effect, the experience of the self in the immanence of life is a wholly other space, since the self engages the affectivity and the fact of life as a *pathos*. Here one returns to the claim that the relations of inter-subjectivity do not exist on the plane of individuality, but rather on a plane of 'phenomenological tonalities' of the originary experience of Life. This means that the relations of inter-subjectivity exist on a plane of ipseity and affectivity. Only on this plane can the self meet an other who is a self and enter into relation. Therefore we will have understood, if Life is an originary ground (*un sol originaire*), that relation is always

---

25 Henry, 'Eux en moi: une phenomenology', p. 202.

accomplished in life. And more, it is life which is the condition and possibility of relation in so far as it is 'capable of bringing forth itself in a self, bearing in it the potential of life and that which can give potentiality to all that is living'.[26] From this proceeds the radical philosophical affirmation:

> the transcendent condition of the possibility of every Self and every conceivable 'I' is to know the immanent generation of absolute Life, revealing itself identically as the condition of the transcendental possibility of the relation of every Self to every other, the condition of the experience of other.[27]

From now on one must recognize that this intimate relationship between the relation to the other and the originary ground (*le sol originaire*) of life no longer permits one to invoke questions relative to inter-subjectivity under any mode of composition or intentionality. In effect, one must henceforth admit the return to life. And so the place of revelation and auto-revelation, dona-tion and auto-donation, in so far as it is also knowledge for the self, is equally so for the other in so far as it shares in the same community of essence, which is Life itself. This leads each self towards an other who is a self, because the self and the other are now in a definitive sense, originally one with the other. But above all, as Michel Henry notes:

> The one is in the other in a sort of interior phenomenological reciprocity in which the place is that of 'Before'. This 'Before' is that which precedes the one and the other and yet remains in them for as long as they are these living Selfs [*des Soi vivant*]. It is this way that each and every conceivable com-munity is born and forms itself in its originary phenomeno-logical potentiality.[28]

---

26 Henry, 'Eux en moi: une phenomenology', p. 204.
27 Henry, 'Eux en moi: une phenomenology', p. 204.
28 Henry, 'Eux en moi: une phenomenology', p. 205.

This affirmation is decisive, and one must apprehend it as the essential thread in the progress of Henry's conceptual work – and notably in his notion of 'reciprocity' – a new expansion, particularly with regard to the notion of a philosophy of language in *Paroles du Christ*. On this view the experience of the other is reconstituted in terms of the source of life, the contents, potencies and virtualities by which life is also a 'a community of the transcendental Self of those living'. But the most obvious mark of this community is 'by essence invisible'. This means that this community is 'strange to the world and to its phenomenological categories' because the contemporaneous notion of Being passes beyond the schemes of space and time (we will return subsequently to this determination). And so in this regard the question of community is posited on the phenomenological plane because Michel Henry prioritizes life as the mode of access to this communal reality and the mode by which it is given. Again, this resounds throughout his philosophical oeuvre, by which he holds 'this unique reality and essence of community and its members . . . is called life' and that 'the essence of community is life, and every community is a community of living beings', which means that 'life is a "how", a mode of revelation and revelation itself'.[29]

It is therefore the 'how' of donation to the members which one must make into the object of elucidation. In other words: how does life give and give itself in such a way that life is auto-donation? This is the question if one agrees to the fact that life returns in such a way so as not to confound the community as life and the members of the community. One must here recognize that Michel Henry distinguishes himself in the way that he poses the question of anteriority in his philosophy of life in the measure to which he holds that 'only living beings – absolute subjectivities – enter into the community which is life'. He insists, forcefully and clearly, on the fact that this movement is part of life and is therefore the point of departure of all his

---

29 M. Henry, 'Pour une phénoménologie de la communauté' in *Phénoménologie matérielle* (Paris: PUF, 1990), p. 161.

reflections on the community of the living. According to Michel Henry, 'the community is nothing other that this assembling of living individuals' and the wish to 'oppose one to the other, the community to the individual, or to establish between them a hierarchical relation is simply non-sense', above all if 'subjectivity is the *principium individuationis*'.[30] There is thus in Michel Henry both an ethics and a politics of community.

For this reason Michel Henry advances the idea that 'community is an affective subterranean surface [*nappe affective souterraine*] and that each one drinks the same water of this source and of this well one is oneself – but without knowledge, without distinguishing oneself, from the other or the *Fond*'.[31] This means that the experience of the other is an experience that escapes thought, and so is above all the experience of this *Fond* of life. Michel Henry writes:

> [that which the living] experiences is identically itself, the *Fond* of life, the other insofar as it is also this *Fond* – thus the living experiences the other in the *Fond* and itself in terms of the unique experience of the *Fond* which the other has. This experience is the other who has the *Fond* in itself as the 'I' has the *Fond* in itself. But neither the 'I' nor the other represent this to themselves. [*Cette épreuve est l'autre qui a le Fond en lui comme le moi a le Fond en lui. Mais cela ni le moi ni l'autre ne se le représentent.*][32]

This orientation of Henrian philosophy metaphorizes the Johannine paternal motif in the direction of the Eckhardian notion of the *Fond*. And it shows how much the notion of 'pathos-with' (*pathos-avec*) is at the heart of the system of thought that forms the 'pathetic community', with the forces and affects that are proper to it, such as for example the colours of a painting, which is not a 'fragmentation of exterior things

---

30 Henry, 'Pour une phénoménologie de la communauté', p. 163.
31 Henry, 'Pour une phénoménologie de la communauté', p. 178.
32 Henry, 'Pour une phénoménologie de la communauté', p. 178.

but the expression of their interior reality'.[33] As Michel Henry notes, there is 'but a single community, situated . . . in an intelligible sphere in which everything is intelligible to the other and to itself on the basis of the primordial intelligibility of pathos'.[34]

Without this new sign all comprehension of the experience of the other collapses into the standard of the appearance of the world, which means that the condition of the possibility of the apparition of a plurality of selves (*des moi*) cannot be made fully or radically. In this way the common content of the communal life of Selves (*des Soi*) is this transcendental life, on the subject of which Michel Henry writes:

> Because what is common in every community is life, therefore the community presents an other essential trait, that of being a community of the living. And it does so in the sense of being the transcendental Self of the living, in the measure to which only in community is the Self possible. And reciprocally, the community is not possible without them, without the primordial Self in which life lives in the self and which contains the potential multiplicity and undefined of every possible 'I'.[35]

If this is so, it is because Life is the condition of the possibility of the community of the living; and yet, as Michel Henry adds, the community is first of all by its very nature religious (because it is invisible), even if it possesses the appearance of appearing in the world (which elsewhere is the cause of dishonesty and lying). And so Life is a stranger to the categories of philosophical reasoning that occupy the world of time and space. Life is an 'intuition of religion'.

Examples such as these are numerous and are scattered throughout Henry's oeuvre. The most powerful of which – but also the most enigmatic and perhaps paradigmatic – is that of the community of the dead. Why? Because it radicalizes his

---

33 Henry, 'Pour une phénoménologie de la communauté', p. 179.

34 Henry, 'Pour une phénoménologie de la communauté', p. 179.

35 M. Henry, 'L'expérience d'autrui: phénoménologie et théologie', in *Phénoménologie de la vie: Sur l'éthique et la religion*, p. 159.

claim, for here all perception seems abolished and naturally finished. And in being abolished it seems that this community does not subsist except in recollection, that is to say, as an object of re-presentation by which no pathos can intervene upon these acts and thoughts. But this is not the case, in so far as Michel Henry holds that 'the dead in our life are identified only as those who have left this world'. This means:

> many are still living whom we can see again and in this way perceive afresh, in such a way that this seeing again does not change their death in us but renders it only more sensible. Likewise, it must be said that the life and death of the other, the interruption of his common Being, is not confined to perception, to its possibility or to its impossibility of fact. We can even posit that the impossibility of perception is the condition of Being in common. Kierkegaard goes so far as to say that Being in common with Christ, what he calls contemporaneity, is more difficult for those who see than for those who do not see. It is here a trait which he calls 'the strange acoustic of the spiritual world'. For he does not want the laws of perception to be the laws of Being in common.[36]

This is certainly an expression of radical thought which cannot be fully commented upon here. Nevertheless, it serves to emphasize the extent and potentiality which phenomenology thus entails for him.

Of Religion: Manifestation and Pathetic Language

The evocation of 'contemporaneity' in the order of community and inter-subjectivity permits the prolongation here of the claim to take into account the question of religion. Michel Henry notes:

---

36 Henry, 'Réflexions sur la *cinquième Méditation cartésienne*', p. 119.

[T]he etymology of the word religion – *re-ligare* – itself offers a clue: it is a bond, a bond between my life and the absolute life. And this bond itself opens to ethics because a way of life determines human life as nothing other than ethics . . . The reason we are alive is to welcome in ourselves this life and to live in it, in multiple ways, in the effort of creation, in the solitude of the cloister or in the simplicity of devotion.[37]

Michel Henry often observes and theorizes the event the 'key words' of phenomenology carry, and are transferable into the conceptual fields of the methodology and discipline of theology and religion. On this account Henry makes a strong but nuanced claim:

What the philosophers call 'the absolute', religion calls God. But if philosophy says that the absolute is life and if John [the Evangelist] says God is life, it is because they speak of the same thing under a different language. The phenomenology of life therefore is not an artificial veneer or philosophy layered upon the doctrinal body of Christianity. Rather, it simply realises that the object of philosophy and religion are identical. And so not by chance did John say that God is not only Life, but equally, God is Love: John gives us an *affective* definition.[38]

The full amplitude of this intellectual effort has yet to be fully grasped. The radical perspectives and new openings of Michel Henry are particularly accomplished in terms of the theological labour that, from now on, cannot be deployed except within a 'phenomenological' commentary of the conditions of the possibility of efficiency. In this regard what one has is a 'knowledge of life', a relation of knowledge of the 'religious type'. Life is 'sacred':

---

37 Henry, *Entretiens*, p. 141.
38 Henry, *Entretiens*, p. 131.

Life is the support of everything that is religious. Why is life sacred? Because knowledge of life is a knowledge absolutely different from the subject–object knowledge which rests on a separation, knowledge of life is a knowledge not implicated in any form of domination. Life is characterised by its own passivity vis-à-vis itself . . . This situation characterises the essence of life and reproduces itself in effect in each instant of life . . . There is therefore an experience of the self which continues, which inhabits all our powers . . . But in regard to this radical power, we are without power. Religions are nothing but different ways of expressing this fundamental non-power which is inscribed in the passivity of my own life. 'I am in life' signifies that this life passes through me, and this is a mystery . . . On the phenomenological plane this passive donation of life to itself is that which poses the question of life with God. For living life is something one receives, which is necessarily the experience of an infinite respect for oneself. Living life is already religion.[39]

The truly moving character of this affirmation, advanced by Michel Henry in 1993, is perfectly consonant with the major conclusions of his earlier texts. Particularly this is so of his most exegetical moments, in which one finds a force of profound and fruitful meditation, summarized by Michel Henry in a citation of Eckhart: 'the joy of the Lord . . . is the Lord Himself'.[40] One must here acknowledge the essential contribution of this Eckhartian sensibility in the claim that 'unity as such determines experience, the self-experience of Being in its self-enjoyment. This fundamental ontological presupposition means that the internal structure of immanence is that of revelation.'[41] Here is not the place fully to address this enigmatic proximity. But holding to a vision in continuity with the Henrian work – and remaining within the framework of reflection on the mode of the operative articulations of transcendence and immanence – one is

39 Henry, *Entretiens*, p. 108–9.
40 Henry, *The Essence*: English at p. 327; French at p. 407.
41 Henry, *The Essence*: English at p. 327; French at p. 407.

pointed to the fact of the great tradition of the three births of the Word. For Henry this again is an Eckhartian motif (see the magnificent pages 417ff. in *L'Essence de la manifestation*).[42] These three births of the Word, originally patristic and prominent in Cistercian spirituality, return significantly in *Paroles du Christ*.[43] Above all one must note the triadic order here: of ordinary language (the 'Word which was spoken'); of interpretive language (the 'Word which is thought but remains inexpressible'); and of phenomenological/pathetic language (the 'Word unthinkable and inexpressible' that 'never departs' and 'remains eternally in the one who speaks it'). These are the moments of historical incarnation, of spiritual incarnation and of the parousia of the eschaton.

This resonance in the Henrian oeuvre is decisive and permits one to grasp that the propositions of language are themselves bound to the modality of the manifestation/showing of language, its logos. This means, 'the primitive Saying [*le Dire primitif*] is never on the side of what is said, on the side of what is shown; rather, it is what shows'.[44] This means that the forms and historical structures, even in the framework of a language that dismisses the condition of the possibility of a phenomenon, are the potencies of all saying, which means that 'one has to explain what this advent is – *this phenomenalisation of pure phenomenality* which defines conjointly the object of phenomenology and the ultimate foundation of every possible language'.[45] Such is this 'other' of language, which is not of this world and which possesses this propriety of speaking 'of the self' because it is about the language (*parole*) of life, so much so that the plane of

---

42 Pages 334ff. in the English translation.

43 M. Henry, *Paroles du Christ* (Paris: Seuil, 2002).

44 M. Henry, 'Material Phenomenology and Language (Or, Pathos and Language)', *Continental Philosophy Review* 32 (1999), pp. 343–65, here p. 345. French: M. Henry, 'Phénoménologie matérielle et langage (ou pathos et langage)' in *Phénoménologie de la vie, 3: De l'art et du politique* (Paris: PUF, 2004), p. 327.

45 Henry, 'Material Phenomenology and Language', p. 345 (French, p. 327).

affectivity, as the essence of life itself, is its most originary and most ultimate referent. In summation, this language of truth precedes and is other to the language of the world because it is not of the world. It is therefore this language that permits one to speak of the world, because it is inhabited by Life itself, by pure affectivity, because it is the 'pure suffering/joy of the self'.

Without doubt it is *Paroles du Christ* in which Michel Henry takes furthest this new pathetic phenomenology of language. Above all the stake of this work rests in the denunciation of the possibility of the duplicity of speech (*parole*) in the critical life of reciprocity, a notion that is too mundane for the speech of the language of life. Christianity is not a 'humanism' nor a human wisdom, because it cannot be reduced to a normative ethic. Such an ethic, if it were to exist for Christianity, would be love, which is permanently marked by the possibility of failure and salvation. And so, otherwise than an ethic, Christianity is a life in regard to God, to the secret will that marks all flesh with the seal of affectivity and the reconstitution to the experience of the 'immanent generation of our life in the infinite life of God'. In this way Christianity opens the community to the disruption of a filiation, socially marginal and naturally clandestine, continuously rediscovered in the 'Language of Life' (*Parole de la Vie*). This confirms the 'affective subterranean surface [*nappe affective souterraine*]' of Being, its *Fond* in an Eckhartian sense. Thus one must turn to the affect, to the pathos, to the radically pathetic nature of inter-subjectivity in order to comprehend the amplitude of the experience of the other. And this circumvention of every noetic presentation of the other drives towards the sole originary and original: Life gives of itself and in itself.

Conclusion: For a Phenomenology that Lives

This detour through Christianity by which phenomenology rediscovers an unsuspected richness provokes a considerable turn by which it is possible to think the Logos, no longer as the horizon of the world, but more radically, as the horizon of Life.

The Logos is not the horizon of the body of the world but of the flesh of life. Michel Henry writes:

> The Incarnation of the Word does not hold everything in historical Time. For the Word made flesh in Christ is the eternal Word of God. It is in Him that all were created, not only the world but also all that is a stranger to the world: our flesh, the ipseity of our Self, our life. When God breathed his life into a fragment of silt, creating this transcendental Self, carnal and living as each man, in this his body was nothing but matter, dust in fact. But his flesh was wholly life. The time of all life in his carnal ipseity appeared to animate something of life. By the incarnation he consented to be a part of this generation in which alone we are capable of understanding creation.[46]

It is of a real self in the process of the generation of a 'First living Self in which Life is revealed to a self'. Which means, according to Michel Henry, there is never an anonymous flesh to which one can ascribe 'non-personality', in so far as no flesh yields to a mundane horizon and all affectivity is that of a self. From this proceeds an important affirmation, once again, in the spirit of Eckhart:

> As soon as flesh is given over to life, it ceases to be this objective body with its strange forms, with its incomprehensible sexual determination, apt to arouse our anguish, delivered to the world, subjected to the question 'why'? For as Meister Eckhart understood: life is without why. The flesh which carries in it the principle of its own revelation does not ask for any other authority to illuminate itself. When in its innocence each modality of our flesh experiences itself, when suffering says suffering and joy says joy, it is Life that speaks in it, and nothing has power against its word [*parole*].[47]

---

46 Henry, 'Incarnation', p. 178.
47 Henry, 'Phénoménologie de la vie', in *Phénoménologie de la vie, 1: De la phénoménologie*, p. 75. English transaltion: 'Phenomonology of Life' in this volume, pp. 258–9.

Surely here it has been shown that the orientation of the phenomenology of life poses the irreparable question of the experience of the other. In effect, if according to the world the body is a body-object and according to life the body is a subjectivity, a subjectivity constituted by impressions and the possibility of experiences, then the experience of the other will be experienced on a second plane, one which is also the plane of flesh, and therefore not the plane of the objective body. In this sense experience must lead, not only to the appearing of the world, but more to the auto-revelation of life. The extent to which philosophy points to the failure of all comprehension of the other through a phenomenology of intentionality – which is nothing other than a metaphysics of representation – illustrates the value of the sorrow of being. This sounds as a warning:

> It is first of all the reduction of the real Being of the other in me to a noetic presentation outside of me; in that this other, in the simplest sense, takes on the quality of a thing perceived by me, a Being other than an ego/'I'. The one who is no longer in me is a wound that I am or the inebreated-ecstasy of a real modification of my transcendental life itself, it is precisely an unreality, the correlative of an intentional aim. [*Celui-ci n'est plus en moi cette blessure que je suis ou l'ivresse d'une modification réelle de ma vie transcendantale elle-même, il n'est précisément qu'une irréalité, le corrélat d'une visée intentionnelle.*] Husserl recognised this reduction of the experience of the other to the unreal and tried to minimise it.[48]

Ultimately this general orientation leads to an evocation, a means of concluding this argument, a connection patiently weaved or inchoately intimated in the logic of life. This is the connection for Michel Henry between phenomenology and Christianity, which returns to the argument that has here been advanced. First of all, one recalls surely that Michel Henry never practised a rationalist reduction of Christianity and did not

---

48 Henry, 'Réflexions sur la *cinquième Méditation cartésienne*', p. 120.

seek to assimilate it to his own philosophy of life. Christianity maintains its status as 'religion' according to a tripartite etymology: *relegere* (the plane of immanence), *religare* (the plane of transcendence) and *religere* (the plane of passivity), which open to a trinity of modalities of the existence to the relation of Life. On the other hand, in a way that has been magnificently explicated by Anne Henry,[49] the relation to Christianity is not of the order of a turn, nor of a 'willed system' or a 'return to tradition'. More naturally, it is about 'authentic mediation', a 'reclaiming of the originary in the way of speculation'. This is discerned particularly in the Scriptures, in 'the' Book, the sedimentation of all writing called to become 'holy writ'. Above all the Scriptures trace, in their letter and spirit, the contours of the relation of all individuals with the absolute, and precisely in so far as they offend they absolve.

But this meditative attitude (in its most philosophical sense) is characteristic of all great philosophy, which follows this thread through the notion of action. For Michel Henry this is 'more essential than thought'. >From this he recognizes:

> In the New Testament it is never said that a 'truth' is a universal truth in the sense of a rational truth, no more is it said that Being is reducible to this kind of truth. For me, truth, in the measure to which it is 'life', contains an ipseity because living is the self-experience of oneself and there is no experience of self that does not belong to a self. Truth is therefore tied, for essential reasons, to individuality. In the celebrated *Prologue* to the Gospel of John, one discovers that God generates a Self by which he experiences himself and is revealed to a self, which is his Word.[50]

This is a recognition, for Henry, and not a turn or occultation to an 'other' Michel Henry. This means that to understand

---

49 A. Henry, 'Vivre avec Michel Henry: Entretien avec Anne Henry' in *Michel Henry: Auto-donation. Entretiens et conferences* (Paris: Beauchesne, 2004), pp. 266–7.

50 Henry, *Entretiens*, p. 131.

Henry one must understand his determination to hold together the two sources of our culture: Graeco-Latin and Judaeo-Christian. So much so for Henry, we 'are the children of this paradoxical, and yet infinitely precious, alliance'.[51]

It is in this sense and for this reason that the freedom of action appears as pure, as pure manifestation and pure revelation. These are the common terms of the labour of phenomenology and theology. It is in this regard that material phenomenology poses, on the plane of absolute immanence, questions that are more radical and essential, questions that are evidently those of God, those that cannot be absorbed into the plane of understanding that claims historical evidence as its proper proof. Christianity is not a *gnosis*, a particular knowledge, which means it is a religion of the 'simple', of the 'little' and that its holy revelation of the Father was hidden from the 'learned' and the 'wise'. Salvation is not obtained through a movement of intellectual comprehension. It is this that explains the decisively particular proposal of the comprehension of material phenomenology, especially if we remain attentive to the notion of rereading:

This belated realization I discovered through the texts of the New Testament. The theses implicated by these texts were those which drove me in the internal development of my philosophy to know: First, the definition of the absolute (God) as Life. Second, the affirmation that the process of life as becoming in a self and as an experience of a self necessarily generated in itself an Ipseity in which precisely it experiences itself and reveals itself as itself – which is its Word, in such a way that this does not happen in terms of it own process but appears as constitutive of its own accomplishment and so contemporaneous with itself: 'In the beginning was the Word'. Third, that which we call the human, that is to say, the transcendental living Self that each of us is, is never of the world. For me, the 'turn to theology' in contemporary

---

51 Henry, *Entretiens*, p. 132.

phenomenology is not a 'deviation' or a denaturalization of phenomenology, rather it is its accomplishment.[52]

Everything is there and it all comes. But if it is in itself, the 'intellectuals' and the 'philosophers' whom Michel Henry evokes as an epigraph to his argument have an immense task of existential import before them. It is a task to be thought through the figure of Nicodemus, for the Scriptures are never far when thought begins to return to the transcendent: *Nicodème, ce 'Maître', dont on sait quel exil intérieur il a accepté d'éprouver, de vivre surtout!*[53]

---

52 Henry, *Entretiens*, p. 154.

53 [I would like to acknowledge my gratitude to Adrian Pabst and Conor Cunningham for their helpful comments on draft versions of this translation. (Trans.)]

10. The World without the Lie

KARL HEFTY

We cannot pretend to assign a place to that which is the condition of
every place . . .
Michel Henry[1]

A reader of Michel Henry's philosophy may conclude that he
has no positive concept of the world. If we encounter any world
at all in his work, we encounter a world defined not as the
horizon of Being, but as the horizon of non-Being. As such, the
world is not a real place and cannot be; and this non-place has
a meaning. The world has the phenomenological sense of a
nowhere: 'ontological milieu of unreality'.[2] Far from the mere
object of a negation, the world in this sense gains the status of a
phenomenality, or manner of appearing, whereby, in the strict
sense, nothing can manifest itself, nothing can give itself, and
nothing can show itself. If it is obvious that there is no place for
the world in this phenomenology, it is equally obvious that
there is no place for phenomenology in this world.

Is this the last word on the world of a philosophy that would
dismantle from within the philosophical inheritance of the

---

1 'On ne peut prétendre assigner une place à ce qui est la condition de
toute place.' M. Henry, *L'essence de la manifestation* (Paris: PUF, 3rd
edn, 2003), p. 597. English translation: *The Essence of Manifestation*
(The Hague: Martinus Nijhoff, 1973), p. 478. (Hereafter *EM*, with
French pagination followed by English pagination in brackets.) Here
Henry refers to Martin Heidegger. See 'Aletheia (Heraklit, Fragment
16)', *Vorträge und Aufsätze*, 5th edn (Pfullingen: Verlag Günther Neske,
1985), pp. 249–74.
2 *EM*, pp. 327, 328 (263, 264).

modern West? Is the philosophy of life resurrected in these ruins merely a chimera, an impossible a priori that surpasses Kant only by contriving a world even *less* accessible and *less* real? After all, a simple negative determination of life's phenomenality can suffice: 'that which is not world'.[3] And the opposition is unambiguous: 'the appearing of life is opposed feature for feature to the appearing of the world'.[4] 'No flesh can appear in the appearing of the world.'[5] 'No life can appear in the appearing of the world.'[6] An ontological dualism of 'reciprocal exclusion'[7] separates two modes of phenomenality that never coincide. Does this situation not arise with the *ego cogito* of Descartes? Can a return to the problem of the ego offer anything but a tired repetition of this episode in the history of western philosophy?

By what determination of thought does the world open itself to philosophical scrutiny? What constitutes the world's truth and renders it accessible to us? Could it be that the truth of the world is nullified and rendered meaningless, not by the false or dubitable, but by a lie? For Henry, an internal necessity in the life of the ego gives it the power of conferring meaning on the

---

3 *EM*, p. 564 (450).

4 M. Henry, 'Phénoménologie et langage (ou, pathos et langage)', *Phénoménologie de la vie, 3: De l'art et du politique* (Paris: PUF, 2004), p. 335. English translation, 'Material Phenomenology and Language (Or, Pathos and Language)', tr. L. Lawlor, *Continental Philosophy Review* 32 (1999), p. 352.

5 M. Henry, *Incarnation: une philosophie de la chair* (Paris: Éditions du Sueil, 2000), p. 59.

6 M. Henry, 'Phénoménologie de la vie', *Phénoménologie de la vie, 1: De la phénoménologie* (Paris: PUF, 2003), p. 62. English translation: 'Phenomenology of Life', tr. N. Hanlon, *Angelaki* 8:2 (August 2003), p. 101, and reprinted in the present volume.

7 *C'est moi la vérité: Pour une philosophie du christianisme* (Paris: Éditions du Seuil, 1996), p. 55. English translation: *I Am the Truth: Toward a Philosophy of Christianity*, tr. S. Emanuel (Stanford: Stanford University Press, 2003), p. 40. Henry also employs the term *exclusion réciproque* to indicate the opposition of appearance and being in the phenomenality of the world. See *Incarnation*, p. 61.

world. By its singular confrontation in each transcendental life, the phenomenality of the ego takes the form of ipseity, in which life gives the ego to itself perfectly. According to Henry, the plenitude of this perfect self-manifestation itself provides the condition for the phenomenality of the world. Although the ego has the power to confer meaning upon the world, the ego is not the source of this power any more than the world is the source of its meaning. The truth of the world and the truth of the ego find their common origin in life's dispossession. In this way, the humility of the power of seeing opens for us in each case and for the first time an absolute world.

Phenomenality, Ipseity, Truth

In more than one sense, phenomenology poses the question of how appearance itself appears. In fact, phenomenology never stops posing the question. The question acquires a rigorous meaning with Heidegger's ambition for total methodological transparency. A clear determination of the meanings of phenomenon as variously showing, announcing, signifying, appearing, and so on, leaves little room for ambiguity. Everything depends upon the position of the question. That is why the methodological conception of phenomenology 'does not characterize the what of the objects of philosophical research as subject-matter, but rather the *how* of that research'.[8] But do we miss the point entirely if we ask whether Heidegger's 'how' has anything at all to do with the question of how anything *can* show itself? Has he left us any room to wonder whether, after all, he simply takes for granted that something *does*? How is it possible that anything shows itself? No one can deny that

---

8 'Er charakterisiert nicht das sachhaltige Was der Gegenstände der philosophischen Forschung, sondern das Wie dieser.' M. Heidegger, *Sein und Zeit* (Tübingen: Max Niemeyer Verlag, 11th edn, 1967), p. 27. English translation: *Being and Time*, tr. J. Macquarrie and E. Robinson (Oxford: Blackwell, 1962), p. 50.

phenomenology always finds itself confronted with the question of its own possibility, but what meaning can this question have?

Michel Henry assigns this first question of phenomenology a new sense. The how of appearance no longer belongs to the order of methodology. The question is now one of knowing how, but the meaning of this question is thoroughly ontological: the possibility of phenomenology is the possibility of a phenomenology of self-manifestation. 'How can the condition for the possibility of every manifestation become itself something manifest?'[9] How does manifestation make manifest everything it manifests? In other words, how does manifestation manifest itself?[10]

Understood in this sense, phenomenality has both universal and concrete meaning, universal because the inquiry concerns the condition for the possibility of *any* manifestation, concrete because this way of being a phenomenon must be a concrete Being. If phenomenality can show itself, can be a phenomenon, phenomenology can attain the condition of its own possibility, namely an original and adequate revelation. The how is not the method, but the content; 'its *Wie* is a *Was*'.[11] 'The 'how' of this revelation is a real Being.'[12] Nevertheless, this content has a peculiar and paradoxical status, because it achieves a concrete meaning in abstraction from the content of all determined phenomena. This provision may seem to disqualify the ego from consideration, but the ego is and must be the real Being in question precisely in so far as it *does not* fall subordinate to any other condition. A philosophy confined to a merely external and structural analysis of the bond that unites the ego to Being has no power here.[13] It belongs to the ego to take up from with-

---

9 *EM*, p. 50 (39).

10 *C'est moi, la vérité, EM*, p. 46 (33).

11 Henry, 'Phénoménologie et langage (ou, pathos et langage)', p. 336. '. . .what allows a phenomenon to be a phenomenon?', 'Phenomenology of Life', p. 100 ('Phénoménologie de la vie', p. 59); 'something capable of appearing', *EM*, p. 50 (39).

12 *EM*, p. 52 (40).

13 *EM*, p. 42 (33).

in this relation. In this precise sense, the ego is a problem that can never go away. Philosophy has no business attempting to solve this problem. It does well simply to see it.

So long as it remains prisoner to the horizon of phenomenological distance, phenomenology cannot see this problem. Phenomenological distance is the form of illegitimate phenomenology, namely of phenomenology that endeavours both to submit to a horizon of presence and to show this horizon. Phenomenology misappropriates ontology and assumes the power of manifestation whenever, outside the problematic of the ego, it presumes both to give us access to things and to be this access itself.[14] Henry defines the horizon of transcendence as the power of giving access conceived of as original remoteness. This remoteness consists in the difference between appearance and being, or in their presupposed coincidence. The philosophy of consciousness remains prisoner to this transcendent horizon.[15] Henry includes among its detainees not only German Idealism, but also the phenomenology of Husserl, Heidegger, Sartre and Merleau-Ponty. Contrary to what one might expect, the problem with consciousness is not a dualism between subject and object, but a pervasive monism. Consciousness is not one term in the relation between subject and object, but 'the commerce which takes place between the terms, it is the Being of this "between"'.[16] Monistic indifference is the consequence of a theory of consciousness that takes this relation as its essence. At the ontological level, this indifference makes the subjectivity of the subject identical to the objectivity of the object. Its failure to preserve the difference between the two forms of phenomenality is also a failure to preserve their unity.

The relation of the ego to itself in ipseity cannot fall subordinate to any horizon of presence, nor can self-presence itself constitute such a horizon, because a horizon by definition escapes every presence. Henry makes startling and seemingly

---

14 *EM*, p. 77 (63).
15 *EM*, n. 22, p. 104 (84).
16 *EM*, p. 105 (85). Cf. Heidegger, *Sein und Zeit*, p. 132 (170).

implausible claims about presence that seem to ignore any condition of Being-in-the-world. Conceived of as original revelation, presence 'exists by itself, without any context, without the support of any exterior and "real" Being'.[17] We would misunderstand this claim, however, if we failed to notice the aesthetic dimension of manifestation as the power for creativity. This power makes no dubious appeal to an absolute freedom of the ego. On the contrary, the power for creativity, which Henry attributes to the ego, begins essentially with non-freedom. 'The meaning of the Being of the *ego cogito* is to confer a meaning upon Being; more fundamentally it is to be the source of this meaning, the absolute origin from which, in every case, the latter springs forth as a free creation.'[18] The power to confer meaning, this meaning at the absolute origin of all meaning, Henry identifies as 'the originary naturing' (*naturant originaire*).[19] The power to confer meaning pertains as much to the nature of meaning as to the meaning of nature. This power is creative and receptive at the same time.[20] The ego receives itself at the same time as it receives each of its powers. This common bond unites the problem of truth and the problem of the ego in an inextricable way. In this sense, it belongs to the ego to 'realize' the condition for the possibility of every phenomenon.[21]

Situation and the Transcendental Illusion

In what sense has philosophy misunderstood the concept of situation? How far has philosophy evacuated this concept of its meaning? For Henry, to be in a situation means to be incapable of assuming a point of view or taking an attitude (*de prendre attitude*) with regard to Being, a point of view outside, above or beside Being, whereby we might take command of the totality

---

17 *EM*, p. 53 (41).
18 *EM*, pp. 32, 33 (26).
19 *EM*, p. 35 (27); 'such a power is as such creative', p. 364 (292).
20 *EM*, p. 210 (72).
21 *EM*, p. 47 (37).

of its possibilities with an all-encompassing intelligibility, as though we might then choose from among them one as our own, and only *then* achieve Being authentically. But the ontological determinations that govern this impossibility of stepping outside Being have remained in confusion. Rather than understanding Being-in-situation just *as* Being, we have interpreted Being-in-situation as a *contingency* in relation to Being.[22] Beginning in this way, however, with a determination of situation as contingency, and thus as limitation, we cannot help but end with the bizarre and ontologically untenable notion of situation as a restriction, as an external imposition upon something more original.

Do the determinations whereby Heidegger arrives at Being-in-the-world show any susceptibility to this criticism? Henry rules out the possibility that the concept of the world promises to open for us, namely the possibility of taking an attitude or having a point of view on our situation. True situation cannot depend for its being *as situation* upon an exterior attitude that we, for one reason or another or no reason at all, happen to assume towards it. By its implicit appeal to transcendence, this ontological duplicity always and in every case condemns the phenomenology of the world to contradiction, because the world, as world, has no power to be itself as world. How far does Heidegger acknowledge this duplicity when he makes recourse not to Being-in-the-world, but to the resolute decision of *Dasein*, who remains, in Heidegger's words, 'free either for authenticity or for inauthenticity'?[23] Henry's answer is unambiguous: 'the *existentiell* determination of the concept of situation has nothing original about it'.[24] In the effort to disclose situation in terms of a more original world, Heidegger still more originally *determines* the situation of Being-in-the-world itself as such.[25]

---

22 *EM*, p. 423 (339).
23 *Sein und Zeit*, p. 232 (English 275).
24 *EM*, p. 433 (347).
25 *EM*, p. 434 (348).

Consider the manner by which *Dasein* finds itself and thereby discovers its Being. As Being-in-the-world, *Dasein* 'is already ahead of itself in each case'.[26] But in what does this basic disparity within *Dasein* consist? *Dasein* must make recourse to a provenance of Being other than Being-in-the-world. 'Once it is a question of determining *Dasein's* Being-in-situation appeal is without doubt made to transcendence, namely, to *Dasein* itself.'[27] In this sense, *Dasein* both is and is not self-founding.[28] Disparity within *Dasein* is the ontological condition for its authenticity. *Dasein* finds its own foundation 'in the not-Being-the-foundation of self of its own Being'.[29] Given that ipseity occupies such prominence in Henry's philosophy, it may seem paradoxical that Henry criticizes Heidegger for making an appeal to the self in order to secure *Dasein*'s Being. Heidegger must make recourse to the self not because he secretly relies upon transcendence, but because he has mistaken its essential meaning. No subsequent resolution can resolve the very splitting of Being that he works so rigorously to avoid. If the power of transcendence always requires reference to a power outside the self, namely to a power that does not constitute the Being of self, the self bears within itself 'unreality as a constitutive element' of its very Being.[30]

A fidelity to the meaning of situation sustains the criticism of Heidegger. For Henry, 'a situation is precisely what cannot be chosen, what we cannot 'accept' or 'refuse''.[31] Transcendence just *is* situated-Being.[32] If Heidegger refuses this transcendence, he does so by redoubling it. But this redoubling is the inevitable effect of building a philosophy upon the phenomenality of the world. In the light of this phenomenality, appearance *can* found nothing at all, in the positive and nihilistic sense of this nothing

---

26 *Sein und Zeit*, p. 228 (English 270).
27 *EM*, p. 439 (352).
28 *EM*, pp. 439–41 (352, 353).
29 *EM*, p. 442 (354).
30 *EM*, p. 358 (288).
31 *EM*, p. 426 (342).
32 *EM*, p. 429 (343).

that anxiety knows the world to be.[33] These criticisms of Heidegger seem to carry the tint of a Sartrean lens. But Henry affirms and perhaps completes this critique of situation later, in *C'est moi, la vérité*, where he explains the transcendental illusion of the ego.

The ipseity of the ego is its mode of givenness to itself, its manner of possessing itself. The transcendental illusion arises when the ego imagines it possesses the life that is given to it. In the transcendental illusion of the ego, this ego takes itself as the ground of its Being. Now the ego attributes to its own power the power to be able to want, to will, to do, and so on, taking itself as its source. It forgets its condition and falsifies it. It forgets life, which in its ipseity gives it to itself and at the same time gives it all its powers and capacities. It falsifies by taking its givenness (including its givenness to itself) as its own work.

> Who, in fact, lifting a weight, does not think that he is the one lifting it; or, taking an object does not think that his own strength is doing so? Liar! How could he exercise this power if Life had not given it to him along with all his capacities? Properly speaking to attribute to yourself what does not belong to you is a theft.[34]

But this transcendental illusion has a truth. The gift by which life (self-giving) gives the ego to itself is in reality one with it. 'In making the ego a living person, life has not made it a pseudo person.'[35] The positive quality of this gift, of the effectiveness of the 'I Can', masks what makes it possible. The phenomeno-logical status of life as invisible, immanent and not of the world, explains the ego's transcendental illusion. In its mode of care, *Dasein* succumbs to this illusion. The ego relates everything in the world only to itself, as outside possibilities, tasks and projects for which it cares. But strictly speaking it is impossible for the ego to care for its true self, because in care the self that

---

33 Anxiety reveals the Nothingness of the world. *EM*, p. 432 (347).
34 *C'est moi, la vérité*, p. 178 (English 141).
35 *C'est moi, la vérité*, p. 178 (English 141).

life generates is absent in principle. Care and ipseity are thus not two forms of behaviour or attitudes; they are two modes of phenomenality.[36]

In care, the properties that ostensibly characterize Being-in-the-world actually fall into contradiction. The relationships of proximity and distance inherent to Being-in-the-world no longer have any meaning, because they amount to the same thing. Thus, as Henry argues in *Incarnation*, the phenomenality of the world is a phenomenality of both difference and indifference: everything that appears is different and yet it makes no difference what appears because everything that appears is the same. This phenomenality is a kind of 'powerlessness', according to Henry, because what appears is incapable of bestowing Being.[37]

The appearing of the world,

> turns away from itself with such a violence, it throws outside with such force . . . that everything to which it gives appearance can never be anything other, effectively, than exterior in the dreadful sense of something which, placed outside, chased as it were from its true Residence, from its original Homeland, deprived of its ownmost possessions, finds itself from that point abandoned, without support, lost – prey to this abandonment from which Heidegger needed to deliver man once he had made of him, as 'being-in-the-world,' a being of this world and nothing more.[38]

Dasein 'exists and can exist only as this foundation from which it is discarded'. In this sense, the philosophy of consciousness,

---

36 Henry already indicates the structure of this impossibility in *L'essence le la manifestation*. 'Insofar as the essence of phenomenality is other than its effectiveness, it rather finds in the latter its own suppression'. *EM*, p. 135 (110).

37 Henry, *Incarnation*, pp. 59–61.

38 'détourne de soi avec une telle violence, il jette au-dehors avec tant de force . . . tout ce à quoi il donne d'apparaître ne peut jamais être autre chose, en effet, que de l'extérieur, au sens terrible de ce qui, mis dehors, chasse en quelque sorte de sa Demeure veritable, de sa Patrie d'origine, privé de ses biens les plus propres, se trouve dès lors abandonné, sans appui, perdu – la proie de ce délaissement auquel Heidegger devait

which includes the philosophy of Heidegger, saves the absolute only by 'throwing it back in a hinter-world' [*le rejetant dans un arriène monde*].[39] Rejection is the ontological meaning of *Geworfenheit*.

Life without a Hinter-world

Henry begins section 34 of *L'essence de la manifestation* with what may now seem an astonishing and incredible affirmation: 'With the determination of the essence of transcendence as immanence, the transcendental rapport of *Being-in-the-world* is no longer simply affirmed but, on the contrary, grasped in its intrinsic possibility.'[40] The phenomenality of inherence, which we have seen Henry describe elsewhere as the *naturant originaire*, he now determines in a decisive way as consciousness of imagination. The phenomenality of life and the phenomenality of the world now find a common moment. Nevertheless, in consciousness of imagination the phenomenality of the world is absent. 'In the manifestation of imagination there resides not the phenomenality of the world but that which makes it possible, that in which this phenomenality arrives at effectiveness.'[41] The world phenomenalizes itself in the act of imagination, or more precisely in the revelation immanent to the act of imagination. This consciousness preserves the division between the

---

livrer l'homme pour en avoir fait, en tant qu''«être-au-monde» un être de ce monde, rien de plus.' 'Phenomenology of Life', p. 101 ('Phénoménologie de la vie', pp. 62, 63). Henry, *Incarnation*, p. 60. I here borrow the translation of Nick Hanlon.

39 *EM*, p. 148 (120).

40 'Avec la détermination de l'essence de la transcendance comme immanence, le rapport transcendental de l'être-au-monde n'est plus affirmé simplement mais saisi au contraire dans sa possibilité intrinsèque.' *EM*, p. 262 (326). The reader should note that Henry uses both *être-au-monde* and *être-dans-le-monde* for Heidegger's *In-der-Welt-sein*. The English translation by Etzkorn, here and elsewhere, renders both as 'Being-in-the-world', without noting the distinction, which is probably merely a stylistic one.

41 *EM*, p. 328 (264).

two modes of phenomenality; not that there are two conscious-
nesses, but that the one does not properly belong to the other.
Both are structural determinations of consciousness itself, not
properties added to it. It is not a question of how consciousness
of one is, in the same moment or event, consciousness of the
other.[42] Consciousness of imagination is 'the phenomenological
reality of transcendence itself'.[43] In this shocking affirmation,
Henry preserves the structure of intentionality, not as the
consciousness of the world, but as the consciousness of consciousness of the world.

We can now see that the world as such has a proper manner of
appearing and even a certain power of manifestation.
'Substituting one phenomenology for another, that of Life or
Logos for that of the world, is not to misunderstand the power
of manifestation that belongs to the latter, but rather strictly to
circumscribe its domain and thus its capability.'[44] The phenomenality of life provides no way of escape from the world; nor
does this phenomenality perform the task of 'a formal and
empty negation of the world'.[45] Indeed, according to Henry, the
phenomenology of life 'does not as such constitute any hinter-
world [*arrière-monde*]'.[46] No longer are we consigned to the
unlivable double-place in which philosophy and theology so
often leave us, either torn between 'two worlds' (*deux mondes*)[47]
or a 'world apart' (*un 'monde' à part*)[48] or displaced in a 'hinter-
world' (*arrière-monde*).[49] On the contrary, Henry sees unfolded,
at the foundation of the world, 'the horizon of a pure world', not
another world, but 'this world without laceration' (*ce monde*

---

42 *EM*, p. 330 (265).
43 *EM*, p. 331 (266).
44 *C'est moi, la vérité*, p. 109 (English 85).
45 *EM*, p. 571 (456).
46 *EM*, p. 414 (332): 'Le milieu ontologique où s'accomplit l'unité de
tous les phénomès n'est pas cependant l'objet d'une affirmation métaphysique et ne constitue comme tel aucun arrière-monde.'
47 *EM*, pp. 507, 508 (404).
48 *EM*, p. 530 (423).
49 *EM*, p. 148, 414, 499 (120, 332, 397).

sans déchirement),[50] in which, in his words, 'is inaugurated our vital communication with the Being of nature'.[51] This vital communication is affection by an act: 'the act which forms the world' (*l'affection originelle de la transcendance non par le monde mais précisément par l'act qui le forme, c'est-à-dire, par elle-même*).[52] On the basis of its submission to this original act of creation, we can affirm, with Henry, that 'the subject is affected outside experience'.[53]

In the pure milieu of this phenomenality, the essence finds nothing to oppose. Following Meister Eckhart, Henry describes this pure milieu as 'the desert of its own foundation'.[54] The poverty of this desert is not the poverty of an empty negation or a provisional renouncement, but is itself essential. Neither merely given nor merely received, place in this way constitutes at once both 'a task and an accomplishment'.[55] Life's desert is the essence of place, which opens onto life 'wherever it takes place'.[56] Henry is in no sense tempted by the Gnostic insistence that I *must* suffer, and it would be an obvious mistake to interpret his argument as any sort of normative injunction. The point is not that I must suffer, but that, at the foundation of my Being, *I can*. Eckhart writes:

> Emptied of things, creatures, himself and god, and if still God could find a place in him to act, this man is not poor with the most intimate poverty . . . since [it] requires that man shall be emptied of God and all his works, so that if God wants to act in the soul, he himself must be the place in which he acts.[57]

---

50 *EM*, p. 362 (291).

51 *EM*, p. 574 (460).

52 *EM*, p. 576 (461).

53 '"le sujet se trouve affecté en dehors de l'expérience" c'est-à-dire indépendamment de l'étant.' *EM*, p. 575 (460). Cf. Edmund Husserl, *Erfahrung und Urteil* (Hamburg: Classen und Coverts, 1948), p. 53.

54 *EM*, p. 402 (322).

55 *EM*, pp. 355, 402 (286, 323).

56 *EM*, p. 415 (332).

57 Eckhart, *Traités et Sermons*, tr. F. A. and J. M. (Paris: Aubier, 1942), p. 257, quoted by Henry in *EM*, p. 390 (313).

Henry is a philosopher of transcendence, but the horizon of the world is not the horizon that marks out definitively the presence or absence of Being, nor is the transcendence of Being reducible to the transcendence of the world's horizon. Place does not gain its essential meaning by reference either to the *cogito* or to the ontological destruction that would make of it a Being-in-the-world. Henry's phenomenological ontology acknowledges that obscurity belongs in principle to the essence of Being. The world may remain *res extensa* in its essence, but it is no longer immediately obvious 'what' the world is. Although this thought makes thinking the horizon of Being its explicit ambition, the ambition is a modest one. The phenomenology of life does not seek to bring the horizon of Being to consciousness in order to surmount it, but 'in order to live it as such, in mystery'.[58] The true Being of place is inscrutable, irreducible; and a 'secret shudder freezes our rapport to the world to its core'.[59] The truth of life,

> truth itself in its original and universal structure, is also tragic, for it signifies the irremediable and the definitive, the inauguration of an absolute world [*un monde absolu*] from which nothing can be taken away, to which nothing can be added, where without detour and without lie, things are what they are, Being is what it is, in this perfect adequation which is Being itself.[60]

---

58 'pour la vivre comme telle dans le mystère.' *EM*, p. 23 (18).

59 'ce tremblement secret qui transit notre rapport au monde et le determine quell qu'il soit, partout et toujours, comme essentiellement affectif.' *EM*, p. 603 (482). I am grateful to Lauren Silvers for suggesting this translation.

60 'Mais cette vérité, celle de la vérité elle-même dans sa structure originaire et universelle, est aussi bien tragique, car elle signifie l'irrémissible et le definitive, l'instauration d'un monde absolu duquel rien ne peut être soustrait, auquel rien ne peut être ajouté, où, sans detour et sans mensonge, les choses sont ce qu'elles sont, l'être est ce qu'il est, dans cette adéquation parfaite qui est l'être lui-même.' *EM*, pp. 361, 362 (291).

11. Phenomenology of Life

MICHEL HENRY

Translated by Nick Hanlon

The phenomenology of life lies within the ambit of that great current of philosophical thinking which originated in Germany at the end of the nineteenth century with Edmund Husserl and that, via major thinkers such as Martin Heidegger and Max Sheler, continued throughout the twentieth century. It still remains very much alive today, notably in France.[1] I would like to show in which ways the phenomenology of life is a tributary of this movement of thought which is one of the most important in our culture, and in what ways it diverges from it.

The originality of phenomenology must be understood on the basis of the objective it has assigned itself. While the other sciences study specific phenomena – physical, chemical, biological, juridical, social, economic, etc. – phenomenology explores what allows a phenomenon to be a phenomenon. Phenomenology investigates pure phenomenality as such. One can confer various names upon this pure phenomenality: pure manifestation, showing, unveiling, uncovering, appearing, revelation, or even a more traditional word: truth. As soon as the object of phenomenology is understood in its difference from the object of other sciences, a further distinction seems to impose itself: that of the phenomenon considered on the one

---

1 'Phénoménologie de la vie' was first delivered as a lecture to the Munich Academy of Fine Arts, 14 November 2000. A month before he died in July 2002, Henry confirmed, in discussion with Joseph and Joëlle Llapasset, his belief that this article conveys the essence of his whole philosophical project.

hand in its particular content, and on the other hand in its phenomenality. Such is the distinction between that which shows itself, that which appears, and the fact of appearing, pure appearing as such. It is the difference that Heidegger formulates in his own way in paragraph 44 of *Being and Time* when he distinguishes truth in a secondary sense as that which is true, that which is unveiled, from, at a deeper level, the unveiling as such as 'the most original phenomenon of truth [*das ursprünglichste Phänomen der Wahrheit*]'.[2]

Another primary intuition of phenomenology is that appearing is more essential than being; it is only because it appears that a thing is able to be. To express this with Husserl, using a formula borrowed from the Marburg School (which I modify slightly): 'Something is inasmuch as it appears [*Autant d'apparaître, autant d'être*]'. I carry this precedence of phenomenology over ontology one step further by saying that it is only if the appearing appears in itself and as such that something, whatever it may be, can in turn appear, can show itself to us.

Despite these various points, however, the phenomenological presupposition of phenomenology still remains wholly indeterminate. The principles of phenomenology tell us that 'something is inasmuch as it appears' and they urge us to go, to quote the famous slogan, 'straight to the things themselves [*zu den Sachen selbst*]'. But the meaning of these principles remains obscure so long as we lack a clear definition of what is meant by the fact of appearing, by the concrete phenomenological mode according to which this pure appearing (i.e. the pure phenomenological matter, so to speak, in which phenomenality as such phenomenalizes itself). Now, if one directs this question towards the founding texts of phenomenology one notes that behind the phenomenological indeterminacy of the principles of phenomenology, a certain concept of phenomenality slips in, the very conception which initially presents itself to ordinary thought and which constitutes at the same time the oldest and least critical prejudice of traditional philosophy. This is the con-

---

2 M. Heidegger, *Sein und Zeit* (Halle: Niemeyer, 1941), pp. 220–1.

ception of phenomenality that is derived from the perception of objects in the world, which is to say, in the final reckoning, the appearing of the world itself.

The reader may not easily accept this idea that the founder of phenomenology, Edmund Husserl, confronted with the explicit question of 'how' objects are given (*Gegenstände im Wie* – 'objects in the how'),[3] answers: via the appearing of the world. Doesn't Husserl, in keeping with tradition, instead refer to the principle of phenomenality to consciousness and thus to a type of 'interiority'? However, we should not forget the essential definition of consciousness as intentionality. Understood as intentional, consciousness is nothing other than the movement through which it throws itself outside: its 'substance' exhausts itself in this coming outside which produces phenomenality. The act of revealing in such a coming outside, in a setting at a distance, is what constitutes showing (*faire-voir*). The possibility of vision resides in this setting at a distance of that which is placed in front of the seeing, and is thereby seen by it. Such is the phenomenological definition of the object: that which, placed in front, is rendered visible in this way. Appearing is here the appearing of the object in a double sense: in the sense that that which appears is the object, so then the mode of appearing at issue here is the mode of appearing peculiar to the object and that which renders it visible, i.e. this setting at a distance on which arises the visibility of all that which is susceptible of becoming visible for us.

At this point a further question cannot be avoided: how does the intentionality which shows or makes visible every thing reveal itself to itself? Could it be by directing a new intentionality upon itself? If so, can phenomenology avoid the bitter destiny of that classical philosophy of consciousness which finds itself bound in an endless regression, obliged to place a second consciousness behind the knowing consciousness (in our case a second intentionality behind the one that we are attempting to

---

3 E. Husserl, *Leçons pour une phénoméologie de la conscience intime de temps* (Paris: Presses Universitaires de France, 1964), p. 157.

wrest from obscurity)? Or else does a mode of revelation exist other than the showing of intentionality, in which phenomenality would no longer be that of the outside? Phenomenology has no answer to this question. Thus a crisis of extreme gravity takes form in it which soon leads to aporia. The very possibility of phenomenality becomes problematic if the principle of phenomenality escapes its grasp. As we know, Husserl could only describe as 'anonymous' that self which in the final instance is constitutive of the way things appear. It is with Heidegger that the appearing of the world is taken to its highest degree of elaboration. From section 7 of *Being and Time* the phenomenon is understood in the Greek sense – *phainomenon*, from the root *pha*, *phos*, which signifies light, so that appearing signifies coming into the light or into clarity, i.e. 'that inside of which something can become visible or manifest in itself'. The world is the ek-static horizon of visibilization inside of which everything can become visible, and the second apart of *Being in Time* declares explicitly that this 'horizon' concerns exteriority, the 'outside of self' as such. The world is identified here with temporality, and temporality is nothing other than 'the originary "outside of self" in and for itself [*Zeitlichkeit ist das ursprüngliche "Außer-sich" an und für sich selbst*].'[4]

There are three decisive traits that characterize the appearing of the world. Their brief enumeration will serve as an introduction to the phenomenology of life itself, whose first thesis will be that no life can appear in the appearing of the world.

1. In so far as the appearing of the world consists in the 'outside of self', in the coming of an Outside, so all that shows itself in it, shows itself outside, as exterior, as other, as different. *Exterior* because the structure in which it shows itself is that of exteriority; *other* because this ek-static structure is that of a primordial alterity (all that which is outside of me is other than self); different because this Ek-stasis is identically a *Difference*, the operation which, opening up the divide of a distance, renders different everything to which this setting at a distance

---

4 Heidegger, *Sein und Zeit*, p. 329

allows to appear – in the horizon of the world. Such an appearing turns away from itself with such a violence, it throws outside with such force (being itself nothing other than this originary expulsion of an Outside), that everything to which it gives appearance can never be anything other, effectively, than exterior in the dreadful sense of something which, placed outside, chased as it were from its true Residence, from its original Homeland, deprived of its ownmost possessions, finds itself from that point abandoned, without support, lost – prey to this abandonment from which Heidegger needed to deliver man once he had made of him, as 'being-in-the-world', a being of this world and nothing more.

2. The appearing which unveils in the Difference of the world does not just render different all that which unveils itself in that fashion, it is in principle totally indifferent to it, it neither loves it nor desires it, and having no affinity with it, it does not protect it in any way. As far as this appearing is concerned, it doesn't matter whether that which appears is a darkening sky of the equality of a circle's radii, a nanny-goat or a hydroplane, an image of a real thing, or even the formula that contains the secret of the universe. Like the light of which Scripture speaks, which shines on the just as well as on the unjust, the appearing of the world illuminates everything that it illuminates in a terrifying neutrality, without distinguishing between things or persons. There are victims and torturers, charitable acts and genocides, rules and expectations, and exactions, and wind, water, earth, and all this stands before us in the same way, in this ultimate manner of being which we express when we say 'This is', 'There is'.

3. However, this indifference of the appearing of the world to that which it unveils in the Difference, which makes everything of it except that which a Father is for his Son, a brother for his brother, a friend for his friends (a friend who knows everything that his brothers know, and first and foremost the first among them: the First Born Son) – this indifference, we should say, hides a more radical destitution. The appearing of the world is not only indifferent to everything it unveils, it is incapable of

conferring existence upon it. It is without doubt this incapacity of the appearing of the world to take account of that which unveils itself in it which explains its indifference towards it. Indifference and neutrality here mean powerlessness, from which they are derived. Heidegger, who first thought of the concept of the world in its originary phenomenological signification as pure appearing, was quite aware of both this indifference (the anguish in which everything becomes indifferent) and this powerlessness. The unveiling unveils, uncovers, 'opens', but does not create (*macht nicht, öffnet*). This is how the ontological destitution of the appearing of the world reveals itself, as itself incapable of setting out reality.

Now this ontological destitution of the appearing of the world does not result from a peculiarly Heideggerian thesis: one finds it already in Kant's *Critique of Pure Reason*. Kant understood what is at stake in the question of the world as phenomenological. This is why the *Critique* consists of an extremely rigorous description of the phenomenological structures of the world. The world is co-constituted through a priori forms of the pure intuition, the intuition of space and of time, as well as through the categories of the understanding. 'Forms of pure intuition' means pure ways of showing (*faire-voir*), considered in themselves, independently of the particular and contingent content (which is designed as 'empirical') of that which they show on any given occasion. 'A priori' means that these pure ways of showing precede all actual experience. Considered in terms more general than those of their specific characteristics (substance, causality, reciprocal action), the categories of understanding have the same fundamental phenomenological signification, that of belonging to showing and of rendering showing possible by assuring its unity. Now, the phenomenological structure of this unifying power is the same as that of the pure intuitions, it is a showing which consists in the fact of placing outside (*poser dehors*) that which becomes visible in this way. According to Kant's decisive affirmation, the forms of intuition and the categories of understanding are both representations. To represent in this sense is experienced in German as *vor-sellen*, which signifies very precisely to 'place in front' (*poser devant*). Now, what is important for us in all this, the recurrent thesis of the *Critique*, is that the phenomenological formation of the world in the conjoined and coherent action of the diverse 'showings' is for ever incapable, by itself, of setting out (*poser*) the reality which constitutes the concrete content of this world – in order to gain access to this reality, Kant was forced to have recourse to sensation.

But the appeal to sensation which can alone give access to reality hides within it an appeal to *life*, that is, to a radically different mode of appearing. Life is phenomenological through and through. It is neither a being (*étant*) nor a mode of being (*être*) of a being. This is not the life about which biology speaks. To tell the truth, modern biology no longer speaks about life. Since the Galilean revolution its object has narrowed to material processes compatible with those studied by physics. As François Jacob expresses it: 'In today's laboratories one no longer enquires about life.'[5]

The only life which exists is transcendental phenomenological life, the life which defines the originary mode of pure phenomenality to which henceforth, for the sake of clarity, we will reserve the name revelation. The revelation peculiar to life stands opposed point by point to the appearing of the world. Whereas the world unveils in the 'outside of self', being only the 'outside of self' as such, such that everything which it unveils is exterior, other, different, the first decisive trait of the revelation of life is that, because it carries no divide or gap within it and never differs from itself, it only ever reveals itself. Life reveals itself. Life is an auto-revelation. Auto-revelation, when it concerns life, thus means two things. On the one hand, it is life which accomplishes the work of revelation, it is everything except a thing. On the other hand what it reveals is itself. This, the opposition between that which appears and pure appearing, which had already been present in classical thought and which

---

5 F. Jacob, *La Logique du vivant: une histoire de hérédité* (Paris: Gallimard, 1970), p. 320.

was then brought to the fore by phenomenology, disappears in the case of life. The revelation of life and that which reveals itself in it are as one.

Everywhere there is life we encounter this extraordinary situation, which is discernible in each modality of life, even in the most humble of impressions. Take, for example, an experience of pain. Because in ordinary apprehension a pain is at first taken as a 'physical pain', one attributed to part of the objective body, let us practise on it that reduction which retains only its painful character, the 'painful as such', the purely affective element of suffering. This 'pure' suffering 'reveals itself to itself,' which means that suffering alone allows us to know what suffering is, and that what is revealed in this revelation, which is the fact of suffering, is indeed precisely suffering. In this modality of our life, the 'outside of self' of the world might well be absent – a fact indicated by the lack of any drive that might separate suffering from itself, such that, driven back against itself, overwhelmed by its own weight, it is incapable of instituting any form of stepping-back from itself, dimension of flight thanks to which it might be possible for it to escape from itself and from that which was oppressive about its being. In that absence of any divide within suffering, the possibility of turning one's gaze upon it is ruled out. No one has ever seen their suffering, their anguish or their joy. Suffering, like every modality of life, is invisible.

Invisible does not designate a dimension of unreality or illusion, some fantastical other world, but exactly the opposite. We have seen that it is the appearing of the *world* which, throwing every thing outside of itself, at the same time denudes it of its reality, reducing it to a series of exterior appearances into which it is impossible to penetrate because they have no 'interior', each merely referring you to another one which is just as empty and devoid of content as itself, in this game of indefinite referrals which is the world. We have seen that, according to Heidegger, the appearing of the world is incapable of creating that which unveils itself in it. By contrast, each of the modalities of life is a reality – one that is abrupt, immediate, incontestable, insuperable. But as soon as I try to see this reality, it disappears. I am certainly able, for the image of my suffering, to re-present it to myself, yet the fact remains that the reality of suffering never exists outside of itself. In the representation of suffering I am only in the presence of a noematic unreality, of the signification 'suffering'. It is only when all distance is abolished, when suffering experiences itself as pure suffer*ing* and joy as pure enjoy*ing*, that we are dealing with actual suffering, that revelation and reality are one.

This brings us to the third characteristic which opposes the revelation of life to the appearing of the world. Whereas the latter differs from every thing that it causes to show itself, in such a way that it is totally indifferent to every such thing, life, on the contrary, keeps within it that which it reveals, it resides inside, in every living being, as that which causes it to live and never leaves it for as long as it lives. This then is a new relationship, foreign to the world, peculiar and interior to life; we must now consider in itself the hitherto unthought relation between life and the living being, without which we can understand nothing of this living being that we are. Foreign to the world, acosmic, invisible, the relation of life to living being is relation of absolute immanence. How could one conceive of a living being that did not carry life within it? But the question equally arises of knowing why there is a living being in life: why is no life possible that might be anonymous, impersonal, foreign to every individuality?

Now, no more than the question of imminence, the question of the relation of life to the living being is not a metaphysical one, an object of speculative constructions or of indefinite debates. It is a matter for phenomenology and more particularly for a phenomenology of life, of which it becomes that central question. It is also an originary question. It obliges us to go back to an absolute life, the Life spoken of by John.

Absolute life is life which has the power to bring itself into life. Life 'is' not, it happens and does not cease happening. This coming of life is its eternal reaching into itself, the process or trial (*le procès*) in which it gives itself to it*self*, crushes itself against itself, experiences itself (*s'éprouve soi-même*) and delights in itself, thus constantly producing its own essence, as far as this consists in this testing experience (*épreuve*) and delight in itself. Now, no experience produces itself as experience or trial of it*self* if it does not generate in its very accomplishment the Ipseity whereby it is able to experience itself and delight in itself. As long as we are not speaking of the concept of life but of a real life, a phenomenologically actual life, then the Ipseity in which this real life comes into itself in experiencing itself is also one that is phenomenologically actual, it is a real Self, the First Living Self in which, experiencing itself, Life reveals itself to itself – its Word. Thus the process of Life's auto-generation is accomplished as the process of its auto-revelation, in such as way that the auto-revelation does not come at the end of this process but belongs to it and is consubstantial with it like an immanent condition of its effectuation. 'In the beginning was the Word.' There is no life without a living being, like this Self that all life carries in it, in so far as it is this experience of self of which we are speaking. But equally there is no Self without this Life in which every Self is given in itself, in such a way that outside of life no Self is possible.

However, doesn't this analysis of absolute life distance us from the phenomenology which seeks to confine itself to the concrete phenomena that we live through, does it not throw us back into speculation, if not into dogma or belief? Haven't we yielded to the 'theological turn of French phenomenology'[6] denounced by Dominique Janicaud?

And yet are we not, we too, living beings? Living beings in the sense of a life which experiences itself, and not just a complex set of material processes which know nothing of themselves? Living beings which are themselves also living Selves? This strange analogy between the internal process of absolute life experiencing itself in the Self of the First Living Being and our own life revealing itself to itself in this singular Self that each of

---

6 D. Janicaud, *Le Tournant théologique de la phénoménologie française* (Combas: L'Eclat, 1991).

us is forever becoming less extraordinary than it seems at first sight if we first of all establish the distinction between them.

Our life is a finite life incapable of bringing itself into self. The Self that this life carries in it is itself a finite Self. As Husserl says in a manuscript of the 1930s, 'I am not only for myself but I am me [*Ich bin nicht nur für mich, aber Ich bin Ich*].' I am not only for myself, i.e. this individual appearing in the world, a thing among things, a man among men, who represents itself constantly to itself, always in a state of care for itself, who only busies itself with things and with others with a view to itself. In order to relate everything to oneself, one must first of all be this Self to whom everything is related, one must be able to say *Ich bin Ich*. But the point is that this *Ich bin Ich* is not at all originary. I am indeed myself, but I am not brought to myself in this me that I am. I am given to myself, but it is not me myself who gives me to me. A Self such as that of man, a living transcendental Self – such a Self is only ever to be found in the 'Word of life' of the first letter of John, whom Paul describes as 'a First Born among many brothers' (Rom. 8.28–30). For we too are born of absolute Life. To be born does not mean to come into the world. Things appear for an instant in the light of the world before disappearing into it. Things are not 'born'. Birth concerns only living beings. And for these living beings, to be born means to come to be as one of these transcendental living Selves that each of us is. It is solely because we have first come into life that we are then able to come into the world.

In this way the nature of our transcendental birth becomes clear. How do we come into life? We come into life in so far as life comes in it*self* (*vient en soi*) and in the same way that life comes in itself. It is because absolute life comes into it*self*, while experiencing itself in the ipseity of the First Living Self which is its Word, that every man given to himself in the ipseity of this life comes into himself as a transcendental living Self. It is for this reason that every life, every transcendental phenomenological life, is marked at its heart with a radical and insurmountable individuality.

Here we should make a historical observation which is laden

with repercussions for our time. Life has been notably absent from the western philosophy inherited from Greece, which defines man through thought. When at the beginning of the nineteenth century life makes, with Schopenhauer, its great return to the European scene, it is life stripped of individuality, anonymous, impersonal, savage, which will establish its rule not only over philosophy but over culture as a whole, conferring upon it its tragic and absurd character, clearing the way to brutal force, to violence, to nihilism.

The phenomenology of life is thus confronted with one last question. We said that in every living being life comes to pass as a Self which belongs to every life and to every determination of life. Thus there is no suffering which might be nobody's suffering. Because God is Life, one must effectively say with Meister Eckhart: 'God engenders himself as myself [*Dieu s'engendre comme moi-même*]'[7] – an abyssal affirmation which suffices to dismiss all the various 'crises of subject' of contemporary nihilism. However, since the latter not only conceives of life as anonymous but also as unconscious, so then, taken in once again by the Greek *phainomenon* which reserves manifestation to the light of exteriority, modernity proves incapable of grasping the invisible in its proper phenomenological positivity.

What does this phenomenological positivity consist in? Consider suffering once more. We said that suffering reveals suffering, but this proposition must be corrected. The auto-revelation of suffering which is accomplished in suffering cannot be the fact of suffering considered in its particular content; it is true that it is accomplished just as well in joy, boredom, anguish or effort. It is in its affectivity in reality that anguish is revealed to itself, in this pathetic auto-impressionality which constitutes the flesh of this suffering as of every other modality of life. This is the reason why these are all affective modalities. There is here, according to the inspired intuition of Maine de Biran, a 'feeling of effort' such that it is only in the trouble of this effort or in its

---

7 Meister Eckhart, 'Sermon no. 6' in *Traités et sermons* (Paris: Aubier, 1942), p. 146.

satisfaction that any form of action is possible, not as an objective displacement which is itself unconscious, but through its affectivity. This affectivity does not designate any particular sphere of our life, it penetrates and founds as a last resort the entire domain of action, of 'work' and thus of economic phenomena, which consequently cannot be separated from the realm of human existence, as it is believed possible to do today.

In the same way, finally, there is a pathos of thought which explains the privilege accorded by classical philosophy to obviousness, to matters that seem self-evident. It is easy to recognize behind this privileging of the self-evident the reign of the visible which dominates the development of our culture, which remains a prisoner of Greek *theoria*. However, the fact is that thought, including rational thought, is only ever given to itself in the pathetic auto-revelation of life, and even Husserl himself, despite his effort to found phenomenological method upon the visibility of the self-evident, had to admit that 'the consciousness which judges a mathematical "state of things" is an impression'.[8]

Against Husserl, then, let us acknowledge the decisive fact that all modalities of life, those of theoretical and cognitive thought no less than others, are affective at their root, and this is because the phenomenological matter in which pure phenomenality originally phenomenalizes is itself an Archi-passibility; every 'self-experiencing' only becomes possible through this Archi-passibility. In John's words, God is not only Life, he is Love. Thus an essential connection is set up between the pure fact of living and Affectivity.

If our various tonalities find their ultimate possibility in the essence of life, it follows in the first instance that they can never be explained solely from the worldly events that we interpret as their 'motives' or 'causes'. We say 'a misfortune has occurred'. This signifies that an objective event – accident, illness, bereavement – has produced a feeling of suffering in a being that is susceptible to suffering, i.e. a living being given to itself in a life

---

8 Husserl, *Leçons*, p. 124.

whose essence is Archi-passibility. Yet why should such a senti-
ment take on the form of this affective tonality rather than
another? How can we fail to notice here that all the modalities
of our life are divided up according to a decisive dichotomy
between modalities lived as positive – impressions of pleasure
or of happiness – and modalities said to be negative – impressions of pain or of sadness? As a result, our entire existence
seems caught in an affective becoming which is not in the least
bit indeterminate, ceaselessly oscillating between malaise and
satisfaction, suffering and joy – with neutral tonalities like
boredom or indifference presenting themselves as a sort of
neutralization of this primitive oscillation.

How, then, can this dichotomy be explained if it does not
result merely from the events of the world, if instead we are
determined to locate its ultimate condition within ourselves? We
have replied to this question. In so far as the essence of 'living' is
'self-experiencing' (*s'éprouver soi-même*) in the immanence of a
pathetic auto-affection without divide or distance vis-à-vis oneself, life is marked with a radical passivity towards itself, it is a
suffering of oneself or a 'self-suffering', a 'self-enduring', a
passivity stronger than all freedom and whose presence we
have recognized in the most modest suffering which is incapable
of escaping itself, driven back to itself in a primordial passion
peculiar to every life and to every living being. It is only because
of this primitive 'suffering' which belongs to every 'self-
experiencing' as the concrete phenomenological mode of its
accomplishment that something like a 'suffering' is possible.

In the accomplishment of this 'self-suffering', however, life
experience itself, comes into it*self*, augments itself with its own
content, delights in itself – it is enjoyment, it is joy. It is clear
that these two originary and fundamental phenomenological
tonalities, a pure 'suffering' and a pure 'enjoying', root themselves a priori in the 'self-experiencing' which constitutes the
essence of every conceivable life. In its turn, the dichotomy made
manifest over the whole of our affective tonalities rests upon this
decision between the two fundamental phenomenological
tonalities. But what is thereby revealed to us, at the same time as

this most profound essence of life, is the a priori and transcendental possibility of the passing of all our tonalities each into each other. This continual slippage of our tonalities – whether it be a case of a continual transformation or of an abrupt change, of a 'leap' – is itself also discernible in the concrete becoming of our quotidian existence. Such a becoming can sometimes seem absurd and incomprehensible when subjected to the vicissitudes of a contingent history or to the palsy of unconscious drives. Thus it was in the eyes of the poet Verlaine when, casting his gaze over the whole of his past existence, he wrote this disillusioned line: 'Old good fortunes, old misfortunes, like a line of geese . . . [*Vieux bonheurs, vieux malheurs, comme une file d'oies . . .*].'[9]

This impression appears superficial, however, once we understand that this potential modification of out multiple modalities is inscribed in an originary possibility of the passage each into each other of the fundamental phenomenological tonalities belonging to the essence of life. And this is because pure suffering is the concrete phenomenological mode according to which the coming of life into itself accomplishes itself, its embracing of itself in pure enjoying and thus the possibility of every conceivable form of happiness and joy, something which in the final reckoning is never anything other than *joie de vivre*, the limitless happiness of existing.

Considered in their specific phenomenological content, suffering and joy are assuredly different, in the same way as are malaise and satisfaction, desire and gratification. It is even this difference, the will to substitute positive modalities for negative modalities, which most often determines action, and this from its most elementary forms (like the immediate impulse of every need to satisfy itself). However, despite their difference and sometimes their violent opposition, suffering and joy as well as their multiple modalizations are united in a more originary

---

9 P. Verlaine, 'Ô vous, comme un qui boite au loin, Cahgrins et Joies', *Sagesse* in *Oeuvres poétiques complètes*, ed. Y.-G. Le Dantec and J. Borel (Paris: Gallimard, 'Pléiade', 1962), p. 247.

identity, which is that of the co-constituent suffer*ing* and enjoy-*ing* of the essence of life and its ipseity.

In order to grasp this most originary identity, however, we must not lose sight of the finitude of our own life, we must perceive our life in its Foundation, i.e. no longer in that place where it seems to us that it experiences itself in a sort of psychological facticity always incapable of recognizing itself, but instead where it is given to itse*lf* in the auto-donation of absolute life, in the place of our transcendental birth. Such was the inspired intuition of Kierkegaard when he understood that it is at the peak of his suffering, at the limit of his despair, that this despair inverts itself into beatitude, when, as he puts it, 'the self plunges through its own transparency into the power which establishes it'.[10]

From the Archi-passivity of absolute Life there further follows that most singular character of the human condition, which is being an incarnated existence. Because the latter is immediately interpreted as an existence in a body it refers us back to the question of the body which, like every fundamental question, refers us in its turn to a phenomenological foundation, that is, to a mode of appearing. Now, the mode of appearing which presents itself here as being evidently that of the body is the appearing of the world, and this in two senses. On the one hand, every body, whether it be our own body or any other body, shows itself to us in the world, taking its phenomenological properties from the phenomenological properties of the world, and first and foremost its very exteriority. However, this worldly body is not only 'exterior', it is a body furnished with several sensual qualities. This means that this body which is seen, touched, heard, etc. presupposes a second body, a transcendental body, which feels it, which sees it, which touches it, which hears it, etc., thanks to the powers of its different senses. In the phenomenology of the twentieth century these powers are understood as so many intentionalities, in such a way that the transcendental body which constitutes the universe is an

---

10 S. Kierkegaard, *Traité du désespoir* (Paris: Gallimard, 1949), p. 64.

intentional body. It is in this second sense that *our* body is a body of the world, in this sense that it opens us to this world itself. The appearing upon which this opening to the world rests is the same as that in which the body-object of the philosophical tradition shows itself to us; it remains in both cases the 'outside of self' as such. Only, as we have seen, the intentionality which causes every thing to be seen (*qui fait voir*) is incapable of bringing itself into phenomenality. This aporia upon which Husserlian phenomenology came to founder is repeated in respect of the body reduced to the intentional body. Each of these features of this transcendental body can only give us that which it gives – seeing, touching, hearing . . . – if it gives itself originally to itself in the giving that it accomplishes. An immanent auto-donation of this type only happens, however, in life, in its pathetic auto-revelation.

Only in this way can we overturn our conception of the body: when we understand that the appearing to which it is consigned is no longer that of the world, but precisely in the fact that this body which is ours differs completely from other bodies which people the universe, it is no longer a visible body but a flesh – an invisible flesh. For in so far as flesh finds its phenomenological foundation in life, it takes from this latter all of its phenomenological properties. It is characterized not only by acosmism and invisibility – which themselves suffice radically to distinguish flesh from the 'body' of the philosophical tradition – but also by this fact, this small fact: that all flesh is the flesh of someone. All flesh is someone's, not just on account of a contingent liaison, but for this essential reason that since a Self is implicated in every auto-revelation of life, it erects itself in all flesh at the same time as life, in the very event which gives life to it*self* – in its transcendental birth. In every respect a tributary of life, flesh takes from this latter its own reality, this pure phenomenological matter of auto-impressionality which is indistinguishable from that of pathetic auto-affection. Flesh is very precisely the pure phenomenological matter of every genuine (i.e. radically immanent) auto-affection, in which life experiences itself pathetically. It is only because flesh is the phenomenological matter of auto-impressionality (which derives its possibility of auto-affection from life) that it finds itself constituting the reality of the whole of our impressions.

Our life, however, is finite life.

Our finite life is only comprehensible on the basis of the infinite life in which it is given to it*self*. Just as our Self, incapable of bringing itself into itself, refers back to the First Living Self, to the Word in which absolute life reveals itself to itself, so too in the same way the auto-impressionality which renders possible every impression and every flesh presupposes the Archi-passibility of absolute life (i.e. the originary capacity to bring itself into itself in the mode of a pathetic phenomenological effectuation). It is only in the Archi-passibility that all flesh is passable, which is to say that it is possible in its turn – this flesh which is nothing other than that: the possibility of a finite life which draws its possibility for the Archi-passibility of infinite Life.

This is where the phenomenology of life can defend its claim that it is able to escape the domain of philosophical tradition. Is it not capable of illuminating certain decisive elements of our culture that belong to its non-Greek source, notably Judaeo-Christian spirituality? Precisely to the extent that all flesh is only given to it*self*, in the Archi-passibility of life, the phenomenology of life unveils the singular link which establishes itself between the two initiatory declarations which mark the famous Prologue of John: 'In the beginning was the Word', 'And the Word was made flesh' (John 1.1–14). We have already explained the first declaration, if it is true that no life is possible which does not imply in itself the Self in which it experiences itself. And if, coming now to the second expression, all flesh is only passible in the Archi-passibility of life in its Word, then the incarnation of the Word ceases to seem absurd, as it seemed in the eyes of the Greeks. On the contrary, we must recognize between Word and flesh much more than an affinity – rather an identity of essence which is nothing other than that of absolute Life. As soon as flesh is given over to life, it ceases to be this objective body with its strange forms, with its incomprehensible sexual determination, apt to arouse our anguish, delivered to the world, indefinitely subjected to the question 'why?' For as Meister Eckhart understood, life is without why. The flesh which carries in it the principle of its own revelation does not ask for any other authority to illuminate itself. When in its innocence each modality of our flesh experiences itself, when suffering says suffering and joy says joy, it is Life that speaks in it, and nothing has power against its word.

This Archi-passibility beyond all passibility but present in it, immanent in all flesh as that which gives it to itself, beyond all sensible or intelligible evidence, what can it be called if not an Archi-intelligibility, an Archi-gnosis whose essence John describes as the coming of absolute Life in the Word (before it makes possible the coming of the Word in a flesh similar to our own)? Thus Johannine Archi-intelligibility is implied everywhere that there is life, it reaches out even to these beings of flesh that we are, taking up in its incandescent Parousia our derisory sufferings and our hidden wounds, as it did the wounds of Christ on the cross. The more purely does each of our sufferings happen with us, the more each suffering is reduced to itself, to its phenomenological body of flesh, so the more strongly we experience in ourselves the limitless power which gives suffering to itself. And when this suffering reaches its limit point, in despair, then, as Kierkegaard puts it, 'the self plunges through its own transparency into the power which established it', and the intoxication of life submerges us. Happy are those who suffer. In the Depths of its Night, our flesh is God. The Archignosis is the gnosis of the simple (*la gnose des simple*).

12. Suspending the Natural Attitude: Transcendence and Immanence from Thomas Aquinas to Michel Henry[1]

CONOR CUNNINGHAM

Glauben ist Sein.
Franz Kafka

Against the temptations presented by what Edmund Husserl calls the natural attitude, we shall argue that only in being thought by God, only in being called by God into existence, and thus being, and so inhabiting the *recollection* of this call, is life possible.

On such a view, being and event, every happening and all existence, requires already to have been in order to be. Otherwise we have what we might call an ontology of *collection*; one that is predicated on the existence of some basic 'stuff', a given, into which we plunge our thoughts, like blades, or arrest with stiff concepts: either Swiss cheese with holes, or a flux with temporary forms of stability cast across its flow. And examples of such 'stuff' range from Thales' water, to Descartes' *res extensa*, and indeed, more recently, DNA, but most importantly for us here, being – *esse* – itself. Though we won't deal with this here, it is arguable that both models involve violence.[2]

---

1 I would like to thank Rudi te Velde and Patrick Riches for very helpful comments on an earlier draft of this paper.

For a list of abbreviations used in the text here, please see p. 287.

2 See C. Cunningham, 'Nothing Is, Something Must Be: Lacan and Creation from No One' in C. Davis, J. Milbank and S. Zizek (eds),

St Thomas Aquinas posits the paradox of being: *life as lived recollection*. In articulating *life as lived recollection* Thomas situates his theology of the paradox of being in remarkable continuity with the patristic Fathers, a continuity continued after him by figures such as Meister Eckhart, Nicholas of Cusa and, perhaps more controversially, Michel Henry. We can consider being in this way, because the radical nature of a Creator requires us to see our being as not belonging to us essentially: our being as 'begged-being', as it were,[3] our being, in itself, is nothing.

In Thomistic terms, this is the real distinction between a creature's essence and its existence, thus each creature remains 'exterior to itself', as Joseph de Finance puts it.[4] Later we will develop some crucial consequences that arise from this ontological *ecstasis*. Returning to the point in hand, any such recollection, or recalling, is not a denigration of nature, or creatures, but quite the reverse. For it is indeed a protective measure, as shall be argued below. Having our being, therefore, only in terms of recollection, rather than collection, precludes ownership; instead we receive that which we are. Consequently, our lives are then understood to be the gift of borrowed existence.

For Aquinas, in terms of the rational soul, this borrowing of existence can rise to the point in which it participates not only in being, by way of its first act, but in terms of operation, in a second perfecting act that invites us into God's self-knowledge. In this regard, Aquinas employs the distinction of *finis operis* ('end of the work') and *finis operantis* ('end of the worker'). This distinction signals both the form of the creature and the proper operation of that form, which completes it, as such, for it speaks of the perfection God intends for the creature.

Theology and the Political (Durham, NC and London: Duke University Press, 2005), pp. 72–101.

3 See Cardinal C. Journet, *Entretiens sur le Mystère chrétien* (Broché, 1988), I: 148.

4 See J. de Finance, *Être et agir dans la philosophie de Saint Thomas* (Paris: Beauchesne, 1945), p. 151, n. 1.

Similarly, Aquinas plays on the ambiguity of the Vulgate's language with regard to Genesis 1.26–27. For, there it reads that man is made 'to the image of God' (*ad imaginem*), and not 'in the image of God', as the King James Version does.[5] We shall return to this dynamic sense of ontology below. What is important for us at this point is to realize that in owning nothing we receive all. Crucially, it is for this reason that Michel Henry echoes the Gospel according to St Luke, wherein we are told that the poor are blessed, for it is they who will receive the kingdom of God.[6] Conversely, to collect being is to haemorrhage all form, and thus lose all objects, indeed materiality itself dissolves in the wake of the endless pursuit of more, which is, of course, a bid for self-possession. Like the prodigal son who demands his part, and so loses all in ruination, as against the son who remains, and to whom it is disclosed by his father: 'Son, thou art always with me, and all I have is thine' (Luke 15.31) – in this way, the Father's is an unbroken good, and that is why you cannot have a 'part', for there is no 'stuff', or *tertium quid*, that would allow for division. Importantly, we suggest that the two sons are the same person, doing so because the second son employs the same logic of possession.[7]

Such possession can indeed appear in how we understand God and it is this form of idolatry that Meister Eckhart brings to our attention in the following quote: 'Therefore I pray to God that he may make me free of God.'[8] What Eckhart here

---

5 The Greek of the Septuagint (*kat' eikona*) accommodates this reading, as it allows for a sense of being 'according to the image', while the Hebrew *be-selem* is less forgiving, as it suggests a sense of place, thus one would be 'in the image'.

6 See M. Henry, *I am the Truth: Toward a Philosophy of Christianity*, tr. S. Emanuel (Stanford: Stanford University Press, 2003), p. 215; also see Luke 6.20.

7 See, A Monk of the West, *Christianity and the Doctrine of Non-Dualism*, tr. A. Moore and M. Hansen (Hillsdale, NY: Sophia Perennis, 2004), p. 27.

8 Meister Eckhart, *Essential Sermons, Commentaries, Treatises and Defence*, tr. and ed. E. Colledge and B. McGinn (London: SPCK, 1981), p. 202.

signals is the radical nature of Christian orthodoxy, one that we might profitably refer to as Christian non-dualism, to employ Vladimir Lossky's phrase.[9] Such an understanding helps to bring to the fore what are arguably our own idolatrous modes of thinking, and so to understand more concretely what it might mean to 'have faith'; that is, be faithful rather than merely believe in God. Indeed it might turn out that this notion of 'belief' is very much at the heart of our problem.

Why? Well for many reasons. Let us take two. The first is that belief in God is somewhat derivative, or secondary. When we ask, do you believe in God? – the form that this takes, presumes that in the absence of an intelligent, and free Creator, existence is an unproblematic concept. In strict terms, consequently, the question of whether God exists is misdirected, to say the least. For even if the answer came back positively, we would have to be cautious in accepting this as a good thing, because the god that is now said to exist seems to be something of a straw-divinity, so to speak, maybe more Homeric than Abrahamic.

So, we have to realize that belief in God's existence presumes belief, which is maybe a flaw of classical theism – for only God can gift faith, for only God gifts the believer, too.[10] In other words, belief cannot be understood as a discreet act, analogous to an object – thus it cannot, as it were, be collected. In connection with this, we see that talk about the existence of a transcendent God is in some sense illusory; or rather it is somewhat epiphenomenal. It is, because talk of God in this way tends to provide a realm for the formation of nature, or of the natural subject, over and against the supernatural, and so on. In this way, the god that we must be rid of is in fact the autonomous subject, who, rather comfortably, rests upon the implied

---

9 See V. Lossky, *Théologie negative et connaissance de Dieu chez Maître Eckhart* (Paris: Vrin, 1973), p. 263. Also, see S. Grant, *Toward an Alternative Theology: Confessions of a Non-Dualist Christian* (Indiana: University of Notre Dame Press, 2002).

10 As Henry says, 'Only God can make us believe in him, but he inhabits our own flesh', *I am the Truth*, p. 233; we shall return to a discussion of flesh below.

significance of solidity – the firm ground beneath their feet that neither needs, nor is affected by, their belief or non-belief in God. Thus theism's articulation of what God is, or what belief in God might be has in some sense accommodated, if not encouraged, the formation or positing of a pure nature: what Cardinal Cajetan called a 'closed whole'.[11] And of course from this position issues forth all the questions about divine intervention, and the now seemingly immiscible relationship between transcendence and immanence, for God now has to enter an alien domain, or so it would seem – and in so doing, becomes not simply supernatural, but unnatural.

Now, Aquinas of course does speak about the existence of God, quite rightly too, but he does so only within certain contexts. As Thomas says:

> To know in a general and confused way that God exists is implanted in us by nature since God is the ultimate happiness of human beings; for a human naturally desires happiness and what is naturally desired by a person must be naturally known to him. This, however, is not to know absolutely that God exists, just as knowing that someone is approaching is not the same as knowing that Peter is approaching even though it is Peter approaching; for there are many who imagine that the perfect good of human beings, which is happiness, consists in riches, and others in pleasures and others in something else. (*STh* I, q. 2, a. 1, ad. 1)

In this way, belief in God does not rule out utter misunderstanding. As the following passage from St Paul's letter to the Romans makes clear:

> For what can be known about God is plain to them, because God has shown it to them. Ever since the creation of the world his eternal power and divine nature, invisible though they are,

---

11 Cardinal Cajetan, *In Primam*, q. 12, a. 1, n. 10, quoted in H. de Lubac, *The Mystery of the Supernatural*, tr. R. Sheed (New York: Crossroad Herder, 1998), p. 140.

have been understood and seen through the things he has made. So they are without excuse; for though they knew God, they did not honour him as God or give thanks to him, but they became futile in their thinking, and their senseless minds were darkened. Claiming to be wise they became fools, and they exchanged the glory of God for images resembling a mortal human being or birds or four footed animals or reptiles. (Rom 1.19–23)

From this we can understand that belief in God, belief in the divine can indeed frustrate faith. This of course supports the thesis that belief is less than univocal. Indeed Aquinas makes the point that belief in God is indeed equivocal. For instance he tells us: 'To believe is said equivocally of the human faithful and devils, faith is not in devils from some infused light of grace; as it is in the human faithful' (*De Ver.* 14.9, ad. 4.); thus the book of James (2.19) tells us: 'Thou believest that there is one God; thou doest well: the devils also believe and tremble.' Aquinas also makes the point, one that echoes the passage from Romans, that 'Perhaps not everyone who hears this word "God" understands it to signify something than which nothing greater can be thought, since some have believed God to be a body' (*STh* I, q. 2, a. 1, ad. 2). And it should be said that what this Anselmian phrase means is not straightforward, because our theological and philosophical imaginations, due to our seduction by the natural attitude, tend to settle on a conception that is often misguided, if not idolatrous, for example, we might consider this greatness in terms of power – power being understood in rather voluntaristic terms, terms that are articulated in the ability to suspend at will an apparently natural order. Against this understanding, Aquinas speaks of the 'dignity of causality' being granted to creatures (*STh* I, q. 24, a. 8, ad. 2). We will return to the question of the ontological status of nature and creatures later, but what we should note for the moment is that if we conceive God in terms of power, we have managed to reduce God to our own level. For the simple reason that divinity becomes a matter of something that I cannot do –

suspend the natural order – rather than it being about someone I am not. The former logically includes me by default – I can't do it, but that inability is not logically impossible, while the former is nonsensical: Peter cannot be Paul – hence it is indeed crucial to know who indeed is arriving over the hill.

Returning to the question of belief, as already indicated, belief can be opposed to faith, as the passage from the Gospel of Matthew (7.21–23) illustrates in stark terms:

> Not everyone who says to me, 'Lord, Lord', shall enter the kingdom of heaven . . . On that day many will say to me: 'Lord, Lord, did we not prophesy in your name, and cast our demons in your name, and do many mighty works in your name?' And then I will declare to them, 'I never knew you; depart from me, you evildoers.'

Or in other words, belief in God is not salvific; it is not, because for Thomas there is no such thing as generic belief. Faith is instead a technical term, having more to do with virtue than the mere assent to a set of propositions. But what is important to realize is that this situation arises from the very nature of Thomas' God, a God who is pure actuality ('Deus est Purus actus', *STh* I, q. 25, a. 2, ad. 1), and who creates out of infinite goodness, doing so because of the natural desire to share that goodness (for instance, see *ScG* I, c. 86, n. 718; *STh* I, q. 44, a. 1, ad. 1). Now, this means that all univocity is disabled. It is, because the very terms arrive with the discussion, as it were. Consequently, God is not simply an inverted form of us. Aquinas tells us in the *Summa Theologiae* that 'We must first ask if God exists; then how he is or how he is not; we must then enquire into his operations, his knowledge, his will and power' (*STh* I, q. 2). The problem here being for us twofold: first, the modern mind tends to stop the process of inquiry at the establishment of existence, it either is or it is not – the rhetoric of efficient causality left on its own, without any notion of finality, which for Aquinas is the cause of causes (*causa causarum*, see *STh* I, q. 5, a. 2, ad. 1); and, second, even if one does proceed to ask about God's knowledge etc., the terms employed tend to assume the pretence of being purely philosophical, which means that a form of the previous problem remains, namely, generic belief in God, and thus our philosophical description of God, assumes a unilateral form: from us to God, and this again raises the problem of univocity.

This comes out well when Thomas explains why we have revelation or, more accurately, why knowledge of the Trinity is necessary:

> In one way it was necessary for the right idea of creation. By saying that God made all things by his Word, we exclude the error of those who say that God produced things by necessity. When we say that in him there is a procession of love, we know that God produced creatures not because he needed them, nor because of any other intrinsic cause, but on account of the love of his own goodness . . . [Revelation is also needed so we can] think rightly concerning the salvation of the human race. (*STh* I, q. 32. ad. 3)

In other words, a proper doctrine of creation requires a correlative understanding of creation and soteriology: they are inextricably linked. And here, crucial to this point, is the understanding of God's triunity and simplicity, the fact of the divine Trinity being wholly Simple: for the correlation of creation and soteriology analogically participate within this uncreated correlation of triunity and simplicity, this radical understanding of non-discrete difference. And so the latter helps us understand the former.

According to Thomas, 'God's relation to the creation is understood as a purely conceptual relation, while the creature's relation to God is real' (*STh* I, q. 45, a. 3, ad. 1); or again, 'Every relation which we consider between God and the creature is really in the creature, by whose change the relation is brought into being; whereas it is not really in God, but only in our way of thinking, since it does not arise from any change in God' (*STh* III, q. 2, a. 7; see also, *STh* I, q. 28, a. 1, ad. 3; *STh* I, q. 6,

a. 2, ad. 1). With regard to the question of change, Aquinas expands on this elsewhere, saying:

> Creation is not a true change, but is a certain relation of the created thing, as a being that is dependent on the Creator for its existence and that connotes succession to previous non-existence. In every change there must be something that remains the same although it undergoes alteration in its manner of being . . . In creation this does not take place in objective reality, but only in our imagination. (*Comp. Theol.* 99; also see, *ScG* II, c. 18, n. 952).

So we now know that God does not act out of necessity, and, also, God's actions involve no change in God – of course, it cannot, because for Thomas God is devoid of potentiality, thus it is impossible for God to change. This divine simplicity, or, in other words, pure actuality, is reflected in the fact that creation is not itself a change, because if creation were indeed a change, then God's action would operate against something extrinsic, a background, as it were. This being the case, God's identity would involve potentiality; moreover, any such potentiality would cast into doubt what indeed was irreducibly God and what was creature. By way of analogy, Aquinas tell us, 'If evil exists, God exists' (*ScG* III, pt. 1, c. 71, n. 10). God as simple, infinite Goodness affords the conceptual space for us to speak about evil, but if God were not pure Goodness, or if God were impotent for a moment, with regard to suffering, say, then we could not in truth pick out evil or suffering (indeed we could not even locate the incarnation), because the terms would be set adrift within a univocal plane that would prohibit any such discernment.

When Aquinas argues that God did not create through necessity he of course precludes a deity cast in the mould of Spinoza's Substance. In addition, when we understand that creation is not a change, we leave a Feuerbachian God behind – because we are no longer employing domestic concepts – as we do when, for example, we speak of generic belief. Here it is important to realize that for Aquinas there are three distinct types of belief with regard to God. First of all, there is 'believe in God' (*credere Deum*), in other words, one would believe in God's existence. Second, one might 'believe God' (*credere Deo*), that is, one trusts God. Lastly, and importantly, Aquinas also uses the notion of *credere in Deum*, and in line with his understanding of the *imago Dei*, being a matter of 'to the image', we might think of this last form of belief as one that is also toward God, just as a creation for Aquinas, is not an 'in-itself', but an ecstatic being-toward God (*esse ad creatorum*; see *STh* I, q. 45, a.3). Indeed it is for this reason that theology is not interested as such in the creature *in se*, but only as it is in relation to both its principle and end, namely, God; consequently, this being-toward God is being toward-being (*ad esse*). Just as Aquinas's Christology is a characteristically high Christology, so too his metaphysics can be characterized as a high metaphysic.

Creation is a relation with God. And this relation is not in God but rather in our understanding, our imagination. To substantiate this claim we should perhaps recall that Aquinas speaks of three types of relation. Logical (*rationis relatio*), or according to reason (*secundum rationem*), when the relation is only in the mind, and real, when the terms themselves cause the relationship. Both real and logical relations are mutual. But the third type is asymmetrical, and this is called a mixed relation. In such cases one term is logical and one is real. According to Thomas, this 'happens whenever two extremes are not in the same order' (*STh* I, q. 13, a. 8). With regard to God and creation, the former is the logical relation, while the latter is the real relation. This being the case we can maybe see how the idea of recollection is useful, because if creation were a change, for instance, then we could in some sense collect it, as it would occupy a discreet moment. But if there is no change in God, then any linear sequence of (efficient) causality is rendered impossible. Thus, it is better to think of God's simplicity in terms of recollection. God creates, acts and causes difference through himself and the metaphor of recollection is mindful of this. This will be developed below.

Before it is, let us very briefly clarify the relation between philosophy and theology, with regard to God. The problem is that God is too different, or is the very possibility of difference itself, in so far as he is pure act. Consequently, God is unthinkable in general terms. But not only does God invent the terms we might employ – the concepts we would be inclined to use, but existence, with all its rocks and moss, all its mud and clouds is the manifestation of God's goodness, and as such it is a personal, original and free communication of that essential goodness. As Aquinas says, 'All creatures are compared to God as artifacts to an artist. Whence the whole of nature is like a certain artifact of the divine nature' (*ScG* III, c. 100). Consequently, our imaginations fail, depending instead on *sacra doctrina*, as already suggested. Yet, on the other hand, if theology were simply to abandon philosophy it would be left with a less than satisfactory historical positivism: we would collect historical data, as opposed to collecting philosophical concepts. Moreover, a sufficient articulation of *sacra doctrina* requires philosophy. Rejecting either the subsumption of theology by philosophy, or a fideistic rejection of philosophy, we must employ natural reason for the use of theology, doing so for fear of once again establishing a dubious dualism of nature and grace. As Aquinas is keen to tell us, 'Grace does not destroy nature, it perfects it' (*STh* I, q. 1, a. 8, ad. 2); and Eckhart echoes this exactly, 'For God is not a destroyer of nature; rather he perfects it.'[12] Yet the language of perfection does not suggest a univocal continuum, but instead an analogical consonance. Thomas expands on this:

> The gifts of grace are added to nature in such a way that they do not destroy it, but rather perfect it. So too the light of faith, which is imparted to us as a gift, does not do away with the light of natural reason given to us by God. Rather, since what is imperfect becomes a representation of what is perfect,

---

12 Meister Eckhart, quoted in B. McGinn, *The Mystical Union of Meister Eckhart* (New York: Crossroad, 2001), p. 66.

what we know by natural reason has some likeness to what is taught to us by faith. (*In De Trin.* 2.3. *responsio*)

And why, we might ask, does natural reason bear a likeness? Quite simply, as Aquinas says, 'We see everything in God and judge everything by him in the sense that it is by participating in his light that we are able to see and judge, for the natural light of reason is a sort of participation in the divine light' (*STh* I, q. 12, a. 11, ad. 3). What is important for us is the notion that to abandon philosophy, or natural reason, or to be able to locate a pure theology, is to perpetrate a similar error of locating a pure philosophy.[13] Analogously, Aquinas feels free to speak of God creating in terms of his will, but also to speak in terms of emanation (see *STh* I, q. 45, a. 1), doing so in a bid to include God's very nature, otherwise a univocity hides in our simple rejection of emanation terminology. It does, because we fear it for bad reasons of our own, in other words, we are still entertaining a less than satisfactory understanding of Creator and creatures, that is, we still think that what is other than God is something that can be collected, as it is external, or discrete, either spatially or temporally. If Augustine tells us to 'love, and do as we will', Aquinas, in a sense, tells us to love, and philosophize as we will. So the likeness that natural reason bears is itself a recollection of God's reason, God's self-knowledge, for how could it be otherwise – there being no pure nature. And what we will see is crucial is that

> Effects proceed from an efficient cause because they pre-exist there; every agent enacts its like. Now effects pre-exist in a cause according to its mode of being. Since, then, God's being is his actual understanding, creatures *pre-exist* then as in his mind, and so as being comprehended, do they proceed from him. (*STh* I, q. 19, a. 4; see also, *In de Div. Nom.* V, ii, 662)

---

13 Cf. C. Cunningham, *Genealogy of Nihilism* (London and New York: Routledge, 2002), pp. 273–4.

From this quote we can see that natural reason bears a resemblance to faith, because God, as an intelligent agent, creates according to his own similitude, therefore all that is bears the imprint of that likeness. Moreover, in terms of recollection – reason recalls faith, doing so, because reason recalls its maker – something it is able to do, because its very existence rests with divine pre-existence. We can see that in relation to God, faith cannot abandon reason – or theology, philosophy, but in utilizing it, it becomes transformed. As Aquinas says: 'Those who use philosophical texts in sacred teaching, by subjecting them to faith, do not mix water with wine, but turn water into wine' (*In De Trin.* 2.4, ad. 5). Indeed Aquinas says that 'It is necessary that natural reason be subservient to faith' (*STh* I, q. 1, a. 8, ad. 2). Why must it be? Well, as Rudi te Velde has said, 'If reason were justified in its claim to autonomy the only way Christianity could affirm its faith would be by rejecting reason.'[14] For such autonomy would then become a counterfeit God, so to speak,[15] as it would offer itself as a competitor. But also, reason left to its own cannot cope with what is most fundamental in life. This is why we see a great deal of philosophy do away with many phenomena, rather than remain in a state of unknowing with regard to their possibility, and the complexity of their existence. From consciousness to colour, we witness a wholesale cull in the name of parsimony – the economy being here one of philosophy's own ability. The consequences of leaving reason to itself are epitomized by the philosophy of Paul Churchland – an advocate of eliminative materialism – who says: 'Could it turn out that nobody has ever believed anything?'[16] Here we see why we cannot simply ask philosophy if it believes in the existence of God, when it does not even believe in belief! It is little surprise, then, when Aquinas says, 'If the

---

14 R. te Velde, 'Natural Reason in the Summa Contra Gentiles', *Medieval Philosophy and Theology* 4 (1994), pp. 42–70, at p. 58.

15 On the notion of a counterfeit God, see W. Desmond, *Hegel's God: A Counterfeit Double?* (London: Ashgate, 2003).

16 P. Churchland, *Matter and Consciousness* (Cambridge, MA: MIT Press, rev. edn, 1988), p. 43.

only way open to us for the knowledge of God were solely that of reason the human race would remain in the blackest shadows of ignorance' (*STh* II.ii q. 22, a. 1, ad. 1). Yet at the same time, to repeat, Aquinas does not reject the use of philosophy, but treats it like the captured woman in the book of Deuteronomy (21.10–13):

> Doctors of Sacred Scripture take from witnesses to truth wherever they may be found . . . Not that their teachings should be appropriated as a whole; the bad parts should be rejected and the good kept. Truth from whatever source is from the Holy Spirit. Deuteronomy 21 speaks figuratively about this where it says that 'if a man sees a young woman among the captives, he should trim her nails and hair; that is, cut off all that is superfluous'. (*Sup. Titum* 1.15, n. 32)

Now, at the beginning of this paper, it was suggested that all that is, only is by participating in God, who is *ipsum esse subsistens*. As Aquinas says:

> The likeness of things in the divine intellect is one which causes things; for whether a thing has a vigorous or feeble share in the act of being, it has this from God above; and because each thing participates in an act of existence given by God, the likeness of each is found in God. Consequently the immaterial likeness in God is a likeness not only of the forms but also of the matter. (*De Ver.* 2.5)

Again, we hear the term likeness. Let us unpack this notion of participation, and in doing so cast light on our notions of transcendence and immanence, and the danger of our natural attitude, with regard to being.

Because our being is not essential to us, there are two complementary ways of looking at being – complementary, because they are saying the same thing – but it is our reactions to these that determine whether it is a question of sin or faith. Because we are created, because all we have is received, it is perpetually the case that in a sense our being is always naked. In other words, we receive our existence. As Anselm says to God, 'You are in no way less, even if they should return to nothing.'[17] Eckhart echoes this: 'He could add the entire world to God and would have nothing more than if he had God alone.'[18] And Nicholas of Cusa says it in even more dramatic terms: 'It is as if an artisan's production dependent on the intention of the artisan, possessed no other existence proper to itself than that of this dependence where existence comes to it, like the image of a face in the mirror, that of itself is nothing either before or after receipt of the image.'[19] Aquinas invokes similar imagery when he refers to creation thus: 'the created things themselves are the mirror of God [*ipsae res creatae sunt speculum Dei*]' – (*De Ver.* q. 12, a. 6). This means that creatures are in a sense nothing, and both Eckhart and Aquinas concur: 'All creatures are one pure nothing. I do not say that they are a little something or anything, but that they are pure nothing';[20] 'each created thing, in that it does not have existence save from another, taken in itself, is nothing' (*STh* 1a, 2ae, q. 109, a. 2). In other words, does the fact that we participate in being, rather than have being essentially, remove the integrity of our existence, is God an ontological bully – giving with one hand while taking with the other? There are of course two possible answers to this question. Let me first take the reaction that fears this ontological nakedness, so to speak. Recall Adam and Eve in the book of Genesis. 'Then the eyes of both were opened and they knew they were naked: and they sewed fig leaves together and made loincloths for themselves' (Gen. 3.7). Maybe this understanding of nakedness causes us to hide from it; doing so perhaps in fine

---

17 St Anselm, *Proslogion*, tr. M. J. Charlesworth (1965; reprinted, Notre Dame: University of Notre Dame Press, 1979), ch. 20.

18 Meister Eckhart, *Omne datum optimum* in *Sermons*, tr. J. Anceleth-Hustache (Paris: Editions du Seuil, 1974–78), vol. 1, p. 65.

19 Nicholas of Cusa, *De Docta Ignorantia*, ch. 2.

20 Quoted in McGinn, *Mystical Union*, p. 105. Eckhart sometimes terms this nothingness of the creature *nuellitas*, but for Aquinas to be a creature means to be an actual being.

clothes, exalted position, or just the chatter of the world. And this is indeed one form of collection, rather than recollection. According to Aquinas, all the powers of the soul are in a sense lacking the order proper to them (see *De Malo* 7, 1). Indeed, he tells us that 'Every sin is contrary to nature' (*STh* I–II, q. 78, a. 3); yet he tells us, 'Every sin is rooted in a natural appetite' (*De Malo* 8, 2); it is, because 'Every sin consists in the longing for a passing good' (*STh* I–II, q. 72, a. 2); we are, it seems, borne along by the senses. And such sin gives rise to a sense of nakedness, because in seeking to find the eternal in the temporal we chase desperately and without hope – because faith is the substance of things hoped for, as the letter to the Hebrews (11.1) tells us. And it is this chase that generates the aforementioned doubt, and in so doing leads us to read creation as being devoid of the divine. Yet for Aquinas's God, there is never some rejected remainder, not even sin. For as Aquinas tells us, 'in a certain sense it is true what Socrates says, namely that no one sins with full knowledge' (*STh* I–II, q. 58, a. 2). In other words, even though we have placed our faith in the transient, we have done so in a form of good faith. As Thomas says: 'since every operation is for the sake of some real or apparent good, and nothing either is or appears to be good except insofar as it participates in some similitude of the highest Good, which is God, it follows that God himself is the cause of any operation as its end' (*STh* I, q. 105, a. 5). So in some vague sense, even the sin of presuming a pure nature as the source of what is valuable, still testifies to the transcendence that is not opposed to the temporal, or the transient, indeed quite the reverse.

If, then, we do not interpret our nakedness negatively – for as God said to both Adam and Eve, 'Who told you were naked?' – we can read it in terms of intimacy (here, I am interpreting sin in strictly ontological terms).[21] As St Augustine said of God, 'But you are deeper than my inmost being and higher than my

---

21 See C. Cunningham, 'Trying My Very Best to Believe Darwin' in C. Cunningham and P. M. Candler (eds), *Belief and Metaphysics*, Veritas Series (London: SCM Press, 2007).

own height' (*Confessions* III, 6, 11). In Thomistic terms – following the first proposition of the *Book of Causes*, which states that 'Every primary cause infuses its effect more powerfully than does a secondary cause' – Aquinas tells us:

> As long as a thing possesses being, God must be present to it, and this in a manner in which it possesses existence. Now, existence in each thing is what inheres in it most intimately and most profoundly. We must thus necessarily conclude that God is in all things, in an intimate manner. (*STh* I, q. 8)

Our nakedness then is one of intimacy – of the very relationship of immanence and transcendence, which cannot, on pain of invoking a third term, be set over and against each other. This intimacy, this non-invasive, divine concurrence, informs the world. As Aquinas tells us:

> In a way God performs all the actions of all creatures, because he gave to natural things the powers through which they can act, not only as the generating gives power to heavy and the light, yet does not conserve it as well. But God also acts as one continuously holding the powers in being. For he is the cause of the power, which has been bestowed not only as the one generating but also with respect to being. So God can be said to be the cause of action insofar as he causes and conserves natural power. (*De Pot.* 3.7)

We can now begin to see how immanence is itself the recollection of transcendence, being so because an agent produces a likeness to itself. Thus we will find the idea of an opposition between God and immanence more and more problematic, to the extent that, following Henry, we can even reverse the order: 'The essence of transcendence resides in immanence'; and any fear we feel from such a reversal will itself be a product of a misguided understanding of transcendence.[22]

---

22 M. Henry, *The Essence of Manifestation*, tr. G. Etkorn (The Hague, Netherlands: Martinus Nijhoff, 1973), p. 380.

Let us turn for a moment to a consideration of knowledge. As Aristotle tells us, 'All men by nature desire to know' (*Metaphysics* 980a, 21); indeed for Aristotle living is to be regarded as a kind of knowledge. Why must it? Well, Aquinas argues that 'God's knowledge causes things. For God's knowledge is related to all created things just as a craftsman's knowledge is related to the things he crafts' (*STh* I, q. 14, a. 8). Joseph Pieper expresses this idea well, 'Only what is thought can be called in the restricted sense "true" but real things are something thought . . . to put it more explicitly, they are real because they are thought creatively, that is, they have been fashioned by thought. The essence of things is that they are creatively thought.'[23] For Aristotle, and Aquinas following him, it is true to say that *omnis scientia bona est.*[24] This seems counterintuitive. But if we for a moment interpret knowledge ontologically, and as always being an imitation of God's Life, namely, his intellect, indeed an imitation of our very creation, then it seems a little less odd. Consequently knowledge does not collect data, but rather is an embodied recollection of divinity itself. Maybe it is for this reason that Aquinas, following Aristotle's *De Anima*, thinks that the soul is in a sense all things; or better, 'Man in a certain sense contains all things' (*STh* I, q. 96, a. 2). Why might this be true? Thomas argues that 'The human soul is a kind of horizon, and a boundary, as it were, between the corporeal world and the incorporeal world' (*In III Sent*. Pro.). Likewise, the soul 'exists on the horizon of eternity and time' (*ScG* II, c. 86, n. 12). Accordingly, the human is for Aquinas a little world (*minor mundus*). Importantly, the human is not just a horizon, but also a frontier (*horizon et continuum*) – we shall return to this below. This being the case, it recalls matter as mindful of God, so to speak. 'Above the human form in the world of generation and corruption, there is nothing more

---

23 J. Pieper, *The Silence of St. Thomas*, tr. J. Murray SJ and D. O'Connor (South Bend, IN: St Augustine's Press, 1999), p. 51.

24 This idea must, however, be set over and against the vice of *curiositas*, consequently knowledge must be accompanied by the virtue of *studiositas*.

perfect. Therefore the end of all generation is the human soul. Matter tends towards it as towards its last' (*ScG*, III, c. 22, n. 7). Consequently, for Aquinas, even prime matter bears a remote, but crucial resemblance to God, the First Cause (see *In de Div. Nom.* IV, ii, 297). Indeed, the usually maligned prime matter is said to desire the Good (see *In de Div. Nom.* IV, ii, 296).[25] Yet there is no doubt that materiality can accommodate a certain idolatry. As Aquinas tells us, the human being 'is distracted by and occupied with sensible things' (*STh* I, q. 94, a. 1). Moreover, sensible objects are the 'chief impediment to the contemplation of God . . . since they plunge the human being very deep into sensible things, consequently distracting her from intelligible objects' (*ScG* III, c. 27, n. 10). But crucially, this ability to distract is itself a sign of the Good:

> In themselves, creatures do not turn us from God, but lead us to Him . . . If they turn men from God, it is the fault of those who use them foolishly . . . And from the very fact that they can thus withdraw us from God proves that they came from Him, for they cannot attract men except by the good found in them and that they have from Him. (*STh* I, q. 65, a. 1, ad. 3)

Hence just as man, as we already know, is made 'to the image of God' (*ad imaginem*) and to the creator (*esse ad creatorum*), so are all things. Hence, as Max Seckler warns us, nature is the very 'domain of operation [*Wirkbereich*] of Grace', thus it must not be thought of as a 'counter-concept [*Gegenbegriff*] to grace but the correlative of grace, [thus it is] created towards grace'.[26] Again, for Thomas, there is no remainder, ontologically speaking – neither sin, nor matter resides outside the divine economy. Thus according to Aquinas:

---

25 On the positivity of prime matter, see C. Fabro, *Participation et Causalité selon S. Thomas d'Aquin* (Louvain: Publications Universitaires, 1961), pp. 413–16.

26 M. Seckler, 'Das Heil der Nichtevangelisierten in thomistischer Sicht', *Theologische Quartalschrift* 140.1 (1960), pp. 38–69, at p. 68.

It is clear that nature is a certain kind of divine art impressed upon things, by which these things are moved to a determinate end. It is as if a shipbuilder were able to give to timbers that by which they would themselves move to take the form of a ship. (*In II Phys.* 14, 268)

If immanence, as a reflection of divine art, is a distended act of recollection (indeed for Henry, transcendence is itself only remembered in immanence), then consequently we have nothing to collect, nothing to possess; here Eckhart's notion of an appropriate detachment (*abgeschiedenheit*) towards things is relevant. This situation is intensified when we realize that the simple 'procession of the divine persons are the cause of creation' (*STh* I, q. 45, a. 6, ad. 1; see also *STh* I, q. 33, a. 3); or indeed, that 'All processions and multiplications of creatures is caused by the procession of the distinct divine persons' (*In I Sent.* d. 26, q. 2.2, see also *In I Sent.* d. 14, q. 2). And, of course, such processions are intransitive, that is, they do not shed their simplicity – for the economic Trinity is in some sense another name for creation, which is itself, if we recall, only real for us, only a change in our imagination, our very lives being the recollection of the divine life: *Esse est similitudo Dei*. Thus, for Henry, our lives are themselves the auto-revelation of divine, transcendental ipseity.[27]

Two aspects regarding immanence come to the fore when we consider knowledge. First of all, as Aquinas says, 'We are not capable of knowing what God is, but we can know what he is not' (*STh* I, q. 3, Pro.). In addition he tells us: 'This is what is ultimate in human knowledge of God: to know that we do not know God' (*De Pot.*, q. 7, a. 5, ad. 14). But again the agent causes its likeness, for immanence reflects this incomprehension, one that actually arises, however paradoxically, from knowability. As Thomas tells us: 'The essential ground of things are unknown to us. We do not even know the substantial forms as they are in themselves' (*In de Anima* I, 1, n. 15); thus

---

27 See Henry, *I am the Truth*, p. 121.

'We do not even know the essence of a fly' (*In symbolum Apostolourum, scilicet 'Credo in Deum'*, exposition, prol. 864). He goes on elsewhere to say that 'Created things are darkness in so far as they proceed from nothing' (*De Ver*. q. 18, a. 2, ad. 5). Yet he is in agreement with the author of the *Book of Causes*, which stipulates that, 'The measure of the reality of a thing is the measure of its light' (*Liber de Causis*, prop. 1.6). How can we resolve what appears to be a contradiction? If we use another quote from Pieper, things may become clearer: 'things are so utterly knowable that we can never come to the end of our endeavours to know them. It is precisely their knowability that is inexhaustible.'[28] Hence we can see that immanence's darkness, its unknowability, is caused by its knowability – this, then reflects God, who is most knowable, yet incomprehensible, even in the Beatific vision. Immanence is again the recollection of its maker, who is so close (for *nihili est distans ab Deo*), that we cannot fix our gaze – the proverbial blinding light – though ontologically speaking an apt description. Accordingly, for Henry, we cannot know God because that would be to make God into an object, which would be to presuppose that God is simply otherwise than us, or that we are otherwise than God. In this way the ultimate distance is the impossibility of distance, the very revelation of which is the incarnation, in so far as Christ is the only true human (see below).

All Knowledge is, then, for us a matter of 'Learned ignorance', to borrow Cusa's phrase. Yet an ignorance that can never be fully wrong, for all knowledge is in act, and all act is imitative of God. As Aquinas tells us: 'The first completely perfect actuality has in itself the whole fullness of perfection, causes actual existence in all things' (*Quaestio disputata de spiritualibus creaturis*, 1c). Moreover, 'What is in potentiality is reduced to actuality only by something that is in actuality' (*In de An*. III, c. 10, n. 185). Consequently, knowledge, in being a move from not knowing to knowing, is a move from potentiality to actuality. But one that requires a prior actuality, other-

---

28 Cf. Pieper, p. 60.

wise the human intellect will never know anything, as it will be left for ever chasing so as to collect knowledge of the merest thing (i.e. the essence of a fly). In this way, God, as *actus purus*, is the sole principle of intelligibility. And in more Augustinian terms, we can maybe understand knowledge to be the non-identical repetition of divine knowledge, that is, recollection (*anamnesis*). Importantly, this idea of recollection is itself a fruit of goodness, as it is an ontological sign of gratuity, and this comes even more to the fore when we consider that God is both principal and end for creatures. Thus we come from God, and we are to return to God. As Aquinas says:

> In the exit of creatures from the first principle, we observe a kind of circular movement owing to the fact that all things return as to their end to that from which they came forth at their beginning. That is why the return to the end must be accomplished by the same causes that led to their emergence from their beginning. (*In I Sent.* d. 14, q. 2, a. 2)[29]

Elsewhere he tells us: 'The ultimate perfection of the rational creature is to be found in that which is the principle of its being; since a thing is perfect so far as it attains to its principle'; because 'When a being finds in another all of the reason for its existence and its goodness, it is impossible that it not love, by nature, this other being more than itself . . . hence everything in its own way naturally loves God more than itself' (*STh* I, q. 60, a. 5, ad. 1). Thus in seeking God, it seeks its own perfection. Again to quote Thomas, 'the proper perfection of things is nothing other than a certain likeness to God, such that, by seeking its own perfection it seeks God' (*STh* I, q. 6, a. 1, ad. 2); or, as Henry might put it, in seeking one's self, we find God. Here we see in the starkest possible terms the non-dualism of Christian theology: God

---

29 On the theme of circularity in Thomas, see P. Rosemann, *Omnes Agens Agit Sibi Simile* (Leuven: Leuven University Press, 1996). Interestingly, Rudi te Velde argues that Aquinas later drops the motif of a circular return of humanity to God via the mediation of the incarnation. See *Aquinas on God* (London: Ashgate, 2006), p. 32, n. 14.

cannot be something alien to immanence, something simply different.

Here, Aquinas makes a telling point: 'As the Philosopher says even falsehoods testify before they stand apart not only from Truth but from one another' (*ScG* IV, 7). Deism, theism, pantheism and panentheism, likewise all the heresies, such as Arianism and Sabellianism, point to a shared inability to have faith in a Creator God – for all reveal a conceptual pride, that domesticates and patronizes transcendence. Thus there can be no strict dualisms, just as there can be no remainders – pure sin, mere matter, utterly wrong knowledge, or simple, univocal being. Rudi te Velde expresses this well, when he says that 'The attribute "being" does not name God prior to the distinction between infinite and finite being.'[30] According to Aquinas, Christ is the 'Word of all things' (*Verbum omnium rerum*). This being so, the Word is 'not merely that by which the arrangement of all creatures takes place; [but] . . . the arrangement itself' (*De Ver*. q. 4, a. 5, ad. 6). We will come back to this. Before doing so, it is important to understand that nature left to itself becomes disordered and consequently loses the very things it thought it best understood; indeed nature itself is lost, as it dissolves (diabolically) under the weight of its supposed autonomy. Again to quote Churchland:

> Consider sound. We know that sound is just a train of compression waves travelling through the air, and that the property of being high pitched is identical with the property of having a high oscillatory frequency. We have learned that light is just electromagnetic waves . . . We now appreciate that the warmth or coolness of a body is just the energy motion of the molecules that make it up . . . What we now think of as 'mental states' . . . are identical with brain states in exactly the same way.[31]

---

30 R. te Velde, *Participation and Substantiality in Thomas Aquinas* (Leiden: Brill, 1995), p. 194.
31 Churchland, *Matter and Consciousness*, p. 26.

In such a world all intentionality has disappeared, and with it all lives. As David Chalmers says: 'you can't have your materialist cake and eat your consciousness too'.[32] Crucially, as Henry says:

> Science believes that it continues to operate in its own proper domain when it reduces these properties to their material physical substrate. What escapes science is that sensible qualities never exist as the simple properties of an object. Before being projected onto that object, they are subjective impressions that in fact presuppose sensibility, that invisible essence of Life that is Christian Truth.[33]

Here, materialism represents what we might call a Zwinglian metaphysics,[34] for our lives have no real presence; instead they are purely symbolic, as a behaviourist would indeed insist is the case. This situation is itself a result of 'reason [becoming] more and more a prisoner to itself', to borrow the words of Pope John Paul II (*Fides et Ratio*, para. 22).

This brings us back to man as both horizon and frontier, to this unique being whom the Fathers called a 'composite nature'. In man we find a unity in difference, a complication of the powers of creatures: he recalls the vegitative and the intelligent, time and eternity.

In so doing, man is, as Thomas says, the 'completion of the universe' (*ScG* I, 86). Moreover, as Henri de Lubac tells us, 'By revealing the Father, and by being revealed by Him, Christ completes the revelation of man to himself.'[35] This signals the fittingness (*convenientia*) of the incarnation. Consequently, as

---

32 D. Chalmers, *The Conscious Mind* (Oxford: Oxford University Press, 1996), p. 168.

33 Henry, *I am the Truth*, p. 37.

34 See C. Cunningham, 'Trying My Very Best to Believe Darwin'; also C. Cunningham and P. M. Candler (eds), *Evolution: Darwin's Pious Idea (Interventions)* (Grand Rapids: Eerdmans, 2008).

35 H. de Lubac, *Catholicism: Christ and the Common Destiny of Man* (San Francisco: Ignatius Press, 1988), p. 264. Cf. *Gaudium et Spes*, 22.

Henry says, 'More original than the truth of Being is the truth of man.'[36] And of course the more we are repulsed by the apparent anthropocentricism of this, the more anthropocentric we are, for man's truth, in so far as man is, is the incarnation. Inspired by such insight, Henry argues that there is no birth in the world. He says, 'In the world, according to Christianity, no birth is possible.'[37] Indeed Christ prohibits the 'natural attitude' to birth: 'Do not call anyone on earth Father; for you have one Father, he in Heaven' (Matt. 23.9).[38]

Eckhart puts it more decisively: 'I am unborn.'[39] Why? Because 'God and I are one', he tells us.[40] Or as Nicholas of Cusa expresses it, God is not other (*Non Aliud*) – and this is not a species of ontotheological arrogance, for we are back to the question of our nakedness. In another provocative passage, Eckhart speaks of the kiss that passes between the humble man and God;[41] indeed the poor can *command* God.[42] For being one with God is the realization of ontological nakedness, what Henry calls a terrifying lack – hence all existence and consequently all knowledge is recollection (both being a consequence and sign of divine simplicity). How could it be otherwise? As Aquinas tells us, 'The first completely perfect actuality has in itself the whole fullness of perfection, causes actual existence in all things' (*Quaestio disputata de spiritualibus creaturis*, 1c).

And we can here see that the virgin birth is the truth of all births, indeed of creation. But the natural attitude seduces us or,

---

36 Henry, *Essence of Manifestation*, p. 41.

37 Henry, *I am the Truth*, p. 59.

38 Jacques Maritain echoes this: 'How can it be that I am born? It is the certitude of being born common to all men, which suppresses in us the blossoming – There is only one solution: I have always existed, this I who thinks; but not in myself . . . nor in some impersonal life. Where, then? It must have been in a being of transcendent personality.' J. Maritain, *Approaches de Dieu* (Paris: Alsata, 1953), pp. 83–86.

39 Meister Eckhart, *A Modern Translation*, tr. R. Blakney (New York: Harper & Row, 1941), p. 231.

40 Eckhart, *A Modern Translation*, p. 232.

41 Eckhart, *A Modern Translation*, p. 242.

42 Eckhart, *A Modern Translation*, p. 242.

better, it sedates us. It is for this reason, as Henry makes clear, that Christ asserts that all those who came before him were thieves, they were so because Christ as the absolute 'Before' ('Before Abraham I am') dissolves the logic of possession, doing so through the ultimacy of divine generosity. Henry rightly brings our attention to the words of St Paul, asking us to believe them: 'What do you have that you did not receive? And if you did receive it, why do you boast as though you did not?' (1 Cor. 4.7).[43] For Henry, this is the great challenge to the ego's transcendental illusion, which exemplifies the great lie of the antichrist, for it is not that the antichrist denies that Jesus is the Christ, believing instead that he is but a man, rather, it is the idea there could be such a thing as a person outside Christ.[44] Our natural attitude is left in the middle of a dilemma.

If we endeavour to live without God, that is, if we posit a pure nature, and thus something which accommodates the logic of possession, of collection, then we will meet our own demise, a demise that we have already witnessed in the words of Paul Churchland. For if we rest our cathedrals on the supposed solidity of the world, they will melt, doing so because quite simply there is no life in the world, and we know this because all such towering cathedrals, which scrape the sky, fail to get off the ground. For like some ripe green apple, the world speeds up the camera, revealing its well-dressed truth: the apple rots and returns to dust. In this way, all such identities are mere placeholders, and any semblance of solidity is the result of temporal parochialism. As Henry says, 'if there existed no other truth than that of the world, there would be no reality at all anywhere but only, on all sides, death'.[45] And let us not rush to think that, here, Henry relies on a dualism, maybe a Gnostic one at that. For Henry is taking his lead from Christ whom we are told came not to condemn the world, but to save it (John 3.17); left

---

43 See Henry, *I am the Truth*, p. 140.

44 'The idea of a specific and hence autonomous human nature . . . is from the Christian viewpoint an absurdity.' Henry, *I am the Truth*, p. 100; also see p. 270.

45 Henry, *I am the Truth*, p. 20.

to itself our natural attitude, like the Prodigal Son, leads to ruination: colour, time, intentional life, free will, nature, materiality, all these perish in the night in which all cows are black. Against such eliminative thinking, we must suspend our natural attitude, and so must refuse our diabolic portion. Instead turning (*metanoia*) to giving thanks to what is always before us, what is always already. As Henry says, 'This Before is that which precedes the one and the other and yet remains in them for as long as they are these living selves [*des Soi vivant*].'[46] And this before is, for Henry, Life itself, the auto-revelation of Life itself, Life's 'absolute before'[47] that is made manifest as our very flesh. On its own, the world is dry and brittle, or more accurately, it can only move to reduce existence to mere dust; flesh for the world is impossible, indeed any such 'prodigal world' knows only the cadaver. But God, as Life, is the gift of our flesh ('Verily I say unto you, unless you eat the flesh of the son of Man, and drink his blood, you have no life in you', John 6.53). In a similar vein, Aquinas tells us that Christ is 'written on our flesh';[48] indeed our 'flesh is the hinge of salvation', as Tertullian rightly insists.[49] Henry radicalizes this insight: 'in the depth of its Night, our flesh is God', thus we can maybe realize the full ontological implications of our lives as one of *anamnesis*. Consequently, if we seek to collect, we decompose, like Mr Valdemar, in one of Edgar Allen Poe's tales, but if we recall anew the very reception we are, and so recognize the truth of Life's auto-revelation, and so are 'configured to God' (*ScG* IV, c. 22), then we can begin to realize that Kafka is correct, *Glauben ist Sein*; the profundity of which leads him dramatically to conclude (and Henry follows him here) that 'the expulsion from Paradise is in its main significance eternal . . . but the eternal nature of the occurrence makes it nevertheless possible that not only could we live continuously in paradise, but that

---

46 M. Henry, 'Eux en moi: une phenomenology' in *Phénoménologie de la vie, 1: De la phénoménologie* (Paris: PUF, 2003), p. 208.

47 Henry, 'Eux en moi: une phenomenology', p. 158.

48 Thomas Aquinas, *Sermon on the Apostles' Creed*, III, 2.

49 Tertullian, *De Resurrectione Mortuorum*, VIII, 2.

we are continuously there in actual fact, no matter whether we know it here or not'.[50] The reason for this being, that 'there is a goal, but no path',[51] as he also puts it, thus our flesh, our being, manifests what Merleau-Ponty calls our 'vertical past'.[52] Our nakedness then is one of intimacy, of the very relationship of immanence and transcendence, which cannot, on pain of invoking a third term, be set against each other. This intimacy, this non-invasive, divine concurrence, informs the world. Thus maybe we can now begin to see how immanence is itself the recollection of transcendence.

Abbreviations

Comp. Theol.	*Compendium Theologiae*
De Malo	*Quaestio disputata de malo*
De Pot.	*Quaestio disputata de potentia*
De Ver.	*Quaestio disputata de veritate*
In I Sent.	*Scriptum super libros Sententiarum Liber I*
In III Sent.	*Scriptum super libros Sententiarum Liber III*
In II Phys.	*Sententia super Physicam Liber II*
In de An.	*Quaestio disputata de anima*
In de Div. Nom.	*Expositio de divinis nominibus*
In De Trin.	*Expositio super librum Boethii De Trinitate*
ScG	*Summa contra Gentiles*
STh	*Summa Theologiae*
Sup. Titum	*Super ad Titum*

---

50 F. Kafka, 'Paradise' in E. Heller (ed.), *The Basic Kafka* (New York: Washington Square, 1979), pp. 168–9.

51 F. Kafka, *Journal Intime*, tr. P. Klossowski (Paris: Grasset, 1945), p. 302.

52 M. Merleau-Ponty, *The Invisible and the Visible*, ed. C. Lefort, tr. A. Lingis (Evanston, Ill: Northwestern University Press, 1968), p. 244.

13. The Thomistic Telescope: Truth and Identity

JOHN MILBANK

Truth and Identity

The question of truth is deeply related to the question of identity and stability. If we think of truth as saying 'what is the case?' as in 'it's true that there's a cat perched on the window-sill', then the cat has to stay still long enough for one to be able to verify this. And there has to be something distinctly recognizable as a cat. Too fast a flash of mere fur would undo everything.

However, we don't necessarily have to have anything to do with cats, who may be too elusive for the cause of truth. We can invent something stable for ourselves by making it sufficiently rigid and treating it always the same way (more or less), like a table that we eat on. Then it seems that we can be sure of saying some true things about the table. Still we may wonder if the table is really as it appears to us to be, securely shaped and coloured, and some people may use it to sit on, thereby redefining it. A more radical recourse is to invent something more abstract like the number 1. This seems more certain and controllable – until we realize that we can only define it in relation to 2, but 1 as twice exemplified in 2 does not seem to be the pure 1 that cannot be multiplied or divided. It quickly appears that the most fundamental self-identical thing is elusive and inaccessible: it would have to be immune to participation and multiplication, but the 1s we know about can be divided and so multiplied into two halves and so forth. Then we resort to a further abstraction. Turning from arithmetic to algebra and logic: whatever 1, the self-identical, is, we do at least know that it cannot be *as* 1 also zero – even if, as 1 it can also be 2, 3, 4 and so forth. This gives us the law of excluded middle or of non-contradiction: 1 cannot be at the same time zero, and *no* 1, no single thing, can be and not be what it is at the same time and in the same respect. If this *were* possible, then even tautologies would not be true, but we do at least know that a standing tree is a standing tree is a standing tree, recursively, *ad infinitum*.

Since the ancient Greeks, just this law has been seen as the foundation of all logic, and so of all truthful discourses. Here at least one has a *formal* truth: modern thought, starting long ago with certain medieval currents, has often hoped to build on this formality towards a secure epistemology and even an ontology. But here a doubt must always persist as to whether one can cross the chasm between logical possibility and given actuality. Is anything more than a thin formal truth available to us?

For the ancients and much of the Middle Ages, things stood otherwise. The law of excluded middle only ruled actuality because there were real stable identities out there in the world. Ralph Cudworth, the seventeenth-century English philosopher and theologian noted that in Plato's *Theaetetus,* Socrates' sceptical interlocutor, Protagoras, by arguing that reality is only material particles in random flux, entailing that our knowledge of them is only the contingent *event* of our interaction with them, renders the law of non-contradiction inoperable.[1] For Socrates points out that if reality and knowledge consist only in sequences of events, then a affecting b must presuppose a_1 affecting b_1 and so on *ad infinitum*. Every item at the same time and in the same respect would already be *not* this item, and our knowledge of something could only be knowledge of this knowledge and so on recursively, such that either we could

---

1 R. Cudworth, *A Treatise Concerning Eternal and Immutable Morality* ed. S. Hutton (Cambridge: Cambridge University Press, 1996), Book I, ch. II, p. 17; Book II, ch. II, 1, p. 33.

never stay still long enough to be subjectively aware, or else our staying still must be an illusion – the illusion of being a subject. Likewise, Aristotle in his *Metaphysics* said that without stable substance the law of non-contradiction cannot hold.[2] One can at least read this assertion to mean that, without stable essences, stable formed matters or *eide* out there in the world, the law of excluded middle cannot be applied to a deprived reality which would then be, like Protagoras's reality, somehow 'really contradictory'. However, I suspect that Aristotle's doctrine of the priority of act over possibility means that, more radically, he thinks that only the actuality of ontological substance makes it true in the realm of logic, which ponders possibilities, that the law of non-contradiction really does hold.

At the very least though, one can see that if this law applies only in the realm of logic, this gives us but a meagre doctrine of truth. It certainly will not allow that things in so far as they 'are' are somehow also 'true', but also it will not allow us to make truthful statements about things as they are, or even as they appear to us to be. So can we be assured that there are real, actual self-identical items in the world? Plato, it seems, was half in agreement with sceptics like Protagoras: the material world was in itself a temporal flux. If it nonetheless exhibited relative stabilities we could rely on, this was because it participated in eternal and immutable archetypes of everything: trees in the *eidos* of tree, just acts in the *eidos* of justice and so on. Aristotle, by contrast, thought that the *eide* were perfectly stable within the material, temporal world, without participation in transcendence. These two views of the forms or *eide* were then synthesized in different ways by later commentators on Aristotle, by the Neoplatonists and then by Islamic, Jewish and Christian thinkers. To say that the world contained *eide* and participation in those supreme *eide* that were divine ideas, was to say that even if the world does not itself think (and most people affirmed even this in the case of the celestial realm, beyond the lunar orbit) it is nonetheless composed of thoughts or the reflection of

---

2 Aristotle, *Metaphysics* 1007a–1035b.

thoughts, which are meanings. Beings themselves are also truths, because they only exist as manifesting themselves in ordered patterns related to ends they seek and the ordered proportions and relations they enter into with other beings.

This view also implies that there is an ordained proportion between things as they exist and our knowledge of things. As knowers we are not like visitors to this solar system from an altogether strange galaxy, making observations and taking notes that reality never intended us to be capable of taking. Instead, for the Platonic–Aristotelian tradition, forms in things exist in order that they may finally be known. For this reason knowledge is not a mirroring of things, a 'representation' of them, but rather it is the process by which forms themselves migrate from matter to a higher mode of being that is intellectual existence. Thus an act of thinking, for Aristotle, was identical with the realization of an objective *eidos* as a thought.[3] But inversely, to have a thought and realize an *eidos* also further fulfilled and unfolded the active capacity of thinking itself. The transition from passive reception to active formation by mind was often debated: did the passively received form really become the active form, or did it rather occasion the sympathetic emergence of the latter? Respectively, these positions can be seen as more Aristotelian and more Platonic. There were many sub-variants, and yet they all rang changes on the same shared theme. Thought, for this model was possible, not on account of the accident of mirroring, based on the example of the eye mirroring light, but rather on account of an arcane ontological proportion, or ordering, or 'convenience' between things as existing and things as known.[4]

---

3 Aristotle, *On the Soul* 429b20–30, 430a5–10.
4 See J. Milbank and C. Pickstock, *Truth in Aquinas* (London and New York: Routledge, 2001), pp. 1–60.

Realism and Nominalism

Already in the Middle Ages however, beginning as far back as the twelfth century with people like Roger Bacon and Gilbert Porreta, this started to seem unsatisfactory.[5] On the traditional model it appears that one can only teach someone to know by sage advice to attend to one's inner light which intuits and judges by nature and without other reason. One could not, under this jurisdiction, teach a fundamental *method*, which says 'accept only the transparently clear and what can be measured and proved and shown to work in a repeated fashion'. So in a long process culminating in the seventeenth century, various thinkers suggested that knowledge was not a kind of communion with being and realization of being, but instead was logical certainty, representational measure and technological experiment.

Often these recommendations were accompanied by a theology which said in effect: 'God has laid down the world with an order that is radically contingent, according to the decrees of his freely willed charity: this order does not necessarily reflect the divine ideas, and embodies no relative necessities of essence. For this reason, our minds do not operate by gathering the ways in which the world symbolizes and participates in God, nor by abstracting out and unfolding pure essences. Instead we are to observe God's gift of Creation in a detached manner (indeed like investigators from another galaxy), and to respond to the divine freedom with free usage of the world for pragmatic ends that we invent and contract with others to observe.'

What was seen as especially mysterious and unnecessarily obscure in the older view was the idea of universal essence: surely besides trees, one does not need to suppose that there is a real *eidos* of tree, even if this only exists *qua* universal in our minds? Isn't our idea of a tree just a generalization from trees,

---

5 See O. Boulnois, *Être et Représentation: Une généalogie de la métaphysique moderne à l'époque de Duns Scot* (xiiie–xive siècle) (Paris: PUF, 1999), pp. 17–107.

which then functions as a cognitive *sign* for trees? This getting rid of universal essences is usually known as 'nominalism' or 'terminism': universals are just conventional names or terms, not natural subsisting realities.

However, we have already seen that the *eide* were traditionally seen as the guarantors of truth, and of the operativity or even reality of the law of excluded middle. How could one now have truth without them? Well, first of all, the entire Platonic–Aristotelian tradition had always hesitated between – or tried to include both – the idea that stable substance resides in a general *eidos* on the one hand, or in an individual substance, on the other, be this material or angelic (God was taken to be beyond the contrast of individuality and generality). The nominalists chose exclusively the latter fork: arguing that the sameness of an individual tree (for example) belonging to a particular species, grown bent in a particular way and so forth, was much more secure than some vague essence of 'treeness'. In the second place, however, they tended to declare (William of Ockham is the best instance) that universal essence as much as flux violates the principle of non-contradiction. For the traditional 'realist' (meaning here the opposite of nominalist) view, the tree *as* individual tree always shows something universal, not in an aspect but *in toto*, and not in terms of a parcelled-out share, because there is (at least for Aquinas and even to a degree for Scotus) no self-standing essence out there in the world apart from individual trees. Concomitantly the universal form 'tree' in my mind as universal also *is* the fulfilled-as-comprehended individual trees. In either case 'universal' and its opposite, 'individual', seem to coincide. Nominalism was in part a strategy for a purged Aristotelianism fully following through on the law of excluded middle.

Ockham and others also suggested that notions of participation and analogy of attribution likewise violated this law: something cannot be at once like and unlike a higher thing, not simply in some isolatable aspect – for then one could parcel out analogy between univocity and equivocity – but truly *as* its whole self. Something similar applied for the nominalists to ideas of real relation: something cannot be *intrinsically* and not just externally and accidentally related to something else without it being itself as not itself.[6] One can notice here how close real relation and universal are to each other as concepts: a real relation implies something in common shared between two things, rendering them what they are. Inversely, if trees embody a universal form of treeness, even though this form does not stand like a totem in the middle of the forest (like a mutant golden fir, as occurs very occasionally in North American evergreen forests), then it means something like the hidden relational community between them. Likewise, the really universal tree in the mind only exists as the really relational (real for the mind's relation to the thing known) intention of all particular trees.

Universal, analogical participation, real relation. These were the three essential components of the realist idea that the world holds together as a kind of arcane harmony ordained by God. In God, the source of this harmony, order was at once actuality and knowledge; the creation echoed this by a reciprocal interplay between being and knowing. Being urged towards knowing; knowing could be distilled from being, but knowing always had to return to the surplus of harmony and potential knowledge that finite being contained and that could be encompassed only by God's infinite awareness. Such an outlook in effect claimed that, as Balthasar today puts it (building upon, but improving, Descartes), that only the awareness that we participate in the divine understanding which always understands more of his creation than we do, ensures that we do not think of our thoughts of things as merely solipsistic elaborations of our own being.[7]

---

6 William of Ockham, *Quodlibetal Questions* 4.12; 5.11; 5.12; 6.9; 6.12; 6.13; 6.14; *Summa Logicae* 1.16.

7 H. U. von Balthasar, *La Theologique I: Vérité du monde*, tr. C. Dumont SJ (Namur: Culture et Vérité, 1994), p. 54. In some ways Descartes is a transitional figure; the 'modern view' of knowledge is more emphatically elaborated by Locke.

As we have seen, this scheme of cosmic harmony was once seen as guaranteeing the operation of the law of non-contradiction, and so the presence of identity, and therefore the presence of truth. Now the nominalists in effect declared that this was, after all, half pagan myth of mysterious and ungraspable fluxions: far from guaranteeing truth, it violated the law of excluded middle itself. They proclaimed a disenchantment in the name of logic, or evidence, or experiment, or human political freedom, but also in the name of the divine freedom and the priority of the divine will, which as self-giving was the will to charity.

So if two accounts of truth were at stake here, so also were two accounts of Christianity – so different that they almost seem like different religions. For the old realistic account, in actuality there is no *bare* being; actual being is accompanied always by value – it shows itself as meaningful truth, just as it communicates itself as goodness. As Hans Urs von Balthasar *almost* says (but see later) in his *Theologik I*, for Aquinas and others truth was more than just representation of being, because it was also being manifesting itself as beauty; likewise the good was more than fulfilment of selfish desire, because it was an aiming for the Beautiful that is objectively lovable in itself.[8] Balthasar (now followed by Gilbert Narcisse) thus rightly draws out the crucial yet latent aesthetic character of the older vision: beauty as 'taking care of herself' (as the English Catholic artist Eric Gill famously put it) was little mentioned, just because it was so fundamentally presupposed and was the real link between being, truth and goodness.[9] Thus in the realist vision, being as value was a free gift, but also a gift of reciprocal exchange of gifts between being and knowing, knowing and willing.

For the new nominalist account, by contrast, the only being one can securely and entirely know is *represented* being, which

---

8 Balthasar, *La Théologique I: Verité du Monde*, pp. 229–34.

9 G. Narcisse, *Les Raisons de Dieu: Arguments de Convenance et Esthétique Théologique selon St. Thomas d'Aquin et Hans urs von Balthasar* (Fribourg: Editions Universitaires Fribourg Suisse, 1997).

is the bare fact of an individual possession of being as self-identical: 'One is one and all alone and ever more shall be so.' A finite thing can now be considered in logical abstraction from its createdness, simply as existing. Already, beginning with Scotus and later extended by Ockham, this bare logical minimal consideration of being nevertheless informed a new minimalist ontology: each thing as existing fully possesses its own being. If it did not, if as existing it only borrowed its existence from a supreme *esse* whom it resembled (as for Aquinas) then *as being* it would also not be, and as *being* finite its actual existence that it possessed would also be infinite. Already Scotus declared that analogy and participation violated non-contradiction.[10] The result was that, for Scotus, while God, as infinite, created finite beings in respect of their particularity and caused occurrence, he did not (as for Aquinas) as *esse* create general abstracted being (in the mode of finite *ens commune*) as such. So being was no longer regarded as intrinsically and ineluctably a gift, and being as finite being no longer reflected the divine infinite harmony which ensured that it was always really an exchange of reciprocities.

However, this did not mean that gift was abandoned. Modern Franciscan theologians characteristically argue that this rather allowed the gift itself to be de-ontologized.[11] Since being is not the gift, *finite* being is pure free gift beyond any supposed existential necessities. Reciprocity is lost, but this is not to be regretted: instead the divine gift to us is purely gratuitous and does not 'return' to God (even though God as replete does not really 'receive' anything for Thomistic theologians either) by way of a created reflection of the divine order.[12]

---

10 Duns Scotus, *Ordinatio* I d. 3, q. 2, a. 2.26; I d. 8, q. 3.121; *Collatio* 24.24. See also William of Ockham, *Quodlibetal Questions* 4:12

11 See O. Todisco OFM , 'L'Univocità Scotista dell'Ente e la Svolta Moderna', *Antonianum* LXXVI (Jan.–Mar. 2001), fasc. 1, pp. 79–110; I. Manzano OFM, in the same issue, pp. 43–78.

12 See also J.-L. Marion, *Étant Donée: Essai d'une Phénoménologie de la donation* (Paris: PUF, 1997).

Likewise, since the created return is in no way naturally elicited, humans make an entirely free response from within a freedom more ontologically outside divine determination than it was for Aquinas. Meanwhile, within the created order, reciprocity and teleology is replaced (already with Scotus) by formal contract and a moral law valuing primarily free personhood.[13]

So now we can see that the debate about truth, which concerns the question as to whether identity resides in the individual only, or also in the essence, is also the debate about the gift. Does the gift arise as free and unilateral beyond being, or does being without the gift lose the reciprocal dimension of the gift, the dimension of gift-exchange which *complements* free unilaterality, just as essence for Aristotle and Aquinas *complements* the self-standing individual? The debate about truth, then, is simultaneously the debate about the nature of goodness and of charity. Those who find essences, analogy and real relations to be contradictory will most likely find the idea of a free gift that expects or hopes for a return to be also contradictory – as likewise violating the law of excluded middle.

Names against Nominalism

So which side is right? And perhaps this is the most fundamental debate within western culture. We can call the Scotist and nominalist way 'Modern Christianity' and suggest that it is in large part responsible for modernity as such (its legacy eventually merging, in Hobbes and Spinoza, with the neo-pagan legacy of Machiavelli). However, 'Modern Christianity' and modernity (the child it has half-parented) has increasingly run into conceptual problems. These are primarily problems with nominalism itself. All its key strategies eventually turned sour. Let me try to summarize this in three instances.

First of all, the idea that a universal is a sign. As John N. Deely's researches have shown, building on the labours of

---

13 See Manzano, 'Individuo y Sociedad en Duns Escoto'.

Jacques Maritain in this regard, the Iberian Thomists in the Baroque Era, especially those of the school of Coimbra in Portugal, and supremely the Portuguese theologian Jean Poinsot (John of St Thomas), produced an effective counter-riposte.[14] Not only is a universal a sign, but a thought as such in its character as an inner word (as Aquinas already taught) is itself a kind of sign. A first encounter with one's first tree would already think it under the sign 'tree' without explicit reference to other trees; one would only see it as an individual tree through the inchoate recognition that there might be other trees of different shapes and sizes that were still trees. Because we only grasp the individual tree via sign of tree in general, the relation of tree to sign of tree must be a *real relation*: we cannot think of a tree without its sign and merely bring the two together *ad placitum*. No, since the tree is only invoked through the sign, the sign must be really and not accidentally related to the tree.[15]

This circumstance does not then apply only to our *concept* of the tree; it applies also to our percept and mental image of the tree. Hence whereas the nominalists said that 'a concept is only a sign', the Coimbrists declared that even a percept and a mental image is a sign. It followed for them that if the rawest material of all thinking still involves a sign-relation, then it can never be a question of 'only' a sign, nor of a merely stipulated relation. If a percept or image is itself a sign, it is in a sense already a faint adumbration of a concept; in consequence a concept as a more abstract and reflexive sign is also indispensable for a more fully developed knowledge even of individuals and is therefore never a 'mere' sign only.

Moreover, for Poinsot we negotiate the actual world in terms of natural signs: the sight of a track and a break in the trees

---

14 See J. N. Deely, *New Beginnings: Early Modern Philosophy and Postmodern Thought* (Toronto: University of Toronto Press, 1994), esp. pp. 53–86.

15 J. Poinsot (John of St Thomas), *Cursus Philosophicus*, I qq 1–6, 646a 9–41 – 693a31. J. Deely (ed.), *Tractatus de Signis: The Semiotic of John Poinsot* (Berkeley, CA: University of California Press, 1985), pp. 116–219.

suggests a way through the forest and so forth. Without these natural signs we would be lost, doomed to pure sylvan errancies, since we cannot recognize the path as path in treading it, unless we first grasp it as sign of a continuous way. These natural signs are therefore instances of cognitive real relations latent in nature herself.

There is also an important further point: while mind is less substantive, as less self-standing, than a physical reality like a tree, its relations to things via concepts which are signs is as real as the tree's relation to the ground on which it depends. This applies *both* to conventional 'stipulated' signs (like the 'King's Head' on an inn signboard) which are said by Poinsot to be 'materially transcendental' (conventional) *and* to natural signs: both types are 'formally' speaking ontological rather than merely 'transcendental' relations, because in both cases the sign-relation is indispensable for thought. Poinsot noted that being and knowledge coincided in God precisely in the mode of relation, as the doctrine of the Trinity finally explicates.[16]

---

16 On the real relation of stipulated signs, see *Cursus Philosphicus* I.q 2 6 58617 – 659633 (*Tractatus de Signis*, pp. 141–2). For the reference to the Trinity, see *Cursus Philosophicus* q. 17, a. 1, 575a19–b28 (*Tractatus de Signis*, p. 83): 'in God relations are not extrinsic denominations but intrinsic forms'; a 3 585a1 – 588b11 (*Tractatus* pp. 103–8). Here, among other arguments, Poinsot denies, against Scotus, that a categorial relation, in the case of the Trinity and elsewhere, can be founded on another categorial relation – this would compromise the radically constitutive character of the relation for the being of its poles, and in effect reduce an ontological relation to a grounding substance that nonetheless never appears, because one enters into an endless regress of relations; or else reduce an ontological relation to a transcendental one, making it the accidental effect of prior relational circumstances which would be themselves transcendental and so on, again in a regress. See also Deely, *New Beginnings*, pp. 67–8. The Peircean infinite regress from signifier to signified that becomes in turn a signifier is certainly not envisaged by Poinsot; nevertheless it is not really a 'Scotist' regress (although Derrida's variant is) because each sign-relation for Peirce is a real relation that reveals a partial *aspect* of essential truth. By comparison, the Scotist chains of relation undo any real relationality.

Nominalism's very names therefore are names on its tomb-stone: we cannot after all obtain proper descriptions before attaching names of a general type.

The Elusive Individual

Let us look in the second place at problems which have emerged with the idea of individual substance.

William of Ockham thought that he had reduced the list of categories to substance and quality.[17] However, if there only

---

Clearly, however, the trinitarian relations exceed even this mode of regress since they are infinite.

Scotus in this respect tends to think of real relations as more 'free float-ing' in relation to their polar extremities than does Aquinas. Hence for Scotus there is a more actual or 'formal' distinction in God between the personal relations and the divine essence than there is for the Angelic doctor. In fact, the relatively free-floating character of the Scotistic rela-tions compromises their substantive character as founded utterly in the really natures of their extreme poles – ensuring that the relation is essential to the being of these poles. It is here significant that for Scotus the personal relations in the Trinity are not really constitutive of the Persons, but are secondarily derived from different modes of procession from the Father (respectively by nature and by will), again in contrast with Thomas. Deely cites a passage where Poinsot declares that these extremely technical considerations constitute *the* point of difference between the Thomist and Scotist schools, yet he fails to observe both that Scotus's account of real relations is weaker than that of Aquinas and that it should be significant that Poinsot builds his radical semiotic upon a Thomistic not Scotist account of relationality. Moreover, despite Poinsot's criticism of the opening of the Scotist relation to a regress that would reduce every ontological relation to a transcendental one, Deely *does* compare the Scotist regress to a Peircean one, which appears clearly incompatible with Poinsot's reading of the subtle doctor. See John of St Thomas, *Cursus Philosphicus*, q. 17, a. 2 579b35 – 580a28 and J. Deely, *Four Ages of Understanding* (Toronto: University of Toronto Press, 2001), pp. 382–5.

17 William of Ockham *Quodlibetal Questions*, 7.2 resp: 'qualities of the third species differ in reality from substance' (unlike relation, action and passion, position, etc.).

exist individuals, the notion of qualities 'attaching' to individuals, and the often accompanying idea that we only perceive individuals in terms of these qualities, seems problematic. Just what is this mysterious 'attachment'? It seems just as occultly sympathetic as essence, real relation and analogy. Qualities ought simply to *be* the individual substance, or else other individual substances accidentally attaching to it, like limpets to a rock. One can read aspects of Leibniz's work as trying to rectify this situation: if a thing and its qualities are the same, then they can be substituted for each other *salva veritate*.[18]

The full reductionist programme however awaited the twentieth century. Then Frege and Russell attempted to reduce every 'is' of predication to the 'is' of pure identity: 'x is y' as in 'this apple is red', is then only comprehensible as x = y where 'equals' spells identity. There must be no obscure and impenetrable attachments. However, as the American Catholic philosopher and religious solitary (educated partly in France) Claire Ortiz Hill has recently well shown, this radical programme is unsustainable.[19] One cannot reduce all the qualitative aspects under which individual things appear to us simply to the things themselves in their bare extensional existence. The tree comes to us sighing, creaking, resistant, concealing, growing and so forth. If we tried to identify all these things we would soon produce nonsense. And why? Because the referent, the tree, is *only* available to us under an infinite multitude of senses or aspects, which in attending to we also *intend*. For this reason, the collapse of the attempt to reduce quality to equality with individual substance entails also the problematization of individual substance as such.

So just as that seeming ally of nominalism, the sign, led back to universal and real relation, so also, as phenomenology has

---

18 See H. Ishiguro, *Leibniz's Philosophy of Logic and Language* (Cambridge: Cambridge University Press, 1990), pp. 17–43.

19 C. Ortiz Hill, *Rethinking Identity and Metaphysics: On the Foundations of Analytic Philosophy* (New Haven: Yale University Press, 1997).

realized, its other seeming ally, the individual substance, proves intrinsically multiple and self-concealing (like the back of the tree that always remains however many times we run round it). Instead of it being the case that there are only atomic things, it turns out that (as George Berkeley already taught) there are only multiple qualities (in fact multiple shared essences) since the tree has no monopoly on sighing. Just how it is that we perceive through all this annual flurry but one tree, is the real mysterious thing: what else can one say but that the mind constructs a kind of analogous holding together that enables it intentionally to reach the real tree? Once nominalism self deconstructs, it seems that analogy lies not only between things but within things as before them, so allowing them to be. Another way of putting this would be to say that there can be no access to ontology without a complex phenomenological detour.

The problem of aspects (as first opened up by Husserl and later considered by both Heidegger and Wittgenstein) seems therefore to ruin individual substance and to disclose the analogical infinity of the particular thing in a way that even older realism had not seen. I hope that we are beginning to realize, then, how the collapse of nominalism does not simply *take us back* to the older realism. It is actually the same with signs: Poinsot already saw that if thoughts are signs, then the signs of culture are lived thoughts and real relations. Beyond Thomas, as Maritain suggested, he started to see human historical culture as essential to the unfolding of our thought and participation in the divine *logos*.[20] (Poinsot's thoughts on intellectual being and signs can supplement attention to the Thomist metaphysics of *esse*, even though – dissenting from Deely here – one can agree with Gilson against Maritain that Poinsot like most of the Baroque Thomists misunderstood this metaphysics.) Deely has plausibly argued that C. S. Peirce linked signs and real

---

20 J. Maritain, *Distinguish to Unite or the Degrees of Knowledge*, tr. G. B. Phelan (Notre Dame, IN: University of Notre Dame Press, 1995), pp. 75–145.

universals in a fashion like that of Poinsot, and to a degree indicates that his claimed kinship with Scotus rather than Aquinas was mistaken.[21] But Peirce added to the counter-nominalist reaction the point that if a universal as real is still a sign, then indeed it is only partial and so *aspectual,* and must always be interpreted by a formally 'third' position which 'abducts' to an absent indicated thing. Although Aquinas also knew that one cannot ever 'survey' the interval between thought and thing, Peirce adds again a more temporal dimension: not only does the *eidos* arrive in the mind like an event, it must always be further

---

21 Deely, *New Beginnings,* pp. 39–109, 183–245; Deely, *Four Ages of Understanding,* p. 385. In the latter place, Deely acutely notes that the foundation for the Coimbrist idea that percept and image, equally with concept, involve the instance of sign, lies in the Thomist version of the *verbum mentis,* and that this point is *not* found in Scotus. I submit that this shows that a radical and realist semiotics has more kinship with Aquinas than with Scotus, yet Deely attributes to the latter a discovery of the formal role of the interpretant (the 'third' position in the semiotic process which is present even if no actual third subject is present) without much textual warrant. Equally he attributes to Scotus a discovery of the place of the signified in the same process (whereas this is already there in Augustine and Aquinas) and with more justification of the idea of the semiotic web, as Scotus speaks of signs being signs of other signs (see *Four Ages,* pp. 376–85).

It should also be noted that already Roger Bacon and later William of Ockham allowed that a verbal sign can directly signify a thing without the mediation of the mental concept. In both cases, however, this revised scheme points less to the necessity of language for thought than to a downgrading of the role of the formal essence as *species* in the act of understanding, and the beginning of the idea of thought as the direct imaging or 'representation' of an external thing. See *Four Ages,* pp. 365–75, 385–91.

See in addition C. S. Peirce, *Reasoning and the Logic of Things* (Cambridge, MA: Harvard University Press, 1992), esp. pp. 14, 46–65; *Philosophical Writings of Peirce,* ed. J. Buchler (New York: Dover, 1955), esp. pp. 74–120, 150–7, 251–90. It is true that Peirce claims to follow Scotus in basing his metaphysics on formal logic and Scotus indeed sought to do this. However, Peirce's semiotic exceeds formal logic – it is really an onto-logic and is not independent of the given character of our mind and our animality, and our relation to the cosmos.

interpreted, in a hermeneutical process that runs to infinity. What guides this interpretation? It can only be for Peirce the will towards more realizations of the Good in the world, which yet assumes that this unfolds further a *real ontological bond* between the sign-universal and the absent original which it conveys to us. In a comparable fashion, Balthasar rightly suggested that already for Aquinas truth was not just Greek *aletheia*, the disclosedness of being, but also Hebrew *emet*,[22] truth as bond or fidelity, or *troth* as one could so nicely say in Old English. One helps to reveal truth in plighting one's troth to being. But the semiotic perspective accentuates this plighting as a renewal through variation of ontological vows in the course of historical time. Truth as event echoes onwards and never quite, in time, fully occurs.

So signs and aspects have started to undo nominalism, and to insinuate a reborn and extended realism: a kind of Thomistic Telescope – the same *organon*, but drawn out and allowing us to see further and more clearly.

Sets or Essences

Now I want to suggest a third new lens for the telescope and this has to do with the question of numbers and sets. As Claire Ortiz Hill reminds us, Frege sought a way out of his reduction of predication to equality via Cantor's mathematical set-theory.[23] Thing and quality could be identified in so far as a qualified thing is one example of a single set of kinds of things: the red apple is identical with the apple since the red apple falls within the set of all apples. One can say that in order to handle qualities, nominalism must turn to sets instead of essences; more suspiciously, one might say that sets are the minimum obeisance that nominalism is forced to render to essences. Already

---

22 Balthasar, *La Thélogique I: Verité du Monde*, p. 39.

23 Ortiz Hill, *Rethinking Identity and Metaphysics*, pp. 2–3, 57–73, 111–16.

though, it had emerged with Cantor himself that sets are afflicted by paradoxes not entirely remote from the third man argument that supposedly undermined the Platonic theory of forms. This is doubly significant, because set-theory not only deals with numbers which are, as we saw, the most primitive paradigms of identity, but also, by treating even natural numbers as primarily sets and instances of sets, seeks to logicize arithmetic and not mystify it as necessarily a revelation of 'real' numbers. Although Cantor in fact made realist affirmations regarding numbers, he did not consider these to be essential for his formalist account of mathematics. In this account numbers are sufficiently defined by their distinctness and insertion into a linear series; as such they are 'intersubjective' for Cantor. While he also considered numbers (outside the bounds of pure arithmetic) as 'transubjectively' imaging physical reality, he nonetheless thought that they only enjoyed a fully real status in themselves in so far as they existed in the mind of God. (Here he cited Augustine; yet for Augustine as for other genuinely Platonizing thinkers, our numbers can only be analogically akin to the divine ideas in their eminently 'quantitative' aspects.)

Thus if nominalism began by saying that universal essences violate the law of excluded middle, now it is threatened by the vaunted discovery (in the paradoxes of set-theory) that so do *individuals* in their most paradigmatic arithmetical and logical instances.

Already in the Middle Ages, Robert Grosseteste and later Gregory of Rimini and others noted the existence of what we today call transfinites: $1 + 1 + 1$ is an infinite series, and so is $2 + 4 + 8 + 16$, yet the latter seems infinitely to grow bigger than the former. Or again, the series of all even integers seems paradoxically to be the same size as the series of all even and odd integers, when both are extended to infinity, even though the continuum of the latter series must from another perspective be considered greater. Cantor, however, argued that this kind of example does not show radically incommensurable transfinite infinities, since the drawing of endless lines across the two infinite series between each respective member establishes the same infinite cardinality which he named aleph-zero.[24] Here he appeared arbitrarily to ignore the increase factor in the medieval examples, or the 'escaping' factor of every next even integer in the modern one (2 is more than 1, 4 than 3 etc.), and he did so because he rejected the idea that the equality or else inequality of two or more series could be a matter of pure choice. The increase factor was thus inconsistently relegated by Cantor to the realm of pure indefinite possibility, even though this factor alone constituted the difference between the two sets which allows one to talk of two 'different' cardinalities that are then deemed to be 'equal'. This opposition to choice in the field of pure arithmetic was also exhibited in his equally dubious rejection of Guiseppe Veronese's claim for the reality of actual infinitesimals.

The Cantorian set-theoretical paradox emerges from his treatment of the problem of the transfinites. His own example of transfinitude depends upon multiplying or subdividing whole digits with different finite quantities to produce different series. A posited increasing or decreasing difference of an individual digit (by fractal multiplication or division) is alone what allows 'diagonalization'. The latter concept indicates the fact that, however far one infinitely subdivides in turn the infinitely sub-divided units of a numerical interval, one can still construct diagonal lines across the vertical lines of the subdivisions to produce an infinite sum of the subdivided units higher than the total infinite sum of all these subdivisions, since any diagonal line drawn across a set of verticals will be longer than any single vertical line. In the situation of infinitely continuous division, this is the case because the diagonal is always one unit ahead of the previous position on the vertical that it has just crossed. This ensures that even the infinite diagonal is always

---

24 R. Grosseteste, *De Luce, passim;* G. Cantor, *Contributions to the Founding of the Theory of Transfinite Numbers* (New York: Dover, 1955). See in addition for most of the details regarding Cantor in this paper, J. W. Dauben, *Georg Cantor: His Mathematics and Philosophy of the Infinite* (Cambridge, MA: Harvard University Press, 1979), pp. 108, 122, 128–31, 143–8, 233–5, 296.

longer than an infinite series of verticals that it has traversed. To the seemingly exhaustive sum of the infinite, the infinite diagonal therefore endlessly adds 'one more'.

This diagonal, usually termed C, is said to diagonalize out of a set which might appear to contain it: C is in this way somehow greater than aleph-zero. Such a set thereby becomes 'non-denumerable'.

It should be noted here that, since aleph-zero denotes a cardinal sum, it indicates an actual and not merely potential infinite; hence the contrast between aleph-zero and C cannot be approximated to that between a finite potential infinite and the real actual infinite in Aquinas's thought. Cantor's relationship to scholastic mathematics was in fact highly ironic: against Aristotelianism he affirmed actual mathematical infinites, and against materialistic determinism he rejoiced in the indeterminism of transfinites. Yet in common with scholastic tradition, he, as a devout Catholic, feared any validation of an immanent, material eternity. Thus Cantor vigorously and incoherently denied that transfinites confirm the existence of infinitesimals, on the basis of the Archimedean principle that a number is a number if a finite or infinite group of them can be added together to produce yet another linear magnitude. Cantor claimed that this principle was demonstrable, thereby denying its traditional status as a pure axiom, which it clearly is, since it aims to define the concept of ordinary number as such and cannot therefore itself be proven within such a linear system.

Cantor sincerely believed that transfinites could once and for all banish such spectres as the infinitesimals. Thus even though they were a form of mathematical actual infinity, he still hoped that they would *take over* the older metaphysically restrictive function of the mathematical potential infinite. By showing the measurable order of actual infinity in the immmanent world, they would rule out of play an infinitely divisable continuum, real infinite magnitudes and real numbers smaller than any arbitrarily small real numbers yet more than zero (infinitesimals). He hoped thereby to confine the immanent actual infinite to the cardinality of aleph-zero and the linearity of increasing or decreasing transfinite cardinal sets. Yet as we have seen, he evades the situation where an advancing or diminishing series simultaneously constitutes and disturbs cardinality, in such a way that one can regard a set equally in terms of a relatively cardinal or a relatively ordinal aspect. Infinitely large or infinitely small numbers are then in the same undecidable case as the transfinites: one can think of the greatest of the infinitesimals simply as having an infinite cardinality, or alternatively one can think of it as linearly advancing to the number 1 in terms of multiplying itself by the imagined smallest of the transfinites (the cardinality of the lowest 'diagonal') which stands in linear contrast to multiplying itself by the next smallest of the transfinites and so forth.

But a similar consideration applies to diagonalization itself. Cantor thought that he had insinuated a kind of order into disorder, since C is the infinite plus 1. However, Kurt Godel later rightly declared that it was undecidable whether C was greater than aleph-zero by a kind of leap, or whether there were an infinity of mediating diagonals between them – that is to say, between the diagonal and the set of all the verticals.[25] This ensures that C is both greater *and* not greater than aleph-zero – that a set contains and does not contain itself – violating the law of non-contradiction. The same can in fact be said for Grosseteste's paradox: 2 + 4 + 8 etc. is and is not bigger than 1 + 1 + 1 etc. Furthermore since, in the case of a numerical set, the set is defined by a numerical series and contains such series, there is recursion here of much the same kind as afflicts Bertrand Russell's famous set of all sets that do not contain themselves. For Russell the set of all apples is clearly not itself an apple – else it could not be claimed to contain all apples – in a way that is less clear for the Platonic form of an apple. And the set of all sets of fruits is likewise not itself a set of fruits. However, the set of all sets of this kind (sets not containing themselves as members) appears to lapse back into the condition of a Platonic form after

---

25 See B. Rotman, *Mathematics as Sign: Writing, Imagining, Counting* (Stanford, CA: Stanford University Press, 2000), pp. 73–4.

all. It would seem that, once again, the set of all sets not containing themselves is not itself an example of what it contains, else it could not be exhaustive and fulfil the very condition for being a set. But on the other hand, if it is not contained by what it contains, it follows that it *is* itself an example of a set not containing itself as a member. An ineluctable but contradictory conclusion then ensues: this set includes itself as an example of itself precisely *because* it does not do so.

These paradoxes only intrude when one invokes the infinite: 'all sets' and 'all sub-sets' etc. Graham Priest plausibly argues that diagonalization has always lurked, whenever it has been seen that the finite can be infinitesimally fractalized – whenever one thinks of a finite thing as containing infinite divisions within itself.[26] Hence the infinite presumed set of divisions inside a grain of sand exceeds the grain; more subtly the inside of a tree is an organic series with infinite potential that could exceed the whole tree like a cancer. Likewise, we cannot say which hybrid of the infinite sub-sets of types of apples will ultimately mutate into another kind of fruit altogether. Much more profoundly, for Aquinas the 'accident' of participated infinite *esse* exceeds the finite essence of a creature.[27] One might say here that Being 'diagonalizes out' of createdness. Or again, Kant resumed and complexified an ancient conundrum – if one imagines a totality, one can immediately imagine the breaching of that totality. Hegel pressed this point against him: all categorial limits can only be established in so far as they are transgressed.[28] Critique based upon the bounds of an available set can always be trumped by a metacritique which points out that the bounds are violated in their very establishment. It is the same it seems with every law, theoretical or practical; it is itself within the law, yet must be above it in order to establish it. It must be implicitly the

---

26 G. Priest, *Beyond the Limits of Thought* (Cambridge: Cambridge University Press, 1995). See Milbank and Pickstock, *Truth in Aquinas*, p. 34; Marion, *Étant Donné*, 'Adveniens extra', pp. 17–21.

27 See Milbank and Pickstock, *Truth in Aquinas*, p. 34; Marion, *Étant Donné*, 'Adveniens extra', pp. 17–21.

28 See Priest, *Beyond the Limits*, pp. 79–123.

exception to its own rules, and so its anarchy keeps pace with and ceaselessly crosses out its own legitimating measure.[29]

Attempts have been made to evade these paradoxes. They all involve an attempt to escape recursion and vicious circularity by treating sets as qualitatively different to what they contain. Russell suggested that aporetic master sets are somehow of a higher *type* than the straightforward set, and that the first horizontal numerical series in Cantor's proof of transfinitude is of a different 'type' from the enclosed vertical sub-series.[30] Claire Ortiz Hill today suggests that sets are more like phenomenological aspects or ontological essences.[31] But this move in Hill's version in effect tends to 're-platonize' mathematics and logic in the sense that it bends sets back into essences, into kinds of things-in-themselves existing in a sphere of pure noetic constitution without any necessary reference to actuality (even if it seeks to evade the Platonism involved in recursion and the problems of the third-man argument).

Thomism, Psychologism and Phenomenology

But should we not simply rejoice – is this not nominalism's self-dissolution and our return to the ancient world of real numbers and real logical essences and so forth? But to rejoice would be to accept the unstable truce of much twentieth-century mathematics, logic and philosophy.[32] In this truce, philosophy has its

---

29 See G. Agamben, *Homo Sacer: Sovereign Power and Bare Life*, tr. D. Heller-Roozen (Stanford, CA: Stanford University Press, 1998).

30 Ortiz Hill, *Rethinking Identity and Metaphysics*, pp. 91–111.

31 Ortiz Hill, *Rethinking Identity and Metaphysics*, pp. 136–53. On aspects in phenomenology, see R. Sokolowski, *Introduction to Phenomenology* (Cambridge: Cambridge University Press, 2000), pp. 17–22. For a fine demonstration that Wittgenstein was also centrally concerned with the question of aspects, see S. Mulhall, *On Being in the World: Wittgenstein and Heidegger on Seeing Aspects* (London: Routledge, 1993).

32 See Rotman, *Mathematics as Sign, passim*.

own proper field of possible logical or phenomenological items to investigate, without having to venture upon philosophical speculation about transcendent being outside eidetic appearances, or else outside the consequences of propositional logic. At the same time, the 'Platonic sphere' of Fregean logical items or Husserlian pure phenomena supposedly gives philosophy a task beyond naturalistic science, whose investigations of the brain might otherwise be taken as displacing the need for philosophy altogether.

Such a prospect was indeed often proposed before the advent of Frege and Husserl, and is again often proposed today. Yet we forget that a non-naturalistic psychologism was entertained by the originally Catholic Aristotelian Brentano, as by the early Husserl himself.[33] For Aristotle as for Aquinas's actualism, logic is a property of actual thoughts, of the *psyche*, if not of the mere material brain as for J. S. Mill. Thomism therefore has no stake in simplistic anti-psychologism, nor in possibilistic and supposedly timeless universal essences that are extra-mental – indeed this mode of immanent Platonism (as found in Frege, Husserl and even in Peirce) is really more Scotist in flavour and long-term inspiration. For Aquinas, by contrast, essences are present as universals only in the *psyche*, and for this reason do not escape the materially grounded *temporality* of the specifically human *psyche* – a temporality that is accentuated when we realize that the noetic essence is also sign, aspect and aporetic set. (And indeed for Platonism and Neoplatonism numbers are but conjectured shadows, in a way that is actually *compatible* with non-Euclidean geometries etc.: it was in fact Proclus who first stressed the constructed, contingently 'problematic' character of Euclid's geometry.)[34]

Just for this reason, a telescopically extended Thomism outmanoeuvres pure phenomenology (phenomenology claiming

33 See M. Kusch, *Psychologism: A Case Study in the Sociology of Philosophical Knowledge* (London: Routledge, 1995).

34 Proclus, *A Commentary on the First Book of Euclid's Elements*, tr. E. R. Morrow (Princeton, NJ: Princeton University Press, 1970).

to be the whole of philosophy) by showing that even its most radical effort at reduction is, as Eric Alliez puts it, 'impossible'.[35] For the temporality of the given phenomenological event ensures that there can be no immanent gnoseological security. No manner of appearing to a consciousness can be permanent or final, since, as Protagoras says in Plato's *Theaetetus*, it cannot escape the way in which our knowing, which is expressive of a unique situated perspective and selective response, has always already altered what appears to it. This applies also to the case of all categorial arch-phenomena postulated as general conditions of possibility for appearing in general – like the ontological difference (Heidegger), the saturated adonation of the subject or the aesthetic object (Marion) or auto-affection (Henry). These overarching frameworks also only appear to awareness in the course of time and if they present to us something that is, indeed, always unavoidable, then at the same time they present us with something that is inherently problematic and irreducibly subject to radically different interpretations.

So when phenomenology claims to be able to present such transcendental phenomena as reductively given to analysis, it can only do so by virtue of a dogmatic treatment of the bounds of finitude, which ignores the fact that the boundary between the finite and the infinite is not itself a clear and given border within finitude. Thus being is seen as the authentic nullity that lies within and beyond mere finite beings; the saturation of the gift within beings is understood as the non-appearing 'call' of the invisible to an equally radically concealed subjectivity, and the auto-affection of the subject is understood as an immediate presence of self to self in the very act of awareness which involves no detour via corporeal sensing or reflexive imagining. Essentially, phenomenology's dubious claim to displace metaphysics is here itself rooted in hidden assumptions derived from a Scotistic metaphysics by way of the Kantian legacy: within the field of being taken as univocal one can posit a clear boundary

---

35 E. Alliez, *De l'impossibilité de la phénoménologie: sur la philosophie française contemporaine* (Paris: J.Vrin 1995).

between finite and infinite, such that the finite is fully comprehensible within its own terms.

Thomism, however, or an 'extended' Thomism, still offers in
the face of this 'modernism' an alternative hermeneutics of being
and knowing in general that is at once 'pre-' and 'post-' modern.
The grammar of 'finite' suggests that it can only be known in
conjunction with the infinite; the phenomenology of finitude
suggests that (as for Aquinas) it is at once radically 'finished' and
yet also 'incomplete' in so far as it limits both actuality and
possibility; a speculative apprehension of finitude (after Eckhart,
Cusa, Bruno and Pascal) suggests that the finite is always
hollowed out by infinitude, just as a grain of sand is endlessly
divisible, and moreover that a limited thing is only definable by
its relations to what lies outside itself – relations which are themselves potentially infinite in scope. Accordingly, one possible
interpretative response to the grammar, phenomenology and
logic of the finite is to argue, after Aquinas, that since, according
to our human *modus cognoscendi* it is always the finite instances
of being, truth, goodness beauty or spirit that makes most sense,
and since, nonetheless, it is also clear that these instances do not
furnish any exhaustive experience of the transcendentals or
the quasi-transcendentals (spirit, knowing, desiring etc. which
coincide with being truth etc in God but not in all finite things),
that we always experience a partial apprehension of realities
whose true home is in the infinite. This hermeneutic ontology
remains truer, one might argue, to the irreducibly murky character of the boundary between finite and infinite by not allowing
that the finite is comprehensible simply in its own terms, or that
one can distinguish infinite from finite merely in terms of an
infinite quasi-quantity or else by a hypostasized negation of all
bounds (as with Heidegger). Instead, this ontology seeks to safe-
guard the judgement that we consistently experience or in some
sense 'see' a *mediation* between the visible and the invisible.
Such a judgement and such an experience remains ineffable: yet
the dogmatic claim for such an ineffability can only be ruled out
by the counter-dogmatism of the Scotist-Kantian legacy within
whose horizon pure phenomenology still stands.

This counter-dogmatism which arbitrarily shelters the finite from the infinite (or vice versa in the case of Levinas and Marion) grounds pure phenomenology as a 'rigorous science'. Once this dogmatism is exposed as such therefore, one can see that such a project is in reality impossible. And given this impossibility, a radical scepticism seems to open to view. The very reasons that render phenomenology impossible, also ensure that its critical bracketing of transcendence is metacritically abolished: since no stable *noemata* appear within the realm of noetic appearing, bracketing loses its alibi and *raison d'être* in terms of any secure, isolatable, self-appearing categorical framework. Without the alibi, the investigative assumption must be that bracketing can never have been where it claims to be according to the witness of a supposed reductive clarity, and instead that our intentions, via signs, directly reach but modify objective worldly realities.

And this presumption, despite its proximity to a hyper-scepticism (because of the presumed modification involved in all knowing), may reopen the path to a genuine security for knowledge grounded in eternal realities, as opposed to the immanent security that is illusorily offered by the foundationalism of most twentieth-century philosophy – a security that, after all, secures only a 'human' knowledge that could be nothing more than perspectival illusion.[36]

---

36 This was grasped by Derrida for phenomenology and by Rorty for analytic philosophy: both writers though lapse into a scepticism that pays negative tribute to what they comprehensively deconstruct. This is because they fail to see that that they have deconstructed the 'metaphysical' (or onto-theological) barrier against 'metaphysics' if one takes this term (anachronistically) to mean the tradition of analogical ontology which referred being to God and not God to being (the Cappadocians, Dionysius, Augustine, Bonaventure, Aquinas, Eckhart, Cusa, Pico, Bérulle, etc.).

Number and the Dynamic Universal

We have seen that the logical and phenomenological 'essences' that reappeared in twentieth-century thought were at once too static and at the same time too little psychic, since they were but whimsically placed beyond the limited naturalness and subjectivity of the human mind. Yet just because this presumed psychologism was suppressed, a 'third realm' of logical beings and *noemata* could be substituted for the assumption that such essences are ontologically real, which follows (one could persuasively argue) from the natural intentional bent of the human mind. Essences could be newly deployed as a barrier against the need for any metaphysics evoking transcendence only because they themselves were the prime counters within a dogmatic metaphysics of immanence.

One can argue that Clare Ortiz Hill is therefore wrong in her Husserlian desire to substitute this sort of essence for the notion of a set. One needs instead something like a new sort of hybrid 'set-essence'. The notion of 'essence' would return because that of 'set' turns out to be aporetic, yet 'essence' remains 'set' because the notion of 'essence' alone does not successfully banish every aporia.

For at this point we need to acknowledge what was *valid* in the nominalist critique of essence, as also of analogy and real relation. Surely they *do* tend to violate the principle of non-contradiction, and we can reconstrue this in terms of the way these concepts involve numeration and the interference of the infinite in the finite. In fact, Aristotle already declared in the *Metaphysics* that the basic paradigm of generic essence is number – which is metaphorically akin to the *stoicheion* of geometry which is an ultimate part of matter (that which remains formally the same however further subdivided).[37] To this degree western philosophy remained Pythagorean. Even if the universal of a tree is not a tree, even if it is only in the mind, is a sign, conveys an unfolding series of aspects and manifests

---

37 Aristotle, *Metaphysics*, 1014a26–1014b15.

the event of the arrival of *eidos* in constantly renewed interpretation, it still, in all these modes, sustains a dimension of numeration and inclusion. Whatever else we are doing in thinking, we are always doing mathematics: distinguishing, dividing, uniting, including, excluding, denumerating, subnumerating, and so forth. The set conceived as type or essence is supposed to evade the breaking of the law of identity thrown up by set-theory, but the nominalists already showed that the notion of essence appears also to violate this law, and in any case the notion of essence has never been free of the notion of number and number entails the idea of a set.

So one should not say that the (paradoxically) recursive set must be replaced by pre-modern essence, but rather that the recursive set is revealed in its contradictoriness as once again essence, which *in turn* we must now reconceive in terms of number and recursive set, as earlier we reconceived it in terms of sign and aspect. Since essence is newly grasped as dynamic, as appearing only in a series of infinite aspects that must always be interpreted as signs of further aspects, essence now possesses in its constitutive multiplicity and eventfulness, an inescapable numerical aspect (in terms of both natural integers and transfinite sets and other actual infinites).

Already, in the seventeenth century, Ralph Cudworth had somewhat renumerized the notion of essence. He sought to reintegrate the new mathematicized physics into Platonic-Aristotelian tradition by introducing a new non-negative fundamental quasi-matter consisting in mathematical and geometric basic elements whose essence lay in pure logical form, not mere material extension. Higher forms of active power (exhibited in the motions of magnetism, planets, plants and animals) beyond this basic level displayed the presence of other ontological realities besides the mathematical *ogkoi* or 'bulks'. These higher forms Cudworth named *dynameis* or 'active principles'.[38] And

---

38 R. Cudworth, *The True Intellectual System of the Universe*, vol. 2 (Bristol: Thoemmes, 1995), pp. 390–4; vol. 2, p. 619: here nature bestows 'a kind of life' in everything; *A Treatise Concerning Eternal and*

yet these were for him manifest primarily in the harmonious and self-sustaining aesthetic patternings of the static 'bulky' mathematical elements. These patternings for Cudworth constituted *real relations* that he termed *scheses*.[39] When we understand the truth, our mind reproduces or sometimes artificially originates such *scheses*. Here a new acknowledgement of the mathematical building blocks of reality goes along with a more flexible and still more relational understanding of the categorial organization *common* to mind and the world, as compared with medieval scholasticism.

Cartesian dualism is thereby, one might argue, benignly plundered by Cudworth. There are two basic kinds of finite being: the bulks and the active principles. However, even the inert and mutually external bulks are the deposits of vital activity, and this activity has hierarchical degrees culminating in human understanding. The latter (foreshadowing Peirce) does not just fully elaborate forms under the guiding lure of the Good (which for Cudworth is identical with the Divine Father

---

Immutable Morality, Book III, ch. I, 3–4, p. 51; ch. II, 4, p. 57; ch. III, 1, p. 57; Book IV, ch. VII, 1, pp. 73–4 and in particular 75. In the latter place, Cudworth mentions the analogy between the active 'anticipatory' power of mind and the 'spermatic or plastic power' in animals that unfolds a virtuality. Later he speaks of the 'vital active principle' in all of nature which produces the 'pipes of Pan, Nature's intellectual music and harmony', which only the active human mind, not the passive senses, can partially reconstitute: Book IV, ch. II, 15, pp. 99–101. For Cudworth's 'Mosaic Atomism', see Book II, ch. VI, pp. 39–40. In his version of the *Prisca Theologia*, Cudworth believed that Moses himself was the first atomist philosopher: this revealed philosophy however – unlike that of the later debased materialist atomists – grasped that if abstract numbers and extensions are fundamental, then even material reality is intellectual: Cartesianism is thought by Cudworth partially to recover this Mosaic perspective. By contrast, for Cudworth even Plato was weak at this point – if secondary qualities are not the upshot of a play of atoms, then the way is supposedly open to the action of pure blind material reality and to 'hylozoist' atheism.

39 Cudworth, *A Treatise,* Book IV, ch. II, 4–13, pp. 86–96; ch. III, 11, p. 111.

as single source of the multiple 'comprehension' of the Son-Logos),[40] but *anticipates* the discovery and invention of new

---

40 Cudworth, *A Treatise*, Book I, ch. III, 8, pp. 26–7: 'Moreover, it was the opinion of the wisest philosophers . . . that there is also in the scale of being a nature of goodness superior to wisdom, which therefore measures and determines the wisdom of God, as his wisdom measures and determines his will, and which the ancient cabalists were wont to call "Crown", as being the top of crown of the Deity. Wherefore although some novelists [innovators] make a contracted idea of God consisting in nothing else but will and power, yet his nature is better expressed by some in this mystical or enigmatical representation of an infinite circle, whose inmost centre is simple goodness, the radii or rays and expanded area (*plat*) thereof all-comprehending and immutable wisdom, the exterior periphery or interminable circumference omnipotent will or activity by which every thing without God is brought forth into existence . . . the will and power of God having no command inwardly . . . either upon the wisdom and knowledge of God, or upon the ethical and moral disposition of his nature which is essential goodness.' (But against Cudworth one must say that this picturesque view is of course too hierarchical to apply to the simplicity of God. In general Cudworth favoured a far too subordinationist-tending view of the Greek patristic *monarchia*, without nevertheless, ever lapsing into Arianism.)

For the notion of *prolepsis*, see *A Treatise*, Book III, ch. III, 1, p. 57; Book IV, ch. I, 1, pp. 73–4. Often Cudworth is read here as anticipating the Kantian a priori, and indeed he sometimes speaks, as in the latter passage, explicitly of an a priori, as if there were a kind of categorial blueprint latent in the mind which (it would seem to follow) one could then critically consider independently of any questions of participation or divine illumination, after the fashion of Locke and Kant. However, one should not consider the idea of 'anticipation' in Cudworth as merely a weakly adumbrated idea of the categorial a priori; instead his more usual way of speaking of its suggests that it is more a notion of an open creative power, such that the *whole* of mind has a fundamentally imaginative, inventive capacity for Cudworth in a way that it did not for Kant. (The same notion is found in other Cambridge Platonists, in particular Nathaniel Culverwell.) At the same time, this more radically creative character does not at all denote the 'construction' of sensations, reducing the material realm to the merely phenomenal; to the contrary, the mind's inventive power resonates with and thereby grasps the divine creative forces at work in the universe, which are the deepest guarantees of its objectivity and materiality. This is clearly shown in Cudworth's comparison of 'anticipation' to reading the alphabet of nature: without forms. For Cudworth as later for Balthasar, the more the mind is self-elaborative, all the more is it receptive.[41]

A modern integration of mathematicized physics and grasp of the numerical dimension of essence is important, since it reminds us that the most 'bulky', seemingly 'material' level is in fact the level most clearly subject to fractal vanishing: the point and the triangle are simply not materially 'there'. It also allows us to realize how higher forms arise through dynamically active and harmonious rearrangement of things. Thereby it renders *eide* both in nature and in us more innovative and productive – nearer in character to forms that are always forming or thinking than just abiding or being thought. That same integration also allows us to see that supposed 'secondary qualities' like colours,

---

prolepsis this script would be meaningless scribble, just as alphabetic writing would be senseless without 'certain inward anticipations that such characters signify the elements of certain sounds and those sounds in turn certain notions or cogitations of the mind' (Book IV, ch. II, 16, pp, 99–100). In this way Cudworth is at once more proto-romantic and yet more metaphysically realist then Kant, and this combination is only possible because of his Platonism: the mind can anticipate the real with a radical inventiveness, and also introduce new artificial forms into the real with their own valid essences, because it is involved in a real recollection of forms and is truly guided by the same divine creative light that shaped (and shapes) the universe.

If, nevertheless, Cudworth sounds at times more proto-Kantian than this, then one can suggest that this is directly related to the absence in his work of any real awareness of a distinction between Plotinian and theurgic Neoplatonism; the 'proto-Kantian' passages seem to develop a Plotinian stress on the autonomous unfolding of the Logos within the soul; the more radically open notion of 'anticipation' can by contrast be related to a more Proclean (and originally Platonic) concern with participation, recollection and disclosure of the divine in the cosmos, as many passages indicate.

It may further be remarked that the later English romantic interest in Plato centring round the 'neo-pagan' Thomas Taylor pursued much more explicitly the theurgic reading. Perhaps this is one crucial reason why the outlook of Shelley, Blake and Coleridge diverges from that of German romanticism; but all this, to my knowledge, has scarcely been researched at all.

41 Balthasar, *La Théologique I: Verité du Monde*, p. 48.

although they are as truly there as quantities (we should here modify Cudworth, who was proto-Lockean in this respect) nonetheless arise as 'events' in the relatively stable habits of our interaction with reality.

Quantities arise in the same way, but unlike colours they involve, as Aristotle realized, our 'common sensing', since no single sense directly grasps quantity. Cudworth insisted that the new atomistic and mechanical physics did not favour either Hobbesian materialism or Cartesian dualism, because both the quantitative and the relational ('schetic') most basic aspects of reality can only be grasped by the mind, not immediately by the senses. Only the mind grasps the *scheses* of thing to thing, part to whole and vice versa, and the ineluctably relational notions of cause and effect, equality and inequality, sign and thing signified, besides the more aesthetic realities of order and proportion which are judged to exist by our minds under the ultimate lure of the good. In consequence, these realities are ultimately intellectual in character – yet while Cudworth rendered the *eide* in the world closer in character to a kind of eidetic thinking process as compared with scholasticism (although this was still only the trace of transcendent divine thought, and he refused the notion of an *anima mundi*), this did not at all mean that he verged towards an idealist subjectivism, even of a Kantian variety. The 'intellectual' character of numerical quantities and real relations was not for him a sign that we ourselves construct apparently given reality, but rather a sign that the universe is 'an intellectual system', since it is created. The understanding of this system more by active mind than by passive sensing does not then point to a pre-organized a priori of mental structure, but rather to the 'anticipatory' power of the mind both with respect to the discovery of nature and the invention of culture. The mind actively grasps the given cosmos, because the obscure signs arising in sensory events provoke a renewed participation in the light of the divine *Logos* that expresses the Paternal goodness and is the creative source of both the cosmos and our finite minds (see note 38 above).

So to see essence as also number can dialectically reinforce one's sense of the dynamic character of *eide* and the closeness of the activity of thought to the changeful character of the cosmos. However, I have said that with number comes also recursive set. This destroys the principle of non-contradiction. So now it seems that realism has failed to secure identity and thereby truth, but nominalism has failed just as dismally. Neither essences *nor* individuals submit to the law of excluded middle. So must we be sceptics? Yet if so, how is it that there appears to be relative identity? As Plato indicated in the *Theaetetus*, the idea that there is only flux and appearance must *also* appear within the flux, and seems thereby to identify a contradictory stable flux and true appearing of this flux to knowledge.[42] As today with supposed 'redundancy' theories of truth, one cannot really cross out truth, or deny the interval between being and truth which being itself opens up, in favour of a reduction of knowledge to one more ontic 'event'. Indeed as Balthasar pointed out (like Adorno), we are only immediately in contact with being because of simultaneous mediation (as in the situation of physical touch). We *know* something is there only to the measure that it resists our knowledge and we also know that there is more to be known, like the back of the tree.[43] We can only speak of being because it shows itself or gives itself as true, and yet in this showing also presents a certain palpable reserve. Thereby, in giving truth it also gives that gap between truth and being which is the never closed future horizon of understanding. Either, then, the relatively stable identities of *eide* are true realities, or else the one paradoxically stable form and truth is the form and truth of formless flux – which finally lacks identity because what it both shows and reserves is an ironic lack of reserve, a concealed as unconcealed nullity. But in neither instance can we any longer appeal to the absolute sway of the law of non-contradiction.

---

42 Plato, *Theaetetus*, 161d1–e5.

43 Balthasar, *La Théologique I: Verité du Monde*, pp. 122–3. On redundancy theories, see Milbank and Pickstock, *Truth in Aquinas*, pp. 1–6; on touch, see *Truth in Aquinas*, pp. 60–88.

Identity beyond Non-contradiction

It seems, then, that the Thomistic telescope must incorporate the perspectives of Nicholas of Cusa. Cusa sought to salvage the Proclean/Dionysian tradition especially associated with the Dominican order, by *admitting* that universals, real relations and participation violate non-contradiction. He also tended to see universals as signs opening up endless perspectives or aspects. Likewise, finite truth was for him (like Cudworth and Peirce) also a continuous task for human artisanal construction, since he also effectively stole from the nominalists the theme of human sub-creation. Whereas, for Ockham, finite spirits, like God, can at least in principle cause finite being,[44] since being is a bare univocal existential that can be posited outside divine creation, in Cusa's writings for humans to create is also to receive something and to surprise themselves, since they only *share* to a limited degree in the divine capacity absolutely to originate.[45] And while we can for Nicholas create triangles or spoons, we nonetheless can only create these as essences: for we must thereafter observe the infinitely unfolding constraints and possibilities of triangles and spoons, which as our own fabricated offspring endlessly take us by surprise and cannot be lawlessly manipulated at our pleasure, just as when we divide or modify things in nature we cannot really change essences – we can cut down trees and genetically modify them; we cannot get rid of the idea of tree that has appeared to us only through real trees growing. The point that even artificial things exhibit essences is elaborated more specifically by Cudworth, who notes that an invented thing like a *horloge* or watch contains certain regular *scheses*, and has a certain regular nature because it is a contrivance of mind – even if the mind that has contrived it cannot at once fathom all the implications of its regularity. (Inversely, for Cudworth, relational regularity in the natural

---

44 William of Ockham, *Quodlibetal Questions*, 1.1; 2.1; 2.9; *Reportatio* 2.6.

45 Nicholas of Cusa, *Idiota: De Mente* in *Opera*, ed. P. Wilpert (Berlin: De Gruyter, 1967), pp. 236–42.

world betrays a certain artificial 'intellectuality', precisely because he has dynamized essence as formation rather than simply form.)[46] This is in fact another disproof of nominalism:

---

46 Nicholas of Cusa, 'On the Summit of Contemplation' (*De Apice Theoriae*) in *Nicholas of Cusa: Selected Spiritual Writings*, tr. H. L. Bond (New York: Paulist Press, 1997), p. 302. Cudworth, *A Treatise*, Book I, ch. III, 4, p. 25; Book IV, ch. II, 4, pp. 85–6 for the *horloge* example. He goes on to adumbrate one of the earliest examples of a 'design argument' on the watch analogy: since nature is regular and ordered like a watch, it must have a creator. However, in two crucial respects Cudworth's argument is subtler than that of later writers like Paley: first of all, he argues that since only the mind, not the senses, recognizes *scheses* of part to part and part to whole – including 'ideas of cause, effect, means, and priority and posteriority, equality and inequality, order and proportion, symmetry and asymmetry, aptitude and inaptitude, sign and thing signified, whole and part' (p. 86) – it follows that these realities are inherently intellectual in character. So whereas, for Paley etc., order is *evidence* of the work of ordered mind, for Cudworth order *immediately* is for us the presence of ordered mind. This contention is powerfully upheld by a usage of Plato's arguments in *Theaetetus* concerning synaesthesia; since certain things are perceived as common to 'sound and colour' (Book III, ch. III, 6, p. 61) such as essence and non-essence, identity, diversity, unity, duality, etc. (note again the link between essence and number here), there are real metaphysical realities perceived by a psychic power beyond the merely sensory.

In a second but related respect also, Cudworth is far more profound than Paley. Along with other thinkers at this period, Cudworth does not see vitalism and mechanism always as opposites. To the contrary, he sees a machine as an automaton, as something 'self-running' and so approaching to perpetual motion. As an automaton, a machine possesses a kind of artificial vitalism, comparable to the active principles of nature and the activity of mind itself. Thus the *horloge* or watch is said *itself* to comprehend 'the logical system . . . of those relative ideas' and not only to be 'measured' by time but itself actively 'to measure' time, by its 'apt and proportionable disposition of certain quantities . . . contemporated together'. In short, Cudworth already takes the paradigmatic machine to be the *computer*. So whereas Paley is saying that the world runs like a machine and therefore we must infer a designer who has imposed this order upon it, Cudworth is saying that the world is like an automatic mind (whose components are eidetic *scheses*) whose mental contribution must intrinsically proceed from an absolute self-subsistent and self-generating thinking principle.

the idea that there can be a 'pure construction' entirely within our control from entirely discrete brutal elements. No, the most basic element, the geometric point, contains the direst mysteries and most inescapable ambuscades.

In sign, aspect (late medieval or renaissance 'perspective') number and *poesis,* Cusa, like Pascal later, recognized the impinging of the infinite at the heart of the finite. (By contrast, Aquinas did not acknowledge an actual as opposed to a possible – or else privated, actual but negatively valued – infinite as truly but contradictorily involved in the finite itself.) Truth, for him, as for the tradition, is the identical, the *non aliud.* But only the finitely identical is subject to non-contradiction, since as bounded it cannot violate its own bounds. In the infinite this does not apply: here the minimum is also the maximum, the hottest the coldest, etc.[47] Here, since the infinite God is all things, including all opposites and yet *simple* as well as infinite, he must be at the same moment and in the same respects these opposites – notice that Cusa needs to affirm in the strongest possible terms, like Aquinas (and unlike Scotus), God's simpleness as well as infinity in order to arrive at the *coincidentia oppositorum.*

However, since the finite is itself invaded and upheld by the presence of the infinite (both in logic and within our phenomenological experience) contradiction collapses identity here also: the point is the circumference of the circle and its centre; the tendency to the infinitely small is also the tendency to the

---

47 Nicholas of Cusa, *On Learned Ignorance (De Docta Ignorantia)* in *Nicholas of Cusa: Selected Spiritual Writings,* tr. H. L. Bond (New York: Paulist Press, 1997), Book I, chs XIII–XXII, pp. 102–20 and *passim.* On the infinite, see also A. Côté, 'Infinité' in J.-Y. Lacoste (ed.), *Dictionnaire Critique de Théologie* (Paris: PUF, 1998), pp. 572–5. (It should also be said that the infinite for Nicholas, unlike Scotus or Descartes, is not something positively thinkable by us, even though it indicates, as for Gregory of Nyssa, a positive and non-relative unboundedness in God himself. Nor can one for Nicholas think of God's infinity without or prior to his other perfections such as goodness, as one can for Scotus.)

infinitely great and so on.[48] For this reason our mathematics, in contrast to the later view of Galileo, cannot really attain to the real components of the divine *mathesis*: perhaps one can suggest, supplementing Cusa and following Grosseteste, that transfinites (besides other actual infinites and irrational numbers) hint at the successive propagation of the actually finite from the true actual simple and qualitative infinite.[49]

As for the Catholic Platonico-Aristotelian tradition in general, so for Cusa, finitude is in flux, and can only borrow relative stabilities of essence and individual substance from the infinite divine ideas, uttered in the *Logos*. However, he adds to this that participation in perfect identity is also participation in perfect non-identity, for the ultimate ontological scenario can always be envisaged the other way round. Only when apparent finite identities collapse in the unbounded is there a stable reality. And then these two metaphysical schemes paradoxically combine: only when the One is itself other to the One and so is Many is it also the One returning to itself as origin. Trinitarian theology allows Cusa to put this in more dynamic terms. The actively possible One is the generation of the actual Many: the Spirit displays this reciprocal bond where absolute becoming and absolute unchanging being are further coinciding opposites.[50] But only in the infinite is there perfect coincidence,

---

48 Nicholas of Cusa, *On Learned Ignorance*, Book 1, chs XIII–XXII, pp. 102–20, and Book 2, ch. XII, pp. 160–6.

49 See Grosseteste, *De Luce*.

50 Nicholas of Cusa, *On Actualised Possibility (De Possest)*, tr. J. Hopkins in *A Concise Introduction to the Philosophy of Nicholas of Cusa* (Minneapolis: Minnesota University Press, 1978), pp. 65–9, 93, 121. Here the Holy Spirit combines the *posse* of the Father and *actualitas* of the Son as *possest*. Later Cusa spoke not of *possest* but of *posse*, meaning absolute originating power or capacity, which is 'incomprehensible'. This is not, however, pure will, nor a purely virtual, logical possibility as for the Avicennian tradition. It transcends both the capacity of self-impulsion that is life and the power to comprehend that is understanding. As the power to be it coincides with the actuality of being, just as it coincides with the actuality of living and of understanding. If *posse* is now the 'highest' attribute, then this is in order to secure ontological

including of the limited and unlimited; between this true infinite and the created explicated finite infinite there is *no* coincidence, as later there is for Hegel. The latter hypostasizes a contradiction that remains contradictory, so that in a way finite and infinite ceaselessly cancel each other out, rendering each a void, and one has (as Hegel admits) a mode of nihilism: Cusa instead invokes a mystery of contradiction which is at the same time its own incomprehensible resolution, and so after all an infinite identity.

It may nonetheless seem troubling that for Cusa the finite, 'explicated', non-simple infinite is still an actual and not merely possible infinite; as such, despite the term *explicatio*, it possesses a cardinality. At this point, the shadow of materialism,

---

equality between the existential, vivifying and intellectual. God's actuality as *esse* is not prior to his self-movement or thought, so the power shown in being is not exhausted by being: indeed life more fully expresses God (and so being as such) than does unqualified being, and intelligence images God still more precisely. Yet intelligence does not give rise to being – as it would if this were a possibilistic ontology; nor does life give rise to being as it would were this a voluntaristic one. Instead these three aspects hint at a greater, ungraspable, powerful unity. In the temporal world it is our mind that most discloses the mysterious trinity of power: in choosing and selecting, the *posse* to be, to live and to understand is 'unfolded'; the mind in understanding 'makes' and this elaborates the '*posse* to become of the makeable' (knowledge) and 'the *posse* of the connection of both' (life). One can infer from this that knowledge as making is neither simply in the power of the maker, nor something ineluctably imposed by the makeable. Rather, 'the connection of both' must be something like aesthetic necessity that elaborates a specifically intellectual mode of life according to a free but specifically patterned motion. Since mind as unfolding most images the divine *posse*, and understanding most corresponds to the Second Person (to follow biblical convention) life to the Third (likewise) and so being to the First, it can be concluded that the spiritual *nexus* of life continues here, as in *De Possest*, to synthesize actuality of being and the possibility of knowledge, even though the term *posse* is now preferred for its greater denotation of simplicity and suggestion of an equalization of the existential dimension with the vivifying and cognitive. See *On the Summit of Contemplation (De Apice Theoriae)* in *Nicholas of Cusa: Selected Spiritual Writings*, pp. 293–303.

monism and pantheism that had hovered over a positive actual infinity ever since Greek antiquity (most of its advocates prior to Plotinus were materialists) seems to re-intrude. However, for Nicholas, every immanent actual infinity is (a) only aspectual, abstracting out some quantitative or else virtual dimension of reality and (b) is always complex and never simple. Nevertheless, it must be recognized that the infinitesimally small and the immeasurably large, together with undecidable factors in sets and diagonals, do indeed 'instantly fade' towards absolute simple infinity, without of themselves in their own peculiar aporetic nature truly encompassing it. In consequence they can be read, or even for a certain insight demand to be read, not as the traces of pantheism, but rather as signs of the creature's created nothingness in itself, and of Augustine's closeness of God to us that is closer than that of ourselves to ourselves.

On this understanding, therefore, finitude reveals itself as a contradictory mystery. Only two rival truths are now possible, even if they can appear alarmingly akin to each other. There is first of all the truth of non-truth of nihilism that will require a mode of faith in nothingness if it is to evade the recursivity of the truth of non-truth. Second, as an alternative, there is the at once conjectured and experienced truth of transcendent metaphysics or theology: this alone now offers us the truth of truth, of a fully ontological truth. For the latter position, every creature exists by diagonalizing out of its finitude through participation in being; humanity is the site of conscious awareness of this exit. A human being can be the living self-aware diagonal, or else can perversely choose to suppress this contradictory reality. Like Cantor's C, humanity is the infinite plus 1, beyond yet not beyond even the infinite aleph-zero extension of the universe. One can try futilely to construe this plus 1 in functional terms as useful to an animal – yet mere *assertion* of non-functionality (as Jean-Luc Marion has often indicated) frustrates any such demonstration and sustains the diagonal excess, while the constant creative eccentricity of the diagonal means that totalizing functional explanation must forever struggle to keep pace with its innovations.

Truth then requires identity. But this is only found in incomprehensible infinite non-identity in which this world incomprehensibly participates. This infinite non-identity is itself the trinitarian play between the infinite *peras* of the One and the equally infinite *apeiron* of the 'complicated' and so simple and ordered Many expressed in the *Logos*. This play spins off from both as their arising unity without surpassing them, in the form of the Holy Spirit which is at once the bond of desire and the freedom of charity. Truth in the creation reflects this infinite exchange, and is to a degree present in the constitutive relational interplay between individuals and universals, and between being as substantial and being as intellectual. This interplay runs also, as we can now see, thanks to the Thomistic telescope, along a temporal axis between nature and culture, and between essence and event, sign and number, substance and aspect.

Truth as the Bond of Being

Balthasar, rather like Cudworth in this respect, affirms that such interplay concerns the Good and the Beautiful as well as the True. To be more precise, though, he actually says that the True is not mere representation, because it is communication of the Good, while the Good is not mere fulfilment of desire because it is the expression of self-giving Being.[51] The Beautiful is supposed for him to be involved in both these excesses. Yet it is hard in a way to see where it finds a place in this scheme. In the end, Balthasar's aesthetic and his presentation of Aquinas's *De Veritate* gives way before a lingering Bonaventuran stress on the priority of the will and the Good. Indeed perhaps because he bases his aesthetics too much upon subjective phenomenological intuition, and too little upon speculative judgement of an ontology, the excess of the invisible in the visible which constitutes for him the lure of beauty is in danger of reducing the notion of visible beauty to a mere sign of an infinite otherness

---

51 Balthasar, *La Théologique I: Verité du Monde*, pp. 229–34.

and gratuity. Then indeed it will seem that the True is the manifestation of Being beyond the mere mirroring of Being, because it also communicates the Good, while goodness is no mere fulfilment of need because it receives the infinite sacrificial one-way gift of Being, which is pure gratuity. One can appreciate how, like Augustine and Cudworth, Balthasar preserves the Platonic notion of a primal Good that sustains even judgements of the True, rendering them in the end precipitations of true desire. However, he at times allows this to mean that the will outruns the ordered distributions of judgements. He ends *Theologik I* by saying that while we cannot comprehend divine truth, truth remains our element, whereas before divine love our cognitive and willing efforts must fall silent and we must simply adore. Love, he says, is more ultimate in God than truth.[52] But are they not co-equal? And is not *theoria* fulfilled in liturgy rather than abandoned by it?

A love beyond even our inkling as to the nature of love sounds like a pure imparticipable manifestation of will. Similarly, Balthasar says that love makes mercy outrun the justice of truth. However, for Aquinas infinite justice as justice was mercy, and mercy remained the infinite just placing or distribution of the reconciled in peace.

By contrast, a lingering Scotist and Kantian conception of mercy as mere subjective gesture persists in Balthasar here. And the same set of positions means that finally for him the one-way unilateral gift triumphs: beyond even the exchange of Father and *Verbum* in the truth, the *Donum* is the excess of free offering in God and to us. It is significant that Balthasar declares that Being is communication of the Good *before relation* – that is to say, before a kind of binding (or *troth*) of Being to this manifestation that would obligate Being in its very freedom.[53] Instead he wants Being to be radically free. But how can this be consistent with the trinitarian giving of the Truth and the Good, of

52 Balthasar, *La Théologique I: Verité du Monde*, p. 285.
53 Balthasar, *La Théologique I: Verité du Mond*, p. 39.

Verbum and *Donum* by the Father who is *esse*, since this *is* a relational communication that is free always as bound in truth?

Here one wonders about the status of Balthasar's metaphysical prolegomena – for in this case starting with the metaphysical transcendentals seems to engender a conflict with the perspective of the theological trinitarian transcendentals which are 'word' and 'gift'. Balthasar rightly says that what is necessary participation from our point of view is free 'revelation' from God's point of view,[54] and one can add that one should be able to say this of revelation *tout court*, since even the revelation in Christ and the Church heightens human participation, and this is necessary to us beyond necessity, in terms of our real supernatural end. He also rightly notes that Aquinas says that every human cognition is an obscure cognition of God – yet by this, as Balthasar knows, Aquinas also means that every human cognition is an obscure anticipation of the beatific vision only reoffered to us by redeeming grace.[55] Therefore, for Aquinas, all participated knowledge occurs remotely by virtue of such grace. This would suggest that metaphysical prolegomena are at best ambivalent, except as conscious anticipations of a trinitarian ontology. It is clear that *in reality* Balthasar's metaphysics would not in general have the shape it does were it not exactly such an anticipation. Yet in this specific instance it seems that the metaphysics of the transcendentals whereby Being gives before relations *governs* the theological ontology of *verbum* and *donum*, such that something in the Holy Spirit is in excess of its substantive relation to the relation of Father to Son. This excess is still the modern 'free gesture' of will, whose background is a Being that is otherwise reduced to a gift-less existential inertia.

However, one can repair Balthasar. He is not consistent in this tendency and at times refuses a Bonaventuran pneumatology.[56]

---

54 Balthasar, *La Théologique I: Verité du Monde*, pp. 238–55.

55 See Milbank and Pickstock, *Truth in Aquinas*, pp. 19–60.

56 Balthasar, *La Théologique II: Vérité de Dieu*, pp. 177–9 and *III: L'Esprit de Vérité*, pp. 152–4. In the latter place, Balthasar refuses the

Rightly he stresses, unlike Jean-Luc Marion, that the *Donum* is both the manifestation of the prior reciprocity in truth of Father and Son *and* that this reciprocity is in itself a passing beyond itself.[57] Without this passing beyond (one can elaborate), the reciprocity between Father and Son might appear to involve a mere symmetry, since the Father *is* engendering and the Son *is* being engendered, according to the logic of substantive relation. Yet since the latter properly implies mutual ecstatic being and not a mutually reflexive self-confirmation through the mirror of the other (a 'doubling' inconsistent with the divine simplicity), the passage of Father to Son and of Son to Father is not just an immediate return in either case, but also a sustained exceeding of any return and so of any merely complicit mutuality. This exceeding of one towards the other therefore is immediately also the exceeding of both by both which gives rise in actuality to the Holy Spirit as the space of possibility for an infinite sharing by infinite others of their mutual love. In this way, the purely relational dyad is only constituted by a constant escaping of the dyad and the symmetry of the Father/Son relation as endlessly renewed by the asymmetry of the third. The third continuously

---

Franciscan distinction of the persons as proceeding respectively 'by nature' (the Son) and 'by liberality' (the Spirit). In the former place though, he seems to endorse a more sophisticated Bonaventuran version of this scheme which distinguishes between exemplarity and liberality. However, exemplarity and *per naturam* are probably equivalent, and the 'surplus' of the Spirit cannot be (as it is for Balthasar) a surplus of love over understanding without making the understanding less than loving. It must rather be something to do with the ecstasy also of understanding beyond the merely dyadic situation (the Peircean need for interpretation by a 'third' outside the closure of the tautologous, or the apodeictic, for example). Also Balthasar in a Franciscan line sees the Son as freely generated by the Father, and refuses the idea that this generation has equally an *intellectual* ground, he denies that the Father can in principle only know himself (and all *esse*), through the Son. If this view is, as Balthasar says 'Hegelian' (but it isn't) then Aquinas – and Gregory of Nyssa, Cyril and Augustine – were all Hegelians.

57 Balthasar, *La Theologique I: Vérité du Monde*, pp. 46, 78–9, and *III: L'Espirit de Vérité*, pp. 216–29; Balthasar, *Theo-Drama Vol. V: The Last Act*, tr. G. Harrison (San Francisco: Ignatius Press, 1998), pp. 105–9.

interrupts the circularity of two and yet this circularity none-theless entirely pivots about this interruption.

Hence although the Father only gives to the Son what the Son returns to the Father, the Son forever receives something new by the excess of the Spirit's spiration in which the Word is breathed out from the Father's mouth. Similarly, although the Father only receives from the Son what he has given to him, he end-lessly receives back something newly inspired by the Spirit's mediation. This constantly renewed asymmetry within the reciprocal relation of Father and Son therefore constitutes the 'moment' of unilaterality that renders the *Donum* truly *Donum* and not just formally equivalent exchange, and at the same time a *Donum* (as Augustine declared) receivable by us as the 'extra' and yet necessary (if we are to realize our supernatural end) gift of deifying grace – just as the Spirit within the Trinity is at once superfluous and yet fundamental.[58] This unilateral moment corresponds, as we saw in the realm of knowledge, to the moment of valid individuality and individual identity that is not exhausted by universal essence.

To sustain this balance regarding the *Donum*, however, one needs to say more emphatically than Balthasar that what exceeds mere representation in the truth is the Beautiful, as this retains the character of truth as measure and yet ensures that truth *as* truth, not as communicated will, exceeds mere copying. Likewise one needs to say that what exceeds satisfaction of desire in the case of the Good is also the Beautiful, because then one can allow that the Good exceeds satisfaction in itself in so far as it is the realized mutual co-dwelling of human or angelic persons, and not merely as the passive receiving of a gift from the excessive source of Being. This ensures that the moment of unilateral giving does not surpass but rather allows mutual reciprocity through asymmetry, since such asymmetrical reciprocity is fundamentally beautiful. In turn, the aesthetic so conceived (here following Balthasar) as balancing a measured manifestness (classicism) and the lure of desire beyond appear-

---

58 Augustine, *De Trinitate*, Book XV, ch. 5, 27–39.

ance (romanticism) cannot reduce beauty to a mere sign of the sublime beyond of the supreme other. Instead, as Balthasar often seems to indicate (when he transcends mere personalism) the invisible here truly is *in* the visible, by another coincidence of opposites (although they only perfectly coincide in the infinite, where the *Logos* is a boundless image).

Repaired in this way, Balthasar's understanding of how truth is aesthetically established in the desire for goodness – the desire to give – blends very well with the Thomistic telescope that newly stresses how truth as realized *eidos* is also truth as anticipation, truth as made, truth as continued event, truth as interpreting signs, truth as receptivity of new aspects.

Together these perspectives suggest that truth is that which opens us to contemplation of the infinite just in so far as it is also that which prepares us for a more harmonious human and cosmic future. Beyond contradiction and non-contradiction, truth only begins to disclose to us an infinite integral identity in so far as it also begins to realize in our finitude the measured exchanges of hope and love which ceaselessly and incomprehensibly blend the same with the different. Truth as disclosure is also troth, the bond of being.

14. Sacramental Aesthetics: Between Word and Flesh

RICHARD KEARNEY

A Phenomenology of Flesh

Husserl blazed a path towards a phenomenology of the flesh when he broached the crucial theme of embodiment in *Ideas* 2, a theme largely ignored by western metaphysics since Plato. This may seem strange given that almost fifteen hundred years of the history of metaphysics comprised what Gilson called the 'Christian synthesis' of Greek and biblical thought. But metaphysics, with few exceptions, managed to take the flesh and blood out of Christian incarnation leaving us with rather abstract conceptual equivalents. It would take Husserl and the modern phenomenological revolution to bring western philosophy back to the flesh of pre-reflective lived experience. Husserl himself, however, for all his talk of returning us to the 'things themselves', remained caught in the nets of transcendental idealism and never quite escaped the limits of theoretical cognition. Heidegger took a step closer to the flesh with his existential analytic of 'moods' and 'facticity', but the fact remains that Heideggerian *Dasein* has no real body at all: it does not eat, sleep or have sex. It too remains, despite all its talk of 'being-in-the-world', captive of the transcendental snare. While Scheler

---

*Some footnotes to this chapter are particularly long, and therefore all notes are to be found on pp. 358–69.

made sorties into a phenomenology of feeling and Sartre offered valuable insights into shame and desire, it was not really until Merleau-Ponty that we got a credible return to the flesh; and not just as cipher, project or icon, but as *flesh itself* in all its ontological depth.

Here at last the ghost of Cartesian and Kantian idealism is laid, as we finally return to the body in all its unfathomable *thisness*. It is telling, I think, that Merleau-Ponty chose to describe his phenomenology of the sensible body in sacramental language, amounting to what we might call – without the slightest irreverence – a eucharist of profane perception. In the *Phenomenology of Perception* (1944), we read:

> Just as the sacrament not only symbolizes, in sensible species, an operation of Grace, but *is* also the real presence of God, which it causes to occupy a fragment of space and communicates to those who eat of the consecrated bread, provided that they are inwardly prepared, in the same way the sensible has not only a motor and vital significance, but is nothing other than a certain way of being in the world suggested to us from some point in space, and seized and acted upon by our body, provided that it is capable of doing so, so that sensation is literally a form of communion.[1]

Merleau-Ponty goes on to sound this eucharistic power of the sensible as follows:

> I am brought into relation with an external being, whether it be in order to open myself to it or to shut myself off from it. If the qualities radiate around them a certain mode of existence, if they have the power to cast a spell and what we called just now a sacramental value, this is because the sentient subject does not posit them as objects, but enters into a sympathetic relation with them, makes them his own and finds in them his momentary law.[2]

We shall have occasion to refer to numerous idioms of transubstantial empathy below. Suffice it for now to note the curious paradox that it is precisely when Merleau-Ponty traces the phenomenological return all the way down to the lowest rung of experience (in the old metaphysical ladder, the *sensible*) that he discovers the most sacramental act of communion, or what he also likes to call 'chiasmus'. The crossing over of ostensible contraries. The most in the least, the highest in the lowest, the first in the last, the invisible in the visible. Here we have a reversal of Platonic and Idealism. A return to flesh as our most intimate 'element', namely, that which enfolds and envelopes us in the systole and diastole of being, the seeing and being seen of vision. Phenomenology thus marks the surpassing of traditional dualisms (body/mind, real/ideal, inner/outer, subject/object) in the name of a deeper, more primordial chiasmus where opposites traverse each other. This is how Merleau-Ponty describes the enigma of flesh as mutual crossing-over in his posthumously published work, *The Visible and the Invisible* (1964): 'The seer is caught up in what he sees . . . the vision he exercises, he also undergoes from the things, such that, as many painters have said, I feel myself looked at by the things, my activity.' So much so that 'the seer and the visible reciprocate one another and we no longer know which sees and which is seen. It is this Visibility, this anonymity innate to Myself that we have called flesh, and one knows there is no name in traditional philosophy to designate it.'[3] It is here, I suggest, that Merleau-Ponty gets to the heart of this nameless matter and descends – in a final return, a last reduction that suspends all previous reductions – to the incarnate region of the 'element':

> The flesh is not matter, in the sense of corpuscles of Being which would add up or continue on one another to form beings. Nor is the visible (the thing as well as my body) some 'psychic' material that would be – God knows how – brought into being by the things factually existing and acting on my factual body. In general, it is not a fact or a sum of facts 'material' or 'spiritual'.

No, insists Merleau-Ponty:

the flesh is not matter, is not mind, is not substance. To designate it, we would need the ancient term 'element', in the sense
it was used to speak of water, air, earth, and fire, that is, in
the sense of a *general thing* midway between the spatio-
temporal individual and the idea, a sort of incarnate principle
that brings a style of Being wherever there is a fragment of
Being. The flesh is in this sense an 'element' of Being.[4]

Returning to examples of painting – Cézanne and Klee – in *Eye
and Mind* (1964), Merleau-Ponty expounds on this chiasmic
model of the flesh as a mutual transubstantiation of the seer and
the seen in a 'miracle' of flesh:

There really is inspiration and expiration of Being, action and
passion so slightly discernible that it becomes impossible to
distinguish between what sees and what is seen, what paints
and what is painted . . . There is no break at all in this circuit;
it is impossible to say that nature ends here and that man or
expression starts here. It is mute Being which itself comes to
show forth its own meaning.[5]

In *Signs* (1960), a collection of essays devoted to questions of
language and art, Merleau-Ponty repeats his claim that the
flesh of art is invariably indebted to the bread of life. There is
nothing so insignificant in the life of the artist, he claims, that is
not eligible for 'consecration' in the painting or poem. But the
'style' which the artist creates converts his corporeal situation
into a sacramental witness at a higher level of 'repetition' and
'recreation'. The art work still refers to the life-world from
which it springs, but opens up a second-order reference of creative possibility and freedom. Speaking specifically of Leonardo
da Vinci, he writes:

If we take the painter's point of view in order to be present at
that decisive moment when what has been given to him to live
as corporeal destiny, personal adventures or historical events,
crystallizes into 'the motive' (i.e. the style), we will recognize
that his work, which is never an effect, is always a response to

these data and that the body, the life, the landscapes, the schools, the mistresses, the creditors, the police and the revolutions which might suffocate painting are also *the bread his work consecrates*. To live in painting is still to breathe the air of this world.[6]

In short, the bread of the world is the very stuff consecrated in the body of the work.

We will return to this aesthetic of transubstantiation in our discussion of Proust below. But before leaving Merleau-Ponty I wish to mention one other intriguing passage in *Signs* where the author – no theologian and certainly no Christian apologist – has an interesting interpretation of Christian embodiment as a restoration of the divine within the flesh, a kenotic emptying out of transcendence into the heart of the world's body, becoming a God beneath us rather than a God beyond:

> The Christian God wants nothing to do with a vertical rela-
> tion of subordination. He is not simply a principle of which
> we are the consequence, a will whose instruments we are, or
> even a model of which human values are the only reflection.
> There is a sort of impotence of God without us, and Christ
> attests that God would not be fully God without becoming
> fully man. Claudel goes so far as to say that God is not above
> but beneath us – meaning that we do not find Him as a
> suprasensible idea, but as another ourself which dwells in and
> authenticates our darkness. Transcendence no longer hangs
> over man; he becomes, strangely, its privileged bearer.[7]

This insight of 'immanent transcendence' is not of course original to Merleau-Ponty. Many Christian mystics – from John of the Cross to Hildegard of Bingen and Meister Eckhart – inti-mated similar things. As have Jewish sages like Rabbi Luria and Rosenzweig, or Sufi masters like Rumi and Ibn'Arabi. Indeed I am also reminded here of the bold suggestion by Teilhard de Chardin that God does not direct the universe from above but underlies it and 'prolongs himself' into it. But what Merleau-Ponty provides is a specific philosophical method – namely, a phenomenology of radical embodiment – to articulate this 'nameless' phenomenon of sacramental flesh. And it is arguable that a number of recent phenomenologists have followed Merleau-Ponty's lead (or parallel path) when seeking to inventory the sacred dimensions of the flesh – I am thinking especially of Jean-Luc Marion's writings on the 'flesh' as a saturated phenomenon in *On Excess* or Jean-Louis Chrétien's phenomenological commentary on the Song of Songs.[8] But Merleau-Ponty has the advantage, in my view, of not only being the first phenomenologist to explicitly identify the sacramental valence of the sensible but also of maintaining a certain methodological agnosticism with regard to the theistic or atheistic implications of this phenomenon. Indeed his philosophy of 'ambiguity' is particularly well suited when it comes to interpreting the sacramental idioms of eucharistic epiphany in Proust, as we hope to show below.

Merleau-Ponty is no Christian apologist in drag, as several of those belonging to the 'theological turn' in phenomenology have been accused. And this chimes well, it seems to me, with the poetic licence enjoyed by artists and writers when it comes to the marvel of transubstantiation in word, sound or image. For poetic licence entails a corollary confessional licence from which no reader is excluded. In this respect, we could say that the phenomenological method – which brackets confessional and other beliefs – is analogous to the literary suspending of same for the sake of all-inclusive entry to the 'kingdom of as-if'. And this suspension of belief and disbelief, I will argue, allows for a specific 'negative capability' regarding questions of doubt, proof, dogma or doctrine, so as to better appreciate the 'thing itself', the holy *thisness* and *thereness* of our flesh-and-blood existence. The attitude of pure vigilance and attention that follows such exposure to a 'free variation of imagination' (the term is Husserl's) is not far removed, I believe, from what certain mystics have recognized to be a crucial preparatory moment for sacramental vision, calling it by such different names as 'the cloud of unknowing' (Julian of Norwich), the 'docta ignorantia' (Cusa) or, in eastern mysticism, the 'neti/neti' (neither this nor that) which paves the way for the highest wisdom of reality.

For reasons of economy, and limited competence, I will be confining my remarks in the second part of this paper exclusively to three modernist writers of fiction. That similar arguments could be made – and perhaps more cogently – with regard to the sacramental vision of musicians, painters and poets is undeniable. Especially when one considers how such artists work more closely with the sensible and carnal than novelists do. But that is a task for others more expert than I in those disciplines.[9]

* * *

Before moving on to a close reading of Proust, however, I wish to mention one other contemporary philosopher – Julia Kristeva – who also has had much to say on the sacramental imagination, especially as it relates to what she explicitly calls an aesthetic of 'transubstantiation' in Proust and Joyce. In *Time and Sense*, Kristeva offers this example, among many others:

> A sensation from the past remains within us, and involuntary memory recaptures it when a related perception in the present is stimulated by the same desire as the prior sensation. A spatio-temporal association of sensations is thus established, relying on a link, a structure, and a reminiscence. Sensation takes refuge in this interwoven network and turns into an *impression*, which means that sensation loses its solitary specificity. A similarity emerges out of all these differences, eventually attaining the status of a general law in the manner of an idea or thought. The 'general law', however, is no abstraction, for it is established because the sensation is *immanent in it* . . . This process keeps the structure from losing its sensorial foundation. Music becomes word, and writing becomes a *transubstantion* in those for whom it creates 'new powers'.[10]

Kristeva links this aesthetic of transubstantiation – that she finds in Joyce and Proust – back to the writings of the later

Merleau-Ponty, which she calls 'mystically significant'.[11] Indeed her notion of a 'general law' of ideational sensation is surely not unrelated to Merleau-Ponty's reference to a 'momentary law' cited above. Most specifically, Kristeva relates the eucharistic aesthetic to the chiasmic relation between the visible and invisible, the inner feeling and outer expression, that Merleau-Ponty describes as a reversible interpenetration of *flesh*. Refusing the dualistic division of spirit and body into two separate substances, both Kristeva and Merleau-Ponty counsel us to rethink flesh more phenomenologically as an *'element,* as the concrete emblem of a general manner of being'.[12] And in this respect, Kristeva keenly endorses Merleau-Ponty's claim that 'no one has gone further than Proust in fixing the relations between the visible and the invisible'.[13] Indeed identifying Merleau-Ponty's model of reversibility with the notion of 'transubstantiation' in Proust, Kristeva sees this miracle of the flesh as a model both for therapeutic healing and for reading literary texts.

Kristeva believes that the reversible transubstantiation of word and flesh expresses itself as a certain catharsis which saves modernist writers like Proust from the prison of linguistic idealism to which purely formalist readings have consigned him.[14] And this, we should not forget, is a linguistic semiotician speaking: 'Although Proust never stops "deciphering", his world does not consist of "signs". At any rate, his world is not made of sign-words or idea-signs and certainly not of signifiers and signifieds.'[15] Proust, Kristeva observes, was disappointed or amused by 'empty linguistic signs' and preferred instead the fluidity of 'atmospheric changes', a 'rush of blood', a sudden silence, an 'adverb springing from an involuntary connection made between two unformulated ideas'.[16] Kristeva finds support for this aesthetic of 'real presence' in the young Proust's aversion to 'signs' and 'strict significations' and points to the fact that Jean Santeuil (Marcel *avant la lettre*) conceives of art as a 'work of feeling' which focuses on a 'sort of obscure instinct of permanent brilliance' or 'lava about to overflow', as well as on 'what is not yet ready to come forth'.[17] The paradigmatic Proustian text, she avers, rises up 'against the abyss between language and lived experience' and operates as a work which expresses 'the vast array of impressions that the hero's sentence strives to communicate (despite his reservations about language) by associating weather, villages, roads, dust, grass and raindrops through a mass accumulation of metaphors and metonymies'.[18]

This, Kristeva surmises, paves the way in Proust 'for the *impression,* which makes up for the weakness of linguistic signs'.[19] And so words are only useful for Proust when they exert an 'evocative power' over our 'sensibility' and display a kinship with a sort of 'latent music' (the terms are Proust's).[20] Resisting the temptations of semiology and Platonism, Proust's eucharistic writing aims for a 'lively physical expressiveness that resists the passivity of the civilised sign'.[21] It strives instead towards a language of the lived body: what Proust called 'the vigorous and expressive language of our muscles and our desires, of suffering, of the corruption or the flowering of the flesh'.[22] Let us now turn to a textual reading of the sacramental aesthetic at work in Proust's major work, *In Search of Lost Time.*

Proustian Eucharists

Sacramental idioms are central to the work of Marcel Proust. Tropes of 'transubstantion', 'resurrection' and 'revelation' occur in several key passages of *In Search of Lost Time*, celebrating the bread and wine of the everyday. These tropes signal a grammar for recovering the timeless in time, as in the famous madeleine episode, but also a grammar of artistic transformation, as in Marcel's final disquisition on the writing process in *Time Regained* (the final volume of the novel). This Proustian transfiguring of passing moments into something mystical and enduring invariably takes the form of a consecration of quotidian experiences of flesh and blood *thisness* and *thereness.* Let us take a more detailed look at some examples.

Food and taste are of course crucial to the epiphany of the madeleine and tea episode, but I would suggest it is another eucharist epiphany at the end of the labyrinthine narrative which brings us closest to Proust's sacramental vision. I refer to the penultimate scene chez les Guermantes when Marcel is left waiting in the library antechamber as a pre-prandial music recital is being performed. Having arrived late, Marcel experiences a cluster of epiphanies as he waits before entering the Guermantes' salon. Here in this antechamber of remaindered time certain achronic moments return to him.

Marcel's first involuntary memory is of entering the San Marco Cathedral in Venice, a site of eucharistic celebration par excellence. This flash of memory is triggered by his stumbling on some uneven cobblestones as he traverses the Guermantes' courtyard. Though he had been unable to take in the sacramental epiphany at the time (when he first visited Venice with his mother) he relives it now many years later here in Paris. We shall return to this momentarily.

This 'miracle of the courtyard' is followed by another involuntary memory brought on by the sound of a spoon striking a plate as a waiter in the dining room prepares the banquet table (for the feast to come). Then we have a third quasi-eucharistic epiphany as Marcel wipes his lips with a starched table napkin, the sensation suddenly recalling a luminous moment in his childhood when he sat in the dining room of the Grand Hotel at Balbec. And, finally, Marcel experiences a very formative (if forgotten) moment in his childhood: fetching a volume of George Sands' novel *Francois le Champi* from the Guermantes' library shelves, he suddenly relives an evening when Maman read this same book to him at bedtime in Combray. And it was this nocturnal reading which coincided, as we know from the opening scene of the book, with the inaugural moment when his mother left the dinner table with Marcel's father and Swann to come and kiss her son Marcel goodnight. Reading and feasting are thus intimately associated with the maternal kiss which set Marcel on his search for lost time, eventually culminating in the composition of the novel of that name.[23]

Samuel Beckett has described this cluster of epiphanies as a 'single annunciation'; and I think this allusion to the miracle of incarnation is telling. For in this scene Marcel comes back to the flesh. He is reminded, at this same Guermantes' party, that most of his loved ones are dead (Robert de Saint Loup, Grandmaman, Maman, Swann, Odette, Francoise), that Charlus is dying, and that he himself (Marcel) has just escaped a brush with death in a sanatorium. Marcel is brought back to earth, so to speak, and sees behind the masks of Parisian show and snobbery to the underlying reality of mortal flesh, transience and passing away. And it is only then, the author seems to imply, that Marcel is ready, at last, after many thousands of pages questing for the perfect work of art, to renounce his elite romantic pretensions and acknowledge that real art is an *art of flesh* – a literary transubstantiation of those contingent, fragile, carnal and seemingly inconsequential moments that our conscious will is wont to consign to oblivion. (One recalls Merleau-Ponty on Da Vinci above.) Marcel can finally assume his vision of 'Combray and its surrounding world taking shape and solidity out of a cup of tea'.[24]

* * *

Julia Kristeva lays special emphasis on the San Marco epiphany, recalling as it does an earlier chapter in the novel, and an earlier moment in Marcel's life, when he visits Venice with Maman. Kristeva interprets this pivotal episode as central to the understanding of Proust's eucharistic aesthetic, combining as it does the various epiphanies of Mamam reading, the madeleine and the stumbling stone. Examining various drafts of Proust's novels and notebooks, Kristeva finds it very significant that Proust described his aesthetic in liturgical terms of 'transubstantiation', 'real presence' and the incarnational mystery of 'time embodied' and 'time resurrected'.[25] She herself uses these same terms, deployed in the Catholic eucharistic rite, to describe the way in which Proust's characters relate to themselves, each other and the textual style of the novel through a mystical model of criss-crossing times:

As combinations of past and present impressions, the characters contaminate one another and fuse their contours; a *secret
depth* attracts them. Like the madeleine soaked in tea, they
allow themselves to be absorbed into Proust's style. These
Proustian heroes and visions will eventually leave us with a
singular and bizarre taste that is pungent and invigorating. It is
the taste of the sense of time, of *writing as transubstantiation.*[26]

Kristeva goes on to cite many scenes which elaborate on this
sacramental idiom of transubstantion in terms of 'translation',
'incarnation', 'metaphor' and 'superimposition'.[27] For Proust it
is the task of the writer to 'search for an object' in which 'each
hour of our life hides', for he believes that each time we achieve
such a task we resuscitate those hidden moments in the form of
epiphanies. In his writings on the aesthetics of Ruskin and
Male, for example, Proust identifies two particular such moments,
a bit of toast that will become a 'madeleine' and a Venetian
paving-stone: namely, two of the key epiphanies of *In Search of
Times Past.* Commenting on the example of the paving stone in
San Marco Cathedral, Kristeva writes:

> Tripping on the stone and then stumbling would thus be a
> way of having faith in the sacred. Indeed the sacred is made
> of stone: a 'living stone, rejected by men but in God's sight
> chosen and precious' (1 Peter 2.4–5) . . . The cornerstone,
> along with its manifestations in Proust's writings, is thus pre-
> sented as a sign of the cult of Jesus, as the real presence of
> essence. The cornerstone appears to have been Proust's
> underlying motif, for between the cathedrals and the Mass
> . . . Proust wished to fathom the mystery of 'transubstantia-
> tion'. He managed to do so by . . . clearing his own path
> through everyday sensations, and by acknowledging an eroti-
> cism that influenced and increasingly overwhelmed the future
> narrator's involuntary memory.[28]

Or again, 'In contact with the "living stone", he (Marcel) himself becomes a "living stone", a "stream of light", a participant
in the sacred, in "transubstantiation."'[29]

Proust himself, of course, describes the coming together of different times and scenes as both 'metaphor' and 'resurrection'. And for Proust these terms are curiously allied if not identical. Both involve the translation of one thing in terms of another. True art, Marcel comes to realize, is not a matter of progressively depicting a series of objects or events ('describing one after another the innumerable objects which at a given moment were present at a particular place'); it occurs only when the writer 'takes two different objects' and 'states the connection between them'.[30] And here we return to Merleau-Ponty's logic of sacramental perception. For it is identification of 'unique connections' and hidden liaisons between one thing and another that enables the writer to translate the book of life (that 'exists already in each one of us') into the book of art.[31] This is how Marcel puts it: 'truth – and life too – can be attained by us only when, by comparing a quality common to two sensations, we succeed in extracting their common essence and in reuniting them to each other, liberated from the contingencies of time, with a metaphor'.[32] That Marcel privileges figures of resurrection and transubstantiation in this work of metaphor reconfirms his sacramental aesthetic.

But let us say a little more about the famous 'The Trip to Venice' episode which follows immediately after the death of Albertine. The scene opens with a golden angel on San Marco campanile 'announcing' a certain 'joy'. Several themes are tightly woven into this short chapter to 'reaffirm Proust's notion of art as transubstantiation'.[33] Combray and Venice, childhood and adulthood, France and Italy, and the two distinct temporal sensations of past and present 'condensed into a metaphor'. The scene plays out a dream of death and rebirth. 'Death plays a role in this condensation. A reference to the grandmother's death echoes Albertine's more recent disappearance, which is now ready to be internalized and transformed into the innermost depths of writing.'[34] Recalling the mother's presence under the window, the narrator confesses an impression of 'getting closer and closer to the essence of something secret'.[35] Kristeva reads this visit to San Marco as pivotal to the entire development of the novel. It is, she claims, a crucial station in the initiatory journey between 'The Death of the Cathedrals' chapter and the concluding volume, *Time Regained*, comprising what she calls a 'voyage toward a *living* meaning'.[36] This is how she interprets the scene:

> The mystery of this incarnate Venice resides in the mother's presence . . . the incorporation of mother and city . . . A strange fusion is established between the mother's body and Venice's body. Sitting and reading underneath the pointed arches of an ogival window, the mother inscribes herself in the beautiful stones of Saint Mark's. The window is identified with 'a love which stopped only where there was no longer any corporeal matter to sustain it, on the surface of her impassioned gaze . . . It says to me the thing that touches me more than anything else in the world: *I remember your mother so well*. Through the magic of this infiltration, the Venetian window becomes the matter sustaining maternal love – the window *is* the love for the mother. The same process applies to the baptistery, where we find devoted women who appear to have been taken right out of a Carpaccio painting: 'She (the mother) has her place reserved there as immutably as a mosaic.'[37]

The word 'fusion' here is telling, I suspect, given the French association with brewing beverages, for example the *infusion* of Linden tea in the madeleine episode. So that we might say that mystical fusion and liquid fusion brush shoulders across memory and time. Nor is it insignificant that Marcel's anamnetic retrieval of the Venice baptistery in the epiphany of the Guermantes' paving stone, is contiguous with the related recall of Maman reading the story of Francois le Champi and his foster mother *Madeleine* Blanchet: a mystical-maternal association which Kristeva makes much of.[38] Kristeva concludes her psychoanalytic reading by suggesting that the Venice scene is best understood as an 'incarnation founded on the love between a son and his mother'.[39] She is well aware of the Marian and

Catholic connotations of this Madonna and Child imagery and deems it highly significant that Proust redrafted the chapter several times and was revising it right up to his death, as witnessed in certain deathbed notes to Celeste Albaret – e.g. 'cross out everything that occurs before my arrival with my mother in Venice'. Hurried by his final illness, Proust concentrated on communicating his own 'aesthetic credo' in this pivotal episode, which, for Kristeva, expresses itself in 'the integration of the spiritual theme with the sensual theme, which includes the love for the mother in the celebration of Venice'.[40]

Proust chose ultimately to emphasize the 'interpenetration between Venice and his mother, between the angel's light and the body'; and this choice 'endures until the final typescript', inviting us to consider the trip to Venice 'as an apotheosis of the madeleine and paving-stone episodes'.[41] For Kristeva, accordingly, Venice powerfully assumes the mystical role of a 'sensual and symbolic Orient', a city that becomes 'maternal and thus stresses its own incarnation'.[42] This, concludes Kristeva, is the 'cornerstone' of Proust's entire eucharistic aesthetic, treating Venice as a 'world within a world' (Proust's words), the very character of 'time embodied'. In this manner the visit to Saint Mark's Baptistery may be read as the crucial link between the 'erotic bindungsroman' – running from Maman and Ghilberte to Albertine – and the annunciation of epiphanies in the 'final pensive pages' of the novel.

* * *

But Venice is not the last station on Marcel's journey; and Maman is not the last object of his affections. On the contrary, by the end of the novel it seems that Maman has been accepted as the 'lost object' par excellence, prompting him to move from an aesthetic of melancholy to one of mourning and resurrection. As the novel progresses I believe that Marcel moves increasingly beyond the various transfers of amorous want and returns to the Madonna of the ordinary universe: Francoise. The menial maid of the opening chapters now returns as 'the Michaelangelo of our kitchen',[43] a quotidian creature capable of transforming a farmyard chicken into a delicious family feast of *poulet roti*. I would even suggest that by the final volume of the novel, *Time Regained,* Francoise – as everyday cook and seamstress – has become Marcel's model for writing the novel. The narrator now confesses, after all, that '[he] should work beside her almost as she worked herself'.[44] This conjecture is confirmed, I believe, if we recall how Francoise is compared to Giotto's *Caritas* in her being as well as her appearance (*pace* Swann) in the opening volume.[45] Replacing the endless litany of elusive metonymic muses – from Maman and Ghilberte to Mlle de Guermantes and Albertine – Francoise reemerges in the end as a post-muse of the everyday microcosm. The ethereal and unreal Albertine transmigrates back, as it were, into the Francoise of flesh and blood. The death of Marcel's exotic fantasy lover is the occasion for the rebirth of the forgotten scullery maid. Curiously, it is Francoise's very qualities of patient craft and endurance, grounded in a sharp sense of mortality and earthiness, that Walter Benjamin celebrates in his famous concluding image of Proust – 'for the second time there rose a scaffold on which the artist, his head thrown back, painted the creation on the ceiling of the Sistine Chapel: the sickbed on which Marcel Proust consecrates the countless pages which he covered with his handwriting . . . to the creation of his microcosm'.[46] Kitchens and cathedrals. Dying and creating. Earthly frailty as the portal to art. Moreover, it is also Benjamin who would observe – whether thinking of the culinary seamstress Francoise or not – that 'the eternal is in any case far more the ruffle on a dress than some idea'.[47]

So where does this leave Mamam? I suspect that by the time Marcel recalls Maman in the final Paris epiphanies – which trigger the involuntary memories of both the Venice visit and the bedtime reading of *Francois le Champi* – it is less a question of 'fusion' than of trans-fusion. Or of 'transversal', as Proust himself uses the term in Marcel's final contemplative musings on time embodied and regained. In other words, rather than embracing a form of immediate or magical union, Proust introduces the preposition *trans* to capture the sense of both identity and difference over time. Transfusion, transversal, translation, transubstantiation.

But a final word on Francoise. If Francoise is indeed Marcel's ultimate guide, it is perhaps no accident that the novel becomes fragmented in a number of different directions in *Time Regained* just when it appeared to reach closure and become whole (in the manner of some Hegelian teleology). Resisting the Hegelian temptation, the book remains undecided as to whether Marcel's projected novel is Proust's *In Search of Lost Time* or not. That is for the reader to decide. Indeed, it is curious how each philosophical reading of Proust – think of those by Ricoeur, Deleuze, Levinas, Benjamin, Ginette, Beckett, De Man, Blanchot, Kristeva, Nussbaum, Murdoch, Girard – manages to *translate* the novel into the reader's own hermeneutic! The ultimate definition, perhaps, of an 'open text'. Or what we might also call – taking our cue from Merleau-Ponty's passage on eucharistic reciprocity and reversibility – a sacramental text.

So, we would argue, the marginalized and mocked Francoise is now retrospectively restored as Marcel's most reliable guide. And we recall that it was this housemaid who was always pointing Marcel away from literature-for-literature and in the direction of literature-for-life. She was the mundane servant who, 'like all unpretentious people', had a no-nonsense approach to literary vainglory and saw through all Marcel's literary rivals as mere 'copiators'.[48] It was Francoise, Marcel now realizes, who had 'a sort of instinctive comprehension of literary work' capable of 'divining [Marcel's] happiness and respecting [his] toil'.[49] And so Marcel ultimately resolves to labour as she did, stitching and threading from bits and pieces of cloth – 'constructing my book, I dare not say ambitiously like a cathedral, but quite simply like a dress'.[50] The Muse is displaced by the maid. The fantasy persona of Albertine, the main source of Marcel's tormented jealousies and deceptions, is finally replaced by the seamstress of the real.

Proust performs a daring return from heroic wanderings to the weavings of the everyday. The marvels of literature are no longer to be sought in monumental basilicas of grandiose design (or in great battle scenes – the novel is set in 1916) but in the intricate weft and warp of ordinary existence. And in this embrace of writing as weaving we find the literary trope of 'metaphor' being allied to that of 'metonymy'. The transformative and synthetic power of metaphor, which turns contingency into essence, is here supplemented by a second moment which returns essence to contingency – that is, to metonymy as a process of displacement and replacement, of humble stitching and restitching, of one thing ceding itself to another in the quotidian play of existence. This double process is what we have been calling transubstantiation. The reversible translation of word into flesh and flesh into word.

This new understanding of writing as a stitching of webs, tapestries, textures, texts – leads Marcel to the insight that he is the 'bearer' of a work that has been 'entrusted' to him and which he will, in time, 'deliver' into other hands (that of the reader). The connotations of pregnancy and birth are pronounced. This intuition of the basic inter-textuality of writing comes to Marcel as a sort of deliverance from his own long fear of death. Affirming that genuine literature is a form of messianic 'repetition' or remembering forward – from natality to mortality and back to natality again – Marcel finds himself 'indifferent to the idea of death'.[51] Learning to die is learning to be reborn. 'By dint of repetition', as he says, 'this fear had gradually been transformed into a calm confidence. So that if in those early days, as we have seen, the idea of death had cast a shadow over my loves . . . the remembrance of love had helped me not to fear death. For I realized that dying was not something new, but that on the contrary since my childhood I had already died many times.'[52] Invoking the scriptural passage about the seed dying in order to flourish, Marcel's authorial self now faces the possibility of being posthumously reborn again as another, as one of those many harbingers of new life, epitomized by Mlle de Saint Loup or, more generally, by his future readers. Natality re-emerges from mortality. So that the final passage of the novel – recalling the dead Albertine and the dying count Charlus – invokes an enveloping movement of Time which swings back and forth, up and down, carrying us towards vertiginous and terrifying summits, higher than the steeples of cathedrals, before eventually returning us to earth again, 'descending to a great depth within . . . '. In short, if time is all too wont to raise mortals 'to an eminence from which suddenly they fall',[53] acknowledging the inevitability of this fall back into the ordinary universe enables fear to become love and literary delusion true writing.

Conclusion

So what is the significance of the fact that our chosen witness of sacramental imagination – Proust – is agnostic, and that the characters who best embody his sacramental vision are women (Maman, Mlle de Saint Loup, Francoise)? Is this not a different kind of eucharistic language to the one which informs our traditional male-dominated liturgies (where usually no women need apply)? This is surely a sacramental vision of a new sort; or at least of the old revisited otherwise. It deploys the poetic licence of fiction to suspend confessional creeds and doctrines in order to offer 'free variations' of transubstantiation, namely the reversible 'miracle' of word-made-flesh and flesh-made-word.

Recalling the canonical definition of transubstantiation as 'the transforming of one substance into another', we may say that we have identified three main kinds in our reading Proust: (1) *intra-textual*, (2) *inter-textual* and (3) *trans-textual*. As instances of the first kind we may cite the numerous examples of one character being transfused into another (Maman into Ghilberte, Albertine and Francoise; Ghilberte into Mlle de Saint Loup; the young Marcel into Marcel the narrator) or one spatio-temporal moment translated into another (as in the madeleine epiphany or the involuntary memories of Maman reading in Combray and Venice recalled years later in the Guermantes' library). As examples of the second (inter-textual) kind, we might cite the transmuting of one narrative into another (e.g. the numerous instances of the scriptural Eucharist transliterated into the eucharistic reenactments of Maman in Venice and Marcel's final epiphanies in the Guermantes' library). And finally, we may identify key examples of the trans-textual model in the transubstantiation of author into narrator, character and reader. This third kind – involving the very process of writing and reading, of configuring and refiguring – is the one high-lighted in the phenomenological analyses of Merleau-Ponty, Kristeva and Ricoeur. And it is with this final model that we encounter an opening of the world of the text towards the post-textual world of the reader, and backwards (by way of implied regress from character to narrator to author) to the pre-textual world of the writer. This acknowledgement, however tentative and mediated, of some extra-textual element – intimating a life of action before and after the text – is in keeping with the sacra-mental paradigm of transubstantiation: a paradigm which, I have been suggesting, testifies to the unbreakable liaison between the body of the text and the bread of life. Or, to revisit the language of epiphany, between word and flesh.

That Proust was an agnostic, apostate and atheist by turn did not prevent him from being haunted by a singularly mystical vision of things. It may, in a paradoxical sense, even have contributed to it by predisposing him to something beyond the reach of most conventional religious codes. (Church history attests a deep complicity between mysticism and atheism.) Proust bears witness, in a unique way, to a mystical sacredness at the heart of the secular world. And for him the mutual transfiguring of material bread and mystical body is anything but 'sacrificial' – in the dogmatic sense of an expiatory victim sacrificed to redeem sins and appease an omnipotent Father. Proust's sacramental aesthetic is far removed from a divine economy of penalty, reward and judgement. But I would argue that it is in keeping with reading of the incarnation as an act of radical kenosis and emptying where the sacred unhitches itself from absolute Being ('equality with the Father', as Paul put it) in order to descend into the heart of finite flesh. So that the birth of the son as an incarnate historical being coincides with the demise of the the Father as Immutable Master of the Universe.

For unless the divine seed dies there can be no incarnational rebirth. Or to put it in the words of the young Jewish mystic, Etty Hillesum, 'by excluding death from one's life we deny ourselves the possibility of a full life'.

Several contemporary philosophers have, I believe, touched on this notion of a post-sacrificial sacredness, or a 'religion without religion' as Caputo and Derrida call it. Caputo's notion of the 'weakness of God' comes close to this, inspired as it is by not only a kenotic reading of Christian incarnation but also by a deconstructionist take on the complicity of mysticism with a certain atheism identified by Derrida in his late essay *Sauf le Nom*. Here Derrida, who claims that he 'rightly passes for an atheist', has this to say:

> The desire of God, God as the other name of desire, deals in the desert with radical atheism . . . The most consequent forms of declared atheism will have always testified to the most intense desire for God . . . Like mysticism, apophatic discourse has always been suspected of atheism . . . If atheism, like apophatic theology, testifies to the desire of God . . . in the presence of *whom* does it do this?[54]

In an intriguing dialogue with apophatic theology, thinkers like Stanislas Breton and Gianni Vattimo have shown how a kenotic moment of 'nothingness' and 'emptiness' resides at the core of a post-metaphysical faith. Faith, says Breton, 'must inhabit the world and give back to God the being he has not'; and speaking more specifically of kenosis he talks of a process that follows 'the descent of the divine into a human form, obedience unto death, the ignominy of the Cross. But at the very moment that the paroxysm of abasement touches the depth of nothingness, the shock of the negative, in its paradoxical power, commands the exultant ascent toward the point of origin.'[55] In the case of Vattimo, kenosis entails a reading of 1 Corinthians 12 (on love) which treats the incarnation as God's relinquishing of all power and authority so as to turn everything over to the secular order. Vattimo considers 'God's self-emptying and man's attempt to think of love as the only law' as two sides of the same coin. And his conclusion, while startling is entirely consistent, namely that secularization is the 'constitutive trait of authentic religious experience'.[56] Copernicus, Freud and Nietzsche need no longer, on this account, be seen as enemies of the sacred but, on the contrary, as 'carrying out works of love'.[57] And I think that Gilles Deleuze is making a somewhat similar point when he declares that we must abandon the sacrificial instinct for scape-goating and instead identify with the lamb: 'The God who, like a lion, was given blood sacrifice must be shoved into the back-ground, and the sacrificed god must occupy the foreground . . . God became the animal that was slain, instead of the animal that does the slaying.'[58]

But it is, in my view, Paul Ricoeur who most poignantly struggles with this post-sacrificial notion of death and resurrec-tion in his final testament, written as he was dying, *Vivant jusqu'a la mort* (2007). Speaking of a certain kind of 'grace' accompanying the experience of death, Ricoeur notes:

> it is not important for this moment of grace that the dying person identifies with a particular religion or confession. Indeed maybe it is only when faced with death that the religious becomes one with the Essential and that the barrier dividing religions (and non-religions like Buddhism) are tran-scended. Because dying is trans-cultural it is also trans-confessional and trans-religious.[59]

Admitting his basic suspicion of 'immediacy and fusion', he makes one exception for 'the grace of a certain dying'.[60] Ricoeur talks about this grace as a 'paradox of immanent transcen-dence', of an especially 'intimate transcendence of the Essential which rips through the veils of confessional religious codes'.[61] To encounter such authentic grace one must, Ricoeur suggests, forgo the will for one's own personal salvation by transferring this hope onto others. He also speaks, in this respect, of renouncing the metaphysical fiction of an otherworldly Being dispensing punishment and reward in some kind of celestial tribunal. Speaking of the great Rhine mystics, Ricoeur says that they only 'renounced themselves' for the sake of opening to the Essential, to the point of being, in their contemplative detachment, incredibly active in the creation of new orders, in teaching, in travelling and tending to the forgotten of this world. By being available like this to the Essential they were motivated to 'transfer the love of life onto others'.[62] God thus becomes a God *after* God, a god of the living rather than of the dead, the dichotomy between 'before' and 'after' death suddenly dissolving.

And so here again we confront the basic spiritual paradox, so oft invoked by Proust, that 'he who clings to his life loses it and he who lets it go gains it'. In this context Ricoeur offers a startlingly refreshing reading of the eucharist as a celebration of blood-as-wine, transubstantiation being taken as a sign of life and sharing rather than a token of sacrificial blood-letting.[63] The eucharistic commemoration of the giving of one's life – 'Do this in memory of me' – thus becomes an affirmation of the gift of life to and for the other rather than an anxiety about personal physical survival after death. In other words, when Christ said 'It is finished', he meant it. He was offering up his own personal life, in a second gesture of kenotic emptying (the first being the descent from divinity into flesh as incarnation), so as to give life to others, in service (Luke 22.27) and in sacrament (the breaking of bread at Emmaus, the cooking of fish for his disciples when he returned – incognito – in the form of the risen servant, and ever after, down through human history, in the guise of feeding the 'least of these'(*elachistos*)). Ricoeur concludes his terminal testament with this remarkable note:

> The Son of Man came not to be served but to serve. Hence the link between *death-rebirth in the other* and *service as gift of life*. And the link between service and feast. The Last Supper conjoins the moment of dying unto oneself and the service of the other in the sharing of food and wine which joins the man of death to the multitude of survivors reunited in community. And this is why it is remarkable that Jesus never theorized

about this and never said *who* he was. Maybe he didn't *know* for he *lived* the Eucharistic gesture, bridged the gap between the imminence of death and the community beyond. He marked a passage to glory (through suffering and death) without any sacrificial perspective.[64]

The fact that Ricoeur calls himself a 'Christian who writes philosophically' rather than a 'Christian philosopher' seems to me significant here. For he is acknowledging the importance of a certain gap, a certain non-confessional space occupied by philosophy and art, which allows us to freely and imaginatively revisit, and at times anamnetically retrieve, the often forgotten, congealed and taken-for-granted resources of traditional religion. God must die so that God can be reborn. Or as Ricoeur puts it, 'we must smash false idols so that genuine symbols can speak'.[65]

In these philosophical accounts by thinkers in the phenomenological tradition, we find the letting go of a certain fixation serving as a *via negativa* which permits the return of a second naivety (Ricoeur): a repetition after the experience of death and nothingness which signals a new kind of 'miracle' and 'resurrection', this time in ordinary events ignored first time round. For Proust these moments of sacramental remembrance occur when Marcel comes to renounce his initial Great Literary Expectations and ultimately acknowledges the muse of the mundane (Francoise) and the grace of a natality which exceeds him (Mlle de Saint Loup). The bread and wine of quotidian existence can then be celebrated in eucharistic epiphanies of the everyday such that hitherto ignored moments are retrieved out of passing time, for a new life which assumes and subsumes death, for a new generation of successors (Mlle de Saint Loup), and for a new community of readers. Unless the seed dies, the wheat cannot grow and the bread cannot be shared.

But this is not apologetics. I am not suggesting that Proust was an advocate of Christian faith or liturgy. I am simply sounding the possibility of a certain post-theistic mysticism embracing a eucharistic aesthetic where the secular and sacred unite. Thus while not wishing to exclude confessional writers from adherence to such a sacramental aesthetic – think of G. M. Hopkins, Bernanos or Claudel, for example – I merely suggest that it is valuable for us in this secular era to consider how certain non-confessional authors deploy an art of transubstantiation to explore a mysticism of *God-after-God,* or as some might prefer to say, of spirituality-after-religion. The 'after' here need not be read as privative but rather as a function of 'ana', that is, of retrieval and resurrection *après coup.*[66] As in ana-mnesis or, as I have proposed elsewhere, in *ana-theism.*[67]

I use the term *anatheism* to refer to the return of the divine in the profane after the eclipse of God (taken in the metaphysical sense of a causal Being of otherwordly omnipotence and theodicy). Anatheism thus signals a *via affirmativa* following the *via negativa* of modern doubt and disenchantment. In this light, the agnosticism of Proust might be read as a sort of 'negative capability' which carves open the possibility of a post-theistic mysticism. That is, the possibility of a God after metaphysics, a God after dogmatism. Meaning what? Meaning an opening towards a God who neither is nor is not but may be – depending on our response to each mystical moment. This signals an attentiveness to infinity embodying itself daily in acts of eucharistic love and sharing. An endless crossing over and back between the infinite and infinitesmal. The highest deity becoming – kenotically, sacramentally – the 'very least of these'. The word made everyday flesh. Ongoing and interminable gift of transubstantiation.

Notes

1 M. Merleau-Ponty, *Phenomenology of Perception* (London: Routledge, 2002), p. 246. I am grateful to John Manoussakis for this reference. See his extended discussion of this theme in *God after Metaphysics: A Theological Aesthetics* (Bloomington: Indiana University Press, 2007).

2 Merleau-Ponty, *Phenomenology of Perception*, p. 248.

3 M. Merleau-Ponty, *The Visible and the Invisible* (Evanston:

Northwestern University Press, 1968), cited in R. Kearney, *Modern Movements in European Philosophy* (Manchester: Manchester University Press, 1986), pp. 88–9

4 Merleau-Ponty, *The Visible and the Invisible*, p. 89.

5 M. Merleau-Ponty, 'Eye and Mind' in R. Kearney and D. Rasmussen (eds), *Continental Aesthetics* (Oxford: Blackwell, 2001), pp. 288f.

6 M. Merleau-Ponty, *Signs* (Evanston: Northwestern University Press, 1964), cited Kearney, *Modern Movements*, p. 85.

7 Merleau-Ponty, *Signs*, pp. 83–4.

8 See also the work of Catherine Keller, *Face of the Deep: A theology of Becoming* (London and New York: Routledge, 2003), and Manoussakis, *God after Metaphysics*. Nor should we omit reference here to Gabriel Marcel's intriguing philosophical reflections on incarnation and embodiment, which exerted a considerable influence on the 'religious' phenomenological writings of Ricoeur and Levinas.

9 See, for example, the work of my colleagues Frank Kennedy on music and Steven Schloesser on painting (especially Rouault) and what he calls 'mystic modernism', *Jazz Age Catholicism: Mystic Modernism in Postwar Paris: 1919–1923* (Toronto: University of Toronto Press, 2005).

10 J. Kristeva, *Time and Sense: Proust and the Experience of Literature* (New York: Columbia University Press, 1996), p. 251.

11 Kristeva, *Time and Sense*, p. 246. Transubstantiation is technically defined as: (a) 'The changing of one substance into another'; (b) 'The conversion in the Eucharist of the whole substance of the bread and of the wine into the blood of Christ, only the appearances (and other "accidents") of bread and wine remaining: according to the doctrine of the Roman Catholic Church 1533' (*The Shorter Oxford English Dictionary*, p. 2349). What fascinates modern writers like Joyce and Proust about this process, according to Kristeva, is that such an act, mixing the secular and the sacred, combines both an 'imaginary' and 'real' character and provides a certain grammar for the transfiguration of flesh into word and vice versa.

12 Kristeva, *Time and Sense*, p. 246.

13 Kristeva, *Time and Sense*, p. 246.

14 See Kristeva, *Time and Sense*, p. 247: '*A state of flesh* appears to underlie the therapeutic act, but it can become a true *therapeutic* act only if language is led to the reversible and chiasmic sensation that supports it' (what Proust calls the 'impression' or 'transubstantiation'). For Kristeva this reversibility of flesh can take the form of (1) a literary act of writing and reading as a 'two-sided sensoriality', or (2) a psychoanalytic act of transference and counter-transference. Interestingly, neither

Proust nor Joyce were insensitive to the powers of psychotherapy, any more than they were to the powers of religion – without practising either. One thinks of Joyce's exchanges with Jung – when he was 'jung and freudened' as he puts it in *Finnegans Wake* – or of Lacan's intriguing pun on Joyce as 'sinthome' (*symptome/saint homme* or 'holy man'). And one recalls the following observation by Proust in *Contre Sainte-Beuve:* 'Reading is at the threshold of spiritual life and can lead us to it though it does not constitute it . . . For someone who is lazy, books play the same role that psychotherapists do for those afflicted with neurasthenia' (cited in Kristeva, *Time and Sense*, p. 385). Kristeva cites and comments on a number of relevant 'mystical' passages from Merleau-Ponty's *The Visible and the Invisible* (pp. 246f.).

15 Kristeva, *Time and Sense*, p. 251.

16 Kristeva, *Time and Sense*, p. 252.

17 Kristeva, *Time and Sense*, p. 252.

18 Kristeva, *Time and Sense*, p. 252.

19 Kristeva, *Time and Sense*, p. 252.

20 Kristeva, *Time and Sense*, p. 252.

21 Kristeva, *Time and Sense*, p. 252.

22 Proust, *Contre Sainte-Beuve*, cited in Kristeva, *Time and Sense*, p. 252. I think Kristeva is close here to the hermeneutic model of extra-linguistic refiguration which Paul Ricoeur speaks of in *Time and Narrative*, vol. 3 (Chicago: Chicago University Press, 1988). See Ricoeur's claim, for example, that 'What a reader receives is not just the sense of the work, but, through its sense, its reference, that is, the experience it brings to language and, in the last analysis, the world and the temporality it unfolds in the face of this experience' (pp. 78–9). Or again in 'Life in Quest of Narrative' in *On Paul Ricoeur: Narrative and Interpretation* (London: Routledge, 1991), p. 26: 'My thesis is here that the process of composition, of configuration, is not completed in the text but in the reader and, under this condition, makes possible the reconfiguration of life by narrative. I should say, more precisely: the sense or the signification of a narrative stems from *the intersection of the world of the text and the world of the reader*' (which is already 'prefigured' by the world of the author).

23 Contrast this inaugural – and ultimately lost – kiss of maternal 'fusion' with the disastrous kiss of 'diffusion' which Marcel experiences with Albertine later in the novel. The closest Marcel may be said to achieve a eucharistic kiss, beyond these two extremes, might be the brushing of his lips on the table napkin chez les Guermantes, which recalls the meal at the Grand Hotel in Balbec, or, perhaps more emblematically, the image of the 'star-shaped' crossroads where the two diverging paths of his youth – le chemin de Méséglise and le Chemin de Swann

– converge almost mystically, chiasmically, 'transversally', in the figure of Ghilberte's daughter, Mlle de Saint Loup, at the final party. But this final kiss is a kiss deferred for others, in the future, just as the final meal chez les Guermantes is a feast postponed: his lips touch the napkin but he does not eat.

It is significant, I think, that Proust's novel does not end with the epiphanies in the library. Marcel does not stay in Guermantes' library and though he takes this occasion to announce an extremely elaborate theory of literature and life, the text does not culminate with theory. Marcel leaves the library and re-enters the everyday universe. And it is here, in the midst of the chaos and commotion of a fragmenting Parisian community, that Marcel has what I consider to be his ultimate epiphany: his meeting with Mlle de Saint Loup (Ghilberte's daughter).

Mlle de Saint Loup appears at the end of the story and leads the author-artist beyond the vain play of mimetic triangles and abstract trinities back to the ordinary universe of generation and gratuity. Was she not, Marcel says of Mlle de Saint Loup – 'and are not the majority of human beings? – like one of those star-shaped crossroads in a forest where roads converge that have come, in the forest as in our lives, from the most diverse quarters?' And he adds: 'Numerous for me were the roads which led to Mlle de Saint-Loup and which radiated around her' (p. 502). Marcel then recalls the two great 'ways' –the Guermantes Way represented by her father, Robert de Saint Loup, and the Méséglise Way represented by her mother, Gilberte, the narrator's first youthful love. 'One of them took me, by way of this girl's mother and the Champs-Elysées, to Swann, to my evenings at Combray, to Méséglise itself; the other, by way of her father, to those afternoons at Balbec where even now I saw him again near the sun-bright sea. And then between these two high roads a network of transversals was set up' (p. 502). >From this emerges Marcel's new vision of life as a large web where the various incidents of time past and time recovered crisscross in a 'network of memories' which give us an 'almost infinite variety of communicating paths'. So that life resurrected in and through literature becomes a palimpsest of chiasmic overlaps and transversals that cannot be brought to a final close. Mlle de Saint Loup sets up a series of reverberations and recollections that resonate out into the future. She is the only character in the novel not 'recalled' from the past as such. She comes to Marcel out of the future as it were, taking him by surprise. And it is precisely by virtue of her 'messianic' advent into Marcel's world that she opens up a new *optique* on the past, the present and the time-still-to-come.

This new *optique* is what Marcel now calls a three-dimensional psychology, one which leads from life to literature and back again. Marcel's recapture of the different planes and elements of his life, following his encounter with Mlle de Saint Loup in the party, makes him realize that 'in a book which tries to tell the story of a life it would be necessary to use not the two-dimensional psychology which we normally use but a quite different sort of three-dimensional psychology'; a perspective which affords, he says, ' a new beauty to those resurrections of the past which [his] memory effected while [he] was following his thoughts alone in the library' (pp. 505–6). Marcel, like Stephen after his library epiphany, is now ready to 'part' with his past so as to regain it. He is prepared to pass from the 'see this, remember' (epiphany 1) to the 'will see' (epiphany 2). And again like Stephen, Marcel will be led to his book and to a life-beyond-the-book by someone with whom he does not actually speak (Molly for Stephen; Mlle de Saint Loup for Marcel). In Ghilberte's daughter, coming to him across the room in the Guermantes' salon, Marcel sees the possibility of rebirth and renewal, another's life beginning again and going beyond his own. This young woman, he realizes, is the incarnation of time lost and regained. 'Time, colorless and inapprehensible time, so that I was almost able to see it and touch it, had materialized itself in this girl . . . still rich in hopes, full of laughter, formed from those very years which I myself had lost, she was like my own youth' (p. 507).

Then comes the moment of decisive *anagnoresis* (see Aristotle, *Poetics*, 4.4.1448). While tempted to rejoin his old ambition to compose a great masterpiece which would 'realize a life within the confines of a book!' – mimetically drawing 'comparisons from the loftiest and the most varied arts' (p. 507) – Marcel says no. He resists the temptation. 'What a task awaited him!' he proclaims, taking his final distance from the persona of the Great Writer, now suddenly displaced into the third person – 'How happy would he be, I thought, the man who had the power to write such a book!'(p. 507). But Marcel now knows he is not this man. He is not one of those Promethean romantic artists whose will-to-power would construct his work 'like a general conducting an offensive', or an architect building a huge vaulted 'cathedral', ensuring one's immortality even in the tomb , 'against oblivion'(p. 508). This Ideal Author of the Ideal Book is not for Marcel. He no longer believes in the Gospel of the Absolute Text. Instead, he resolves on a far more modest proposal: to begin a work which will serve not as a text in-itself and for-itself – the Grand Illusion of the self-sufficient-Book – but rather as a pretext for the renewed and resurrected life of his readers. Marcel's critical conversion is marked by the seemingly innocuous phrase, 'But to return to my own case . . .'. The word 'But' is all important here. The full passage reads as follows: 'But to return to my own case, I thought more modestly of my book and it would be inaccurate even to say that I thought of those who would read it as "my" readers. For it seemed to me that they would not be "my" readers but the readers of their own selves, my book being merely a sort of magnifying glass like those which the optician at Combray used to offer his customers – it would be my book, but with its help I would furnish them with the means of reading what lay inside themselves. So that I should not ask them to praise me or to censure me, but simply to tell me whether "it really is like that", I should ask them whether the words that they read within themselves are the same as those which I have written' (p. 508). The author dies unto himself so as to be reborn in and through his readers. Marcel's literary *metanoia* is complete. The die is cast. This ultimate epiphany expresses itself in a series of descriptions of writing as discovery and disclosure – midwifery, pregnancy, childbirth, mining, incubation, detection, listening, diving, excavation, repetition, revelation. Indeed it confirms Samuel Beckett's own conclusion that for Proust, 'the only fertile research is excavatory' (S. Beckett, *Proust* (New York: Grove Press, 1970), p. 25). The old romantic delusion of art as some fiat of omnipotence gives way to a more humble profession. To an aesthetics of passion rather than imposition, of receptivity rather than volition, of humility rather than hubris. Epiphany as anaphany. In a word, ana-aesthetics.

24 Cited in Kristeva, *Time and Sense.*

25 Kristeva, *Time and Sense*, p. 101.

26 Kristeva, *Time and Sense*, p. 23.

27 Kristeva, *Time and Sense*, pp. 102, 106, 108, 133, etc.

28 Kristeva, *Time and Sense*, p. 106.

29 Kristeva, *Time and Sense*, p. 108. Kristeva cites this telling passage from Proust's *Contre Sainte-Beuve*: 'Crossing a courtyard I came to a standstill among the glittering uneven paving-stones . . . In the depth of my being I felt the *flutter* of a past that I did not recognize; it was just as I set foot on a certain paving-stone that this feeling of *perplexity* came over me. I felt an invading *happiness*, I knew that I was going to be enriched by that *purely personal thing, a past impression, a fragment of life in unsullied preservation* (*suddenly*, I was flooded by a stream of light). It was the sensation underfoot that I had felt on the smooth, slightly uneven pavement of the baptistery of Saint Mark's' (p. 107).

30 M. Proust, *In Search of Lost Time, vol. VI: Time Regained*, tr. A. Mayor and T. Kilmartin (New York: Modern Library Paperback, 1999), p. 290.

31 Proust, *In Search of Lost Time, vol. VI*, p. 291.

32 Proust, *In Search of Lost Time, vol. VI*, p. 290. Gilles Deleuze makes the point in *Proust and Signs* (London: Athlone Press, 2000) that Proust's epiphanic experience of 'essences' requires the 'style' of art and literature to be brought to expression. Proust speaks here of 'a qualitative difference in the way that the world looks to us, a difference that, if

there were no such thing as art, would remain the eternal secret of each man' (M. Proust, *In Search of Lost Time, vol. III*, tr. C. K. S. Moncrieff and T. Kilmartin (Vintage, 2000), p. 895). In *Time Regained* Proust famously describes the move from the inner secret essence within each life to the style of literary art as an act of 'translation'.

Deleuze refers to a 'final quality at the heart of the subject' due to the fact that the essence 'implicates, envelops, wraps itself up in the subject' (*Proust and Signs*, p. 43) and so doing constitutes the unique subjectivity of the individual. In short, essences may be said to individualize by being caught or inscribed in subjects in what Proust referred to as a 'divine capture' (*In Search of Lost Time, vol. I: Swann's Way*, p. 350). The epiphanic translation of essence is also described by Proust as a 'perpetual recreation of the primordial elements of nature' (*In Search of Lost Time, vol. I*, p. 906), implying that the essence retrieves the birth of time itself at the beginning of time. Invoking the Neoplatonic idea of *complication* – referring to an original enveloping of the many in the One prior to the unfolding of time (*explicatio*), Deleuze suggests that it is to this original timeless time, complicated within essence and revealed to the artist, that Proust points when he writes of 'time regained'. And, one might add, it also has echoes of Leibniz's view that each created monad represents the whole created world. Is this not close to what Proust is getting at when he writes of 'Combray and its surrounding world taking shape and solidity out of a cup of tea' (*In Search of Lost Time, vol. I*, p. 51). But in Deleuze's reading of Proust, essence can only recapture this original birth of the world through the 'style' of art – expressing that 'continuous and refracted birth', that 'birth regained' in a substance (words, colours, sound) rendered adequate (Deleuze, *Proust and Signs*, p. 46).

I think this can be linked with Walter Benjamin's suggestion that Proust's involuntary memory is 'closer to forgetting than what is usually called memory', for it is only when we can forget conventional time that we are open to the capture or recall of originary timeless time. Following Proust's hint that 'the only true pleasures are the one's we have lost' (*In Search of Lost Time, vol. VI*, p. 222), Benjamin defines the root of Proust's 'elegiac happiness' in terms of 'the eternal repetition, the eternal restoration of the original, the first happiness' which occurs in literature (*In Search of Lost Time, vol. VI*, p. 200). Benjamin, like Deleuze, argues that the Proustian translation of essences – which I call epiphany – is only available through the mediation of literature. Indeed Benjamin goes so far as to claim that 'the image of Proust is the highest physiognomic expression which the irresistibly growing discrepancy between life and literature was able to assume' ('The Image of Proust' in *Illuminations* (London: Pimlico, 1999), p. 197). Proust's use of literary metaphor extended the usual understanding of this trope to mean not just one thing standing for another – a notion deconstructed by Paul De Man's famous reading of Proust – but one thing standing for the world. Or as Benjamin put it, 'an experienced event is finite' but an involuntarily 'remembered event is infinite because it is only a key to everything that happened before and after it' ('The Image of Proust', p. 198).

By contrast, my own reading of Proustian transubstantiation as a two-way crossover between literature and life follows the more hermeneutic reading of Paul Ricoeur (*Time and Narrative*, vol. 2) and of Kristeva cited above. As Ricoeur puts it, Marcel's 'decision to write has the capacity to transpose the extra-temporal character of the original vision into the temporality of the resurrection of time lost' (*Time and Narrative* p. 145); and in so doing it opens up a return journey to the life of the reader, refigured by the text towards new possibilities of being in the lived world. The reading of the text invites the reader to repeat the 'spiritual exercises' performed by the narrator in and through the text, so that 'the process of composition, of configuration, is not completed in the text but in the reader and under this condition makes possible the reconfiguration of life by narrative' (Ricoeur, 'Life in Quest of Narrative', p. 26). In short, the hermeneutic reading espoused by Ricoeur, Kristeva and myself construes epiphany as a double translation between life and literature. Proustian translation would thus take the form of a bilateral 'transversal' from life to literature and from literature to life. This seems faithful to Proust's own chiasmic image of the 'star-shaped crossroad' where 'roads converge . . . from the most diverse crossroads' (*In Search of Lost Time, vol. VI*, p. 502).

33 Kristeva, *Time and Sense*, p. 112.

34 Kristeva, *Time and Sense*, p. 112.

35 Kristeva, *Time and Sense*, p. 112.

36 Kristeva, *Time and Sense*, p. 113.

37 Kristeva, *Time and Sense*, p. 113.

38 Kristeva, *Time and Sense*, pp. 3–22, 116. Kristeva also identifies revealing nominal associations here with Marie Madeleine in the Scriptures.

39 Kristeva, *Time and Sense*, p. 114.

40 Kristeva, *Time and Sense*, p. 115.

41 Kristeva, *Time and Sense*, p. 115.

42 Kristeva, *Time and Sense*, p. 116.

43 Proust, *In Search of Lost Time, vol. II*, p. 23.

44 Proust, *In Search of Lost Time, vol. VI*, p. 432.

45 Proust, *In Search of Lost Time, vol. I*, p. 95.

46 Benjamin, 'The Image of Proust', p. 210.

47 W. Benjamin, *The Arcades Project* (London: Harvard University

Press, 1999), p. 69. One might also mention here John Caputo's notion of holy 'quotiedianism' in *The Weakness of God: A Theology of the Event* (Bloomington: Indiana University Press, 2006), pp. 155f.

48 Proust, *In Search of Lost Time, vol. VI*, p. 509.

49 Proust, *In Search of Lost Time, vol. VI*, p. 509.

50 Proust, *In Search of Lost Time, vol. VI*, p. 509.

51 Proust, *In Search of Lost Time, vol. VI*, p. 509.

52 Proust, *In Search of Lost Time, vol. VI*, p. 509. The point is not that epiphanies never happened before the library scene; it is that Marcel was not yet ready to see and hear them for what they really were. He had not yet, to cite Deleuze, been fully trained in his 'apprenticeship to signs'. And it is not until such apprenticeship is accomplished, through his recapitulative awareness of 'being-towards-death' in the library, that Marcel can finally acknowledge the preciousness of even the most banal and discarded events through the lens of time recaptured (*le temps retrouvé*). Art is less a matter of romantic creation than of epiphanic recreation. For, as Marcel asks, 'was not the re-creation by the memory of impressions which had then to be deepened, illumined, transformed into equivalents of understanding, was not this process one of the conditions, almost the very essence of the work of art as I had just now in the library conceived it?' (Proust, *In Search of Lost Time, vol. VI*, p. 525). Such epiphanic understanding marks the moment of *anagnoresis*. Otherwise put, time has to be lost before it can be recovered. Unless the seed dies, accidents cannot be retrieved as essences, contingencies as correspondences, obsessions as epiphanies. Only through the veil of mortality, can the sacred radiate across the profane world which the arrogant repudiate as ineligible for art. It is only after he renounces his promethean Will-to-Write that Marcel's previously in-experienced experience is re-experienced in all its neglected richness. (And the greater the neglect the greater the richness.) For it is precisely the rejected and remaindered events of Marcel's existence which return now, in and through literature, as 'resurrections'. The three personas of Marcel – as character, as narrator and as author – seem to crisscross here for the first time, like three Proustian Magi recognizing that the deepest acts of communion are to be found in the most fortuitous acts of ordinary perception.

53 Proust, *In Search of Lost Time, vol. VI*, pp. 530–1. So what do these Proustian conclusions tell us about epiphany? They indicate, I suggest, that epiphany is a process which is 'achieved' in a series of double moves. First, that of mortality and natality. Second, that of metaphor (the translation of one thing into another) and metonymy (the disclosure of new meaning through the accidental contiguity of contingent things). Third, that of constructing and deconstructing.

Moreover, it is in this last double-gesture that the text surpasses itself and finally reaches out towards its future readers. For if we begin with the notion that literature 'constructs' an epiphany based on the recreation of impressions recalled in involuntary memory, the literary text in turn 'deconstructs' itself in order to allow for the recreation of the reader. That is how Francoise's sewing works – stitching and unstitching, weaving and unweaving, endlessly. In a form of hermeneutic arc, the text configures an epiphany already prefigured by a life which is ultimately refigured by the reader (see Ricoeur, *Time and Narrative*, vol. 2, especially the section entitled 'The Traversed Remembrance of Things Past' in Chapter 4). And this reader is one who not only co-creates the text with the author but re-creates it again as he/she returns from 'text to action'. So that if epiphany invites a first move from life to literature, it re-invites us come back again from literature to life.

Walter Benjamin identifies the weaving motif of textuality in Proust thus: 'For the important thing for the remembering author is not what he experienced but the weaving of his memory, the Penelope work of recollection' ('The Image of Proust', p. 202). Benjamin interprets this Penelope trope in terms of a textual process of weaving–unweaving, forgetting–remembering, composing–disrupting, which manages to reveal the extraordinary in the ordinary. Once again, Penelope's fidelity to the epiphanies of the everyday is affirmed: 'Can we say that all lives, works and deeds that matter were never anything but the undisturbed unfolding of the most banal, most fleeting, most sentimental, weakest hour in the life of the one to whom they pertain' (p. 203). Or again: 'Proust's most accurate, most convincing insights fasten on their objects as insects fasten on leaves, blossoms, branches, betraying nothing of their existence until a leap, a beating of wings, a vault, show the startled observer that some incalculable individual life has imperceptibly crept into an alien world. The true reader of Proust is constantly jarred by small shocks' ('The Image of Proust', p. 208). This emphasis on the microscopic and minuscule is repeated at the level of language itself where Proust offers us a subatomic investigation of society in terms of exploring the reverberations and associations of the most everyday words and phrases, what Benjamin calls 'a physiology of chatter' (p. 206). This reminds me, in turn, of Camus' observation that 'all great deeds and all great thoughts have a ridiculous beginning. Great thoughts are often born on a street corner or in a restaurant's revolving door' ('The Myth of Sisyphus' in G. Marino (ed.), *Basic Writings of Existentialism* (New York: The Modern Library, 2004), p. 448); a passage followed by his curious eucharistic allusion to the finding in the 'body, affection, creation', the 'wine of the absurd and the bread of indifference on which [the rebel] feeds his greatness' (p. 478). I am also reminded here of the telling passage in Aristotle's *On the Parts of Animals* (645a15–23), where he writes: 'Every realm of nature is marvelous: and as Heraclitus, when the strangers who came to visit him found him warming himself at the furnace in the kitchen and hesitated to go in, is reported to have bidden them not to be afraid to enter, as even in that kitchen divinities were present, so we should venture on the study of every kind of living thing without distaste; for each and all will reveal to us something natural and something beautiful.'

54 J. Derrida, *On the Name*, Stanford: Stanford University Press, 1995), pp. 35f.

55 S. Breton, *The Word and the Cross* (New York: Fordham University Press, 2002), pp. 114, 84f.

56 G. Vattimo and R. Rorty, *The Future of Religion*, ed. S. Zabala (New York: Columbia University Press, 2005), p. 35.

57 Vattimo and Rorty, *The Future of Religion*, p. 36. See also in this regard, J.-L. Nancy, *La Déclosion: Déconstruction du Christianisme* (Paris: Galilée, 2005).

58 G. Deleuze and F. Guattari, *A Thousand Plateaus* (Minneapolis: University of Minnesota Press, 1987), p. 122.

59 P. Ricoeur, *Vivant jusqu'à la Mort* (Paris: Editions du Seuil, 2007), p. 45.

60 Ricoeur, *Vivant jusqu'à la Mort*, p. 45.

61 Ricoeur, *Vivant jusqu'à la Mort*, p. 47.

62 Ricoeur, *Vivant jusqu'à la Mort*, p. 76.

63 Ricoeur, *Vivant jusqu'à la Mort*, p. 90.

64 Ricoeur, *Vivant jusqu'à la Mort*, p. 91.

65 P. Ricoeur, 'The Critique of Religion' in C. Regan and D. Stuart (eds), *The Philosophy of Paul Ricoeur* (Beacon Press, 1978), pp. 213f. Ricoeur also talks about the related notion of returning to a second naivety of authentic faith after the dogmatisms and prejudices of one's first naivety have been deconstructed and purged.

66 See J.-F. Lyotard on the notions of 'post' and 'ana' – which he links specifically with a postmodern attitude to time and history – in *The Postmodern Condition* (Manchester: Manchester University Press, 1984). Lyotard does not, however, consider these terms in any mystical or eucharistic light. We might also note the importance here of not only the Platonic model of *ana-mnesis* but also the Aristotelian idea of *ana-gnoresis*, a special kind of re-cognition through poetic awareness whereby we recall something previously forgotten and realize how different things are connected, how 'this' relates to 'that' etc. See the *Poetics* 4.4.1448f and *Rhetoric*, 1.2.23.1371f.

67 See my development of this ana-theistic aesthetic in the related texts, 'Epiphanies of the Everyday: Toward a Micro-Eschatology' in J.

Manoussakis (ed.), *After God: Richard Kearney and the Religious Turn in Phenomenology* (New York: Fordham University Press, 2006); R. Kearney, 'Traversing the Imaginary: Epiphanies in Joyce and Proust' in *Traversing the Imaginary: Richard Kearney and the Postmodern Challenge*, (Evanston: Northwestern University Press, 2007); and my discussion of the eschatological temporality of the Palestinian formula in both Judaic and Christian messianism, as it relates to a certain literary hermeneutics, in 'Enabling God' in *After God*, and in 'Hermeneutics of the Possible God' in I. Leask and E. Cassidy (eds), *God and Giveness* (New York: Fordham University Press, 2005). I extend the discussion of the sacramental aesthetics of Proust to include those of Joyce and Virginia Woolf in 'Sacramental Imagination: Eucharists of the Everyday', forthcoming 2008.

15. Heidegger, Dilthey, and 'the Being-Question': Towards a Critical Appraisal of Heidegger's Use of Hermeneutic Phenomenology[1]

CYRIL MCDONNELL

Introduction

In his 1925 lecture course *History of the Concept of Time: Prolegomena*, Heidegger tells his students:

> As superior as his analyses in the particular certainly are [in *Ideen I* and *II*], Husserl does not advance beyond Dilthey. However, at least as I [Heidegger] see it, my guess is that even though Dilthey did not raise the question of being and did not even have the means to do so, the tendency to do so was alive in him. (*HCT* 125)[2]

---

1 This essay is a revised and extended version of a paper, under the title 'Dilthey, Heidegger, and Levinas', delivered at a Conference on 'Phenomenology and Transcendence' in Nottingham University (2 September 2005). I wish to thank the participants of that conference, in particular Branko Klun, Felix O'Murchadh, James McGuirk and Regina Swartz, for their interest in and kind reception of that paper.

2 M. Heidegger, *History of the Concept of Time: Prolegomena*, tr. T. Kisiel (Bloomington: Indiana University Press, 1985); M. Heidegger, *Prolegomena zur Geschichte des Zeitbegriffs, Gesamtausgabe (GA)* vol. 20, ed. P. Jaeger (1979); M. Heidegger, Lecture Course, Marburg 1925. Henceforth abbreviated as *HCT*.

In this paper, I want to take seriously Heidegger's *disclaimer* to his students that he is doing something new with the tradition of phenomenology and phenomenological research inaugurated by Husserl, and deal with his claim that *he is doing something new* with the tradition of hermeneutic-phenomenological research inaugurated by Dilthey.[3] I intend to demonstrate that if we follow Heidegger *philosophically* down the path of his appropriation of Dilthey's manner of thinking, then it becomes quite clear that it is Dilthey (and not Husserl, nor Aristotle) who is Heidegger's real philosophical mentor in Heidegger's so-called 'phenomenological decade' of 1917–27.[4] This paper in fact makes a stronger claim; it argues that Heidegger uses *implicitly* central features of Dilthey's hermeneutic-phenomenological method of enquiry, in particular Dilthey's interest in the experience of language, in order to *correct* Husserl's manner of phenomenological reflection: that is to say, Heidegger uses Dilthey to read Husserl *against* Husserl. This is why Husserl could see and did see (much to his disappointment) both overt and covert attacks on his own particular position in philosophy and phenomenological research in the unfinished text of Heidegger's *Being and Time*,[5] whether that author inscribed

---

3 Assessing the extent to which Heidegger develops Husserl's position in phenomenology, or the extent to which Husserl either accurately or inaccurately understands Heidegger's position in phenomenology, therefore, will not be of primary interest in this article. Others have attempted this. Cf. Burt C. Hopkins, 'The Husserl–Heidegger Confrontation and the Essential Possibility of Phenomenology: Edmund Husserl, *Psychological and Transcendental Phenomenology and the Confrontation with Heidegger*', *Husserl Studies* 17 (2001), pp. 125–48.

4 Cf. T. Sheehan, 'General Introduction. Husserl and Heidegger: The Making and Unmaking of a Relationship', in E. Husserl, *Psychological and Transcendental Phenomenology and the Confrontation with Heidegger (1927–1931): The 'Encyclopaedia Britannica' Article, The Amsterdam Lectures, 'Phenomenology and Anthropology' and Husserl's Marginal Notes in 'Being and Time' and 'Kant and the Problem of Metaphysics'*, tr. and ed. T. Sheehan and R. E. Palmer (Dordrecht: Kluwer Academic Press, 1997), pp. 1–32.

5 M. Heidegger, *Being and Time*, tr. J. Maquarrie and E. Robinson (Oxford: Blackwell, 1962, 2000). Henceforth abbreviated as *BT*.

such attacks there wittingly, or not.[6] The phenomenological manner of thinking advanced by Heidegger in *Being and Time*, therefore, is both better read and better evaluated in terms of its appropriation of Dilthey's manner of thinking than in terms of a result of any philosophical engagement with Husserl in *Auseinandersetzung*, as several commentators and critics, including Heidegger himself, profess.

There are three sections in this paper. The first section outlines Heidegger's general appropriation of some tenets of Dilthey's expansive thought that are most relevant to an evaluation of Heidegger's overall 'path of thinking' about 'the Being-Question'. The second section reconstructs Heidegger's specific deployment of Dilthey's hermeneutic method in the formulation of 'the Being-question' and its relation to *Dasein* in *Being and Time*.[7] The final section contains an evaluation, *pace* Levinas, of Heidegger's partial and highly selective use of Dilthey's idea

---

6 'In order to come to a clear-headed and definitive position on Heideggerean philosophy, I devoted two months to studying *Being and Time*, as well as his more recent writings. I arrived at the distressing conclusion that philosophically I have nothing to do with this Heideggerean profundity, with this brilliant unscientific genius; that Heidegger's criticism [of my work], both open and veiled, is based upon a gross misunderstanding [of my work]; that he may be involved in the formation of a philosophical system of the kind which I have always considered my life's work to make forever impossible. Everyone except me has realised this for a long time.' E. Husserl, 'Letter to Alexander Pfänder, January 6, 1931', tr. B. Hopkins, in Husserl, *Psychological and Transcendental Phenomenology and the Confrontation with Heidegger (1917–1931)*, Appendix 2, p. 482.

7 Heidegger's use of hermeneutics in *Being and Time* continues to baffle commentators. According to one commentator: 'It is noteworthy then, that *Being and Time* does so little to clarify the nature of hermeneutics, so little to explain to the puzzled reader how ontology could be a matter of hermeneutic interpretation.' W. Blattner, 'Ontology, the A Priori, and the Primacy of Practice' in S. G. Crowell and J. Malpas (eds), *Transcendental Heidegger* (Standford: Standford University Press, 2007), pp. 10–27 (p. 24). Once Heidegger's appropriation of Dilthey's hermeneutic manner of thinking is understood, however, this part of Heidegger's hermeneutic philosophy is less puzzling.

of hermeneutic phenomenology in the elaboration of 'the Being-Question'.

Heidegger's General Appropriation of Dilthey's Manner of Thinking

It is well known that Heidegger's development of Dilthey's historical-hermeneutic approach in the direction 'the Being-question' (*die Seinsfrage*) and its relation to *Dasein* in the 1920s usurped, most controversially, Husserl's entire idea of transcendental phenomenology.[8] Heidegger, however, was not entirely committed in his own retrieval of 'the question of the meaning of Being' to continuing into the early decades of the twentieth century in philosophy all of the essential elements or features initiated in the late eighteenth and early nineteenth century by the Historical School of Thought.[9] On the contrary, it is arguably the case, as Philip Rosemann has shown, that Heidegger's philosophical position is so decidedly against our ability to take, or to reach the question of the meaning of Being as a genuinely historically conditioned question at all, that his 'path of thinking' (*Denkweg*) about 'the Being-question' displays a

---

8 I. M. Fehér, 'Phenomenology, Hermeneutics, *Lebensphilosophie*: Heidegger's Confrontation with Husserl, Dilthey, and Jaspers' in T. J. Kisiel and J. van Buren (eds), *Reading Heidegger from the Start: Essays in His Earliest Thought* (New York: State University of New York, 1994), pp. 73–89 (pp. 87–8). Cf., also, C. R. Bambach, *Heidegger, Dilthey, and the Crisis of Historicism* (New York: Cornell University Press, 1995). Cf., also, Heidegger's remarks on the 'lack of history' that characterizes Husserl's phenomenology and the task of 'activating' and retrieving 'the genuine sense of the past' in phenomenology in his 'Wilhelm Dilthey's Research and the Struggle for a Historical Worldview (1925)', tr. C. Bambach, in M. Heidegger, *Supplements: From the Earliest Essays to 'Being and Time' and Beyond*, ed. J. van Buren (Albany: State University of New York Press, 2002), pp. 147–76, esp. p. 175.

9 W. Brock, *An Introduction to Contemporary German Philosophy* (Cambridge: Cambridge University Press, 1935), pp. 20–3.

profoundly ahistorical understanding of history.[10] Heidegger was not quite interested in developing all of the features of Dilthey's particularly expansive philosophy of life (*Lebensphilosophie*) either.[11] According to Dilthey, 'the religious thinker, the artist, and the philosopher create on the basis of lived experience.'[12] Heidegger, *qua* philosopher, however, appears to be interested only in those (lived) experiences that say something to him about the question of the meaning of Being itself and its relation to *Dasein*, by which Heidegger means, the awareness of the 'there' (*Da*) of 'Being' (*Sein*), and in which I find myself implicated as a being in Being and as a being who has some implicit 'understanding of Being' (*Seinsverständnis*). This 'understanding of Being', Heidegger notes in *Being and Time*, extends not only to oneself and the world but also to one's fellow human being.[13] It is, nevertheless, an intrinsic feature of our experience of being a being in Being that such an experience, like all of our experiences (*Erlebnisse*), as Dilthey argued and as Heidegger agrees, cannot but be lived (*er-lebt*) and somewhat understood. Thus Heidegger concludes, pushing Dilthey's manner of thinking towards a topic that Dilthey himself did not address, that '[the meaning of] Being can be something unconceptualised [*unbegriffen*], but it never completely fails to be understood [*es ist nie völlig unverstanden*]' (*BT* 228).

The centrality of what Heidegger calls 'the hermeneutic of the facticity of *Dasein*' in the formulation and elaboration of 'the question of the meaning of Being' in *Being and Time*, then,

---

10 P. W. Rosemann, 'Heidegger's Transcendental History', *Journal of History of Philosophy* 40:4 (2002), pp. 501–23. Cf., also, Heidegger, *HCT* p. 138, as clear evidence that 'historical research' is not and *cannot*, according to Heidegger himself, be his concern in his '*genuine repetition*' of the question of the meaning of Being.

11 Cf. Heidegger's remarks on Dilthey's philosophy of 'life' in *Being and Time*, § 10, pp. 72–3.

12 W. Dilthey, *Poetry and Experience: Selected Works*, vol. 5 (Princeton: Princeton University Press, 1996), p. 225.

13 Scant treatment of one's own fellow human being is given in *Being and Time*, or in other works after that, by Heidegger.

clearly indicates that Heidegger employs *some version* of Dilthey's manner of thinking in his own philosophical researches into 'the question of the meaning of Being'. It also indicates, it seems to me, some direct influence of Dilthey's manner of thinking on Heidegger's own effort to find new words and new meanings of words that Dilthey was unaware of, such as, for instance, the very term *Dasein* itself.[14] In Dilthey's well-known triad, human experience (*Erlebnis*) contains implicitly some form of understanding (*Verstehen*) and that understanding is completed and raised to a higher level of meaning in expression (*Ausdruck*). 'Each of these consequent phases', therefore, 'is a step in a creative process', but what remains in this process, as de Boer notes, is 'the orientation to the individual, which is not 'crossed out', but 'raised' and 'intensified' [in its meaning].'[15] This, of course, occurs in the interpretation of any thing, for, it 'too, is tuned to the individual, whether this be a psychical experience, an act, a literary work or an object of culture'.[16] Heidegger, however, seems to apply this general triadic-hermeneutic model of understanding to his own *methodological* use of the very term *Dasein* itself – whether hyphenated as *Da-Sein*, or not – for, in *Heidegger's interpretation* of that term, *Dasein* expresses the meaning of its own experience and its own '(pre-)understanding of Being', even though this new meaning that Heidegger gives to and sees in (t)his term '*Dasein*' never featured, hitherto, in the German language.[17] From all of this, therefore, I think that we can conclude, and conclude in fairness to Heidegger, that Heidegger is only interested in those tenets and themes that he found in Dilthey's expansive writings (or in anybody else's

---

14 *BT* § 7c, 'The Preliminary Conception of Phenomenology', pp. 58–63.

15 T. de Boer, *The Rationality of Transcendence: Studies in the Philosophy of Emmanuel Lévinas* (Amsterdam: Giegen, 1997), p. 174.

16 De Boer, *The Rationality of Transcendence*, p. 174.

17 Schelling, for example, does talk about God as *als reines Dass* and Brentano wrote a book *Vom Dasein des Gottes* but such would be unintelligible in the context of Heidegger's meaning and use of such terms in his philosophy of *die Seinsfrage* and its relation to *Dasein*.

writings for that matter that he happened either to encounter or to choose to read) that would help him *methodologically* 'to raise anew the question of the meaning of Being' and its relation to *Dasein*, his topic in philosophy, his task in phenomenology and phenomenological research, and his contribution to hermeneutic phenomenology. If this is the case, however, then Heidegger's famous retort in the Introduction to *Being and Time* about *Husserlian* 'phenomenology', that 'higher than actuality stands possibility' – reiterated in his 1969 Supplement to 'My Way to Phenomenology (1962)'[18] – is really being directed *against* Husserl's concept of phenomenology, as the latter excludes any such possibility, and in favour of a possibility inherent within *Dilthey's* concept of phenomenology, though this is not explicitly stated as such by Heidegger.

There is, then, a general but nonetheless definite conceptual ambiguity, to which I would like to draw attention, in Heidegger's use of the terms 'phenomenology' and 'descriptive psychology' in *Being and Time*, 'My Way to Phenomenology', and especially in his 1925 lectures on *The History of the Concept of Time: Prolegomena* where Heidegger portrays a more intimate philosophical connection between Dilthey's 'Descriptive Psychology' and Husserl's 'Descriptive Psychology', and speaks of an 'an inner kinship' between Husserl's manner of thinking in the *Logical Investigations* (1900–01) and Dilthey's manner of thinking in his 1894 Academy essay 'Ideas towards a Descriptive and Analytic Psychology' (*HCT* 24).[19]

---

18 M. Heidegger, 'My Way to Phenomenology' in Heidegger, *On Time and Being*, tr. J. Stambaugh (New York: Harper & Row, 1972; Chicago: University of Chicago Press, 2002), pp. 74–82 (p. 82).

19 Heidegger even *stresses*, almost in the same breath, the point that 'the decisive move' towards the 'idea of a *descriptive psychology*' that begins in Franz Brentano's *Psychology from an Empirical Standpoint* (1874) not only 'had a profound impact on Dilthey [in the 1894 Academy essay]' but also that 'the truly decisive aspect of Brentano's way of questioning is to be seen in the fact that Brentano became the teacher of Husserl, the subsequent founder of phenomenological research' (*HCT* 20–3).

It is true that both Dilthey and Husserl (and Brentano of the Vienna period) called their work 'descriptive psychology', but identity in terms is not equivalent to identity in concepts. There is no 'inner kinship', whatsoever, between Dilthey's manner of thinking adopted in the Academy essay of 1894 and Husserl's manner of thinking adopted in the *Logical Investigations*. Any 'inner kinship' between both forms of analyses is, at most, negative in character; that is to say, both Dilthey and Husserl's forms of analyses do not avow the applicability of the method of the natural sciences in the study of the meaning of experiences that are characteristically lived by humans – the experiences of human normative acts of logical reasoning *as such* being Husserl's selected topic of investigation, the whole of 'life' being Dilthey's topic of investigation. Such 'an inner kinship' between Dilthey's analysis of (lived) experiences from the point of view of their structural totality and inherent historical (and linguistic) depth-dimension in 'Ideas towards a Descriptive and Analytic Psychology' and Husserl's analysis of the (lived) experiences of a normative logical consciousness *as such* from a descriptive-eidetic psychological point of view, as presented in the second volume of the *Logical Investigations*, is 'an inner kinship' that is entirely fabricated by Heidegger. This is why Dilthey was particularly impressed by the first volume of the *Logical Investigations*, the *Prolegomena*, wherein 'naturalism in the particular form of *psychologism*, specifically psychologism in the particular field of logic' (*HCT* 116) is refuted, and yet less than impressed by the descriptive-eidetic-psychological analysis of the experiences of (abstract, ahistorical) *logical consciousness as such* in the second volume, comprising, in two parts, the Six Logical Investigations, and which, as Heidegger notes in 'My Way to Phenomenology', are 'three times as long' as volume one.[20] Nevertheless, this is why Dilthey is correct to compare in his letter to Husserl, alluded to and quoted by Heidegger in his 1925 lectures, 'their [Husserl–Dilthey] work to boring into a mountain from opposite sides until they break through and

---

20 Heidegger, 'My Way to Phenomenology', p. 76.

meet each other' (*HCT* 24). But their work bore into the same mountain (=*Erlebnisse*) from opposite sides, and when they meet each other, it is Husserl who must break through to Dilthey, not Dilthey to Husserl.

Dilthey begins with what Husserl leaves out, namely, with the lived nature of experiences themselves in all their particularity and totality as founded and rooted in historical, linguistic, social, personal, temporal and mundane existence. Meaning is to be found within those experiences themselves, and not by way of either factual inner perception or eidetic intuitive inspection of intentional consciousness and its contents in inner reflection, as advocated by the Brentanean–Husserlian school of descriptive a priori psychology from about the mid-1870s onwards.

Dilthey's starting point is a simple starting point, but it is important to note that it is a standpoint that resides *outside* of 'the natural standpoint' (*die natürliche Einstellung*) as depicted by Husserl. According to Dilthey, human experiences are characterized by a desire to understand such experiences, and when we understand the meaning of such experiences we endeavour to express that meaning in language, which itself is a product of human activity and human interactivity. Things (*Dinge*), from Dilthey's point of view, therefore, cannot be regarded simply as lying-there-in-stock (*vorhanden*) with an existential and essential meaning, whether attention is directed towards them, or not, as fostered in the thesis of the natural standpoint because the very meaning of those things presented to our experiences necessarily depends upon the particular way in which the meaning of such things is interpreted and articulated *in* our experiences of them. The chair at the top of the wedding table facing the bride, the electric chair awaiting the condemned man, the wheelchair presented to the patient recovering from an operation, are never 'initially' seen as chairs that are somehow first given as things given to acts of outer perceptual-sense experience, and which later obtain their meaning via the achievements of the sense-bestowing activity of one's own actual intentional consciousness (as Husserl's analysis of 'thing-perception' in *Ideas I* demonstrates). This is 'an *un*natural' way for a human being to experience the world, even through identifiable acts of outer perceptual-sense experience, as Heidegger stresses in *The History of the Concept of Time*, following Dilthey. The (hypo)thesis of the natural standpoint, nevertheless, is *a* way of looking at the world, and *a* way of interpreting the world of things given to outer perceptual-sense experience from a decidedly non-human point of view, no more and no less; and it is a way that depends upon the linguistic expressions and historical evolution of the natural-scientific community, as well as metaphysical hypotheses about the nature of the human being in that world of things. Our actual experiences – and experiences are things that cannot but be lived – however, are simply not things given to acts of outer perceptual-sense experience (*Sein als Ding*) or reducible to (conscious) experience immanently perceived (*Sein als Erlebnis*), the twin poles of Husserl's 'Being-talk' (*Seinsrede*) in the transcendental reduction (*Ideas I*, §46). This is exactly what Heidegger is alluding to, without mentioning Husserl's *Ideas I* by name, when he concludes in *Being and Time*:

> Our everyday environmental experiencing [*Erfahren*], which remains directed ontically and ontologically towards entities within the world, is not the sort of thing that can present [the lived experiences of] Dasein in an ontically primoridial manner for ontological analysis. Similarly our immanent perception of experiences [*Erlebnissen*] fails to provide a leading-clue [*Leitfaden*] which is ontologically adequate. (*BT* 226)

A different way of addressing and explicating the meaning of experiences – and not just the reflective consciousness of experiences – therefore, is needed in phenomenology and phenomenological research.[21] This is Heidegger's critical conclusion against Husserl, as it had been Dilthey's too, and before

---

21 Cf. Heidegger, 'My Way to Phenomenology', p. 77.

Heidegger. A different leading clue is needed, if we are to go back to the things themselves of experiences (*zu den Sachen selbst*). And just as Dilthey had found before Heidegger, Heidegger too finds in our actual experience of language and hermeneutics a much more reliable 'rod and staff' (*Stab und Stecken*)[22] – though Heidegger says this of his reading of Brentano's 1862 doctoral thesis on Aristotle's metaphysics – in the *reading* of any text in philosophy, including his reading of 'the master's' [Husserl's] texts.

Heidegger, therefore, had solved his 'main difficulty' (*eine Hauptschwierigkeit*) concerning how the manner of reflection that called itself 'phenomenology' is to be conducted, and with which he struggled for many years, as he recalls in 'My Way to Phenomenology', when reading and rereading Husserl's texts in phenomenology, both the *Logical Investigations* and *Ideen I* and later *Ideen II*.[23] The way to do phenomenology is to hear what is expressed in the words themselves. In Heidegger's way of doing phenomenology, then, 'hearing' what is expressed in the written word must re-place, and so, dis-place 'seeing' that which is deposited in actual intentional consciousness and its objectivities. This includes a fortiori, 'seeing' that which is retrievable in and through consciousness's reflection upon itself, as Husserl had stipulated in his way of doing phenomenology.[24] Or, perhaps more accurately speaking, for Heidegger, it is only through hearing what is expressed in the written words that seeing what is talked about is made present, in an analogous manner to the way in which the apostles recognized Jesus *only after he spoke*, i.e. upon hearing his words they saw him (though the analogy cannot be pressed too far here in

22 Heidegger, 'My Way to Phenomenology', p. 74; English translation 'chief help and guide' modified.

23 Heidegger, 'My Way to Phenomenology', p. 76.

24 Heidegger, of course, will give this 'living now' of *Ideas I*, § 77 a distinctively Kierkeagaardian temporal interpretation on top of his appropriated Diltheyean-historical interpretation, with the net result of overriding 'historicality' by 'temporality' in Division Two of *Being and Time*.

Heidegger's method for the authority of the text itself is the final court of appeal, not the author of the text). Here, then, Heidegger's alignment to Dilthey's hermeneutic starting point overwrites *methodologically* the Husserlian starting point in phenomenology and phenomenological research, with Husserl's and Brentano's idea of 'descriptive psychology', as a matter of fact, 'losing in competition' (*Besiegtwerden im Wettstreit*), if I may borrow a phrase from Brentano's Vienna lectures in *Descriptive Psychology*.[25] All of this, therefore, both confirms and advances Dilthey's conclusion that 'because our mental life finds its fullest and most complete expression only through language, explication finds completion and fullness only in the interpretation of the written testimonies of human life'.[26]

The following commentary that Heidegger makes in his 1925 lectures, purportedly, on Husserl's theory of expression and perception in the Sixth Logical Investigation, '§37 The Fulfilling Function of Perception: The Ideal of Ultimate Fulfilment' (*Logical Investigations*, 761–64) bears testimony to the extent to which Heidegger has already incorporated and internalized this methodological switch and leap (*Sprung*) in his critical reading of Husserl's texts, for, as Heidegger explains to his students:

> It is . . . a matter of fact that our simplest perceptions and constitutive states are already *expressed*, even more, are *interpreted* in a certain way. What is primary and originary here? [Heidegger rhetorically asks, and he answers.] It is not so much that we see the object and things . . . but rather the reverse, we see what *one says* about the matter. (*HCT* 56)

---

25 F. Brentano, *Descriptive Psychology*, tr. and ed. B. Müller (London: Routledge, 1995), pp. 5–6.

26 W. Dilthey, *Gesammelte Schriften*, vol. III, p. 217; 'The Hermeneutics of the Human Sciences' in K. Mueller-Vollmer (ed.), *The Hermeneutics Reader: Texts of the German Tradition from the Enlightenment to the Present* (New York: Continuum, 1985; Oxford: Basil Blackwell, 1986), pp. 148–64.

Because Heidegger situates the above commentary as being a commentary on Husserl's theory of expression, some commentators have been led to believe – wrongly, in my opinion – that here Heidegger is unearthing something that is embryonic in Husserl's thought (in particular in the Sixth Logical Investigation).[27] Such is clearly not the case. Rather, what Heidegger is defending above is a version of Dilthey's views on the priority of the way linguistic acts of meaning contain the highest step in the expression of meaning in human experience – including the expression of meaning that is contained and present in, at the most basic and simplest level of meaningful acts of perception, the perception of things given to outer perceptual-sense experience – and not Husserl's position in the Sixth Logical Investigation, for whom 'Signitive acts constitute

---

27 Cf. T. Kisiel, 'On the Way to *Being and Time*: Introduction to the translation of Heidegger's *Prolegomena zur Geschichte des Zeitsbegriffs*' in T. Kisiel, *Heidegger's Way of Thought: Critical and Interpretative Signposts* (London & New York: Continuum, 2002), pp. 36–63 (p. 38). Cf., also, D. Moran, 'Heidegger's Critique of Husserl's and Brentano's Accounts of Intentionality', *Inquiry* 43 (2000), pp. 39–66 (p. 58). Kisiel does recognize in his earlier study *Genesis* (1993), nevertheless, that 'It is well known that the [Husserlian] phenomenological "principle of all principles" gives the primacy to intuition [over expression]. Less noted [by Husserl?] in this context is the inseparable intentional relation between intuition and expression, that is, between intuitive fulfilment and *empty* intending. All of our experiences, beginning with our most direct perceptions, are from the start already expressed, indeed interpreted [as in Heidegger's Diltheyean inspired reading of Husserl]. This Diltheyean emphasis of the intentional structures described by Husserl in the *Logical Investigations* is the seminal insight of Heidegger's hermeneutic breakthrough in 1919' (*Genesis*, p. 49). This Diltheyean emphasis, however, on the way 'immediate experience . . . is already contextured like a language' (*Genesis*, p. 49) is precisely one that is *not described by Husserl at all* in the *Logical Investigations*, nor could he or does he describe it so because of Husserl's unphenomenological theory of language (e.g. animating marks on a page) and his assertion of the way the description (the linguistic sign) of the intended object gives away to the intended object itself *and drops out* in the immediacy of intuitive fulfilment in consciousness in Husserl's theory.

the lowest step: they possess no fullness whatever' (§ 37, 761, my emphasis).[28] It is this very fact of our linguistic experience – and language is an experience – whereupon meaning is expressed in and through the words we use and where meaning is 'fulfilled' and 'completed', however not fully articulated or fully capable of articulation, such meaning is therein, that Dilthey uses against Husserl's phenomenological manner of proceeding. It is not a phenomenological fact, as Husserl leads us to believe in the Sixth Logical Investigation, that linguistic acts of meaning in themselves are 'empty' intending acts requiring 'intended objects' – whatever ontological status the latter objects may have – to complete their meaning. (Nor is it a phenomenological fact of linguistic experience that words *qua* marks on a page are animated by a sense-bestowing intentional consciousness, as Husserl suggests in his theory of language, and which he transfers over to his theory of perception in his objection to Brentano's understanding of 'physical phenomena' as 'immanent sense data' e.g. as 'reds' rather than as the red of the rose, or as 'sounds' rather than as the song of the singer, i.e. as sensations actively interpreted through objectivating acts.)[29]

---

28 If Heidegger had actually provided this passage from the *Logical Investigations*, in addition to his 'gloss' or 'interpretation' of that passage, his students would have been more able to see that Heidegger is merely 'alluding' to Husserl's position and 'critiquing' that position as well. It is worth remembering what Schleiermacher writes about the literary device of 'allusions'. He notes: 'Allusions always involve a second meaning, and if a reader does not catch the second meaning along with the first, he misses one of the intended meanings, even though he may be able to follow the literal one. At the same time, to claim that there is an allusion where there actually is none is also an error. An allusion occurs when an additional meaning is so entwined with the main train of thought that the author believes it would be easily recognised by another person.' F. Schleiermacher, *Hermeneutics and Criticism*, tr. A. Bowie (Cambridge: Cambridge University Press), p. 23.

29 'I hear a *barrel organ* – the tones sensed are interpreted *as those of a barrel organ*' (Husserl, *Logical Investigations*, p. 860). 'I do not see colour sensations but coloured things; I do not hear sound sensations but the song of the singer' (Husserl, *Logical Investigations*, p. 569). Husserl's view on the sense-bestowing (*Sinngebung*) function of the

In the above passage from the Sixth Logical Investigation that Heidegger is alluding to in his 1925 lecture course, therefore, Heidegger is really 'correcting', rather than 'elucidating' (for his students) Husserl's theory of expression and perception. And Heidegger is correcting Husserl's position on phenomenological grounds, or, more precisely stated, on grounds that are based upon our very own experience of language itself – just as Dilthey had corrected Husserl beforehand (but of which Husserl appears to have taken no notice). Heidegger is certainly not 'developing' *philosophically* prefigured possibilities inherent in Husserl's Sixth Logical Investigation. Heidegger, after all, is not an authority on the interpretation of anybody else's text, or, for that matter, his own texts, even if, as commentators have noted, 'Heidegger himself has been at pains to point this out, [. . . that] his hermeneutical phenomenology already finds its foundation in Husserl's Sixth Investigation Section 37' and that he is engaging 'in *Auseinanderseztung* with Husserl, his mentor in the phenomenological decade 1917–1927.'[30] If Heidegger is

---

intentional activity of consciousness in the constitution of the meaning of objects presented *via* acts of outer perceptual-sense experience, however, is *Husserl's theory* (and not Brentano's), and it is a theory which Husserl derives from his view of the way in which consciousness animates and interprets the meaning of a word ('marks' on a page),which he transposes onto his analysis and understanding of the meaning of perception. Cf. de Boer, *The Development of Husserl's Thought*, tr. T. Plantinga (The Hague: Martinus Nijhoff, 1978), p. 163, and D. Moran, *Edmund Husserl: Founder of Phenomenology* (Cambridge: Polity Press, 2005), p. 128. Dilthey, as was well known at the time, was highly critical of just such a theory because it is based upon an *unphenomenological* understanding of the experience of language (as Dilthey argues *against* Husserl).

30 Moran, 'Heidegger's Critique of Husserl's and Brentano's Accounts of Intentionality', p. 58. Commentators on the Husserl–Heidegger *philosophical* relationship should really take with a pinch of salt both the later and the early remarks conveyed in Heidegger's self-interpretation that Husserl is the one with whom he engages philosophically in *Auseinandersetzung*. If we take *Auseinandersetzung*, with Derrida, to mean 'a debate that harries and worries things so as to question them or call them into question, *most closely*, efficiently, and effectively, *in effect*,

correcting Husserl's position on *phenomenological* grounds of the experience of language, as Dilthey did before him, and if this is what Heidegger is doing with (Husserlian) phenomenology in his 1925 lectures, then is there not a case to be made for the argument that it is Dilthey, and not Husserl, contrary to the Heidegger's own self-interpretation and self-evaluation, who is Heidegger's real *philosophical* mentor during Heidegger's so-called phenomenological decade of 1917–27?[31]

It seems to me that this case can be made, and that this case can be made at two levels, first at a general level of discussion about Heidegger's philosophy and second at a very particular level of discussion of Heidegger's elaboration of 'the Being-Question' in *Being and Time*. At a general level, Heidegger's declared interest and explicit stress in *Being and Time*, and in many other earlier and later works, on what is *said* about Being and on what is *written* about Being as a matter that both contains and raises both the meaning and our understanding of life-experiences to a higher level of comprehension – however unnoticed such an 'understanding of Being' may be for some, or however actively forgotten such an issue may be for contemporary philosophers, such as Dilthey, Husserl, Scheler, Nietzsche and the likes – testifies to Heidegger's practical adherence to Dilthey's triadic-hermeneutic model of experience–understanding–expression in his methodological retrieval of the question of the meaning of Being in phenomenology and phenomenological research. The second case, which is to be made at a very particular level of interpretation, requires a more detailed

---

indeed, starting from a comprehensive, understanding, patient, and tireless reading – a generous reading' (Jacques Derrida, *On Touching – Jean-Luc Nancy*, tr. Christine Irizarry (Stanford: Standford University Press, 2005), p. 21), then this cannot be said of Heidegger's reading of Husserl's Sixth Logical Investigation in his 1925 Summer Semester lecture course, but it can be said of his 'generous' reading of Husserl's text *through* Diltheyean spectacles.

31 Another prime contender for this mentoring, of course, is Aristotle, or at least Heidegger's hermeneutical-phenomenological reading of Aristotle. Cf. W. A. Brogan, *Heidegger and Aristotle: The Twofoldness of Being* (Albany: State University of New York, 2005).

philosophical reconstruction of Heidegger's *advancement* of Dilthey's manner of thinking in the actual formulation and elaboration of 'the Being-Question' and its relation to *Dasein* in *Being and Time*. The following section attempts this.

Heidegger's Appropriation of Dilthey's Thought in the Elaboration of 'the Being-Question'

That the question of the meaning of Being must find its origins in 'ontic experiences', testifies to Heidegger's deference to Dilthey's general hermeneutical-phenomenological investigations into the meaning of life experiences. Though Heidegger begins his philosophizing with Dilthey's stance in hermeneutic phenomenology, he clearly does not end with Dilthey. It is of importance, therefore, to distinguish three things in Heidegger's appropriation of Dilthey's manner of thinking in the elaboration of 'the Being-Question', namely: (i) the influence of Dilthey on Heidegger's starting point in philosophy, (ii) the question of the meaning of Being that Heidegger discerns about our life experiences of the meaning of Being that Dilthey is oblivious to (as much as other thinkers are, from Parmenides to Husserl), and (iii) the precise nature and extent of the influence of Dilthey's manner of thinking in Heidegger's argument for the ontic-ontological priority of *Dasein* in the formulation of 'the Being-Question'.

Heidegger's starting point

Heidegger's starting point in *Being and Time* appears to be straightforward and innocuous, at least as it is presented by him. According to Heidegger, '(e)verybody understands 'the sky *is* blue,' "I *am* happy," and similar statements' (*BT* 23).[32]

---

32 *BT*, p. 23, translation modified. Heidegger continues, however, to note that such average understanding of Being demonstrates that it is incomprehensible: 'Allein diese durchschnittliche Verständlichkeit demonstriert nur die Unverständlichkeit.'

Heidegger, therefore, starts with the meaningfulness of certain basic everyday linguistic experiences. Herein, Heidegger starts with Dilthey, or, perhaps more accurately speaking, Heidegger starts by drawing our attention to particular linguistic statements that already express meaning about things that are, about that-which-is (*das Seiende*). It now follows from this starting point – statements about that-which-is – that if everybody understands the emphasis that Heidegger puts on the verb to be in these statements, namely, that the sky '*is*' blue and that I '*am*' happy, then in addition to and in distinction from some understanding of that-which-is as referred to by such statements, in this instance, the sky and being in a happy mood, 'something like the Being of that-which-is [*das Sein des Seienden*]' is also understood in 'this expression', however implicitly. What Heidegger is not doing here, then, is giving an argument either for or against the existence (or continued existence) of the external world, or an argument either for or against the existence (or continued existence) of the inner world, the inner world of experiences that no-one else has direct access to. This is not his concern. That the sky *is* blue and that I *am* happy would lead Augustine, for example, to distinguish radically the outer and the inner world, and to develop, accordingly, an appropriate method of 'interiority' to examine the human condition. Heidegger, however, is not interested in following Augustine (completely) down this particular methodological line of existential-philosophical inquiry. Likewise, Heidegger is not concerned with the question of the 'exteriority' of the external world, as his (in)famous comment in *Being and Time* that 'the "scandal of philosophy" is not this proof [of the external world] has yet to be given, but that such proofs are expected and attempted again and again' (*BT* 249) makes crystal clear; as his equally famous retort makes clearer, that *Dasein*, unlike Leibniz's monads, does not need windows to look out onto the world since where else do I experience my being except from being-in-the-world (*BT* § 43).

By starting with linguistic statements that already express meaning about that-which-is, whether that-which-is is of an inner or outer nature, Heidegger's starting point in *Being and Time* actually evades any questions pertaining to the existence of the inner or outer world. This is not to imply that in this starting-point Heidegger is advocating some form of meditation on a platonic universal of Being, for, as he insists – and as he was to later correct himself in *Introduction to Metaphysics* – the meaning of Being must always be understood, and can only be understood, and is only understood in relation to actual experiences of 'that-which-is' (*das Seiende*), to 'ontic experiences' just as Dilthey had stressed.[33] Hermeneutic focus has to begin and return to 'ontic experiences' themselves. Indeed, Dilthey's stress to Husserl on this very point may well account for Husserl's rather enigmatic self-evaluation of the influence of conversations he had held with Dilthey in 1906 in the transition of his own thought from the descriptive-eidetic psychological analyses of the *Logical Investigations* (1900–01) to the position of transcendental idealism (that occurred around 1907–08), first documented in *Ideas I* (1913),[34] because in the reduction 'the meaning of Being as thing [*Sein als Ding*]' given to *actual acts of outer perceptual-sense experience* and 'the meaning of Being as (conscious) experience [*Sein als Erlebnis*]' given to *actual acts of immanent perception* is the focus of his meditation on the meaning of Being.[35]

---

33 Cf., also, *HCT*, pp. 90–1.

34 Dilthey died in 1911, and so could not have read Husserl's version of transcendental idealism in *Ideas I*. If he were alive, he no doubt would have pointed out the thoroughly ahistorical nature of that position too, just as he had to Husserl about the latter's earlier position in the *Logical Investigations*, in particular the second volume of descriptive-eidetic analyses of the experience of an ideally logical-normative consciousness *as such*.

35 Thus Heidegger's remarks in *HCT* about why 'a fundamental problem [the question of the meaning of Being] is left unposed and must remain unposed in it [he means, as is evident from the context, in 'the work of the two leading researchers in phenomenology today, Husserl and Scheler'] and why it must, what conditions must be fulfilled in order to pose it, and how this leads to a more radical definition of the task of phenomenological research. This problem is the *basic phenomenological*

Heidegger, however, is not concerned with the meaning of Being as thing given to outer perceptual-sense experience or with the meaning of Being as (conscious) experience immanently perceived, rather he is concerned with the linguistic fact that in understanding the meaning of statements about that-which-is – whether such statements refer to things given to outer sense perception, experiences immanently perceived, moods, dispositions, tools, God, Gods, or whatever – this understanding also presupposes some understanding of the meaning of Being itself. This is what I am calling Heidegger's starting point. It is a starting point that is clearly 'overlooked', 'pre-supposed', 'unthought', 'jumped over' by Husserl in his reduction – a reduction, it must be noted, as Husserl himself explicitly tells us, marks a return to 'genuine talk of Being [*Seinsrede*]' (whatever are the conclusions he arrives at in that return). This is why Heidegger can point out (correctly) to his students in his 1925 lectures that the question of the meaning of Being is not only raised in Husserl's philosophical position but also answered – the meaning of Being is to be (pre-)determined in and through an analysis of things given to outer sense perception and of (conscious) experience immanently perceived – and so, the question of the meaning of Being as a question (*als Frage*) itself *gets lost* precisely through the reduction. In other words, the question of the meaning of Being is left 'un*thought*' (implicit) and yet also '*un*thought' (not thought by the author) and so in this double sense this issue is hermeneutically 'unreduced' in Husserl's philosophical 'reduction'. And yet the particular method of reductions, both the transcendental and the eidetic reduction, and the particular

---

question of the *sense of being*, a question which an ontology [such as Husserl's transcendental reduction in *Ideas*, for example,] can never pose but already constantly presupposes and thus uses in some sort of answer [to the question of the sense of Being], grounded or otherwise. The immanent critique of the natural trend of phenomenological research allows the question of being to arise. A partial answer to this question is in fact the real theme of this course' (pp. 90–1). See some critical evaluations of his answer on pp. 395–6 of this chapter.

manner of thinking (reflection) advocated by Husserl within these reductions, can never in principle tackle the question of the meaning of Being itself, the very thing (*die Sache selbst*) that grounds in the first place Husserl's meditation on Being in the *Seinsrede* of his reduction. The problem, as far as Heidegger can see, is not just with Husserl's 'talk of Being', however; it is a problem with anybody's explicit 'talk about the Being' of that which is (*Sein des Seienden*), and that problem has existed from time immemorial, i.e. from Parmenides onwards.[36]

From a Diltheyean hermeneutic-methodological point of view, the problem for Heidegger seems to be this. In understanding the meaning of the statements 'the sky *is* blue' and 'I *am* happy', the meaning of Being itself is indeed thought in such experiences but it is not thought *out of that thought*; that is to say, the meaning of Being lies at once both un-*thought* (implicit) and *un*-thought (not thought by the author) *in* the understanding of such statements. It is as if in *becoming aware* in my actual experiencing of the fact that the sky *is* and that I *am*, or that you *are* and that the world *is*, or that 'the stone ''is''' or that 'the lecture hall is illuminated' etc., these very awarenesses point to the fact that I must have already somehow forgotten (in my memory, as Augustine would add in Book X of the *Confessions*) the very thing itself (*die Sache selbst*), that is, the source of the intelligibility of those statements, namely, that the sky *is understood* by me *to be* a being in Being and that *I understand* myself *to be* a being who understands that I *am* a being in Being.[37] Recall Book 10 (17) of the *Confessions*, where Augustine remarks, 'I hid in my memory not their images but the realities.'[38] And recall Augustine's well-known remarks

---

36 Cf. *BT*, pp. 47–8.

37 Husserl speaks about such 'becoming aware' in the Sixth Logical Investigation, but Husserl's concept is of an entirely different nature and in an entirely different context from Heidegger's starting point and Heidegger's concern and argument about the question of the meaning of Being.

38 Cf. J. McEvoy, 'Does Augustinian *Memoria* Depend on Plotinus?' in J. J. Cleary (ed.), *The Perennial Tradition of Neoplatonism* (Leuven: Leuven University Press, 1997), pp. 383–96.

from *De Trinitate* (and often quoted by Heidegger in his lectures in the 1920s):

> while there are three in numbers, existence, life and understanding, and though the stone exists and the animal lives, yet I do not think that the stone lives or that the animal understands, whereas it is absolutely certain that whoever understands also exists and is living. That is why I have no hesitation in concluding that the one which contains all three is more excellent than that which is lacking in one or both of these.[39]

It is this 'understanding of *Being*' – which Heidegger insists extends equally to the world, to myself, and to my fellow human being – that withdraws, hides and is forgotten in our very understanding of and experiencing of the things themselves that is expressed in such everyday statements as 'the sky *is* blue', 'I *am* happy', and so forth.[40]

---

39 There is, therefore, in Augustine's method of 'interiority' much more involved than reaching an understanding of one's own individual existence in Being. As one commentator points out, 'Augustine's demonstration of God's existence begins precisely where his refutation of the sceptics ended, that is, from the certainty that he exists, lives and understands, and proceeds by a very detailed line of reasoning to the conclusion that God exists. A careful analysis of this process of argumentation shows that it contains five steps.' J. McBride, *Albert Caus: Philosopher and Littérature* (New York: St Martin's Press, 1992), p. 36. This author then proceeds with admirable acuity to detail Augustine's line of reasoning (pp. 36–7). Cf., also, Tarsicius J. van Bavel, 'The Anthropology of Augustine', *Louvain Studies* 5 (1974), pp. 34–47 (p. 35).

40 Such a pre-ontological understanding of Being that is deposited in our ontic experiences of that-which-is would have been as hidden from Parmenides as it would have been from Plato as it was from Aristotle and Aquinas – and so in the unfolding of the history of western metaphysics, from Parmenides to Husserl. And so, it also goes without saying that this 'pre-ontological understanding of Being' has absolutely no connection with Husserl's Sixth Logical Investigation and the latter's phenomenological elucidation of Kant's thesis 'Being is not a real predicate' that unfolds therein. Notwithstanding Jacques Taminiaux's meticulous investigations into this matter, I find Heidegger's own 'suggestions' philosophically misleading.

Because the meaning of Being is not thought but implicit, and this is precisely how Heidegger following Dilthey understands the 'unthought' (*das Ungedacht*), this points to *the possibility* of retrieving that meaning, but such a retrieval (*Wiederholung*) can only be enacted and set in operation hermeneutically. Thus Heidegger *can* now argue in *Being and Time* that *the only way* in which 'ontology' – where 'ontology' means post-Kantian study of the way the meaning of the living word of 'Being' is understood – is possible is 'as [hermeneutic] phenomenology'. This statement on Heidegger's part, therefore, cannot, without gross distortion of its significance, be turned around, as it has been by commentators, to suggest that Heidegger really meant 'only as ontology is phenomenology possible', where 'ontology' refers to classical metaphysics and 'phenomenology' refers to Husserlian (eidetic or transcendental) phenomenology. Rather, it means that the only way in which the question of the meaning of Being can be resurrected from oblivion and kept alive 'today' (*heute*), which is Heidegger's desire in the opening sentence of *Being and Time*, is by actively engaging in a hermeneutic reading of texts in the history of philosophy that deal with this matter[41] in order to relive the experience and understanding of Being itself that has been deposited and expressed in and through their written word but which has been left unthought. Thus in Heidegger's starting point, 'hearing' that which is unthought (in any talk about that which is) methodologically replaces 'seeing' that which is revealed in and through the 'seeing'. This is why it is only by way of hermeneutic-phenomenology that [post-Kantian] ontology is possible.

---

41 This applies in all of Heidegger's reading of the texts of any other contemporary thinker, poet, politician that purports to address and express our understanding of the meaning of Being in a person's life, in a society, or in a nation. Heidegger's selection is not as innocent or arbitrary as it might seem, then, and this can call into question his entire approach to 'the Being-question', but such is outside the scope of this paper. Cf. H. Ott, *Martin Heidegger: A Political Life*, tr. A. Blunden (London: Fontana Press, 1993).

Heidegger's 'Being-question'

Heidegger's starting point that there is an implicit (unthought) issue concerning the meaning of Being deposited in our everyday understanding of statements about that-which-is, nevertheless, is not identical to the question that he raises about this starting point in philosophy. Heidegger's 'Being-*question*' is simply this. If our understanding of everyday statements such as 'the sky is blue' and 'I am happy' implies that 'something like Being' is also understood and also meant in those statements, then what is that meaning of Being upon which the intelligibility of such simple statements rests? And where does the understanding of that meaning of Being that is evidently deposited and implicitly expressed in the statements and in these linguistic experiences come from, as I depend upon it in order to make such statements intelligible? This is Heidegger's 'Being-*question*'. Here, however, Heidegger's appropriation of Dilthey's thought seems to run aground, for the very fact that we all live in a vague and general understanding of Being – as important as this Augustinian anthropological postulate is both to Heidegger's starting point and to Heidegger's elevation of the ontic-ontological priority of *Dasein* in 'fundamental ontology' – this, in itself, does not and cannot a priori give us any solace or direction as to where an answer to this question that Heidegger is putting about such an experience can be found. The facticity of the understanding of Being that is exhibited in our everyday statements about the being of things-that-are is not enough, it offers no clue. Analysing those mundane-linguistic experiences will not lead to a recovery of 'the Being-question'. Rather, if the question of the meaning of Being is to be retrieved and reawakened and addressed *as a question*, then a different kind of experience containing its own understanding of the questionable nature of the meaning of Being itself needs to be found and brought into play. Here Heidegger advances Dilthey's thought in a direction that is clearly of no concern to Dilthey but of central significance to Heidegger. And Heidegger believes that he has found just such 'a phenomenal basis' that makes the meaning of Being 'worthy of questioning [*frag-würdig*]' in the anticipatory awareness, in the present, of my own death in the future (*Vorlaufen zum Tode*), as disclosed from within the particular mood of *Angst*.

In the anticipatory awareness, in the present, of one's own death, the questionable appearance of the meaning of Being becomes unavoidable because in that awareness the statement 'I am' both means and expresses at once an understanding that that I am, that I am not-to-be, that not-to-be is part of what it is to be an 'I am who am', and that my mode of being harbours no self-guarantee is being at all, yet is (fact), hence, why. Saying 'I am' in the mood of *Angst* in anticipatory awareness of one's own death, and understanding what that statement means, therefore, both contains and expresses *a different kind of particular experience* of the meaning of Being in comparison to such similar statements as 'the sky *is* blue', or 'I *am* happy', or 'Give me a glass of water, I am dying of thirst'. Heidegger believes that the anticipatory awareness of my own death in the present, and of my own death only, brings us *methodologically* to 'the Being-question' (*BT* 235). Dilthey, of course, could not regard any such inner 'brooding' over one's own death, from a methodological point of view, as a requirement of historical-hermeneutic research into the meaning of our life experiences or of death, and indeed it would be improperly invoked as such, if it were. And yet, it is not invoked by Heidegger as a historical-hermeneutic possibility in *Being and Time* either, rather it is invoked in that essay as an existential-methodological task (requirement), for, 'this possibility [disclosed in *Angst*] must not be weakened; it must be understood *as a possibility*, it must be cultivated *as a possibility*, and we must *put up with* it *as a possibility*, in the way we comport ourselves towards it [in such brooding over death]' (*BT* 306). Herein Heidegger gives Dilthey's manner of thinking a particularly Kierkegaardian-existentialistic twist in the methodological elaboration of 'the Being-question', and it is one that sets Heidegger's project outside of the bounds of Diltheyean hermeneutic phenomenology and inside the bounds of the future memory inscribed in Easter liturgical rites of Christian religious experience of 'Remember man that thou are dust, and onto dust thy shalt return.'[42]

The ontic-ontological priority of Dasein in 'the Being-question'

Strictly speaking, therefore, it is really only in and through the experience of the tenuousness of being and the accompanying questioning of that presence in the understanding of that Being that is evoked in the understanding of one's own being as a being-for-death, in the mood of *Angst*, for *that* individual being in *Dasein*, that *Dasein*, in Heidegger's scheme of thing, exhibits its ontic-ontological priority in 'the Being-question'. In fact, Heidegger explicitly tells us that 'we [he] have [has] chosen to designate this entity as 'Dasein', a term which is purely an expression of its Being [*als reiner Seinsausdruck*]' (*BT* 32).[43] What Heidegger seems to be saying here is that the meaning of this term is *purely* determined by the underpinning meaning of the particular experience itself, and not the accorded meaning of linguistic convention, and it expresses what is understood in that experience from out of itself, namely, the questionable presence of the meaning of the tenuousness of Being itself, i.e. the understanding of the essence of finite being in human (lived) experience of being itself. This is a highly creative use of language by Heidegger – what other German understands the term *Dasein* in the way Heidegger understands it as an expression depicting the awareness of the 'There' of 'Being', in which I find myself implicated as a being in Being who only in and through questioning the very meaning of Being itself makes 'the structural totality' of *Dasein* visible? And yet the meaning that Heidegger gives to this term *Dasein* and his use of language in

---

42 Cf. M. Heidegger, *The Concept of Time*, tr. W. McNeill (Oxford: Blackwell, 1992), bilingual English–German edition, containing M. Heidegger, *Der Begriff der Zeit: Vortrag vor der Marburger Theologenschaft Juli 1924*, ed. H. Tietjen, with postscript (Tübingen: Niemeyer, 1989).

43 Cf., also, *HCT*, § 17.

this way is strictly in accord with Dilthey's philosophy of life, and with the expression of part of life's meaning that we mortals are all to familiar with, namely, the contingency of Being. This underlines Heidegger's characteristic existentialistic rendering of Dilthey's triadic structure of *Erlebnis-Verstehen-Ausdruck* in his famous depiction in *Being and Time* of the human being as a being whose own being is the matter at stake for *that* being in the way that being expresses itself and goes about itself (*es geht um*) in its being-in-the-world. Thus it is Dilthey's manner of thinking, albeit radically modified through Kierkegaardian glasses, that is at work in the meaning that Heidegger *gives* methodologically to *Dasein*, and not Husserl's manner of thinking or Husserl's theory of perception, nor Aristotle's *phronesis*, nor Plato's *eros*,[44] nor what can be seen via listening to the normative power of Greek or German etymological terms (as Heidegger himself conceded, later, to Fr Richardson). If this is the case, then the particular 'understanding of Being' that is constitutive of *Dasein*'s ontic-ontological priority in the formulation of 'the Being-question' is one place where a relevant evaluation of Heidegger's philosophy can, and perhaps should, begin.

Towards a Critical Evaluation of Heidegger's Use of Hermeneutic Phenomenology in 'the Being-question'

According to Heidegger, the 'understanding of Being' that is definitive of *Dasein's* mode of being-in-the-world differs from any understanding of Being that is gained in and through cognitive-reflection on beings as beings (*das Seiende*). In point of fact, identifying and pointing to beings that either come into existence or go out of existence cannot add to or subtract from *Dasein's* 'understanding of Being' because such indications

---

44 Cf. R. Rojcewicz, 'Platonic Love: Dasein's Urge toward Being', *Research in Phenomenology* 27 (1997), pp. 103–20, esp. pp. 118 and 120.

presuppose some understanding of Being *already there* for *Dasein*, but deferred in the process. It is a central contention in Heidegger's formulation and elaboration of 'the Being-question', therefore, that there is 'an understanding of Being' that is always and already present *implicitly* in *Dasein*, back behind of which we cannot go, i.e. that we cannot think, when addressing 'the question of the meaning of Being' in phenomenology and phenomenological research. Heidegger thinks that this position in phenomenology and phenomenological research is unchallengeable and unquestionable, for, as noted above, pointing to beings in *their* being will *obstruct* the issue at hand, or at least it will lead to a fundamental *mis*-targetting of the issue at hand that Heidegger wishes to address in his 'Being-question'. 'Doesn't insistence on what is,' Heidegger asks rhetorically in his late lecture 'The End of Philosophy and the Task of Thinking', 'block access to what-is?' (*Versperrt die Insistenz auf dem Beweisbaren nicht den Weg zu dem, was ist?*)[45] Insistence on what is deflects attention from *the way* what is, is. Hence, insistence *by us* on the being of the being of beings, deflects attention from the 'understanding of Being' that is already presupposed, according to Heidegger, as a precondition both for, to and in any such ostentation.

For Heidegger, then, questions pertaining to the 'understanding of Being' and to the being of the being of beings must be kept not only distinct but also unrelated. The former belong to phenomenology, the latter remains outside of phenomenological remit. The 'understanding of Being' and the being of the being of beings, therefore, are entirely different concepts of being in Heidegger's starting point in philosophy. Heidegger himself clearly *recognizes* this distinction in *Being and Time*. Heidegger, in fact, *insists* on this distinction in *Being and Time* because his 'path of thinking' about 'the Being-question' and its relation to *Dasein* clearly requires it. Heidegger, however, does not explore any further this distinction in *Being and Time* (or in

---

45 M. Heidegger, 'The End of Philosophy and the Task of Thinking', in Heidegger, *On Being and Time*, pp. 55–73 (p. 72).

later works). Heidegger's starting point and finishing point in philosophy and phenomenological research, therefore, remains asserted, and the same, namely:

> Entities *are* [Heidegger's emphasis], quite independently of the experiences by which they are disclosed, the acquaintance in which they are discovered, and the grasping in which their nature is ascertained. But Being 'is' only in the understanding of those entities to whose Being something like an understanding of Being belongs. (*BT* 228)

In order for Heidegger to maintain this position, Heidegger must acknowledge, as de Boer has acutely pointed out, *that there is* a being [small 'b'] of the being of entities that *precedes* the Being of the understanding of Being [big 'B'].[46] Heidegger does not turn to the significance of this first being of the being of entities that is not reducible to the understanding of Being of those entities deposited in *Dasein* in his 'path of thinking' about 'the Being-question'. The being of the being of entities is set aside, and not returned to in the development of Heidegger's thought, as it had been set aside and not returned to in the development of Husserl's thought either. Recall Husserl's famous transcendental reduction. Outside of all that we can know and actually do know about things given to outer perceptual-sense experience, there is 'nothing' of any intelligible or sensible nature to know 'in itself'; there is only 'nonsensical thought'.[47] *That* such things or entities *are* is not a matter for phenomenology and phenomenological research. Likewise, outside the apodictic knowledge of the existence of a currently lived psychical-act experience (and its intentional object, if it exists) in an act of immanent perception – and whose non-existence is inconceivable – lies *its* existence; but *that* such an experience exists (in its facticity as Dilthey understands it) in immanent

---

46 T. de Boer, *The Rationality of Transcendence: Studies in the Philosophy of Emmanuel Lévinas* (Amsterdam: Giegen, 1997), p. 119.

47 De Boer, *The Rationality of Transcendence*, p. 119. Cf., also, de Boer, *The Development of Husserl's Thought*, pp. 338ff., 369, 381.

perception is not a matter for phenomenology and phenomenological research in Husserl's definition of phenomenology. The
facticity of lived experiences is to be ignored because their
meaning is not susceptible to scientific analysis and scientific
generalizations or conceptual analysis in any form in Husserl's
eidetic eyes. There can be no eidetic science of the 'thisness' of
this particular experience here and now. And since the essential
features of such lived-experiences is all that counts, the very
lived nature of the particular experiences themselves in their
uniqueness must be passed over and not be entertained as a
matter for philosophy and phenomenological research. This is
what Heidegger, influenced by his reading of Dilthey, means
when he says to his students in his 1925 lectures that 'the being
of the intentional [acts of consciousness] . . . *gets lost precisely
through them* [i.e. *both* the eidetic and the transcendental
reductions' (*HCT* 110). And yet Heidegger himself does not
return to this facticity of the life experiences of *Dasein*. That I
exist, that you exist, that you die, that I die are not the concern
of Heidegger's phenomenology either, but my understanding of
myself as a being-for-death is. Outside of one's own actual
understanding of oneself as a being-for-death, then, that you
are murdered, or that blood-lust and domination 'exists' (not in
Heidegger's sense of that term) is not the concern of *Dasein* in
Being and Time. It is at this point that Levinas, inspired by
Dilthey's philosophy of life, raises the following, critical question within both Husserlian and Heideggerean phenomenology
and phenomenological research: is not the very anonymous
existence of things that are and of experiences that are a presupposition itself requiring and inviting a hermeneutic investigation? This investigation, however, would lie both beyond and
outside the dual limits set by Husserl in the transcendental
reduction on the 'understanding of Being' as thing given to
outer sense perception and on the 'understanding of Being' as
(conscious) experience immanently perceived, and outside
the existential-phenomenological limit set by Heidegger on
'the understanding of Being' *as that which is hermeneutically
deposited and revealed in anxious anticipation, in the present,*

of one's own death in *Dasein*, whose own being, and own being
alone, remains the root of 'the understanding of Being' *and* the
sole matter at stake that needs to be thought in philosophy and
phenomenological research. If Heidegger is right, and if our
'understanding of Being' extends equally to the world, to myself
and to my fellow human being, then the critical question that
Levinas raises is how can I reach '*an* understanding of Being'
that is not mine but shareable and for the good of our human
existence, and *therefore* for the good of our human understanding? Focusing on *Dasein* – i.e. on the awareness of the 'There'
(*Da*) of 'Being' (*Sein*), in which one finds oneself implicated as a
being in being and as a being-for-one's-own-death – methodologically excludes a prioristically such an *ethical* (or 'metaphysical' in Levinas's sense) possibility within phenomenology
and phenomenological research. Heidegger's insistence on the
ontic-ontological priority of 'the understanding of Being' in
Dasein as the back behind of which we cannot think, then, is
itself a presupposition, an assertion that needs to be tested for
its phenomenological credentials.

If 'the understanding of Being' that I possess, and in which I
live, move and have my being, extends equally to the world, to
myself and to my fellow human being – as Heidegger suggests –
then the very existence of the other human being and of that
being's understanding of Being has at least the potential to call
into question 'the understanding of Being' that *I have* acquired
(and *can* acquire) about the world, about myself and about my
fellow human being. Would not my concern for the being of
another shatter the concern that I actually can have and do have
about that which is at stake in my own being a being in Being?
'Do not do unto others, that you would not have done to yourself' (Matt. 7.12; Luke 6.31) is a familiar injunction recorded in
the Bible but it is one that is rooted in human 'ontic' experiences. So, who are the 'others' that is referred to here? Clearly
'the other' is not *merely* an empirical other given to acts of outer
perceptual-sense experience through perspectival variations,
nor the 'other' who plays a necessary role in the dialectical constitution of the consciousness of the self in relation to the other,

whether conceived in Hegelian or Husserlian dialectical manner, nor the 'other' whom I hold in friendship and she in friendship to 'me', as Aristotle and Aquinas would have it. Rather, the other that is spoken of 'not to be done as one would have done to oneself', is he and she who have been *othered* in society: the poor, the widow, the orphan, the leper, the marginalized.[48] This is what is expressed and understood and meant in this biblical injunction, and it has a universality of meaning, albeit not arrived at or as clearly seen in eidetic ideation as Husserl would like, or in existential brooding about one's own death as Heidegger would like, but nonetheless it contains a universality all the same, 'for those who have eyes to see it'.[49] In this invocation to serve the other, the other, Levinas remarks, takes 'the me' (*le moi*) in me as hostage or pledge (*otage*) of his and her responsibility; this is an 'ontic experience' and it is an 'ontic' experience whose meaning is expressed and documented in biblical verse and in everyday life experiences. 'Biblical verses do not function here as proof but as testimony of a tradition and an experience. Don't they have as much right as Hölderin and Trakl to be cited?'[50] And, of course they do, if you follow Dilthey's revolutionary philosophy of life, for, 'The religious thinker, the artist, and the philosopher create on the basis of lived experience.' Hence the expression and understanding of life experiences that are written about and spoken about by the prophets in the psalms and in the stories of the New Testament invite the reader to engage both in and with a person's reflection on his and her own self understanding. Here, however, there can be no 'science' of human self-understanding, only hermeneutic 'retrieval' and 'interpretation' of the significances of the way of life that unfolds *in* and *through* human experiences themselves.

---

48 Cf. T. de Boer's excellent treatment of this in 'Beyond Being: Ontology and Eschatology in the Philosophy of Emmanuel Levinas', *Philosophica Reformata* 38 (1973), pp. 17–29 (pp. 23–4).

49 De Boer, *The Rationality of Transcendence*, pp. 169–83.

50 E. Levinas, 'Without Identity' in *Humanism of the Other*, tr. N. Poller (Illinois: University of Illinois Press, 2003), pp. 58–69 (p. 66).

Outside of my actual experiences lies the very existence of my fellow human being, but this is an experience, and it is an experience that must be thought. And outside of that the God who calls me to be responsible before the other, for the other, to the other, is also an experience, an experience recorded in the Old and New Testaments, and an experience that must be thought. A true existential humanism is a humanism of the other, then, but such a humanism of the other is only intelligible in light of affirming a relation to a third, to He, who is present, in addition to you and me, as Absolutely Other, 'who can never be seized directly and always remains a "He"'.[51]

If Levinas is right, then we should be able to go back to Heidegger's *Being and Time* to traces where Heidegger acknowledges, but does not listen to, the word of God. And, indeed, there is documentary evidence in *Being and Time*. At a critical point in his analysis of death, Heidegger declares that even if one were assured of one's whither and thither, the meaning of the tenuousness of being experienced in *Angst* cannot be cancelled, struck out, denied in the affirmation of such a Creator God.[52] In *Introduction to Metaphysics*, Heidegger takes a different view. He suggests that affirming the existence of a Creator God would cancel the questioning of the meaning of Being, as an answer to that question has been accepted.[53] But is Heidegger correct? If

---

51 De Boer, 'Beyond Being', p. 24, and, as de Boer continues, 'For this Levinas uses the term "illéité", which is derived from *il, ille*.' Cf. also, E. Levinas, 'Signification and Sense' in *Humanism of the Other*, pp. 9–44 (pp. 41–2).

52 Cf. *BT*, p. 175.

53 This is what lies behind Heidegger's famous remark in 1953 that if he were to be called by faith he would have to 'shut up shop'. 'Report of a session of the Evangelical Academy in Hofgeismar, December 1953', tr. J. Greisch in R. Kearney (ed.), *Heidegger et la question de Dieu* (Grasset, 1988), p. 335. Cf. also, J. Derrida, *Of Spirit: Heidegger and the Question*, tr. G. Bennington and R. Bowlby (Chicago and London: The University of Chicago Press, 1991), p. 115, n. 3. Walter A. Brogan says that Heidegger hints at this as early as in his 1922 Aristotle essay 'and queries whether the idea of a philosophy of religion is not itself contradictory, even though his own courses had more than once bore this title', *Heidegger and Aristotle: The Twofoldness of Being*, p. 12.

the tenuousness of not only mine but of all particular finite beings in being is dependent on an act of the will of a Creator God, would this not leave the contingency in being that is experienced more questionable, and not less questionable? It is certainly not anchored ontologically in any necessity, and it is certainly not anchored hermeneutically in an already necessarily deposited meaning, however unthought, in texts that need to be read in order to raise anew the question of the meaning of Being, as Heidegger's path of 'thinking' about the 'Being-question' does. It certainly would require, however, engaging in addressing the unthought in Heidegger's own understanding of the certainty of faith as opposed to questioning, in favour of the way faith questions thought.

16. Love of Enemies for a Lover of Wisdom, or, Can a Phenomenologist be a Philosopher?

FELIX Ó MURCHADHA

Common to both Christianity and Philosophy is the insight that love is a relation of desire disclosing or revealing essential truth. This insight is born out of the very practice of philosophy and the revelation of Christ.[1] The love of wisdom and the love of Christ begin in the mood of wonder. However, wonder gives rise to different, indeed conflicting, experiences of desire and in consequence different accounts of love between philosophy and Christianity. While Greek philosophy is motivated to over-come wonder, Christianity is the practice of living in wonder, living, as St Paul says, in this world as if not of this world. The ambivalence of Christian being-in-the-world expressed here shapes a non-Greek understanding of desire. It should come as no surprise then that when the writers of the Christian Scrip-tures came to account for the love which is this relation of desire, they spoke not of *eros*, but tended rather to use the verb *agapao* or – most especially in Paul and John's letters – a noun found previously only in the Septuagint translators of the Hebrew Scriptures, *agape*. The significance of this linguistic usage in terms of a difference in Christian and Hellenistic accounts of

---

1 I use this term to signify the significance of Jesus of Nazareth to Christianity, not to make any theological claim as to the truth of this significance.

love was at one time stressed highly by biblical scholars and theologians;[2] textual analysis has since uncovered a much more varied picture.[3] While the results of such philological research are indispensable in a study of the type attempted here, they must remain in the background. The concern of this paper is phenomenological, not so much to argue for a clear distinction of *eros* and *agape* as to show an irreducible tension between them and demonstrate the phenomenological basis of this tension in the structure of desire. More specifically the concern is to understand that phenomenon indicated in the command, 'love your enemies'. Such a command is incomprehensible if we are to understand love as *philia* or as *eros*, as these terms are described and as they operate in Plato and Aristotle.[4] If that is so, and if this command is not simply a hyperbolic inflation of Christian love but lies at its core, then the question poses itself whether it lies outside, external to and incommensurable with, the love of wisdom. If it does so, then two possible consequences can follow: either we accept Christianity in its inner motivation to be incompatible with 'philosophy' or we ask whether the Christian account of love poses philosophical questions for us outside the realm of philosophy understood as Greek. The first option does not allow Christianity to disrupt the philosophical enterprise. But this raises a difficult question: how can we account *philosophically* for this exclusion? Why is it that certain texts and those alone, which express certain experiences and those alone, are beyond philosophical reflection (either above or below it makes no difference here)? This question is all the more pressing as these texts and these experiences centre on a claim to truth and to universal truth. It is one of the major achievements of the

---

2 The most influential figure in this respect was Anders Nygrens. See his *Agape and Eros* (Philadelphia: The Westminster Press, 1953).

3 For an account of that debate, see C. Osbourne, *Eros Unveiled: Plato and the God of Love* (Oxford: Clarendon Press, 1994), ch. 2.

4 In this case at least Nygrens' statement that 'there is no way not even one of sublimation which leads from *eros* to *agape*' (*Agape and Eros*, p. 50) is correct.

so-called 'theological turn' in recent French phenomenology[5] – but really the roots of this are to be found in the origins of phenomenology itself – to take this question seriously. I do not see how the exclusion of original Christian experience and the texts which express it can be justified philosophically. Hence, only the second option is open, one which calls 'philosophy' itself into question. Schematically the question of this paper may be posed in this way: is the love (*philia*) of wisdom necessarily erotic, or can it be – perhaps must it be – also, perhaps primarily, agapeic?

Divine Love and Creation

In Luke's account of the 'Sermon on the Plain' the four beatitudes and four curses are structured in terms of a series of reversals.[6] The reversals are not to be understood as referring to this present world and the next future world, but rather to the immanence of this world and the transcendence of God. In this world appears that which is not of this world, which transcends it. The kingdom of God belongs to the poor, those whose desire transcends the mere worldliness of things. The beatitudes and curses chart a series of reversals in terms of oppositions between rich and poor, hungry and well fed, laughing and weeping. The final beatitude sums up the previous three: 'Blessed are you when people hate you' (Luke 6.22).[7] The curses conclude with:

---

5 This re-evaluation of Christianity in relation to the philosophical tradition stretches beyond those such as Levinas, Henry, Chretien and Marion (the targets of Janicaud's polemic) who stand explicitly within the Judaeo-Christian tradition. Badiou, Nancy and Derrida have from more or less explicitly atheistic positions taken up Christian themes and texts.

6 In the following I concentrate on Luke's account of the Beatitudes rather than that of Matthew, because the structure of reversal found in Luke is not present in Matthew and the emphasis on the non-reciprocity of the lover of enemies is not as strong in Matthew as it is in Luke.

7 All biblical quotations are taken from the *New Jerusalem Bible* (London: Darton, Longman & Todd, 1985).

'Alas for you when everyone speaks well of you' (Luke 6.26). Desire should not be for the love of people in the world any more than for satisfaction from things of the world. In effect Christ is calling those 'who are listening' (Luke 6.27) to be prepared to be hated.

The oppositions which structure the beatitudes and curses suggest conflict. But the logic of reversal extends to conflict itself: instead of responding to hate with hate, the relationship is reversed by responding to it with love: 'Love your enemies, do good to those who hate you . . . ' (Luke 6.27). Hate is to be responded to with love. The command to love is itself paradoxical, all the more so a command to love one's enemies. To love is to do good (*kalos*). *Kalos* means beautiful or noble; used as an adverb it means right or appropriate (*en kalo*: in the appropriate place). To love my enemy is to act towards him in an appropriate way. Appropriate to what? Not to the enemy as such, but rather to the one called (Jesus is speaking directly to his disciples, unlike in Matthew where on the mountain he addresses the crowds).[8] The command to love can best be understood as an expression of love.[9] In other words, the command, 'love your enemies', expresses the love Jesus has for those to whom he is speaking. This is not so much a commandment in the sense of the Law, but rather a *declaration* of love. Christ is described by Paul as having died for those who were his enemies: those who were turned away from God (Rom. 5.10). >From the mouth of Christ, to love your enemies amounts to saying, 'love as I love you'.

Further on in the passage it states: 'if you love those who love you what credit (*charis*) can you expect?' (Luke 6.33). Such 'love' – so the logic of this passage suggests – is actually no love at all. Love is measured not by reciprocity, but by non-reciprocity, by a giving with no expectation of return: 'love your enemies and do good to them, and lend *without any hope of return*' (Luke 6.35). In respect to enemies love is without

8 Luke 6.20: 'fixing his eyes on his disciples he said . . .'.
9 Cf. P. Ricoeur, 'Love and Justice' in *Figuring the Sacred* (Minneapolis: Fortress Press, 1995), pp. 324–9.

hope of return, your enemy remains your enemy, the gift of love is without recipient. Nor is there any appeal here to notions of a common humanity grounding the love of an enemy. Nor finally, *pace* Aquinas, can we say that we should love the enemy for the sake of the one who is truly lovable, namely God in whose image he is.[10] The love of enemies is direct, not indirect (as Aquinas's solution would have it), directed at those who are other than me. I am not the object of my love in any form, there is no notion of becoming one in love. In love the other remains other, remains beyond the reach of my love.

Love without reciprocation is for Christianity the very measure of love, because in the Christian sense there is nothing higher than love: love is not a servant of knowledge, as it is for the Greeks.[11] Nor can love take its model from knowledge in the sense of an appropriation of its object. Love rather is a gift which first God bestows. It is the example of the self-less love of Christ, of a sacrifice, to which any response is uncertain. This gift may be taken up, but the giving of the gift does not depend on its being taken up. If it were so that the gift was given in the expectation of its being taken up, then love would be in the service of something else.

Certain implications can be drawn out here. First, the imitation of Christ is central to this account. The plausibility of the account derives from the example of Christ: God's love of sinners is manifest both in creation and in the incarnation,[12] to listen to Christ is to follow his example in loving one's own enemies. If it is only through Christ that one can know God, it is only through following his example that one can know Christ. In that case the practice of following Christ is itself the highest knowledge. Second, there is nothing in the sinner, which

---

10 Thomas Aquinas, *Summa Theologica* 2.2, q. 23, a. 1.

11 Cf. on this issue, M. Scheler, *Love and Knowledge* (Chicago: University of Chicago Press, 1992), p. 190.

12 The parallel of creation and incarnation is clear in Paul: 'Yet for us there is one God, the Father, from whom are all things and for whom we exist and one Lord, Jesus Christ, through whom are all things and through whom we exist' (1 Cor. 8.6).

gives good reason for the love being shown him. If anything the sinner is hateful. There is then no correspondence in nature between the act of love and the one loved, nor is love given in the expectation of such correspondence. Similarly in the case of enemies, love is not given on the basis of a correspondence between lover and beloved, rather it is given precisely in the lack of such correspondence. Third, the desire, which characterizes this relation of love is not one of fulfilling a lack, if it were this account of love would lead to despair not to blessedness. Rather, this is a love manifest in acts in which the self gives of itself beyond any demands of justice.

Such an account of desire and love is scarcely conceivable within the erotics of Greek philosophy. Plato's statement, 'the gods do not philosophize', is never contradicted in Greek philosophy.[13] The gods do not philosophize because the gods are already wise. Hence, they do not love wisdom. But as there is nothing higher that can be loved than wisdom, it follows that the gods do not love. For Plato to love is to desire what is lacking. This desire is for appropriation, for becoming oneself in gaining love's object. The lover wishes to become the object of her love. Ultimately the lover wishes to be wise. Love in this understanding is an ascent, one which motivates the ascent from the cave. It is a violent desire struggling against the materiality of existence, but itself prefigured in that very materiality. It is this that allows Plato to move from that love common to everyone (*pandemos*) to the heavenly love.[14] But this heavenly love is as much a worldly love. The word Plato uses here, *ouranous*, can just as easily be translated as worldly. This is no contradiction: the love of which Plato speaks is a love for the worldliness of the world: light, sky, the divine domain as opposed to the dark materiality of the earth.[15] This is a love,

---

13 Plato, *Symposium*, 204a1.

14 Plato, *Symposium*, 180–181.

15 In this sense Heidegger's polemos of earth and world (sky) repeats key Platonic structures. See M. Heidegger, 'Origin of the Work of Art' in *Off the Beaten Track* (Cambridge: Cambridge University Press, 2002), pp. 23–33.

which moves upwards not downwards. There is then an imitation of the divine here, but not of divine love. Love, rather, is in service of the imitation, it is that which makes human beings strive to imitate the divine. This structure does not merely relate to the divine: at every level from the sensual to the highest intellectual there is a relation of love with that which corresponds to the nature of the soul. The sensual soul yearns for the things of the senses, the intellectual soul for the immaterial things, ultimately for the divine. This yearning is rooted in lack, but a lack which is prefiguring: the senses lack the things of the senses, the intellect the things of the intellect. Hence, the relation of love is that between the same: for such a love there can be no stranger. Furthermore, the love of wisdom is a love of that knowledge which characterizes wisdom. That is the knowledge of necessary and eternal truths. Divine knowledge is of such truths, which see beyond the contingencies of the lower earthly world to their higher necessity. To see the world through divine eyes is to see it as a world in which nothing is lacking. The striving of eros leads to the disclosing of a world in which there is no lack and hence no love. Love evaporates in knowledge/wisdom.

The account of love in Luke stands in opposition and contradiction to such Platonic erotics. This opposition is fundamental and has fundamental consequences. To briefly indicate what these may be in a scriptural context before turning to some phenomenological reflections in the next section, I will refer to two Pauline passages from 1 Corinthians and from Romans.

The line in 1 Corinthians, which introduces the so-called 'hymn to love', is standardly translated as: 'now I am going to put before you the best way of all [to set your mind on spiritual things]' (1 Cor. 12.31). This does not mean that he is outlining the best way among many possible ways. The Greek is *eti kath' hyperbolēn hodon. Hyperbole* means exaggeration beyond measure. One could translate here as 'beyond excess'. This is a way, which is not simply excessive, but is out of all relation to anything within the economy of human life. He is not making a comparative statement but rather saying that the way of love is beyond all measure within that economy. The way of love, that love expressed in the command to love one's enemies, is a way beyond the worldly economy. But it is for all that a command to act in the world. It concerns actions towards enemies. Who then are my enemies? We are familiar with what appears to be the opposite question posed of Christ, who are my neighbours (Luke 10.29)? Christ responds to this question with the story of the good Samaritan: my enemy is my neighbour.[16] In effect my neighbour is commensurate with my enemy: the world is not divided up into friends and enemies, the enemies referred to in the command are not an identifiable group of people.[17] The imitation of Christ is the imitation of one who is in the world, but rejected by the world. As God's love is for all in the world, which turns away from him, the love of enemies is for all that which turns away from me, that is, which turns away from the light of the world in which all things are manifested to me.

Understood outside of the strictly ethical domain, that which turns away from me is not confined to the realm of other people, what we might call the realm of inter-subjectivity. Things as much as people, to the extent that they stand outside me, turn away from me as well as towards me. This brings us to the second passage, Romans 8.19–23:

> the whole of creation is waiting with eagerness for the children of God to be revealed. It is not for its own purposes that creation had frustration imposed on it, but for the purpose of him who imposed it with the intention that the whole creation itself might be freed from slavery to corruption and brought into the same glorious freedom as the children of God. We are all well aware that the whole creation, until this time [*achri tou nun*], has been groaning in labour pains.

---

16 For an acute phenomenological analysis of this parable, which, in its implications, conflicts with the position being articulated in this article, see K. Held, 'Ethos und die christliche Gotteserfahrung', *Archivio di Filosofia* (2001), vol. 69 (1–3), pp. 247–61.

17 In this and other respects Carl Schmitt's reading of the injunction to love one's enemies is distortive. Cf. C. Schmitt, *The Concept of the Political* (New Brunswick: Rutgers, 1976), p. 29.

This is a passage in which every word calls for commentary. It is relevant to the concerns of this paper because it brings together the history of salvation: creation, fall, redemption and the second coming. It is the love of God which is expressed in all of these and which is fully revealed in the final glory. What is striking of course about this passage is that the history of sin, the fall, salvation, redemption, final glory, are not confined here to humanity but concern all creation. For all creation time is not a neutral, indifferent measure, but rather one of loss and hope. The mention of this time is an abbreviation of what went before in verse 18: *tou nun kairou* – in this present kairos. All of creation is included in the kairological event of the incarnation and the eschatological promise of the second coming.[18]

The imitation of Christ is the imitation of the incarnational love of God. If that love is the creative love of God, the love that creates what it does not lack and which thus makes possible enemies, then it is a love for all creation. The place of humankind is a key one, of course. Its sin brought about frustration and corruption, through a human being salvation is gained. But here it is the commonality of human and non-human which is being emphasized, right down to the promise of the same glorious freedom for both. According to St Bonaventure, salvation came through a human being because a human being brought together the lower and higher in nature.[19] This is a basically Greek thought, but one which is being employed in a non-Greek context: the *historical destiny* of the world centres on humankind. The event of the incarnation reveals *agape*, reveals a divine love and a divine desire as the meaning of that history, a meaning which displaces human beings in relation to creation by reference to an event within the world, which is not of the world.

Love of enemies is a love of that which is insufficient to that love. It offers no fulfilment, no satisfaction of lack. There is no

18 There are clear echoes here of Isaiah 11.6: 'The wolf will lie down with the lamb/the panther lie down with the kid.'
19 See Z. Hayes, 'Christology – Cosmology', *Spirit and Life* 7 (1997), pp. 51–5.

commonality of nature between the lover and the beloved. This love is neither motivated by the object of love nor by the nature of the lover. God's love is without condition because God is love (*ho theos agape estin*) (1 John 4.8). Love originates in God, that is, in God's free giving. This giving is creation itself. Hence, the negative ontological thesis *creatio ex nihilo* can be translated positively as *creatio ex caritate* – creation out of love. The insufficiency here is absolute: all creation is out of love, out of a groundless giving to which the love of enemies responds in imitation.

Phenomenology, Agape, Prayer

Agape is indissolvably intertwined with revelation. Revelation, it may be argued, can only be taken on faith. But to leave matters there is to ignore that revelation is possible only to the extent to which it is meaningful. The account of *agape* and desire, to the extent to which it is meaningful, must be open to philosophical reflection. But in this case such reflection concerns philosophy itself in its inner erotic movement. The philosophical task then is to bring *eros* and *agape* into relation with one another. Many questions arise in such an attempt. Is there a language in which that relation can be accounted for and perhaps adjudicated? Is this a language of reason or of faith or of neither one nor the other? Is the desire to bring together and adjudicate itself erotic? Can we speak of desire and love without *having* desire and love, and if desire and love are split do we know from which desire, in which love, we are speaking? To face these questions directly would require more space than the confines of this paper allows. I will, therefore, approach them obliquely by posing the question in the title of this paper: can a phenomenologist be a philosopher? This question becomes pertinent to the issue of faith and reason because phenomenology since Husserl has remained committed at least to this: that the description of phenomena should be compelling, not in the way of rational argument, but rather in the sense which Husserl designates as *Ausweisung* – literally, that it can demonstrate to all who consider it that it is a true description of phenomena in their showing.[20] Before (in both senses) reason and faith, there are phenomena, there are appearances appearing in their own manner of appearance to somebody.

There are phenomena only if there is access to that which appears in its appearing, hence the importance of method in phenomenology. The phenomenological method for all its apparent constructions is a method of waiting. It is a method in the middle voice. Phenomenology is concerned to *let* what is appear as it is. To let appear is to be prepared to be surprised. It is to be prepared to be surprised at the intimate level of the disclosure of the appearing of an appearance to me. Such preparedness for surprise, for that which seizes from above, beyond the dominant gaze, is – it might be argued – implicit in the experience of wonder that lies at the roots of philosophy itself. But it is clear in Aristotle's account that to say that philosophy begins in wonder is to say that it begins in lack of knowledge.[21] Hence, as philosophy's goal is to gain knowledge of first principles, philosophy aims to overcome wonder. This assumes a final goal of knowledge, which in principle is possible, because all knowledge is worldly, all knowledge has its source in that which is commensurate with human experience. Ironically, it is in exploring human experience that phenomenology encounters phenomena which are incommensurate with – not measurable in terms of – human experience and transcend that experience in a radical manner. The question now is what desire and what love allows for this encounter.

It is undeniable that the practice of phenomenology has been guided by the erotic principle of lack and fulfilment.[22] Yet,

---

20 E. Husserl, *Ideas Pertaining to a Pure Phenomenology and to a Phenomenological Philosophy: First Book*, tr. R. Rojcewicz and A. Schuwer (The Hague: Springer, 2001), § 136.

21 Aristotle, *Metaphysics*, 982b11–22.

22 Arguably both Husserl's dream of rigorous science and Heidegger's project of fundamental ontology are both characterized by such a motivation.

there is here too a moment where this desire and love break down. This breakdown does not herald the limit of phenomenology, but rather the limit of the erotic within the project phenomenology sets for itself. To put the thesis most strongly, phenomenology discovers, due to the very sense of its project, nature as created, nature namely as gratuitous, as originating in a love – givenness – for which there is no sufficient reason. For this origin there is no natural reception, as it receives what is beyond nature, beyond nature but yet within nature, ultimate yet contingent, excessive and invisible.

The erotic desire of phenomenology is inherent in the importance it grants to intentionality. As Husserl conceives it, intentional consciousness, when in doubt as to the meaning of its object, remains unfulfilled. Something is missing. What is missing is the object itself in its givenness. Consciousness strives to make up this lack. Indeed, there is a striving already there in an implicit and unacknowledged way before the conscious ego is activated at all. The tendency of the object coming towards the subject is responded to by a turning towards the object, which is pre-predicative, pre-conscious. In this context Husserl speaks of the attractiveness of the object and the ego yielding to its stimulus even at this preconscious level.[23] For Husserl, the cogito's interest is in its intentional objects, this is in the end a cognitive interest striving to *know* its object, whether in a theoretical or in a carnal sense. For Husserl fulfilment of such intentional consciousness is in principle possible, albeit constituted temporally and inter-subjectively. What Husserl calls the internal horizon of the object can be brought to intentional consciousness. Yet Husserl recognizes too the excessiveness of the object to intentional consciousness. One of the key insights of Husserl's early phenomenology is that the object is perceivable in itself only in and through its adumbrations: it manifests itself in its adumbrations. Hence, the object though 'in person' is

---

23 E. Husserl, *Ideas Pertaining to a Pure Phenomenology and to a Phenomenological Philosophy: Second Book*, tr. R. Rojcewicz and A. Schuwer (Dordrecht: Kluwer, 1989), p. 225.

never present in anything but a finite mode. The presence of the object is never one of pure transparency in accordance with the cognitive model (despite the fact that Husserl in his own interpretations of his analysis tended towards such a model), but rather the presence of an object which never fully satisfies the intentional consciousness but rather intensifies it, in a manner which suggests the movement of desire towards an object.[24]

This movement is an erotic one, which seeks fulfilment in the object. But what Husserl's analyses show us is that this erotic drive is both inspired and refused by the object in its ambiguity. The object shows itself and withdraws in its self-showing. The withdrawal is the appearance of the excess of the object, the excess of its givenness over that which is given to intuition.[25] Such excess points to the primacy of desire: desire as opposed to need is not fulfilled in its object, but hollowed out by it.[26] What this shows is that the drive of eros finds its limit in the excess of the givenness of the object. That excess is not accountable in erotic terms and yet it is precisely the object in its excess which provokes that drive. Desire begins in affectivity, in the passivity of being acted upon by the object. This being acted upon is itself a gift, a gratuitous giving of the object. The object, however, as acting upon me is not the object of erotic drive but the 'subject' of agapeic gift. The name for this 'subjectness' of the object is creaturehood. As that which is in excess of any correlation to consciousness the object reveals itself as in excess of its worldliness. In its discovery of the object as given, as irreducible in its appearance to the horizons of the world, phenomenology –

---

24 See R. Barbaras's insightful account in *Desire and Distance: Introduction to a Phenomenology of Perception* (Stanford: Stanford University Press, 2006), pp. 109–14.

25 This is in effect the core of Marion's critique of Husserl. See his 'Being and Phenomena' in *Reduction and Givenness* (Evanston: Northwestern University Press, 1998), pp. 49–53.

26 The term is Levinas's. See his 'God and Philosophy' in *The God who Comes to Mind* (Stanford: Stanford University Press, 1998), p. 67.

against its initial programme – uncovers the object as in the world but not of the world, i.e. as created.

Fulfilment in terms of intentional consciousness means that the object is disclosed as corresponding to an intention: fulfilment is in terms of an object, an entity of which certain aspects remain hidden and absent. This hiddenness and absence of the object is not something lacking in the object in the sense of that which cannot satisfy the desire for the object. Rather, it is an excess of the object perceived. Hence, the givenness of the object remains insurmountable, the subject cannot be adequate to that givenness. Understood in terms of the erotic tradition of philosophy this would mark philosophy as tragic. But such an understanding is not true to the object in its givenness. As given, the object exceeds the intentional gaze and must do so.

Understood as created in terms of the intersection of *eros* and *agape* the perception of things and of persons poses, in line with Romans 8.19–23, no fundamental difference: in both cases what is disclosed is the limit posed by created things not in terms of their lack of satisfying potential, but precisely as being in excess of all possible satisfaction, as being double: objects of erotic drive and 'subjects' of excessive gift.

Within the Christian tradition creation has been understood agapeically as a radically initiatory act, i.e. an act not of moulding pre-given matter, but of bringing into being. Such *creatio ex nihilo* we have already reformulated as *creatio ex caritate*. Love is nothing in the sense of being without sufficient reason. In terms of such love, all things are equally groundless as they have their source in the love of God (subjective and objective genitive), which is without reason. Leibniz understands *creatio ex nihilo* in terms of that 'being which carries within itself the reason for its own existence',[27] but that is to understand creation in terms of sufficiency. *Creatio ex nihilo* understood as *creatio ex caritate* is absolutely contingent, it is a contingent act

---

27 G. W. Leibniz, *Theodicy: Essays on the Goodness of God, the Freedom of Man, and the Origin of Evil*, ed. A. Farrer (La Salle: Open Court, 1985), p. 127.

which opens up the history of creation. But if that love is without measure – and its manifestation in the world knows no worldly measure, although its glory can appear to me only in the world and hence in being – then it is bestowed as much on one being as on an other. The hierarchy of beings, as Leibniz shows,[28] is based on the principle of sufficient reason; in relation to love it loses its basis. Phenomenologically speaking the appearing of a rock on a hillside, a rose in a garden, a person in suffering has no priority one against the other. Understood as created, no thing in the world is privileged, only events enacting that creation can give place to that which breaks with the economy of the world.[29] This leads not to indifference but rather to singularity. The manner of givenness differs from one phenomenon to the next; the task of phenomenology is to allow them to come to speech. The hiddenness of phenomena, the invisibility of what gives itself, brings constative speech to breaking point. What is left is not silence, but a speech which is attentive to silence, which awaits and lets appear. Such speech is not a discourse of cause and effect, but rather of phenomena as they give themselves. Such discourse is prayerful. Prayer is fundamentally hymnal: all prayer sings praise. To praise is to give glory, that is, to let the splendour of that which is appear to me. In this sense the discourse of phenomenology is fundamentally doxological. It attempts not to explain things within a system in which they have a sufficient reason, that is, a reason outside of themselves, but rather attempts to describe things in the singularity of their appearance. This singularity of appearance is the splendour of things. To allow to appear in splendour is to allow the excessive givenness of that which appears to appear as it is, that is, as this singular thing. In its openness to the singularity of appearance phenomenology tends towards an overcoming of erotic striving in its acknowledgement of that in

---

28 G. W. Leibniz, *Leibniz's Monadology*, ed. N. Rescher (Pittsburgh: University of Pittsburgh Press, 1991), § 36 and § 37.

29 Cf. Y. Lacoste, 'Batir, Habiter, Priere', *Revue Thomiste* 87 (1987), p. 380.

the world which is not of the light of the world. In this sense phenomenology sees things, all things, in relation to an instance in terms of which all things are equal, all things are frustrated, all things are fallen into the ambiguity of their worldly appearance. But this fallenness is that which all things have in common, not as a shared property, but rather as an *event* to which all things are related and can be understood in terms of such a relation.

In this sense phenomenology regains a fundamental moment of Christian thinking, namely the rejection of the dualism of Greek philosophy. The event of the incarnation brought to its ultimate moment that which all things share, namely a relation to the world and a relation beyond it. In associating with sinners Christ brings into communion the unapproachable light that no worldly eye can see and the impenetrable darkness that remains in excess of all possible friendship. In reaching the invisible phenomena in the entity, phenomenology in its own terms enacts this communion. Phenomenology understood in its inner movement is a denial of dualism for reasons which in the end are Christian not Greek: things in the world surge towards us not as body or mind but as material entities imbued with spirit, i.e. historical and temporal possibility. This points us back to the duality which Paul sees not between body and mind, but rather between, on the one hand, the body in its enrapture with the superficial reality of things (*sark*) being in the world as a self-moving entity (*psyche*), and, on the other hand, the body which lets appear its spiritual source (*pneuma*).[30] But this source is not in conflict with the body, but rather holds out the ultimate possibility for the body. As Paul tells us, the point is to spiritualize all things. The body is not a prison to escape, but rather that which can be transformed. Phenomenology not alone allows us to think this, but in its own movement leads to such an understanding: material beings in their appearance break with the

---

30 Cf. Paul in 1 Corinthians 15.44. On this theme, see J. Mensch, *The Beginning of the Gospel according to John* (London: Peter Lang, 1992), pp. 185–204.

immanence of the world in the temporality of their appearing.[31] This temporality, this event character of appearance – in Paul's terms the kairos – is that which escapes the erotic gaze. It is that which lies at the core of the singularity of appearance itself.

In the World, Not of the World

The love of enemies is ultimately the love of material creation, of that which shares in historical possibility, in which hope is embedded. The love of enemies is that which gives meaning to hope, a hope in the singular possibility of every material being to be itself, to appear as itself. Love and desire remain split. The object of phenomenology remains double. Between *eros* and *agape* it is phenomenologically impossible to choose. This reflects the relation of things to the world and to that which is beyond the world's light. In asking the question of the appearing of appearance, phenomenology places the philosopher in a position of waiting. Its attitude is a prayerful one faced with absence, given over to the disproportionality of that of which it awaits, directed towards the coming to be of that which appears. In this position between *eros* and *agape* phenomenology negotiates in desire the movement of that which is in the world but not of the world and does so only to the extent that the phenomenologist herself imitates a love of enemies, which turns towards that which turns away from her.

---

31 Cf. J.-L. Marion, *Being Given* (Stanford: Stanford University Press, 2002), p. 139.

17. *Anamnesis* as Alterity?

IAN LEASK

Jean-Louis Chrétien's stunning analyses have already empha-sized, to those of us who are interested, something of the 'vio-lently difficult and intensely aporetic' nature of *anamnesis*[1] – a description that would seem to run counter to Levinas's well-known objections to Platonic recollection. What this paper examines, however, is the possibility that Levinas himself – *despite* himself, perhaps – has already indicated something of that same aporetic structure.

Specifically, the paper consists of three distinct yet related segments: (1) a broad outline of Levinas's 'standard' objections to *anamnesis*; (2) a broad outline of Levinas's depiction of Husserl (on temporality) as a kind of modern apotheosis of the supposed narcissism of 'anamnetic' western thought; (3) close focus upon Levinas's readings of Husserl's phenomenology of internal-time consciousness. As we shall see, there is an intrigu-ing ambivalence to the last of these, to the extent that – in crucial respects – this treatment goes strongly against the grain of his more typical reading of Husserlian 'narcissism'. As such, we shall also see, this (untypical) aspect of Levinas's treatment begs questions of his own wider schema, and might even take us to the threshold of a 'positive' phenomenology of *anamnesis*.

---

1 J.-L. Chrétien, *The Unforgettable and the Unhoped For*, tr. J. Bloechl (New York: Fordham University Press, 2002), p. 2. French: *L'inoubliable et l'inespéré* (Paris: Desclée de Brouwer, 1991), p. 2.

Levinas on *Anamnesis*

In Levinas's 'standard' account of western thought, *anamnesis* is a foundational faultline that runs a fateful and incremental course. In the beginning (so to speak), it means that the Socratic *psyche* – spoken to and guided by the 'daemon' with which it coincides – (re-)discovers that it already possesses all of its knowledge and that it cannot encounter 'anything really foreign [*véritablement étranger*]' within itself (PII 51/78).[2] Accordingly, this circularity confirms the soul as self-sufficient, as its own *arche*; it seems that, ultimately, there is nothing heteronomous for it or to it. What Socratic teaching amounts to is thus, for Levinas, '[the] primacy of the same' – in other words, the conviction that I should 'receive nothing of the Other but what is in me, as though from all eternity I was in possession of what comes to me from the outside' (*TI* 43/13). Socratic innateness is, in short, the 'sovereign expression' of the self's self-containment.

For Levinas, of course, such self-containment provides, as well as the starting point, the goal or *telos* for philosophy's overall odyssey (and odyssey is surely the operative term here). Indeed, according to Levinas, the very 'evolution' of western thought is nothing less than the progressive modulation of 'anamnetic' structures – structures outlining return, unity, co-incidence – to the point where transcendence might be rendered wholly *immanent*: the Good, the One, are eventually overcome (as supposedly 'wanting' or 'one-sided') by the ever-greater self-assertion of the western soul.[3] *Geist* 'finding itself' (in a long

---

2 For a list of abbreviations of works cited in this chapter, see p. 432. Page numbers are given for both English and French versions.

3 See esp. PT, p. 11/40: 'The evolution of Western thought, freeing [*libérant*] itself from the transcendence of the One, but finding it again [*retrouvant*] in the unity of the system and immanence of transcendental unity. The return in immanence – in the world that is perceived, embraced, mine – of the very large and quasi-formal structures of the neo-Platonic schemata, the contours of which can still be clearly discerned in the set of modern Hegelian or Husserlian themes.'

travail that turns out to be: the way home), *Geist* realizing itself as the Identity of Thought and Being, as Absolute – such Hegelian depictions are (merely) the most thorough inflation of that ancient transmutation of the unknown into the recollected. *Anamnesis* already prescribes – fatefully – philosophy's foreclosure; its effect is to 'exclude the transcendent, encompass [*englober*] every other in the same, and proclaim the philosophical birthright of autonomy' (PII 48/75).

Furthermore, and accordingly, this 'birthright of autonomy' provides the crucial foundations not only for Hegelian panlogicism, but also for the succeeding phenomenological investigation that might fancy itself free of grandiose metaphysical assumptions. Indeed, it seems fair to suggest that, for Levinas, the phenomenological priority afforded intentional re-presentation provides a *post*-Hegelian articulation of what the Socratic *psyche* has always 'stood for': autonomy without precedent; the anticipation of all surprise; the gathering of all that is into 'simultaneousness'. As with Socratic self-examination, so 'the "act" of [phenomenological] representation discovers, properly speaking, nothing before itself': it establishes 'a pure present without even tangential ties with time' (*TI* 125/98). Re-presentation rules out any possible exteriority, anything 'beyond its own instant'; pure presence takes precedence. Far from being challenged, then, philosophical narcissism is sanctified – or so Levinas would have it – by the now 'perfected' technical armoury of Husserlian phenomenology.

Levinas on Husserl on Temporality

It is perhaps worthwhile being more precise about what Levinas means in this last respect. *Qua* contemporary re-presentative of an age-old narcissistic circularity, Husserlian phenomenology (so he claims) betrays the truth of its pedigree *via* a volitional drive always to render temporal disparity present within a simultaneousness, or conjunction, brought about by the subject's knowing grasp; it is this 'making-present' that seems to be, for Levinas, the most telling (and most dubious) phenomenological reflex. By (re-)discovering presence as the work of consciousness, that is to say, the Husserlian ego establishes, or reduces, the time of consciousness to the consciousness of time:[4] the 'primordial intrigue [*l'intrigue primordiale*] of time' (DR 164/88–89) is dismissed, or at least subordinated, by the imposition of a re-presentational frame. Accordingly, past and future become merely 'retained or anticipated presents [*presents retenus ou anticipés*]' (FOTO 138/25); intentional consciousness maintains control – in terms of the present. Re-presentation is 'not *marked* by the past but *utilizes* it as a represented and objective element' (*TI* 125/98); it denies its own enduring, its own temporal succession, by converting exteriority into its noemata – thereby reducing alterity to the production of meaning-bestowing thought. ('Such is the work', Levinas declares, 'of the Husserlian *epoche*' (*TI* 125/98).) For Levinas, Husserlian temporal analysis assumes that time has 'exhausted itself [*s'épuisait*] in its way of making itself known or of conforming to the demands [*exigences*] of its manifestation' (FOTO 138/25). Hence:

> The constitution of time in Husserl is also a constitution of time in terms of an already effective consciousness of presence in its disappearance and in its 'retention', its immanence, and its anticipation – disappearance and immanence that already imply what is to be established, without any indication being given about the privileged empirical situation to which those modes of disappearance in the past and imminence in the future would be attached. (OUJ 209/59)

In short, Husserl forces the alterity of time into a violent Procrustean containment. His thought thereby becomes – as far as Levinas is concerned – a kind of consummation of *anamnesis*: the quintessential privileging of the present, 'the integration of

---

4 See, for example, DR, p. 163/88.

all that is *other* into . . . the synchrony – or the a-temporal – of the system' [*PT* 12/40].[5]

Levinas on Husserl on Primal Impression

Unsurprisingly, we find some of Levinas's most concentrated attention to Husserlian temporalization in the analysis he provides, in *Otherwise than Being* (*OB*), of the 'absolute' primal streaming, the realm of the proto-impression (or primal impression), which Husserl takes to be the basis of conscious life itself. Needless to say, this apparent self-temporalizing of the acts of consciousness is regarded (in *OB*) with deep suspicion: although such a primal realm might seem beyond objectification, beyond intentionality, and beyond (or beneath) self-coincidence, its 'true status', Levinas maintains, is more to do with guaranteeing the prestige of autarchic consciousness. For Levinas, it is not just that 'the primal impression is . . . not *impressed* without consciousness' (*OB* 33/41) – a point which might suggest a distinction between the intrinsic nature of primal impression and the 'secondary' role of consciousness. It is also, and more significantly, that the intrinsic nature of primal impression is itself confirmation of the 'hegemony of presence' – it is, Levinas would have it, the absolute source and beginning of all temporal modification, the spontaneous centre which is *indifferent* to protention and retention. As such, primal 'streaming' becomes 'the prototype of theoretical objectification' (*OB* 33/42); it is as if the primacy of 'presence' is *already confirmed* by this notion of origin and creation. (Proto-impression precedes all else – even its own possibility. Its presence is *pure*.) The primal impression might seem, 'initially', to be beyond intentionality – but it is always 'fitted back in the normal order' and is never on 'the hither side of the same or of the origin' (*OB* 33/42). Accordingly, 'the non-intentionality of the primal retention is not a loss of consciousness' (*OB* 34/43) – for 'nothing can be produced in

---

5 Translation modified.

a clandestine way [*à l'être clandestinement*]', '[n]othing enters incognito into the Same' (*OB* 33/42), 'nothing can break the thread of consciousness' (*OB* 34/43). The (negative) significance of Husserl's internal-time analysis could hardly be greater, then: the Husserlian interpretation of proto-impression is, Levinas claims, 'certainly the most remarkable point of this philosophy in which intentionality "constitutes" the universe' (*OB* 33/42). This, it would seem, is how the Husserlian primal impression provides a kind of foundation for that 'consummation' of *anamnesis* which Levinas finds in Husserl's wider promulgation of presence.

* * *

If such an assessment seems unequivocal, however, it is not. Or, more accurately, it is not the full statement of Levinas's attitude towards Husserlian time-consciousness (however typical it may be). For we also find, in Levinas's 1965 essay 'Intentionality and Sensation' (IS), a reading of Husserlian 'absolute streaming' which may not quite contradict his general approach, but which certainly throws into question some of the central contentions we have just noted.

The 1965 essay is designed as a general (although intensive) survey of the significance of intentionality's corporeal 'basis' – and, not surprisingly, given this context, consideration of proto-impression is at the centre of Levinas's treatment. Here, though, the treatment of proto-impression is startlingly different from its counterpart in *Otherwise than Being*. Initially, Levinas stresses how Husserl's *The Phenomenology of Internal Time-Consciousness* (PITC), overall, is in no sense 'the deduction or construction of time starting out from an atemporal gaze [*d'un regard intemporal*] embracing the proto-impression and its pale modifications' (IS 142/44); on the contrary, Levinas will have it, *The Phenomenology of Internal Time-Consciousness* shows the proto-impression – pure of all ideality, 'nonideality *par excellence*' (IS 144/46) – to be more like a kind of immanent disjunction 'within' consciousness. The Husserlian proto-impression is, fundamentally, *non*-coincidence, 'presenting' itself only in terms of its own departure or deviation from the present. Its 'structure' is itself divergence – so that the proto-impression 'in itself' is always already beyond itself, always already the event of 'dephasing'. The proto-impression is not 'in sequence'; it is more a transgression of continuity, a fundamental *lapse*.

(In this respect, it is more than instructive to compare (a) Levinas's claim here that '[a]n accentuated, living, absolutely new instant – the proto-impression – already deviates from that needlepoint [*pointe d'aiguilee*] where it matures [*mürit*] absolutely *present*' [IS 142/43]), with (b) his more typical suggestion, found elsewhere, that stable identity or presence is characterized by its demarcating, or, rather, its being, 'a *point* or an *instant* . . . pure *where*, pure *when* and pin*point*' [PP 31/19]. The significance of proto-impression, as described in 1965, is, we might say, that it 'misses the point' – or, more particularly, that any point misses it, that it cannot be pin-pointed.)

For the Levinas of 'Intentionality and Sensation', then, the pro-tention and retention which 'attach' to any proto-impressional instant are never adequate to, and are overflowed by, sensation-al flux: adequation, presence and recuperation are 'defeated', so to speak.[6] (There is a kind of constitutive gap, Levinas suggests, between sensation-event and proto-impression: the former *both precedes and succeeds* the latter; this, in turn, seems to found the 'diachrony stronger than structural synchronism [*plus forte que le synchronisme structural*]' (IS 148/52) which Levinas finds at the core of Husserlian embodiment.)

Furthermore, and perhaps most significantly of all, Levinas's reading of genesis and 'origin' here seems (*contra* the reading in *OB*) to undermine rather than bolster the autonomy of the subject: absolute primal streaming can certainly be seen as source, beginning, or creation, as *genesis spontanea*; yet, far from this confirming the primacy of presence and theoretical objectification, what arises 'in' this origin only serves to *confirm* alterity, the un-present-able. There is, Levinas insists, 'unfore-seeable novelty' arising within this origin; any fulfilment is

---

6 See IS, 144/46–7.

'beyond all conjecture, all expectation, all germination, and all continuity, and consequently is wholly passivity [*toute passivité*], receptivity of an "other" penetrating [*pénétrant*] the same . . .' (IS 144/47). (This, in turn, shows 'the essence of all thought as the reserve of a fullness that escapes [*échappe*]' [IS 145/46–7.) It would seem, in other words, that the conscious-ness of time does not overwhelm or suppresses the time of consciousness; rather, *and as Husserl himself shows*, the con-sciousness of time is 'always already' the time of consciousness – and so is 'always already' lapse, dispersion, iteration, alterity. Husserl, according to this reading, uncovers 'an irreducible otherness strong enough to resist the synchronization of the noetico-noematic correlation' – in this case, the irreducible *self-*otherness of our 'absolute subjectivity'. (In Husserl's own words, cited here by Levinas: 'das Zeitigende ist gezeitigt' – 'that which temporalizes is [already] temporalized'.[7]) The answer to Levinas's central question in 'Intentionality and Sensation' – 'Is there diachrony within intentionality?' (IS 143/45) – is there-fore an unambiguous 'Yes': as he will conclude, it is this 'diver-gence from . . . ' that is nothing less than '[t]he mystery of intentionality' (IS 145/47).

Summary and Conclusion

To sum up and clarify. First, Levinas's 'standard' and general position is that, with its desire for fulfilment, accomplishment, unity, return and co-incidence, *anamnesis* effectively determines the fundamental character of the entire philosophical quest; as such, he maintains, *anamnesis* establishes the structures that will allow for the eventual overcoming of that 'powerless [*impuissante*] and pious nostalgia for the transcendence of the unattainable' (PT 14/41) which, initially, was also a funda-

---

7 Levinas cites the 'remarkable' formulation provided by G. Brand, *Welt, Ich und Zeit: nach unveröffentlichen Manuskripten Edmund Husserls* (The Hague: Martinus Nijhoff, 1955), p. 75.

mental (and distinct) aspect of the philosophical life. In other words, the transcendence that was so central to Platonic thought (the Good, the One) is swallowed up, made immanent, by the historical unfolding of what was also so central to Platonic thought – recollection. One aspect of the Platonic legacy overcomes the other.

Husserlian phenomenology, as we have also seen, is generally taken to be as much the 'outcome' of this historical development as is the Hegelian system: as far as Levinas is concerned, Husserlian re-presentation seems to be a kind of ultimate expression of the philosophical drive to reduce all externality to the immanence of subjectivity; this reduction means that 'the identity of pure consciousness carries within itself, in the guise of the "I think", understood as intentionality . . . all "transcendence", all alterity' (PT 11/40). In other words, Husserl supposedly details, describes *and completes*, the development of philosophical self-sufficiency and autonomy: with phenomenology, even absence is merely anticipated possession, 'grasping before the grasp'. Intentionality gets whatever it wants; transcendence gives way to immanence.

However, this depiction of Husserl still has to accommodate the issue of Husserlian 'absolute' consciousness – and, as we have just seen, Levinas's position, in this regard, is far from clear-cut. Certainly, *Otherwise than Being* has it that Husserl's analysis of proto-impression is *fundamental* for the whole edifice of the narcissistic, re-presentational ego; but, against this better-known assessment, there is also the 1965 suggestion, in 'Intentionality and Sensation', that self-temporalization is beyond pin-pointing, beyond grasping (even as anticipation), beyond the ideality of any idea. It is this 'alternative' Husserl who raises hugely important issues – not just about Levinas's philosophical relationship with Husserl, but, more significantly, about Levinas's wider depiction of the supposedly 'autonomous' and narcissistic western soul 'conversing with itself', rendering all alterity present to its grasp, and thereby confirming the 'primacy of the Same'. The 1965 essay seems – implicitly, at least – to question any such assumption. Here, after all, we glimpse the possibility that 'self'-temporalization is not strictly speaking, *self*-temporalization at all – more a kind of 'structural' alterity, a 'knotted intrigue', within and yet not 'of' the self. And here, *as Levinas himself is wholly explicit in stating*, we glimpse the possibility that, deep within immanence, within apparently 'indistinct sedimentation and thick alluvium' (IS 149/53), we find nothing less than *transcendence* (understood literally, as what Levinas terms 'a passing over, an over-stepping', a 'going-beyond-itself-within-itself', 'the zero point of representation [that] . . . is beyond [*au-delà*] this zero' (IS 148/51)). Self-examination may so often lead to consummated narcissism; but it can also gesture towards a *non*-coincidence, a *non*-ideality and a *non*-adequation, 'always already' at the very core of the human soul.

The significance of this alternative depiction of Husserl – which is also, and more importantly, an alternative depiction of selfhood as such – becomes all the clearer if we contrast it with what we might term the 'standard' Levinasian depiction of the self 'prior to' or 'before' encounter with the Other person. In 'Philosophy and Transcendence', for example, Levinas makes quite plain his suspicions of any notion of the philosophical 'before' (outside of the context of the Other human, that is): the 'before', he tells us, 'come[s] down to the priority of an idea that in the "deep past" of innateness was already a present correlative to the *I think*, and that – retained, conserved, or resuscitated in the duration of time, in temporality taken as the flow of instants – would be, by memory, re-presented' (PT 31/44). So often, it seems, any appeal to a 'before' is about asserting what Levinas terms 'the privilege of the *I think*, "stronger" than time, and gathering the scattered temporal shadows into the unity of transcendental apperception, the firmest and most formal of forms, stronger than any heterogeneity of contents' (PT 31/44). 'True transcendence' comes only *via* (or in terms of) ethical responsibility to the Other: 'the face of one's fellow man [is] the locus in which transcendence calls an authority with a silent voice in which God comes to mind [*vient à l'idée*]' (PT 5/39), he announces; meanwhile, 'anamnetic' narcissism is a kind of block, a barrier, that such 'true transcendence' must surmount.

The contrast with 'Intentionality and Sensation' could hardly be greater, then. After all, the 1965 work suggests an alterity 'within' the self – but *an alterity that has nothing to do with the other human's face, call or demand*. It signifies an 'originary field' of 'lost time', beyond intentionality, beyond reduction to presence. It undermines the assumption of 'the privilege of the *I think*, stronger than time [*plus 'fort' que le temps*] . . . , stronger than any [*toute*] heterogeneity of contents' (PT 31/44). And it indicates *transcendence* at the 'core' of selfhood – a transcendence glimpsed precisely in terms of an overflowing of our own temporalizing (which means that 'our own' temporalizing is never quite 'our own'). In short, it shows that the Levinasian 'Immemorial' is not *necessarily* unique to the effect of the Other: now, it seems, a 'transcending, pre-original diachrony which by-passes the present' is also how we might refer to '*self*'-temporalization.[8]

Might it be, then, that – before Chrétien, and perhaps with greater *phenomenological* rigour – Levinas describes something remarkably close to *anamnesis*? This may appear a tenuous suggestion: Socratic recollection and the Husserlian instantaneous proto-impression are surely wholly distinct, categorically separate; and 'transcendence' is surely a quite different term in Platonic and phenomenological contexts. Nonetheless, the linkage is (at least in part) Levinas's own: recall that, in his 'standard' critique, Levinas portrays Husserlian proto-impression as 'certainly the most remarkable point of this philosophy in which intentionality "constitutes" the universe'; and he portrays Husserl's time-thinking in general as a completion or consummation of Socratic *anamnesis* – the triumph of 'technical' simultaneousness. The efficacy of Levinas's own historical

---

8 The 1965 essay has received comparatively little attention – a lacuna in Levinas scholarship that seems all the more striking, given its significance. For a rare exception to this general rule, see R. Bernet, 'Levinas's Critique of Husserl' in *The Cambridge Companion to Levinas*, ed. S. Critchley and R. Bernasconi (Cambridge: Cambridge University Press, 2002), pp. 82–99, esp. pp. 91–3.

narrative would seem to be challenged, therefore – *by Levinas himself* (*c.* 1965): re-assessing Husserlian 'selfhood' provokes – *mutatis mutandis* – significant questions about the supposedly 'fateful' ancient origin from which it emerges *and which it supposedly consummates.*

However, the most significant point here is not just to do with a kind of inverted historical logic. What is more important, surely, is that Levinas's fine-grained and nuanced phenomenological attention (in its 1965 form, at least) reveals certain structural features of selfhood vis-à-vis temporalization – lapse, dispersion, divergence; the mark of an irrecuperable 'before'; fundamental diachrony – that, in Chrétien's terms, are precisely the 'structural' features of *anamnesis.* Perhaps, if we follow Levinas's phenomenological leads, we might begin to appreciate all the more what Chrétien's remarkable labour has been trying to establish – namely, that, as Plato puts it (at *Phaedrus* 249c, for example), *anamnesis* confronts us not with self-transparency, but with ultimate mysteries.

Abbreviations

DR   E. Levinas, 'Diachrony and Representation' in *Entre Nous: On Thinking-of-the-Other*, tr. M. Smith and B. Harshav (London: Athlone, 1998), pp. 159–77; 'Diachronie et Representation', *Revue de l'Université d'Ottowa* 55.4 (1985), pp. 85–98.

FOTO E. Levinas, 'From the One to the Other: Transcendence and Time' in *Entre Nous: On Thinking-of-the-Other*, tr. M. Smith and B. Harshav (London: Athlone, 1998), pp. 133–54; 'De l'un à l'autre: Transendance et temps', *Archivo de Filosofia* (1983), 51, 1–3, pp. 21–38.

GDT   E. Levinas, *God, Death, and Time*, tr. B. Bergo (Stanford University Press, 2000).

IS   E. Levinas, 'Intentionality and Sensation' in *Discovering Existence with Husserl*, tr. R. Cohen and M. Smith (Evanston: Northwestern University Press, 1998), pp. 135–50; 'Intentionalite et sensation', *Revue Internationale de Philosophie*, 71–72, fasc. 1–2 (1965), pp. 34–54.

OB   E. Levinas, *Otherwise than Being or Beyond Essence*, tr. A. Lingis (The Hague: Nijhoff, 1981); *Autrement qu'être ou au-delà de l'essence* (The Hague: Nijhoff, 1974).

OUJ   E. Levinas, 'The Other, Utopia, and Justice' in Jill Robbins ed., *Is it Righteous To Be?* (Stanford University Press, 2002), pp. 200–10; 'L'autre, utopie et justice', *Autrement* 102 (Nov. 1988), pp. 50–60.

PII   E. Levinas, 'Philosophy & the Idea of Infinity' in *Collected Philosophical Papers*, tr. A. Lingis (Dordrecht: Kluwer, 1992), pp. 47–59; 'La philosophie et l'idee de l'Infini', *Revue de Métaphysique et de Morale* 62 (1957), pp. 241–53.

PITC   Edmund Husserl, *The Phenomenology of Internal Time Consciousness*, ed. Martin Heidegger, tr. J. S. Churchill (Indiana University Press, 1964).

PP   E. Levinas, 'Philosophy and Positivity' in Regina Schwartz (ed.), *Transcendence: Philosophy, Literature, and Theology Approach the Beyond* (New York and London: Routledge, 2004); 'Philosophie et Positivité' in Jean-Luc Marion (ed.), *Positivité et transcendance: suivi de Levinas et la phenomenologie* (Paris: PUF, 2000), pp. 19–34.

PT   E. Levinas, 'Philosophy and Transcendence' in *Alterity and Transcendence*, tr. Michael Smith (London: Athlone, 1999), pp. 3–38; 'Philosophie et transcendence' in *Encyclopédie philosophique universelle* (Paris: Presses Universitaires de France, 1989), pp. 38–45.

TI   E. Levinas, *Totality and Infinity: An Essay on Exteriority*, tr. A. Lingis (Pittsburgh: Duquesne University Press, 1969); *Totalité et Infini: Essai sur l'extériorité* (The Hague: Nijhoff, 1961).

18. 'The Words of the Oracle': Merleau-Ponty and the 'Philosophy of Freudianism'

MAURO CARBONE

In his Preface to Angélo Hesnard's *L'œuvre de Freud et son importance pour le monde moderne*, Maurice Merleau-Ponty insisted on certain 'new motives' driving Hesnard to turn his attention to Freud's work. A few pages later Merleau-Ponty himself admitted that such a turn in his own work towards

> a philosophy that is now perhaps more mature, and also to the growth of Freudian research – precisely in the direction taken by Doctor Hesnard – that today leads me to express a different relation between phenomenology and psychoanalysis, the implicit philosophy of psychoanalysis itself, and in the long run makes me less indulgent than Doctor Hesnard generously is toward my own earlier attempts.

Nevertheless, this did not stop Merleau-Ponty from noting that the critiques he had in the past levelled against Freudian psychoanalysis 'still seem true to me'. A few pages earlier, he had summarized them (such as they were set out in an 'early work' which we can presume to be the *Phenomenology of Perception*). At issue were the critiques of those who, like him, 'consider the Freudian unconscious as an archaic or primordial consciousness, the repressed as a zone of experience that we have not integrated, the body as a sort of natural or innate complex, and communication as a relation between incarnate beings of this sort who are well or badly integrated'.

The Preface to Hesnard's book is contemporary with Merleau-Ponty's last three courses at the Collège de France, courses dedicated to the 'concept of nature'. Occurring in the academic years of 1956–57 and 1959–60, one of the courses was significantly entitled 'Nature and Logos: the Human Body', which focuses precisely on our body 'as the root of symbolism'. Precisely in describing 'the emergence of symbolism', Merleau-Ponty refers to what he had qualified a few years earlier, in the summary of another course on 'The Problem of Passivity'. His qualification was:

> Freud's most interesting insight was – not the idea of a second 'I think' which could know what we do not know about ourselves – but the idea of a symbolism which is primordial, originary, the idea of a 'non-conventional thought' (Politzer) enclosed in a 'world for us,' which is the source of dreams and more generally of the elaboration of our life.

The definition of symbolism upon which Merleau-Ponty here insists with respect to the human body motivates the fundamental place psychoanalysis occupies within the course: 'symbolism – not in a superficial sense, i.e., a term representing another, holding the place of another, – but in the fundamental sense of: expressing of another'.

In his conclusion to the preparatory notes for the course, several pages are once again dedicated to psychoanalysis. Merleau-Ponty wrote them for the previous year's course, entitled 'Philosophy Today', and as yet they have not been translated into English. In order to better understand these pages, however, we must first recall the intention lying behind this course.

Similarly to the working notes in *The Visible and the Invisible*, the 'course outline' begins with the observation of 'our state of non-philosophy', concerning which these notes propose that 'never has the crisis been so radical'. It is a matter, the notes explain, of a 'crisis of rationality in relations between men', as well as 'in our relations with Nature', both of which reflect the 'consequences of the development of technology [*technique*]'.

These course notes, then, concentrate on the attempt to identify the multiple 'cultural symptoms', 'that attest to [one] same crisis situation, i.e., at once the peril and the possibility for the rebirth of philosophy in Western ideology: poetry, music, painting, and psychoanalysis'.

In psychoanalysis, as in the other 'cultural symptoms', Merleau-Ponty recognizes an ambivalent flux between: 'the psychoanalysis that is a symptom of decadence, whether it posits a separate unconscious or opposes it to conscious control; [. . . and the] psychoanalysis that, on the occasion of disintegration, rediscovers a deeper unity: unconscious thought as the non-conventional thought of the I as profoundly related'.

A few pages earlier Merleau-Ponty explains this ambivalence between two understandings of psychoanalysis: (1) as a positivistic explanation of the sexual by the I; or (2) an understanding in which the 'sexual' upon which everything rests is thought not to be 'genital' because human desire itself is thought of as entirely different from every automatic function.

The continuity of thought that ties these notes to those 'earlier attempts' Merleau-Ponty mentions in his Preface to Hesnard's book here become evident. Here one finds this continuity as much in the critiques levelled (as early as *The Structure of Behavior*) against the causalistic temptations of the psychoanalytic language as in the interpretation of the Freudian 'pansexualism' formulation in the *Phenomenology of Perception*.

On both of these subjects, at the beginning of the very long footnote concluding the chapter on 'The Body in its Sexual Being' of *Phenomenology of Perception*, Merleau-Ponty wrote: 'one can no more get rid of . . . psychoanalysis by impugning "reductionist" conceptions and causal thought in the name of a descriptive and phenomenological method'. Rather, he continued, this method can contribute to the formulation of psychoanalysis 'in another language'. In fact, precisely in that chapter of *Phenomenology of Perception*, Merleau-Ponty had tried to formulate the Freudian 'pansexualism' in a non-causalistic way: 'There is interfusion between sexuality and existence, which means that existence permeates sexuality and *vice versa*, so that it is impossible to determine, in a given decision or action, the proportion of sexual to other motivations, impossible to label a decision or act "sexual" or "non-sexual".' Here I would like to underline that Merleau-Ponty used 'the phenomenological notion of *motivation*', which in a previous chapter of the same work he qualified, with Husserl, as a 'fluid' concept, explaining that 'to the degree that the motivated phenomenon comes into being, an internal relation to the motivating phenomenon appears; hence, instead of the one merely succeeding the other, the motivated phenomenon makes the motivating phenomenon explicit and comprehensible, and thus seems to have pre-existed its own motive'.

Therefore, 'whatever the theoretical declarations of Freud may have been,' Merleau-Ponty specified that when the former described what we heard the latter calling the 'interfusion between sexuality and existence', 'it would be a mistake to imagine that' psychoanalysis 'is opposed to the phenomenological method; psychoanalysis has, on the contrary, albeit unwittingly, helped to develop it by declaring, as Freud puts it, that every human action "has a meaning", and by making every effort to understand the event, short of relating it to mechanical circumstances'.

In the late period of Merleau-Ponty's thought this motivation becomes linked with his new interest in psychoanalysis as one of the 'cultural symptoms' within which he sees the operation – in an implicit manner – of a 'new ontology' that, by virtue of the ambivalence mentioned above, struggles to find an appropriate philosophical formulation. Merleau-Ponty will now seek to make this new and appropriate formulation, especially in his last two courses of the year 1960–61, which were interrupted by his sudden death: 'Philosophy and Non-Philosophy Since Hegel' and, even more explicitly, 'The Cartesian Ontology and the Ontology of Today'.

437

The 'new motives' of this interest in psychoanalysis outlined in the Preface to Hesnard's book rest upon a conviction that that which is qualified as 'the implicit philosophy of psychoanalysis itself' will help to delineate the contours of an '*ontology of today*'. Merleau-Ponty sought to give an explicit philosophical formulation to this '*ontology of today*' in his last courses at the Collège de France. The continuity between this new evaluation of psychoanalysis and the critiques and interpretations he had proposed in the past becomes particularly apparent in a passage contained in the course notes we are in the process of examining. Here, Merleau-Ponty decides in favour of this evaluation precisely because of the interpretation of Freudian 'pansexualism' that had been his previously:

> The true (+ comprehension) formulation is that not everything is sexual, but that there is *nothing* that is not sexual, there is *nothing* that is *asexual*. The progression past the genital is not an absolute distinction or break in the ontological character of sexuality . . . [rather] it is a major contribution to our relation to being.

In the same text Merleau-Ponty adds that '[psychoanalysis] outlines a philosophy . . . if it allows itself to be guided by the relation with being such as it appears in mankind'. And 'Philosophy of Freudianism' is precisely the title of a working note in *The Visible and the Invisible*, a note that is among the most important for our comments here.

The working note begins by reiterating the critique of the causalistic interpretation of what Freud defines as 'the connection between the impressions of the artist's childhood and his life-history on the one hand and his works, as reactions to those impressions, on the other'. However, the note points out that this causalistic interpretation is but a 'superficial interpretation of Freudianism'. If such an interpretation is obviously to be avoided, it is generally more a matter, as the note indicates, of making 'not an existential psychoanalysis, but an *ontological* psychoanalysis'.

The development of the preceding elements of critique and interpretation of psychoanalysis in the 'new motives' therefore encouraged the passage in Merleau-Ponty's thought from the existential perspective one encounters in the *Phenomenology of Perception* to the ontological perspective that inspires his later reflections. In other words, what promotes this development – and, of course, nourishes it – is the deepening of the notion of a 'proper body'. A notion which, if it implies the *correlation* between a perceiving subject and the perceived world, nevertheless remains within the '"consciousness"–"object" distinction', as *The Visible and the Invisible* also admits. And so it is with the notion of 'flesh' that Merleau-Ponty manages to designate the common ontological texture that intertwines our body, with the other's and with the things of the world, enveloping them all in a horizon of *co-belongingness* within which subject and object are not yet constituted such that every body and every thing is simply given as a *difference* with respect to others.

The working note to *The Visible and the Invisible*, which we are in the process of examining, proposes that if read from a certain perspective, 'the philosophy of Freud is not a philosophy of the body but of the flesh', the latter being understood precisely as the common horizon within which all beings belong. And it is to this common horizon that the note suggests a Freudian overdetermination of the symptoms that Merleau-Ponty insisted upon in the *Phenomenology of Perception*, where he contended that 'Freud himself, in his concrete analyses, abandons causal thought'. It is precisely as intertwined in the *flesh* of Being that 'any entity can be *accentuated* as an emblem of Being', as the note to *The Visible and the Invisible* explains. And, overdetermined in this manner, it can lead to 'the fixation of a "character" by investment of the openness to Being in an Entity – which, henceforth, takes place *through this Entity*'.

Let us then recall and reread from this perspective the affirmation whereby, within 'the circular movement of our lives . . . everything symbolizes everything else' – which accredited the '*psychoanalytic intuition*' in *Cezanne's Doubt* – as well as the reminder of the Freudian overdetermination of all symptoms, which also appears in this text, and, more generally, the totality of the commentary, developed in this same text, on the famous essay by Freud entitled *Leonardo da Vinci and a Memory of His Childhood*. Moreover, this latter essay is of particular interest because it intersects in a significant manner with two Freudian writings dedicated to the theme of 'fetishism'. Indeed, on the one hand, this text was written the same year (1909) during which Freud presented to the Vienna Psychoanalytic Society his hypotheses *On the Genesis of Fetishism*; and, on the other hand, he will state that this essay already put forth the explanation of fetishism presented by him in a writing published on this subject in 1927.

As we know, the 'childhood memory' to which the title of Freud's essay makes reference was recounted by Leonardo in the midst of his scientific work on the flight of kites, as this 'memory' concerned precisely the figure of a kite that had landed on his crib and hit him in the mouth with its tail: a figure that is evoked, according to Freud, by the drapery of Mary's cloak in *St Anne with Two Others*.

On the basis of this 'childhood memory' (*Kinderheitserinnerung*), Freud is impelled to attempt to decipher the *enigma* of Leonardo's character. However, despite its title, Freud's essay supposes that 'the scene with the vulture would not be a memory of Leonardo's but a phantasy [*Phantasie*], which he formed at a later date and transposed to his childhood', or, to be more exact, the later, phantasmic elaboration of a double reminiscence: that 'of being suckled and being kissed by his mother'.

According to the perspective Merleau-Ponty now adopts, as in the case that inspired this 'memory', an experience of *initiation* occurs as soon as there is an encounter with a being, an entity, which, in so far as it is taken from the ontological horizon of the flesh, is *accentuated* as an opening of a '*dimension* of being', according to an expression that recurs in our working note to *The Visible and the Invisible*.

In an experience of initiation, in a being, an entity ends up *dimensionalizing* itself as 'an essence'. This occurs when this being has *been revived in a creative manner* (according to the Merleau-Pontyan expression 'creative revival', that also appears in the essay on Cezanne) within an association such that the being turns out to be *overdetermined*. As it is explained in another working note to *The Visible and the Invisible*, a note that is fundamental for this problem, 'there is no association that comes into play unless there is overdetermination, that is, a relation of relations, a coincidence that cannot be fortuitous, that has an *ominal* sense'.

Merleau-Ponty therefore warns us against a *simply associationistic* interpretation of the '"associations" of psychoanalysis', seeking rather to think 'association as initiation': this is what the title of one of his notes on the writer Claude Simon proposes significantly. I quote it here in its entirety:

> The red of the gunner's badges (Claude Simon: text in *Lettres françaises*) – it says this and that to him – one says: by association. It's not that, nor *Verschmelzung* etc. It's that there is a force of meaning in the texture of this red, a qualitative texture, first of all. Then, the experiences of which it re-awakens the feeling have been lived *through* it (as things are experienced through their names) and that's the reason – that archaic structure is the reason – why it will always be the mediator of those experiences. Because our experience is not a flat field of qualities, but always subject to the invocation of some fetish or other, always reached through the intercession of some fetish or other.

The initiation is therefore not initial. It can give itself only '*through*' the *revival* of an experience in another, but it can nevertheless not be resolved in the simple *association* of the two, since it is *always* a matter of a '*creative* revival' – and this even if, by virtue of a 'retrograde movement of the true', we tend to consider the sense as pre-existing in the experience, whose 'force of meaning' in reality consists only in an anticipation *for* the revival that follows. The initiation is thus accomplished in the *between* that lies between the experiences that are associated with it, and that is why it gives itself as an 'overdetermination' with respect to both of them.

This is possible since, as we saw in the note on Claude Simon, 'our experience is not a flat field of qualities', that is (to return to the working note to *The Visible and the Invisible* on the 'Philosophy of Freudianism'), in so far as it possesses this 'ontological capacity' that Merleau-Ponty defines as the 'capacity to take a being as representative of Being'. Indeed, it is by virtue of this capacity that a being can be 'dimensionalized' and thereby 'overdetermined' as an essence – that is to say, in Greek terms, as an *idea* – but also as a 'fetish', as the note on Claude Simon suggests.

From this perspective, we can therefore say that fetishism reveals itself to be a special, and in some cases pathological, instance of our 'ontological capacity'. Now, it can be understood as such, as we have seen, not by a 'philosophy of the body, but of the flesh'. And it is precisely on the level of this philosophy that Freud seems to position himself in his presentation *On the Genesis of Fetishism*.

Borrowing several observations proposed by Krafft-Ebing, he begins by admitting that 'ultimately anything can possibly become a fetish'. Nonetheless, and in disagreement with the one who invented the term 'fetishism', Freud subsequently affirms that fetishism does not derive from a memory, but that it is tied to the repression of an impulse: 'a type of repression' – he explains – 'which is instituted by the splitting of the complex. A portion is genuinely repressed, while the other portion is *idealized*, what in our case is specifically *raised to a fetish*.'

That is why Freud, with respect to this issue, writes of a 'partial repression' (*partielle Verdrängung*) of the representatives tied to the repressed impulse: precisely because it is partial, this repression produces a peculiar 'elevation of a portion of the repressed complex to an ideal', and this is what, in his opinion, fetishism consists of.

It is here necessary once more to emphasize the manner by which Freud refers the representatives on which this repression is effected to various impulses, such as the visual impulse in the case of a clothes fetishism, and the olfactory impulse in the case of a shoe or hair fetishism. These beings thereby find themselves 'accentuated' (we could say with Merleau-Ponty) as so many emblems of Being.

In the brief article Freud devotes to *Fetishism* eighteen years later, fetishism is again correlated to the partial repression of an object of which it is the idealized preservation. But Freud's interest is here focused on the *object* of this repression – indicated in a univocal manner in 'the woman's (the mother's) penis' – rather than on the *genesis of fetishism*, as the title of his 1909 presentation appropriately indicated. Fetishism henceforth appears tied in a causalistic manner to the castration complex, and this is the primary reason why this article seems to be based upon a 'philosophy of the body' – in some aspects of the objective body even more than of the lived body – rather than upon a 'philosophy of the flesh'.

Merleau-Ponty never seems to have referred explicitly to *Fetishism*. Nonetheless, Freud's article shows also another aspect in which Merleau-Ponty focused his criticisms of psychoanalysis, criticisms that he borrowed in particular from the work of Georges Politzer. By categorizing the 'repressed' as that which is 'denied (which would be to say unknown)', as Merleau-Ponty observes in the course notes devoted to psychoanalysis examined above, Freud's article seems to characterize the unconscious as a 'second consciousness', an 'adequate thought hidden' by the I in order to defend itself from it. But Merleau-Ponty's notes remind us that this characterization leads to affirming the 'postulate of the priority of the conventional, of the priority of the thinking subject', whereas the perspective to which Merleau-Ponty arrived led him to an *ontological* generalization of primordial symbolism through which we have already seen him referring to the 'non-conventional thought' of Georges Politzer.

In this light, if we consider that Freud is referring in the article in question to his essay on da Vinci, then we can reasonably propose that what inspires such a recapture is precisely the orientation of psychoanalysis that Merleau-Ponty criticized in that very essay, namely, the orientation whereby we see psychoanalysis signify a cultural symptom of decadence.

As we have indicated, such an orientation, in Merleau-Ponty's opinion, explicitly reintroduces a philosophy of consciousness by positing the separation between the conscious and the unconscious. In order to retain the sense of the word 'unconscious' as 'the index of an enigma', as Merleau-Ponty wants to do in his Preface to Hesnard's book, such a separation must necessarily be avoided. Here, once more, we must return to the working note of *The Visible and the Invisible* entitled 'Philosophy of Freudianism', where he recommends: 'The Id, the unconscious – and the Ego (*correlative*) to be understood on the basis of the flesh.'

During the important conference devoted to the unconscious which took place at Bonneval in 1959, Merleau-Ponty points to a model of such a 'correlation', one which allows us 'to unravel the negative in the positive and the positive in the negative'. As he highlights in the conclusion to his summary on the 'Problem of Passivity', the notion of 'negative magnitude' illustrated by Kant, allows one to 'recognize an articulation, a simultaneity of presence and absence', since it consists precisely in the idea of a reciprocal implication of the positive and the negative.

It is according to a similar dynamic, I think, that Freud, in his 1909 presentation, describes the 'partial repression' that engenders fetishism. Conversely, the orientation underlying his 1927 article contains a few affirmations to which it would be possible to refer the words Merleau-Ponty employs in his Preface to Hesnard's book in order to reaffirm his critical remarks on psychoanalysis: 'We refused, as we always will, to grant to that phallus which is part of the objective body, the organ of micturition and copulation, such power of causality over so many forms of behavior.'

On the other hand – that same passage goes on to say – from psychoanalysis, 'we learned . . . to discern an imaginary phallus, a symbolic phallus, oneiric and poetic'.

These last two adjectives return in the conclusion of the last summary composed by Merleau-Ponty – that of the previously mentioned course on 'Nature and Logos: The Human Body' – in order to designate what he defines there as 'powers' of the flesh. And this flesh is for philosophy the 'condition without which psychoanalysis remains anthropology', as the working note to *The Visible and the Invisible* warns.

Indeed, the flesh – since it ties our body to that of others and to the things in the world – is shot through with a 'logic of implication or promiscuity' that Merleau-Ponty praises Freud for having indicated (even if Freud did not always know how to describe it in an appropriate manner). Dreams, as well as the 'free associations' of psychoanalysis, hint at this logic (this is why they should be interpreted solely in an associationistic manner), and both attest to the fact that they deal in a logic constantly *operative* within the 'carnal' relationships our body maintains with others and with things.

It is precisely to such an operative (*fungierende*) 'logic of implication or promiscuity' that Merleau-Ponty refers his eventual characterizations of the unconscious 'as perception that is imperception', as the 'feeling itself, since feeling is not the intellectual possession of "what" is felt, but a dispossession of ourselves in favor of it, an opening toward that which we do not have to think in order that we may recognize it'. This is the opening to which conscious thought cannot but remain *essentially* 'correlated'.

If, then, such a 'logic of implication or promiscuity' constitutes the framework of the sensible of which it makes the 'oneiric world of analogy', it is for this very reason that it reveals how the 'poetic' power of the flesh can also be qualified as a 'power *poietical* of worlds'.

The poetic and oneiric powers *of the flesh* – powers that *do not belong to us* – are *powers of primordial symbolization*, they are the powers by virtue of which the others and the things we experience acquire a *dimension* (in the sense Merleau-Ponty ascribes to this word) and a mythical temporality, sedimenting themselves in our unconscious. This is why Merleau-Ponty characterizes the unconscious as an 'archaic structure', not only

445

in the note on Claude Simon cited previously, but also in his Preface to Hesnard's book, where an analogous expression – 'archaic or primordial consciousness' – appears as Merleau-Ponty synthesizing his own previous interpretation of psycho-analysis (thus displaying an important element of continuity).

Even 'our waking relations with objects and others especi-ally' – he therefore writes in the summary of his course on the 'Problem of Passivity' – 'have an oneiric character as a matter of principle: others are present to us in the way that dreams are, the way myths are'. Indeed, the poetic and oneiric powers of the flesh are also *mythopoietic* powers that, as such, introduce an *operative mythicity* in the 'logic of implication or promiscuity' through which our relations with others and with things are continually animated.

Just as in the case of the kite for da Vinci, in our experience these powers are vested in certain beings through which we open up onto Being and which, for that reason, become its 'emblems'. They are the figures not of an *origin* having occured in the past once and for all, but of an 'originary' that, although subject to 'the retrograde movement of the true', *operates* in an explosion 'which is forever', enveloping our relations with others and with the things in a decisive and inextinguishible mythical halo. For this reason, our experience will never cease to take up in a creative manner these emblems as though they were – as we can read in *Cezanne's Doubt* – 'the words of the oracle', which is ultimately nothing other than the words of myth. >From this perspective, Merleau-Ponty writes in the Preface to Hesnard's book that psychoanalysis 'returned our myths to us'. Indeed, it is in this that, in the course notes, Merleau Ponty indicates the contribution psychoanalysis can make to a non-nihilistic resolution of this 'crisis' of which it is at the same time one of the 'symptoms'. He writes:

[Psychoanalysis] can be the deepening, the enrichment of cul-ture or the aggravation of the crisis, depending on whether it accentuates the objectivistic and technician spirit from which it emerges . . . or whether it is this spirit recognizing its limits, the spirit of rediscovering our archaeology as not being made up of decisions on the part of the I or *Erlebnisse* of consciousness – Mythical time = time before time or before things, and still present.

If, then, the crisis of our epoch can have a positive outcome this will mean, among other things, that psychoanalysis will have succeeded in reconfiguring the mythical heritage of the western tradition in terms that allow us to continue to think it as our own.

19. On the Critiques of Pairing and Appresentation by Merleau-Ponty and Levinas

TIMOTHY MOONEY

It is hardly an exaggeration to state that the fifth of the *Cartesian Meditations* is the most contentious of Husserl's later writings. As Paul Ricoeur has observed, the preceding meditations made the world as phenomenologically reduced draw its existence-sense from me alone, amounting to the most radical expression of a new idealism.[1] Accepting that the world of the naive natural attitude carries the sense of being there for all of us, Husserl in this last meditation endeavours to unearth the intentionalities, syntheses, motivations and evidences by which I fashion and verify the original sense of another ego, of another subject who perceives that world and me also. The difficulty of this task is signalled in his remark that the sense of every such 'Other' is of a being whose existence transcends mine radically.[2]

1 P. Ricoeur, *Husserl: An Analysis of His Phenomenology*, tr. E. G. Ballard and L. Embree (Evanston: Northwestern University Press, 1967), p. 10.
2 *Husserliana I. Cartesianische Meditationen und Pariser Vorträge*, ed. S. Strasser (The Hague: Martinus Nijhoff, 2nd edn, 1963), pp. 122–3, 126; English: *Cartesian Meditations*, tr. D. Cairns (The Hague: Martinus Nijhoff, 1960), pp. 90–91, 94. To be abbreviated as *Hua I*. The last meditation in this work does not of course mark Husserl's final position on the Other, a position that was never worked out to his own satisfaction. For a comprehensive study of the investigations in his late manuscripts, see J. R. Mensch, *Intersubjectivity and Transcendental*

In the French phenomenological scene, one of the first extended critiques of this procedure of explicating the sense of the alter ego was set out by Maurice Merleau-Ponty in *Phenomenology of Perception* (1945).[3] Some sixteen years later, Emmanuel Levinas – who had been instrumental in introducing the writings of Husserl to a philosophical audience in France – formulated further criticisms in *Totality and Infinity*, his own *magnum opus*.[4] Both thinkers share the view that Husserl's notions of pairing and appresentation, which follow on from his reduction to the sphere of ownness, are deeply problematic. Their reasons for holding this view provide fair illustrations of their respective concerns.

The first thinker sees the various moves in the Fifth Meditation as aberrations from an original project of returning to the phenomena themselves, though one of them might be salvaged – he is open to an alternative account of pairing, while rejecting what he takes to be the notion of analogical apperception. The second thinker, by contrast, understands each move as exemplifying a philosophy that has culminated in a total suppression of alterity, following in the dismal tracks of a tradition that has privileged intelligibility throughout its history, to the extent that all its exceptions have been notable ones.[5] He jettisons

---

Idealism (Albany: SUNY Press, 1988). Since Merleau-Ponty and Levinas do not refer to these writings in their critiques, I end my positive account of Husserl on the Other with his Fifth Meditation.

3 *Phénoménologie de la perception* (Paris: Gallimard, 1945). English: *Phenomenology of Perception*, tr. C. Smith (London: Routledge and Kegan Paul, 1962). To be abbreviated as *PP*.

4 E. Levinas, *Totalité et Infini: Essai sur l'extériorité* (The Hague: Martinus Nijhoff, 1961). English: *Totality and Infinity: An Essay on Exteriority*, tr. A. Lingis (Pittsburgh: Duquesne University Press, 1969). To be abbreviated as *TI*. Whereas Husserl for the most part uses the upper case 'Other' to denote the alter ego, Levinas always uses it to denote the transcendence of the human existent. Things are deployed in the lower case.

5 Though it is comparatively well known, it should be noted here that the characterizations of Husserl's phenomenology by Levinas in *Totality and Infinity* show a remarkable inattentiveness to his earlier and more

pairing and appresentation in the service of an approach that would recognize and foreground the inability of representation to capture or even approximate to the infinity of the Other.

In this essay I hope to demonstrate that the criticisms made by these thinkers are persuasive in part, though they fail to do justice to Husserl's conception of appresentation in particular. It has fallen to Jacques Derrida and other commentators to provide a more accurate interpretation of this notion and of its ultimate value. I begin my first section by referring to some of Husserl's remarks about encountering the Other in *Ideas II* and *The Crisis*, following this with an outline of his procedure in *Cartesian Meditations*. In my second section, I lay out the criticisms of pairing and appresentation by Merleau-Ponty and Levinas. In the third and fourth sections I expand upon these criticisms, but chiefly strive to show what their respective authors distort, dismiss prematurely, fail to reconstruct, and pass over altogether.

Husserl's Account from Ownness

In the second book of *Ideas*, Husserl's studies of the constitution of phenomena follow on from his method of reduction. In the naive but ineradicable natural attitude, each of us believes that he or she is an item in an external world that always claims independent existence. Husserl brackets or suspends this sense of the world in the *epoché*, putting it into inverted commas. The question is then no longer of its truth or falsity, but of explicating how it is constituted by consciousness as a meaningful and credible claim in the first place. Crucial to such explication is the avoidance of the naturalistic presumption that in ordinary perception we encounter bare physical things to which we then

---

nuanced readings, commencing in 1930 with *Théorie de l'intuition dans la phénoménologie de Husserl* (Paris: Librairie Vrin, 1963). English: *The Theory of Intuition in Husserl's Phenomenology*, tr. A.Orianne (Evanston: Northwestern University Press, 1973).

ascribe value predicates.[6] The true world of experience is of useful, beautiful or horrible things, and more fundamentally of people that are strange and familiar, friends and enemies and never indifferently present.[7]

The surrounding world in which we naively experience others is prior to the material nature of scientific theory, and is first entitled the life-world in a supplement to *Ideas II*.[8] In *The Crisis of European Sciences*, Husserl embarks on a genealogy of the modern scientific materialism and mind–body dualism that he sees as having distorted this intersubjective life-world. He notes that classical science from the seventeenth century onwards utilized the conceptual model of completely determined (pure and precise) bodies in an absolute, geometrical space and time as the standard for understanding the behaviour of worldly bodies.[9]

This model originated with Galileo's thought-experiment of a perfect sphere on a perfect plane, which if moved would continue to infinity in a straight line.[10] From Galileo onwards, claims Husserl, the success of mathematical physics has led

---

6 *Husserliana IV. Ideen zu einer reinen Phänomenologie und phänomenologischen Philosophie: Zweites Buch*, ed. M. Biemel (The Hague: Martinus Nijhoff, 1952), pp. 182, 183. English: *Ideas Pertaining to a Pure Phenomenology and to a Phenomenological Philosophy, Second Book*, tr. R. Rojcewicz and A. Schuwer (Dordrecht: Kluwer, 1989), pp. 191, 193. To be abbreviated as *Hua IV*.

7 *Hua IV*, pp. 176, 190 (tr. pp. 185–6, 200).

8 *Hua IV*, pp. 191, 374–6 (tr. pp. 201, 384–5).

9 *Husserliana VI. Die Krisis der europäischen Wissenschaften und die transzendentale Phänomenologie*, ed. W. Biemel (The Hague: Martinus Nijhoff, 2nd edn, 1962), pp. 38–9. English: *The Crisis of European Sciences and Transcendental Phenomenology*, tr. D. Carr (Evanston: Northwestern University Press, 1970), pp. 39–40. To be abbreviated as *Hua VI*.

10 If we imagine a perfectly circular body thrown on a perfect horizontal plane, according to Galileo, we can conclude that this body will move along the plane with a uniform and perpetual motion, provided the plane is extended infinitely. *Dialogues Concerning the Two New Sciences*, tr. H. Crew and A. de Salvio (London: Macmillan, 1914), p. 244.

scientists to throw a garb of mathematical ideas over the life-world, to the extent that its method of prediction is conflated with true being.[11] Such was the situation already inherited by Descartes:

> In his view of the world from the perspective of geometry, the perspective of what appears to the senses and is mathematizable, Galileo *abstracts* from subjects as persons leading a personal life; he abstracts from all that is in any way spiritual, from all cultural properties which are attached to things in human praxis. The result of this abstraction is the things purely as bodies; but these are taken as concrete real objects, the totality of which makes up a world that becomes the subject matter of research. One can truly say that the idea of nature as a genuinely self-enclosed world of bodies first emerges with Galileo. A consequence of this, along with mathematization, which was too quickly taken for granted, is the idea of a self-enclosed natural causality in which every occurrence is determined unequivocally and in advance. Clearly the way is thus prepared for dualism, which appears immediately afterward in Descartes.[12]

Concurring that the world is mechanically determined, Descartes could only preserve qualities of freedom and spontaneity on the part of consciousness by taking the latter as making up a distinct realm of its own. Other thinkers regarded these qualities as illusory add-ons to the mechanistic world picture, and took the alternative route of physicalistic naturalism.[13]

On Husserl's view, already sketched out in *Ideas II*, the living body of a man or animal is a concrete totality. Incapable of fragmentation, it is not a material being in the natural scientific sense, and cannot be comprehended in this manner. The human or animal psyche, furthermore, is not something that is bound

---

11 *Hua VI*, pp. 51–3 (tr. pp. 51–3).
12 *Hua VI*, pp. 60–1 (tr. p. 60, slightly emended).
13 *Hua VI*, pp. 63–4 (tr. pp. 63–4).

to this living body in an external relation, standing next to or inside the former. Our experiential life informs us that the body and psyche are fused together throughout. Taken in themselves they are mere abstracta, moments of the one integral being without independent existence. Consciousness is not a Cartesian container of ideas, and it is not something private that is shut off from others.

When we see the smiling face and hear the soft words, we are experiencing a person's love for us. When we see the child singing and splashing in the bath, we are experiencing his or her enjoyment and exuberance. Lived experiences are not behind their faces and postures, but shown in and through them. Whenever we see a human person dancing, chattering, laughing and crying, we are seeing a body that is distinctive because it is 'filled with soul' through and through. The apprehension of a human being is such that this sense permeates the body. There is no question here, says Husserl, of a temporal sequence in which we would first apprehend the body and then the person. Rather we perceive the living body of the person in the one blow.[14] And every person that we encounter manifests a singular style. Though each personal life has its typicality, it is different in each case, for it is the typicality recognizable from that person's past comportment, and unique to him or her.[15]

For Husserl, however, the problem of the 'Other' (or other ego) is not solved by such descriptions. He realizes that there is still something genuinely hidden and elusive about the Other, something that the Cartesians had grasped without getting it right. What this is, according to Husserl, is the other's consciousness *as he or she lives it*, from his or her perspective. We experience an alter ego, another consciousness in the world, but we do not see it from within, from his or her point of view.[16] He could have added that such alterity unnerves us all on at least *some* occasions. Thus we enquire about the suddenly ecstatic,

---

14 *Hua IV*, p. 240 (tr. p. 252).
15 *Hua IV*, pp. 270–2 (tr. pp. 283–4).
16 *Hua I*, pp. 123, 139 (tr. pp. 91, 108–9).

troubled or violent person, wondering about what is going on in his or her mind. The phenomenon of the Other is of a being that is both accessible and inaccessible, and it is this last sense that requires explication.

Husserl already touches on his solution in the Göttingen Lectures of 1910–11, suggesting that the Other's experiences are appresented, that is to say, given with his or her living body by analogy with my own experiences.[17] In the fifth of the *Cartesian Meditations*, we find Husserl's worked-out attempt to elucidate the full sense of the Other who is experienced originally in everyday life. To this end, he proposes a second and quite different reduction to that of naive world-belief. In his first reduction, Husserl is adamant that nothing given in the natural attitude of belief is lost, no phenomena whatsoever of things or of persons or of the world. Only what is completely preserved in suspension, as it were, can be explicated properly.[18] In his second reduction, he specifically excludes all of the experiences that I as both transcendental, sense-constituting subject and embodied person have ever had of Others, including the sense that the world is there for all of us. I can no longer even conceive of myself as being alone, as the last survivor of a disaster, since this would presuppose the prior apprehension of them.[19] This reduction must depart radically from all otherness:

> Thus we abstract first of all from what gives men and brutes their specific sense as, so to speak, Ego-like living beings and

---

17 *Husserliana XIII. Zur Phänomenologie der Intersubjektivität: Texte aus dem Nachlass. Ester Teil: 1905–1920* (The Hague: Martinus Nijhoff, 1973), pp. 1–3, 62–4, 111 n. 1, 154–5, 224–7. To be abbreviated as *Hua XIII*.

18 *Husserliana III.1. Ideen zu einer reinen Phänomenologie und phänomenologischen Philosophie: Erstes Buch*, ed. K. Schuhmann (The Hague: Martinus Nijhoff, rev. edn, 1976), pp. 63–6. English: *Ideas Pertaining to a Pure Phenomenology and to a Phenomenological Philosophy, First Book*, tr. F. Kersten (The Hague: Martinus Nijhoff, 1982), pp. 59–62. To be abbreviated as *Hua III.1*.

19 *Hua I*, pp. 124–5 (tr. pp. 93–4).

consequently from all determinations of the phenomenal world that refer by their sense to 'others' as Ego-subjects and, accordingly, presuppose these. For example all cultural predicates. We can say also that we abstract from everything *'other-spiritual,'* as that which makes possible, in the 'alien' or 'other' that is in question here, its specific sense. Furthermore, the *characteristic of belonging to the surrounding world*, not merely for others, who are also given at a particular time in actual experience, but also *for everyone*, the characteristic of being there for and accessible for everyone, of being capable of mattering or not mattering to each in his living and striving – a characteristic of all Objects belonging to the phenomenal world and the characteristic wherein their otherness consists – should not be overlooked, but rather excluded abstractively.[20]

The culmination of this abstractive reduction is in what Husserl calls the 'sphere of ownness'. The sense of the objective world gives way to the world as 'mere nature', and in this realm, one body stands out with utter uniqueness. This is my body, which is not merely extended in space, but a living, animate organism. I govern or command it at will, being able to move it immediately. Through it I can lay hold of things and transform them. It is the locus of outer and inner sensations, the latter embracing heat and cold, familiar aches and pains and twinges and kinaesthetic experiences, constant and prominent sensations of movement and of my current posture. I feel my feet and hips as well as the ground in walking, for example, and I feel on my neck the weight of my head leaning forwards.[21]

My body is also the 'absolute here' of perceptual experience. I have a relative here that is made up of the range of objects that I can reach without changing my position through walking or climbing. Every other place is there, but loses its 'thereness' when I come to occupy it. Be they near or far, however, the

---

20 *Hua I*, pp. 126-127 (tr. pp. 95-96, slightly emended).
21 *Hua I*, p. 128 (tr. p. 97).

things of nature fan out from my body like spokes from the hub of a wheel. As absolute here, my body is the centre of orientation or 'zero-point' for everything else. In my dealings with these things and with myself, according to Husserl, I sometimes objectify my body, perceiving my own animate organism reflexively. I feel one hand through the other and see it with my eyes, so the functioning organ becomes an object and vice versa. As David Bell has noted, the point is that I know what it looks like as well as feels like to walk or pick up something or scratch an itch and so on.[22]

When I perform self-objectification, reflectively objectifying myself in this manner, continues Husserl, I come to understand myself as a worldly object, as an animate organism whose exterior is being seen by me myself the sense-constituting and embodied ego. I have not performed a reduction to a sphere of ownness so stripped down it could never be known as such once I had actually reached it. In the sphere of radical solitude, in other words, I retain the capacity to make an own–alien distinction, a distinction between what belongs to my sphere of ownness and what lies outside it. In seeing my corporeal outside reflectively, with my own eyes, I realize that the boundary between mere nature and me myself is marked out by the edge of my living body, by where it ends.[23]

Let us now assume that another person enters my own perceptual sphere visually. The task is to explain how I would get from that body there to the sense of encountering another ego. I cannot call on the intersubjective acquisitions of everyday life. These have been excluded by the second reduction, since they are to be uncovered rather than presupposed tacitly. What would first occur, maintains Husserl, is the apprehension of a sensuous configuration similar to my own, such that my consciousness would be led to spontaneously 'pair' each of them, namely, that visible body over there with my own body that is

22 *Hua I*, pp. 128, 145–6 (tr. pp. 97, 116–17). See also D. Bell, *Husserl* (London and New York: Routledge, 1990), pp. 223–4.

23 *Hua I*, pp. 129–32 (tr. pp. 98–102).

livingly present to me (and which I have previously objectified). Pairing is a 'passive synthesis of association', passive in that two sensuous configurations appear prominently in my consciousness, motivating it to associate them together prior to any active intervention by my ego.[24]

Pairing lays down the ground for that 'analogizing apperception' or 'appresentation' by which I grasp that the other body is a living animate organism that is governed by another ego.[25] And this is all that pairing does – there must be further and peculiar evidences for giving that body there these senses in analogical appresentation. What I would notice is that in its behaviour it is moving like I move, turning round, picking things up and scratching like I do. All these incessantly changing yet harmonious forms of comportment indicate to me that the body over there is an animate organism, which I apprehend as an analogue of my own. This is one side of analogical apperception. Yet the question also arises, according to Husserl, as to why this animate organism is experienced as the body of another, that is, of another ego, and not as a second animate organism of mine within my sphere of ownness.[26]

The answer proffered by Husserl is that I can only currently perceive from here, and never from there. I have to move to convert a there into a here – they cannot be present in my sphere of ownness at the same time. In seeing the other animate organism, I am seeing a being that is there while I am here, and that can occupy positions that I did formerly. And this absolute here of mine always has a particular content in relation to its systems

---

24 *Hua I*, pp. 142–3 (tr. pp. 112–13).

25 *Hua I*. As Michael Theunissen has pointed out, the members of the original pair are in each case *Körper* rather than *Leib* – they are my physical body and the other one. The pair is not made up of living bodies, of animate organisms or psychophysical unities, since that would presuppose what is to be established. This goes against any reading that tries to assimilate pairing into analogical appresentation. *The Other: Studies in the Social Ontology of Husserl, Heidegger, Sartre and Buber*, tr. C. Macann (Cambridge, MA: The MIT Press, 1984), pp. 62–5.

26 *Hua I*, pp. 140, 143–4 (tr. pp. 111, 113–14).

of appearance, that is, to the perceptual functions of my own animate organism. I have certain kinaesthetic sensations if I am lying on the branch of a tree and looking straight downwards, for example, such as the pressure on my stomach and the weight of my head on my neck. But the current movements of the animate organism over there, such as walking or running or turning around, do not provide me with the appropriate kinaesthetic sensations.[27]

All those harmonious and recognizable things occurring in and by way of that animate organism over there, moreover, are not being accomplished by me, either immediately or mediately. A further fundamental characteristic of my living body, as we have seen, is that it is the only animate organism that I govern immediately. Through it I can effect mediate changes on things, but only from here. To see all those other movements – taking place continually and fluidly and at a distance – in the light of my own bodily evidences is to grasp that there is another ego governing immediately that animate organism there, an analogue of my ego. This is the obverse side of analogical apprehension, the appresentation of an alter ego, once again an absolute here, but a different one located there.[28]

From observing its comportment in places familiar to me, I also appresent the Other as experiencing the same nature and ultimately the same world as me. I apprehend that I would see what he or she is seeing if I were currently standing over there. Through empathic experience, continues Husserl, I can gradually feel myself into the higher activities of this alter ego going beyond mere bodily governance, activities like sadness and cheerfulness that are recognized from my own conduct in similar circumstances. And a remarkable fact that will soon strike me is that the Other can look back at me and hear me and so forth. My animate organism can enter his or her field of perception, so that I am experienced as his or her Other.[29] In the

---

27 *Hua I*, pp. 146, 148 (tr. pp. 116–17, 119–120).
28 *Hua I*, pp. 140, 146, 151 (tr. pp. 110, 116–17, 122).
29 *Hua I*, pp. 148–9, 152–3, 158 (tr. pp. 119–120, 123–5, 130).

succeeding sections of the Fifth Meditation, Husserl seeks to explicate the ways in which we can proceed to constitute communally a socio-cultural life-world.

The Critiques by Merleau-Ponty and Levinas

Writing on the idea of a generative phenomenology after Husserl, Anthony Steinbock has set out succinctly many of the criticisms that have been made of the former's procedure of constituting the sense of the Other from within the sphere of Ownness. Among these are the feasibility of the overall Cartesian framework, the one-sided relation of foundation enjoyed by the ego with regard to the alter ego, and the feasibility of a static method – which is not concerned with a genesis taking place in time – for such a task. The lack of attention to linguistic communication in Husserl's constitutive analysis is noteworthy, and the layer of culture that appears at the end of the meditation is an ad hoc, tacked-on addition.[30] Steinbock adds that Merleau-Ponty's insights are instructive in this regard, in particular his contention that the problem of the Other is always a particular case of some others, with the alien consciousness only being accessible within a constellation of others.[31]

In *Phenomenology of Perception*, Merleau-Ponty's starting point is a commitment to the phenomenological ideal of unprejudiced description. To go back to the things themselves is to return to the world that precedes the theoretical constructions of natural science, whose naturalistic presuppositions have infected empiricism and idealism alike. Influenced heavily by

---

30 A. J. Steinbock, *Home and Beyond: Generative Phenomenology after Husserl* (Evanston: Northwestern University Press, 1995), pp. 68, 75.

31 Steinbock, *Home and Beyond*, p. 75. On this point, see M. Merleau-Ponty's *Le visible et l'invisible, suivi de notes de travail*, ed. C. Lefort (Paris: Gallimard, 1964), p. 113, n. 1. English: *The Visible and the Invisible, followed by Working Notes*, tr. A. Lingis (Evanston: Northwestern University Press, 1968), p. 81, n. 14.

Husserl's *Crisis*, Merleau-Ponty decries the 'objective thought' that underlies scientific naturalism. The working hypothesis of modern science, taken over uncritically by philosophy, is of worldly reality as a determined totality of causal processes. For objective thought, these processes can be analysed mathematically into ultimate simples or elementary variables, the combinations and proportions of which explain the processes in question.[32]

Once dualism incorporated the living body into a physiological mechanism, the ego as taken as a transcendent cause of the latter's movements, initiating them from without because, precisely as ego, it had nothing in common with nature. Dualism thus perpetuated and amplified objective thought – to the extended mechanical body it opposed a thinking stuff, the ultimate unit of psychological analysis.[33] As a machine or automaton, observes Merleau-Ponty, the body ceased to be the visible expression of someone's being, so that the perception of another's body could not really be of that person. The other was an ego that could only be apprehended indirectly, as the result of an inference. The fate of the living body was to become an exterior without an interior, and of the subject to become an interior without an exterior. It could not be determined as anything more than a rational and impersonal consciousness, since it was no longer individuated or particularized by its body. Hence the singularity as well as the internal unity of the body-subject was passed over.[34]

It will be of little surprise to learn that Merleau-Ponty has great admiration for the descriptions of experiencing another person that are set out in *Ideas II*. We will recall how Husserl refuses to separate body and psyche, and refers to the singular style manifested by each person that we encounter perceptually. He recognizes that a free consciousness could never have an internal relationship to a machine-like body. Merleau-Ponty

---

32 *PP*, pp. ii–iii, 139, 402 (tr. pp. viii–ix, 120, 350).
33 *PP*, pp. 60–1, 66–7 (tr. pp. 49, 54–5).
34 *PP*, pp. 67–8 (tr. pp. 55–6).

stresses that this is something that the Cartesians were quite correct about. Their mistake was to abandon the internal relationship of psyche and living body instead of the automaton.[35] But if Husserl recognizes that the Other's body is filled with soul through and through, he goes on to forget it, or rather to neglect it seriously, in the last of the *Cartesian Meditations*.

In the account of pairing that follows the reduction to ownness, according to Merleau-Ponty, we find Husserl most obviously abandoning his commitment to unprejudiced description and falling into objective thought, namely, into a provisional dualism that violates the originary phenomenon of the Other.[36] He sunders the Other's living body into an outside – a similar sensuous configuration to my body that is paired with mine – which then receives from me the sense of an animating ego inside it. It supposedly gets this sense via analogical appresentation because in self-objectification I had grasped what the living body looks like as well as feels like. For Merleau-Ponty, after Max Scheler, Husserl's reasoning by analogy presupposes what it wants to explain, the original character of my experience of the Other.[37] This hidden presupposition lands his account in its deepest difficulties.

Merleau-Ponty agrees that our bodies are paired in ordinary experience, and that I know what it looks like to walk or wince or touch hands and so on, but his point is that I did not learn

---

35 *PP*, p. 403 (tr. p. 351).

36 I have elucidated some of the consequences of this provisional dualism in 'Husserl's Others', *Yearbook of the Irish Philosophical Society*, vol. 3 (2002), pp. 102–10. I also suggest that the 'novel reduction' to the sphere of ownness found in *Cartesian Meditations* bears some remarkable similarities to the earlier thought-experiment, set out in *Ideas I*, of consciousness as a residuum following the annihilation of the world.

37 *PP*, p. 404 (tr. p. 352). In the same place Merleau-Ponty points out that it was Scheler who already observed that reasoning by analogy in relation to the Other presupposes what it wants to explain. Though he does not cite the relevant text, he is almost certainly referring to Scheler's *The Nature of Sympathy*, tr. P. Heath (New Haven: Yale University Press, 1954), pp. 238ff.

the latter from looking at myself or from my kinaesthetic sensations. I first obtained such awareness through my earliest observations of others. Studies of early childhood – which Merleau-Ponty will examine in detail in 'The Child's Relations with Others' – have shown that at fifteen months, a baby is already familiar with common patterns of behaviour on the part of adults. If I pretend to bite the finger of a baby at this age, he or she reacts by opening his or her mouth. What biting looks like has an immediate, intersubjective significance – from the inside, the baby feels its own jaw and teeth as an apparatus to bite with, and my jaw and teeth from the outside as an apparatus beginning to execute this operation. Put another way, the baby perceives my intention in my body (that of biting), its own intention in its body (that of stopping the bite with its jaw), and hence my intention in its body.[38]

This would seemingly force us to abandon Husserl's notions of self-objectification, pairing and appresentation. For Merleau-Ponty, pairing does take place, but is built out of passive syntheses that give every other's body immediately *as* an animate organism, one that is correlated with my own animate organism from infancy, prior to any reflexive act of self-objectification

---

38 *PP*, pp. 404–5 (tr. p. 352). In his later essay, which was delivered as an extended lecture from the late *Cours de Sorbonne* on child psychology, Merleau-Ponty notes that, in his imitation of facial expressions, 'The child's visual experience of his own body is altogether insignificant in relation to the kinaesthetic, cinesthetic, or tactile feeling he can have of it. There are numerous regions of his body that he does not see and know except by means of a mirror . . . To understand how the child arrives at assimilating the one to the other, we must, rather, suppose that he has other reasons for doing so than reasons of simple detail. If he comes to identify as bodies, and as animated ones, the bodies of himself and the other, this can only be because he globally identifies them and not because he constructs a point-for-point correspondence between the visual image of the other and the interoceptive [internally unified] image of his own body . . . At first the child imitates not persons but conducts.' 'The Child's Relations with Others', tr. W. Cobb in *The Primacy of Perception and Other Essays*, ed. J. M. Edie (Evanston: Northwestern University Press, 1964), pp. 116–17. To be abbreviated as *PrP*.

and without any reasoning by analogy. Now there are aspects of this that Husserl could agree with – he might accept much of this story of one's pre-rational awareness of others, but point out that it is excluded in the reduction to ownness. Merleau-Ponty's retort, however, is that it cannot be washed out of consciousness methodologically:

> Through phenomenological reflection I discover vision, not as a 'thinking about seeing,' to use Descartes' expression, but as a gaze at grips with the world, and that is why for me there can be another's gaze; that the expressive instrument called a face can carry an existence, as my own existence is carried by my body, that knowledge-acquiring apparatus. When I turn towards perception, and pass from direct perception to thinking about perception, I re-enact it, and find at work in my organs of perception a thinking older than myself of which these organs are merely the trace. In the same way I understand the existence of other people. Here again I have only the trace of a consciousness which evades me in its actuality . . . Between my consciousness and my body as I experience it, between this phenomenal body of mine and that of another as I see it from the outside, there exists an internal relation which causes the other to appear as the completion of the system. The other can be evident to me because I am not transparent to myself, and because my subjectivity draws the other in its wake . . . [my] perspective itself has no definite limits, because it slips spontaneously into the other's, and because both are brought together in one single world in which we all participate as anonymous subjects.[39]

Merleau-Ponty's argument is that my earliest consciousness of others cannot be excluded by any procedure because it comprises an internal relation between us that is both prior to and beyond the reach of reflection. The immediate evidence of every other is part of my lack of transparency to myself precisely

---

39 *PP*, pp. 404–6 (tr. pp. 351–3, slightly emended).

because it is grounded in the irreducible opacity of my bodily existence in babyhood. All of the passive syntheses that stretch back into infancy constitute a fund of experience that reflection continually draws on without actually revealing. This fund supplies 'a communication more ancient than thought'. It makes up, as Merleau-Ponty also puts it, 'a kind of original past, a past which has never been a present'.[40]

Crucial to the irreducible correlation of my body with the other's body is the fact that it preceded my identification of myself and of the other, for as a baby I had as yet no comprehension of the own and the alien. We were anonymous existences of which my present body is the ever-renewed trace. In Merleau-Ponty's view, the reduction to ownness prior to pairing is already an example of objective thought. Husserl assumes I can isolate how my body looks to me without ever experiencing others; in other words, that self-appearance and other-appearance are latently self-contained, merely awaiting their thoroughgoing separation. I would then go from the first to the second in my function as sole constituting agent.[41]

A further presupposition that Husserl fails to thematize in the Fifth Meditation is language, which does not translate thought, but accomplishes it. The denomination of objects – among them what is mine and what is yours, what is own and alien – does not follow upon recognition, but is itself their recognition. Language is our common, open-ended and mutually illuminating fabric. It provides me with more detailed articulations of

---

40 *PP*, pp. 280, 294 (tr. pp. 242, 254).

41 *PP*, pp. 402, 406 (tr. pp. 350, 354). Here the influence of Scheler is particularly evident. We do not construct representations of others' experiences from immediately given data that would be provided by those of our own, says Scheler. 'What occurs, rather, is an immediate flow of experiences, *undifferentiated as between mine and thine,* which actually contains both our own and others' experiences intermingled and without distinction from one another. Within this flow there is a gradual formation of ever more stable vortices, which slowly attract further elements of the stream into their orbits and thereby become successively and very gradually identified with distinct individuals.' *The Nature of Sympathy*, p. 246.

meanings originating in gestures, expressing nuances of emotional life as well as more abstract theoretical cognitions. Interwoven with and enriching my understanding of bodily expressions, it is a fundamental ground of empathic awareness. Language constitutes the consummate reciprocity between oneself and others – thus I find speech opening me up to thoughts and points of view that are not my own and beyond my initiative. When my views are contested, furthermore, thoughts are drawn out of me that I had no idea I possessed. Without reciprocity there could be no alter ego, since the world of the one would swallow up the world of others.[42]

Even if Husserl were not to cut himself off from the resources of language and early childhood, the adequate explanation of the alter ego would in Merleau-Ponty's eyes remain elusive. There are difficulties inherent in our perception of others, he remarks, that do not all stem from objective thought. Nor are they all dissolved by the recognition of the significance of gestural and linguistic behaviour. I experience at a distance what others live first hand, and our situations cannot be superimposed on each other. I may state that I know someone and like him, but I am aiming beyond perception 'at an inexhaustible ground which may one day shatter the image that I have formed of him'.[43] This is the price of their being other people with other and unique perspectives. Yet if there are to be misunderstandings and surprises, not to mention struggles to negate and kill alien presences, 'all must have some common ground and be mindful of their peaceful co-existence in the world of childhood'.[44]

When we turn to Levinas in *Totality and Infinity*, we find a critique of Husserl that is distinguished by its severity. His phenomenology of things and of the Other is understood as a continuation of western philosophy's suppression of the infinite

---

42 *PP*, pp. 207–9, 217–18, 407, 410 (tr. pp. 178–9, 186–7, 354, 357).

43 *PP*, p. 415 (tr. p. 361).

44 *PP*, p. 408 (tr. p. 355).

alterity of the Other. The tradition has valorized Being as the totality of the One, first as the impassive existence of nature or matter and then as the synthetic activity of a subject or 'I think'. Philosophical thought renders the Other intelligible in its panoramic gaze. In the pitiless light of rational comprehension, alterity is represented as and reduced to attributive and numerical differences. Intelligibility is the event of representation, the freezing of the Other into universal categories and concepts. The thinker effecting it remains the same, that is, fundamentally unchanged and unmoved, having determined the Other without being surprised or discomfited.[45]

For Levinas, the Other is not the repeatable token of a type, for he or she is singular, a one-off existent that can never be again. The Other's transcendence is first signified through his or her face, in the nudity and vulnerability of the visage or living body that faces me. The face is signification par excellence, the way in which the presence of the Other exceeds every idea of the Other in me. Within the world, it nonetheless points to the infinity beyond the world and beyond my grasp, to the astonishing richness of an existence to which no 'I' and no science can ever be adequate.[46] The Other also signifies his or her unsurpassable alterity in discourse, contesting still further any typologies I might use to capture him or her. Language gives me what I have never known, showing the Other as my teacher. No one has shown better than Merleau-Ponty, remarks Levinas, the incarnate and revelatory character of speech, whose significations commence with no antecedent representations.[47]

Levinas is also influenced by the former's understanding of passive synthesis as leaving a trace of the Other in one's current awareness, a past that was never present.[48] Yet he holds that what feeds into Merleau-Ponty's work, namely, Husserlian

---

45 *TI*, pp. 13, 96–9, 251–2 (tr. pp. 43, 124–6, 274).
46 *TI*, pp. 21–2, 188, 238–40 (tr. pp. 50–1, 213, 261–2).
47 *TI*, pp. 45–6, 169, 180–1 (tr. pp. 73, 195, 205–6).
48 This notion is broached in *Totality and Infinity*. See, for example, p. 102 (tr. p. 129). Its employment is far more evident in the closing pages of Levinas's 1963 article 'La trace de l'autre', reprinted in *En*

phenomenology, breaks open the way to the Other's radical or 'metaphysical' exteriority for the first time. From *Logical Investigations* onwards, Husserl rejects the theory of mental images in his account of the intentionality of consciousness, distinguishing the act of representation from its object. He brings forward the idea of a signification and luminosity intrinsic to the intuited content as such, and hence not the product or possession of a thinking subject.[49] He avoids naturalistic psychologism, and goes on to recognize that the living body cannot be reduced to the world of causally fixed things. Like Merleau-Ponty, Levinas concurs with the Husserlian critique of the mathematization of the world. The view of living bodies as extended things determined mechanistically is a theoretical abstraction and not an original intuition.[50]

Yet no sooner does Husserl expound the idea of intentionality, claims Levinas, than he privileges the notion of representation, arguing that the basic intentional acts on which all other ones are founded are objectifying acts, that is, acts whose unique function is to present objects, and whose syntheses of identification involve object constitutive meaning intentions being fulfilled by corresponding intuitions. Each object, while distinct from consciousness, is nevertheless made into its product, since it is the result of an endowment of meaning by consciousness.[51] Intentionality is an aiming at the visible, the

découvrant l'existence avec Husserl et Heidegger (Paris: Vrin, 2nd edn, 1967), pp. 97–202. English: 'The Trace of the Other', tr. A. Lingis in M. C. Taylor (ed.), *Deconstruction in Context: Literature and Philosophy* (Chicago: University of Chicago Press, 1986), pp. 354–9. In the face of the Other, according to Levinas, we find the trace of an utterly bygone past, an utterly passed absent.

49 *TI*, pp. xvii, 96 (tr. pp. 29, 123). See also *Husserliana XIX.2. Logische Untersuchungen*, Band II/2, ed. U. Panzer (The Hague: Martinus Nijhoff, 1984), pp. 370–1, 414. English: *Logical Investigations*, tr. J. N. Findlay and ed. D. Moran (London: Routledge, 2001), vol. 2, pp. 90, 113. To be abbreviated as *Hua XIX.2*.

50 *TI*, pp. 166, 183, 205, 267 (tr. pp. 192, 208, 229, 291).

51 *TI*, pp. 95–6 (tr. pp. 122–3); *Hua XIX.2*, pp. 397–400, 514, 584–5 (tr. pp. 104–5, 167, 217–18).

latter comprehended as that which falls under an idea. Vision, on this interpretation, 'is essentially an adequation of exteriority with interiority: in it exteriority is reabsorbed in the contemplative soul and, as an *adequate idea*, revealed to be a priori, the result of a *Sinngebung*'.[52]

The turn to transcendental phenomenology with its bracketing and reduction of the natural attitude does not ameliorate matters in any way, for the *epoché* is regarded by Levinas as characteristic of representation, with its very possibility defining representation. What Husserl leaves bracketed to return to in each case is the *noema*, the object *as* it is intended and not the intended object. The represented has now been reduced explicitly to its meaning.[53] Worldly objects are not of course given to consciousness in their totality, for they always have hidden aspects that go beyond each perceptual representation. What is emptily intended in a noema – that is to say, predelineated as what the object will give beyond its current givenness – makes up the noema's horizon. The idea of a horizon, according to Levinas, plays a role equivalent to the concept in classical idealism. An existent arises from a ground that goes beyond it, and the surplus of the existent over its givenness is progressively absorbed by knowledge.[54] Here is marked the return to the intelligibility of the tradition:

> In clarity the exterior being presents itself as the work of the thought that receives it. Intelligibility, characterised by clarity, is a total adequation of the thinker with what it thought, in the precise sense of a mastery exercised by the thinker upon what is thought in which the object's resistance as an exterior being vanishes. This mastery is total and as though creative; it is accomplished as a giving of meaning: the object of representation is reducible to noemata . . . Clarity is

---

52 *TI*, pp. 270–1 (tr. pp. 294–5).

53 *TI*, pp. 98, 100 (tr. pp. 125, 127); *Hua III.1*, pp. 203–6 (tr. pp. 214–17).

54 *Hua III.1*, p. 91 (tr. p. 94); *TI*, pp. 15, 272 (tr. pp. 44–5, 295).

the disappearance of what could shock. Intelligibility, the very occurrence of representation, is the possibility for the other to be determined by the same without determining the same, without introducing alterity into it; it is a free exercise of the same . . . To be sure, representation is the seat of truth: the movement proper to truth consists in the thinker being determined by the object presented to him. But it determines him without touching him, without weighing on him – such that the thinker who submits to what is thought does so 'gracefully,' as though the object, even in the surprises it has in store for cognition, had been anticipated by the subject.[55]

As this would suggest, the exclusion of alterity is already brought about in the first reduction. What the second reduction to ownness accomplishes is a compounding of the damage. When Husserl comes to treat of the living body, his noematic approach admits of no limits. In the living body I identify myself as existing here, situated at home with myself. This absolute 'here' is the site of the 'I can', of that active and vital body that grasps and manipulates and appropriates things. It affords the means of possessing other existents, and herein lies its very sense – the first philosophy of the body finds its transparency in its power.[56]

---

55 *TI*, pp. 96–7 (tr. pp. 123–4).

56 *TI*, pp. 7–8, 16, 103 (tr. pp. 37–8, 46, 130). In the second of these places Levinas comments that it did not take Heidegger long to condemn the destiny of those sedentary peoples who extended the reach of the 'I can' through technological power. In denouncing all this, however, Heidegger goes on to exalt pre-technological powers of possession: '[h]is analyses do not start with the thing-object, to be sure, but they bear the mark of the great landscapes to which things refer. Ontology becomes ontology of nature, impersonal fecundity, matrix of particular beings, inexhaustible matter for things . . . Heideggerean Ontology, which subordinates the relationship with the Other to the relation with Being in general, remains under obedience to the anonymous, and leads back inevitably to another power, to imperialist domination, to tyranny . . . in the enrootedness to the earth, in the adoration that enslaved men can devote to their masters.'

For Levinas, the primordial sphere of ownness in which the living body is explicated in such a manner amounts to a variation on the theme of the same. Self-objectification is merely a modulation of an unalterable 'I' that is experiencing itself from within, staying calm and unaffected throughout the process. This cogito is monadic, modelled as it is on the closed and windowless monads of Leibniz.[57] It embraces my body, and from within it I constitute the Other's body as another object, and again from within, comprehend this object as an alter ego mirroring my own, remaining composed and undisturbed in so doing. What is truly reductive about all this, according to Levinas, is that the Other is taken as another worldly thing, such that the analysis 'dissimulates, in each of its stages which are taken as a description of constitution, mutations of object constitution into a relation with the Other'.[58]

Levinas already discerns a problem with the body in its putative ownness. Husserl's positing of an elevated, upright and able body is, so to speak, lopsided. Even if one accepts his thought experiment of a world that is mine alone, one finds him passing over the world of nourishment. The world that I live *from* reverses the order of meaning-constitution, being its condition and its antecedence. Passed over too is the body as an intersection of physical influences. The body-master invoked in the 'I can' bears the ongoing possibility of becoming a body-slave, of passing from the freedom of health to the encumbrance of sickness. Even in health my body contests its adequate or transparent representation – the objectification that proceeds from the centre of the thinking being is marked by opacity and made eccentric in its original contact with the earth. This was the profound insight of Descartes in his last meditation. He refused to ascribe to the data of his body and of other bodies the status of clear and distinct ideas, showing his superiority over Husserlian phenomenology.[59]

---

57 *TI*, p. 185 (tr. p. 210); *Hua I*, p. 125 (tr. p. 94).
58 *TI*, p. 39 (tr. p. 67).
59 *TI*, pp. 102–3, 138 (tr. pp. 129–30, 164); *Oeuvres de Descartes*

Far worse is the objectification of the Other's body in terms of things, for these can never manifest any radical exteriority and separation. The depth of a thing, states Levinas, 'can have no other meaning than that of its matter, and the revelation of matter is essentially superficial', however much the façade of the thing may have been endowed with beauty through some work of art.[60] It is only the relation with the Other that cuts across the vision of forms, for it alone introduces radical and true transcendence. The inexhaustible surplus of signification over representation in the Husserlian sense is found in the epiphany of the face. Both in itself and in its speech, it precedes the giving of meaning and overflows the intention that would try to envisage it. One must employ the language of constitution and of horizons in order to show their limits, and yet '[t]he shimmer of infinity, the face, can no longer be stated in terms of consciousness, in metaphors referring to light and the sensible'.[61]

On Merleau-Ponty's Critique

When they are read against Husserl's texts themselves, there is sufficient evidence to show that the criticisms voiced by Merleau-Ponty and Levinas are persuasive in certain respects. In the case of Merleau-Ponty, his critique of pairing is well made, indebted though it is to Scheler. There is no way of bypassing the infant's perception of bodily intentions in others prior to the comprehension of self and others. But there is a still further objection to the Fifth Meditation that the Merleau-Ponty of *Phenomenology of Perception* might make. One of his strategies, taken from Bergson, is to examine pathological cases of

---

VII: *Meditationes de Prima Philosophia*, ed. C. Adam and P. Tannery (Paris: CNRS and Vrin, 1964), pp. 83. English: *Meditations on First Philosophy*, tr. J. Cottingham in *The Philosophical Writings of Descartes*, vol. 2 (Cambridge: Cambridge University Press, 1984), pp. 57–8.

60 *TI*, p. 167 (tr. pp. 192–3).

61 *TI*, p. 182 (tr. p. 207).

bodily functioning in order to silhouette the normal performances that we take for granted.[62]

Such cases became all too frequent during and after 1914.
Merleau-Ponty observes that whilst these cases can show up
normality by contrast, here the relationship with normality
ends. Wounds and illness lead to the constitution of different
forms of life with a narrower range of activities and slower
execution times, but with their own internal coherence for all
that. Thus a patient as body-subject is found sharpening the
surviving senses and developing different bodily practices to
substitute for those that are damaged or destroyed. All these
reactions to abnormal situations are pathological in themselves.
This is not to denigrate them, but it is to recognize that injured
bodies cannot be taken as models for healthy and undamaged
ones. To illustrate the latter through the former is not to
exemplify the latter.[63]

What is interesting here is that the objection to the applicability of injured cases to normal cases seems to carry into
Husserl's sphere of ownness. Even if we grant for the sake of
argument that self-appearance can be separated from other
appearance, the ensuing subject that objectifies its living body
in complete and utter solitude would not be doing so in the
ordinary or everyday manner. Merleau-Ponty might make the
point that its self-appearance would be effectively abnormal or
pathological in relation to our everyday self-appearance. And
anything abnormal or pathological cannot serve to explicate or
unpack our ordinary or everyday experience of the Other, or at
the very least to do so reliably.

There is not even the guarantee that abnormal objectification
would allow me to pair my body with the Other's. A baby does
not yet apprehend her self and others, and hardly knows her
reflection. In the sphere of ownness I have no grasp whatsoever

---

62 *PP*, pp. 119, 152–3, 158 (tr. pp. 102–3, 131, 136). For Bergson's
own analyses of pathological cases, see *Matière et mémoire* (Paris: PUF,
5th edn, 1908). English: *Matter and Memory*, tr. N. M. Paul and W.
Scott Palmer (New York: Zone Books, 1988).

63 *PP*, p. 107 (tr. pp. 107–8).

of mirrors. These are cultural products that we learn to recognize as reflecting our bodies. I am not yet aware of what it is like to look at myself looking in a mirror, where I appear to myself like Others appear to me. All I ordinarily see of my body, as Merleau-Ponty remarks, is the fronts of my limbs and torso, and of my head the bulk of my nose and the edges of my eye-sockets.[64] My visual appearance to myself is radically different from that of the Other, since this appearance is not of a figure arrayed in front of me over there. This ordinary appearance would not be sufficient to initiate pairing as a passive synthesis of association.

Now the account of pairing proffered by Husserl may be resistant to this critique. The abnormality of his procedure might not pose a problem if one interprets him as seeking to show that I as subject can still constitute the Other when stripped of my usual resources, and seeking to show nothing else. His aim would be to unearth the powers of constitution inherent in transcendental subjectivity, not to reconstitute the

---

64 *PP*, pp. 107–8 (tr. pp. 91–2). Writing on the child, Merleau-Ponty states that 'In order for there to be an exact consciousness of the image in relation to the model, it seems necessary for there to be some understanding of the role of the mirror. In so far as the mirror is not at all understood, to the extent that the child expects to find in the back of it something like the objects which outline themselves on its surface, he has not yet understood the existence of the reflection . . . If a child under six months of age does not yet have a visual notion of his own body (that is, a notion that locates his body at a certain point in visual space), that is all the more reason why, during this same period, he will not know enough to limit his own life to himself. To the extent that he lacks this visual consciousness of his body, he cannot separate what *he* lives from what *others* live as well as what he sees them living . . . To recognise his image in the mirror is for him to learn that *there can be a viewpoint taken on him* . . . The passage from the interoceptive *me* to the visual *me*, from the interoceptive *me* to the "specular *I*" (as Lacan still says), is the passage from one state of personality to another' (*PrP*, pp. 131, 135–6). It can be argued that Merleau-Ponty is giving far too crucial a role to the specular image. Following Gail Soffer, it will be argued in the main text that the baby has other means of separating what he lives from what others live.

steps we take in ordinary naive experience. In *Ideas I*, he already claims that, given harmonious continua of experiences for consciousness, nothing whatsoever is lacking to constitute a world.[65]

This interpretation of Husserl's stated task would nonetheless be mistaken. It is true that he explicitly views his procedure in the Fifth Meditation as a static one, not being concerned with a genesis going on in time. But it is also true, and indicated at the outset, that he wishes to uncover the intentionalities, syntheses, motivations and evidences by which I ordinarily fashion and verify the original sense of another ego.[66] He quite clearly understands his task as being to explicate systematically the hidden moments that make up one's ordinary constitution of the Other by a different path. The objection made from abnormality, therefore, is targeted in the final analysis at a task that Husserl specifically sets for himself.[67]

There is another way in which Husserl can be defended, however, and it may let one rescue certain aspects of his account. On such a line of defence, I need not learn what I look like in a mirror to pair our bodies. There are other similarities that can be established which are not abnormal in any significant sense. Even in ordinary experience my hands and forearms and feet look much like those of the Other. There could be a number of similarities that are halting and laborious to establish, but sufficient to effect the pairing of bodies. In a manu-

---

65 *Hua III.1*, pp. 104–5 (tr. pp. 110–11).

66 *Hua I*, pp. 122, 123, 136 (tr. pp. 90, 91–2, 106).

67 In this different path, Husserl wants to *both* uncover my ordinary constitutive performances *and* show what is possible from within my own resources. This is not to deny my dependence on Others in ordinary experience, only to show what I contribute to such experiences. I must therefore get rid of the illusion 'that *everything I*, qua transcendental ego, *know as existing in consequence of myself*, and explicate as *constituted in myself*, must *belong to me as part of my own essence* . . . I must first explicate *my own as such, in order to understand that, within my own, what is not my own likewise receives existential sense* – and does so as something appresented analogically'. *Hua I*, pp. 175–6 (tr. pp. 149–50).

script from 1913, Husserl writes of the infant perceiving the aforementioned similarities. He suggests that they must in fact be perceived if the infant is to distinguish his body from those of others.[68] In this light I hope to show how aspects of Husserl's later account of pairing can be retained and reconstructed, along with his notion of appresentation.

As already remarked, Merleau-Ponty does not regard all the difficulties inherent in perceiving others as rooted in objective thought or dissolved in the understanding of gestural and linguistic behaviour. I only see at a distance what others live first hand, and I must first have apprehended their separate existence to know this, splitting the anonymous correlation of our living bodies found in early awareness. How this apprehension takes place is of course a complicated story, and its moments can be glimpsed in their unity. It involves facial, figural and vocal recognition, the infant learning to associate her visible hands and fingers with particular kinaesthetic and tactile sensations, and later on the understanding of words. Gail Soffer observes that one route leading to the distinction between – and the awareness of – the own body and the alien body is opened when the infant sees a hand pick up her rattle, but is disappointed in her kinaesthetic and tactile expectations. A related one is when the infant is attaining mobility, but cannot move any of the movable appearances there.[69]

Bits of this story pop up in Husserl's sphere of ownness, but are decontextualized and misplaced, missing our original correlation and not being applied to infants as in his earlier manuscripts. The author of *Phenomenology of Perception*, on the other hand, can follow more of this story. He would accept that splitting must precede pairing. Our bodies have been perceived as living yet anonymous from the outset, and as soon as the own and the alien are distinguished, that is, perceived as distinct

---

68 *Hua XIII*, p. 71, referred to and summarized by G. Soffer in 'The Other as Alter Ego: A Genetic Approach.' *Husserl Studies* 15 (1999), p. 156.

69 Soffer, 'The Other as Alter Ego', p. 158.

living bodies, the own can be paired with the alien, pairing sup-
posing a prior contrast.[70] The ground has been laid for the
recognition of the 'I' and the 'you' that arrives with linguistic
competence. But even this latter stage of recognition is remarkably naive of itself, and Merleau-Ponty portrays it as follows:

> The perception of other people and the intersubjective world
> is problematical only for adults. The child lives in a world
> which he unhesitatingly believes accessible to all around him.
> He has no awareness of himself or others as private subjec-
> tivities, nor does he suspect that all of us, himself included,
> are limited to one certain point of view of the world. That is
> why he subjects neither his thoughts, in which he believes as
> they present themselves, without attempting to link them to
> each other, nor our words, to any sort of criticism. He has no
> knowledge of points of view. For him men are empty heads
> turned towards one single, self-evident world where every-
> thing takes place, even dreams, which are, he thinks, in his
> room and even thinking, since it is not distinct from words.
> Others are for him so many gazes which inspect things, and
> have an almost material existence, so much so that the child
> wonders how these gazes avoid being broken as they meet.[71]

By points of view Merleau-Ponty means the particular horizons
of perception coming with our experiences and personalities

---

70 Martin Dillon has shown that Merleau-Ponty subsequently
affirms a reconstructed version of pairing: 'Husserl said that the perception of others is like a "phenomenon of coupling." The term is anything
but a metaphor. In perceiving the other, my body and his are coupled,
resulting in a sort of action which pairs them. This conduct which I am
able only to see, I live somehow at a distance. I make it mine; I recover it
or comprehend it. Reciprocally, I know that the gestures I make myself
can be the objects of another's intentions. It is this transfer of my intentions to the other's body and of his intentions to my own, my alienation
of the other and his alienation of me, that makes possible the perception
of others.' *PrP*, p. 118, quoted in M. C. Dillon, *Merleau-Ponty's
Ontology* (Evanston: Northwestern University Press, 2nd edn, 1997),
p. 118.
71 *PP*, pp. 407–8 (tr. p. 355).

that we bring to the world. The child that he portrays is of course aware of points of view in the narrower and indeed elementary sense of the different spatial perspectives that we can have on things. 'Daddy, daddy, come and look,' says my little son at the funfair. I am another empty head turned towards the world, and he assumes that if I come to *see* what he has seen from his former spatial perspective, I will *feel* the same way about it, being just as entranced and excited as he was and is. Projection is as immediate as introjection for the child, and he has as yet no understanding, as Gail Soffer puts it, of what he might experience from that same spatial perspective if he were I.[72]

A question can now be posed that runs like this: admitting that Husserl in his last meditation misses our primordial bodily correlation and splitting and gets pairing wrong, what is so bad about claiming that analogical apprehension or appresentation takes place after the operation of splitting? Appresentation could be involved in the awareness that there is some independent source of that body's movements, and could actually be coextensive with pairing, both temporally and logically. Pairing our moving bodies and appresenting the source of those movements could be two sides of the one process. This would of course fall short of the awareness of another animating consciousness, an awareness that is itself coextensive with self-consciousness, each running with the competent use of indexicals and names.

Putting it another way, why should Husserl's appresentation be debarred from doing work? It, or something very like it, has already taken place for the child that Merleau-Ponty describes. He is at least aware that there is another who sees, and who can see what he sees if he comes to occupy the same perspective. Now the reason advanced for its disbarment, we may recall, is that the other's living body is given to me in infancy without any reasoning by analogy. As Martin Dillon has remarked, Merleau-Ponty only lets analogical reasoning come into

---

72 Soffer, 'The Other as Alter Ego', p. 164.

play when I try to think myself into another's viewpoint in a thematic exploration of empathic identification. Yet Dillon goes on to note that Husserl is careful to avoid this view of analogical apprehension.[73] He takes it to occur before any thematic exploration of this nature. It is an assimilative apperception, 'but it by no means follows that there would be an inference from analogy. Apperception is not inference, not a thinking act.'[74]

Husserl contends that appresentation is operative in the ordinary perception of objects, and it is the understanding of something as indirectly co-present. It is the taking of something to be present in and through something else. Indirect co-presence is quite distinct from direct co-presence. What is directly co-present makes up the perceptual background of a perceived figure. When I enter the kitchen to make a cup of tea, for example, I initially focus on the kettle, and the worktop and cup and cupboard around it are directly co-present. Yet the hidden side of the kettle is also appresented as being there, since it is taken as possible to perceive as soon as I pick up the said kettle and turn it round to fill it.[75]

Analogical appresentation is the apprehension of something as co-present by way of indication, where that something appears as an analogue of something directly present to me. As we saw, I appresent another ego governing the other living body as an analogue of my bodily governance. In terms of evidence, there is a huge difference between the appresented contents in our two examples, which Husserl sets out in full relief on several occasions. The appresented aspects of our kettle can become directly present in a future experience, whereas the alter ego cannot. The latter is never given directly or originally, though its appresented sense is continually verified by the Other's behaviour, in so far as his or her behaviour consistently warrants and confirms the initial giving of the sense.[76] The

---

73 Dillon, *Merleau-Ponty's Ontology*, p. 116.
74 *Hua I*, p. 141 (tr. p. 111).
75 *Hua I*, p. 141 (tr. p. 111).
76 *Hua I*, pp. 144, 148 (tr. pp. 114–15, 119).

initial giving of the sense, however, is a perceptual performance. As David Smith has rightly emphasized, appresentation is not regarded as being merely operative in perception, but as itself a peculiar form of perception. He reminds us that Husserl sets out his view quite adamantly:

> [A]ppresentation as such presupposes a core of presentation. It is a making present combined by associations with presentation, with perception proper, but a making present that is fused with the latter in the particular function of 'co-perception.' In other words, the two are so fused that they stand within the *functional community of one perception*, which simultaneously presents and appresents, and yet furnishes for the total object a consciousness of its being itself there. Therefore, in the object of such a presentive-appresentive perception (an object making its appearance in the mode, itself-there), we must distinguish noematically between that part which is genuinely perceived and the rest, which is not strictly perceived and yet is indeed there too. Thus every perception of this type is transcending: it posits more as itself-there than it 'actually' makes present at any time . . . at bottom absolutely every perception, indeed every evidence, is thus described in respect of a most general feature, provided only that we understand 'presenting' in a broader sense.[77]

This passage helps us understand how sense-giving or analogical appresentation is not a thinking act, in the sense of not being thought through or reflexive. Dillon's interpretation is instructive here – I do not deliberately predicate of the other's body a quality of subjective experience extrapolated from my own life.[78] Again, this would be to presuppose what is to be explained, to

---

77 *Hua I*, pp. 150–1 (tr. p. 122), quoted in part by Arthur David Smith in *The Routledge Philosophy Guidebook to Husserl and the Cartesian Meditations* (London and New York: Routledge, 2003), p. 228.

78 Dillon, *Merleau-Ponty's Ontology*, p. 116.

employ terms that the account is to establish. Nor is appresentation a form of inference, where this comprises reasoning from
premises to conclusions. It is rather pre-inferential in the sense of
being an association made by the infant by virtue of perceptual
evidence, or better, by virtue of what the infant's perceptions are
pointing to or indicating. At a certain stage the Other attains
co-givenness *as* an analogue, rather than *by* analogy. One
cannot create the Other, says Husserl, but only find him.[79] All of
which suggests that his project of constituting the Other from
within must be qualified. Sense-giving is prompted or motivated
by that living body there, and is not a spontaneous production.

To admit this, however, should not tempt us to strip away
too much from the side of the constituting body-subject. For the
Other to be able to appear as an analogue, for analogical apprehension to occur in the first place, we have noted that our infant
or young child must have a minimal appreciation of what it
looks like and feels like to do certain things, say for hands to
grasp and pick up a rattle. Husserl realizes this – it is the origin
of such appreciation that he misses in the sphere of ownness.
And one is helped greatly in understanding this general point by
Thomas Nagel's insight that there is something that it is like to
be a certain consciousness.[80] Returning to the child who takes
me to see as he does from the same place, it can of course be
stressed that what it is like, and what can be appresented, grow
over time. Introjective and projective appresentation evolve
into empathic appresentation, so there is no suggestion that the
earliest appresentation is a one-off event.

---

79 *Hua I*, p. 168 (tr. p. 141). Bernard Waldenfels has illuminated this
point extremely well. 'It is not the case that the self-transgression [in
appresentation] is ascribed to the I as an active operation. Experience is
an event, not an activity. Like everything experienced, the alter ego
becomes constituted in me and does not issue forth from me and is not
left to my discretion.' See 'Experience of the Alien in Husserl's
Phenomenology' in *Phenomenology*, vol. 20 (1990), p. 27.

80 T. Nagel, 'What is it Like to be a Bat', *The Philosophical Review*
83 (1974), pp. 435–50.

There need be no suggestion that analogical appresentation is immediate or self-contained. I as appresenting adult have borrowed from the others of original and anonymous correlation and from the language I have heard. What this mediate experience has allowed me do, nonetheless, is to give back something of what I have received, to find as if for the first time those others that were always there with me. One could summarize this reconstruction of Husserl's account with Merleau-Ponty's help, if not his agreement, as follows: I proceed from original correlation to body splitting, and from there to pairing, of which appresentation could be the obverse side, or at least something that occurs soon afterwards.

The reconstruction in question does more violence to the Fifth Meditation than to *Ideas II* or the manuscripts. But then this last meditation shows the signs of its heritage and its open-ended character. Husserl writes, for example, of contrastive pairing, a phrase that is redolent of the comparison that calls on splitting. Contrastive pairing takes place necessarily, and gives myself the character of being 'my' self. In yet another remarkable passage, he reminds us that in our ordinary de facto experience, that visible body over there is seen as the body of someone else, and not merely as an indication of someone else. The body that is seen by me and the body that is constituted by the alter ego are identified. Such identification is an enigma. But Husserl asserts that the enigma only appears when two spheres or points of view – his and mine – have already been distinguished. And this distinction, he adds, presupposes in its turn that the experience of someone else has done its work.[81]

On the Critique of Levinas

Reconstruction is not an endeavour that springs to mind when we come to consider Levinas's critique. I remarked above that he interprets Husserl's reduction to the sphere of ownness as the

---

81 *Hua I*, pp. 144, 150 (tr. pp. 115, 121).

culmination of a philosophy of representation. This sphere and everything that takes place inside it amount to a thoroughgoing suppression of alterity. For all the hyperbolic character of Levinas's prose, which is easy to dismiss, it seems to me that he too makes some persuasive criticisms of the Fifth Meditation. But I hope to show that these criticisms are best understood as ones of emphasis. This is how Husserl chiefly succumbs to them. Appresentation itself and the more general theory of horizonal intentionality do not suppress alterity as charged.

To defend Husserl against the Levinasian critique, it is necessary to return to *Logical Investigations*, where it is claimed that founding intentional acts are acts of objectification. It is true that Husserl sees the object has the result of a meaning-endowment by consciousness, but it is also true that affectivity plays an ever-greater role as this thought develops. The theory of passive synthesis takes these sense-giving acts as themselves reactive, the results of prompts from transcendent actualities. This much is already found in the last meditation. But in the end, as Levinas would respond, the constituted object falls under the idea, its exteriority being absorbed into the contemplative soul whose idea is adequate to it.

This interpretation can be contested by Husserl in its turn. His initial exposition of objectifying acts informs us that the synthesis of identification of an objectifying act by means of intuition can always turn into a synthesis of frustration, where the putative grasp of the object, as he puts it, is refuted. The sense-giving act is seen to be inadequate.[82] Levinas, as we have seen, nonetheless attributes to Husserl the reabsorption of exteriority into consciousness in newer and wider sense-givings. The later conceptions of noema and horizon foreground the power of consciousness to anticipate whatever the object may hold in store, cushioning and taming surprises in advance. If we are to defend Husserl, therefore, we have to ask, as Jacques Derrida has done, whether he finally summarized adequation,

---

82 *Hua XIX*.2, p. 585 (tr. p. 218).

and rendered the horizons of experience into the all-embracing conditions of available objects.[83]

Already in *Ideas I*, Husserl informs us that all objects are determinable, but can never be fully determined. Our syntheses of identification always leave open the possibility of new and novel determinations that frustrate our horizonal expectations, however much the latter have been revised and enriched.[84] Although we do have the idea of objects as completely determined things-in-themselves, this is an 'Idea in the Kantian Sense', a regulative and asymptotic idea that can only be approached, and never reached. Each object maintains its transcendence, as found in the sense that it can always present something more and something new to us. And what warrants this sense is not some other sense, but intuition itself – external experience alone can verify or nullify the sense of external experience, a thesis also found in *Cartesian Meditations*.[85] The novelty given in experience, furthermore, can shock us quite radically, being recalcitrant to our horizonal anticipations. It is even conceivable that the order of objects and of the world as a whole could break down without return.[86]

---

83 J. Derrida, *L'écriture et la différence* (Paris: Seuil, 1967), p. 177. English: *Writing and Difference*, tr. A. Bass (Chicago: University of Chicago Press, 1978), p. 120.

84 *Hua III.1*, pp. 13–14, 346–7 (tr. pp. 8–9, 358). It is worth noting that the term 'object' has a wide extension for Husserl, but not one with the character of a Procrustean bed. An object is any existent to which consciousness can attend, and may be just as much an ideal truth or factual event as a thing. *Husserliana XVIII. Logische Untersuchungen, Band I*, ed. Elmar Holenstein (The Hague: Martinus Nijhoff, 1975), p. 231. English: *Logical Investigations*, tr. J. N. Findlay and ed. D. Moran (London: Routledge: 2001), vol. 1, p. 145; *Hua I*, pp. 92–3 (tr. p. 57). Husserl stresses that each species of object has its own modes of givenness. 'It is countersensical', he remarks, 'to treat their essential peculiarities as deficiencies, let alone to count them among the sort of adventitious, factual deficiencies pertaining to "our human" cognition.' *Hua III.1*, p. 176 (tr. p. 187).

85 *Hua III.1*, pp. 100–2, 331 (tr. pp. 106–7, 342–3); *Hua I*, p. 97 (tr. p. 62).

86 *Hua III.1*, p. 103 (tr. p. 109).

The importance of Husserl's horizon, as Derrida notes, is twofold. It cannot itself be properly objectified, since we can never uncover all the expectant and attendant meanings involved in objectifying acts. Those transcendent existents that are objectified, moreover, are never grasped adequately.[87] A horizon is not just what is emptily intended in the noema. It includes passive syntheses of association and the tacit aware-ness of one's ability to move round a thing, turn one's head, and so forth. For Derrida, each horizon is enlisted without end in new and provisional objectifications, which keeps it from all totalization. No one has been more determined than Husserl to show 'that vision is originally and essentially the inadequation of interiority and exteriority', wherein 'the perception of the transcendent and extended thing is essentially and forever incomplete'. The awareness that thought is infinitely inade-quate to the infinite, and even to the finite 'distinguishes a body of thought careful to respect exteriority'.[88] Contrary to Levinas, Derrida makes a strong case for interpreting the theory of hori-zonal intentionality as uniquely respectful of the irreducibility of the other to the same, and more specifically, of the other appearing *as* other for the same.[89]

---

87 *Hua I*, pp. 81–3 (tr. pp. 44–5). In one place, Levinas does say that 'Notions held under the direct gaze of the thought that defines them are nevertheless, unbeknown to this naive thought, revealed to be implanted in horizons unsuspected by this thought; these horizons endow them with a meaning – such is the essential teaching of Husserl . . . What does it mat-ter if in the Husserlian phenomenology taken literally these unsuspected horizons are in their turn interpreted as thoughts aiming at objects! What counts is the idea of the overflowing of objectifying thought by a forgot-ten experience from which it lives. The break-up of the formal structure of thought (the noema of a noesis) into events which this structure dis-simulates, but which sustain it, constitutes a *deduction* – necessary and yet non-analytical' (*TI*, pp. xvi–xvii (tr. p. 28)). This a strange passage indeed, forgotten in his own sweeping condemnation of horizons, and forgetting that passive syntheses of association in horizons *enable* thoughts to aim at objects, being pre-intentional and pre-objective.

88 Derrida, *L'écriture et la différence*, pp. 176–7 (tr. pp. 120–1, emended).

89 Derrida, *L'écriture et la différence*, p. 178 (tr. p. 121).

Defend Husserl's overall account of intentionality as one may, and as Derrida does, one must still come back to the exclusionary reduction of the Fifth Meditation. Once we enter the sphere of ownness, the Levinasian case must surely gain more purchase. The self-objectification that takes place in this sphere, according to the prosecution, is of a living body at the disposal of consciousness, noematically transparent in its ability to seize and possess other existents. Now, there is little doubt that Husserl does explicate my own body in its active aspects. But this is only for the task in hand, and there is no suggestion, at least so far as I am aware, of these senses embracing the body or of their being transparent to consciousness. One must look to parts of his other writings to establish this, and can justify doing so by the fact that still other parts have been used to build up the case against him.

As so often before, *Ideas II* is helpful in marking out Husserl's rounded view. The living body can never be transparent to me – the same body that serves as the means for perception obstructs me in the perception of it itself. I cannot take a distance from it and perceive it in the one blow, and the point of transformation of causal processes that impinge on my body into conditional processes that motivate me is hidden. Husserl is not so far from the more modest Descartes as Levinas thinks.[90] He proceeds to make it very clear that the opacity of the living body does not supervene on a consciousness that would be transparent if only freed from such opacity. One cannot objectify one's horizons properly, as stated above, with past experiences and noematic senses eluding adequate comprehension. These sources constitute the ego as a substrate of habitualities. It is never an empty and undetermined pole of experience, a thesis reaffirmed in the fourth of the *Cartesian Meditations*.[91]

Husserl also alludes to the living body as an intersection of physical influences, being in no way insensitive to its vulnera-

---

90 *Hua IV*, pp. 159–60 (tr. pp. 167–8).
91 *Hua IV*, pp. 276–9, 300 (tr. pp. 289–91, 313); *Hua I*, pp. 100–1 (tr. pp. 66–7).

bility and fragility. My skills must be kept at work lest I lose them, and even recovery from illness can leave me with much to relearn. I may be faced with incurable conditions, for example with a nervous disorder that destroys the mastery of my limbs beyond repair. Here the 'I can' is converted into the 'I cannot', and in that respect, as Husserl puts it, I have become another. Normality is never more than normality for a certain age, pre-supposing a minimal degree of health and fitness and so on.[92] Wherever and whenever we are damaged by physical existents, furthermore, a purely mechanical description will immediately fail. I may slice my finger with a knife, bleed copiously and be engulfed in burning pain. To talk of a thing's surface being split by a wedge and emitting fluid is hardly appropriate to the phenomena. Once again Husserl shows himself close to Descartes, who does not think that I survey my injured body like the sailor a broken ship.[93]

Staying mindful of these qualifications, Levinas would not be unreasonable in making the case that the whole direction of the reduction to ownness undoes them. Husserl does not just fore-ground the body in its active and healthy aspects, but tries to leave out of account its habitual character in so far as it has been entwined with Others. Left out also from the sphere of ownness is the vulnerability and fragility of the body. We seem to be lumbered after all with an unhappy semblance of Levinas's picture. The latter is of an embodied consciousness that maintains its composure amid self-objectification, goes on to force the experience of the Other into object constitution, and suffers no significant disturbance in so doing.

The question is whether Husserl's embodied consciousness matches cinematically this entire picture, preserving its character and its composure through its experience of the Other. I do not think it does, and provide some reasons below. Nor do I think that seeing the Other's body as a worldly object is false,

---

92 *Hua IV*, p. 254–5, 276 (tr. pp. 266–7, 288).
93 *Hua IV*, p. 160 (tr. p. 168); *Oeuvres de Descartes VII*, p. 81 (tr. p. 56).

providing it is not seen as a *mere* extended thing. Such is the tendency identified by Merleau-Ponty in the original account of pairing. When we rework that account, however, we remain faced with the other living body as an intersection of physical influences, animated but still a thing. But to start with object or thing constitution is not to prevent the Other's living body being experienced as a *unique* thing, whether for the infant, the adult of *Ideas II*, or even one's embodied ego in the sphere of ownness. Husserl affirms that different objects give themselves differently. On his principle of principles, everything given intuitively must be accepted as what it presents itself as being.[94]

Derrida notes that for Husserl, the Other's body gives itself as unique and *also* as an empirical object.[95] Crucially, the path to the Other's transcendence, to his or her radical exteriority or separation, *must* be by means of such an object. Immediately prior to his explication of appresentation, Husserl states that neither the alter ego nor his lived experiences are given to me originally. If they were directly accessible, the Other would merely be another moment in my conscious stream, and he and I would be the same. Radical separation is a very condition of there being the Other that I can then encounter. And it is precisely because I can never experience the Other first hand – from his or her point of view – that there must be a certain mediacy of intentionality making me aware of this viewpoint.[96]

For Derrida, the avowal of mediation as being required to give the ego *with* the object confirms and respects separation and exteriority.[97] He contends that one of the great strengths of Husserl's story (unassisted by reconstruction) lies in its blending of the alterity of bodies with the alterity of the Other. We will recall that Levinas has two closely related objections to reducing the relation with the Other to object constitution. He or she is radically different from things, and things cannot

---

94 *Hua III.*1, pp. 51, 176 (tr. pp. 44, 187).
95 Derrida, *L'écriture et la différence*, p. 169 (tr. p. 115).
96 *Hua I*, p. 139 (tr. p. 109).
97 Derrida, *L'écriture et la différence*, p. 182 (tr. p. 124).

manifest true exteriority and separation. Levinas equates things with inanimate objects displaying lifeless facades, possessing nothing beyond bare matter. But Husserl does not reduce the sensuous configurations prompting sense-givings to valueless matter.[98] Nor does he reduce objects naturalistically to *res extensa*, as seen in *Ideas II* and *The Crisis*. After he pairs my body with a separate sensuous configuration, according to Derrida, he still avoids, rather than evades, the difficulties created by the Levinasian narrative:

> Bodies, transcendent and natural things, are others in general for my consciousness. They are outside, and their transcendence is the sign of an already irreducible alterity. Levinas does not think so; Husserl does, and thinks that 'other' already means something when things are in question. Which is to take seriously the reality of the external world . . . in the case of the other as transcendent thing, the principled possibility of an originary and original presentation of the hidden visage is always open, in principle and a priori. This possibility is absolutely rejected in the case of Others . . . But without the first alterity, the alterity of bodies (and the Other is also a body, from the beginning), the second alterity could never emerge. The system of these two alterities, the one inscribed in the other, must be thought together: the alterity of Others, therefore, by a double power of indefiniteness. The stranger is infinitely other because by his essence no enrichment of his profile can give me the subjective face of his experience *from his perspective*, such as he has lived it. Never will this experience be given to me originally, like everything . . . which is *proper* to me. This transcendence of the non-proper is no longer that of the entirety, always inaccessible

---

98 *Husserliana XI. Analysen zur passiven Synthesis. Aus Vorlesungs-und Forschungs-manuskripten (1918–1926)*, ed. M. Fleischer (The Hague: Martinus Nijhoff, 1966), pp. 149–52, 162–5. English: *Analyses Concerning Passive and Active Synthesis: Lectures on Transcendental Logic*, tr. A. J. Steinbock (Dordrecht: Kluwer, 2001), pp. 196–9, 210–13.

on the basis of always partial attempts: transcendence of *Infinity*, not of *Totality*.[99]

The double givenness of analogical appresentation, as viewed by Derrida, is very far from signifying the assimilation of the Other into the same. He thinks a transcendence of infinity is indicated genuinely.[100] But Levinas could well enquire whether the transcendent Other of Derrida's Husserl has really escaped assimilation, albeit at a distance. Radical separation is not yet radical alterity. What is appresented, after all, is an alter ego. This is an analogue of my ego, and it is Husserl himself who writes of apperception as assimilative.[101]

In spite of this, assimilation does not have to be assigned the negative and totalizing connotations of Levinas, who translates it as a swallowing of the Other *in* the same. Husserl speaks of it as merely accommodating the sense of one member of a pair to that of the other, motivated by the appearance itself.[102] Nor is the assimilation in appresentation a dead end *at* the same. It is better understood as a springboard which, in showing how the Other is like me, paradoxically opens up the possibility of recognizing what is radical in his or her alterity or transcendence. The awareness of another consciousness, as we shall see below, opens up my own conscious life. But one can discover something even more radical in explicating the Other, according to Husserl. He regards the Other as more than a psychophysical unity or soulful body in the world. It is ultimately a transcendental subject for the world.[103]

Few recent readers of Husserl understand better than Derrida the character of this claim. Using Eugen Fink's formulation, Derrida notes that appresentation opens the way to understanding the Other as another 'origin of the world'. For Husserl, each

---

99 Derrida, *L'écriture et la différence*, pp. 182–3 (tr. p. 124, slightly emended).

100 Derrida, *L'écriture et la différence*, p. 182 (tr. p. 124).

101 *Hua I*, p. 141 (tr. p. 111).

102 *Hua I*, p. 147 (tr. p. 118).

103 *Hua I*, p. 123 (tr. p. 91).

ego can gain the awareness that is beyond the world, that its original relation to the world is more than that of a world-immanent man or woman. The ego can distinguish itself from the world and from its mundane, engaged self, whether or not it ever actually does this. It is never apart from the world or from human being, but can know itself as the original theatre in which everything mundane attains presence, including the very belief that it is in the world and that it is the ego of a man or woman who is bringing a unique, unrepeatable standpoint to that world.[104] But to recognize this of the Other, as Derrida notes, I would have to appreciate that the Other is another ego like mine. There must be some commonality, some assimilation of the Other to the same, if his or her radical alterity is ever to be acknowledged as such.[105]

Remarkable as it might be, the recognition of the alter ego as another origin of the world or transcendental subject would be extremely rarefied. It is certainly absent in most ordinary life and in the initial experience of the Other, even if it is prepared for by such appresentation, rightly interpreted by Derrida as the opposite of 'victorious assimilation'.[106] Levinas's critique focuses on the earlier act of appresenting another ego, taking as the work of an unalterable awareness that retain its composure through the experience of the Other. But my capacity to be disturbed as well as surprised in this first experience of the Other is allowed for by Husserl. I mentioned his claim that novel

---

104 *Hua I*, pp. 116–17 (tr. pp. 83–4).

105 Derrida, *L'écriture et la différence*, pp. 183–4 (tr. p. 125). See also Fink's 'The Phenomenological Philosophy of Edmund Husserl and Contemporary Criticism', tr. and ed. R. O. Elveton in *The Phenomenology of Husserl: Selected Critical Readings* (Chicago: Quadrangle, 1970), pp. 95ff. Supported by Husserl, Fink contends that one must go through the phenomenological reduction to appreciate properly that the ego is an origin of the world. But the procedure is at least a possibility for this or that ego. It may be added that the awareness by the Other of his or her unrepeatable standpoint – and unrepeatable world – is brought out beautifully by the last words of the dying replicant in the penultimate scene of *Blade Runner*.

106 Derrida, *L'écriture et la différence*, p. 182 (tr. p. 124).

experiences frustrating completely my horizonal anticipations would shock me deeply. In his account of perceiving from own-ness, he would accept that the primal awareness of another embodied ego looking out on the world from another stand-point would itself be shocking, as would the realization that I have been turned into an object within its visual field. As Bell remarks, all of this amounts to the decentring of egocentric space, since it loses the mere nature radiating out from me alone.[107]

A novel perception that shocks and surprises does not play about the surface of my awareness, for the abstractive reduction to ownness does not provide a disinterested spectator. Ownness is not the sphere of the same portrayed by Levinas, not that of a purified ego that remains unchanged in experiencing the Other. To change a horizon and change a conviction, says Husserl, is to change oneself, even as a lone person. One is no longer the being who habitually expected such and such and was thus and so decided.[108] It is true that he describes the ego within the sphere of ownness as monadic, and the alter ego as mirroring this monad. Leibniz is here invoked quite explicitly. But I do not remain unchanged in the acts of mirroring, adds Husserl, for it is a two-way process, and therefore not a mirroring proper. The Other is not an analogue in the usual sense, and not a dupli-cate of me. Every pairing, appresentation and empathic experi-ence uncovers new possibilities of understanding, letting new features of my psychic life emerge and evolve in its similarities and differences.[109] This is the psychic life of a singular person.

---

107 Bell, *Husserl*, pp. 222–3.

108 *Hua IV*, p. 311 (tr. p. 324); *Hua I*, pp. 100–1 (tr. pp. 66–7).

109 *Hua I*, pp. 125, 146, 149, 166–7 (tr. pp. 94, 117, 120, 139–40). Leibniz's monad is closed and windowless, and its development unfolds its preformed nature. Yet it only develops and changes through its per-ceptions, whose type and strength differentiate it from other monads. Furthermore, mirroring is already a two-way process for Leibniz, and each monad that reflects all the others still constitutes a unique and unre-peatable standpoint on the world it helps to make up. Rejecting the notion of closed and preformed monads brings us closer to the view that

Though I am always subject to changes I manifest a unique style of my own in their midst, and so too does the personal, embodied life of the Other.[110]

Husserl's experience of the Other, then, may be read as allowing for and even implying radical exteriority, transcendence and alterity. The Other can shock and change me, arriving on the scene as my teacher. It is undeniable, however, that these features do not strike the reader of the Fifth Meditation. One very partial explanation is the extreme sobriety into monotony of Husserl's style of writing. One should not criticize his style any more than the hyperbolic prose of Levinas, which so often looks like its equal and opposite reaction (to use symmetrical language). And of course the absence of excitement in a style of writing does not entail the absence of excitement in the experiences it is endeavouring to describe. But it remains the case that Husserl, who has a genius for reaching new and piercing insights, has a further and rather unfortunate genius for submerging them in turgid prose.

This is a very partial explanation because, irrespective of its style, the last meditation never refers to shock, or to surprise, or to wonder. It is hardly enough to allow for them, or even to imply them by dint of insights set down in the preceding meditations and other works. It always reads *as if* I remain composed in the midst of everything that happens in the sphere of ownness. Levinas is on to a genuine problem of emphasis, whatever the inflationary conclusions that he draws. This is supported, I think, by the example provided by Husserl of an experience that *could* shock and surprise. When I perceive the Other's living body and apperceive his or her ego, he says, these senses must be confirmed continually by harmonious behaviour, indeed by behaviour that is *incessantly* harmonious. Otherwise it will become experienced as a pseudo-organism.[111]

Husserl endeavours to set out. 'Monadology' in G. H. R. Parkinson (ed.), *Leibniz: Philosophical Writings* (London: Dent, rev. edn, 1973), pp. 179–95.

110 *Hua I*, pp. 101, 162-163 (tr. pp. 67, 135–6).
111 *Hua I*, p. 144 (tr. p. 114).

Jane Howarth is quite right in noting that this puts us in mind of science-fiction scenarios where humanoid robots 'give themselves away' by behaving in ways not expected of a human.[112] But I think that Husserl's example gets the phenomenon wrong. Unless I am badly deceived, androids and terminators do not yet populate the life-world. Imagine that, after a first glimpse, a series of perceptions establishes that a certain Other is not a dummy or scarecrow. If his behaviour becomes strange or discordant later on, again I understand him as sick, or mad, or as a person I never really knew after all. I do not understand him as a robot or machine. We saw Merleau-Ponty write of the other person having an inexhaustible ground that may one day shatter the image I have formed of him. Such a description of the Other would not be out of place in *Ideas II*, but it finds a colder house in the Fifth Meditation, particularly in those last sections on the life-world.

In all these pages there is the absence of what Bernard Waldenfels has called the strange bewilderments of everyday life.[113] And one longs for even a fleeting reference to the Other's ability to surprise and shock us humanly, positively and wondrously. In the world that we find, we can be beaten, betrayed and murdered. But we can also be enchanted with love, humbled with kindness, suffused with pity, in short, overcome by the Other in an astounding variety of ways. The Other as the other person is never a 'wonder of wonders' for Husserl, in spite of the extraordinary subtlety, novelty and respect shown in his analyses. That dignity is reserved for the consciousness comprising the pure ego or transcendental subject after the first reduction.[114]

---

112 M. Hammond, J. Howarth and R. Keat, *Understanding Phenomenology* (Oxford: Blackwell, 1991), p. 217. These scenarios are set out very well in the robot stories of Isaac Azimov.

113 Waldenfels, 'Expereince of the Alien', p. 19.

114 *Husserliana V. Ideen zu einer reinen Phänomenologie und phänomenologischen Philosophie: Drittes Buch,* ed. M. Biemel (The Hague: Martinus Nijhoff, 1952), p. 75. English: *Ideas Pertaining to a Pure Phenomenology and to a Phenomenological Philosophy, Third Book,* tr. T. E. Klein and W. E. Pohl (The Hague: Martinus Nijhoff,

His approach is transcendental and universalistic, and in his concern to avoid psychologism, relativism and naturalism, he certainly runs the risk of devaluing facticity and singularity. This brings us back to the problem of emphasis that Levinas can well criticize. Derrida spots this problem too, remarking that Husserl always navigated between the Scylla and Charybdis of logicizing structuralism and psychologistic geneticism.[115]

Husserl was nonetheless aware, as note above, that each personal life has its own typicality. And this he does not purport to comprehend. In 'Philosophy as Rigorous Science', he sets out the ambition of phenomenology to be a pure science of essences. Yet, to give an essence a place in the world of individual being, he says, 'is something that . . . a mere subsumption under essential concepts cannot accomplish. For phenomenology, the singular is eternally the *apeiron*.'[116] He sketches the limits of an approach that Levinas revolts against and Merleau-Ponty helps to reconstruct. In the Fifth Meditation, Husserl admits the problems of birth and death and of our psychophysical genesis have not been touched.[117] His use of a static approach allows prejudices of objective thought to colour his descriptions in a fashion that *Ideas II* is largely free of. For all that, the development of this last meditation has come to include Merleau-Ponty, Levinas and diverse Others. I believe it was Wellington who once said that, apart from a battle lost, the saddest sight is a battle won. *Cartesian Meditations* has become the site or field of a happier and ongoing battle, not to command and control, but to cast a partial light on the Other whose existence transcends mine radically. A story of birth and not of death.

1980), p. 81 (tr. p. 43)64. Husserl adds that this wonder disappears as soon as the light of phenomenology as an eidetic science falls on the pure ego. Wonder is inconceivable, whereas a problematic cast in the form of scientific problems is conceivable.

115 Derrida, *L'écriture et la différence*, p. 235 (tr. p. 158).

116 E. Husserl, *Philosophie als strenge Wissenschaft* (Frankfurt: Klostermann, 1981), p. 43. English: 'Philosophy as a Rigorous Science' in *Phenomenology and the Crisis of Philosophy*, tr. Q. Lauer (New York: Harper & Row, 1965), p. 116.

117 *Hua I*, pp. 168–9 (tr. p. 142).

20. Towards an Ethically Inspired Fundamental or First Theology

MICHAEL PURCELL

The *Dreamer* in William Langland's 'Vision of Piers Plough-man' is seeking direction, and is pointed towards *Learning*, the cousin of *Lady Study*, the wife of *Intelligence*. Eventually, *Lady Study* sends the *Dreamer* on his journey, remarking:

> Theology has always caused me a lot of trouble. The more I ponder and delve into it, the darker and mistier it seems to me to be. It is certainly no science for subtle invention, and without love it would be no good at all. But I love it because it values love above all else; and grace is never lacking where love comes first.

Certainly, Langland would not have had the benefit of exposure to Husserl's phenomenological reduction; nor would he have had the opportunity of reflecting on Levinas's notion of 'the anteriority of the posterior' when, indicating a certain prevenience of grace, he notes that 'grace is never lacking where love comes first'. Theologically, regarding love, we *can* love because we are loved first, and this being loved first translates into the notion of grace as prevenient. But let us leave this to the side, important though this insight is.

In this essay, I would like to consider the notion of fundamental or first theology in its relation to phenomenology and theology. Phenomenology and theology have an uneasy relation, particularly since Janicaud's criticism of the theological turn in French phenomenology.[1] For Janicaud, phenomenology and theology are always two and never one. Levinas attracts particular criticism: phenomenology, as Levinas develops it, is contaminated by majestic theological claims which rise in the background. Levinas transgresses the limits of phenomenology, and strays into an *excess* that has no phenomenological legitimacy. Yet, it seems to me, the difficulty of phenomenology's attitude towards theology is twofold: first, there is an undifferentiated and confined understanding of theology on the part of phenomenology; second, phenomenology, as access to the phenomenon as it gives itself, struggles with excess. On the theological side, there are often uncritical and exaggerated claims made by theology without any phenomenological legitimacy. Thus do phenomenological access and theological excess come into conflict.

Fundamentally, the difficulty is the opposition between *access* and *excess* and how one might account phenomenologically for a phenomenon that gives itself as access. But this is not only an opposition between phenomenology and theology; it also embraces such things as aesthetics, affectivity, hope and desire, and even faith. How can one have a phenomenology of that which transgresses the limits of the phenomenal – not because it is non-phenomenal, but because the object in its very phenomenality gives more? This remains a fundamental phenomenological challenge: how does one gain access to excess? What I would like to argue is that Levinas's understanding of ethics not only as first philosophy but also as first theology offers the possibility of an encounter between phenomenology and theology. Such an encounter is also one that implicates practical involvement in the phenomenal world. Theologically, it concerns a working for justice on the basis of a fundamental theological development of responsibility for the other and others on the basis of ethics.

---

1 See D. Janicaud, *Phenomenology and the Theological Turn: The French Debate* (New York: Fordham University Press, 2001), and also D. Janicaud, *Phenomenology 'Wide Open': After the French Debate* (New York: Fordham, University Press, 2005).

In short, ethics, both as first philosophy and first theology, intends not only interpretation but also transformation in order that responsibility might become incarnate as justice.

So, to make a beginning: theology does cause a lot of trouble. It inhabits 'dark and misty' areas: no sooner have its kataphatic utterances about God ushered in controversy and catastrophe than it has to retreat and apophatically unsay what it has just said. Although Langland would refuse it, theology today is often perceived as a science of 'subtle invention' and arguments that are arcane and detached are often termed 'theological'. Moreover, among theologians, theology disperses and diversifies itself into every area of human life. Thus, almost mirroring Heidegger's *regional ontologies*, the theological environment is populated by regional theologies with unacknowledged or unarticulated presuppositions. Thus we have the theology of the environment, of death, of economics, of art, of sex and gender; and all of these theologies which have a fundamental existential import take their place alongside the great dogmatic theological themes in the Christian tradition: creation, soteriology, Christology, ecclesiology, sacramentology. Yet in all of this, an adequate consideration of theological foundations seems to be lacking.

To take 'revelation' as an example: Christianity is a 'revealed religion' (but let us not forget it is also incarnate). Revelation is the sole ground of theology, and is fundamental to Christianity. The difficulty is that revelation can be condensed into content, with the emphasis on what is believed rather than the act of believing. At its extreme, this ends up in a fundamentalism which might be described, following Levinas, as kindergarten theology. Thus, 'Jesus loves me, this I know, because the Bible tells me so.' This would be a perplexing theology for phenomenology. I take consolation in the words of Roger Burggraeve: 'It is not the case that what the Bible says is true because it is in the Bible, but rather that it is in the Bible because it is true.'[2] This

---

2 R. Burggraeve, 'The Bible Gives to Thought: Levinas on the Possibility and Proper Nature of Biblical Thinking' in J. Bloechl (ed.), *The*

seems to me more adequate both at a fundamental phenomenological and theological level since it considers revelation in terms
of a subject capable of a possible revelation. Theologically, what
we are not speaking of here is a Gnosticism or a Docetism which
bypasses the world, but the excess of any enfleshed person who
presents a challenge to access. The world in which we live and
move and have our being is a phenomenal world.

Yet, Levinas also mistrusts theology, viewing it as a conceptual framework which seeks to contain God, or is an evasion of
ethics and commitment to the world, even though, in *Otherwise
than Being*, he will articulate a possible philosophical access to
the divine in terms of a religion of responsibility. Yet later,
in interview, Levinas will admit that ethics is not only first
philosophy but also first theology:

> We have been reproached for ignoring theology; and we do
> not contest the necessity of a recovery, at least the necessity of
> choosing an opportunity for a recovery of these themes. We
> think, however, that theological recuperation comes after the
> glimpse of holiness, which is primary.[3]

Such '[a]n original ethical event . . . would also be first theology'.[4] For Levinas, it is the excess that ethics brings to reason
that provokes thought, whether phenomenological or theological. Ethics is not only 'first philosophy' but also 'first' (or
fundamental) 'theology'.

---

*Face of the Other and the Trace of God: Essays on the Philosophy of
Emmanuel Levinas* (New York: Fordham University Press, 2000),
p. 166.

3 E. Levinas, *Of God who Comes to Mind* (Stanford: Stanford
University Press, 2nd edn, 1998), p. ix.

4 Levinas, 'The Awakening of the I' in *Is it Righteous to Be?*
(Stanford: Stanford University Press, 2001), p. 182.

Fundamental Theology

Within theology, one can distinguish *fundamental, systematic,* and *practical* theology. As David Tracy writes, 'Each theologian often seems dominated by a single concern'[5] and these often result in particular theologies. But the fundamental question – the question of foundations – remains. In what sense can theology be considered *fundamental?* Tracy, in *The Analogical Imagination,* clarifies the distinctions within theology in terms of the various publics which theology seeks to address. Theology is *fundamental,* and *systematic,* and *practical.* By and large, these three areas respond to the *academy,* the *Church* and *society.* What is needed is clarity in the theological project which involves recognizing 'the existence of three distinct but related disciplines in theology: fundamental, systematic, and practical theologies' (*AnIm* 55).

Fundamental theologies speak, but not exclusively, to the academy. *Fundamental* theologies seek 'to provide arguments that all reasonable persons . . . can recognise as reasonable', and therefore has recourse to 'experience, intelligence, rationality, and responsibility'. Fundamental theologies privilege that critical enquiry which is 'proper to its academic setting'. Although related to systematic and practical theological approaches, and sharing their concerns, fundamental theologies tend to 'abstract themselves from all religious 'faith commitments' for the legitimate purpose of critical analysis of all religious and theological claims' (*AnIm* 57). Further, with regard to meaning and truth claims, fundamental theologies, in attempting to have a genuinely public character, have a concern with the 'adequacy or inadequacy of truth claims' of a tradition, and will engage with other disciplines in the humanities. Thus, fundamental theology is often spoken of as 'philosophical theology'.

Systematic theologies tend to address themselves to and operate from within the ecclesial community – the Church –

---

5 D. Tracy, *The Analogical Imagination* (London: SCM Press, 1981), p. 54 (hereafter *AnIm*).

which is a specific 'community of moral discourse and action' (*AnIm* 57). Systematic theologies tend to speak from within a tradition and address themselves to a more confined audience and are therefore less public. Their task is the re-presentation and reinterpretation of the key moments and tenets of a particular tradition to maintain its transformative potential. 'Creative and critical fidelity' to the tradition is a key concern. Systematic theologies tend to have a hermeneutic approach to a religious tradition, often by way of 'hermeneutic retrieval'. In other words, how might key doctrines and the theology which supports them be articulated anew if the fundamental language of theology finds itself changed?

Practical theologies address themselves to the wider public of society and its political, economic, cultural and pastoral concerns. Their theoretical concern is less explicit, and they regard praxis as a counterbalance and a spur to theory. A key concern of practical theologies is 'the ethical stance of commitment to and sometimes even involvement in a situation of *praxis*' in a personal way (*AnIm* 57). Practical theologies will seek to bring the tools of the various disciplines of the social sciences and humanities to bear on situations of ethical or religious import (for example, 'racism, classism, elitism, anti-Semitism, economic exploitation, environmental crisis', as Tracy suggests).

The relation between *fundamental* and *systematic* theology is similarly argued by Avery Dulles who, in *Models of Revelation*, argues that what he attempts is a 'fundamental theology of revelation'. 'By fundamental theology,' he writes:

I do not here mean a pretheological discipline that proceeds, as the classical apologetics aspired to do, by the 'unaided light of reason.' Rather, I mean a properly theological discipline which is, however, predogmatic. Fundamental theology is theological because it is not a mere preamble but an integral part of the critical and methodic reflection on Christian faith. Beginning from within the Christian tradition, it seeks to spell out what is implied by the stance of faith. Fundamental theology, however, is predogmatic because . . . it does not rest on a finished theory regarding revelation and its mediation through tradition and ecclesiastical pronouncements. Rather, by fashioning such a theory, it contributes to the foundations for dogmatic theology.[6]

But, let us attempt to go phenomenologically and theologically further.

Heidegger on Phenomenology and Theology

Heidegger is a necessary detour for a consideration of the relation between phenomenology and theology, and also the existentiality of faith. He delivered his lecture on 'Phenomenology and Theology' in 1927 at Tübingen, and then, in 1928, a further lecture at Marburg on 'The Positivity of Theology and Its Relation to Phenomenology'. For Heidegger, theology is a positive science, yet also implicated is a confinement of faith to a content to be believed (*fides quae*) rather than faith as an act of believing (a *fides qua*), and a separation of the existentiality of faith from the existentiality of human existence. Within a strict phenomenology, the possibility that faith might be a particular intentionality is not made clear.

Heidegger's great contribution to phenomenology was his transposition of Husserlian phenomenology into an existential mode, and this perhaps has been the most characteristic and continuing trait of Heidegger's reception in France. Yet, the existentiality of human existence – the fact of *Dasein* finding itself always and already as *in-der-Welt-sein* – is not only a phenomenological challenge but also and fundamentally a theological challenge. How do both phenomenology and theology, as methods, give an account of human existence *as such* and in such a way that is both phenomenologically and theologically adequate? For while method enables the appearing of

---

6 A. Dulles, *Models of Revelation* (New York: Orbis Books, 1992), p. 15.

the object, the object challenges the method to be adequate to its appearing *as such*. Method is both structure and stricture. The problem with existence is that it seems to know no bounds, and this tendency towards and beyond any limit – *Dasein* as transcendence – demands both phenomenological and theological articulation.

'Phenomenology and theology'

How, then, does Heidegger understand theology? He implicitly recognizes the existentiality of Christian existence when he distinguishes between 'Christianness' (*die Christlichkeit*) and the historical appearance of 'Christianity', and when, in his Preface, he comments that '[t]his little book might perhaps be able to occasion repeated reflection on the extent to which the Christianness of Christianity and its theology merit questioning; but also on the extent to which philosophy, in particular that presented here, merits questioning'.[7] By the 'Christianness of Christianity' is to be understood something akin to Hans Küng's notion of 'being a Christian' (*Christ sein*), that is, of the meaning and deployment of Christian existence. However, Heidegger does not view theology as a fundamental enterprise; in other words, he does not see theology's task as uncovering the fundamental existential structures of human existence. Rather, as a *positive science*, theology '*as such is absolutely different from philosophy*' (PhTh 50). Its *positum* is faith. In fact, since theology has a specific object in view (faith), it has more in common with other positive sciences and their regional ontologies, such as chemistry or mathematics, than it does with philosophy. Only philosophy is fundamental. It may seem that theology and philosophy inhabit the same domain and intend the same object, namely 'human life and the world' (PhTh 51) but they proceed from different points of view: 'The one proceeds from the principle of *faith*, the other from the princi-

---

7 M. Heidegger, 'Phenomenology and Theology' in J. D. Caputo (ed.), *The Religious* (Oxford: Blackwell, 2002), p. 49 (hereafter PhTh).

ple of *reason.*' (PhTh 51). Theology is a positive science and, as such, it is 'absolutely different from philosophy' (PhTh 51). Heidegger proceeds by considering theology from three aspects: (1) it positive character; (2) its scientific character; (3) its possible relation, as a positive science, to philosophy.

Yet, in so far as faith is primarily an act before ever it is a content, I would argue, that theology is not simply a positive science. Faith is a particular intentionality – 'a way of existence' – that opens on to things yet to come. In this, faith is little different from hope and love. Can a strict phenomenology account for an intended future integral to the present, or is it only a backward glance to a description and interpretation of slaughter, and politics remains that by which we are duped?

Heidegger on the positive character of theology

What constitutes the positive character of theology – the *positum* of Christianity that is 'in some way already disclosed', or, that is given in the manner of its self-disclosure? *As it is given* or *gives itself,* it is phenomenologically accessible. But, let us remember that not only are the various ways of intending and gaining access to an object key in any phenomenological method, but also the object itself also guides access. This is what Jean-Luc Marion responds to when he speaks of the givenness of the 'saturated phenomenon'.[8] Heidegger recognizes this when he argues that, the *positum* of Christianity is not Christianity as

---

8 See J.-L. Marion, *In Excess: Studies of Saturated Phenomena* (New York: Fordham University Press, 2002). Marion stresses that the 'primacy of givenness' places the phenomenological project in question. Not only is phenomenology adequation, but adequation itself is also summoned to be adequate. Thus Marion can raise the question of the relation between phenomenology and theology: phenomenology is entitled to ask theology why it fails to read 'the events of revelation' phenomenologically but insists on 'privileging ontic, historic, or semiotic hermeneutics'. On the other hand, theology is entitled to ask phenomenology to consider the meaning (*sens*) of what gives itself. 'What does *to be given* ultimately signify?' Givenness is not always self-evident, but 'being more essential, might also remain the most enigmatic' (p. 29).

such, but Christianness, and Christianness is a distinctive mode of existence which is articulated in terms of faith and faithfulness.

> The essence of faith can formally be sketched as a way of existence of human Dasein that . . . arises *not from* Dasein or spontaneously *through* Dasein, but rather from that which is revealed in and with this way of existence, from what is believed . . . [and that] is imparted specifically to individual human beings factically existing historically . . . or to the community of these individuals existing as a community. (PhTh 52–3)

Three aspects are worth noting. First, Heidegger acknowledges that faith is a certain human existential in which 'one's entire existence [*Dasein*] – as a Christian existence – [is placed] before God', and that this 'being placed before God means that existence is reoriented in and through the mercy of God grasped in faith' (PhTh, 53). Faith is 'the mode of existence that specifies a factical Dasein's Christianness as a particular form of destiny'. It is *'the believing-understanding mode of existing in the history revealed'* (PhTh 53). Faith, then, as a mode of existing should find its place in any existential analytic of *Dasein*. Faith is also historical, cultural and communitarian, and so belongs to the factical existence of *Dasein* in the world.

Second, faith, or the attitude of belief, is a particular intentionality or comportment – a 'way of existence' – by which the one who believes gains access to reality as it *gives itself* and gives itself *as such*. Implicated here is faith as response to prevenient givenness.

Third, 'that which is revealed' calls forth existence as a particular intentionality. Faith is an intentionality which, before ever it falls into being a content to be believed, is provoked as a particular attitude of response to what gives itself. One might say that faith is an attitude, provoked by an excess which enables access.

Heidegger on the scientific character of theology

Theology is also *scientific*. 'Theology is the science of faith' [*die Wissenschaft des Glaubens*]' and this 'says several things' (PhTh 54). First, theology is the science of that which is disclosed 'in faith'. But what is disclosed in faith is not a content, but an attitude of believing. Theology, then, is 'the science of the very comportment of believing, of faithfulness' and 'faith, as the comportment of believing, is itself believed, itself belongs to that which is believed' (PhTh 54). Faith, as a particular intentionality, can be the proper object of an investigation which is properly phenomenological, for what is to be investigated is not that which is believed, but the believing itself. Thus, one can argue that, although that which is believed (*fides quae creditur*) may be excessive, believing itself (*fides qua creditur*) offers *access* and can therefore be the proper object of a fundamental phenomenological and theological enquiry.

Now, it seems to me that in presenting faith as 'a mode of historical Dasein, of human existence, of historically being in a history that discloses itself only in and for faith' and arguing that '[t]he transparency of faithful existence is an understanding of existence and as such can relate only to existing itself' (PhTh 54), Heidegger has not so much undertaken a theological turn in phenomenology as a fundamentally phenomenological turn in theology. In taking as its object that 'faithful existence' which gives rise to theology, theology places itself in question, and places itself in question in respect of its foundations, even though Heidegger perhaps does not explicitly address this. For Heidegger, theology is primarily *systematic*: it situates believing in the context of the 'substantive content' of theology. One can only 'do theology' from within 'Christianity'. Thus we read:

> it thus becomes evident that, because it is a conceptual interpretation of Christian existence, the content of all its concepts is essentially related to the Christian occurrence as such. *To grasp the substantive content and the specific mode of being of the Christian occurrence, and to grasp it solely as it*

is testified to in faith and for faith, is the task of systematic theology. (PhTh 55)

The task of systematic theology is to relate the *fides quae creditur* (which here corresponds to 'substantive content') to *fides qua creditur* (which here is 'the specific mode of being' of Christian existence'). Theology, as systematic, 'seeks solely to bring clearly to light the intrinsic *systema* of the Christian occurrence as such' (PhTh 55).

However, considered fundamentally, theology is a phenomenology of faithful believing. It is *Christianness* (*Christlichkeit*) or *Christian existence* (*christliche Existenz*) as such, rather than *Christianity*, which is the fundamental concern of theology. Theology radicalizes itself, and so displays its scientific character, when it seeks to uncover its own transcendental conditions.[9] For '[t]heology is not speculative knowledge of God', nor is it 'a form of the philosophy of religion applied to Christian religion' (PhTh 56), nor is it the history of doctrine. Rather, in taking its point of departure in the 'faithfulness' (*Gläubigkeit*) of 'faithful existence' (*gläubigen Existenz*), theology is an 'interpretation of faithful existence', for faith is 'the essential constitutive element of Christianness' (PhTh 58). Indeed, 'all theological concepts necessarily contain *that* understanding of being that is constitutive of human Dasein as such, insofar as it exists at all' (PhTh 58).

But then would theology not only be 'a fully autonomous ontic science' (PhTh 57), but also be more fundamentally *ontological*, and belong to the existential analytic of *Dasein*? Such a fundamental theology might look very much like a phenomenology of human existence.

---

9 'The more unequivocally theology disburdens itself of the application of some philosophy and its system, the more *philosophical* is its own radical scientific character' (PhTh, p. 55).

Heidegger on the relation of theology, as a positive science, to philosophy

Heidegger continues by considering the relation of theology, as a positive science, to philosophy. The faith by which one believes – which is a particular and provoked phenomenological access – allows that which is believed to show itself. It is this faith by which one believes that needs to be scrutinized (both theologically and phenomenologically). Heidegger hints at this falteringly when he writes:

> As a science theology places itself under the claim that its concepts show and are appropriate to the being that it has undertaken to interpret. But is it not the case that that which is to be interpreted in theological concepts is precisely that which is disclosed only through, for, and in faith? (PhTh 57).

Here one must begin to part company with Heidegger. Certainly, the task of theology is to interpret 'that which is disclosed . . . through, for, and in faith', but perhaps not only. Fundamentally, the one who is capable of receiving such a disclosure or revelation is also the object of an enquiry which has to be as much phenomenological as theological. Faith is an attitude of believing, a particular attunement which enables access to what might not be accessed apart from faith. Faith is an intentionality, even though it seemingly aims at an object which cannot be the target of any phenomenological intention. In so far as it is intentional, the act of believing should be the proper object both of phenomenological and theological enquiry. In this regard, faith is no different from either hope or love whose very intentionalities enable access to what might otherwise not be reached. The difficulty in Heidegger is that faith is seen as a closed system, rather than as part of the existentiality of being *Dasein*.

The ongoing phenomenological difficulty is the relation of *access* to *excess*. Excess challenges method as access, and access must adequate itself to the excess that gives itself. This is a phenomenological problem. Heidegger argues that, as ontology, 'philosophy does provide the *possibility* of being employed by theology as a corrective' (PhTh 59) and also that 'there is no such thing as Christian philosophy' (PhTh 60). Theology remains a positive science and, though it considers the act of believing, it remains confined within Christianity. It is philosophy that is fundamental. Evident here is Heidegger's ongoing restriction of theology to the science of what is believed rather than the existentiality of believing. Yet, if, as Heidegger argues, it is the phenomenon of 'Christianness' or 'Christian existence' which is the proper object of theology, by which theology becomes a fundamental consideration of faithful Christian existence, then theology cannot proceed other than phenomenologically. 'Phenomenology is always only the name for the procedure of ontology, a procedure that essentially distinguishes itself from that of all other, positive sciences' (PhTh 60).

Fundamental Theology (Rahner)

We asked above, *how might key doctrines, and the theology which supports them, be articulated anew if the fundamental language of theology finds itself changed?* Let us consider Karl Rahner briefly, for this will lead to an appreciation of Levinas's ethics as a philosophy of religion as responsibility which approximates to 'first theology'.[10]

Rahner begins his *Hearer of the Word: Laying the Foundations for a Philosophy of Religion* with the question, 'What do we mean by philosophy of religion?'[11] Rahner's method, although often described as transcendental, can equally be described as an existential phenomenology, the starting point of

---

10 For a considered exposition of Levinas and religion as responsibility, see J. L. Kosky, *Levinas and the Philosophy of Religion* (Bloomington: Indiana University Press, 2001).

11 K. Rahner, *Hearer of the Word* (New York: Continuum, 1994), p. 1 (hereafter *HW*).

which is a consideration of the human person as a hearer of the word. Whereas 'positive theology' takes as its starting point 'God's freely proffered self-revelation', which is accepted in faith with a view to understanding – and it is perhaps this understanding of theology which is evident both in Levinas and his critics – Rahner proposes a movement counter to such a theology from above. A positive theology, based on faith, would proceed, writes Rahner,

> from above to below, from a study of the believer, influenced by revelation and the light of faith (hence from 'theology') to a metaphysical analysis of 'natural' humanity, i.e., of the knowledge we possess when we abstract from revelation and the light of faith. In other words, from the totality to a residual part, from theology to the philosophy of religion. This way of proceeding would quite naturally lead us to stress the distinction between theology and the philosophy of religion. (*HW* 6).

What Rahner draws attention to is the fact that both theology and philosophy proceed by way of a method which aims at an object, and 'by a law under which it investigates its objects' (*HW* 1). For Rahner such a method is both phenomenological and existential, and the questions which both philosophy of religion and theology raise cannot be taken further 'without touching on some of the most existential concerns of the human person' (*HW* 1). Thus, Rahner will proceed 'in the opposite way', that is, 'from ourselves and our natural knowledge, not to supernatural theology . . . but to an analysis of our capacity for hearing God's revelation' (*HW* 2), a capacity which only knows itself in a moment of response, but a capacity which is also both historical and cultural.

Rahner is keen to associate fundamental theology with the enterprise of philosophy of religion. Religion is a phenomenon. As such, it is an area to which phenomenology cannot be blind or deaf. Religion is not super-added to human life; it is an aspect of human life, and it has a sincerity, in the sense in which

Levinas uses the term in *Existence and Existents*.[12] There is not first a natural religious disposition to which a supernatural element is added. There is always and already an existential openness to excess. The human existential is always and already supernatural, a supernatural existential. In so far as the human *existentiell* is the point of departure for philosophy of religion, both philosophical phenomenology and theology find a common focus as they then attempt to articulate the human *existential* as religion. Such an enterprise is fundamental. Yet, within the phenomenon of religion there is 'room for an eventual theology'. Rahner notes, 'the philosophy of religion becomes the sole possible natural foundation for theology' (*HW* 8). Philosophy of religion, properly understood, becomes the 'only pre-theological way of grounding theology' (*HW* 9). Such a pre-theological way is both existential and phenomenological, and opens on to fundamental theology.

For Rahner, however, theology cannot decide what religion will be, for theology cannot circumscribe the action of God and the guise and manner in which such a self-revelation might happen, or 'how God will establish the relation between God and humanity'. Theology has no other starting point than the human person who asks the question about God and the things of God, although such a starting point, through reflection and reduction, may find that it already has a prevenient history. The posterior is always and already anterior. Grace is always prevenient. For Rahner, the task of a fundamental theology is to lay bare the transcendental conditions within the subject which give the possibility of hearing the word. As Levinas might say, in terms of the anteriority of posteriority, theology, which, as thought, is always a beginning, discovers something older than itself and on which it depends.

Further, Rahner stresses the notion of the one who is a hearer of the word as also being a *capax infiniti*. It is this concern with the one who is so constituted as capable of hearing a possible

---

12 E. Levinas, *Existence and Existents* (The Hague: Martinus Nijhoff, 1978).

word – the one whose potential is *obediential*, and whose existence is a capacity for the infinite (*capax infiniti*) – that is the concern and the mark of fundamental theology. Humanity is created with the infinite as goal in mind. Transcendence is the mark of humanity, but, for Rahner, transcendence is neither evasion nor escape from the world but always by way of the detour which is the world, and this involves commitment to the world. Transcendence finds itself incarnate, and for Rahner, as for Tertullian, it is the flesh that is the hinge of salvation. *Caro cardo salutis*. Now, if the human person is constituted or created in such a way that he or she is open to a revelation, capable of receiving a word from another who is excessive or infinite, then one might say that the human person is to be understood as *response* to an initiative which is not of his or her own devising. But further, being incarnate, any response can only be by way of *responsibility* – a responsibility both imposed and undertaken in the concreteness of incarnate flesh, even to the point of suffering and death *for the other*.

Fundamental theology as phenomenology

It is worthwhile taking the notion of fundamental, or 'first', theology further, since it helps clarify the scope of doing theology with Levinas, as well as differentiates the concerns of theology which, as we have seen, is often viewed from outside as undifferentiated, yet, as a discipline to be differentiated from philosophy which must employ scientific rigour. This, it seems to me, is at the core of Janicaud's critique: theology lacks the rigour of Husserlian phenomenology. Theology attempts too much, is excessive in its claims, is methodologically flawed, and relies on faith as foundational. In this, Janicaud is following Heidegger. Said otherwise, for Janicaud, theology (and a phenomenology that turns towards theology) is excessive and invests the phenomenal with a significance that the phenomenal can neither bear nor sustain.

Yet, the notion that there could be a 'saturated phenomenon',

---

a phenomenon that is 'phenomenal!' becomes the phenomenological problem in need of a critical phenomenological resolution. The perduring debate between phenomenology and theology is misplaced. The point of departure is the phenomenon of the human, which is both a phenomenological and a theological starting point. Theology, in its phenomenological beginnings, is not so much an attempt to answer the question of God, as an attempt to render an account of the one who is able to ask the question of God. In its beginnings, theology is a theological anthropology, a philosophy of religion, a phenomenology. The faith which rises majestically in the background, according to Janicaud, is not fundamental, but it is a fundamental possibility. Heinrich Fries summarizes the notion of fundamental theology well when he writes:

> Fundamental theology treats the fundamentals, the foundations of theology. Under 'fundamental' and 'foundation' is meant the presuppositions and conditions for the possibility of theology. Such presuppositions and conditions are not invented or constructed arbitrarily, or brought in from the outside; they are rather required by the subject itself, theology.[13]

The presuppositions might be supposed to be transcendental, but transcendental in such a way that they not bypass but recognize the necessity of the historical and the cultural nature of enquiry. It might be argued that Rahner's theological approach, responding as it does to Kant's transcendental enquiry into the scope and limits of human knowledge (and Maréchal's response to this), relies too heavily on transcendental enquiry. As David Tracy notes:

> If theology is to continue to have a systematically apologetic task, and if that task is to prove adequate to the contempo-

---

13 H. Fries, *Fundamental Theology*, tr. R. J. Daly (Washington, DC: Catholic University of America Press, 1996), p. 3.

rary postmodern situation, then new criteria for the task are needed. Traditional modern fundamental theologies relied too exclusively on transcendental inquiry – and, too often, models of that inquiry not explicitly related to the questions of language (and thereby plurality and historicity) and questions of history (and thereby ambiguity and postmodern suspicion, not merely modern critique).[14]

This need for fundamental theology to go beyond its transcendental and apologetic confines is evident also in Francis Schüssler Fiorenza, who recognizes a twofold goal in traditional fundamental theology, namely, 'defending the Christian faith in general and in providing the foundation of Christian theology'. Thus, it could be distinguished from systematic theology not just in terms of 'fields of study' but also in terms of 'fields of arguments'.[15] Traditionally, fundamental theology based itself on two claims: 'a distinct method and distinct criteria of truth'.[16] The first, more methodological, involved 'the transcendental, existential, or phenomenological analysis of the religious dimension of human experience', while the second involved 'the attempt to correlate this experience with the content of the Christian faith, or more specifically, with Christian revelation'.[17] Faith would be the counterpart of the response to revelation. It is the relation of faith and response that perhaps epitomizes the problem of the relation of phenomenology and theology, of which Janicaud is so critical. Referring to Rahner, Fiorenza notes that Rahner makes use of a phenomenological and transcendental method to move from the implicit to the explicit. For Rahner, fundamental theology and systematic theologies differ in goal and method. Fundamental theology

---

14 D. Tracy, 'The Uneasy Alliance Reconceived: Catholic Theological Method, Modernity and Postmodernity', *Theological Studies* 50 (1989), p. 560.

15 F. S. Fiorenza and J. P. Galvin (eds), *Systematic Theology Roman Catholic Perspectives*, vol. 1 (Minneapolis: Fortress Press, 1991), p. 269.

16 Fiorenza and Galvin (eds), *Systematic Theology*, p. 270.

17 Fiorenza and Galvin (eds), *Systematic Theology*, p. 276.

'presupposes nothing of Christianity and has the task of providing all Christian truths', while systematic theology, on the
other hand, 'presupposes the community's faith and has the
task of showing that a statement is legitimate in that it is held in
the faith convictions of the community and exists in conformity
with Scripture and tradition'.[18]

The problematic relationship between phenomenology and
what exceeds the phenomenal while yet remaining phenomenal
finds a fundamental aporia in Levinas. In 'Meaning and Sense',
Levinas argues that the other person has a unique or singular
meaning (*sens*) which is beyond any cultural signification
(*signification*) by which the singular other might be delimited.
Although certainly and necessarily historical and cultural, the
significance of the other person goes beyond the particular
situation in which he or she is encountered, and, in this sense,
the other person is his or her own sense.[19] The phenomenological and fundamentally theological problem is how one gives an
account of the excessive in phenomenological terms, and how
method adequates itself to the given as it gives itself. David
Tracy is certainly correct to draw attention to the need for any
transcendental inquiry – whether philosophical or theological –
to acknowledge the historical and cultural reality of incarnate
humanity, and the need to push a transcendental *Denkform*
into the praxis that provokes it.

This is also what Levinas draws attention to in his critique of
the theory of intuition in Husserl's phenomenology when he
criticizes Husserl for being overly theoretical in his method.[20]
For Levinas, transcendental inquiry is an enquiry into founda-

---

18 Fiorenza and Galvin (eds), *Systematic Theology*, p. 278.

19 See E. Levinas, *Basic Philosophical Writings* (Bloomington: Indi-
ana University Press, 1996), pp. 33–64. Originally published as 'La
Signification et Le Sens' in *Humanisme de l'autre homme* (Paris: Fata
Morgana, 1973).

20 See E. Levinas, *The Theory of Intuition in Husserl's Phenomenology* (Evanston: Northwestern University Press, 1973). For Levinas,
practical and axiological life also have an intentional character and offer
access to the object (see p. 158).

tions, yet that enquiry is summoned to give an account of its method when confronted by its object. For Levinas, that object is the other person who shatters thought and summons it further to make further sense of the fragments that remain. Fundamentally, both phenomenology and theology are challenged by the ethical encounter with the other person who, though coming 'after thought' – yet never an 'afterthought' – is found to be prevenient to and provocative of thought, and perhaps the yet-to-be-discovered foundation of any transcendental enquiry. Thought, though a point of departure, is not the absolute origin. Thought, as intentional, is always a 'thinking of'. Yet, the intentional object which is the correlate of thinking is not only that of which thought thinks, but also that *by which* thought can think. Tracy recognizes this when he reflects:

> God's shattering otherness, the neighbour's irreducible otherness, the othering reality of 'revelation,' not the consoling modern communality of 'religion,' all these expressions of otherness come now in new post-modern and neo-orthodox forms to demand the seriousness of all thoughtful theologians.[21]

Bringing theology in its transcendental operation into fruitful confrontation with alterity is the serious task of fundamental theology. There is a fundamental need to confront the transcendental with the ethical, and require of thought (whether in its phenomenological or theological guise) to give an account of its origins. This is not to subvert or enslave subjectivity, but to give it an unpredictable foundation on the basis of which it must respond.

---

21 D. Tracy, 'Theology and the Many Faces of Postmodernity', *Theology Today* 51 (1995), p. 108.

Fundamental Theology and Praxis (a Liberation Perspective)

The caution with which Levinas approaches theology has already been noted. Theology is for him altogether too theoretical, too dogmatic, too divorced from the actuality of the ethical encounter with the other, although theology might be redeemed on the basis of response and responsibility to the other person. Thus, ethics is 'first theology'. Theology – like phenomenology – has its provocative point of departure in the face-to-face encounter with the other person. Yet, there can be no encounter which is disincarnate. The necessary detour of any enquiry – phenomenological, theological or transcendental – is by way of the flesh, which is the stark reality or nakedness of the other person. Flesh is the fundamental meeting point of phenomenology and theology.

It is worth dwelling on the importance of praxis both in theology and phenomenology, for praxis situates thought in intersubjectivity, and thus the fundamental ethical thought which accompanies encounter and provokes thought does not so much resemble the initial theoretical question of Kant's *First Critique* – '*What can I know?*' – but rather confronts us with the more practical, and ethically fundamental question: '*What must I do?*' In a book that deserves further recognition and reading – *Theology and Praxis*[22] – Clodovis Boff (brother of Leonardo) addresses the relation between object and method in theology, and notes the 'crucial dialectical relationship' between epistemology and theory. Fundamentally, this is the difficult relation of phenomenological access to its excess. Husserl sought a phenomenology that would overcome the epistemological gap between the knowing subject and the object known by situating the beginning of phenomenological enquiry in the object as it is given in consciousness. Phenomenological access is key, but access is confronted by excess. In terms of adequacy:

---

22 C. Boff, *Theology and Praxis: Epistemological Foundations* (Maryknoll, NY: Orbis Books, 1987), p. 91 (hereafter *ThP*).

while access limits excess, 'the facts' challenge phenomenology as access to be more attentive and adequate to the excess that accompanies 'the facts'. Referring to Heidegger, Boff notes that, for Heidegger, 'it is always the object that ultimately determines the method', and so, 'instead of imposing a particular method on a particular object . . . we should rather let the object of our research be manifested to itself' (*ThP* 91–2).

Now, in terms of the theological enterprise, this means for Boff a distinction 'between the real and awareness of the real' (which is the distinction in the relation between immanence and transcendence, both of which are co-implicated phenomenologically, for the phenomenological object is the real object). But, it also means, 'on the level of awareness, a distinction . . . between faith and theology' (*ThP* 92–3). Boff approaches these distinctions from the perspective of the socio-political, yet the distinction between access and excess is equally important for both phenomenology and theology. How does one both phenomenologically and theologically access the excess in the phenomenon of human existence. For Boff,

> Philosophical mediation is (extrinsically) constitutive of a 'first theology' in the measure that it concerns the humanity of the Christian human being and the divinity of the God of Jesus Christ. (*ThP* 222)

Boff, interestingly, distinguishes a first theology and a second theology within his project of liberation theology, and also the relation between them. While second theology applies the notion of salvation to the human situation and articulates the human desire for and experience of liberation and political transformation in terms of the theological conception of salvation and with reference to 'biblical content and . . . under biblical dominance', first theology 'contributes intrinsically to [the] constitution of second theology'. Indeed, second theology neither 'excludes [n]or replaces first theology' (*ThP* 79). But, what is required is a deepening of the foundations of first theology, that discourse by which believers are called to give an account of their faith in a revealing word. This is a discourse that implicates a reflection of the very possibility of a revelation, whether transcendentally or phenomenologically. It is a fundamental discourse, which may classically have been articulated as 'natural theology' or 'philosophy of religion' or 'theological anthropology'. It can perhaps also be spoken of as 'phenomenology'.

In view of Janicaud's criticism of the theological turn in French phenomenology and his insistence that phenomenology and theology are always two and never one, I would rather say that phenomenology and theology find themselves necessarily consorting in the same bed. Neither is the consort of the other, nor can offspring of their coming together be legitimized. Yet there is a possibility of a new and creative discourse in which any bastard is not rejected outright but is to be understood. Between phenomenology and theology, there is a difference in perspective. Theology is a point of view, but it is a founded point of view. Were it not so, it would simply be a 'superfluous reduplication of another discourse' by which it ends by 'acting as the ideological substitute for a science that is not there' (*ThP* 80). For example:

> in order to posit a relationship between, for example, salvation and liberation, we need first of all to secure the theological content to be ascribed to the concept of 'salvation.' For theology, the real content of 'salvation' has nothing in common with the equally real content assigned by the social analyst to 'liberation,' even taking the latter content at the absolute limit of its extention and intensity. Social liberation may be as radical as you please, but it will never be the salvation offered by God. There obtains between the two a difference of order, or nature, and not simply of degree. There is no 'quantum leap' that can bridge this gap. (*ThP* 80)

The theological notion of 'salvation' and the social notion of 'liberation' can only be related analogically. But, '[t]his does not mean that *real* salvation has nothing to do with *real* liberation'.

It means 'only and precisely' that 'in order to have an *idea* of (God's) salvation, we can certainly make use of the *idea* of (human) liberation' (*ThP* 80). And this is precisely where 'first theology has its work cut out for it', for the 'scope and limits of a first theology appear where the question arises: What does the *fact* (and now no longer the idea) of (real) liberation have to do with the *fact* (not the idea) of (real) salvation?' (*ThP* 80). The answer is both clear and complex: 'If I may be permitted to speak in Platonic terms, first theology is the "transcending" gaze that, though situated in the empirical world, pierces its limits, contemplates the divine realities, and says: "God's salvation is *like* human liberation"' (*ThP* 81).

This is a fundamental starting point. How might access 'pierce its limits'? This is the phenomenological and theological point of departure. The true life may be elsewhere, but we are in the world (as Levinas will argue in *Totality and Infinity*), and it is from here that a beginning is made in us. This is fundamental. From its initial fundamental gaze, theology seeks a return glance, which would be a dogmatic theology:

> Then for its part, second theology is the return glance, which although certainly in the world, yet from a standpoint within those divine realities returns to the world and, seeing this world 'divinely,' says: 'Human liberation is God's salvation' . . . To say then that the theological gaze (of first theology) is necessarily 'mystifying,' merely because it loses real liberation from its sights – understand 'real' to mean historical, political, human liberation – is to fail to grasp that what is being drawn upon here is an equation of metaphysical, transcendental values, whereas the real, by contrast, is the historical. Such a procedure is itself the effect of an abstraction. (*ThP* 81).

In truth, 'theology cannot practice a *real* abstraction from the world, for it is inevitably incorporated into the world' (*ThP* 18). Theology always and already finds itself incarnate. Further, theology itself is a meaning-bestowing discourse, 'a theory revealing the truth of a meaning' (*ThP* 82). Its discourse is 'that of a transcendental reflection, having the function of guaranteeing the possibility of a revelation, and hence of the faith which corresponds to that revelation' (*ThP* 80).

Theology, Praxis and Ethics as First Theology

The methodological implications of praxis for both phenomenology and theology are also implicated when Leonardo Boff simply states that '*Theology is praxis*'. As praxis, theology is responsive. Theology, fundamentally, responds to need and demand rather than imposing structures or meaning. The facts speak *for and from* themselves, and, in speaking, require a response. (Perhaps one can recognize here, in terms of a Marxist critique, Levinas's statement in *Existence and Existents* that 'the great force of Marxist philosophy, which takes its point of departure in the economic man . . . [is] the sincerity of intentions'.[23] Leonardo Boff identifies this phenomenological approach in the work of Gustavo Gutiérrez.[24] Gutiérrez, Boff argues, recognizes that the theology of liberation is 'not so much a new theme for reflection as a *new way* to do theology'. '*Theology is praxis*.' It is a 'critical reflection on historical *praxis*', 'a new epistemological field', 'a new grammar of interpretation and action'.[25] Theology is not the original fact or datum with which the Church operates. Theology is a second-order discipline whose thought is provoked by and founded on

23 Levinas, *Existence and Existents*, p. 45. The full quote is: 'The great force of Marxist philosophy, which takes its point of departure in economic man, lies in its ability to avoid completely the hypocrisy of sermons. It situates itself in the perspective of the sincerity of intentions, the good will of hunger and thirst, and the ideal to struggle and sacrifice it proposes, the culture to which it invites us, is but the prolongation of these intentions.'

24 See L. Boff, 'The Originality of the Theology of Liberation' in M. H. Ellis and O. Maduro (eds), *The Future of Liberation Theology* (New York: Orbis Books, 1989), pp. 38–48.

25 L. Boff, 'The Originality', p. 38.

the order of experience. Further, theological reflection requires that initial silence and contemplation which precedes action, for silence 'precedes any responsible speaking about God'.[26] For Leonardo Boff, such contemplation is 'the mysticism of eyes open on the world, the mysticism of ears attentive to the cry of the oppressed'.[27] A theology undertaken with eyes closed to the world would run the risk of evading the world and the challenges it presents, and would fall prey to Levinas's criticism of mysticism in the Jewish tradition. A mysticism which is attentive to the human situation and which refuses to close its eyes to human misery and injustice is not a flight from the world and does not avoid the detour of the relation with the other person. God is to be found in human relations, and particularly as the counterpart of the justice that we render to the other person. God arises in ethical encounter, and so ethics becomes first theology, as well as first philosophy. Levinas himself recognized this implicit and fundamental ethical origin of theology in liberation theology.

Ethics, as first theology, would show a commitment to the world, and would be practical and transformative and not merely interpretative. Levinas himself hints at this when, at the beginning of *Totality and Infinity*, he alludes to Rimbaud: 'True life is lacking. We are exiles from this world really.' ('La vraie vie est absente. Nous ne sommes pas au monde.') But immediately he negates these: 'The true life is absent.' But we are in the world.' ('La vraie vie est absente. Nous sommes au monde.')[28]

---

26 L. Boff, 'The Originality', p. 41.

27 L. Boff, 'The Originality', p. 38. See also, R. Haight, 'The Logic of Christian Response' in Ellis and Maduro (eds), *The Future*, pp.147–8: 'Praxis points to conscious, intentional, and thematised practice. Praxis refers to human action that is not simply blind, but which emerges out of critical reflection and theoretical thought . . . Praxis is the enactment, realisation, and actuality of an only logically prior faith.'

28 E. Levinas, *Totality and Infinity* (The Hague: Martinus Nijhoff, 1979), p. 33. See A. Rimbaud, *First Delirium: The Infernal Bridegroom*, tr. P. Schmidt (London: Harper & Row, 1976), p. 229. French: *Une Saison en Enfer, Délires 1* in *Oeuvres completes* (Paris: Gallimard, Bibliothèque de la Pleiade, 1963).

We are in a world, whose foundations and structures are summoned to be other than they are and to be otherwise; responsibility opens on to a justice which demands a transformation of *this world*, a transformation which involves a responsible conversion to the other person which is as much personal as it is structural. 'Responsibility is what first enables one to catch sight of and conceive of value.'[29] So we read: 'When I spoke of the overcoming of Western ontology as an "ethical and prophetic cry" in "God and Philosophy", I was in fact thinking of Marx's critique of Western idealism of a project to understand the world rather than to transform it.'[30] Again, in response to a question concerning whether or not he has a philosophy of history:

I think that an event of unlimited responsibility for another is something other than a vocative, a summons of no consequence; it certainly has a historic meaning, it bears witness to our age and marks it . . . I do think that the *unlimited* responsibility for another, as an enucleation of oneself, could have a translation into history's concreteness.[31]

How might such a translation into concreteness happen? For Levinas, it is in the movement from responsibility to justice. Alluding to liberation theology, he recalls a gathering with students, mainly from Latin America, in Leuven, Belgium:

They spoke to me of what was happening there [in Latin America] as of a supreme trial of humanity. They questioned me, not without irony: where would I have encountered concretely the Same, preoccupied by the Other to the point of undergoing a fissioning of itself? I replied: at least here. Here,

29 E. Levinas, *Otherwise than Being, or Beyond Essence* (The Hague: Martinus Nijhoff, 1981), p. 123.

30 E. Levinas in *Dialogues with Contemporary Continental Thinkers* (Manchester: Manchester University Press, 1984), p. 69.

31 Levinas, *Of God who Comes to Mind*, p. 81.

in this group of students, of intellectuals who might very well be occupied with their internal perfection and who nevertheless had no other subjects of conversation than the crisis of the Latin American masses. Were they not hostages? This utopia of conscience found itself historically fulfilled in the room in which I found myself. That history should be concerned by these utopias of conscience, I believe seriously.[32]

Again, on being asked, in relation to the same encounter, whether 'the ethical relation is entirely utopian and unrealistic':

This is the great objection to my thought. 'Where did you ever see the ethical relation practiced?' people say to me. I reply that its being utopian does not prevent it from investing our everyday actions of generosity or goodwill towards the other . . . This concern with the other remains utopian in the sense that it is always 'out of place' (*u-topos*) in this world, always other than the 'ways of the world'; but there are many examples in the world. I remember meeting once with a group of Latin American students, well versed in the terminology of Marxist liberation and terribly concerned by the suffering and unhappiness of their people in Argentina. They asked me rather impatiently if I had ever actually witnessed the utopian rapport with the other that my ethical philosophy speaks of. I replied, 'Yes, indeed – here in this room.'[33]

Ethics as First Theology

'An original ethical event . . . would also be first theology.'[34] At the outset, we indicated an undifferentiated and confined

---

32 Levinas, *Of God who Comes to Mind*, pp. 81–2.

33 R. Kearney, 'Dialogue with Emmanuel Levinas' in R. A. Cohen (ed.), *Face to Face with Levinas* (Albany: State University of New York Press, 1986), pp. 32–3.

34 E. Levinas, 'The Awakening of the I' in *Is it Righteous to Be?*, p. 182.

conception of theology, which did not recognize the distinction between a theology that is dogmatic and a theology that is fundamental. This lack of distinction leads to the confused debate between phenomenology and theology. It is all too apparent in Heidegger, Janicaud and also (but perhaps to a lesser extent) in Levinas. Although Levinas mistrusts a theology that would be either dogmatic or mystical, he nonetheless opens latterly the possibility of a first theology that would be ethically inspired and motivated.

There is a need for a recovery of the sense and scope of a fundamental theology that takes as its point of departure the human existential. Theology, along with phenomenology, addresses itself to the human existential and the phenomenon of existence, with its faith, its hope and its charity – all of which have no clearly identifiable object. But this does not mean that faith, hope and love are aimless, errant and erring intentionalities. Faith, hope and charity are provoked. The object as it appears in consciousness is always the phenomenological starting point, but that object is intended *as* believed in, or hoped for, or loved. As believed in, or hoped for, or loved, the object intended is excessive, and it may be that faith, hope and love offer an access to a world yet-to-come, which is not out of this world, but is this world otherwise.

What Levinas offers by suggesting that ethics is not only first philosophy but also first theology is that there is a way of bringing into dialogue phenomenology and theology such that they are *not* 'always two' and, while 'never one', they do have a shared interest in incarnate or enfleshed existentiality. The confrontation that both phenomenology and a fundamental theology must undergo is the ethical excess of the other person, and the ways of access. Further, ethics as 'first theology' is not simply another good idea which remains interpretative rather than transformative. The encounter with the other person is not only the provocation of thought but also of action. It is the very *fundament* of theology, for in the encounter with the other person God comes to mind (*Dieu vient à l'idée*).

Sources and Acknowledgements

The editors and publishers also wish to thank the following for permission to reprint previously published material:

Joeri Schrijver's chapter first appeared in 'Metaphysics and Particularity in Contemporary Philosophy (Heidegger, Levinas and Marion)', in L. Boeve, M. Lamberigts, T. Merrigan (eds.), *Theology and The Quest for Truth* (BETL, 202), Leuven: Peeters, 2006, pp. 259–83.

Philipp Rosemann, editor of *The American Catholic Philosophical Quarterly*, kindly gave us permission to reprint John Milbank's 'Truth and the Thomistic Telescope', which previously appeared in *American Catholic Philosophical Quarterly*, 2006 , vol. 80 , no. 2 , pp. 193–226.

Also, we would like to thank Seán O'Boyle of Columbas Press for allowing us to reprint Philipp Rosemann's article, 'Postmodern Philosophy and J.-L. Marion's Eucharistic Realism', which was first published in Maurice Hogan SSC and James McEvoy (eds), *The Mystery of Faith: Reflections on the Encyclical Ecclesia de Eucharistia*, Blackrock, Co. Dublin: Columba Press, 2005, pp. 224–44.

Lastly, we would like to thank Peter Hallward and the editors of *Angelaki* for permission to reprint Michel Henry's article, 'Phenomenology of Life', trans. Nick Hanlon, which first appeared in *Angelaki*, August 2003, vol. 8, no. 2, pp. 97–110.

Name and Subject Index

Absolute, 13–14, 16–19, 423
actuality, 33, 266, 268, 280,
    284, 289–290, 294–295, 310,
    313, 325, 331, 376, 463, 516,
    521n27
Adorno, Theodor, 321
aesthetic experience, 123,
    126–127, 129, 131, 133, 151,
    154–155, 157–158, 160, 162,
    164–166, 170, 173
affective experience, 1, 19–20
affectivity, 206, 212, 221–222,
    252–253, 416, 482, 496
agape, 404–406, 412–413,
    416–417, 420
aletheia, 24, 60, 304
Alliez, Éric, 312
Alston, W.P., 13
analogia entis, 185
anamnesis, 145n13, 281, 286,
    421–424, 426, 428, 431–
    432
angst, 62–63, 394–395, 402
apodictic knowledge, 398
apperception, 116n6,430, 449,
    457, 478, 489
Aquinas, St. Thomas, 90, 135n2,
    261–262, 264–284, 286, 293,
    295–298, 299n16, 300,
    302–304, 307, 309, 311, 313,
    314n36, 324, 328–330,

391n40, 401, 408,
Arendt, Hannah, 35
Aristotle, 60, 126n19, 277,
    290–291, 297, 311, 315, 320,
    371, 380, 385n31, 391n40,
    396, 401, 405, 414
art, 12–13, 17, 124, 128–129,
    152, 156, 158, 160, 162, 167,
    171, 279, 337, 341, 344, 346,
    349, 357–358, 363–364,
    366n52, 471, 497
atheism, 80, 102, 316n38,
    353–354
Augustine, St., 14–15, 19,
    110n69, 140, 271, 275,
    303n21, 305, 314n36, 327,
    329, 330n56, 332, 387, 390,
    391n39
authenticity, 22, 32, 35, 36n11,
    37–39, 41, 43, 47–49, 54, 62,
    233–234
auto-affection, 206, 254,
    257–258, 312
auto-donation, 214, 256–257
auto-generation of life, 202
auto-revelation, 203, 209–210,
    213, 223, 247, 250, 252–253,
    257, 279, 286

Bacon, Roger, 292, 303n21
Barth, Karl, 14–15

beatific vision, 86, 107–108, 280, 330

Beaufret, Jean, 27

Beckett, Samuel, 343, 350, 360n23,

Beierwaltes, Werner, 91n11

being-in-the-world, 12–13, 22, 24, 27–28, 31, 33–34, 36, 51–53, 60–61, 63, 73, 75, 82, 139, 143, 148, 195, 196n59, 232–234, 236–237, 245, 387, 396, 404

belief, 5, 151, 204, 250, 263–269, 272, 339, 454, 490, 504

Bell, David, 491

Benjamin, Walter, 349, 363n32, 366n53

Bergson, Henri, 471

Berkeley, George, 302

biology, 210, 247

Biran, Maine de, 202, 252

Blanchot, Maurice, 42, 350

Blond, Phillip, 184n30, 185–193

Boff, Clodovis, 516–517

Boff, Leonardo, 520–521

Bonaventure, St., 140, 314n36, 412

Borges, Jorge Luis, 123, 126n19

Bowie, Andrew, 153

Brentano, Franz, 115, 311, 375n17, 376n19, 377, 380–381, 383

Breton, Stanislas, 197n65, 354

Bultmann, Rudolf, 20

Burggraeve, Roger, 497

Cajetan, Thomas Cardinal, 264

Cantor, Georg, 304–308, 310, 327

Caputo, John, 90, 354, 365n47

care, 6, 23, 25, 72–73, 143, 148, 235–236, 251, 295

Chalmers, David, 283

charity, 15, 17, 95, 106, 292, 295, 297, 328, 524

Charles, Maxime Fr., 93

chiasmus, 336

Chrétien, Jean-Louis, 177n6, 339, 406n5, 421, 431–432

Christianity, 60, 79, 86, 90, 92, 187, 202–203, 218, 221, 223–225, 272, 284, 295, 297, 404–405, 406n5, 408, 497, 502–503, 505–506, 508, 514

Churchland, Paul, 272, 282, 285

community, 12, 34–35, 43, 65, 68, 96, 101, 103, 130, 210, 213–217, 221, 294, 356–357, 360n23, 379, 479, 499–500, 504, 514

Copernicus, Nicolaus, 355

Council of Nicea, 132

Cudworth, Ralph, 289, 316–317, 318n40, 319–320, 322, 323n46, 328–329

Da Vinci, Leonardo, 117, 337, 344, 443, 446

Dasein, 22–34, 36–38, 40–45, 47–48, 53–55, 60–63, 139, 148, 233–236, 334, 372–376, 379, 386–387, 393, 395–400, 501–502, 504–507,

de Chardin, Teilhard, 338

de Lubac, Henri, 106n57, 283

Deely, John N., 297, 299n16, 302, 303n21

Deleuze, Gilles, 350, 355, 363n32, 366n52

Derrida, Jacques, 58–59, 69, 75, 88, 178–179, 299n16, 314n36, 354, 384n30, 406n5, 450, 482, 484–485, 487–490, 494

Name and Subject Index

Descartes, René, 57, 91–92, 94, 228, 260, 294, 324n47, 452, 463, 470, 485–486
desire, 18–20, 92, 99, 110, 139–141, 144, 146–148, 168–169, 181–182, 192, 245, 255, 266, 277–278, 295, 315, 328–329, 332–334, 340, 342, 354, 378, 392, 404–407, 409, 412–417, 420, 428, 436, 496, 517
Dilthey, Wilhelm, 370–388, 392–394, 396, 398–399, 401
divine transcendence, 1, 14, 17, 136, 176, 185, 191
Dorés, Gustave, 118
doxology, 175, 194–195, 198–199
dualism, 202, 228, 231, 270, 282, 285, 317, 320, 336, 419, 451–452, 460–461
Dulles, Avery Cardinal, 500

Eckhart, Meister, 200, 219–222, 239, 252, 259, 261–262, 270, 274, 279, 284, 313, 314n36, 338
economy of exchange, 149
Elgar, Edward, 25
end of metaphysics, 50, 65, 70
epistemology, 1, 97n28, 175, 184n30, 192, 289, 516
eros, 396, 404–405, 410, 413, 416–417, 420
eschatology, 3, 20, 194
Eucharist, 1, 85, 93, 95–110, 335, 339, 341–344, 348, 350, 352–353, 356–358, 359n11, 360n23, 366n53, 368n66; as Blessed Sacrament, 92, 96–97, 99, 107

excluded middle, 289–290, 293, 295, 297, 305, 321

facticity, 22–23, 25, 31, 36–39, 46, 63, 82–83, 256, 334, 374, 393, 398–399, 494
fallenness, 23, 25, 54, 61–62, 100, 419
Fides et Ratio (encyclical), 84–85, 88, 284
Finance, Joseph de, 261
finitude, 33, 38–42, 44–45, 48, 59, 61, 69, 83, 100, 138–139, 147, 256, 312–313, 325, 327, 333
Fink, Eugen, 3, 489, 490n105
Finkielkraut, Alain, 72
Fiorenza, Francis Schüssler, 513
flesh, 2, 6, 15, 17–18, 69, 119, 187, 191n51, 196n61, 198, 202–203, 209, 221–223, 228, 252, 257–259, 263n10, 286–287, 334–339, 341–342, 344, 349, 351–353, 356, 358, 359n11, 439–440, 442–446, 511, 516
Foucault, Michel, 88, 102
Fourth Lateran Council, 18
Franck, Manfred, 153
Frege, Gottlob, 301, 304, 311
Freud, Sigmund, 43–44, 46, 355, 434–440, 442–445
Fries, Heinrich, 512

Gadamer, Hans-Georg, 151–168, 170–173
Galileo, 325, 451–452
German idealism, 13, 231
gift, 76–77, 96–99, 103, 105–106, 148, 190, 198–199, 235, 261, 263, 270, 286, 292, 295–297, 312, 329–330, 332, 356, 358, 408, 416–417

Gill, Eric, 295
Gilson, Étienne, 91–92, 302, 334
Godel, Kurt, 308
Gregory of Rimini, 305
Grosseteste, Robert, 305, 308, 325
Gutiérrez, Gustavo, 520

Haar, Michael, 59
Habermas, Jürgen, 35, 39
Hamann, Georg, 156
Hegel, Georg Wilhelm Friedrich, 1, 20, 86–88, 154, 160, 309, 326, 330n56, 350, 401, 422n3, 423, 429
Heidegger, Martin, 8–11, 13–16, 19, 21–73, 76, 79–82, 87–90, 93, 101–102, 105, 134–135, 139, 141–143, 147, 153, 174, 177, 179–183, 186, 229, 231, 233–237, 241–242, 244–246, 248, 302, 312–313, 334, 370–377, 379–382, 383n28, 384–403, 409n15, 414n22, 469n56, 497, 501–505, 507–508, 511, 517, 524
Henry, Michel, 176, 177n6, 201–205, 207, 209, 211–240, 261–262, 279–281, 283–286, 312, 406n5
Heraclitus, 111, 137, 366n53
hermeneutics, 18, 36, 79, 152–154, 156, 167, 169, 173, 313, 368n67, 372n7, 380, 503n8
Hesnard, Angélo Théodose, 434–436, 438, 444, 446
Hildegard of Bingen, 338
Hill, Claire Ortiz, 301, 304, 310, 315
Hillesum, Etty, 354
Hobbes, Thomas, 297, 320

horizon, 30, 64, 66, 68, 84, 135–136, 152–154, 166, 172–173, 179–182, 221–222, 227, 231, 238, 240, 244–245, 277, 283, 310, 313, 321, 415–416, 439–440, 468, 471, 476, 482–485, 491
Horner, Robyn, 80
Howarth, Jane, 493
humanism, 402

Ibn'Arabi, 338
icon, 100–101, 106, 111–112, 118–119, 129–130, 132–133, 184n30, 335
iconography, 128n22, 132
idol, 16, 18, 20, 100–101, 111, 112n2, 118–119, 131, 133, 158, 357
image-consciousness, 116, 120–121, 124, 127, 132
inauthenticity, 29, 34–37, 39, 47, 54, 61–62, 233
incarnation, 17, 52, 83, 98–99, 161, 187, 191n51, 202, 220, 222, 258, 268, 280, 281n29, 283–284, 334, 343–344, 347–348, 353–354, 356, 359n8, 360n23, 408, 412, 419
infinite, 3, 17, 61, 97–98, 146–147, 182, 219, 221, 258, 266, 268, 282, 294, 296, 299n16, 301, 305–309, 312–316, 318n40, 324–329, 331, 333, 358, 360n23, 363n32, 465, 484, 511
intentionality, 11, 114–115, 178, 180, 184n30, 208–211, 213, 223, 238, 243–244, 257, 283, 415, 425–426, 428–429, 431, 467, 482, 484–485, 487, 501, 503–505, 507

internal-time consciousness, 421, 426

intersubjectivity, 10, 17, 516

intuition, 6, 14, 26, 40, 118, 123, 125, 135n3, 178, 202, 205, 216, 242, 246, 252, 256, 328, 351, 382n27, 416, 440, 467, 482–483, 514

invisible, 4–6, 18, 66, 77, 82, 100, 176, 178, 181, 186, 190, 199, 207, 214, 216, 235, 248–249, 252, 257, 264, 283, 312–313, 328, 333, 336, 341, 415, 419

ipseity, 197, 206, 212, 222, 224–225, 229, 231, 234–236, 250–251, 256, 279

Islam, 12, 290

Jacob, François, 247

Janicaud, Dominique, 5, 174, 176–177, 183, 187n36, 250, 406n5, 495–496, 511–513, 518, 524

John of the Cross, St., 14, 134–135, 143–146, 149, 338

John Paul II, Pope, 84, 283

John, St., 196n61, 202, 218, 224, 249, 253, 259

Judaism, 99

Julian of Norwich, 339

Kafka, Franz, 41, 204, 260, 286

kairos, 62, 412, 420

Kautsky, Karl, 47

Kierkegaard, Søren, 62, 87, 217, 256, 259, 394

Krafft-Ebing, Richard Freiherr von, 442

Kristeva, Julia, 340–342, 344–348, 350, 353, 359n11, 359n14, 360n22, 363n29

Langland, William, 495, 497

language, 66, 70, 72n55, 83, 86, 88–89, 100, 108, 114, 133, 144, 146, 153, 167, 171, 204, 208, 214, 218, 220–221, 270, 303n21, 335, 337, 341–342, 352–353, 359n14, 360n22, 366n53, 371, 378, 380–381, 382n27, 383–385, 395, 413, 436, 464–466, 471, 481, 492, 500, 508, 513

law of non-contradiction, 289–290, 295, 308, 321

Leeuw, Van der, 128

Leibniz, Gottfried, 301, 363n32, 387, 417–418, 470, 491

Lenin, Vladimir, 47

Levinas, Emmanuel, 10, 16, 20, 42, 44, 50–52, 63–83, 175–184, 186, 314, 350, 359n8, 372, 399–402, 406n5, 421–432, 449–450, 465–468, 459n56, 470–471, 481–482, 484–492, 494–498, 508–511, 514–516, 519–522, 524

Life, 203, 207, 209, 212–213, 216, 218–219, 221–222, 224–225, 235, 238, 247, 249–253, 256, 258–259, 277, 283, 286

life-world, 176, 337, 451, 459, 493

Lossky, Vladimir, 263

Louth, Andrew, 168

Löwith, Karl, 32

Luria, Rabbi Isaac, 338

Machiavelli, Niccolo, 297

manifestation, 27, 65n33, 66, 97–98, 123, 133, 175, 185, 198–199, 205, 209, 220, 225, 229–232, 237–238, 241, 252,

270, 329, 331, 345, 418, 424
Maréchal, Joseph, 512
Marion, Jean-Luc, 50–51,
  63–64, 68–69, 70n49, 73,
  75–82, 85, 90–97, 99–103,
  105–110, 148, 176, 177n6,
  180n16, 184n30, 186, 312,
  314, 327, 331, 339, 406n5,
  416n25, 503
Maritain, Jacques, 284n38, 298,
  302
materialism, 272, 283, 320, 326,
  451
mathematics, 9–10, 305, 307,
  310, 316, 325, 502
McIntosh, Mark A., 151–152,
  157–159, 161, 163–173
Meinong, Alexius, 13
Merleau-Ponty, Maurice, 176,
  186–187, 189, 231, 287,
  334–341, 344, 346, 350, 353,
  434–446, 449–450, 459–467,
  471–473, 475–477, 481, 487,
  493–494
metaphysics of presence, 59,
  89–91, 96
Mill, John Stuart, 311
Mitsein, 33–35, 44–46, 48
monism, 231, 327
mysticism, 93, 143–144, 339,
  353–354, 357–358, 521

Nagel, Thomas, 480
Narcisse, Gilbert, 295
National Socialism, 22, 32–33,
  35–36
natural attitude, 30, 134, 260,
  265, 273, 284–286, 448, 450,
  454, 468
negative theology, 92–93, 105
Neoplatonism, 91, 311,
  318n40

Nicholas of Cusa, 261, 274, 284,
  322
Nietzsche, Friedrich, 46, 50, 88,
  90, 93, 102, 139, 355, 385
nihilism, 25, 35, 84–85, 88, 252,
  326–327
nominalism, 293, 297, 300
nothingness, 11–12, 105, 196,
  235n33, 274n20, 327, 354,
  357

Olivier, Lawrence, 125, 130,
ontotheology, 60, 187
Otto, Rudolf, 14–15

Pannenberg, Wolfhart, 154
pansexualism, 436–438
parousia, 17–20, 104, 220, 259
Pascal, Blaise, 15, 18–19, 313,
  324
Paul, St., 198, 251, 264, 253,
  404, 407, 408n12, 410,
  419–420,
Peirce, C.S., 299, 302–304, 311,
  317, 322, 330n56
perception, 1–7, 9–10, 13, 15,
  17, 100, 113–115, 118–123,
  126, 132, 161, 175, 177,
  185–191, 192n52, 193,
  195–196, 198–200, 211–212,
  217, 243, 335, 340, 346,
  366n52, 378–379, 381–384,
  388–389, 396, 398–399, 417,
  450, 458, 460, 463, 465, 471,
  476, 478–480, 484–485, 491,
  493
perceptual faith, 187–190, 193,
  197
phantasy, 120–127, 130–131,
  133, 440
phenomena, 1, 4–5, 7–9, 31,
  76–78, 94, 114, 120,

123–124, 128, 152, 176, 178,
181, 183–184, 187, 230, 241,
250, 253, 272, 311–312, 383,
413–414, 418–419, 449–450,
454, 486
phenomenality, 4, 7–10, 12, 20,
66, 176, 180, 184n30,
198–199, 207, 209, 220,
227–231, 234, 236–239,
241–244, 247, 253, 257, 496
Picasso, Pablo, 118
Pickstock, Catherine, 108
Plato, 30, 58–59, 86, 289–290,
312, 316n38, 318n40, 321,
323, 334, 391n40, 396, 405,
409, 432
Plotinus, 14, 327
Poe, Edgar Allen, 286
Poinsot, Jean, 298–299,
302–303
Politzer, Georges, 435, 443
Porreta, Gilbert, 292
postmodernism, 84–85, 87, 90
presence, 6, 9n4, 12, 14, 17–20,
57, 59, 61, 76–77, 80, 89–91,
95–97, 99–102, 104,
106–108, 110, 115–116, 131,
189, 231–232, 240, 249, 254,
283, 295, 312, 316, 323–324,
335, 341, 344–347, 354, 395,
416, 423–427, 431, 444,
465–466, 478, 490
present-at-hand, 50, 56, 61
Priest, Graham, 309
principle of sufficient reason,
418
Protagoras, 289–290, 312
Proust, Marcel, 338–346,
348–350, 352–353, 356–358,
359n11, 359n14, 360n23,
363n32, 366n53, 368n67
Pseudo-Dionysius the

Areopagite, 93, 105, 110n69,
314n36
psychoanalysis, 434–439, 441,
443–447
psychologism, 8, 311, 315, 377,
467, 494
pure givenness, 176

Radical Orthodoxy, 90
Rahner, Karl, 163, 508–513
Ramberg, Bjorn, 156
Raphael, 117
rationalism, 85, 87, 91
realism, 302, 304, 321
reciprocity, 213–214, 221,
296–297, 331–332, 350, 407,
465
Richardson, William, 36, 396
Ricoeur, Paul, 177n6, 350, 353,
355–357, 359n8, 360n22,
363n32, 368n65, 448
Rosemann, Philip, 373
Rosenzweig, Franz, 338
Rumi, 338
Russell, Bertrand, 8, 301, 308,
310

Santeuil, Jean, 341
Scheler, Max, 7, 11, 15, 334,
385, 388n35, 461, 464n41,
471
Schillebeeckx, Edward, 96
Schleiermacher, Friedrich Daniel
Ernst, 15–17, 19, 153, 383n28
scholasticism, 317, 320
Schönberg, Arnold, 12
Seckler, Max, 278
Sesto, Cesare de, 117
Sheehan, Tom, 27
signs, 6, 107–108, 112n2, 115,
137, 196, 298–299, 302,
303n21, 304, 314, 316, 320,

322, 327, 333, 341–342, 366n52, 481
Simon, Claude, 441–442, 446
Smith, Arthur David, 479
Smith, James K.A., 83
Socrates, 275, 289
Soffer, Gail, 473n64, 475, 477
Sokolowski, Robert, 116, 124n16, 131
sphere of ownness, 449, 455–457, 459, 461n36, 470, 472, 475, 480–481, 485–487, 491–492
Spinoza, Benedict de, 268, 297
spiritual experience, 151–153, 155, 157–159, 161–164, 166–168, 170, 172–173
state-of-mind (*Befindlichkeit*), 22–23, 36
Steinbock, Anthony, 459
supernatural, 136, 149, 263–264, 330, 332, 509–510
synthetic perception, 2
Szondi, Peter, 153

tabula rasa, 91
Tertullian, 286, 511
theism, 263, 282
thrown projection, 22–25, 32, 45–46
Tracy, David, 499–500, 512
transcendental ego, 3, 474n67
transcendental reduction, 379, 388n35, 398–399
transference, 44, 359n14
transubstantiation, 97, 337–341,

344–346, 350–353, 358, 359n11, 363n32
truth; as correspondence, 51–53, 63–64, 66, 77, 81–82; as uncoveredness, 53, 55–56

unconscious, 252–253, 255, 434, 436, 443–445
understanding (*Verstehen*), 22, 375

Vattimo, Gianni, 354
Veronese, Guiseppe, 306
virtue, 45, 266, 277n24
visible, 2, 4–6, 18, 65–66, 69, 100, 174, 177, 182, 186, 197–199, 207, 243–244, 246, 253, 257, 313, 328, 333, 336, 341, 395, 456, 460, 467, 475, 481
Visker, Rudi, 68, 70
von Balthasar, Hans Urs, 15, 152, 156, 294–295, 304, 319, 321, 328–330, 332–333

Wagner, Richard, 25
Waldenfels, Bernard, 480n79, 493
Weinsheimer, Joel, 169
Welte, Bernhard, 139
wholly other, 14, 202
William of Ockham, 293, 300, 303n21
Wittgenstein, Ludwig, 26, 112n2, 302, 310n31